IMAGES OF W

BURMA
VICTORY
1944–45

RARE PHOTOGRAPHS FROM WARTIME ARCHIVES

Jon Diamond

Pen & Sword
MILITARY

First published in Great Britain in 2022 by
PEN & SWORD MILITARY
An imprint of
Pen & Sword Books Ltd
47 Church Street
Barnsley
South Yorkshire
S70 2AS

ISBN 978-1-39900-853-2

A CIP catalogue record for this book is available from the British Library.

Typeset by Concept, Huddersfield, West Yorkshire, HD4 5JL.
Printed and bound in the UK by CPI Group (UK) Ltd, Croydon, CR0 4YY.

MIX
Paper from responsible sources
FSC® C013604

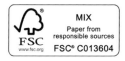

Pen & Sword Books Limited incorporates the imprints of Atlas, Archaeology, Aviation, Discovery, Family History, Fiction, History, Maritime, Military, Military Classics, Politics, Select, Transport, True Crime, Air World, Frontline Publishing, Leo Cooper, Remember When, Seaforth Publishing, The Praetorian Press, Wharncliffe Local History, Wharncliffe Transport, Wharncliffe True Crime and White Owl.

For a complete list of Pen & Sword titles please contact
PEN & SWORD BOOKS LIMITED
47 Church Street, Barnsley, South Yorkshire S70 2AS, England
E-mail: enquiries@pen-and-sword.co.uk
Website: www.pen-and-sword.co.uk

Contents

Acknowledgements

This archival photograph volume in the 'Images of War' series is dedicated to the multinational Allied Armed Forces' service members who fought, who were wounded and who perished during the hellacious land and air combat to defend north-eastern India and recapture Burma from Imperial Japanese rule. In addition, in a true engineering and construction feat, a new Ledo or 'Stilwell' Road was built across northern Burma to reconnect with the Old Burma Road in order to augment supply to China with war matériel for its ongoing defence during its protracted war with Japan.

We ponder, upon viewing these photographs, about the heroic sacrifice made to maintain freedom over military aggression, hegemony and brutality, lest we forget. The author is indebted to the able assistance of the archivists at both the United States Army Military History Institute (USAMHI) at the United States Army War College in Carlisle, Pennsylvania, the Still Photo Section of the National Archives and Records Administration (NARA) in College Park, Maryland, and the Library of Congress Photograph Room in Washington, D.C. Their diligence is much appreciated as they maintain and safeguard these superb historic images for the present tome as well as for future viewers.

Abbreviations

AA – Anti-aircraft
AAA – Anti-aircraft artillery
ABDA – American-British-Dutch-Australian
ADC – Aide-de-camp
AT – Anti-tank
ATC – Air Transport Command
CAI – Chinese Army of India
CBI – China-Burma-India
CG – Commanding General
C-in-C – Commander-in-Chief
COS – Chief of Staff
DSO – Distinguished Service Order
FEAF – Far East Air Force
GOC – General Officer Commanding
HMS – His Majesty's Ship
HQ – Headquarters
IJA – Imperial Japanese Army
IJN – Imperial Japanese Navy
IR – Infantry Regiment
LCI – Landing Craft, Infantry
LMG – Light Machine Gun
LOC – Lines of Communication
LRP – Long-Range Penetration

MG – Machine Gun
MMG – Medium Machine Gun
NCAC – Northern Combat Area Command
NEI – Netherlands East Indies
OSS – Office of Strategic Services
PIAT – Projector, Infantry Anti-Tank
PoWs – Prisoners of War
QF – Quick-firing
RA – Royal Artillery
RAC – Royal Armoured Corps
RAF – Royal Air Force
RE – Royal Engineers
RN – Royal Navy
SB – Stretcher-bearer
SEAC – South-East Asia Command
SMLE – Short Magazine Lee Enfield
TB – Tank Battalion
US – United States
USA – United States Army
USAAF – United States Army Air Force
USN – United States Navy
USS – United States Ship

Chapter One

The IJA's 1942 Conquest of Burma and the 1943 Allied Response

Within the British Empire, Burma was the land link connecting India and Malaya. If the British bastions of Malaya and Singapore were to fall to the Japanese, then India might be assaulted via an overland offensive through Burma after Imperial Japan's Pacific and South-East Asian blitzkrieg against Allied possessions commenced on 7 December 1941. However, Burma's harsh terrain was counted on as being an Allied force-multiplier to protect India from Japanese invasion.

Burma is surrounded by mountain ranges and covered in thick jungle (see Map 1). Four rivers flow south into the Bay of Bengal and the Andaman Sea. The Irrawaddy and its major tributary, the Chindwin, rise in the Himalayas to the north; to the east flow the Sittang and Salween. All were serious military obstacles. Central Burma's valleys – only passable to vehicles in the dry season – open into thickly wooded plains dotted with low hills. Hydrated flat land possessed peasant-cultivated rice paddies. South of Mandalay and Shwebo, arid terrain has sparse vegetation. The Pegu Yomas' (mountains') jungle hills lie between the Irrawaddy and Sittang rivers. The Arakan Yomas, rising to 3,000ft, separate Burma from the west coastal Arakan. In the monsoon season, the muddy fields are impassable to wheels or tracks and the *chaungs* or streams flood. Near the coast, the tracks are fringed with mangrove swamps, so watercraft is the only practical way of ferrying men and stores. In the Arakan, the steep razor-backed hills are covered in dense forest. The Tenasserim, comprising mainly tropical rainforest, is situated in southern Burma from the lower Salween to the Kra Isthmus near Thailand.

As for transportation routes (see Map 5), the major Rangoon to Mandalay railway ran north along the course of the Sittang River and continued north through Shwebo, Wuntho, Indaw and Mogaung, then on to its terminus at Myitkyina. At Mandalay, the railway branched east through Maymyo to Lashio, then reaching the Burma Road. There were two shorter railway branches east of the Irrawaddy River: the first through Meiktila to Myingyan, and the second from Pyinmana north-west to

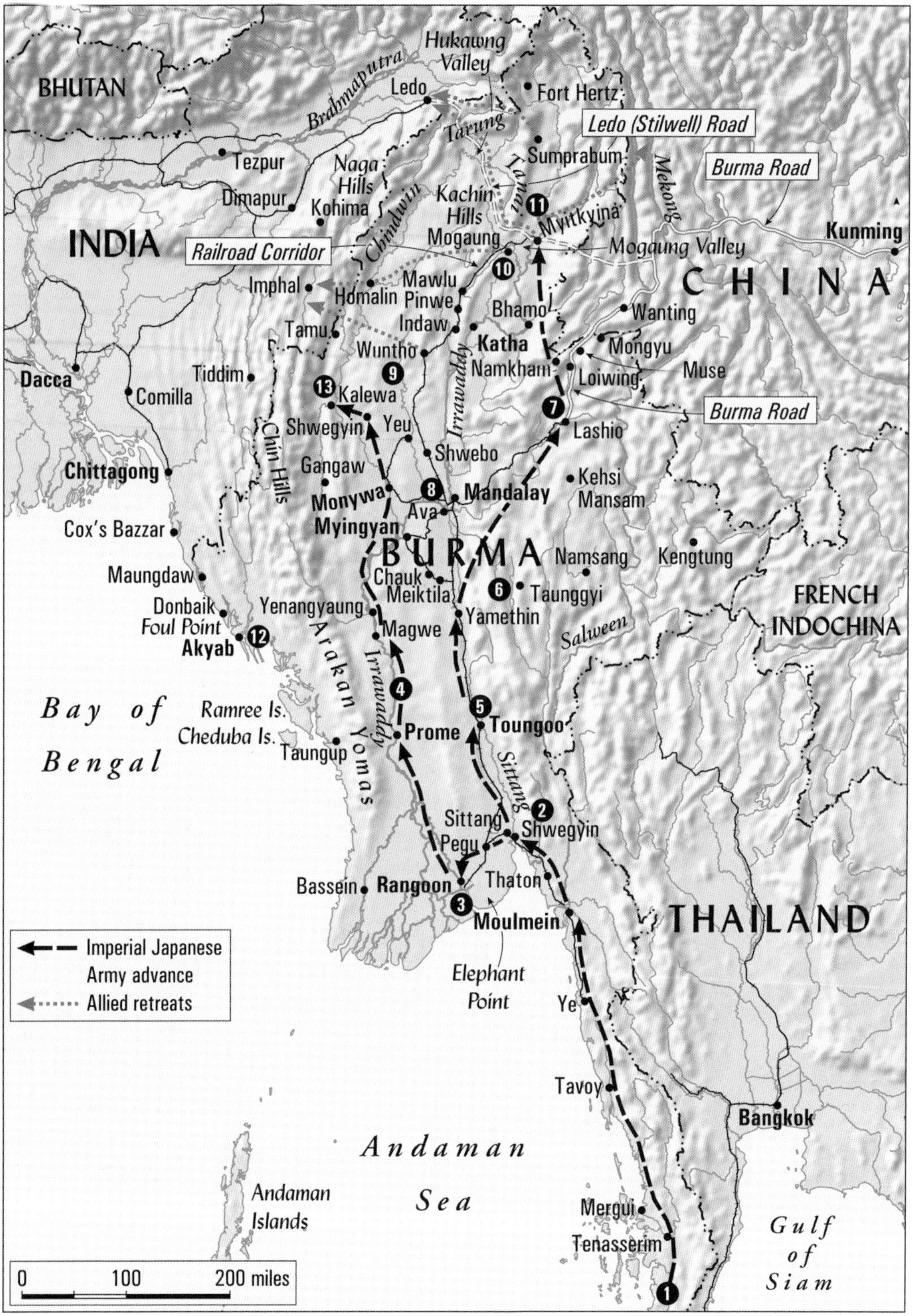
BHUTAN
Hukawng Valley
Brahmaputra
Ledo
Fort Hertz
Ledo (Stilwell) Road
Tarung
Sumprabum
Tezpur
Naga Hills
Tanai
Mekong
Burma Road
Dimapur
Kohima
Chindwin
Kachin Hills
Myitkyina
Kunming
INDIA
Railroad Corridor
Mogaung
Mogaung Valley
Mawlu
Imphal
Homalin
Pinwe
Bhamo
CHINA
Wanting
Tamu
Indaw
Katha
Mongyu
Wuntho
Namkham
Muse
Loiwing
Dacca
Tiddim
Comilla
Kalewa
Irrawaddy
Burma Road
Shwegyin
Yeu
Lashio
Chin Hills
Shwebo
Chittagong
Gangaw
Kehsi Mansam
Monywa
Mandalay
Ava
Cox's Bazzar
Myingyan
BURMA
Namsang
Kengtung
Maungdaw
Chauk
Meiktila
Taunggyi
FRENCH INDOCHINA
Donbaik
Yenangyaung
Yamethin
Foul Point
Akyab
Magwe
Salween
Arakan Yomas
Irrawaddy
Bay of Bengal
Ramree Is.
Cheduba Is.
Taungup
Prome
Toungoo
Sittang
Sittang
Shwegyin
Pegu
Bassein
Rangoon
Thaton
Moulmein
THAILAND
Imperial Japanese Army advance
Allied retreats
Elephant Point
Ye
Tavoy
Bangkok
Andaman Sea
Andaman Islands
Mergui
Tenasserim
Gulf of Siam
0
100
200 miles
1
2
3
4
5
6
7
8
9
10
11
12
13

Map 1. Situation after Japan's Invasion of Burma, January–May 1942.

❶ On 15 January 1942, the IJA 33rd and 55th divisions from Thailand invade Burma's Tenasserim, the strip of southern Burma in the Kra Isthmus and seize airfields at Mergui and Tavoy to bomb Rangoon's port and British convoys. Moulmein, at the Salween River's junction with the Andaman Sea, fell on 30 January. During February, the IJA 33rd and 55th divisions drive westwards towards Rangoon, passing through the Allied Salween and Bilin River lines. **❷** On 22–23 February, the IJA 33rd and 55th Divisions defeat the 17th Indian Division at the Battle of the Sittang Bridge, south of Toungoo, on 22–23 February. A premature Allied demolition of the Sittang River's bridge on 23 February strands two 17th Division brigades and vehicles on the river's eastern bank, leaving Rangoon open for the IJA. **❸** On 5 March, Lieutenant General Sir Harold Alexander, new C-in-C Burma, realizes that Rangoon cannot hold against the IJA 33rd and 55th divisions moving overland through Pegu with the port's oil refineries seized by a Japanese Commando seaborne attack. Alexander's Rangoon garrison retreats north up the Prome Road through the Irrawaddy Valley to protect the oilfields at Yenangyaung. On 8 March, the IJA 33rd Division enters a deserted Rangoon with the IJA 18th and 56th divisions landing by sea. **❹** In mid-March, a reinforced IJA 33rd Division drives north towards Prome. On 19 March, BurCorps, comprising the remnants of the 17th Indian and 1st Burma divisions with the attached 7th Armoured Brigade under Lieutenant General William Slim defends Prome, but crumbles under a Japanese attack on 1–2 April, forcing a withdrawal. Within days, the IJA 33rd Division captures Yenangyaung's oilfields after Slim ordered their destruction on 15 April before retreating. Although the 1st Burma Division was broken as a fighting force at Yenangyaung, General Sun Li-jen's 38th Chinese Division briefly counterattacked on 20 April inflicting many Japanese casualties, but Slim called off the counterattack. **❺** The IJA 55th Division continuing its advance north on to Mandalay attacks the 200th Chinese Division at Toungoo from 24–30 March. The Japanese entered Toungoo on 1 April. **❻** The IJA 56th Division with armour envelops the Chinese flank at Taunggyi and advances north through the Shan States to sever roads to Yunnan Province to prevent Chiang's armies in Burma from retreating. Stilwell's Chinese 200th Division counterattacks the IJA 56th Division on 23–24 April, recapturing Taunggyi to allow the Chinese 5th Army to escape northwards. **❼** The IJA 56th Division resumes its northward advance and occupies Lashio on 29 April to sever the Burma Road as resistance from the Chinese 6th Army's 55th and 93rd divisions collapses. **❽** On 23 April, Alexander orders Chinese forces east of the Mandalay railway to withdraw north-east to defend the road through Lashio, while directing Slim's BurCorps plus Sun's 38th Chinese Division to cross the Irrawaddy at Shwebo on 25 April so as not to get trapped by a defence of Mandalay. **❾** In early May, after the fall of Mandalay and Monywa, Slim's BurCorps and Sun's 38th Chinese Division continue retreating west to the Chindwin River to cross into India near Tamu. Myitkyina is captured by IJA forces on 8 May 1942. **❿** In early May, Stilwell tries to re-establish contact with the retreating Chinese troops, but while at Indaw learns that the Japanese blocked the railway to Myitkyina. So he leads a group of more than 100 soldiers and Burmese nurses westwards to get to the Chindwin River. This 'Walkout' commenced on 6 May with Stilwell crossing the river at Homalin and reaching Imphal on 20 May with Japanese columns in pursuit. **⓫** The Chinese 22nd Division retreats from the Myitkyina area back to Ledo, India. Other Chinese divisions – the 55th, 93rd, 96th and 200th – retreat to the north-east into China. **⓬** Akyab Island on the Arakan coast is captured by the Japanese on 4 May. **⓭** Kalewa, near the Indo-Burmese border, is captured by IJA forces on 14 May. The Japanese occupation of Burma is near-complete except for a British garrison at Fort Hertz in the far north from which British-led Kachin rebels clash with patrols of the IJA 18th Division's 114th IR garrisoning Myitkyina near Sumprabum.

Kyaukpadaung. Another railway branch started north-east of Rangoon and then turned south-easterly through Moulmein and the Tenasserim crossing into Thailand. A fourth railway branch from Rangoon paralleled the Irrawaddy River's eastern side and ran north-west to Prome.

The Rangoon-Mandalay motor road moved north-eastward to connect with Lashio and the Burma Road, which was the main LOC for the United States to supply the Chinese, who were fighting the Japanese for most of the 1930s. From Mandalay, an all-weather road paralleled the railway to Myitkyina through Shwebo, Wuntho and Indaw. Non-all-weather roads emanated north from Myitkyina to Sumprabum and south-west to Mogaung. There were many minor roads throughout but, like the Kamaing Road in the Hukawng and Mogaung valleys, they were no more than dirt tracks.

Japanese Invasion of Burma

Japan's Burmese invasion from eastern Thailand started a week after their Pearl Harbor attack as IJA units captured Victoria Point's airfield on Burma's southern tip. By mid-January 1942, the Japanese had seized other airfields at Mergui and Tavoy in the Tenasserim. The IJA 15th Army's 33rd and 55th divisions waited along the Thai border until Malayan operations were nearing completion to begin the major Burmese invasion on 20 January. Rangoon, Burma's capital and major port, Prome and Toungoo, the Yenangyaung oilfields, and Mandalay, central Burma's major city were Japan's principal objectives. On 18–19 April, the IJA 33rd Division drove into the oilfields at Yenangyaung as the British attempted to destroy them. The inglorious Allied retreat throughout Burma was now in full throttle, enabling the IJA to capture the entire country within weeks as Japanese troops were on both banks of the Chindwin River on 27 April, leaving eastern India in precarious straits. A divided Japanese high command rejected a plan to invade Assam, one of India's north-eastern provinces, as being logistically impractical. The Burmese conquest was complete at a cost of 4,597 Japanese killed and wounded.

China's supply line for almost a decade of combat with the IJA was through Rangoon and a railroad link via Mandalay with the Chinese frontier at Wanting. From there a fair-weather track to Kunming and Chungking was built in 1938 by 200,000 labourers. With Rangoon occupied and the Burma Road severed by the IJA, the Allies would now have to supply Chiang Kai-shek's forces via an air-transport route over the Himalayan Mountains, 'the Hump', to keep them fighting the Japanese.

The Allies in Burma, 1941–42

Britain's military presence in Burma was to protect north-eastern India's industrial areas and maintain the overland route with China, the 'Burma Road'. Britain's Indian army troops in Burma at the onset of hostilities were only the 1st Burma Division and the 13th Indian Brigade. Fearing a Japanese attack from Thailand, the 16th and 46th Indian infantry and the 17th Indian Division arrived to bolster the defences. These formations lacked jungle experience. The 17th Indian Division was previously trained for North Africa and as it was of better quality than the 1st Burma Division, it held the Salween River line covering Rangoon.

The swift Japanese south-east Burma advance overran the Salween and Bilin River lines to confront Britain's new Sittang River defences. These Allied defensive positions were soon in near collapse, so a withdrawal across the river was issued for 23 February 1942; however, a premature detonation of explosives destroyed the bridge, stranding many British-Indian troops and vehicles on the river's eastern side. Rangoon's evacuation was imminent with General Sir Harold Alexander's arrival on 5 March to assume the Burma army command. Alexander ordered the British-Indian garrison to leave Rangoon for Prome on 6 March, destroying many important sites before the IJA entry on 8 March.

The 5th, 6th and 66th Chinese armies (each equalling a British division) moved into Burma from Yunnan Province during February–April 1942 to stem the Japanese advance. Chiang Kai-shek placed Lieutenant General Joseph W. Stilwell (sent to China by President Roosevelt) as an independent commander of these Chinese forces. Stilwell arrived at Lashio on 14 March after meeting the *generalissimo* on 6 March at Maymyo. Stilwell contemplated a counteroffensive; however, that plan disintegrated when the Chinese failed to stop the Japanese at Toungoo after a ten-day stand.

Alexander realized that his weakened forces could not defend the Mandalay-Lashio road (the major link with China), as well as Mandalay proper and the Yenang-yaung oilfields. To retard Burma's complete capitulation to the Japanese, British and Indian forces designated 'Burcorps' comprising the 17th Indian and the 1st Burma divisions' remnants along with the 7th Armoured Brigade were placed under Lieutenant General William J. Slim on 19 March. Slim's defensive line at Prome was attacked by the IJA on 1–2 April, forcing an Allied withdrawal on 2 April. Simultaneously, the Japanese advanced north from Rangoon to Mandalay. On 3 April Slim ordered a defence of the Yenangyaung oilfields north of Prome, but these fell to the Japanese on 18–19 April.

On 18 April Field Marshal Archibald Wavell, C-in-C India, ordered Alexander to prepare for a withdrawal from Burma starting with the majority of British-Indian troops in Mandalay to begin crossing the Irrawaddy River on 25–26 April for their retreat to the Chindwin River and Assam. Alexander's forces withdrew towards Kalewa, which Wavell stocked with supplies before the monsoon's start on 15 May. The last British-Indian troops left Burma on 20 May, as Alexander's command ended after a 1,000-mile retreat with his forces suffering 10,036 casualties, of which 3,670 were killed and wounded and the remaining 6,366 missing.

Chiang's ground and American volunteer air forces combating the Japanese were isolated from resupply both by sea through Rangoon and overland across the Burma Road, located south of Myitkyina, and now relied on the treacherous Himalayan Mountain air supply route ('the Hump') from the air depots in India's north-eastern provinces of Assam and Manipur to the Chinese south-western province of Yunnan due to terrain, bad weather, unreliable C-46 and C-47 transport aircraft and Japanese fighter sorties from the now IJA-occupied Myitkyina airfields.

Japanese Plans

In September 1942, Lieutenant General Renya Mutaguchi, commander of the IJA 18th Division, told Lieutenant General Shōjirō Iida, the commander of the IJA 15th Army, that northern Burma's jungles and mountainous terrain prevented his division from being supplied for a tentative IJA 15th Army invasion of Assam and seizure of air depots there that were supplying the Chinese via 'the Hump' air supply route. By early 1943, only skeleton forces of the IJA 18th and 33rd divisions simply garrisoned northern Burma and the Chindwin River.

In February 1943, 'Chindit' commander Brigadier Orde Wingate (see below for details) with his 77th Brigade's LRP columns during Operation LONGCLOTH demonstrated to Mutaguchi that a large force could cross the Naga Hills and Chindwin River separating India and northern Burma. On 27 March Mutaguchi was promoted to lead the IJA 15th Army in northern Burma, and after scrutinizing Wingate's tactics across the main north-south grain of the rivers and mountains, he concluded that his Japanese troops could be mobile for an Assam invasion with pack transport only during the dry season. Mutaguchi's revelation, along with intelligence of the British build-up at Imphal, convinced him that his IJA 15th Army must eventually attack Imphal and Kohima to pre-empt a large-scale Allied invasion of Burma from India in 1944. On 11 April, Mutaguchi was given the single task of planning the Imphal and Kohima offensives, Operation U-GO (see Chapter 4). The best course would be to attack the British before they had time to complete their preparations for an offensive and capture their base at Imphal, thereby preventing them from launching an offensive into Burma. By summer 1943's end, the IJA was planning an Indian offensive to capture Imphal and Kohima during the early dry season of 1944. Mutaguchi overruled the new IJA 18th Division commander, Lieutenant General Tanaka, from planning a contemporaneous major Hukawng Valley offensive since logistical support would not be provided with Operation U-GO's preparation.

Allied Plans

After Stilwell's 'Walkout' from Burma to Assam in early 1942, his preoccupation with Myitkyina's recapture was apparent as he remarked at an Indian press conference in April: 'I claim we got a hell of a beating. We got run out of Burma and it is humiliating as hell. I think we ought to find out what caused it, go back and retake it.' To this end, since the autumn of 1942, US army engineers led by Brigadier General Lewis Pick began the Ledo Road (to be rechristened the 'Stilwell Road' or 'Pick's Pike') construction project intended to cross a reconquered northern Burma and ultimately link with the old Burma Road in China's Yunnan Province. With Myitkyina and its airfields in Allied hands, ATC transports could fly a lower, broader route to China. Also, with Myitkyina's recapture, the Ledo Road and its companion pipelines could link with the pre-war communications net of northern Burma with Myitkyina becoming a huge Allied supply depot.

To get to Myitkyina, Stilwell would have to move south down the Hukawng valley and across the Jāmbu Bum ridge into the Mogaung valley. The southern exit from the Mogaung valley was within marching distance of Myitkyina and the Irrawaddy valley that forms much of central Burma. The principal barrier between Stilwell and Myitkyina was the IJA 18th Division's three veteran regiments of Burmese combat. Tanaka hoped that monsoon rains in May–June 1944 would stall any advance by Stilwell's Sino-American forces (see below) in northern Burma. Also, in the Hukawng valley, Tanaka possessed advantages, such as terrain familiarity, his 6,300 troops, along with his divisional field mountain artillery regiment possessing 75mm mountain guns and 150mm howitzers.

Colonel Orde Wingate was summoned by Wavell to utilize his new LRP tactics to disrupt Japanese LOC in Burma. Wavell shared Wingate's views for a different type of specially-trained and physically-conditioned British infantryman to re-enter the jungles and mountains of northern Burma in 1943 to combat the victorious IJA forces there. For the first LRP invasion of northern Burma in February 1943 (Operation LONG-CLOTH), one of Wingate's battalions was from the 13th (King's Liverpool) Regiment, which had been on coastal defence duties in England before being drafted out to serve as garrison troops in India. City-bred, mostly married and over 30 years of age, many were physically unfit and had no liking for the arduous task that lay ahead. Wingate espoused that if ordinary British family men could be properly trained for specialized jungle warfare behind enemy lines, then any fit English infantryman could be trained to combat the vaunted Japanese soldier. Along with a new martial spirit, now Brigadier Wingate's new British infantryman, to be called Chindit (a mispronunciation of the Burmese word for the lion, 'Chinthe'), would possess RAF radio communications for air supply for the LRP without ground LOC. Burma's jungle canopy and mountains would obscure the Chindits' movements. Wingate formed his Chindits as the 77th Indian Brigade in July 1942.

However, enthusiasm for the Chindit training regimen and state of readiness of the troops for the entry into Burma was mixed. Chindit subordinate officers, although sometimes critical of their commander's martinet tactics, believed that Wingate never recklessly wasted his troops on the battlefield with the exception of leaving critically-wounded Chindits behind to be cared for by Burmese villagers or worse, the clemency of the Japanese. This unfortunate situation was to be remedied during 1944's Operation THURSDAY.

Wavell's First Arakan Campaign Starts in Mid-December 1942

In July 1942, Field Marshal Count Hisaichi Terauchi, commander of the IJA Southern Area Expeditionary Army Group, was ordered to prepare for an offensive stretching from Imphal in Assam to Akyab in the Arakan. These IJA manoeuvres were to distract the Allies from reinforcing the use of airfields in Assam and eastern India to hinder air supply to China.

Wavell, C-in-C India decided to open a limited offensive in the Arakan, a western Burma coastal plain interlaced with rice paddies, streams and jungle-covered hills. Its intent was to serve as an Allied morale-booster by seizing the initiative from the enemy in this area of Burma for any future IJA invasion of India. To take Akyab Island, a locale called 'Foul Point' and its IJA guns at the tip of the Mayu Peninsula would have to be captured by the 6th British Infantry Brigade. The IJA 55th Division held the Arakan, and the numerically-superior British 14th Division was assigned to capture this area. The British 14th Division's advance started in December 1942. By January 1943, small British mechanized units reached 'Foul Point', but IJA reinforcements stopped the 6th British Infantry Brigade's advance for a month, despite British tanks, with an elaborate log bunker system. 'Foul Point' remained in Japanese hands as the British advance towards Akyab Island stalled. In mid-March 1943, a reinforced 6th British Infantry Brigade moved against IJA positions at Donbaik, near the Bay of Bengal coastline, with a preliminary artillery and mortar bombardment of the enemy's fortifications. As the IJA 55th Division received reinforcements and advanced on British positions, no further attacks on Donbaik were made. Lieutenant General Slim's HQ was hastily sent to the Arakan in early April 1943, just as IJA 55th Division troops were assaulting the 6th British Infantry Brigade's rear as it was pulling back from Donbaik. An IJA 55th Division regiment was nearly decimated by the 6th British Infantry Brigade's mortar and artillery fire, briefly raising Allied morale. However, the IJA 55th Division had defeated Wavell's battalions and brigades during the campaign. Slim pulled back his forces in mid-May 1943 to the original starting-point of October 1942. British battle casualties numbered 2,500 with many more ravaged by malaria. Slim's main concern was to now rebuild the morale of the British and Indian formations again.

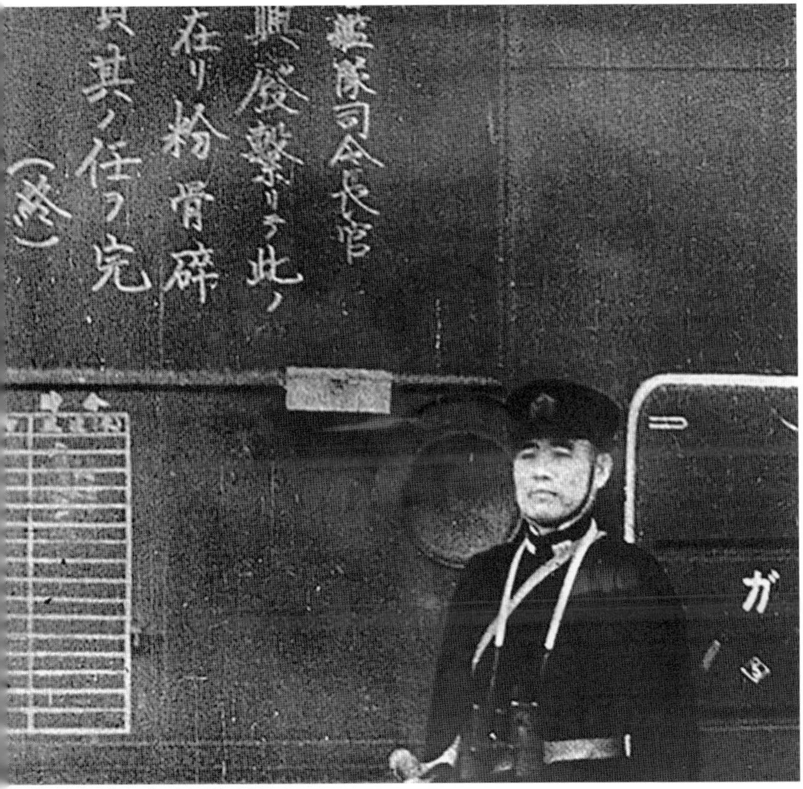

An IJN officer watches a bomber take off from the carrier *Shokaku*, one of six that participated in Admiral Chūichi Nagumo's surprise attack on Pearl Harbor and other US military installation sites on Oahu on 7 December 1941. The Japanese lost twenty-nine aircraft during the two waves of aerial assault. *(NARA)*

USN seamen search for survivors amid the wreckage of the USS *West Virginia* at the Pacific Fleet's anchorage at Pearl Harbor on 7 December 1941. Among many USN vessels attacked, four battleships were sunk and another four damaged. More than 2,400 Americans perished in the attack, with in excess of 1,000 wounded. *(Library of Congress)*

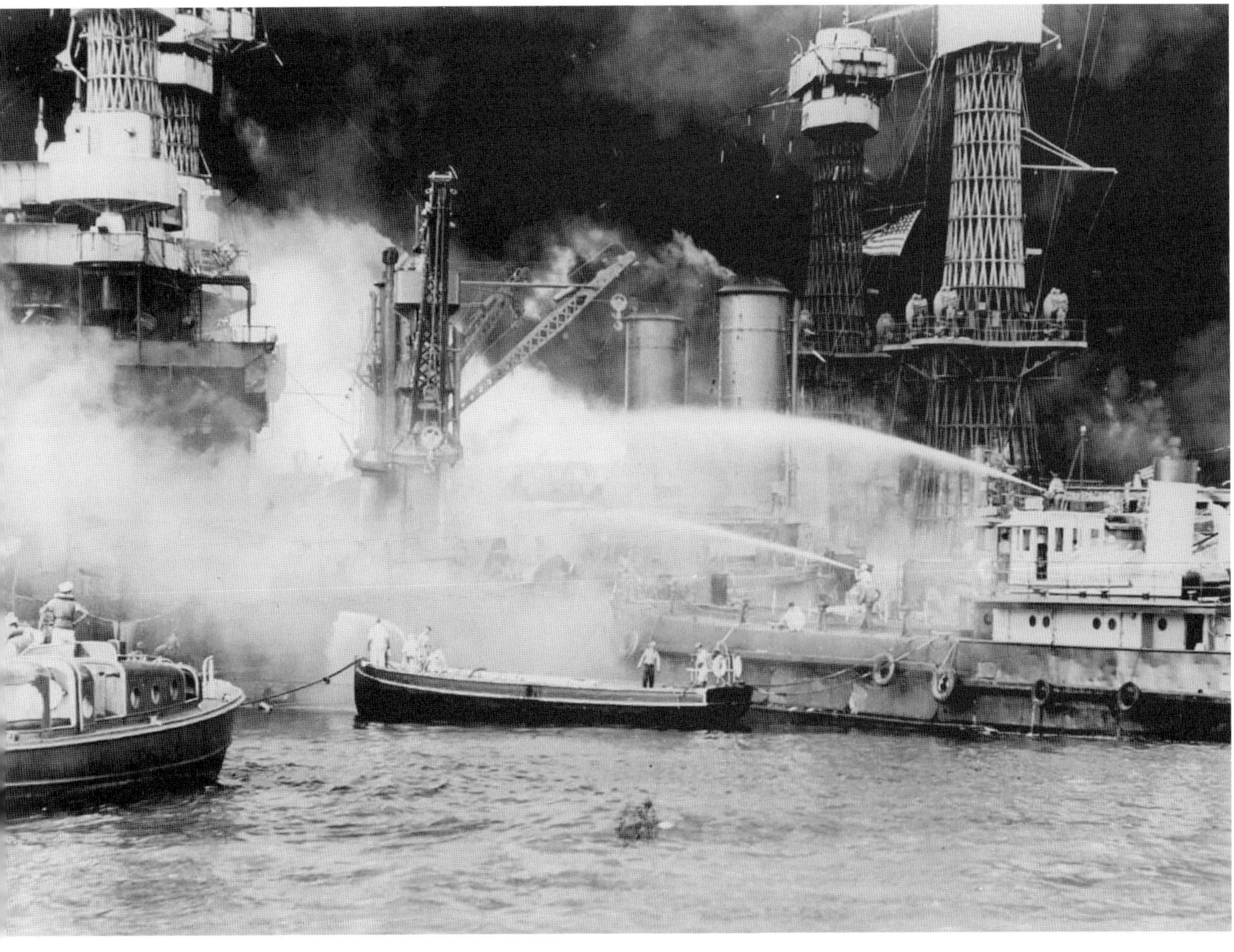

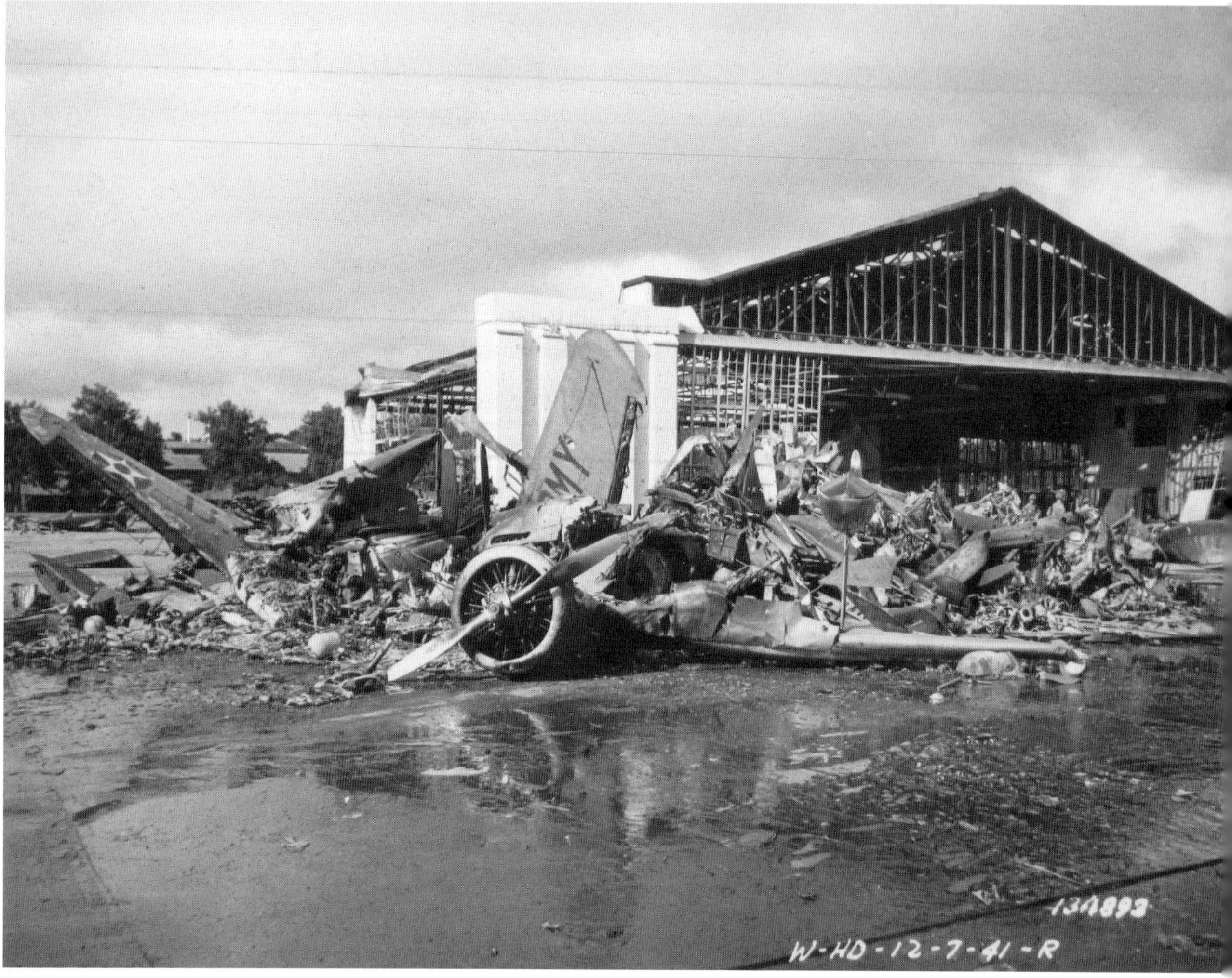
134893
W-HD-12-7-41-R

Destroyed USAAF fighters are seen here after the Japanese attack on Oahu's Wheeler Field. More than 185 US aircraft in total were destroyed and another 155 damaged on the ground at Wheeler (above), Hickam and Bellows Fields as well as Kaneohe, Ford Island and Barbers Point Naval Air Stations. The Marine Corps Air Station at Ewa was the first US military installation hit during the attack with all forty-eight aircraft destroyed on the ground. *(NARA)*

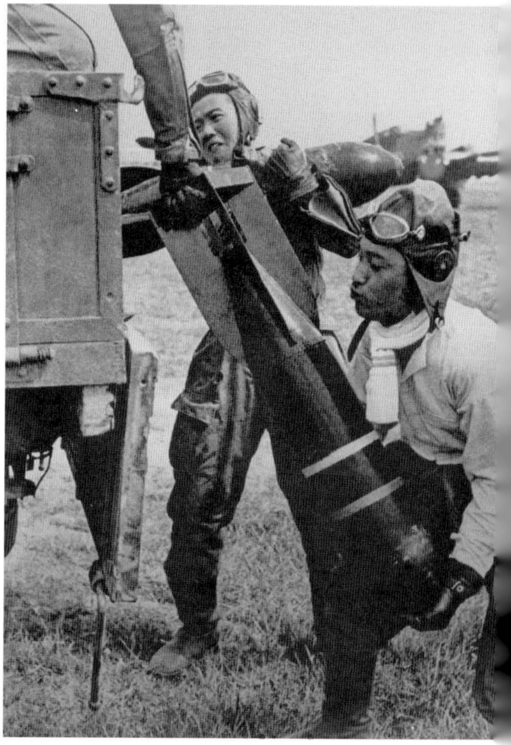

Two IJN airmen unload bombs from a truck at a French Indochinese airfield for a 10 December 1941 attack on the Royal Navy (RN) battleship HMS *Prince of Wales* and the battlecruiser HMS *Repulse* off the east coast of Malaya in the South China Sea. More than 800 RN sailors died in the assault and Singapore's British Eastern Fleet was severely weakened. Eighty-eight IJN Mitsubishi G4M (Betty) and G3M (Nell) twin-engined, medium land-based horizontal and torpedo bombers of the *Genzan*, *Kanoya* and *Mihoro* Air Groups participated in the devastating attack. Four Japanese aircraft were destroyed and another twenty-eight damaged by RN AA. *(NARA)*

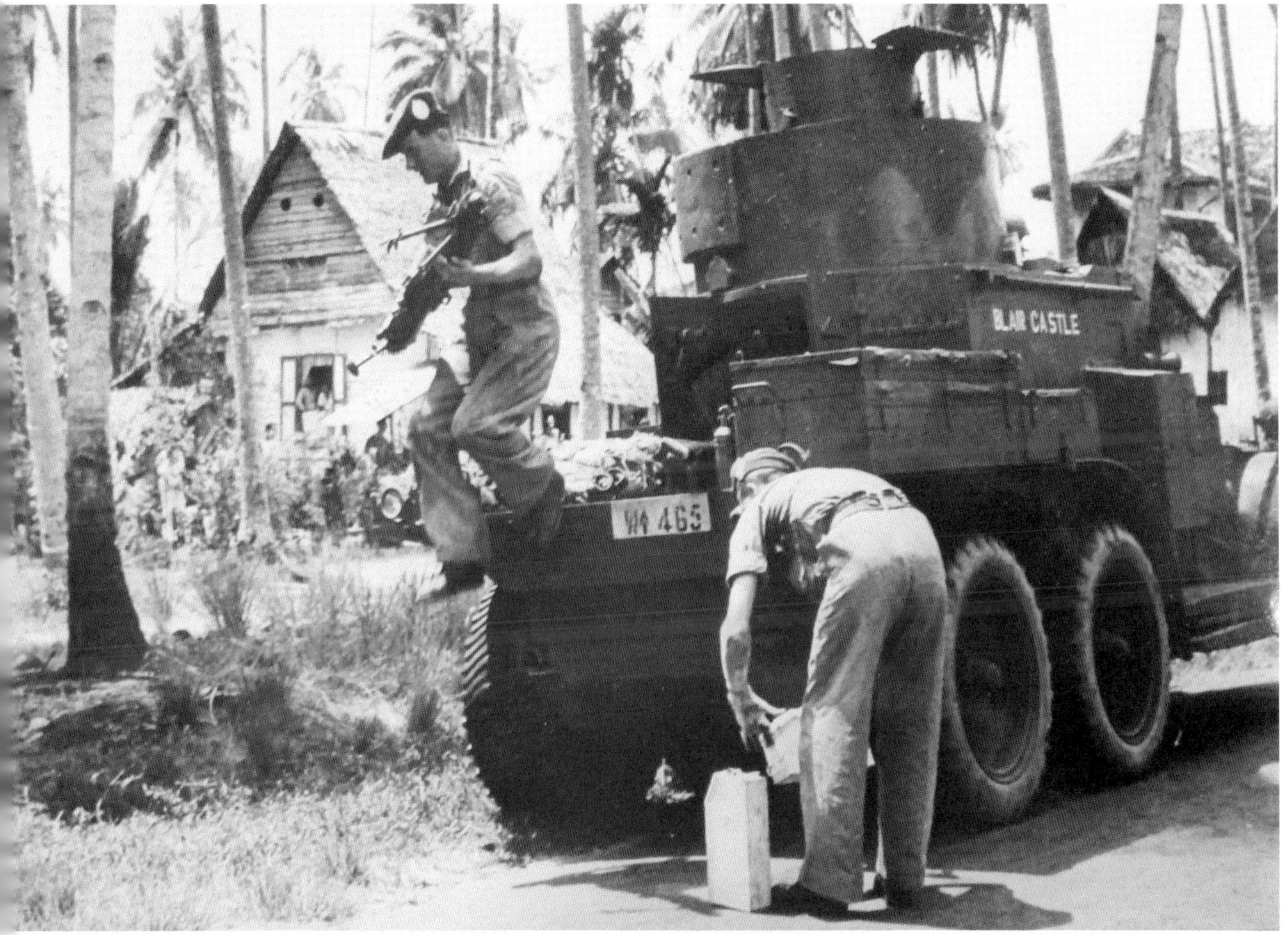
BLAIR CASTLE

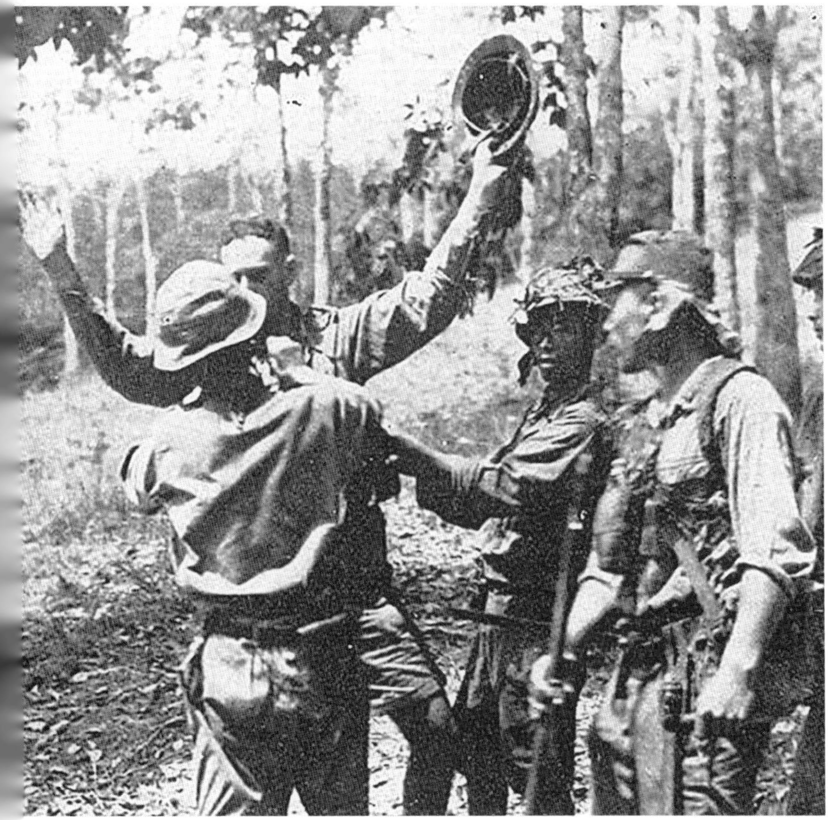

An Argyll and Sutherland Highlander infantryman jumps from his Lanchester armoured car in Malaya with a Vickers Mk 1 MMG. The other Highlander (right) readies a water can, which enabled continuous firing, and an ammunition box. *(Library of Congress)*

Japanese infantrymen search a Commonwealth soldier in the jungles of Malaya in early 1942. British and Australian troops were often surrounded by enemy forces via jungle tracks while Allied soldiers remained near major roads enabling their capture. *(Author's collection)*

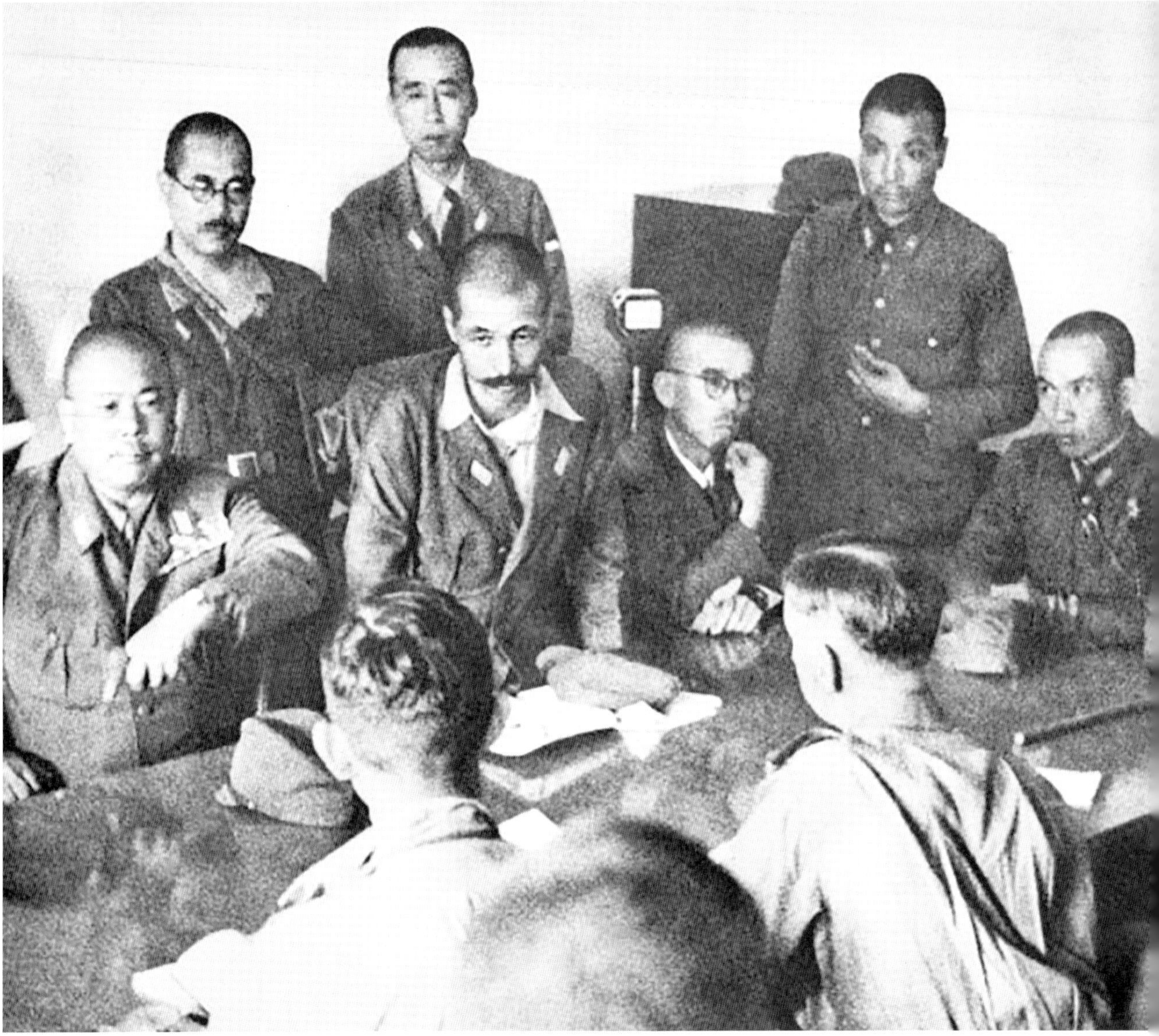

(**Above**) Lieutenant General Arthur Percival, Singapore's CG (far right, back to camera) surrenders to the IJA 25th Army commander, Lieutenant General Tomoyuki Yamashita (far left, seated) at Bukit Timah's Ford Factory on 15 February 1942. Singapore's reservoirs were captured and Yamashita bluffed Percival that the Japanese had inexhaustible artillery ammunition to continue further bombardment. *(Author's collection)*

(**Opposite, above**) Field Marshal Archibald Wavell (second from left) arrives at Batavia in the Netherlands East Indies (NEI) for the American-British-Dutch and Australian (ABDA) conference in early 1942. Wavell as the ABDA commanding officer set up his HQ in Lembaing on Java on 15 January 1942 in order to oversee all Allied forces in the Far East; however, the ABDA command was abandoned on 22 February 1942 after Hong Kong, Singapore, Malaya and the NEI had all fallen to the Japanese. *(USAMHI)*

(**Opposite, below**) Several destroyed US P-35 fighters are destroyed at Nichols Field, located to Manila's south near Cavite Navy Yard on 10 December 1941. The Japanese enjoyed free rein over Luzon's skies with the elimination of the majority of the FEAF at Clark and Iba Fields (on Luzon's west coast) two days earlier. *(NARA)*

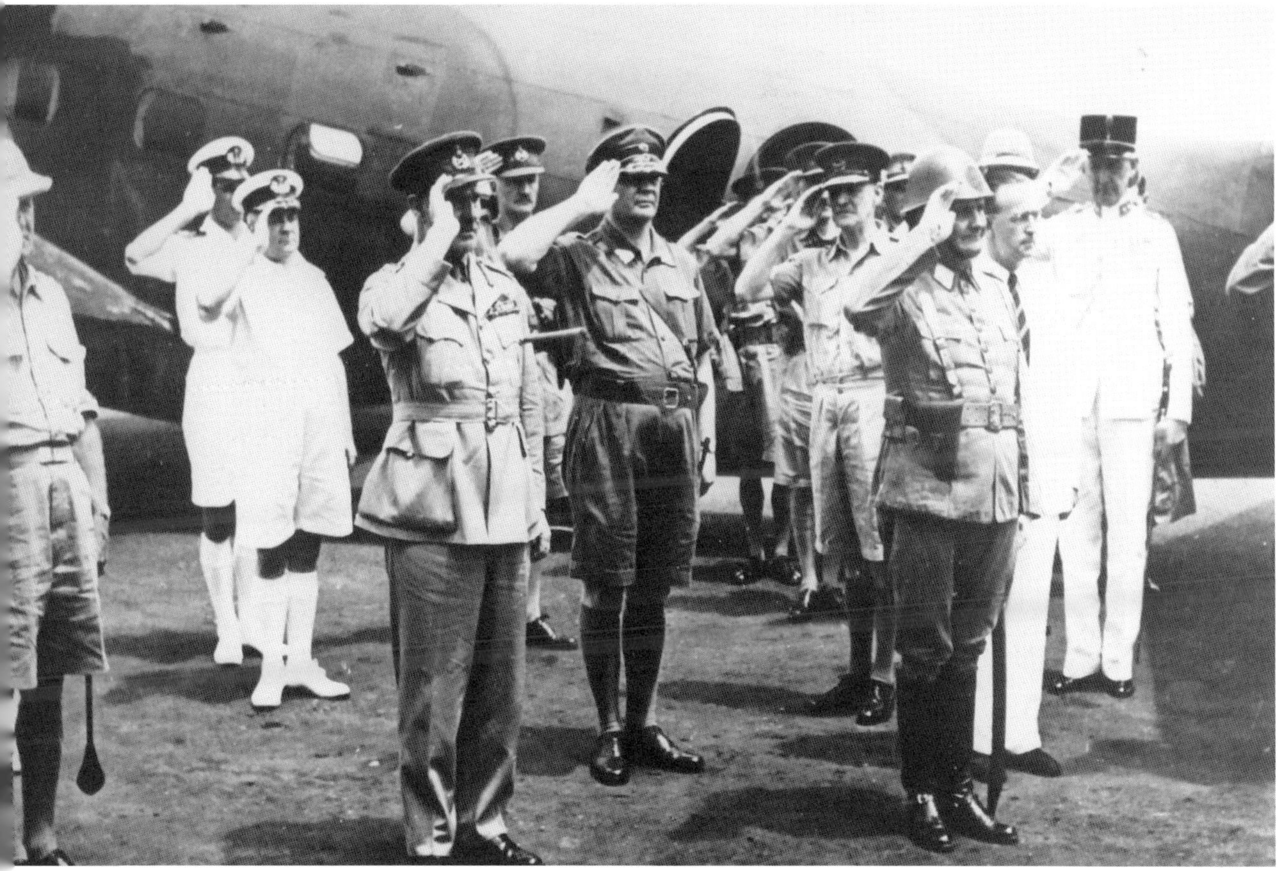

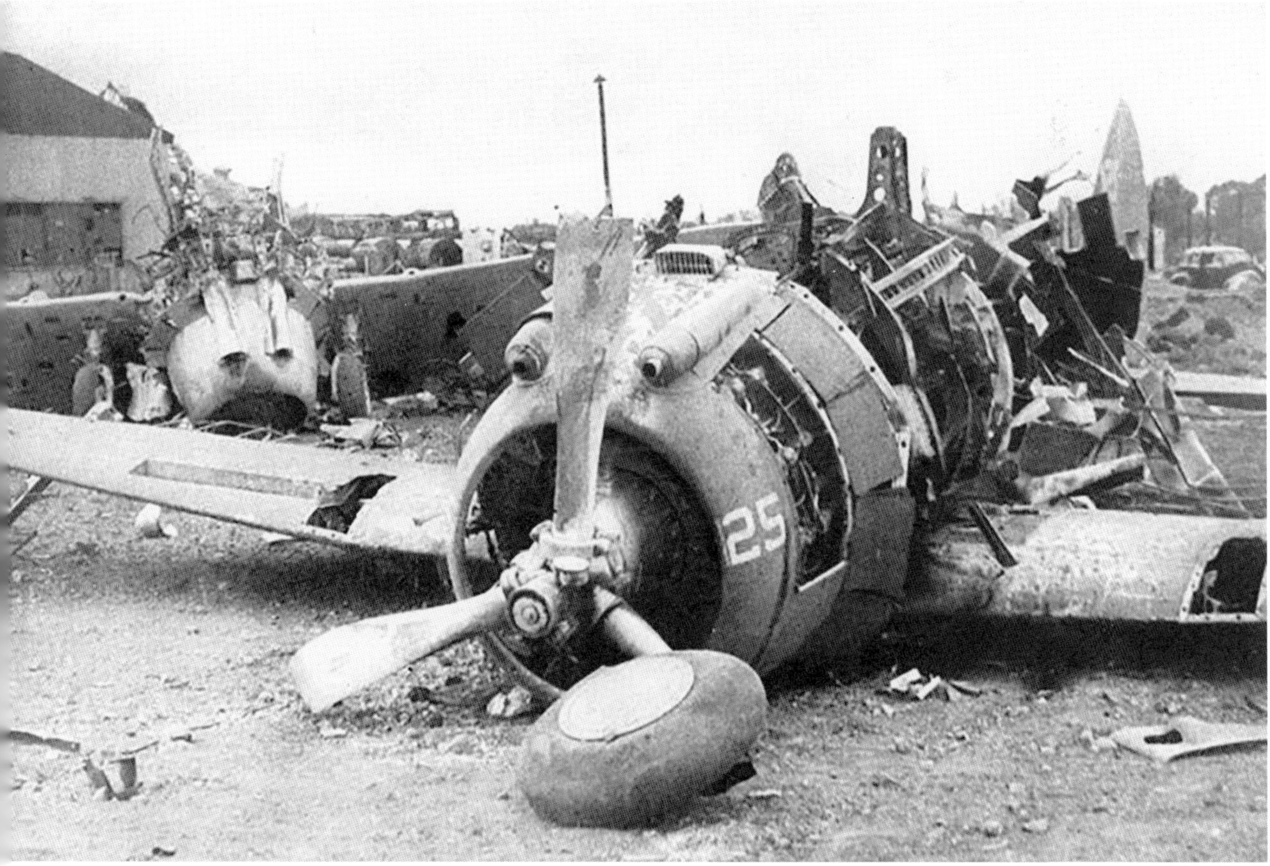
25

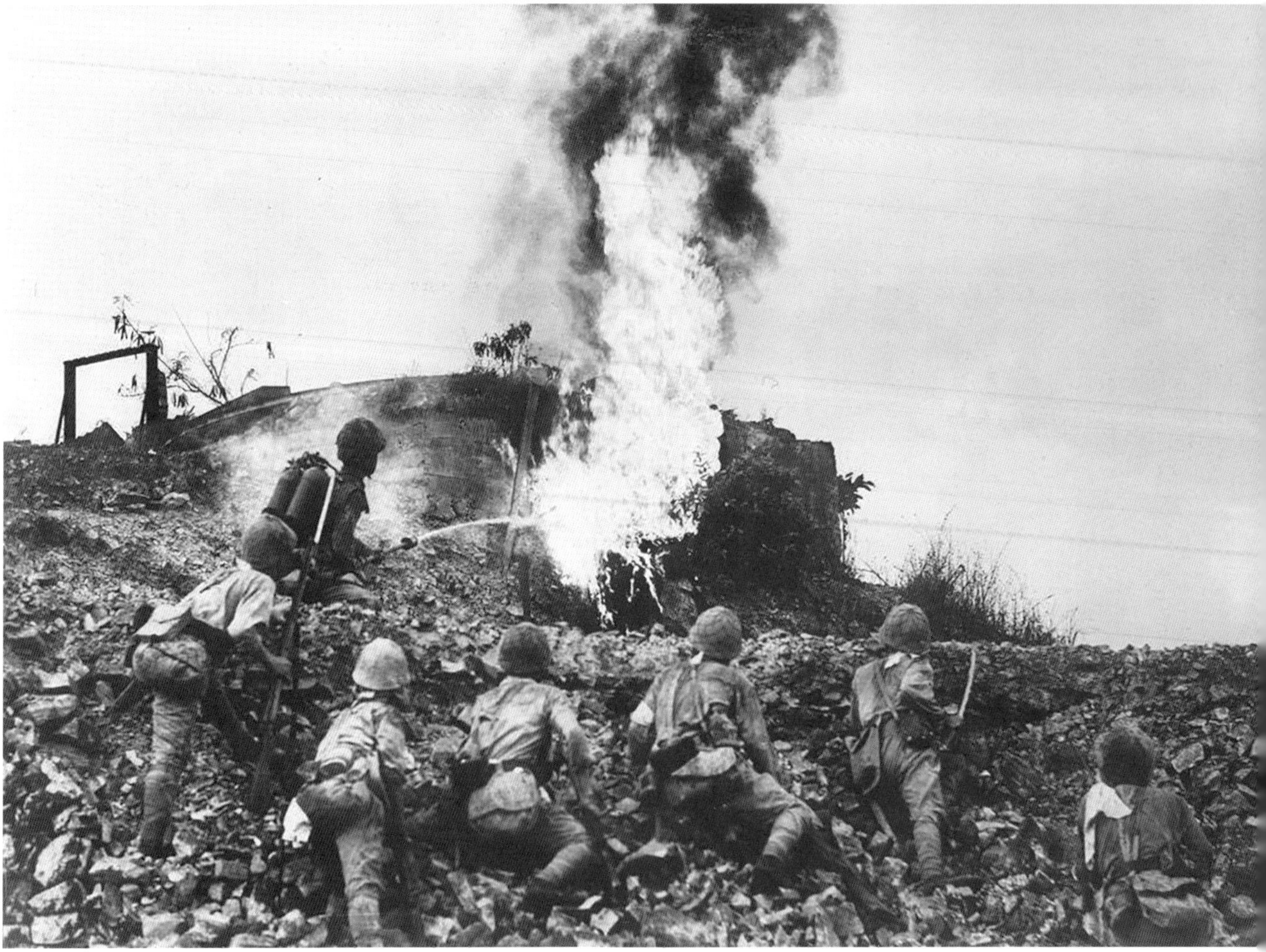

Japanese assault troops utilize a flame-thrower against an American pillbox on the Orion-Bagac Line in late January 1942. This Filipino-American defensive line formed a continuous position across Bataan, enabling physical contact between the Filipino-American North and South Luzon Forces defending the peninsula. *(Author's collection)*

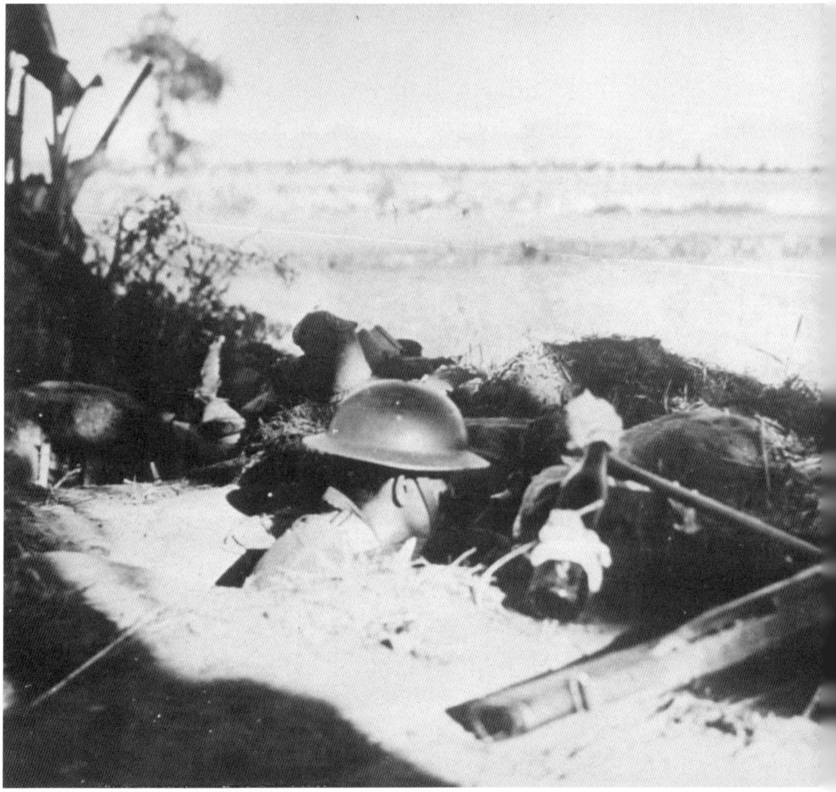

A US army soldier on Bataan holds a gasoline-filled glass bottle with a cloth wick ('Molotov Cocktail') to be used as a last-ditch AT weapon against Japanese tanks in early 1942. *(NARA)*

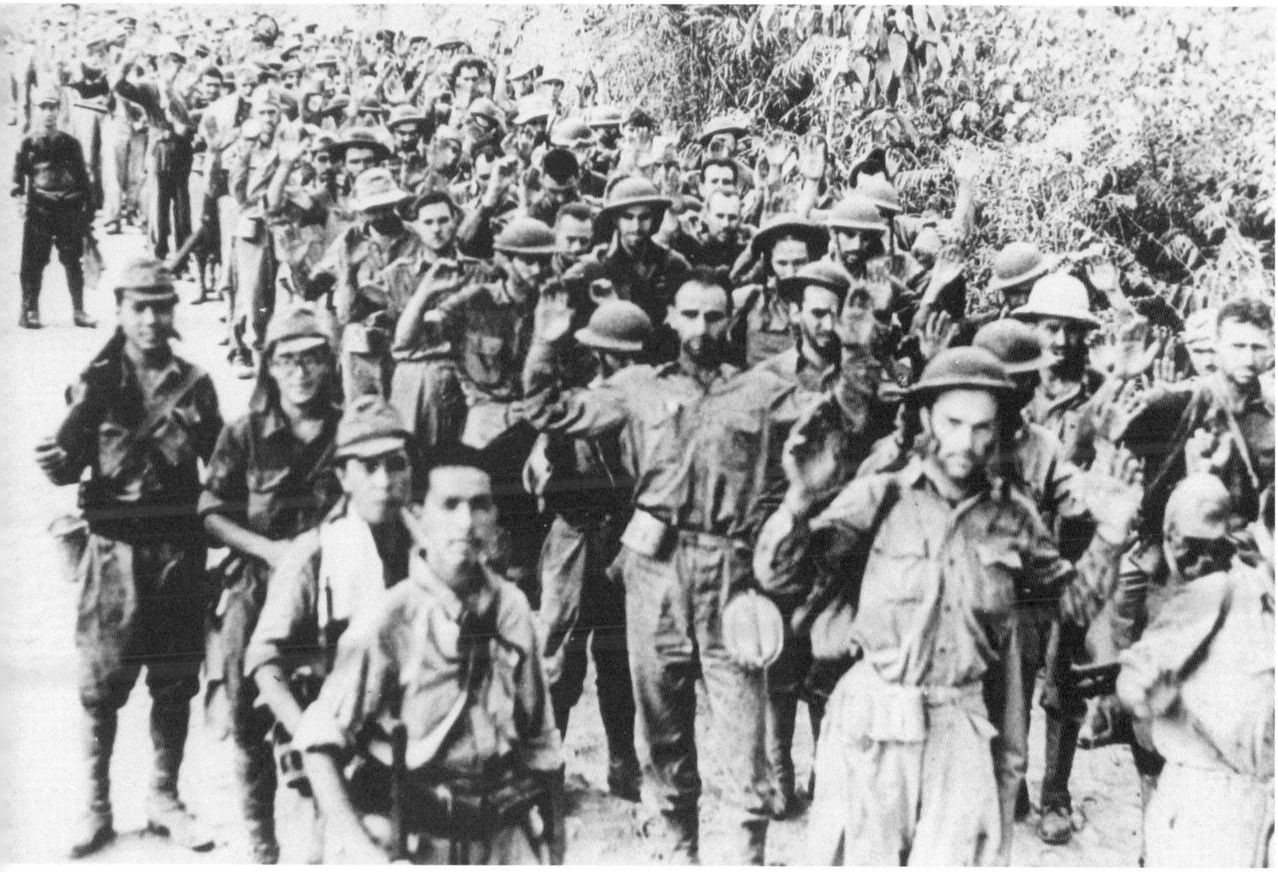

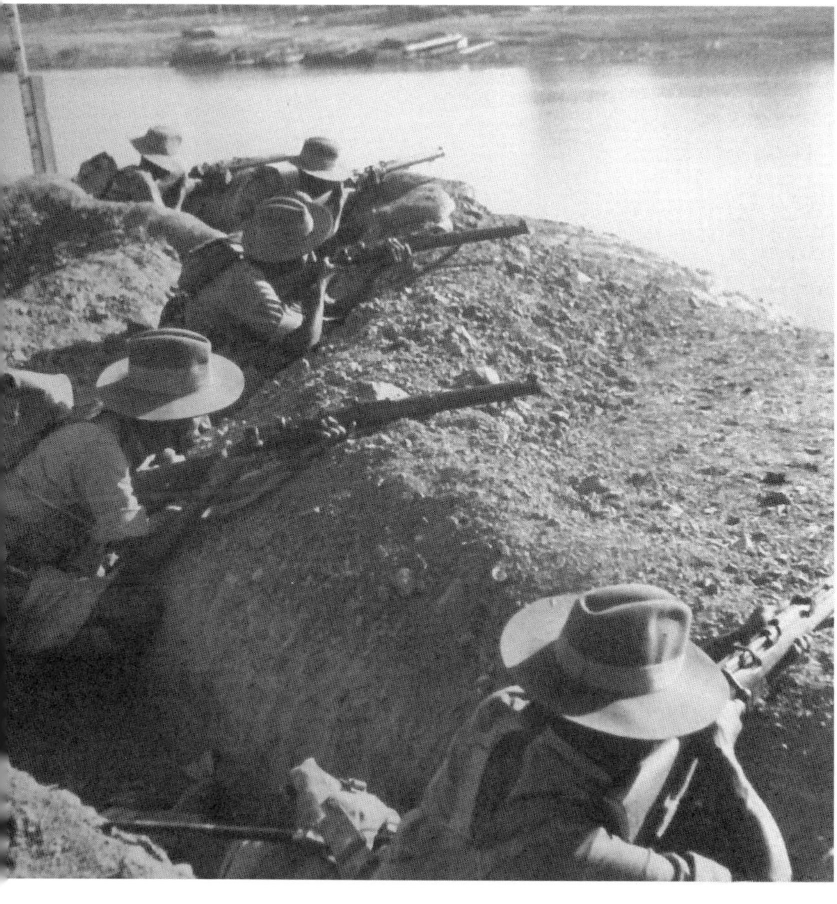

On 9 April 1942, about 12,000 Americans and 63,000 Filipinos became PoWs under the IJA 14th Army. Never anticipating this large number of Philippine army PoWs, the Japanese did not have food or shelter for such a volume of prisoners, many already half-starved and rife with disease. *(NARA)*

Indian troops in their defensive positions on the Sittang River await the Japanese assault. On the night of 22/23 February 1942, a controversial order was given, based on a miscommunication, to blow up the great bridge across the river, stranding large numbers of British and Indian troops still on the eastern side of the river. *(NARA)*

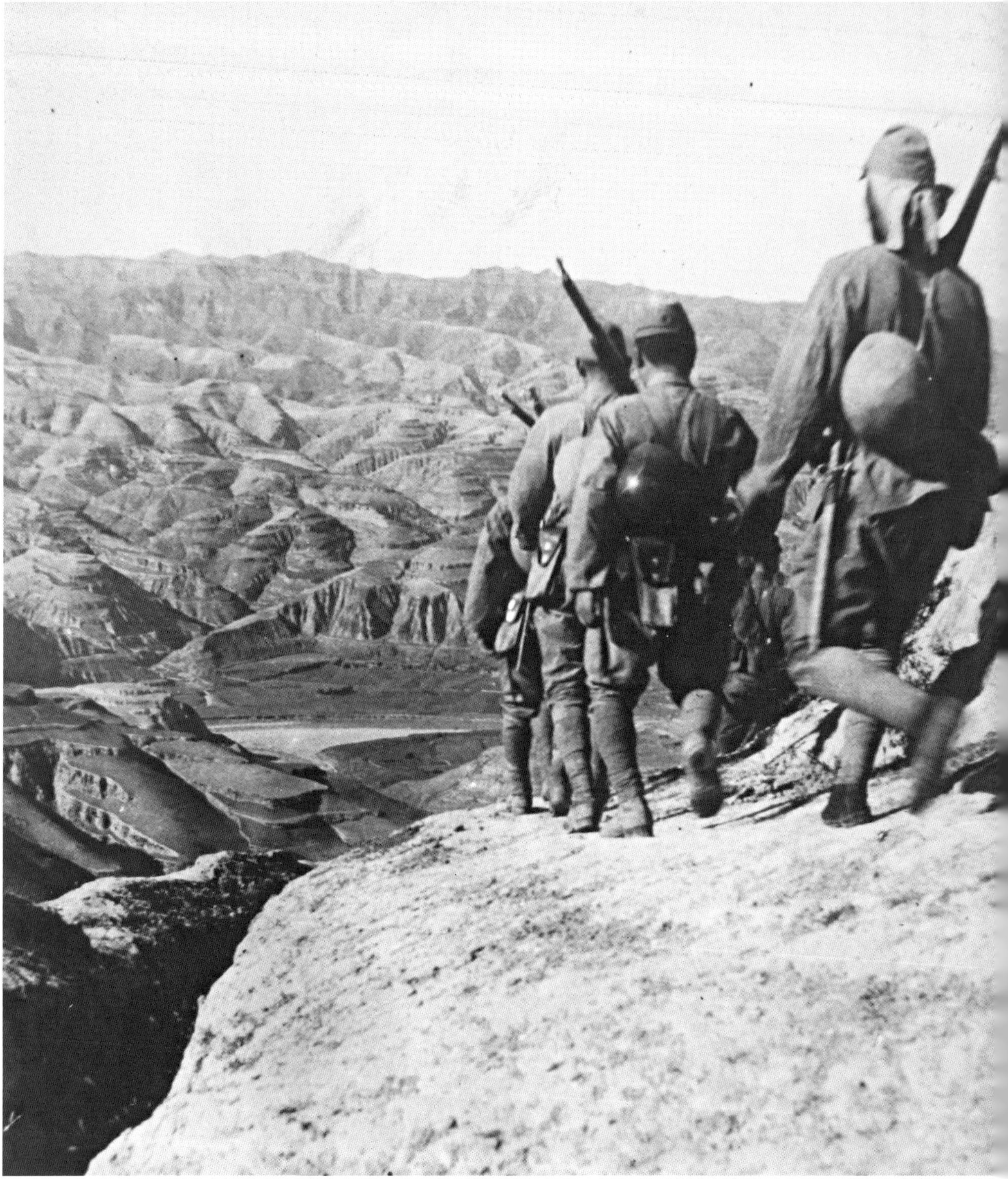

Japanese infantry patrolling through Burma's hills and valleys during the occupation in early 1942. Rather than invade eastern India, the Tokyo high command ordered garrisoning and patrolling amid the inhospitable terrain that precluded LOC for an offensive. *(NARA)*

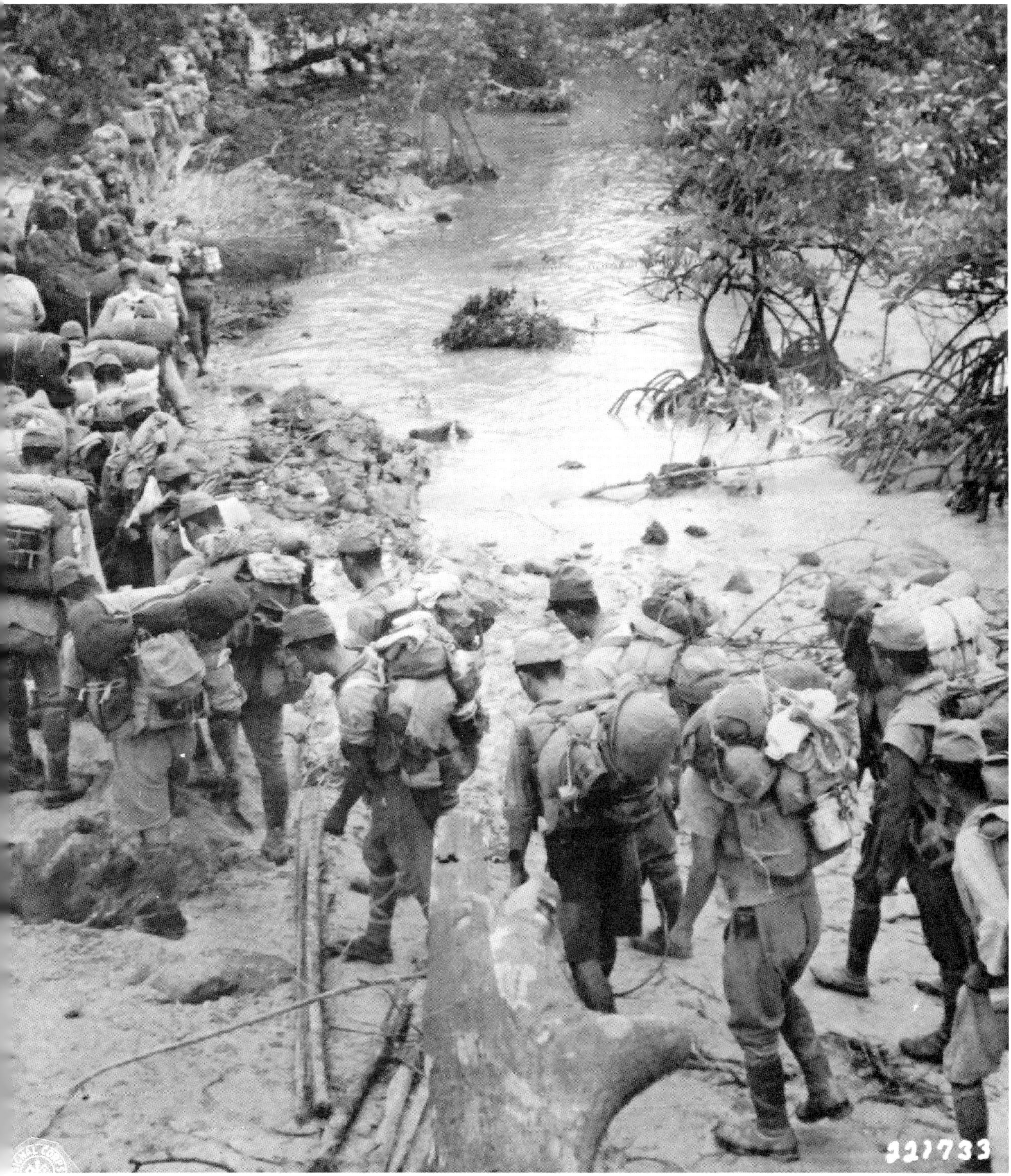

Japanese soldiers march along a Burmese *chaung* in 1942. During the dry season, these waterways were not obstacles but with the monsoon rains, the *chaungs* became raging torrents prohibiting mobility. (*NARA*)

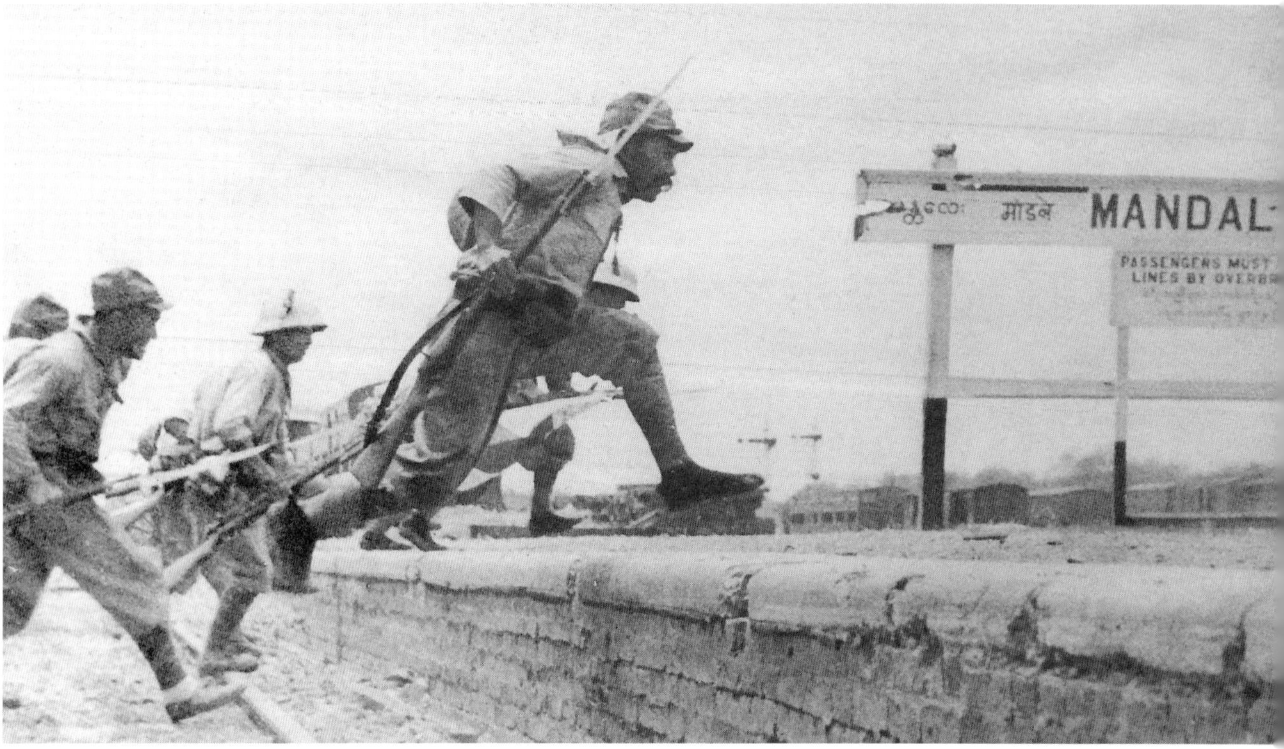
MANDAL
PASSENGERS MUST
LINES BY OVERBR

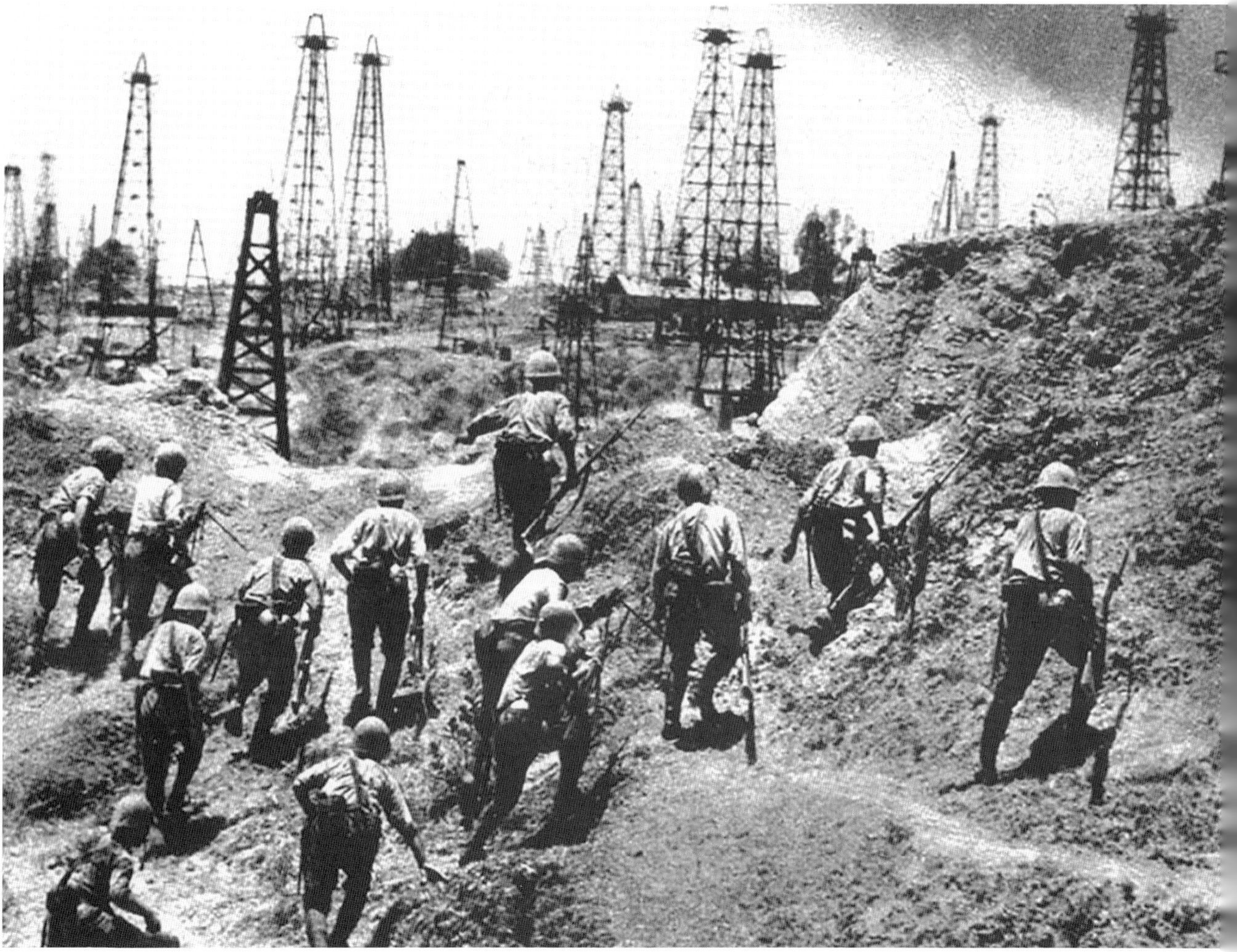

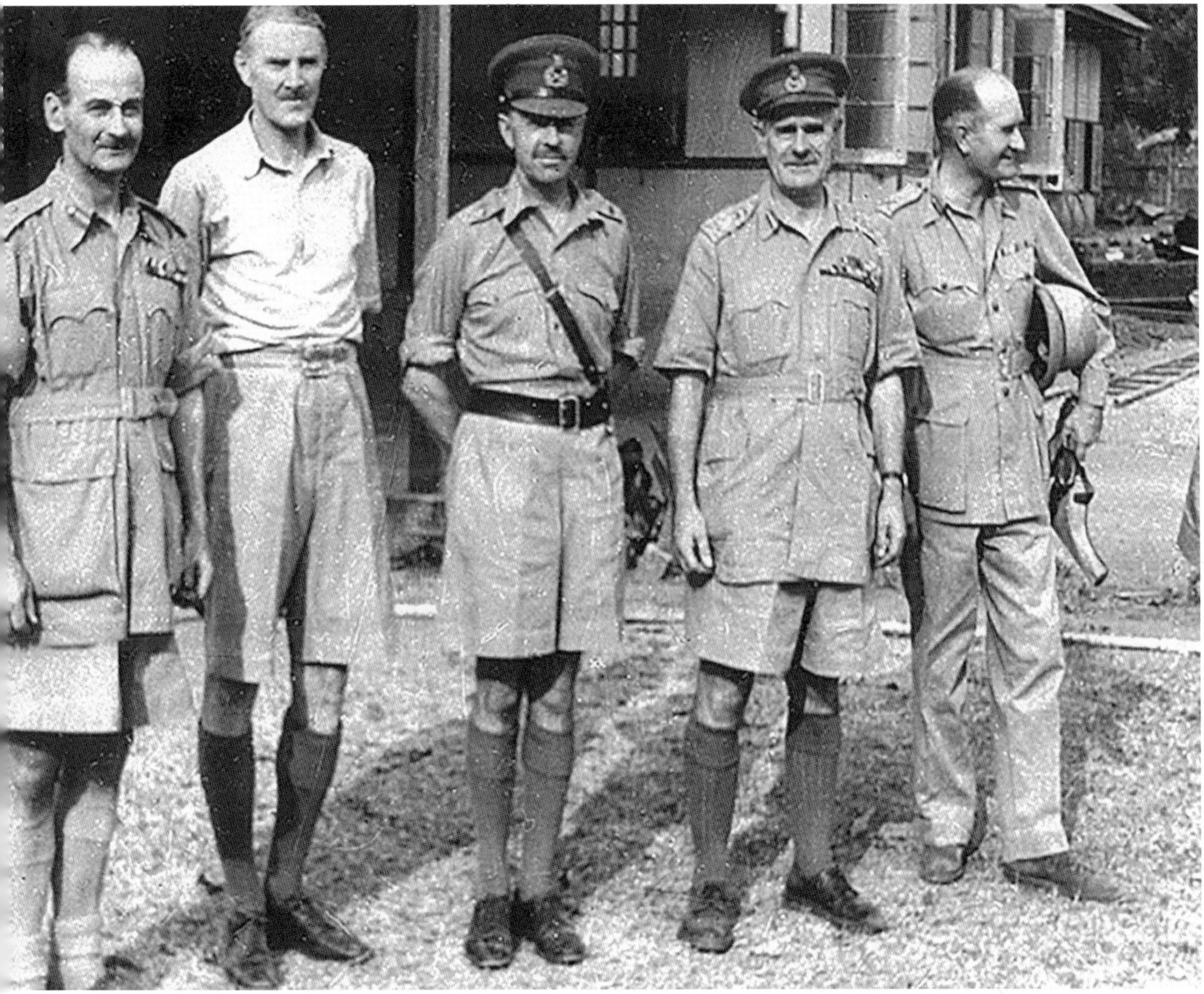

(**Opposite, above**) A Japanese officer leads an infantry detachment towards Mandalay, which was finally evacuated on 29 April 1942 after the central Burmese city was all but burned out. The IJA 18th Division advanced along Mandalay's main road and railway axis and then moved east to cut the Burma Road. *(Author's collection)*

(**Opposite, below**) Japanese infantry capture the Yenangyaung oilfields. The British had to destroy the oilfields there before they fell into Japanese hands while also continuing production until the last possible moment. At 0100 hrs on 15 April 1942, Lieutenant General William Slim, commanding Burcorps, gave the demolition signal with millions of gallons of oil becoming a vast conflagration. *(Author's collection)*

(**Above**) The principal British commanders in Burma and India are assembled in early 1942 before the rout. Lieutenant General Sir Harold Alexander (centre), noted for his unflappable leadership style, was to supervise Britain's longest retreat throughout Burma. Field Marshal Archibald Wavell, C-in-C India (right of Alexander) planned and secured Britain's first victory of the war against the Italians in Libya (Operation COMPASS) and in Ethiopia in 1940–41. He was sent to India in late 1941 with the losses of Greece and Crete. Lieutenant General William Slim of the Indian army (far right) led British, Indian and Gurkha forces out of Burma to eastern India in 1942 and rebuilt the multinational force into a fighting machine that would first hold off an IJA 15th Army attack at Imphal and Kohima in the spring of 1944 and then launch an offensive to recapture Burma from the Japanese. *(Author's collection)*

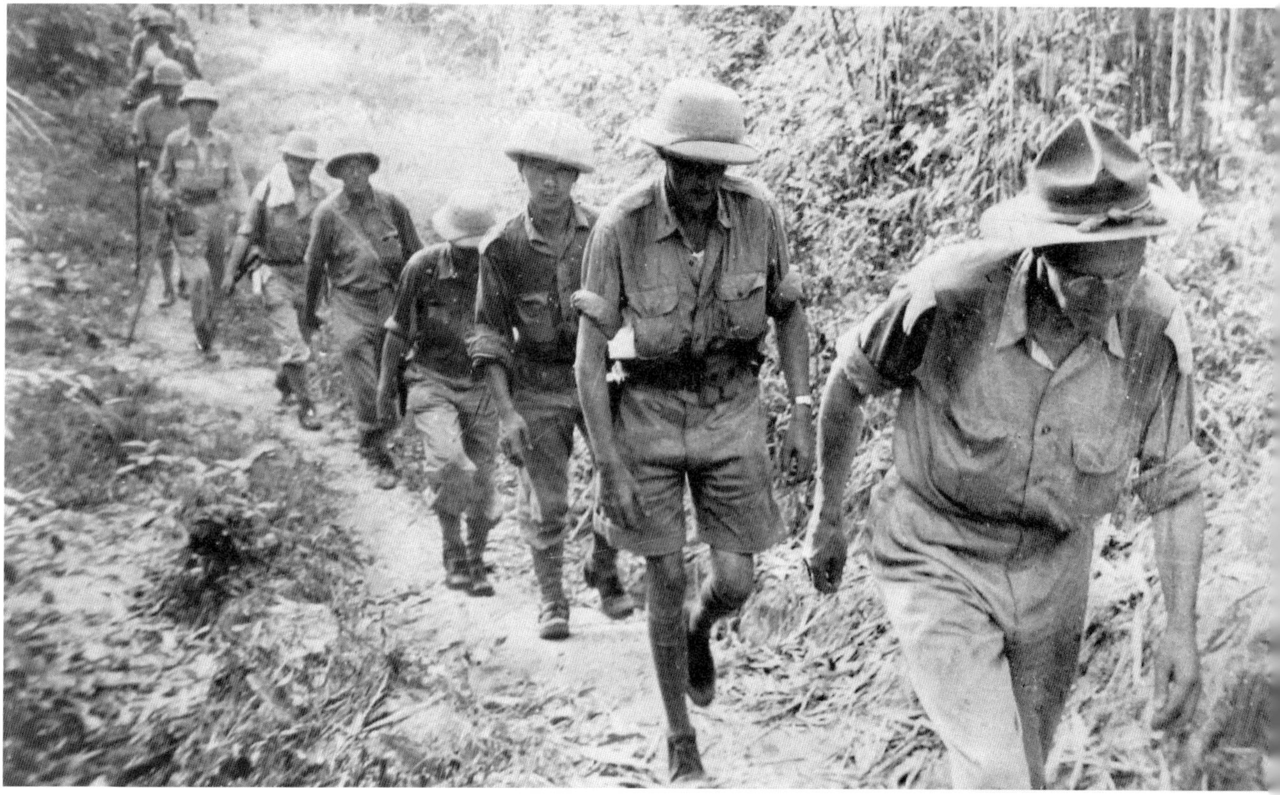

Lieutenant General Joseph W. Stilwell leads the 'Walkout' from Burma in the spring of 1942. After learning that the Japanese had outstripped his withdrawal towards Myitkyina, Stilwell and a party of 114 British, American and Burmese trekked overland and by waterways, crossing the Chindwin River in dugouts and ferries at Homalin, hours before a Japanese cavalry detachment arrived there. Stilwell extricated his entire party to India with march discipline. *(NARA)*

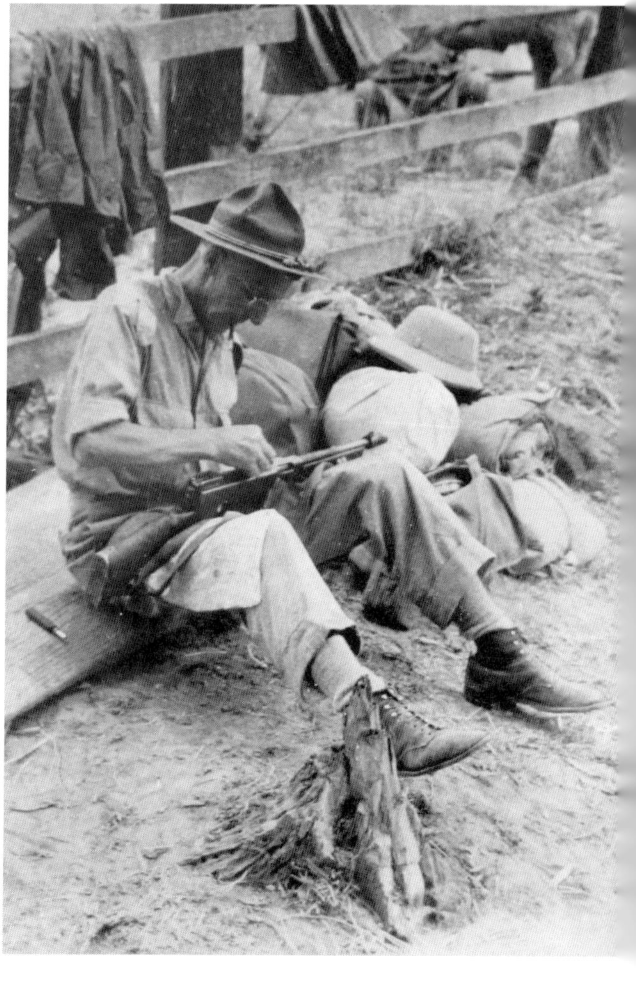

Foremost an infantryman, Stilwell cleans his 0.45in-calibre Thompson (SMG) near Homalin before crossing the Chindwin River to Assam, India. Stilwell, a West Point 1904 graduate, served in the Philippines during the Moro Insurrection, was a chief intelligence officer for General John Pershing's St. Mihiel offensive during the First World War, was the army's initial Intelligence Division's Chinese language officer in Peking, and an informal engineering adviser to China during the 1920s. In 1924 he commanded a battalion of the 15th Infantry Regiment in Tientsin, China during one of his two Chinese tours of duty. At Tientsin in 1924, he initially met his mentor, George C. Marshall, the future US army chief of staff, and in the 1930s served with him at Fort Benning's Infantry School. *(NARA)*

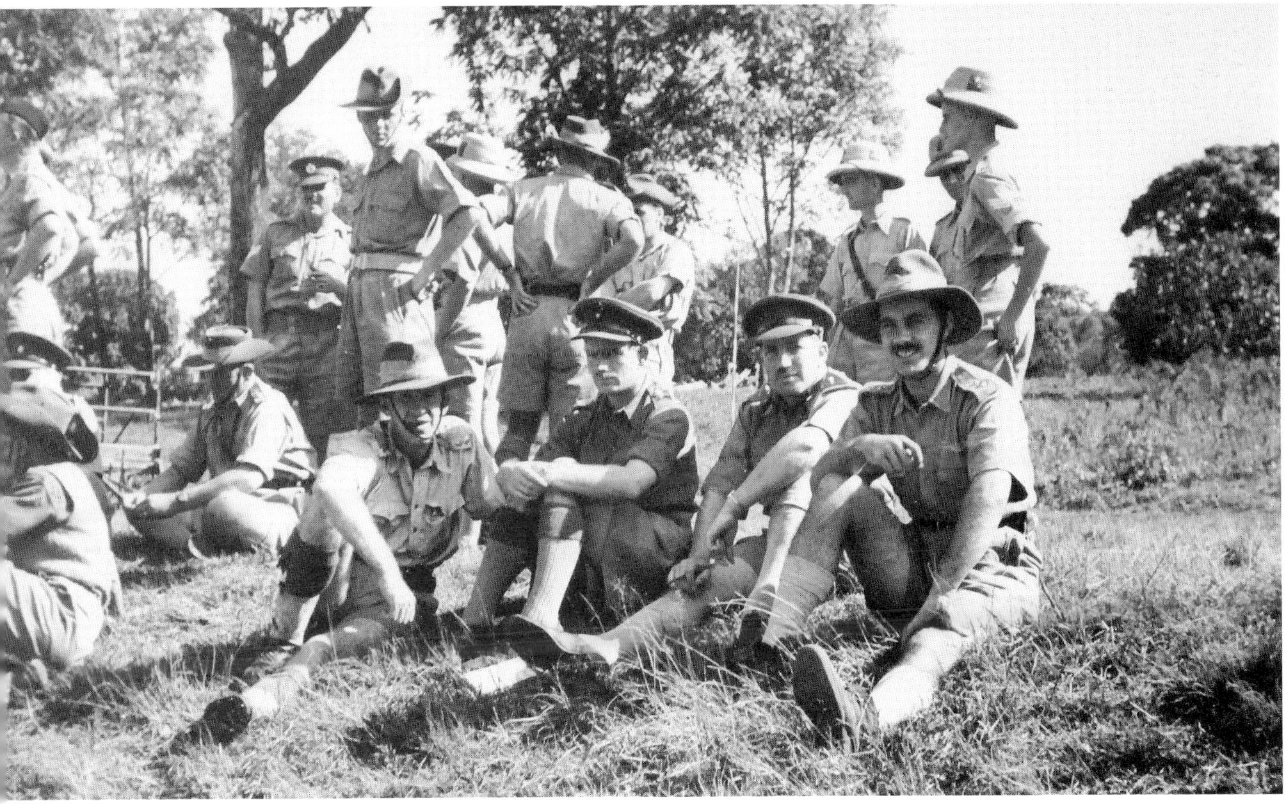

Major Michael Calvert (second from right) seated at the Bush Warfare School in Maymyo, Burma, early 1942. Calvert went from Australia to Burma in late 1941 to be chief instructor and then commandant of the Commando training school at Maymyo, with the task of raising the efficiency of the Chinese guerrillas fighting the Japanese in demolition and sabotage methods. Orde Wingate first met Calvert there, but with the rapid Japanese advance across Burma, Wingate's attempt to foment a British-led Burmese guerrilla-style insurrection against the Japanese was futile. *(USAMHI)*

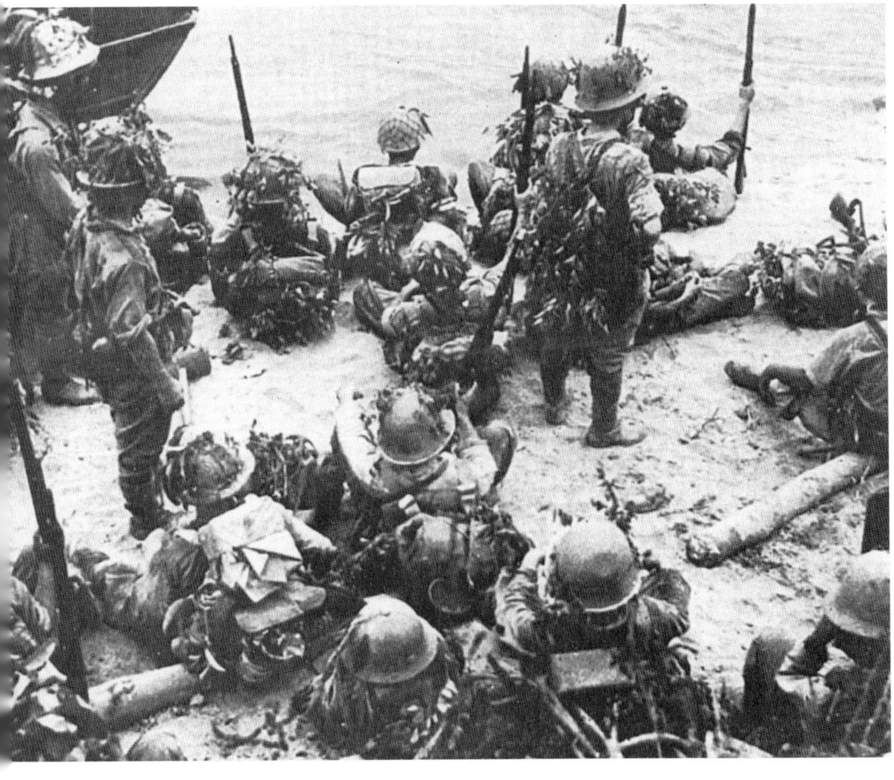

A Japanese platoon rests along the sand on the Burmese side of the Chindwin River during the spring of 1942 after having driven the Allies out of Burma. This was to become the IJA's furthest point west during the blitzkrieg throughout the Pacific and Asia. *(Author's collection)*

Major General Claire Chennault is shown here. Captain Chennault, then a retired US Army Air Corps officer, served as Chiang Kai-shek's military adviser, forming the American Volunteer Group (AVG) of 300 fighter pilots and ground crew to combat Japanese planes over the skies of China and Burma. By November 1941, an AVG squadron (Flying Tigers) of thirty Curtis P-40B Tomahawks aided the British at Toungoo in Burma, while two other squadrons stayed at Kunming, China. From 23 to 29 January 1942, the Japanese lost fifty planes over Rangoon to the AVG and RAF planes. By late February, the few surviving P-40 Flying Tiger aircraft were withdrawn from southern Burma. Chennault was reinstated into the USAAF and later became head of the US Fourteenth Air Force. His relationship with Stilwell was bitter due to strategic differences of opinion as to how to utilize American air power and Chennault's close alliance with Chiang Kai-shek. *(NARA)*

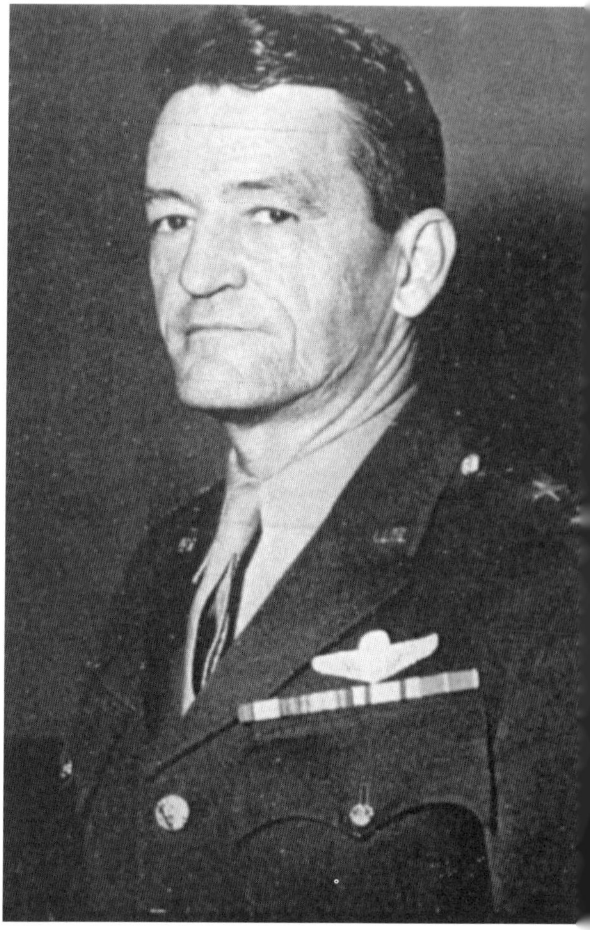

A Curtis P-40B Tomahawk single-seat fighter (nicknamed Flying Tiger because of its shark's teeth painted on the fuselage's front) lands at an airfield in Kunming, China in early 1942. Armed with four MGs, the P-40B had a maximum speed of 350 mph and an altitude of 32,000ft. The plane could climb to 15,000ft in just over five minutes. *(NARA)*

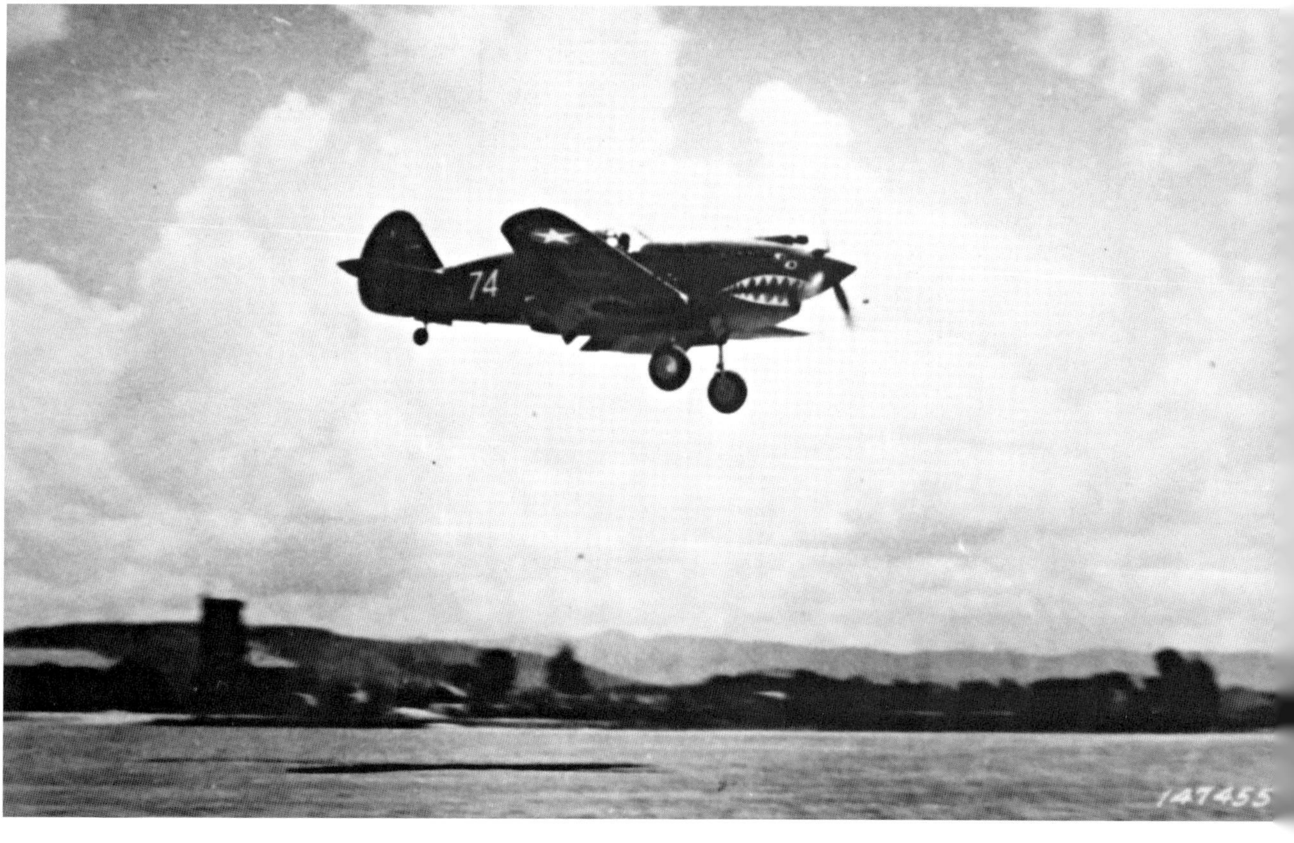
74
147455

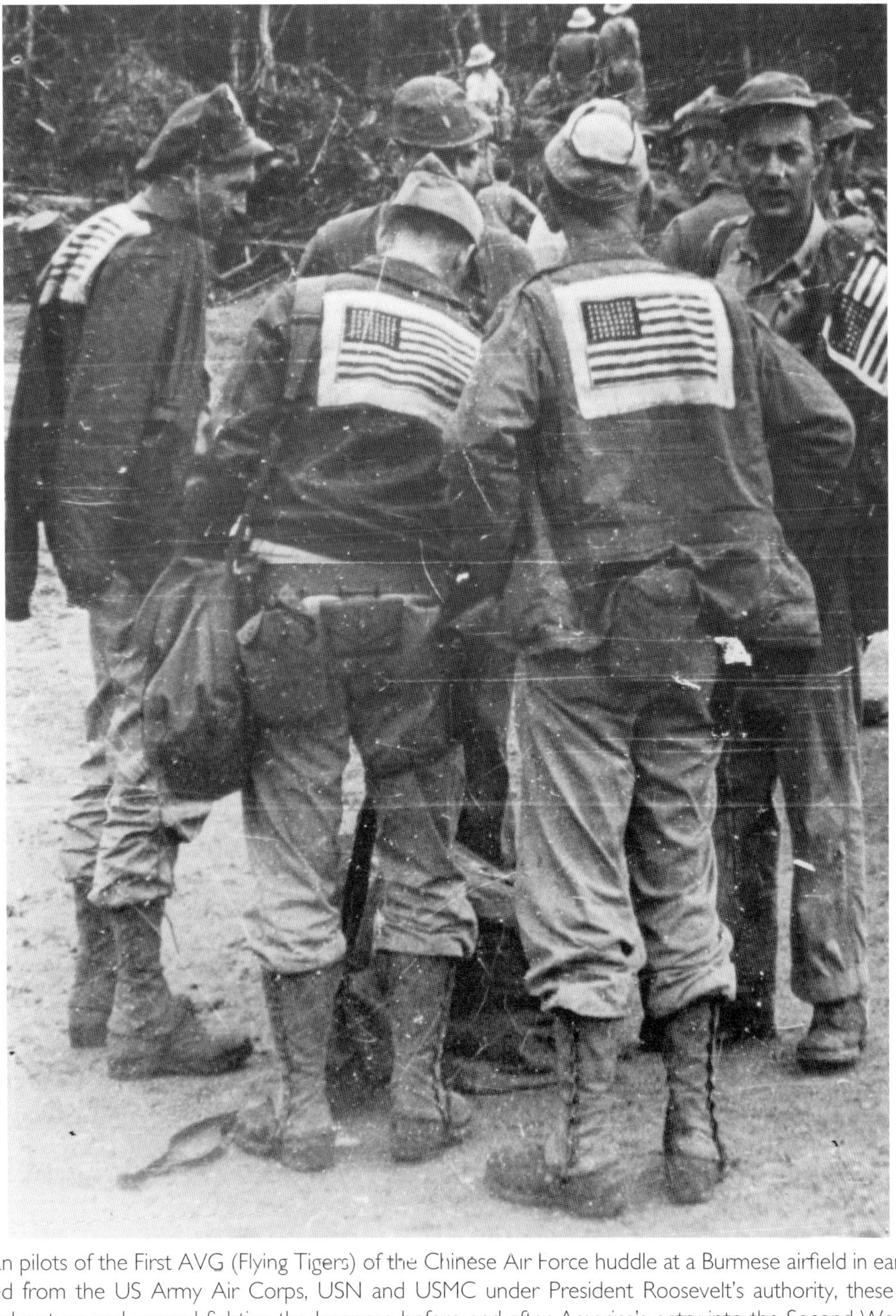

American pilots of the First AVG (Flying Tigers) of the Chinese Air Force huddle at a Burmese airfield in early 1942. Recruited from the US Army Air Corps, USN and USMC under President Roosevelt's authority, these aviators sought adventure and reward fighting the Japanese before and after America's entry into the Second World War. Led by Brigadier General Claire Chennault and flying Curtis P-40B Tomahawks with Chinese insignia, the Flying Tigers arrived in China in April 1941. On 4 July 1942, the AVG was redesignated as the USAAF's 23rd Fighter Group to be absorbed into the US Fourteenth Air Force. *(NARA)*

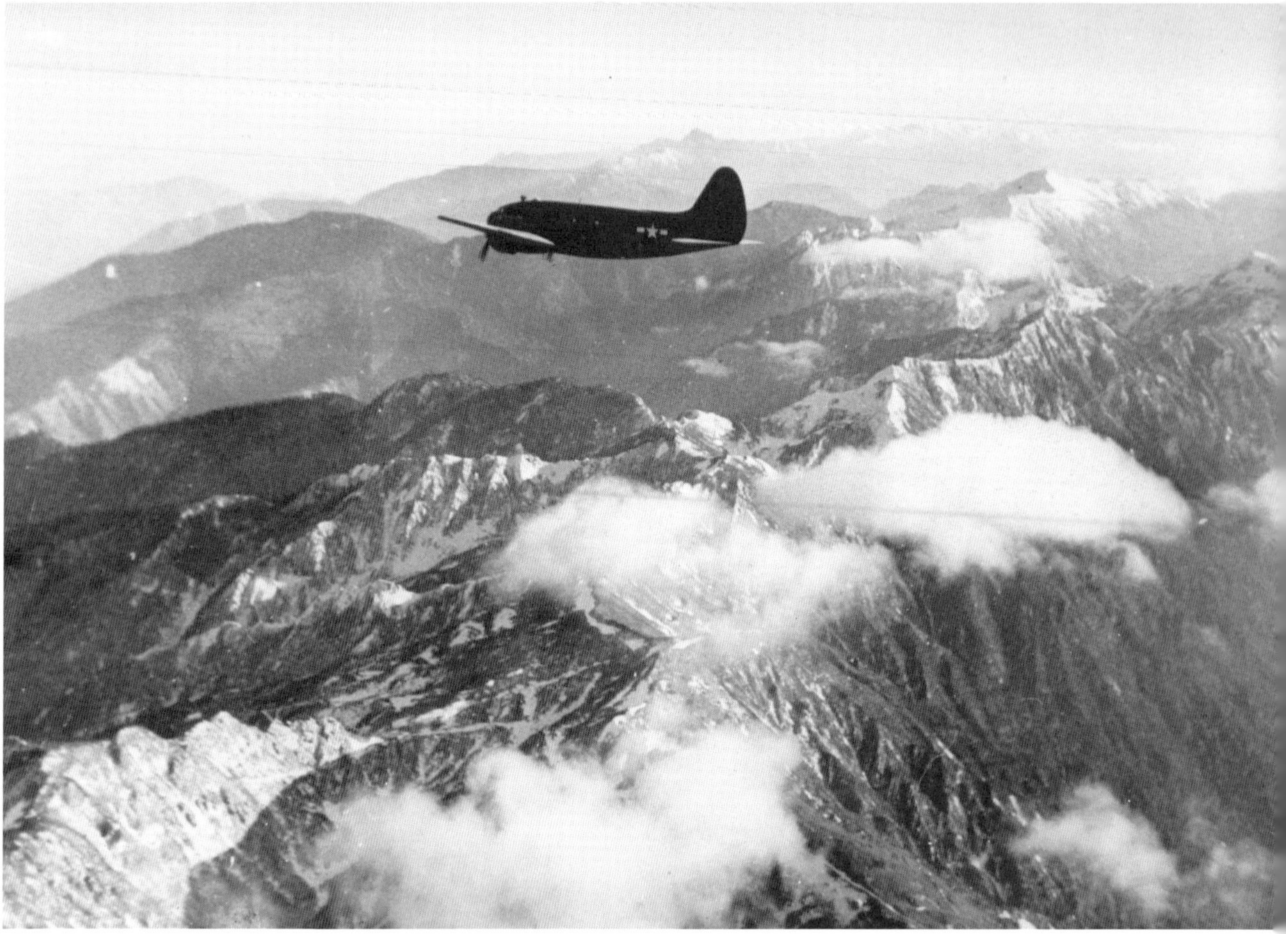

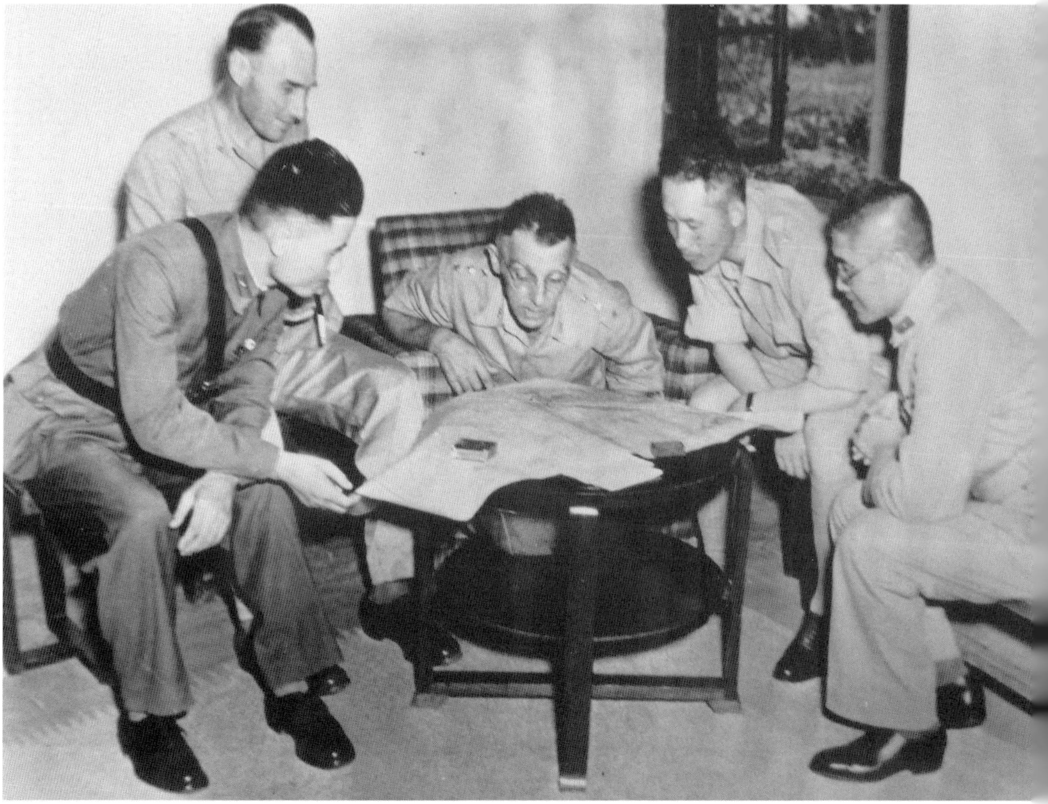

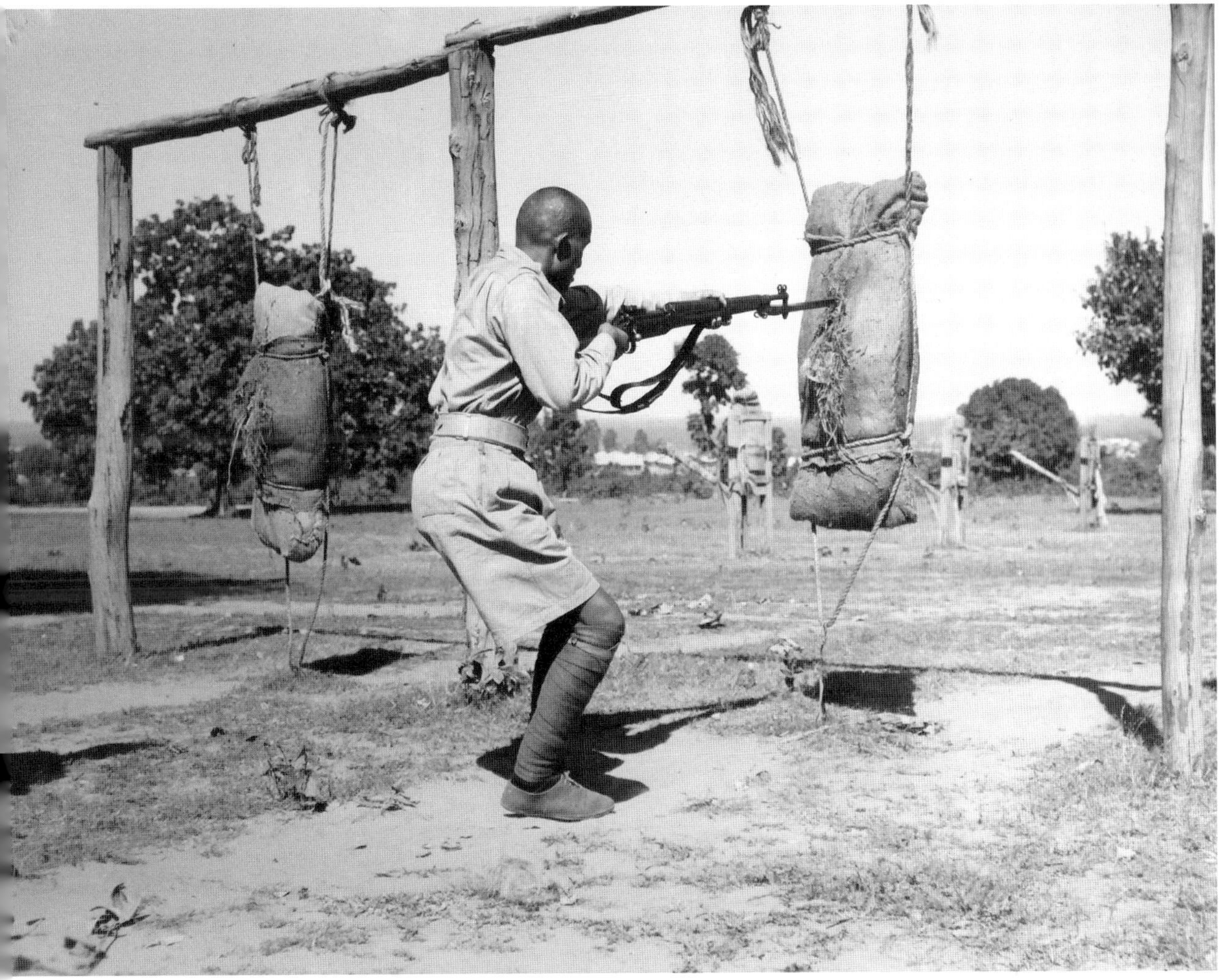

(**Opposite, above**) A C-47 Dakota aircraft of the ATC flies the treacherous 'Hump' run over the snow-capped Himalayan Mountains from the air depots of Assam to Yunnan in south-western China. IJA fighters stationed at Myitkyina were not able to completely interdict the route as the C-47s flew a more treacherous northerly route. *(NARA)*

(**Opposite, below**) Lieutenant General Stilwell, CBI theatre CG meets with subordinate officers in Ramgarh, India. From left to right are General Yan, COS of the Chinese Expeditionary Force; Major General Franklin Sibert, CG Stilwell's Branch Office in India; Lieutenant General Sun Li-Jen, the Chinese 38th Division commander that was to bear the brunt of the fighting in the Hukawng Valley during the 1943–44 northern Burma offensive; and Major General Liao Yao-hsiang, the Chinese 22nd Division commander. Liao's 22nd Division followed up on the 38th Division's success in the Hukawng Valley by capturing Taro. Both Sun and Liao had their divisions trained at Ramgarh after their escape from Burma in 1942. *(NARA)*

(**Above**) A Chinese infantryman at Stilwell's Ramgarh, India training facility for his CAI, a major striking arm of his NCAC, practises bayoneting with a long sword bayonet fitted to his Enfield P-17 rifle. Initially the remnants of the Chinese 38th and 22nd divisions that fought in Burma in 1942 were brought to Ramgarh for reinforcement, refitting, rearming and training. *(USAMHI)*

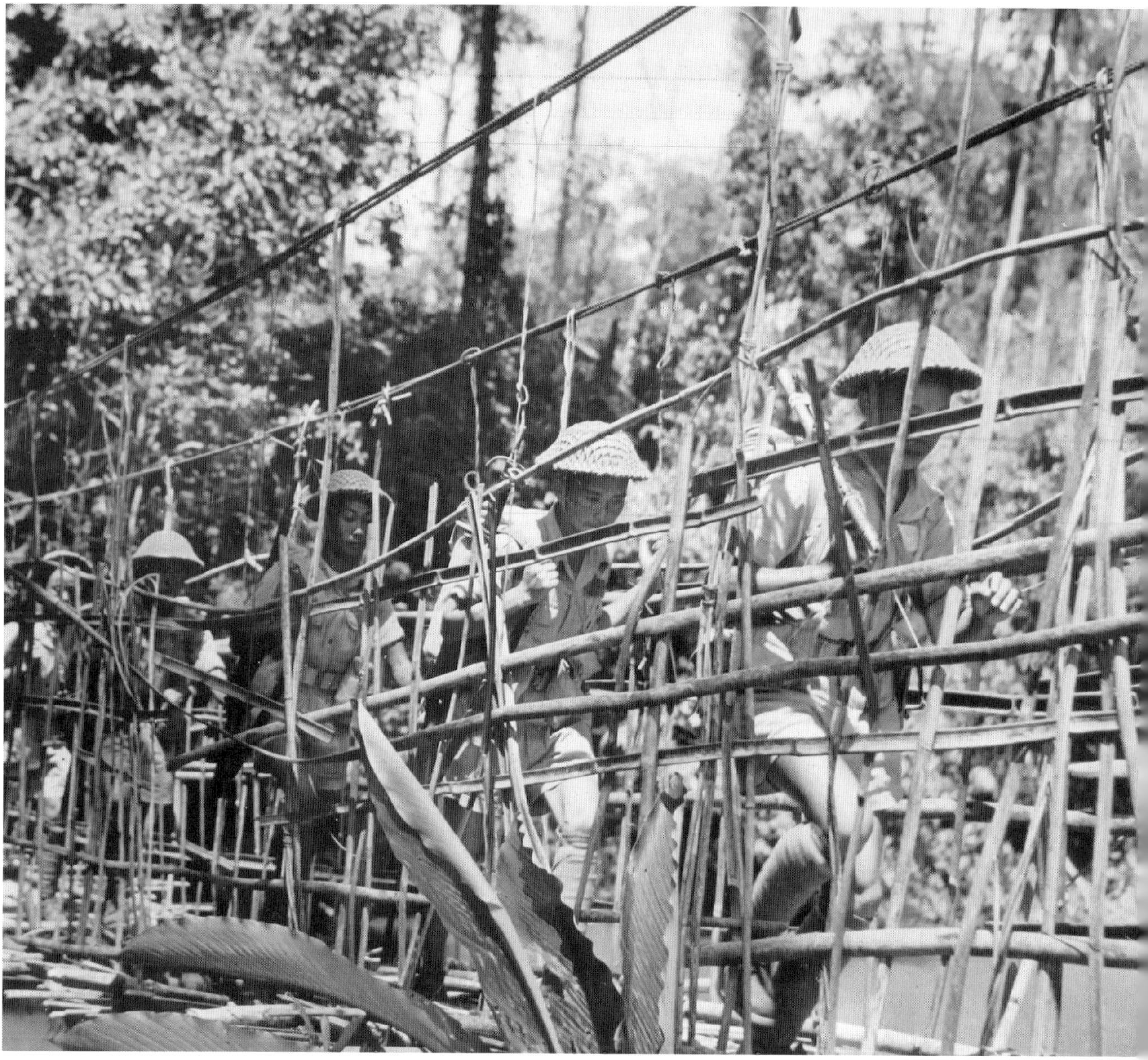

(**Above**) Chinese troops cross a bamboo suspension bridge in the Naga Hills, situated between Ledo and Kohima, on the trek to IJA 18th Division fortified positions along the Tarung River at the northern end of the Hukawng Valley. These bridges were constructed quickly with local materials by accompanying engineers. *(NARA)*

(**Opposite, above**) A Chinese M3 Stuart light tank of the 3rd Company 1st Provisional TB moves up a road after having been in contact with Japanese artillery and mortar fire throughout the previous night near Walawbum on 4 March 1944. Its main armament was a 37mm gun and it had two 7.7mm machine guns with thicker armour than its Japanese counterparts. *(NARA)*

(**Opposite, below**) A destroyed IJA Type 95 *Ke-Go* light tank is seen here from the rear with a Burmese pagoda (background). The thinly-armoured *Ke-Go* had a crew of four. There was one 37mm gun and two 7.7mm machine guns, one forward and one aft. The *Ke-Go*'s commander had to operate the gun in addition to his normal duties, impeding its combat effectiveness. *(USAMHI)*

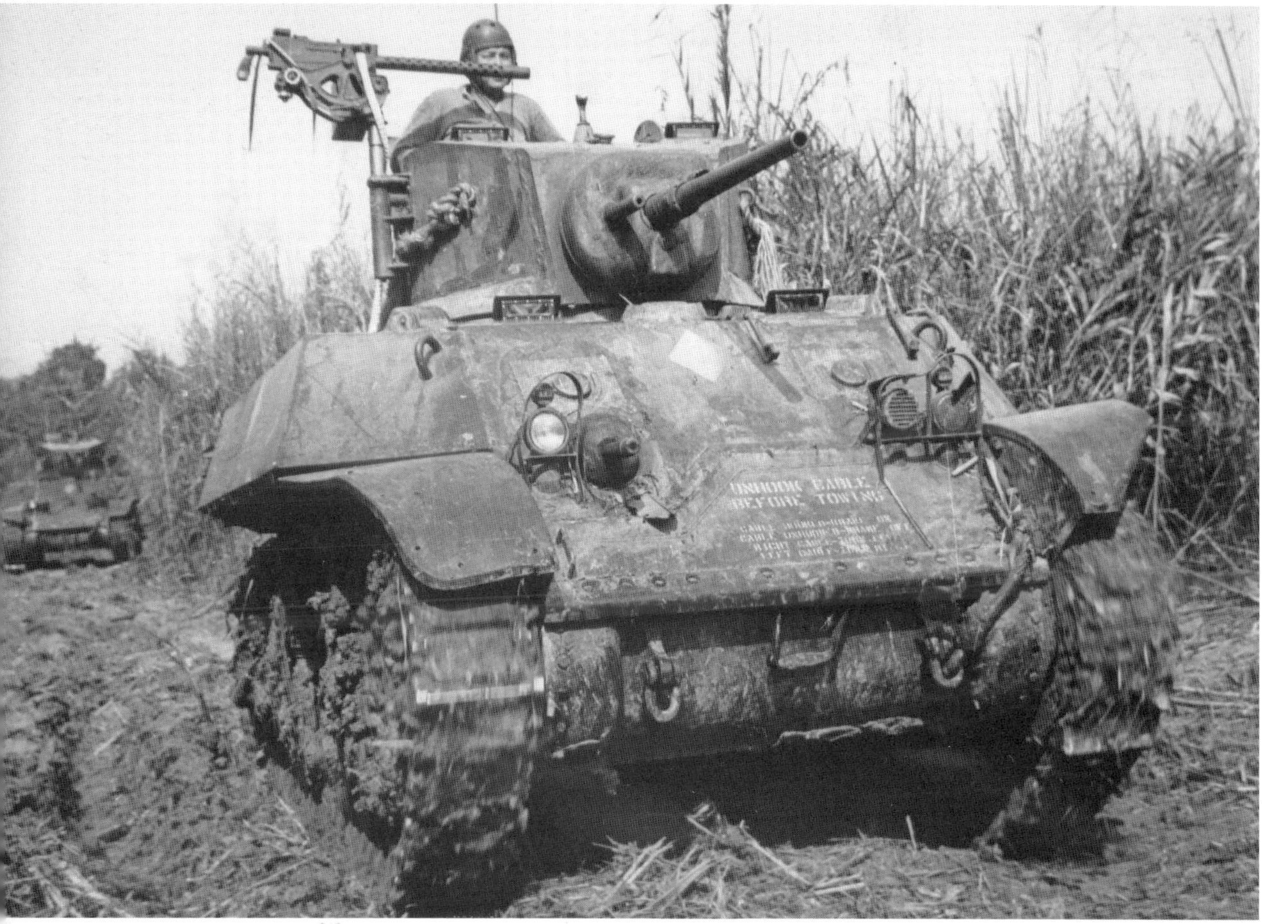
UNHOOK CABLE
BEFORE TOWING

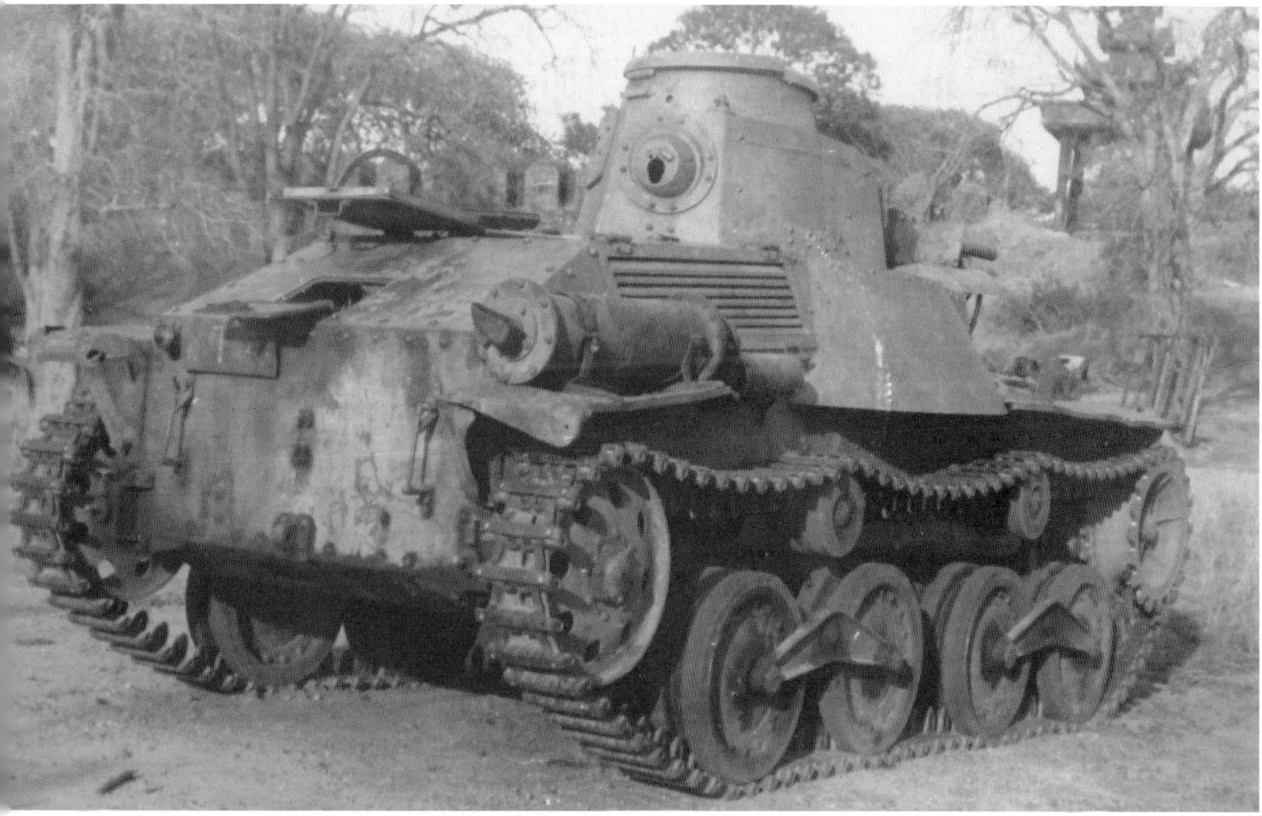

Lieutenant General William Slim inspects 70th British Division troops at Ranchi, India in 1942. Slim was a second lieutenant in the Royal Warwickshire Regiment and was seriously wounded at Gallipoli in August 1915. In the autumn of 1916, he was a captain in the West India Regiment sent to Mesopotamia. Wounded again and awarded an MC, he was sent to the Indian Army HQ as a staff officer. Between the wars, he served as battalion adjutant for the 6th Gurkha Rifles, learning Gurkhali and Urdu. In 1939, he fought the Italians in Abyssinia while commanding the 10th Brigade and then went to Iraq and Syria as an acting major general in command of the 10th Indian Division. When Alexander arrived in Burma in February 1942 to command all Allied forces, he appointed Slim to command Burma Corps (Burcorps) in March 1942. During the Burma retreat, Slim kept his units intact fighting rearguard operations. In the summer of 1942, Slim commanded XV Corps comprising the 14th and 26th Indian divisions. The

14th Division defended the India-Burma border while the 26th Division provided internal security in India as rebellion was fomenting. General N.M.S. Irwin, CG Eastern Army, took Slim's two Indian divisions and gave the future XIV Army CG the 70th British Division and 50th Armoured Brigade at Ranchi. There, Slim commenced intensive jungle training for these formations for future offensive operations in Burma. In March 1943, when Wavell's First Arakan Campaign under Irwin's leadership stalled, Slim was concerned about the low state of morale in the Arakan and he realized that the Japanese infantryman was far better-trained and exhibited more elan than his British or Indian Army counterparts. In October 1943, Slim was appointed Acting GOC, Eastern Army after Irwin was sacked for the dismal outcome of the First Arakan Campaign. (*Author's collection*)

(**Above**) Field Marshal Archibald P. Wavell greets men of the 20th Indian Division in India in 1942. He graduated from Sandhurst in 1900. In September 1914 Wavell commanded a section of the Directorate of Military Operations, but was soon appointed brigade major in the 9th Infantry Brigade in France. In June 1915, Wavell was wounded at the Second Battle of Ypres with a splinter from a German shell destroying his left eye. After some other postings in Scotland and France, Wavell was appointed personal liaison officer with his mentor General Edmund Allenby, C-in-C of the Egyptian Expeditionary Force. Wavell entered Jerusalem in December 1917 and advanced to Damascus with Allenby. In 1939, he became C-in-C Middle East after having served as GOC Palestine in 1937, where he quelled the Arab Revolt with the help of a young major, Orde Wingate. Wavell and Lieutenant General Richard O'Connor (CG Western Desert Force) launched Operation COMPASS in December 1940, smashing the Italian Tenth Army in Cyrenaica from December 1940 to early February 1941. The losses of Greece and Crete, despite defeating the Italians in Ethiopia and Somaliland, ended Wavell's Middle East tenure and he was sent to India as C-in-C in 1941. After the humiliating defeats of British and Commonwealth forces in Asia and the Pacific, some believed that Wavell grossly underestimated the fighting quality of the Japanese soldier even after the loss of Malaya and the massive capitulation of British and Commonwealth forces at Singapore on 15 February 1942. Thus, Wavell realized that extensive retraining of his Indian army formations was necessary. He tried to defeat the Japanese in an area where there was a reasonable chance of success, so he launched the First Arakan Campaign in the winter of 1942–43 after troop-training in India for amphibious operations. (*Author's collection*)

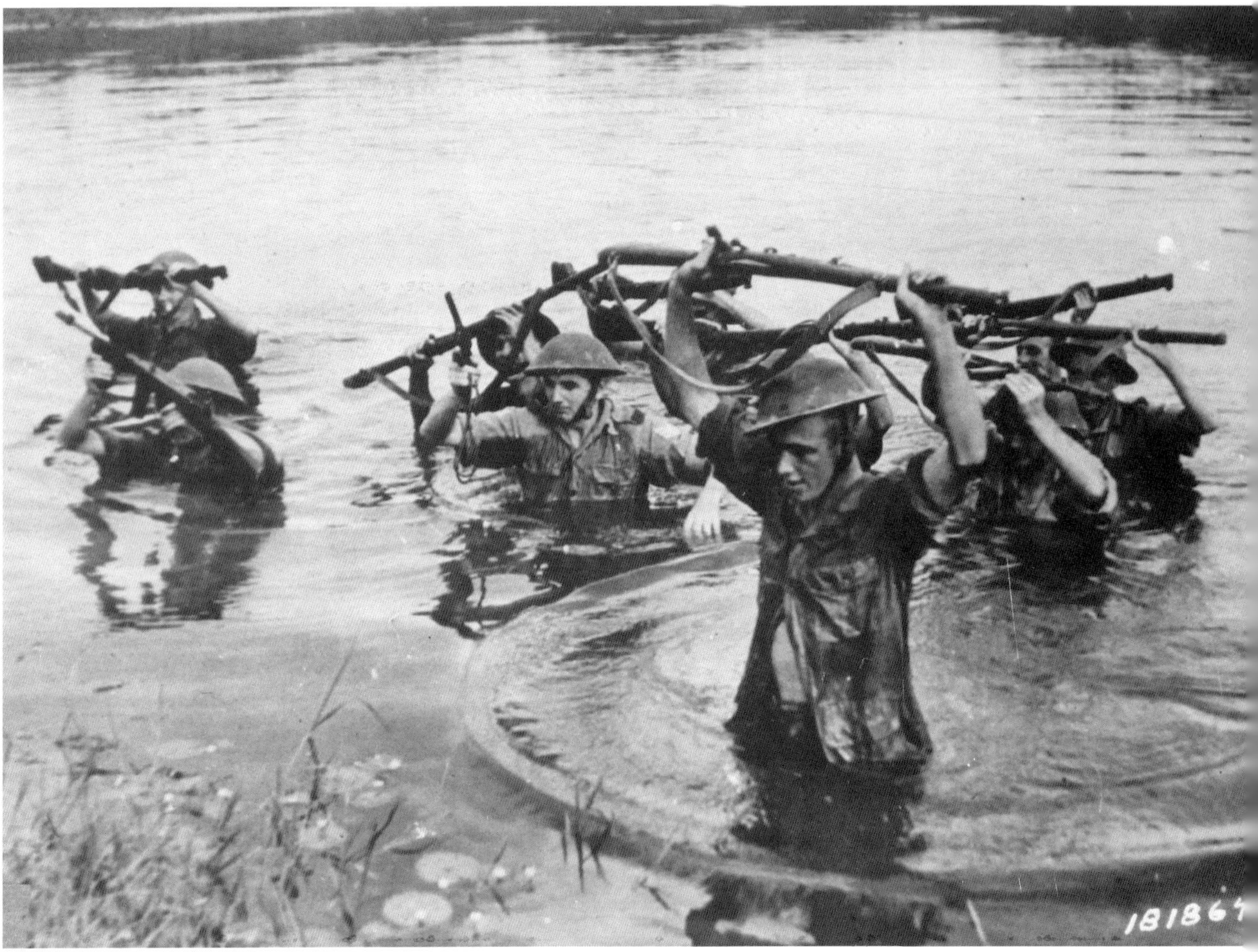
181867

(**Above**) A British infantry patrol emerges from chest-high water after crossing a *chaung* in the First Arakan Campaign in late 1942–43. In September 1942, Wavell ordered Lieutenant General N.M.S. Irwin, GOC Eastern Army, to capture Akyab Island with its airfields and reoccupy the upper Arakan. The 14th Indian Division advanced to Cox's Bazar from Chittagong on the Bay of Bengal and then halted to establish supply depots there. It was not until December that the 14th Indian Division continued its advance down the Mayu Peninsula, a narrow strip of flat land laced with dozens of swamps, tidal creeks, jungle-covered hills and *chaungs*, which ends at 'Foul Point', a less than 10-mile stretch of water that had to be crossed in order to reach Akyab Island. The 14th Indian Division's movement was slow, with sappers building many bridges over the *chaungs* which were vulnerable to Japanese air attack. *(NARA)*

(**Opposite**) A British sergeant leading a 6th British Infantry Brigade patrol is seen here at the edge of a mangrove swamp during the First Arakan Campaign in early 1943. On 25 March, the IJA 55th Division launched an offensive against the 14th Indian Division, causing a change in divisional command. On the night of 5 April, the IJA 55th Division broke into the 14th Indian Division's forward area and overran the HQ of the 6th British Infantry Brigade, resulting in the death of that unit's commander, Brigadier Cavendish. Slim sent elements of his XV Corps' tank brigade to support the British attack on Donbaik near the Bay of Bengal coast. Unfortunately the tanks were Valentine infantry tanks that mounted 2-pounder main turret guns which were ineffective against Japanese bunkers. On 14 April, Lieutenant General Irwin, GOC Eastern Army, passed all operational control of the battle to Slim. *(NARA)*

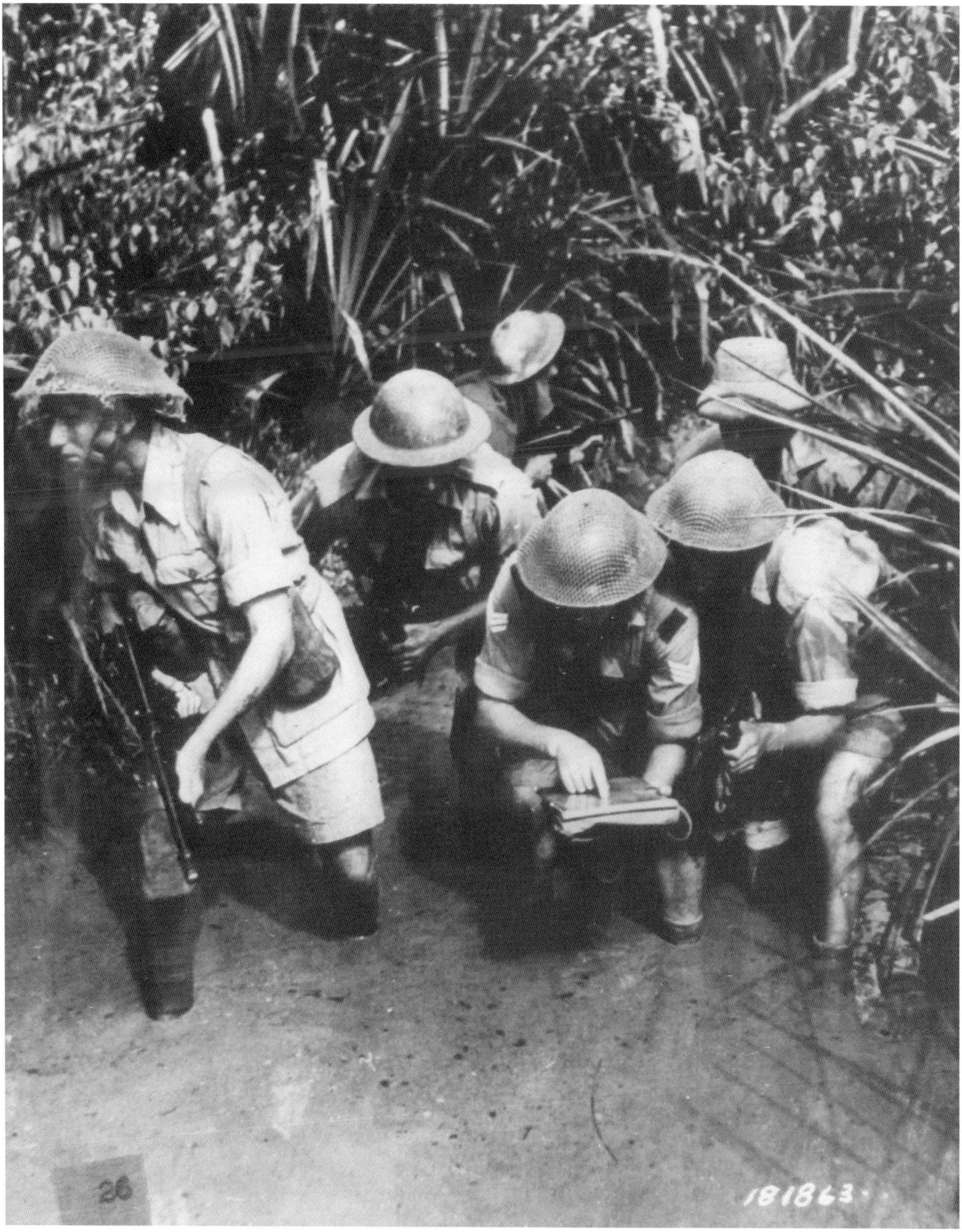
26
181863

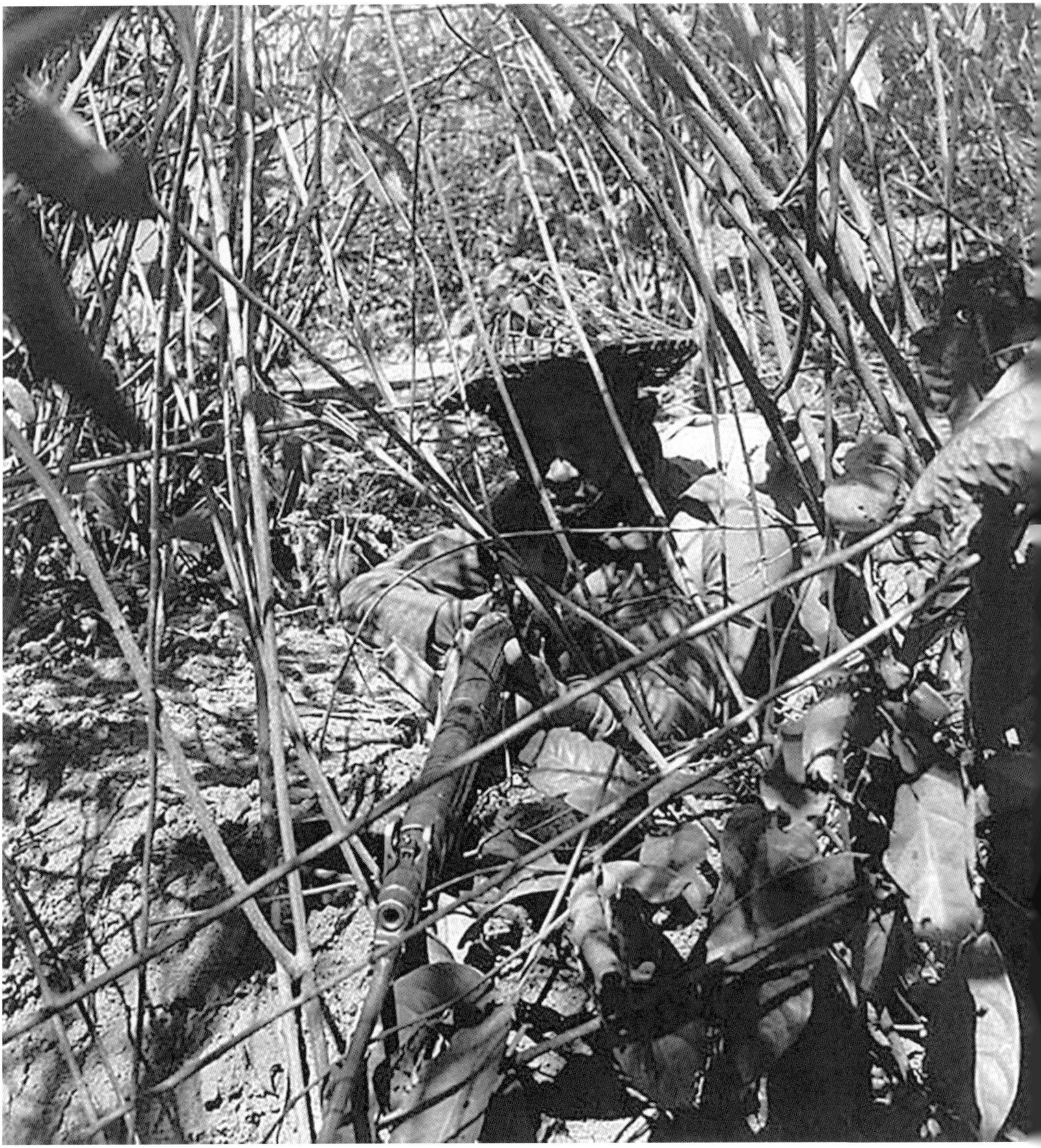

A 14th Indian Division Gurkha infantryman takes cover in thick Arakan vegetation awaiting an IJA attack. In mid-April 1943, Slim, as the XV Corps' commander and in operational control of the Arakan offensive, withdrew the 14th Indian Division back to Cox's Bazar, the starting-point four months earlier, in order to lure the Japanese into a trap. The entire 14th Division was demoralized after failed frontal assaults on Japanese bunkers and the encircling tactics of the enemy to get behind them. The 14th Division never returned to front-line duty and spent the rest of the war as a training division in India. *(NARA)*

Major General Orde C. Wingate, 'Chindit' or 'Special Force' leader aboard his aircraft to visit his brigades' forward areas during Operation THURSDAY in 1944. Graduating from the Royal Military Academy, Woolwich as a gunner, he learned Arabic and used family connections for a Sudan Defence Force posting from 1928 to 1933. Wingate met Wavell (GOC Palestine) in pre-war Palestine in 1936 and it was during the 1937 Arab Revolt that Wingate won a DSO after forming Special Night Squads of British soldiers and Jewish paramilitary volunteers to disrupt Arab insurgent attacks on the Iraq Petroleum Company's pipeline to Haifa. Later in September 1940 Wavell, now C-in-C Middle East, asked Wingate to form an irregular force of Ethiopian 'patriots' to combat the Italians in the Abyssinian highlands in Gojjam Province in May 1941 and restore Emperor Haile Selassie to his throne. Colonel Wingate was summoned by Wavell, C-in-C India, to go to Maymyo, Burma to organize Chinese guerrillas at the Bush Warfare School to fight the Japanese, but the enemy juggernaut precluded his efforts. Back in India, Wavell tasked Wingate to organize LRP units to operate deep behind enemy lines and disrupt their LOC. Although Operation LONGCLOTH's 1943 brigade-sized outcomes were mixed, Wingate strove to form the 3rd Indian Division with multiple Chindit brigades for Operation THURSDAY in northern Burma in early 1944 using revolutionary air resupply and strongholds. (NARA)

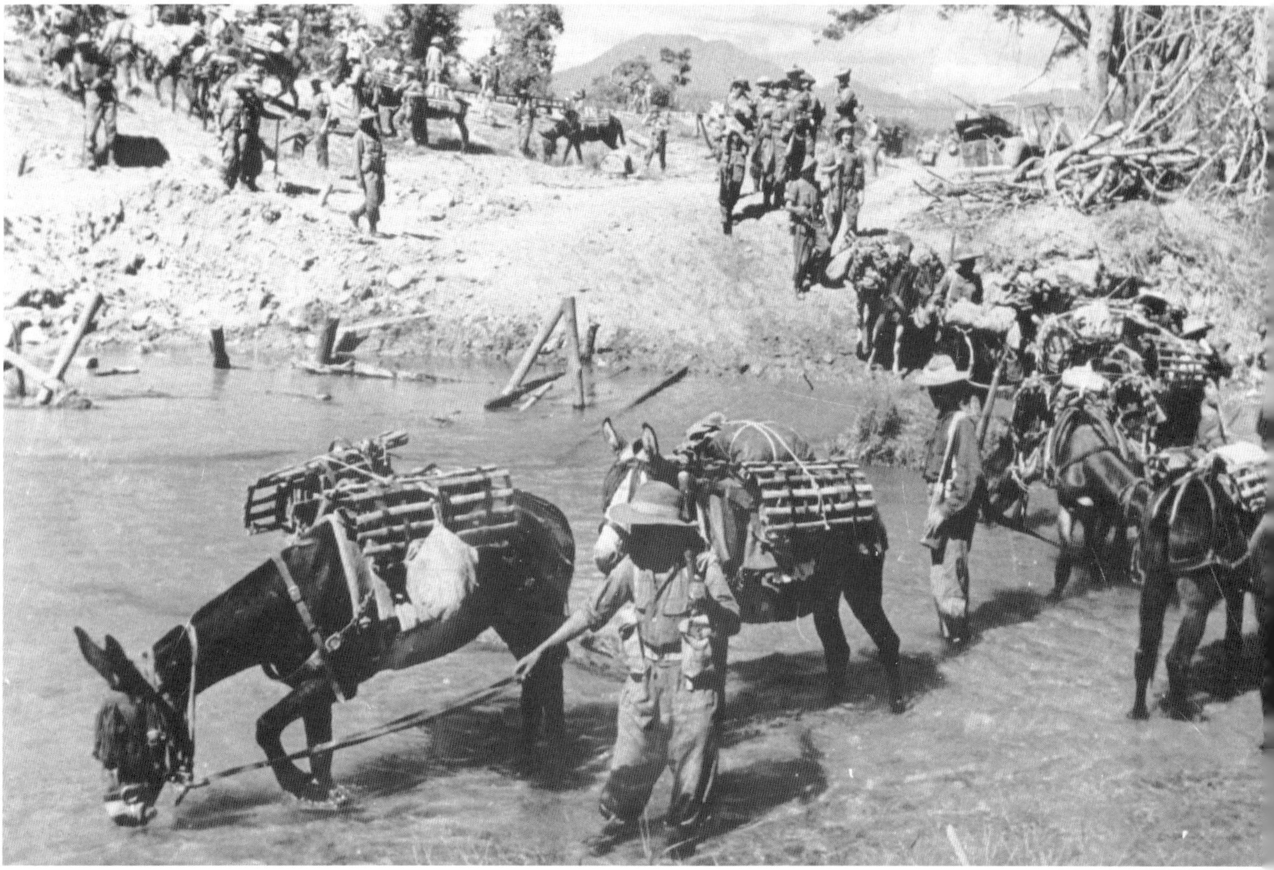

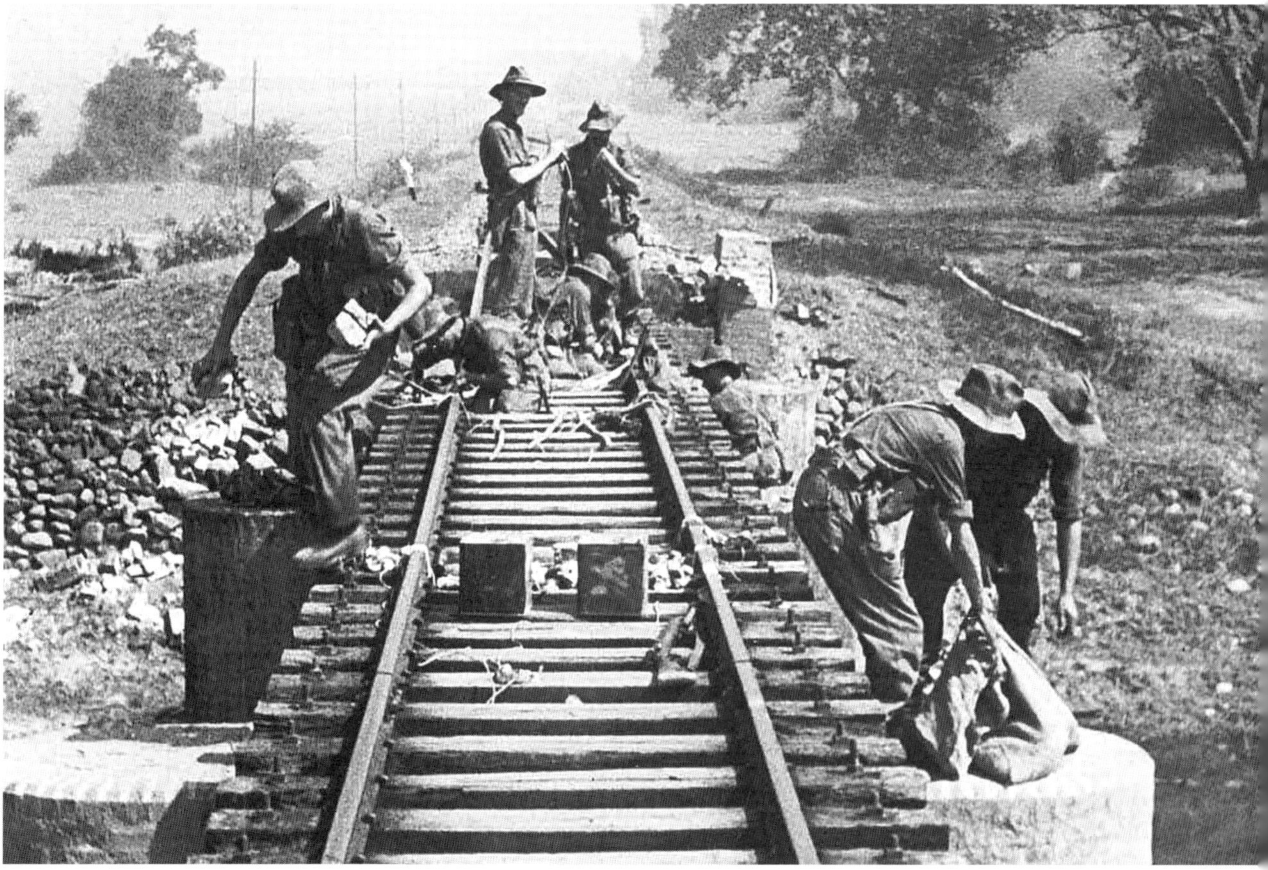

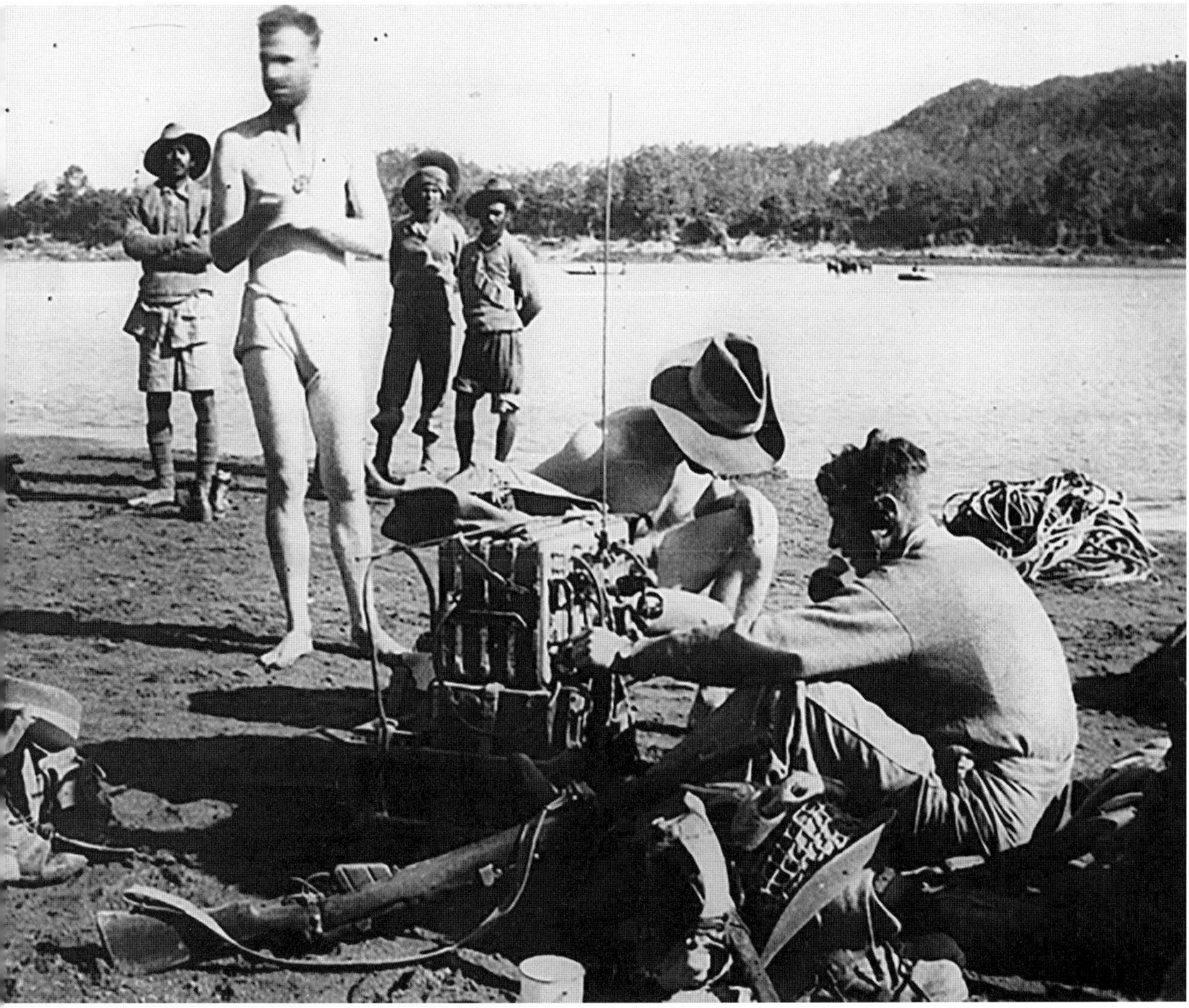

(**Opposite, above**) Chindit infantrymen lead their mule train across a fordable Burmese *chaung*. In these Chindit columns, 'first line' mules carried heavier equipment while 'second line' pack animals transported wireless sets, additional ammunition and other items during Operation LONGCLOTH in 1943. *(NARA)*

(**Opposite, below**) Chindit sappers from Major Michael Calvert's Column No. 3 lay explosives along railway tracks and concrete bridge abutments during Operation LONGCLOTH in 1943. As the explosives were being placed, lorried Japanese infantry attacked the Chindits from Indaw. A sharp fire-fight ensued at the Nankan railway station, which was repulsed by Calvert's troops' mortar and MG fire. *(Author's collection)*

(**Opposite, above**) Chindit signallers attempt to contact the rear echelon for an ATC parachute drop of supplies for the 77th Indian Brigade Southern Group on the Irrawaddy River during Operation LONGCLOTH in late March 1943. The Southern Group acted as a diversionary body, with its target destination being the Myitkyina-to-Mandalay railway that paralleled the Irrawaddy River. By the first week of June, 2,180 Chindits returned to India, often in small groups, out of the 3,000 that had entered Burma on 8 February at the start of Operation LONGCLOTH. *(Author's collection)*

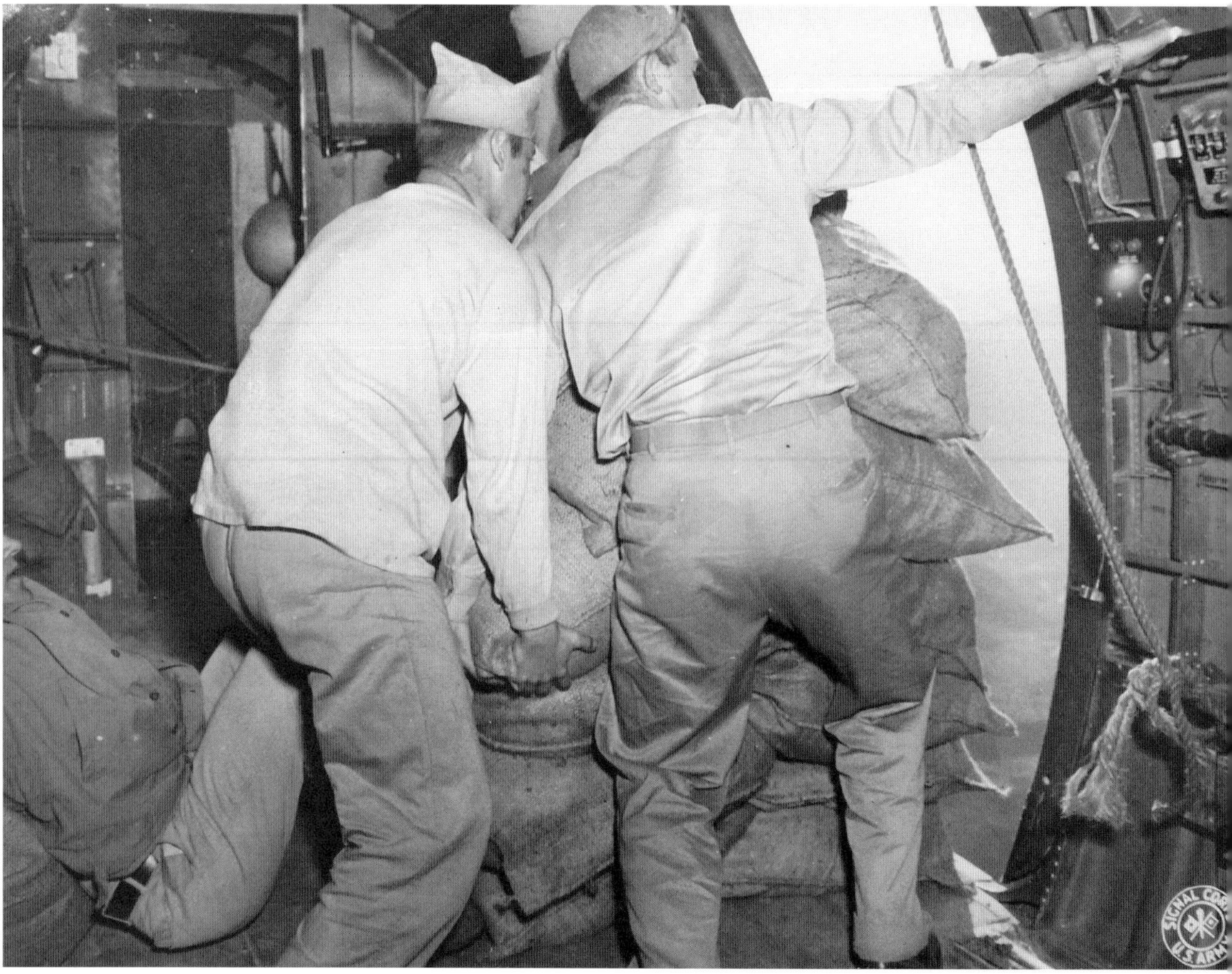

An American aircrew pushes out feed bags as free-fall drops from a C-47 Dakota transport from relatively low altitude to sustain the pack animals during Operation LONGCLOTH. Despite these airdrops, Chindit columns were often isolated from resupply due to radio-signal malfunction, extreme range for C-47 Dakota transports and ensuing aerial interdiction. These supply problems and others compelled Wingate to order his Chindit column to withdraw from Burma. *(USAMHI)*

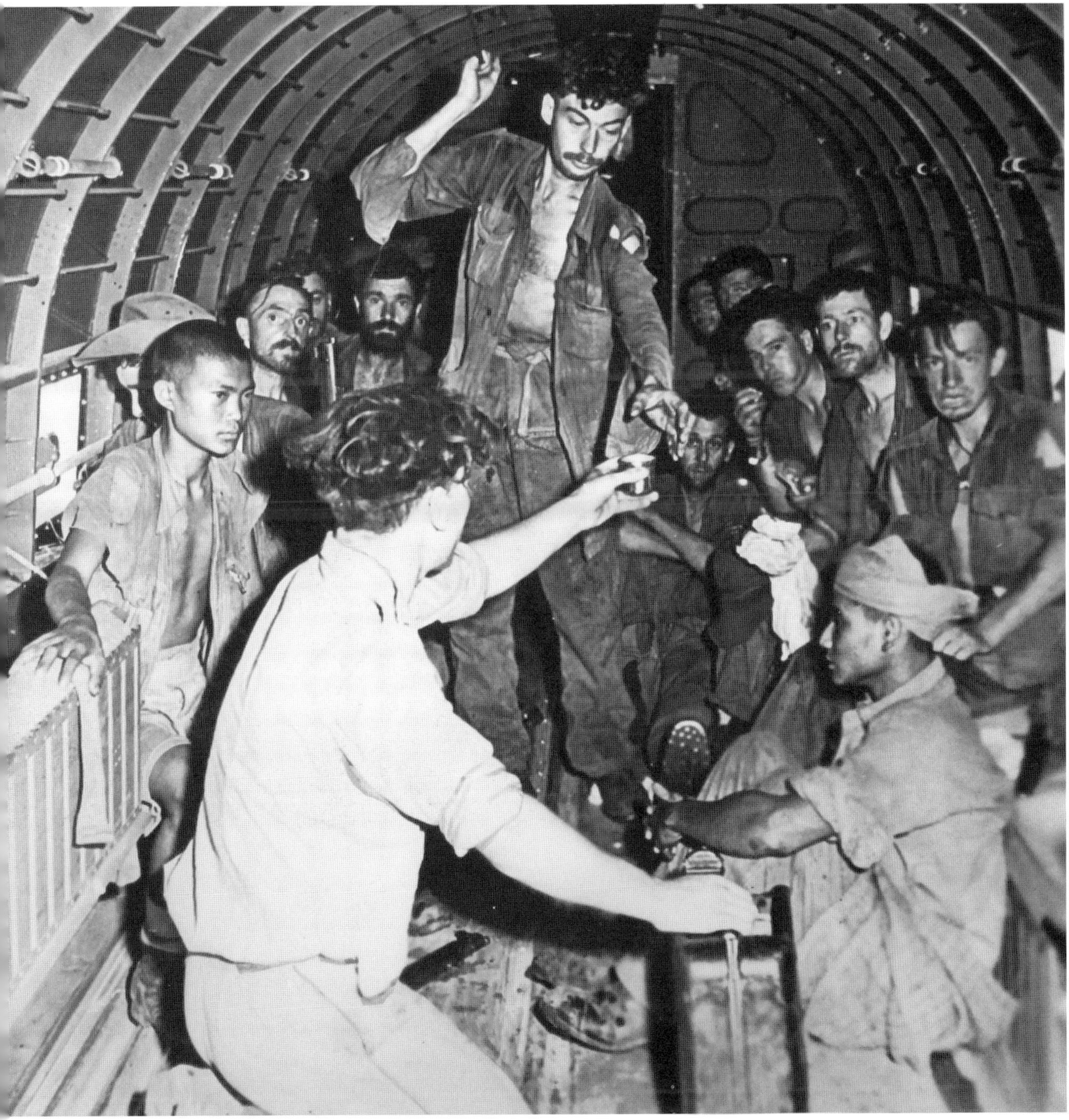

Surviving wounded and diseased Chindits from Major Walter Scott's Column No. 8 are transported back to India in a transport plane after the conclusion of Operation LONGCLOTH. Although Wingate's 1943 LRP invasion of northern Burma received controversial and mixed reviews, Churchill viewed it as a morale-booster as it showed ordinary British and Gurkha soldiers capable of fighting the vaunted Japanese jungle fighters in rough Burmese terrain. Operation LONGCLOTH had sown the seeds in Churchill's and Wingate's fertile minds for an even larger LRP in early 1944, Operation THURSDAY.

(Library of Congress)

Chapter Two

Wingate's Operation THURSDAY and Stilwell's Myitkyina Assault, 1944

After the Allied Quadrant and Sextant Conferences in August and November 1943 respectively, the Combined Chiefs of Staff (CCS) ordered Stilwell to utilize his Ramgarh-trained Chinese 38th and 22nd divisions along with the 5307th Composite Unit (Provisional), also known as 'Galahad' or 'Merrill's Marauders', to move through the Hukawng Valley and across the Jāmbu Bum to capture the railway and airfield hub at Myitkyina and the railway town of Mogaung, both being vital for completing the Ledo Road and opening a ground LOC with an all-weather road and a gasoline pipeline to Yunnan Province, China.

Coincident with Stilwell's mission in northern Burma and with CCS support, Major General Orde Wingate planned a larger second Burma LRP invasion (Operation THURSDAY) for March 1944 with six brigades of the 3rd Indian Division or 'Special Force'. Wingate would utilize Waco glider-borne as well as C-46 Commando and C-47 Dakota transports for air-landing of infantry and supplies, stronghold defensive areas to amplify Japanese LOC interdiction, and the First Allied Air Commando's (under the control of Colonels Philip Cochran and John Alison of the USAAF) aerial attack and resupply capabilities to revolutionize remote combat without any direct sea or land-based LOC. State-of-the-art long-range radio communications per-formed by RAF signallers would coordinate the air drops to patrolling Chindit columns. In early January 1944, Stilwell asked Wingate to move 'Galahad' that the Chindit leader had trained in India up to the Hukawng Valley, which was agreed to. Wingate was instructed to aid Stilwell's advance force from Ledo and to create a favourable situation for the Chinese to advance from Yunnan across the Salween River and to inflict maximum confusion, damage and loss on the enemy forces in northern Burma.

Wingate envisioned that his designated strongholds would be operational within thirty-six hours after air-landing and such defended locales would enable columns to retire into them for safety and then set out on raids from their perimeters. With

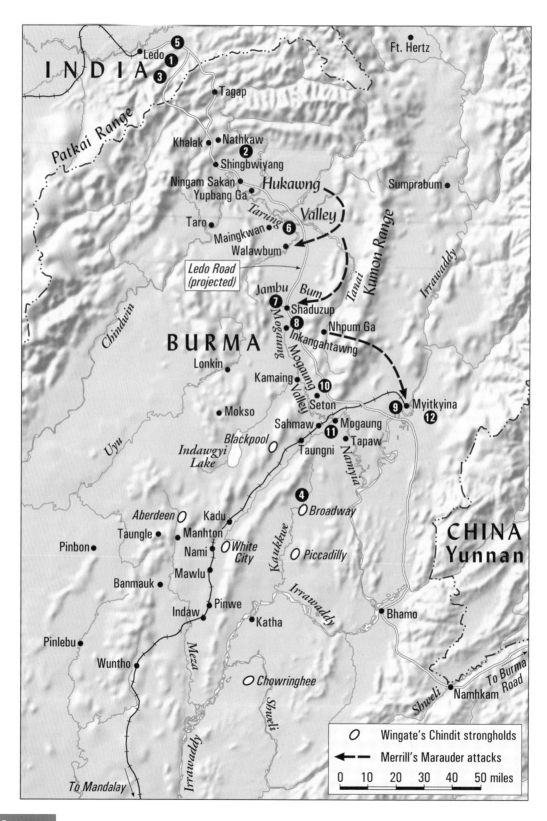

INDIA

Ft. Hertz

⑤ ● Ledo ①
③

Tagap

Patkai Range

Khalak ● ● Nathkaw
②
● Shingbwiyang

Ningam Sakan *Hukawng* Sumprabum ●
Yupbang Ga

Taro ● *Tarung* *Valley*
Maingkwan ● ⑥
Walawbum ●

Ledo Road
(projected)

Jambu *Bum*
⑦ ● Shaduzup
⑧ ● Nhpum Ga
Inkangahtawng

BURMA

Mogaung

Lonkin ●

Kamaing ● *Mogaung* ⑩
⑩ *Valley*
Seton ⑨ ● Myitkyina
● Mokso Sahmaw ● Mogaung ⑫
⑪ ● Tapaw

Blackpool ○ Taungni ●

Indawgyi *Namyia*
Lake

Uyu

④
○ Broadway

Aberdeen ○ Kadu
Taungle ● Manhton ● ○ Piccadilly
Pinbon ● Nami ● ○ White
● Mawlu City

Banmauk ● *Kaukkwe*

Indaw ● Pinwe *Irrawaddy*
● Katha ● Bhamo

Pinlebu ●
Meza

Wuntho ● **CHINA**
Yunnan

○ Chowringhee
Shweli To Burma
Road
Irrawaddy Namhkam ●

Shweli

To Mandalay

Legend:

○ Wingate's Chindit strongholds

◄ - - Merrill's Marauder attacks

0 10 20 30 40 50 miles

Kumon Range

Irrawaddy

Tanai

Chindwin

Map 2. Wingate's Chindit and Stilwell's NCAC Operations, 1943–44. ❶ The Chinese 38th Division leaves India in December 1943 for northern Burma's Hukawng Valley as the military vanguard of the Ledo Road's construction to their rear. **❷** At the Tarung River, elements of the Chinese 38th Division confront IJA 18th Division entrenched units and become encircled in late December by Japanese reinforcements at Yupbang Ga. On 24–25 December, Stilwell directs Chinese infantry and artillery reinforcements to break the enemy's encirclement and within four days the Japanese withdraw from Yupbang Ga. The Chinese 38th and now the 22nd divisions' advance continues down the Hukawng Valley. **❸** The Chindit 16th Indian Infantry Brigade, under Brigadier Bernard Fergusson, marches south from Ledo, India on 5 February 1944 well to the west of Shingbwiyang and crosses the Chindwin and Uyu rivers to establish a stronghold ('Aberdeen') in the Meza River Valley on 10 March, just to the north of Manhton on the Meza River and 25 miles to Indaw's north-west. From 'Aberdeen' the Chindits were to attack the Bonchaung Gorge, the Meza River Bridge and capture the airfield at Indaw on the 'Railway Corridor'. On 27 April, the 16th Brigade finally captures Indaw's airfield but being only a fair-weather airstrip, Fergusson's Chindits are air-lifted out in early May and 'Aberdeen' is abandoned. **❹** After coconut logs are identified by aerial reconnaissance at the proposed 'Piccadilly' air-landing site, Brigadier Michael Calvert and Wingate decide to glider-land the entire 77th Indian Infantry Brigade into another site, 'Broadway', on 5–6 March and construct an airfield and stronghold there. On 6–7 March, a second glider airlift lands the advance guard of Brigadier W.D.A. 'Joe' Lentaigne's 111th Indian Infantry Brigade into Chowringhee's landing field 50 miles to 'Broadway's south-west between the Shweli and Irrawaddy rivers. 111th Brigade units march north-west across the Irrawaddy and Meza rivers to near Baumauk to assist the 16th Brigade, which arrives in the Indaw area on 20 March. On 9 March, Calvert takes five 77th Indian Infantry Brigade columns from 'Broadway' to establish a stronghold called 'White City' to block the railway and motor-road at Henu to Mawlu's north. On 24 March, Wingate dies in a plane crash and Lentaigne now commands the Chindits. In early May, Lentaigne's 111th Indian Infantry Brigade establishes a new railroad block at 'Blackpool' to 'White City's north and Taungni's west, which replaces the 'White City' and 'Aberdeen' strongholds as the monsoon makes those strongholds non-all-weather airfields untenable for requisite reinforcement, resupply and wounded evacuation. 'Blackpool' was to deny the Japanese use of the 'Railway Corridor' to Mogaung's south-west as a rendezvous with Stilwell's Chinese troops heading south from Kamaing was hoped for. The 'Blackpool' stronghold, not as well-defended as 'White City', was evacuated by 25 May after strong IJA attack. Although 'Blackpool' hindered the IJA LOC for more than two weeks, its abandonment enabled Japanese reinforcement towards Mogaung and Myitkyina with 5,000 infantry with artillery. **❺** In February 'Galahad' ('Merrill's Marauders') marched from Ledo into Burma via the Patkai Range's Pangsau Pass. 'Galahad' was to hasten the Hukawng Valley offensive as the Chinese advance slowed on the Americans' right flank. **❻** From 23 February to 4 March, 'Galahad' moved towards Walawbum, 12 miles south-east of Maingkwan, as its first mission. After clashes with the Japanese on 3 March, 'Galahad' forced the IJA 55th and 56th divisions to retreat on 5–8 March to the Jāmbu Bum to avoid annihilation by American and Chinese infantry with Chinese armour. **❼** In mid-March, Stilwell manoeuvred to force Japanese infantry and artillery off the Jāmbu Bum separating the Hukawng and Mogaung valleys. 'Galahad's 1st Battalion with the Chinese 38th Division's 113th IR behind made a shallow envelopment to block the Kamaing Road, the main Japanese LOC, at Shaduzup, south of the Jāmbu Bum. After intense combat, the Japanese withdrew from Shaduzup on 29 March. **❽** On 15 March, Stilwell ordered a second, wider envelopment with 'Galahad's 2nd and 3rd battalions (with OSS Detachment 101 Kachin guerrillas) establishing another block on the Kamaing Road near Inkangahtawng, 8 miles south of Shaduzup, necessitating an 80-mile trek across the steep western slopes of the Kumon Range for 'Galahad' troops with their pack animals. On 23 March, elements of 'Galahad's 2nd Battalion clashed with the Japanese dug in at Inkangahtawng and reinforcing elements of the IJA 18th Division's 55th and 114th IRs. 'Galahad' also blocked 800 Japanese troops moving north-east on 26–28 March from Kamaing towards Nhpum Ga to the east of Inkangahtawng. The Japanese laid siege to 'Galahad's positions within the Nhpum Ga perimeter on 30 March with continued Japanese artillery and mortar fire from 31 March to 2 April. On 9 April, other 'Galahad' relieving reinforcements from Shaduzup broke the IJA three-battalion siege at Nhpum Ga with the remnants of the IJA 114 IR retreating to Myitkyina. **❾** Colonel Charles Hunter (Merrill's deputy) divides the remaining fit Marauders into H (Colonel Hunter), K (Colonel Kinnison) and M (Colonel McGee) Forces between the Tanai River and the Kumon Range north of Nhpum Ga. On 28 April, H and K Forces move south-east across the Kumon Range from Naubum towards Ritpong, with K Force reaching the latter site on 5–6 May. M Force crosses to the Kumon Range's east in early May. After fire-fights with IJA units, H Force resumes a southerly advance towards the western Myitkyina airfield on 11 May with K Force following. On 15 May, H Force crosses the Namkwi Hka, a tributary of the Irrawaddy River coursing around Myitkyina, to attack and seize the Myitkyina airfield in a *coup de main* assault on 17 May. **❿** On 19 May, Chinese 22nd and 38th division troops, having crossed the Jāmbu Bum behind the 'Marauders', encircle IJA 18th Division forces in Kamaing and establish a block in Seton just to the south-east to prevent Japanese troops from reinforcing Mogaung and Myitkyina from the west. **⓫** From 2 to 12 June, Calvert's remaining 77th Indian Infantry Brigade's 2,000 troops are grouped into three battalions to attack Mogaung's entrenched IJA positions, which are reinforced by elements of the IJA 53rd Division's 128th and 151st IRs. By using his Chindits as conventional infantry for Stilwell, Calvert's ranks are almost decimated, but they manoeuvre into Mogaung with the assistance of reinforcing Chinese troops with artillery arriving on 16–18 June. Mogaung fell to the Chindits and Chinese on 26 June. **⓬** The town of Myitkyina on the Irrawaddy River is captured by Stilwell's Allied forces on 3 August after a seventy-eight-day siege of Japanese trench lines. The Japanese received small amounts of supplies and reinforcements via a ferry service across the Irrawaddy River and from the west until Mogaung fell on 26 June.

---

supply and relief, these strongholds could become virtual offensives on their own with 25-pounder field and Bofors 40mm AA guns for defence against enemy infantry, artillery and air attack. Also Wingate's strongholds would have newly-constructed airstrips for light liaison and heavier transport aircraft so the wounded could be evacuated, thereby providing an immediate morale-booster in contrast to Operation LONGCLOTH in 1943.

For Operation THURSDAY, which was to begin in March 1944, Wingate's core element of Chindits for this second LRP operation was six brigades: the 14th and 23rd brigades from a reorganized British 70th Division (a veteran, battle-hardened formation); Brigadiers Calvert's and Lentaigne's 77th and 111th brigades respectively; and Brigadier Fergusson's 16th Brigade. The sixth and final brigade was the 3rd West African Brigade from the 81st West African Division. Wingate's 'Special Force' numbered 23,000 men.

Roosevelt's planners in February 1944 stated that the reoccupation of Myitkyina would enable an increased air-lift to China as well as increase the protection of the air route. Stilwell expressed his confidence that his Sino-American force could seize

Myitkyina by the end of this dry season. However, Churchill and the British high command differed from Roosevelt advocating the improvement of the air route since they were dubious about the Ledo Road construction through 500 miles of jungles and mountains into China after merging with the Old Burma Road. Churchill abhorred the prospect of a large-scale campaign in northern Burma and preferred combating the IJA in the south of Burma with its port of Rangoon as the more valuable strategic goal. The US Army Chief of Staff Marshall, although supportive of Stilwell, also realized the potential pitfalls of a northern Burma campaign to capture Myitkyina with concurrent construction of a new major motor road as it was situated at the end of the thinnest of supply lines while simultaneously combating the Japanese.

Into the Hukawng Valley

Brigadier General Haydon Boatner, commander of the CAI and Stilwell's deputy, ordered Lieutenant General Sun Li-jen to move three battalions of his Chinese 38th Division's 112th IR into the Hukawng Valley on 5 October 1943 to shield the advancing Ledo Road construction crews. The Tanai River flows north-west until it meets the Paktai Range where it becomes the Chindwin River. The Tarung River flows south-west to enter the Tanai River near the village of Yupbang Ga. Both the Tarung and Tanai rivers were in the direct path of the US engineers building the Ledo Road and the former river had to be cleared of IJA 18th Division garrisons in order to provide the work crews safe access to the Shingbwiyang clearing in the northern Hukawng Valley.

Stilwell wanted to move down the Hukawng Valley into the Mogaung Valley with the Japanese-occupied Jāmbu Bum ridge separating the two valleys and then on to Myitkyina in the broad Irrawaddy Valley before the spring monsoon. Stilwell realized that his campaign in northern Burma was 'to go in through a rat hole and dig the hole as we go.' Myitkyina, the northernmost major IJA garrison and air base, was located on the railroad and the Irrawaddy River, 40 miles north-east of Mogaung. A road continued southward from Myitkyina to connect with the old Burma Road into Yunnan, China. The terrain for Stilwell's northern Burma campaign was forbidding, with jungle growth and mountain ranges that slowed advances down to as little as 1 mile an hour.

The IJA 18th Division's 55th and 56th IRs were deployed in the Hukawng Valley, while the 114th IR was stationed at Myitkyina. Lieutenant General Tanaka, the 18th Division CG, also regarded the Hukawng Valley as an awful combat locale with many rivers turning the landscape into a marshy quagmire by the monsoon, creating a nest for cholera and malaria. In early November 1943, Tanaka moved the main strength of the IJA 18th Division from Ningbyen toward Shingbwiyang, the exit of the mountain road on the India-Burma border, to destroy any Sino-American advance from Ledo, India.

On 30 October 1943, units of the IJA 55th and 56th IRs fought the Chinese 112th IR along fortified positions along the Tarung River's fords at Yupbang Ga with an entire Chinese company destroyed by 2 November. The remaining surrounded Chinese waited for relief from the other Chinese 38th Division IRs. Stilwell arrived at Shingbwiyang on 21 December 1943 and personally directed the attacks that stalled at Yupbang Ga with the mine-strewn Tarung River fords taken from the IJA on 14 January 1944.

Stilwell next sent Sun's 38th Division to capture the village of Taihpa Ga where the Tarung River flows into the Tanai River south-east of Yupbang Ga. This IJA strongpoint resisted until 1 February as the Japanese used 75mm and 150mm artillery pieces along with well-fortified entrenched positions. Contemporaneous with the Taihpa Ga assault, elements of Major General Liao Yao-hsiang's Chinese 22nd Division crossed the Tanai River to the west on 9 January and advanced downriver towards Taro on 30 January, where it confronted elements of the IJA 55th IR. Liao's forces encircled and overwhelmed the IJA 55th IR, clearing the Taro Plain.

The 5307th Composite Unit, Provisional ('Galahad' or 'Merrill's Marauders')

On 6 January 1944, Brigadier General Frank Merrill, with Colonel Charles Hunter as his deputy, took command of 'Galahad'. On 21-22 January, Stilwell sent his 1st Provisional Tank Group (eighty tanks) to drive down the Kamaing Road with the Chinese 22nd Infantry Division following. Maingkwan, 15 miles south of Taihpa Ga, was Stilwell's next main IJA base in the Hukawng Valley to attack. 'Galahad', after a march from Ledo, arrived at the front on 20 February and from 23 February–2 March conducted a wide envelopment onto Walawbum along the eastern side of the Hukawng Valley as Chinese infantry and armour frontally advanced at a hesitant tempo south-eastwards on to Maingkwan and then Walawbum. Stilwell's intent was to trap the bulk of the IJA 18th Division in the southern Hukawng Valley. On 3–5 March, the IJA 56th IR probed 'Galahad's positions overlooking Walawbum. On 6 March, after repelling an IJA *banzai* charge leaving more than 400 enemy soldiers killed, Chinese infantry and armour linked up with 'Galahad', but the remaining IJA 18th Division units escaped, which irked Stilwell as Tanaka on 15 March dug in on the Jāmbu Bum at the southern end of the Hukawng Valley before the Mogaung Valley was entered.

Into the Mogaung Valley

To force the IJA off the Jāmbu Bum, Stilwell on 12 March 1944 ordered 'Galahad' and elements of the Chinese 38th Division to make another pair of envelopments over a two-week interval south of the Jāmbu Bum at Shaduzup and Inkangahtawng, the latter 8 miles further south. Once positioned, roadblocks were to pinch the IJA forces in between. The more southerly 'hook' to Inkangahtawng necessitated an 80-mile eastward trek across the steep Kumon Range.

On 26 March 1944, 'Galahad's 1st Battalion commanded by Colonel William Osborne and guided by Kachin guerrillas led by Lieutenant James Tilly of the OSS Detachment 101 arrived at Shaduzup on schedule for the northerly 'hook' at a tributary of the Mogaung River. By 27-28 March, the Sino-American force with their Kachin guides stealthily insinuated itself between 300 IJA troops in Shaduzup and 500–600 more repelling IJA counterattacks. 'Galahad' fired their mortars and used hand grenades until Chinese infantry with pack artillery relieved them at dawn on 29 March. At Shaduzup, 300 IJA 18th Division soldiers were killed, so Tanaka withdrew to the south-west to bypass 'Galahad's 1st Battalion Kamaing roadblock.

Inkangahtawng and Nhpum Ga

'Galahad's 2nd and 3rd battalions left Walawbum on 12 March 1944 and three days later were joined at the village of Naubum by Captain Vincent Curl and 300 Kachin guerrillas of OSS Detachment 101. Moving across the Kumon Range from 15–21 March, this force arrived at Inkangahtawng on 23 March, establishing a block on the Kamaing Road. If the Allies eventually captured Kamaing, 2,000 IJA troops in the vicinity could be isolated from Myitkyina.

Units from 'Galahad's 2nd Battalion, under Lieutenant Colonel McGee, clashed with a company of dug-in Japanese infantry on 23 March at Inkangahtawng. The next day, Japanese reinforcements were dispatched to the south from Shaduzup and 'Galahad'; patrols retreated after finding Inkangahtawng's entrenchments too strongly fortified. Then McGee's 2nd Battalion was heavily attacked, compelling a retreat across the Mogaung River from the Inkangahtawng roadblock. The Japanese also counterattacked with a 1,600-man force from Kamaing on 24 March to get around 'Galahad's flank and move north-east into the Tanai River valley. Stilwell ordered 'Galahad' to prevent this IJA thrust from extending beyond Nhpum Ga, situated between the Kumon Range and Inkangahtawng. 'Galahad' delayed the Japanese movement towards Nhpum Ga from 26 to 28 March.

The Japanese attacked Nhpum Ga in force on 30 March 1944, digging in for a siege. The fighting at Nhpum Ga raged until 9 April with 'Galahad's 2nd Battalion surviving only due to air resupply. Colonel Hunter redirected the 'Galahad's 1st and 3rd battalions to Nhpum Ga, which arrived on 7 April to break the siege on 9 April. Three IJA battalions were destroyed at Nhpum Ga and the IJA 18th Division remnants withdrew to Myitkyina to hold the western airfield and town on the Irrawaddy River. Despite the victory at Nhpum Ga, 'Galahad' was exhausted after fighting over 500 miles of jungle and riddled with malaria, dysentery and scrub typhus. Stilwell was determined to maintain 'Galahad' past its promised ninety-day limit for his final thrust to Myitkyina.

Capture of the Myitkyina Airfield on 17 May 1944

Stilwell's plan to capture Myitkyina, 'End Run', employed 'Galahad's 1,400 survivors (from an original 2,997 troops), OSS-led Detachment 101 Kachin guerrillas, and Chinese 150th and 88th IRs from the 50th and 30th divisions respectively (not Ramgarh-trained) to strike from Nhpum Ga in a flanking move to the east across the Kumon Range. The first phase was a *coup de main* seizure of the western Myitkyina airstrip with additional Chinese reinforcements and heavy weapons to be flown in after its capture to complete the occupation of Myitkyina town.

Colonel Hunter had 7,000 men for 'End Run', which he divided into H, K and M forces. H Force, led by Hunter, comprised the 150th Chinese IR, 'Galahad's 1st Battalion (commanded by Colonel Osborne), and the 3rd Company of the Animal Transport Regiment along with a battery of 75mm pack howitzers detached from the Chinese 22nd Division. K Force, under Colonel Henry Kinnison, comprised the 88th Chinese IR and 'Galahad's 3rd Battalion (led by Lieutenant Colonel Charles Beach). M Force (under Lieutenant Colonel McGee) had 'Galahad's 2nd Battalion survivors and 300 Kachins. K Force left for the Kumon Range on 28 April followed two days later by H Force on 30 April. M Force started its trek on 7 May, covering the open southern flank.

On 5 May Kinnison attacked Ritpong, taking four days for the Japanese defenders to fall to the Chinese 88th IR. H Force overtook and passed through K Force on 10 May at Lazu, about 35 miles north-west of Myitkyina. On 12 May K Force feigned an attack on Nsopzup on the Irrawaddy north of Myitkyina. Later that day, Kinnison's troops clashed with an entrenched reinforced Japanese battalion at Tingkrukawng, but were unable to overtake the IJA force. Kinnison was ordered to disengage and follow Hunter's unexposed southward trail towards Myitkyina. H Force arrived undetected 2 miles from the principal western Myitkyina airstrip on 15–16 May, finding only 100 Japanese and Burmese labourers there. At 1000 hrs on 17 May, Hunter sent in the Chinese 150th IR, which captured the airstrip within forty-five minutes. Hunter wanted to secure the airfield's perimeter, so he requested airlifted reinforcements at 1530 hrs. C-47 transports with guns and ammunition but no infantry started on their way to Myitkyina airfield within minutes of Hunter's communication.

Only one battalion of the Chinese 89th IR arrived in transports and gliders from Ledo late on the afternoon of 17 May, leaving Hunter without sufficient fresh infantry and supplies to mount an effective assault against Myitkyina town immediately after the airstrip's seizure, transforming the campaign into a seventy-eight-day siege rather than another *coup de main* capture of Myitkyina town. Of the 1,310 'Galahad' troops that reached Myitkyina airfield on 17 May, more than half were evacuated to rear-echelon hospitals by 1 June. Only 200 of 'Galahad's 1st Battalion were present at the fall of Myitkyina town on 3 August.

The Siege of Myitkyina Town, 18 May–3 August 1944

On 18 May Hunter, the Sino-American ground force commander at the airfield, faced two under-strength battalions of the IJA 114th IR and other ancillary units totalling 700 Japanese in Myitkyina town. The IJA 56th Division, from the Salween front, reinforced Myitkyina town throughout the remainder of May more quickly than the Allies and the ensuing battle comprised trench warfare with attacks on and retreats from nearby villages rather than manoeuvre. The peak number of Japanese forces totalled 4,600 men with reinforcements from Nsopzup, Mogaung and Bhamo as Stilwell's intelligence officers sensed that the IJA garrison was stronger than expected. The June rains interfered with Allied resupply and reinforcement operations at the Myitkyina airfield. Coupled with increasing Allied manpower losses, infantry attacks were halted and the classic siege warfare tactic of tunnelling was implemented with a battle of attrition producing progress measured in yards.

With Mogaung's capture by the Chindits and Chinese at the end of June, Myitkyina was no longer an isolated Allied base along the Irrawaddy River. When the remnants of 'Galahad's 3rd Battalion captured the northern airfield at Myitkyina on 26 July, Japanese resistance was noticeably weaker. On 3 August, Myitkyina town was finally captured, costing the Americans a total of 2,207 casualties while the Chinese suffered 4,344 casualties. The Japanese incurred 790 killed, 1,180 wounded and 187 captured. Approximately 600 IJA troops were able to be withdrawn from Myitkyina.

The Chindit 77th Brigade at Mogaung, 2–25 June 1944

Orde Wingate, the Chindit organizer and leader, died in a fiery plane crash on 24 March 1944 and Major General W.D.A. 'Joe' Lentaigne assumed command of the Chindits. Lentaigne abandoned the Chindit LRP concept and Wingate's stronghold guidelines, exemplified by his ordering Brigadier Michael Calvert's 77th Brigade to cover Stilwell's left flank by taking Mogaung, the railway town south-west of Myitkyina, by direct assault as conventional infantry.

On 29 May, Calvert signalled Lentaigne his wish to remain near the new Chindit stronghold of 'Blackpool' after his brigade had already withdrawn from both the 'White City' and 'Broadway' strongholds (see Map 2) and resume LRP methods to harass the Japanese. Calvert's request was denied and he moved north-east towards Mogaung, lacking conventional artillery and relying solely on 3in mortars (the 77th Brigade used 60,000 mortar bombs to capture Mogaung). Calvert eliminated a direct frontal assault as 77th Brigade combat casualties and disease since their glider air-landing at 'Broadway' on 5 March 1944 at the start of Operation THURSDAY had thinned their ranks. Instead, remnants of the 77th Brigade advanced on a narrow front against Japanese outposts and occupied villages.

Elements of the IJA 128th IR of the 53rd Division began to arrive at Mogaung from Myitkyina during the early days of June 1944 to strengthen Mogaung's eastern defences against the 77th Brigade. With other elements of IJA infantry and artillery units along with ad hoc ones, Mogaung had 3,500 entrenched Japanese soldiers.

On 8 June 1944, Calvert ordered his Chindits to capture the Pinhmi Bridge over the Wettauk *chaung* to the eastern side of Mogaung. After his initial assault was repelled with heavy casualties, other Chindits forded the *chaung* elsewhere and captured the bridge from behind on 10 June. By 12 June, four battalions of the IJA 53rd Division faced Calvert, who awaited Chinese reinforcements for the Mogaung assault.

On 11–12 June 1944, Calvert's 550 effective Chindits of the 77th Brigade, many with malaria and trench foot, attacked the Mogaung River railway bridge and an area called 'Courthouse Square'. Chinese troops of the 38th Division's 114th IR arrived on 18 June, along with artillery which they used on the Japanese over the next four days. Mogaung was effectively surrounded, with the Chinese reinforcements preventing any further Japanese troops from reinforcing Mogaung from Myitkyina town.

Calvert planned to attack on 23 June, after aerial assault against the Japanese in Mogaung. Despite fighter-bomber sorties, concealed Japanese machine guns exacted a high toll on the 500 attacking Chindits: 60 dead and 100 wounded. On 24 June, the remaining Chindits and Chinese reinforcements finally captured the railway station's red-brick building in Mogaung and the Japanese evacuated the town the next day. Stilwell's rear at the Myitkyina airfield was now secure from a Japanese attack from Mogaung. The 77th Brigade suffered more than 50 per cent casualties and had only 300 fit soldiers out of the original 3,000 Chindits to follow Stilwell's order to join the battle at Myitkyina.

The taking of Myitkyina on 3 August 1944 continued to bring the Ledo Road and pipeline closer to the Old Burma Road. Ultimately, further Allied advances down the 'Railway Corridor' and south to Bhamo coupled with a Chinese offensive from Yunnan enabled the Ledo (or Stilwell) Road to effectively end the Japanese land blockade of China. On 2 October, one of the two pipelines was in operation from the Indian refineries via Ledo to Myitkyina. However, after a month-long smouldering political firestorm between Stilwell and Chiang Kai-shek over control of Lend-Lease supplies, Roosevelt was forced to recall Stilwell from the CBI theatre on 18 October.

(**Opposite, above**) Major General Orde C. Wingate (left) is seen here standing with Colonel Philip Cochran, USAAF (right), one of the commanders of Operation THURSDAY's First Air Commando Group in early March 1944. The two officers briefed pilots and Chindit commanders of the airlifts by gliders from Lalaghat and Hailakandi, India to landing zones in Burma. Cochran assured Wingate that the Chindits had only to 'dream up' ideas and the First Air Commando would make them operational. (*NARA*)

(**Opposite, below**) At an Indian airfield an ox is being loaded onto a C-47 transport for air-lifting into Burma for Operation THURSDAY. Sure-footed mules were prized for hauling the heavier weapons and ammunition, while oxen were used for cart and heavy signal sets transport. (*NARA*)

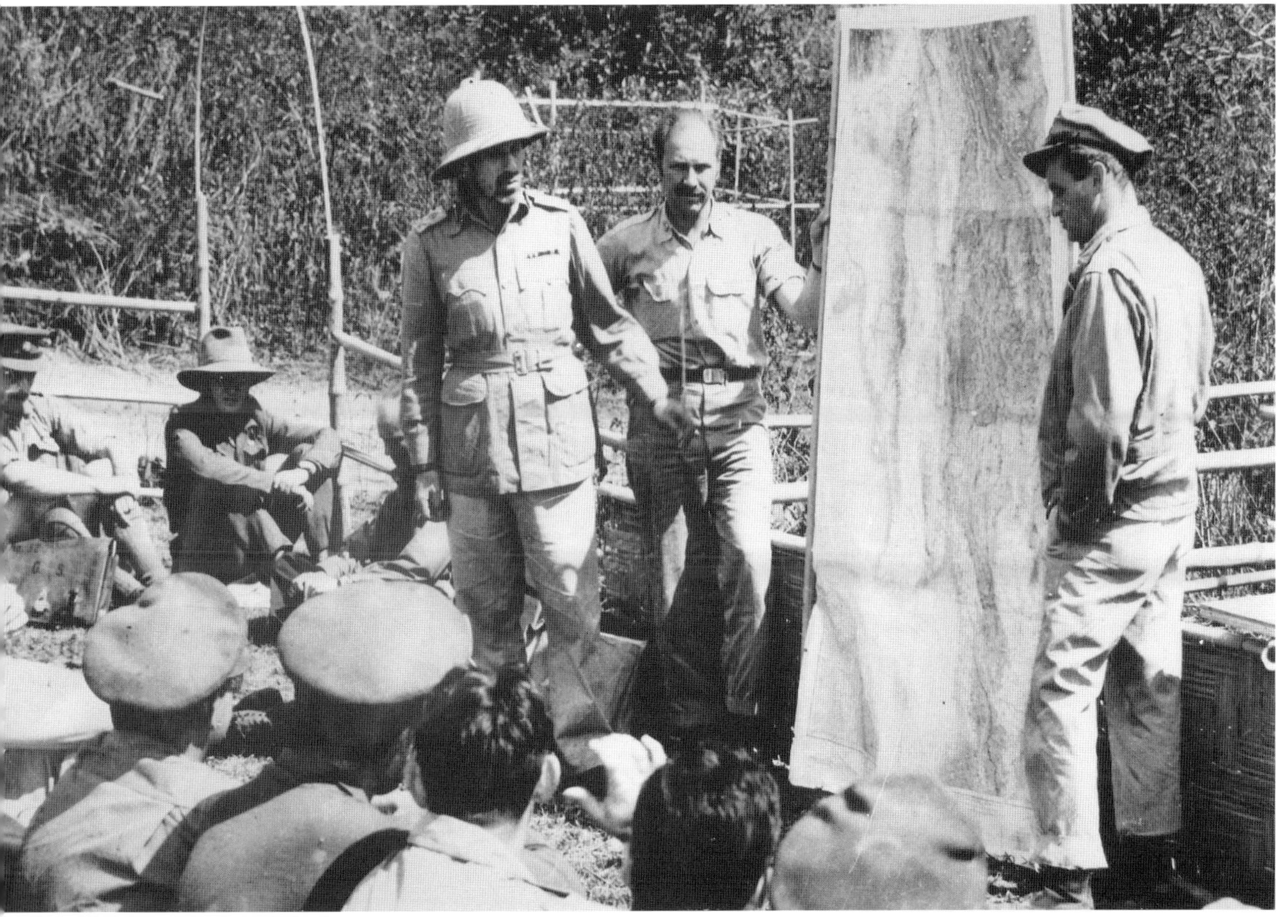

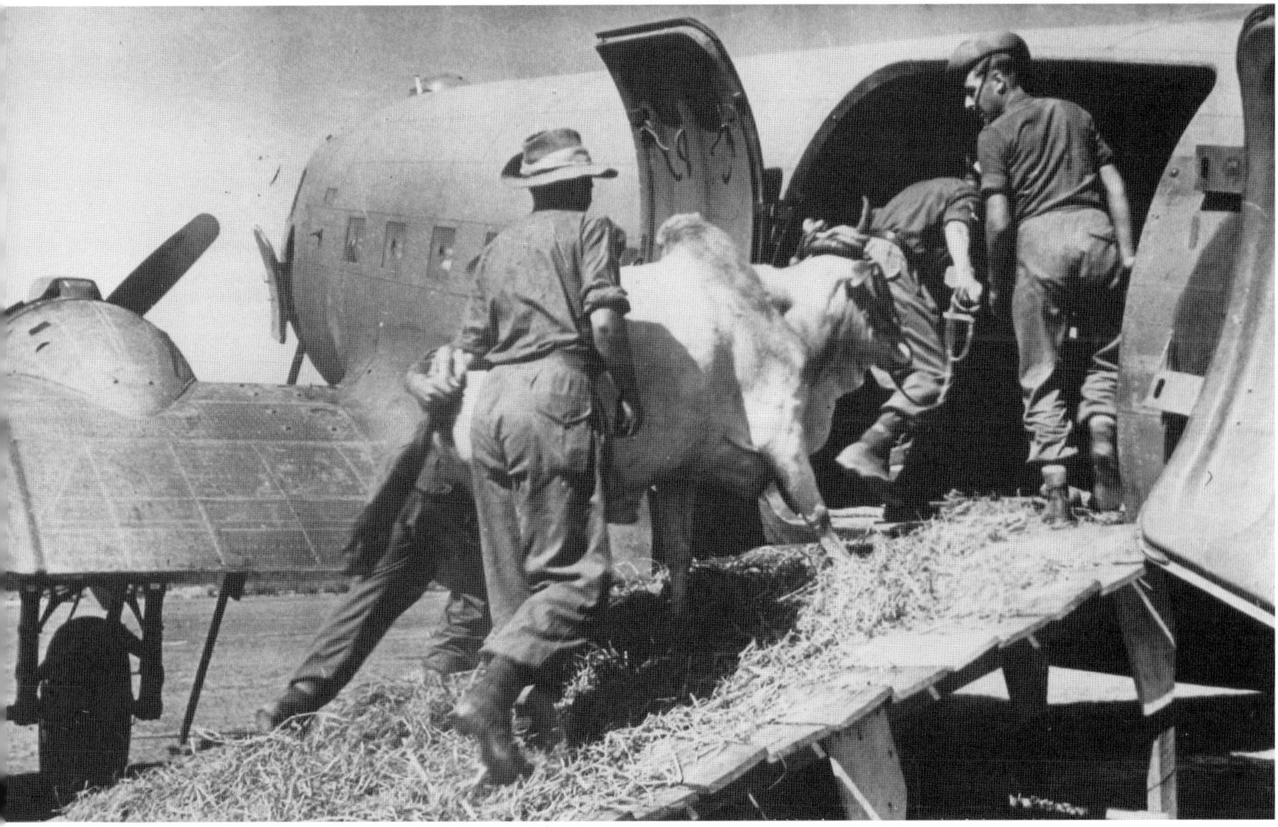

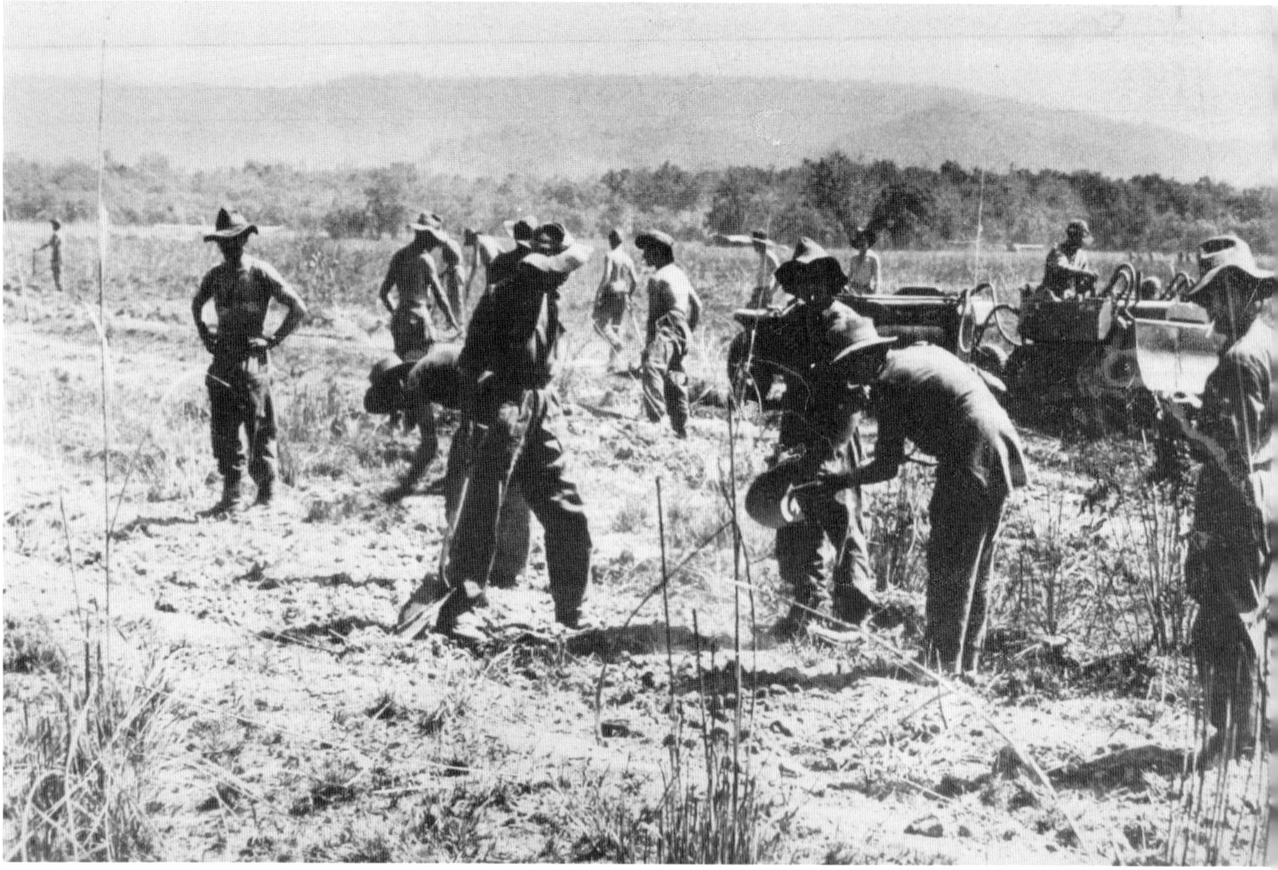

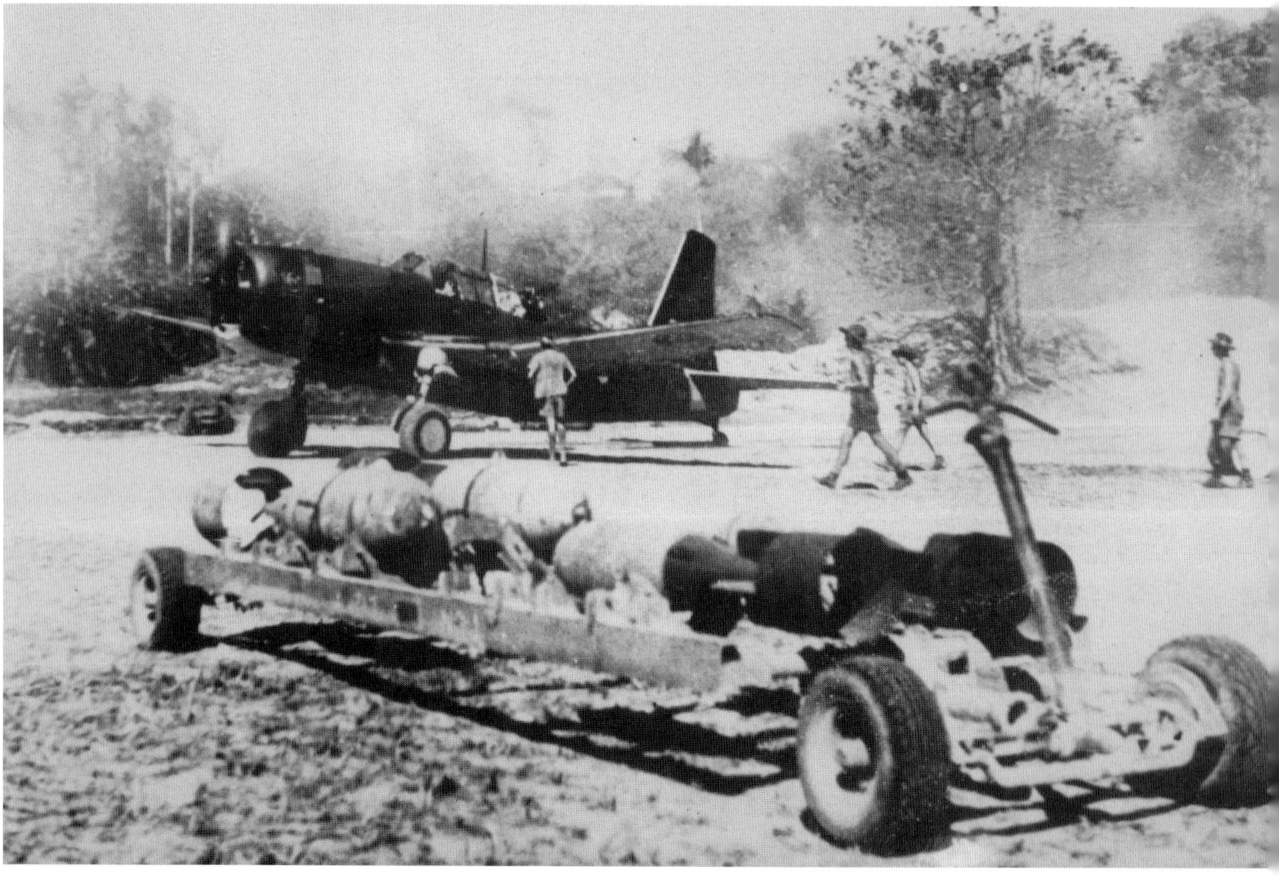

A wounded Chindit infantryman, aided by fellow 'Column' members, awaits evacuation from the airstrip at 'Broadway' stronghold during Operation THURSDAY in March 1944. Stinson L-5 Sentinel liaison aircraft evacuated wounded from airstrips to Assam or from the larger stronghold airfields via C-47 Dakota aircraft. Air evacuation of critically wounded or ill Chindit infantrymen was a notable distinction from Operation LONGCLOTH in 1943, where Wingate controversially left wounded Chindits behind to be aided by Burmese villagers or to the clemency of their Japanese captors. (NARA)

(**Opposite, above**) Brigadier Michael Calvert's 77th Brigade's Chindits use shovels to smooth furrows, which caused many Waco glider crashes at the stronghold 'Broadway's landing field on 6 March 1944. A small bulldozer with an attached scraper (background) was hastily implemented to improve the landing field to prevent further Chindit reinforcement-laden glider crashes. Eventually C-47 Dakota transports landing at 'Broadway' enabled a rapid stronghold build-up of ordnance and AA defence to repel an anticipated IJA infantry and air attack. Accidental glider crashes on the way to 'Broadway' in either western Burma or Assam created an unplanned diversion and caused Japanese attention to shift away from the landing zones. (NARA)

(**Opposite, below**) An RAF Vultee A-31 Vengeance returns to Assam after a dive-bombing sortie in close support of Chindit infantrymen in the Burmese jungle during Operation THURSDAY during the spring of 1944. This American-built aircraft was a two-seater dive-bomber with a range of 1,400 miles. Its armament was impressive as an infantry support weapon ('Wingate's flying artillery'), including six 0.50in-calibre fixed forward-firing MGs in the leading edges of the wings. The plane also had a rearward-firing 0.50in-calibre MG in the rear cockpit for defence against IJA fighters. In order to attack IJA troop concentrations, the A-31 had an external bomb load of two 500lb bombs seen here on the bomb ammunition trailer (foreground). (NARA)

(**Above**) Brigadier Michael Calvert, 77th Indian Infantry Brigade commander during Operation THURSDAY, directs one of the last operations conducted by his brigade. In the background is the red-brick building at the Mogaung railway station. Next to the brigadier is Lieutenant Colonel Freddie Shaw, commanding officer of the 3/6th Gurkha Rifles, while Major James Lumley looks on cradling an American M1 carbine, while the two others shoulder their SMLE rifles. The officers wore no rank insignia lest they be inviting targets for Japanese snipers. On 24 June, after the Japanese were finally driven from Mogaung by the Chindits and Chinese, the BBC broadcast that a Sino-American force captured Mogaung. Calvert sent a message to Special Forces HQ, copied to Stilwell, saying 'the Americans have captured Mogaung, 77th Brigade is proceeding to take Umbrage'. (*Author's collection*)

(**Opposite, above**) After the capture of Mogaung by Calvert's 77th Brigade on 27 June 1944, Chindit infantrymen used the narrow-gauge Mogaung-Myitkyina railway to reinforce Stilwell's Sino-American force locked in a protracted siege of Myitkyina town. The 77th Brigade was decimated as a fighting unit after Mogaung and it would not be until August that the survivors were evacuated to India after its five-month campaign in northern Burma. (*NARA*)

(**Opposite, below**) Ramgarh-trained Chinese infantrymen slog through the mud leading a mule train through the Hukawng Valley in early 1944 during Stilwell's northern Burma offensive to attack Myitkyina on the Irrawaddy River. The mud aided the IJA 18th Division's defence in the Hukawng Valley as it delayed the Chinese advance; however, Stilwell believed that his Chinese 38th and 22nd division generals were purposely moving slowly on orders from Chiang Kai-shek. To hasten the arrival at the Myitkyina airfield before the monsoon, Stilwell employed his 'Galahad' or 'Merrill's Marauders' on a number of envelopments to get around the Japanese defensive positions. (*NARA*)

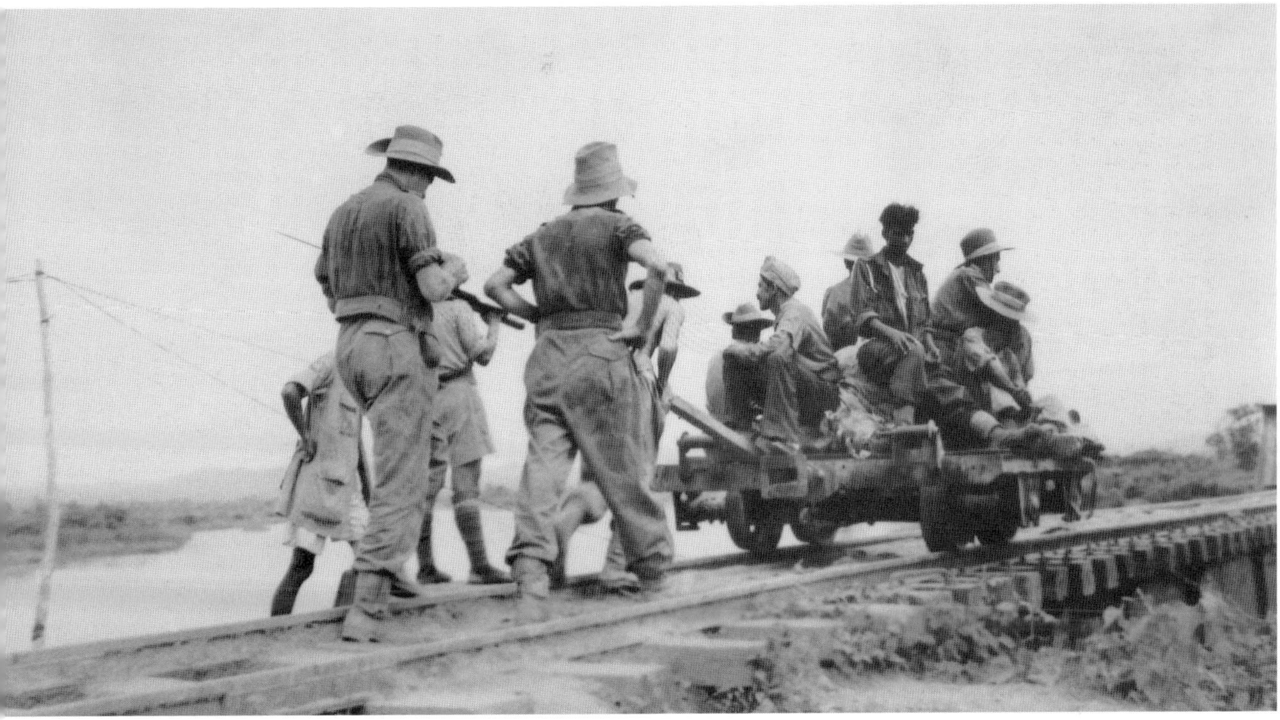

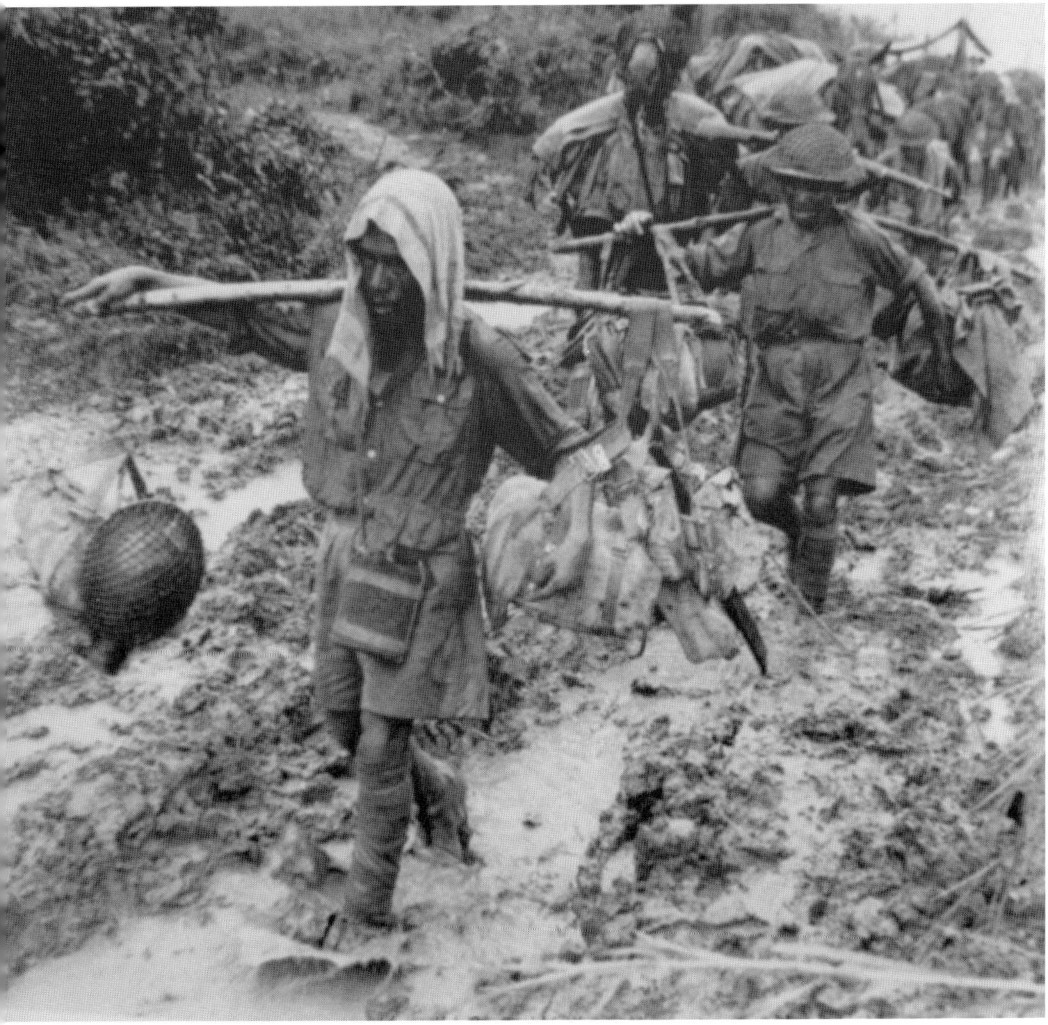

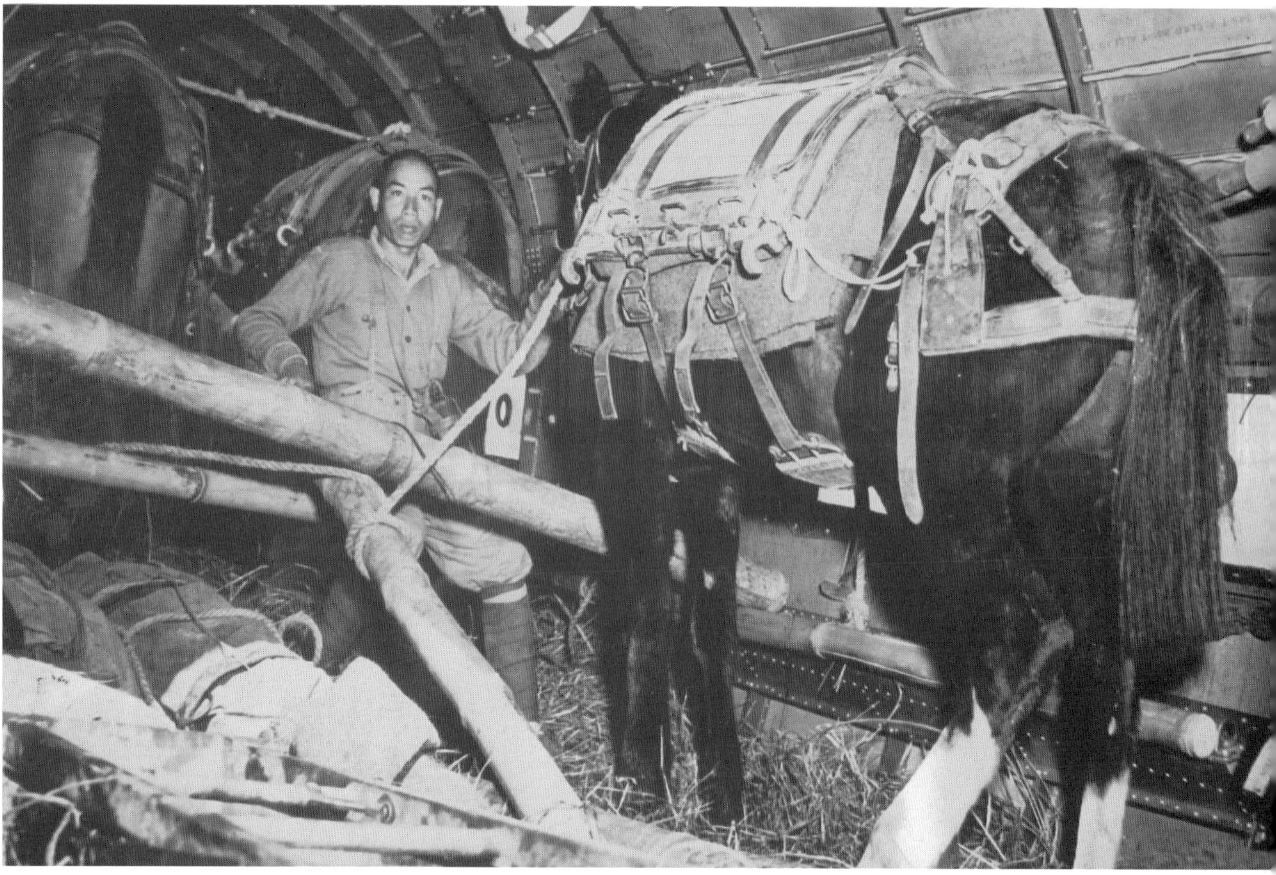

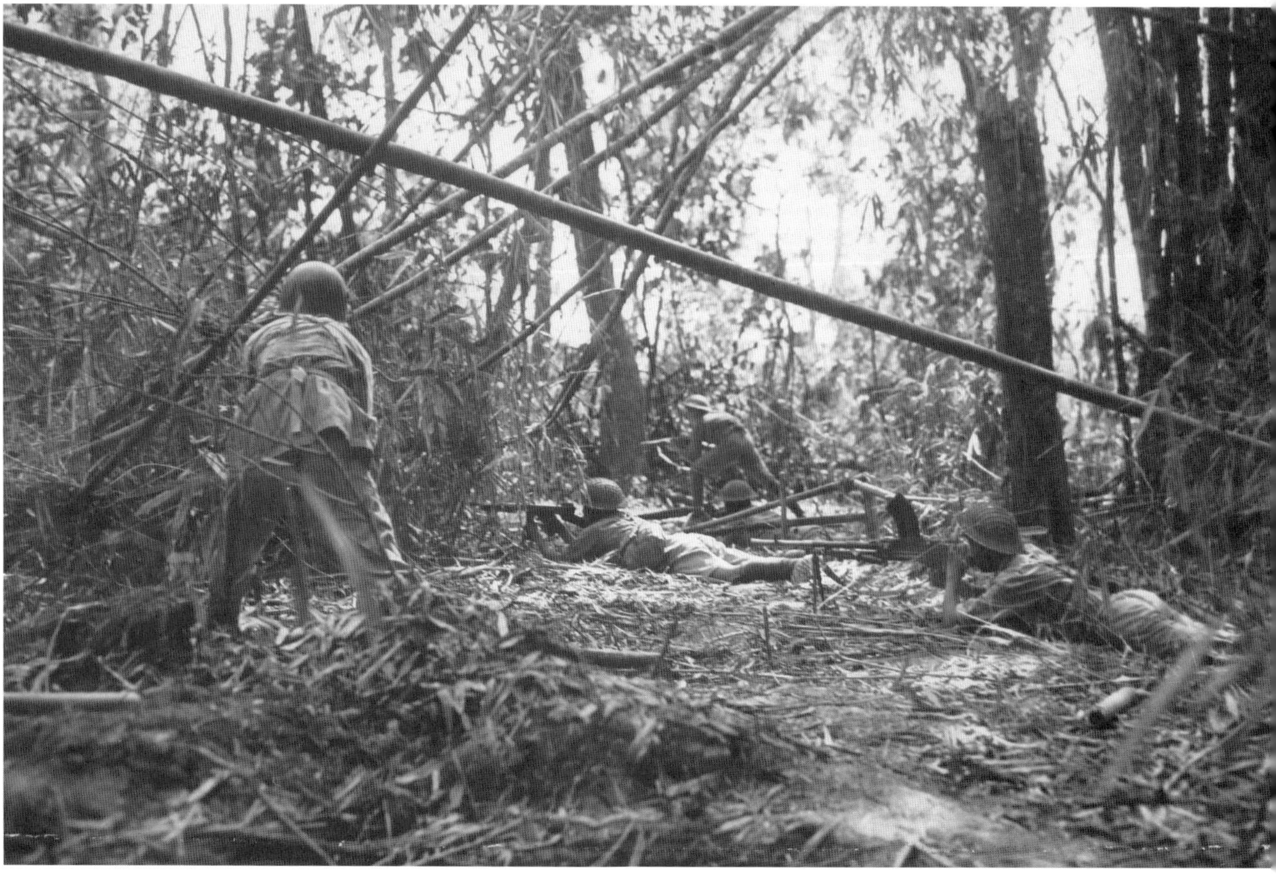

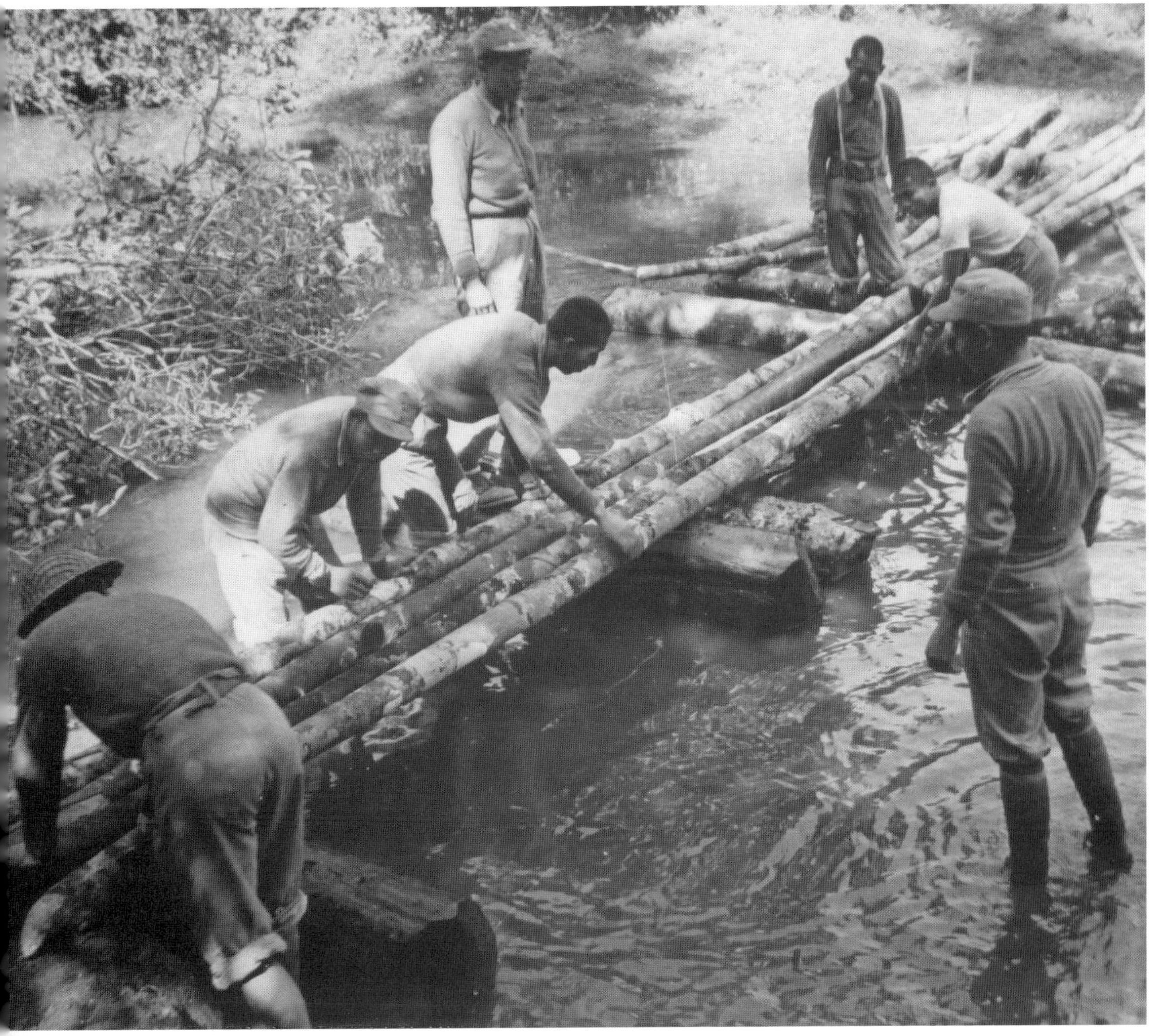

(**Opposite, above**) A Chinese muleteer tends to his pack animals in the fuselage of a C-47 Dakota transport as they are airlifted to the Myitkyina airfield. These sure-footed animals were prized for their sturdiness and load-carrying capacity to get supplies to the front lines from the Myitkyina airfield, which was captured by Stilwell's Sino-American force on 17 May 1944. *(NARA)*

(**Above**) Ramgarh-trained Chinese engineers build a sapling footbridge across one of northern Burma's innumerable *chaungs* or streams. In addition to these military sappers, Chinese and Burmese civilians were employed along with American combat engineers on the massive construction of the Ledo Road that was to eventually link up with the Burma Road to supply the Chinese in Yunnan Province. *(NARA)*

(**Opposite, below**) Ramgarh-trained Chinese infantrymen armed with a variety of British and American weapons combat elements of the IJA 18th Division in a Hukawng Valley fire-fight. The Chinese also had to employ mortars and artillery to dislodge the entrenched Japanese positions along the Hukawng Valley's rivers. *(NARA)*

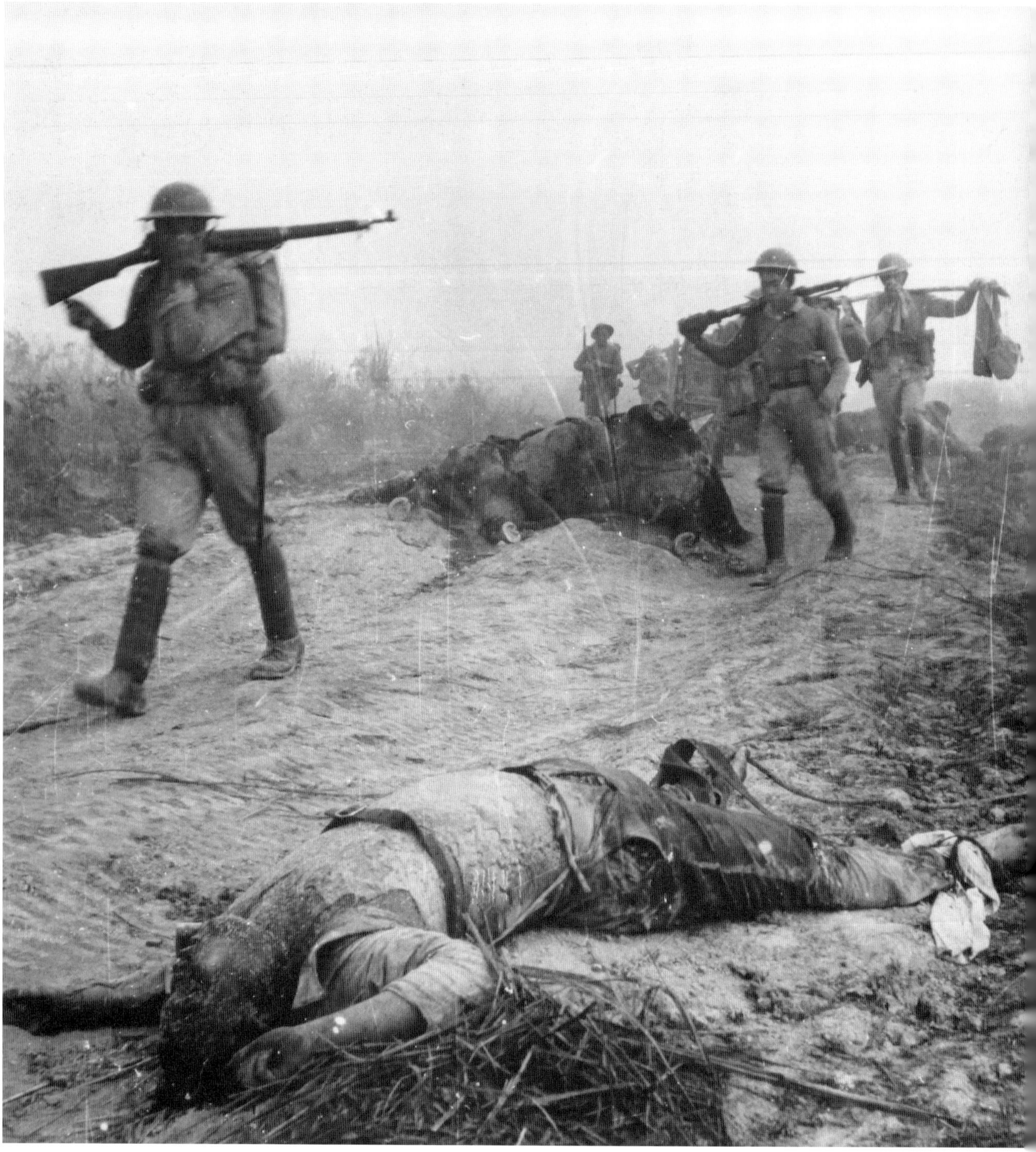

A column of Ramgarh-trained Chinese infantry passes a Japanese corpse and a dead horse on a trail to Myitkyina in May 1944. After attacks on IJA defences in the Hukawng Valley, south of the Jāmbu Bum and along the Kamaing Road, a Sino-American force led by Colonel Charles Hunter captured the Myitkyina airfield in a *coup de main* attack on 17 May 1944. (NARA)

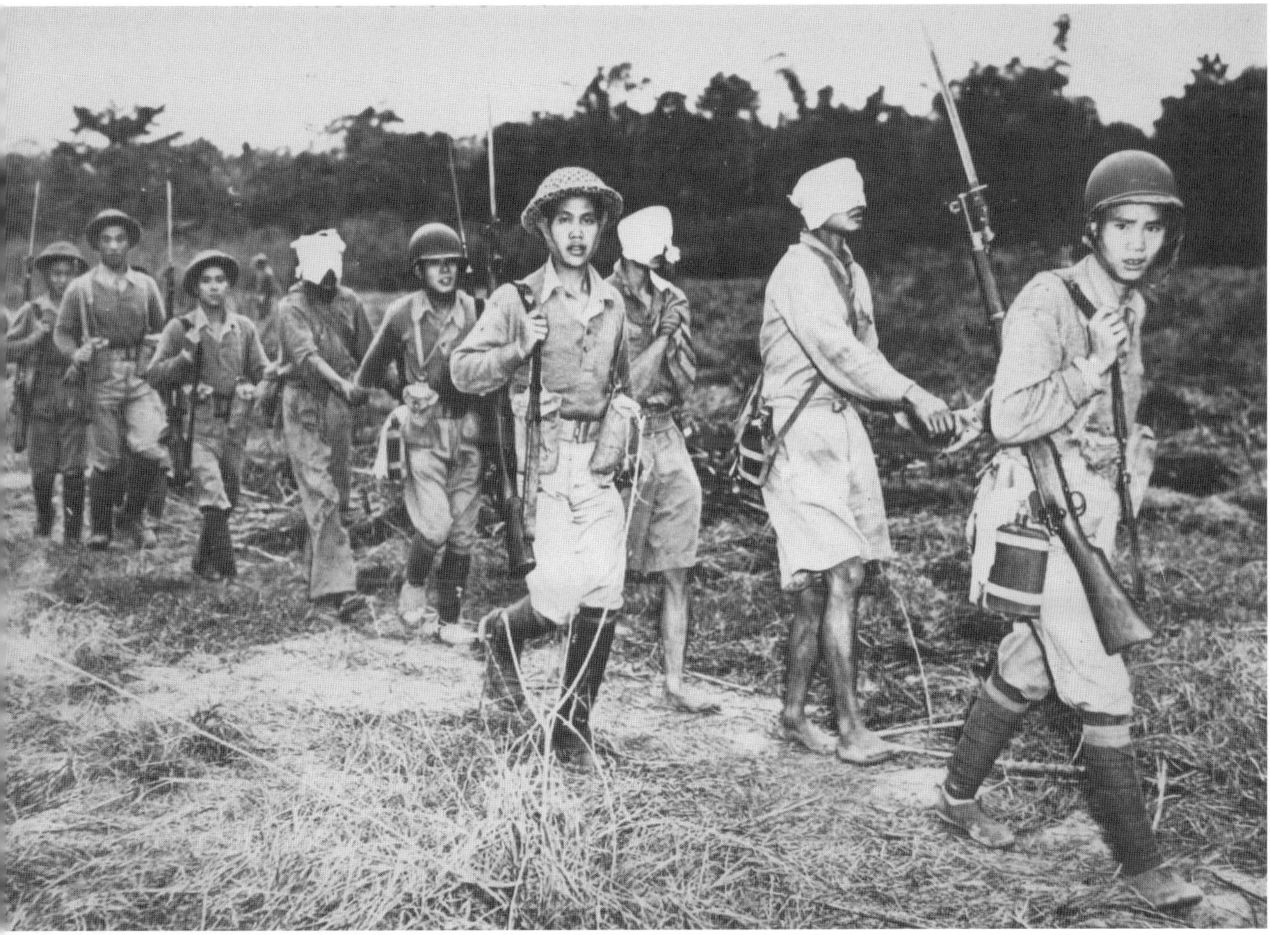

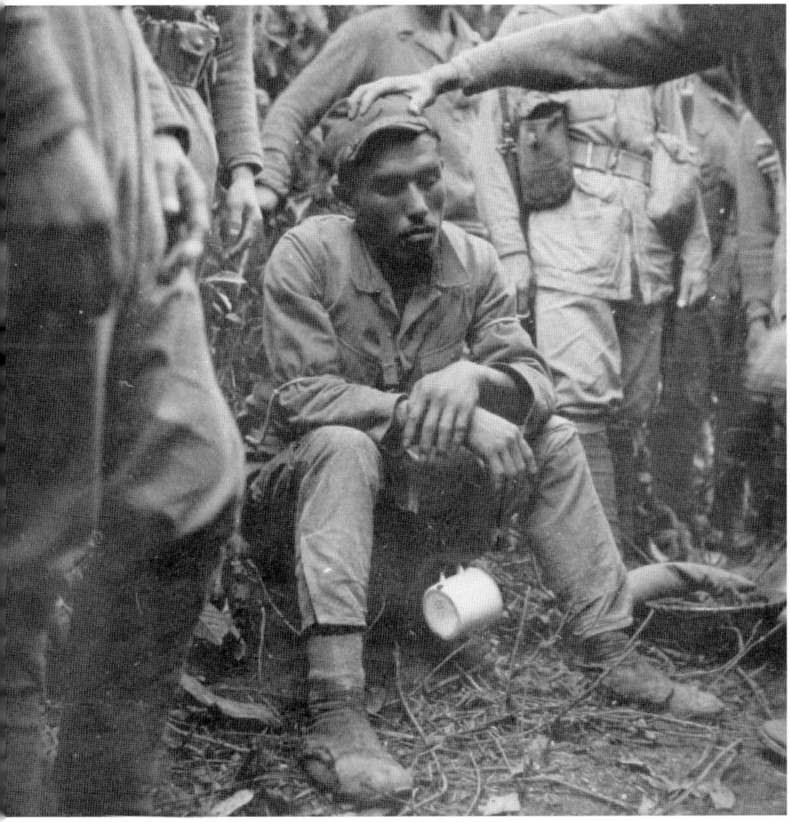

Chinese soldiers escort Japanese prisoners in northern Burma during Stilwell's Sino-American offensive through the Hukawng and Mogaung valleys on the trek to Myitkyina during the first half of 1944. *(NARA)*

An IJA 18th Division infantryman is shown here after capture in the Hukawng Valley in early 1944. His appearance and uniform show that he was not starving or dishevelled. This would be in sharp contrast to the Japanese captured later during the siege at Myitkyina or after the Chindits' capture of Mogaung. *(NARA)*

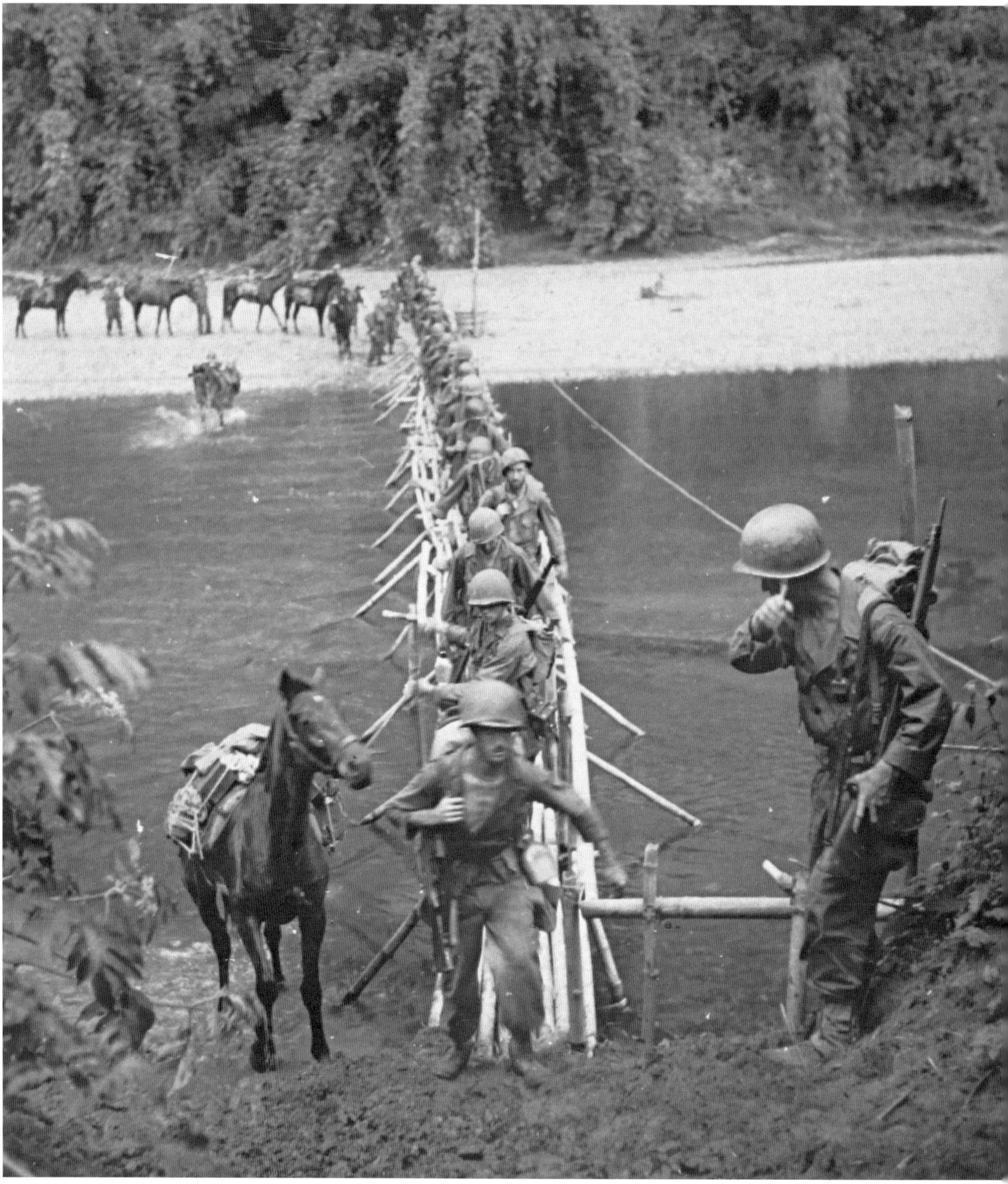

A column of infantrymen and their pack animals from the 5307th Composite Unit (Provisional), known as 'Galahad' or 'Merrill's Marauders', crosses a northern Burmese stream over a wooden footbridge during one of their Hukawng Valley envelopments against elements of the IJA 18th Division in early 1944. *(NARA)*

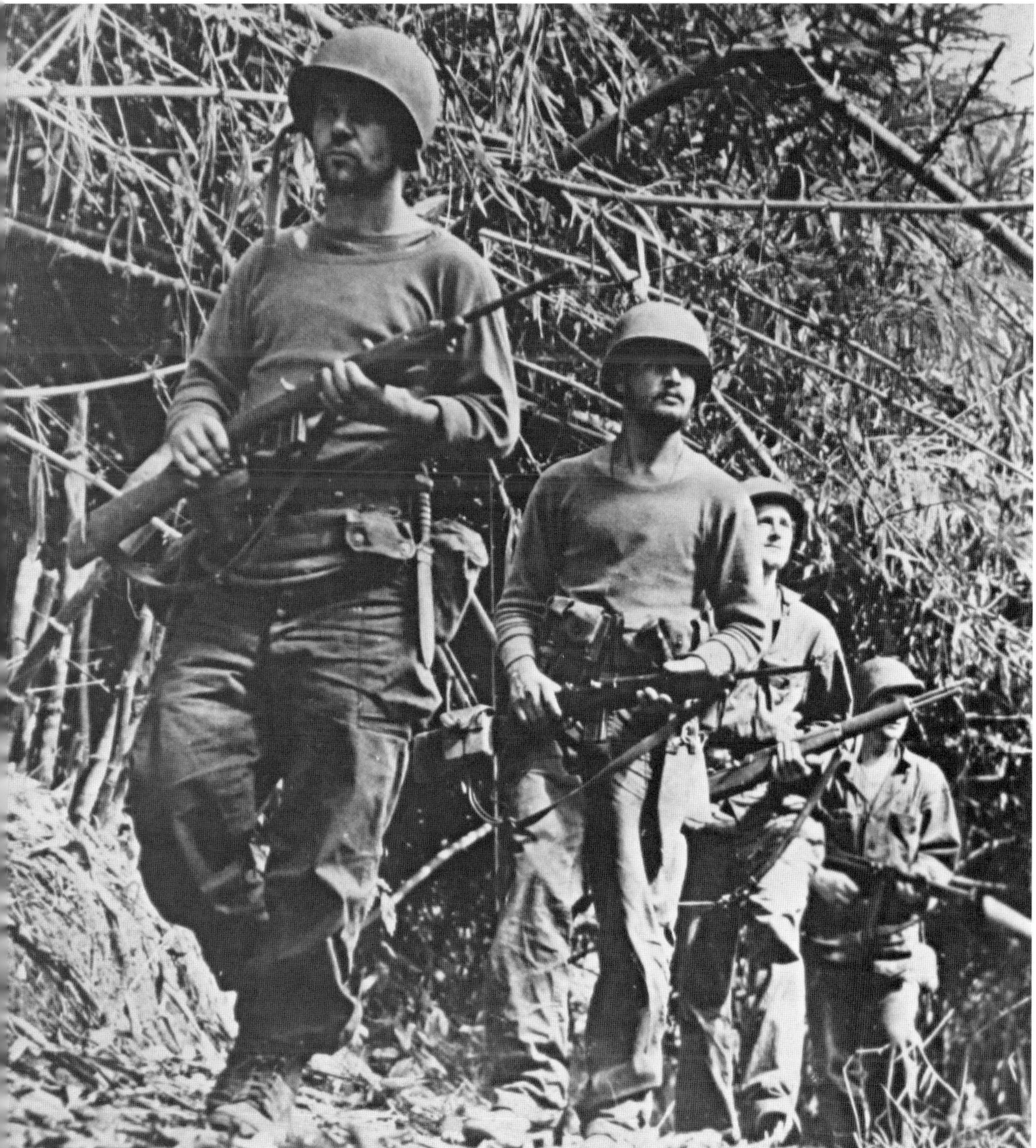

An iconic photograph showing a lightly-kitted 'Galahad' patrol armed with M1 semi-automatic carbines, an M1 Garand semi-automatic rifle and the rear member carrying a Thompson 0.45in-calibre SMG. These reconnaissance patrols were to detect enemy positions and find alternative jungle tracks around them. *(NARA)*

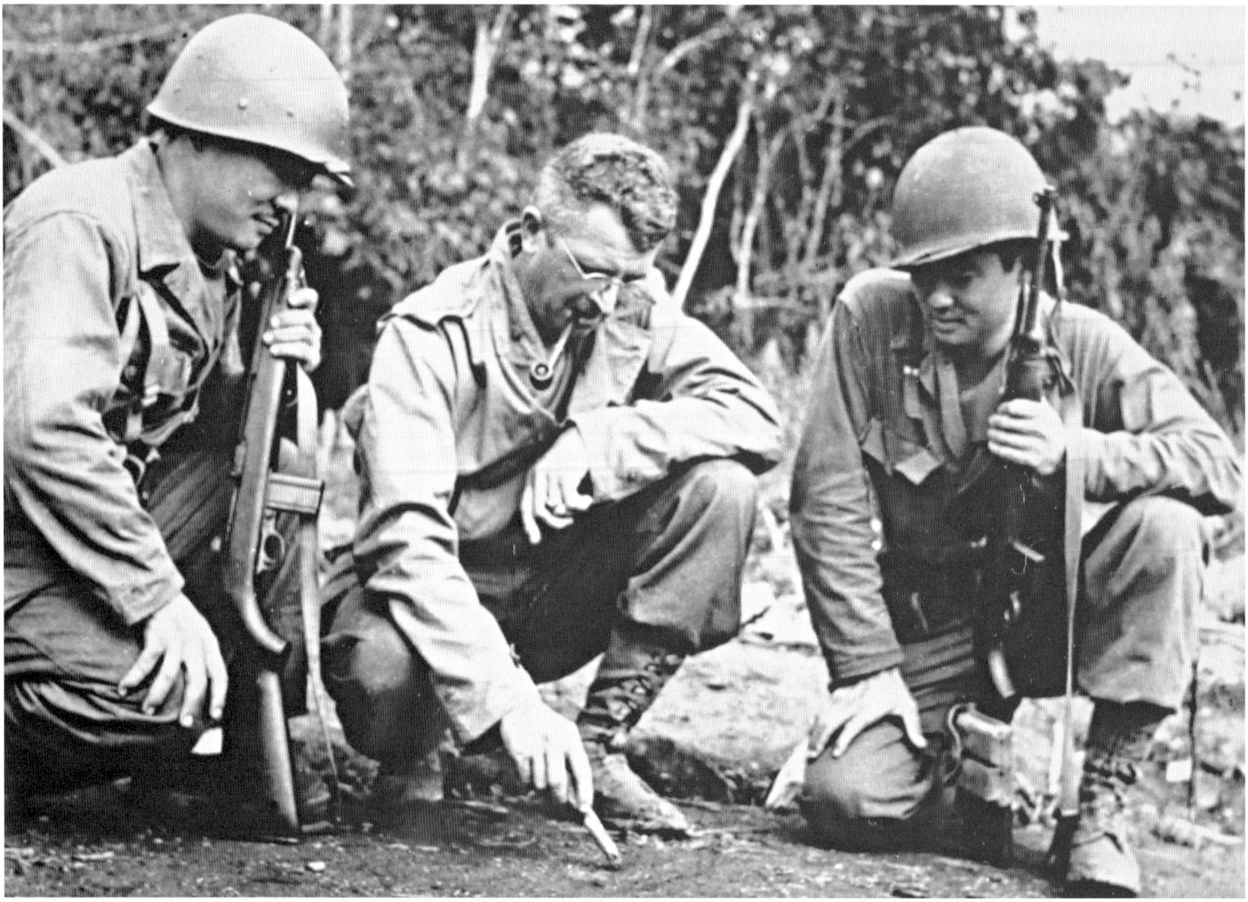

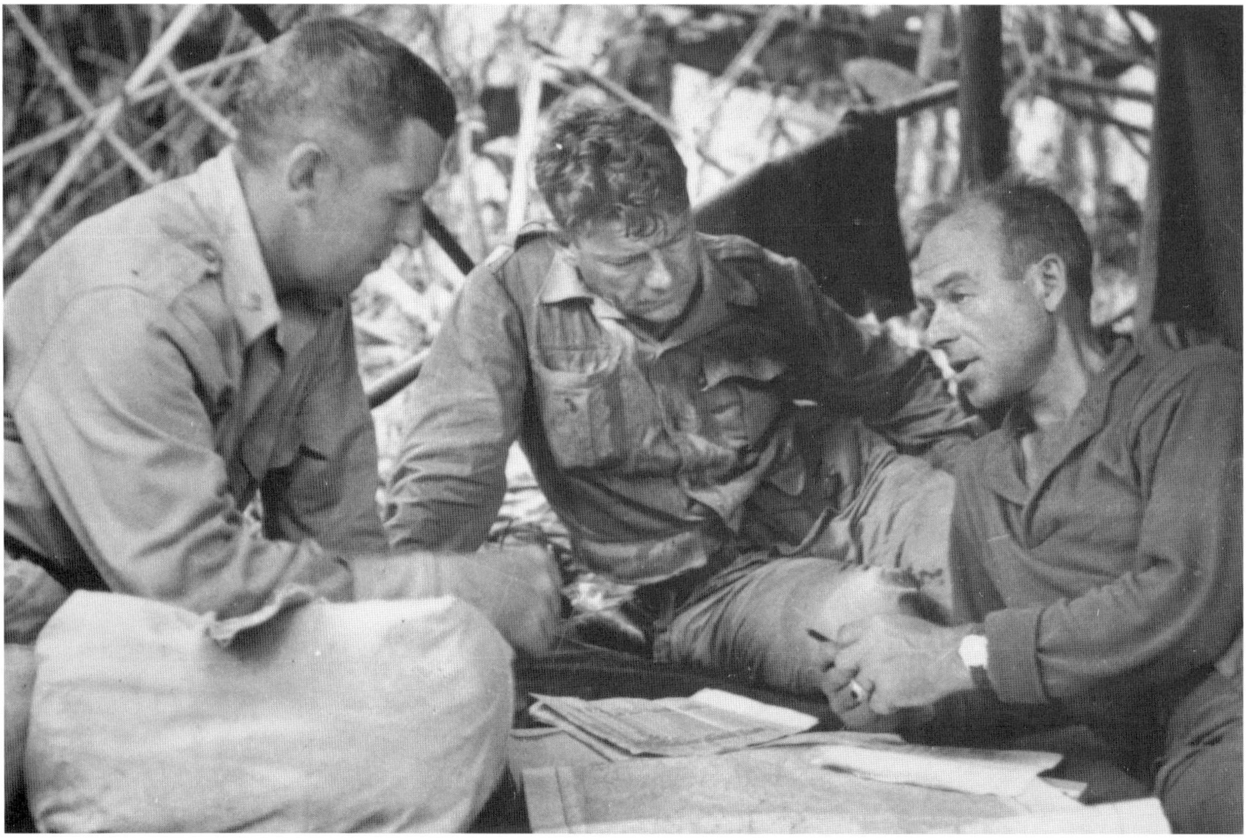

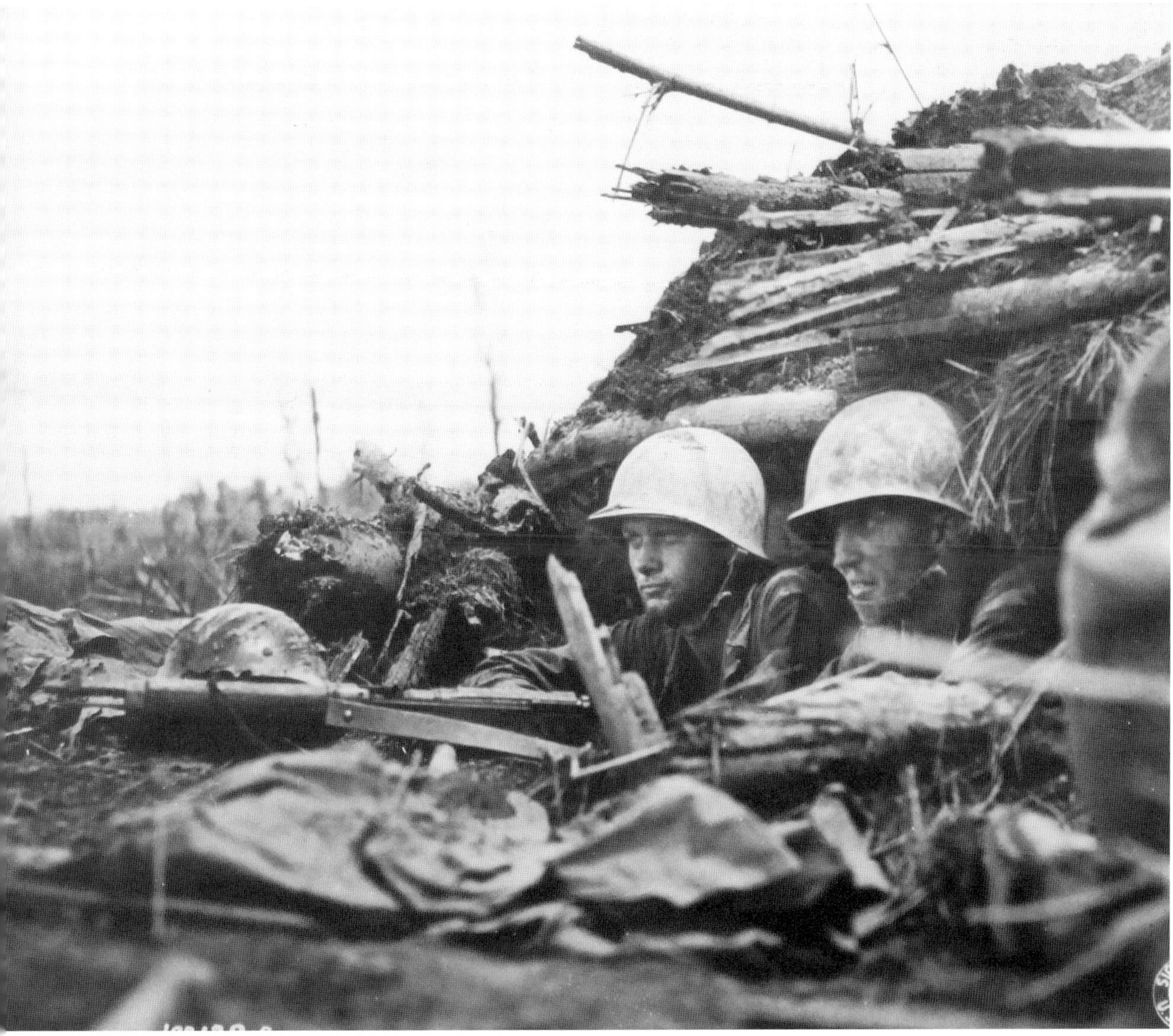

(**Opposite, above**) Brigadier General Frank Merrill (centre) confers with two of 'Galahad's 3rd Battalion's Nisei interpreters, Sergeant Herb Miyazaki (left) and Sergeant Akiji Yoshimura (right), near the Kumon Range in the Mogaung Valley in early spring 1944. The Nisei interpreters, including another Sergeant Roy Matsumoto in the 'Galahad's 2nd Battalion, were invaluable as they intercepted Japanese communications and plans by tapping into enemy telephone lines. *(NARA)*

(**Opposite, below**) Colonel Charles Hunter (right) discusses plans for the Myitkyina airfield attack with Major Frank Hodges (left) and Lieutenant Colonel William Combs (centre) at Naubum in late April 1944. Combs, a liaison officer with the Chinese, would die on 24 June 1944, five weeks after the successful capture of the Myitkyina airfield while trying to warn a green American combat engineer unit of a Japanese ambush. *(NARA)*

(**Above**) American soldiers peer out of a captured enemy pillbox along the siege lines around Myitkyina town after the airfield was captured on 17 May 1944. A discarded enemy helmet and chipped bayonet lie discarded on the ground in front of them. *(USAMHI)*

After the capture of the main western airfield at Myitkyina on 17 May 1944, Stilwell (centre) confers with Merrill (second from left) and the Myitkyina attack force leader Hunter (back to camera) as photographers record the meeting. Stilwell's L-5 Sentinel liaison aircraft (background) shuttled him to different locales. *(USAMHI)*

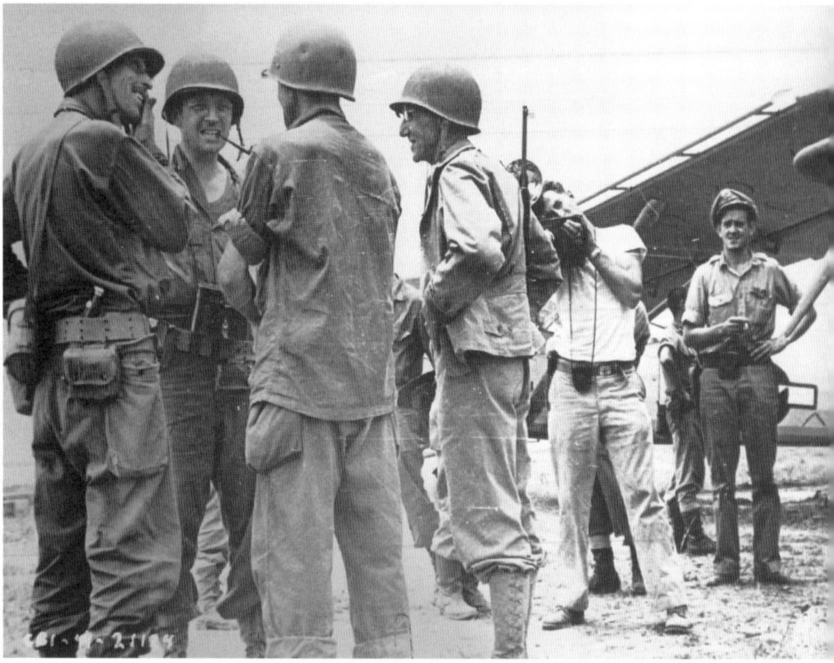

An American airborne engineer of an AAA company mans a 0.50in-calibre MG while a fellow soldier readies another box magazine of ammunition to defend the Myitkyina airstrip from IJA aerial attack. A C-47 Dakota transport sits idle in the background. *(USAMHI)*

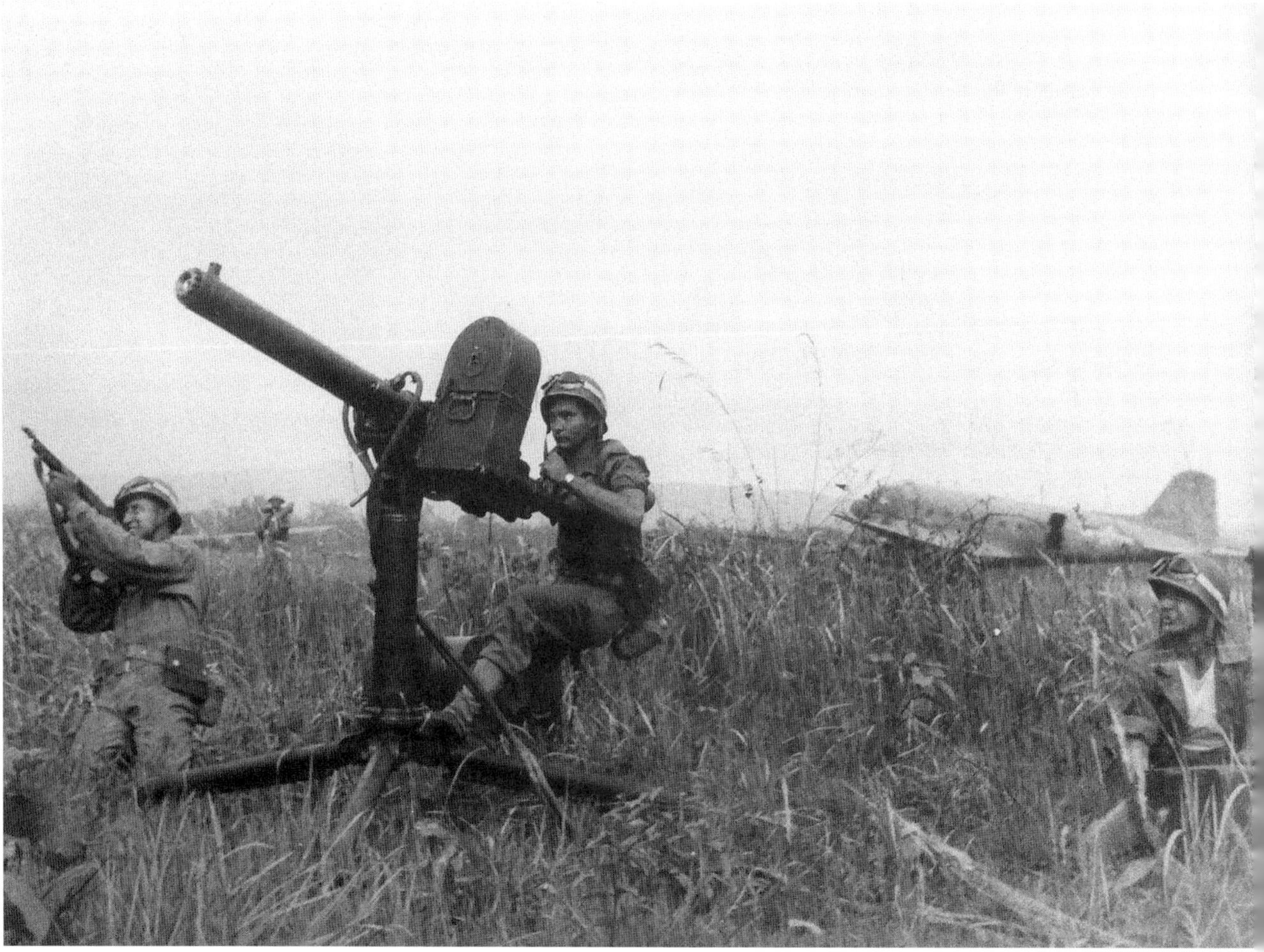

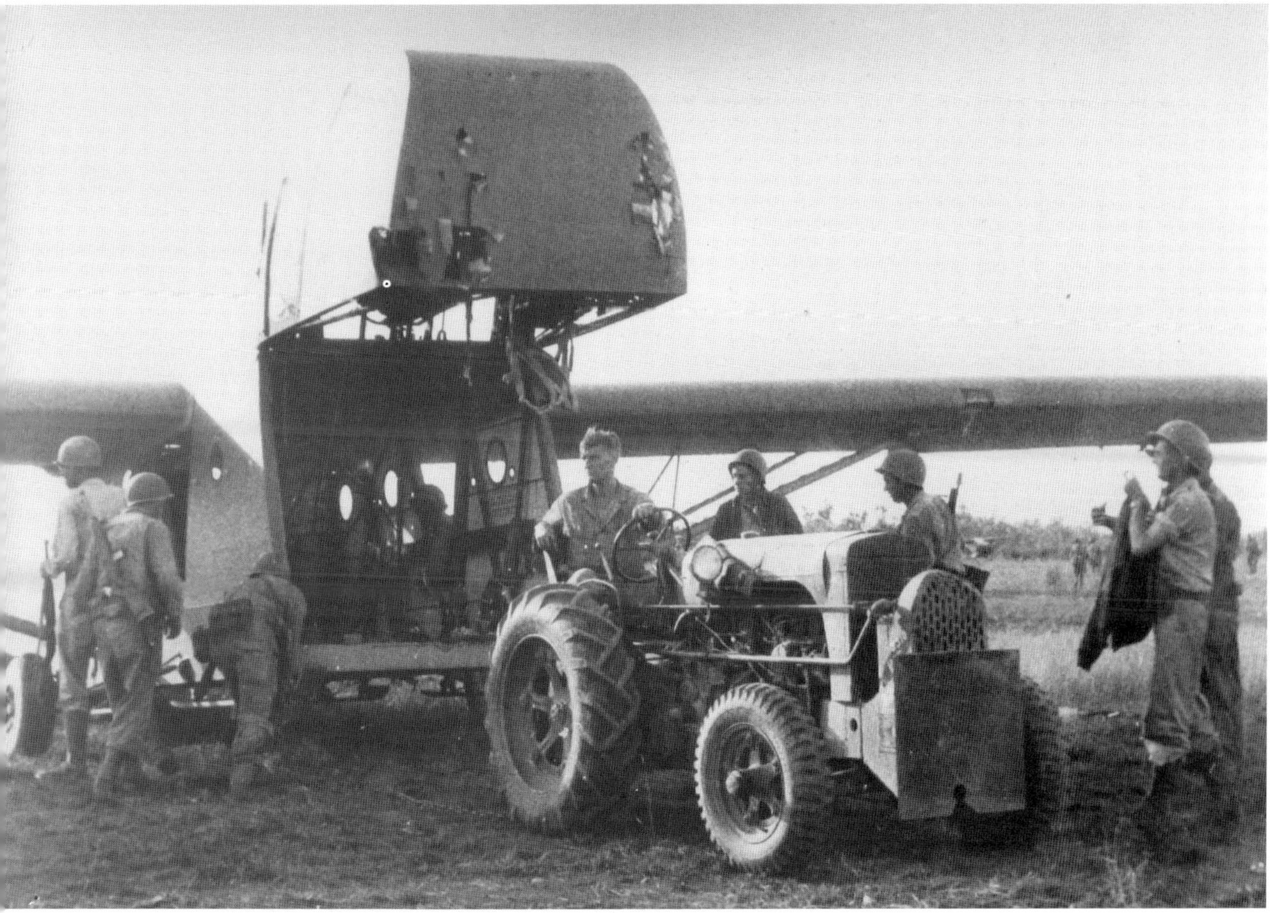

A tractor is unloaded from the nose of a Waco glider at the Myitkyina airfield within days of its capture on 17 May 1944. Equipment such as this tractor was vital to the maintenance and rebuilding of the airfield's runways for larger transport aircraft to land and to house Allied fighter-bombers. *(NARA)*

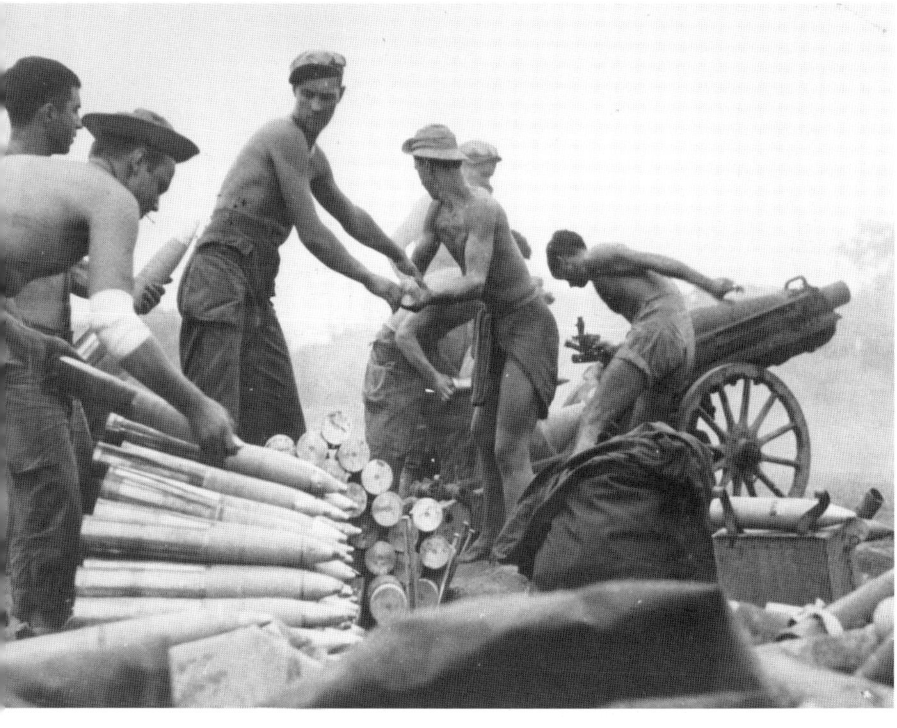

A 'Galahad' 75mm pack howitzer crew in action at the Myitkyina airfield bombarding Japanese positions in an arc around the town on the Irrawaddy River in the late spring of 1944. Such ordnance was air-landed by Waco gliders as the pack howitzer was shipped in component parts to be rapidly reassembled. Some 75mm rounds are stacked in the foreground. *(NARA)*

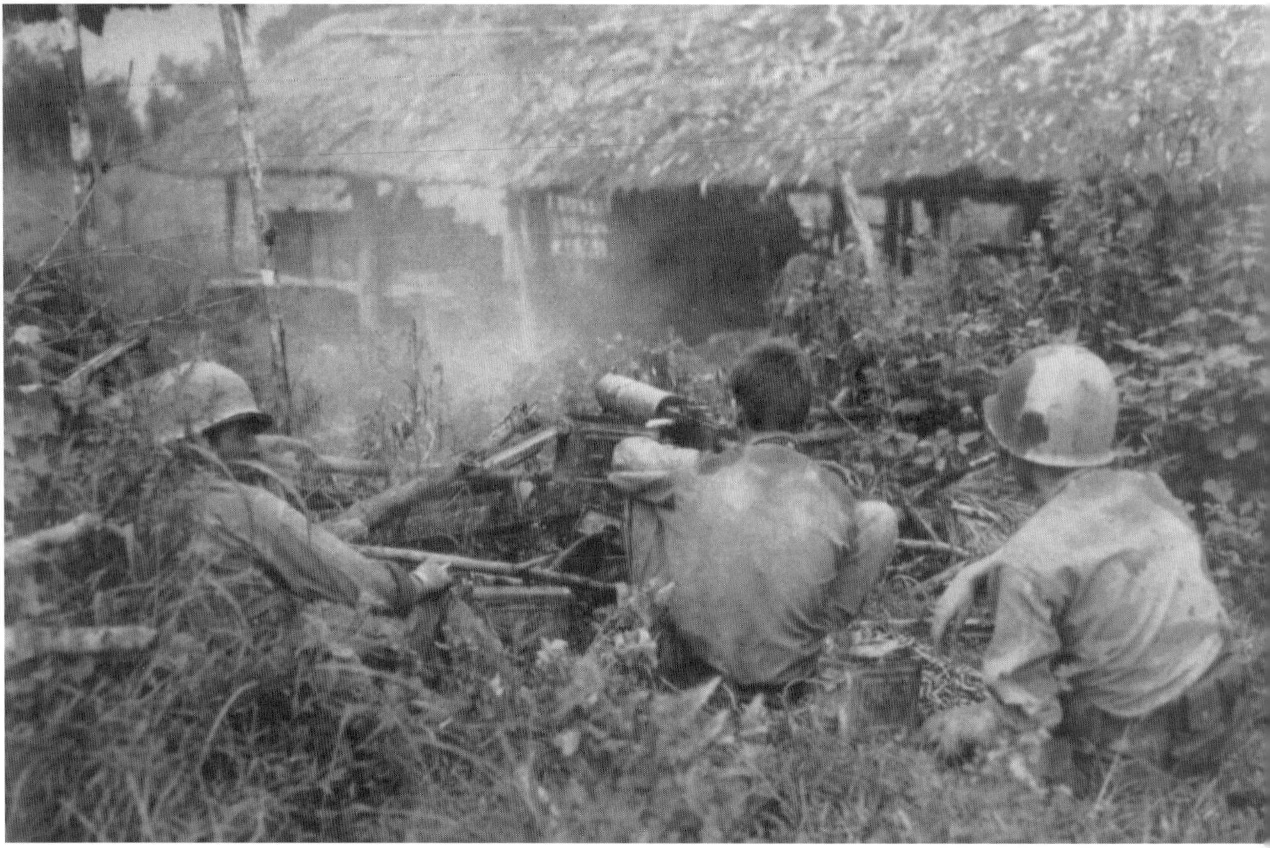

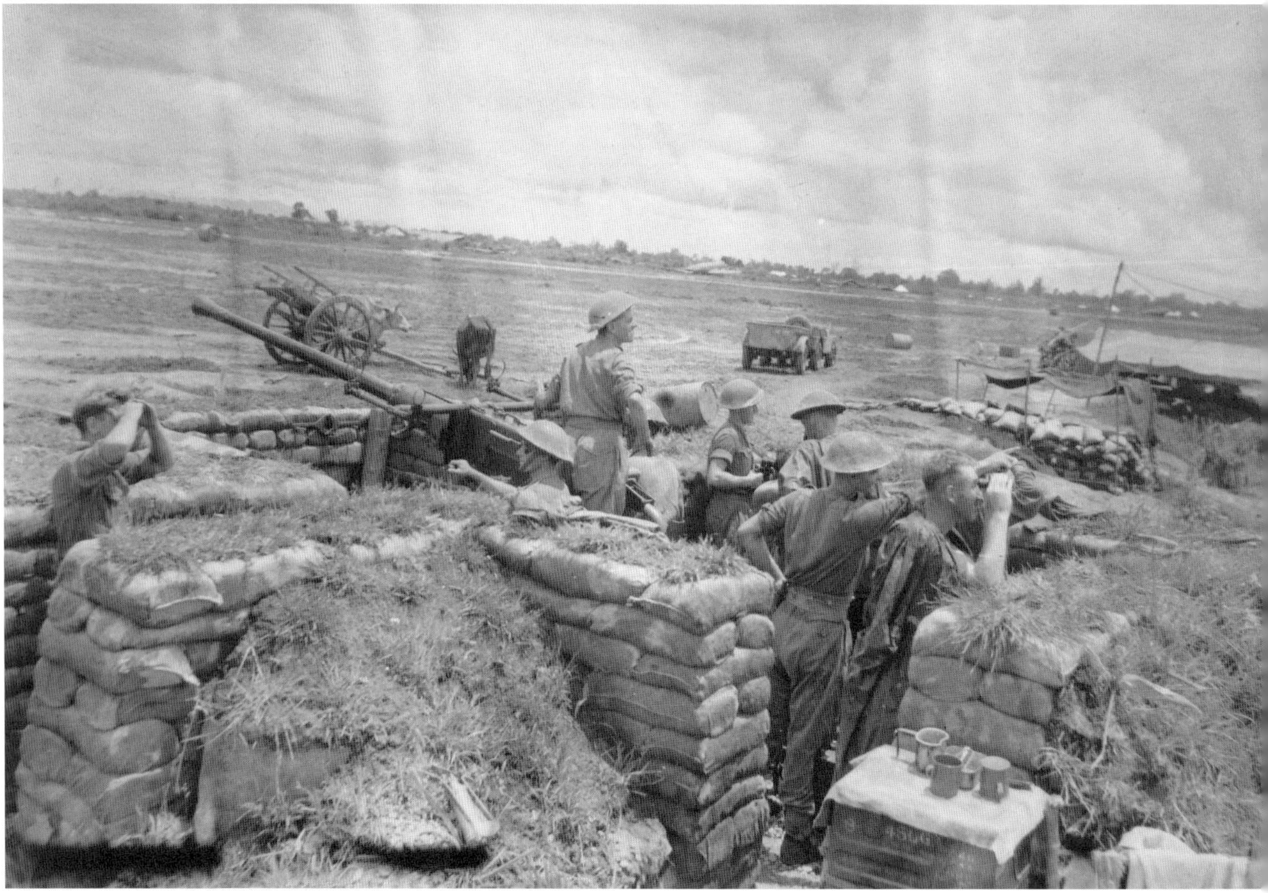

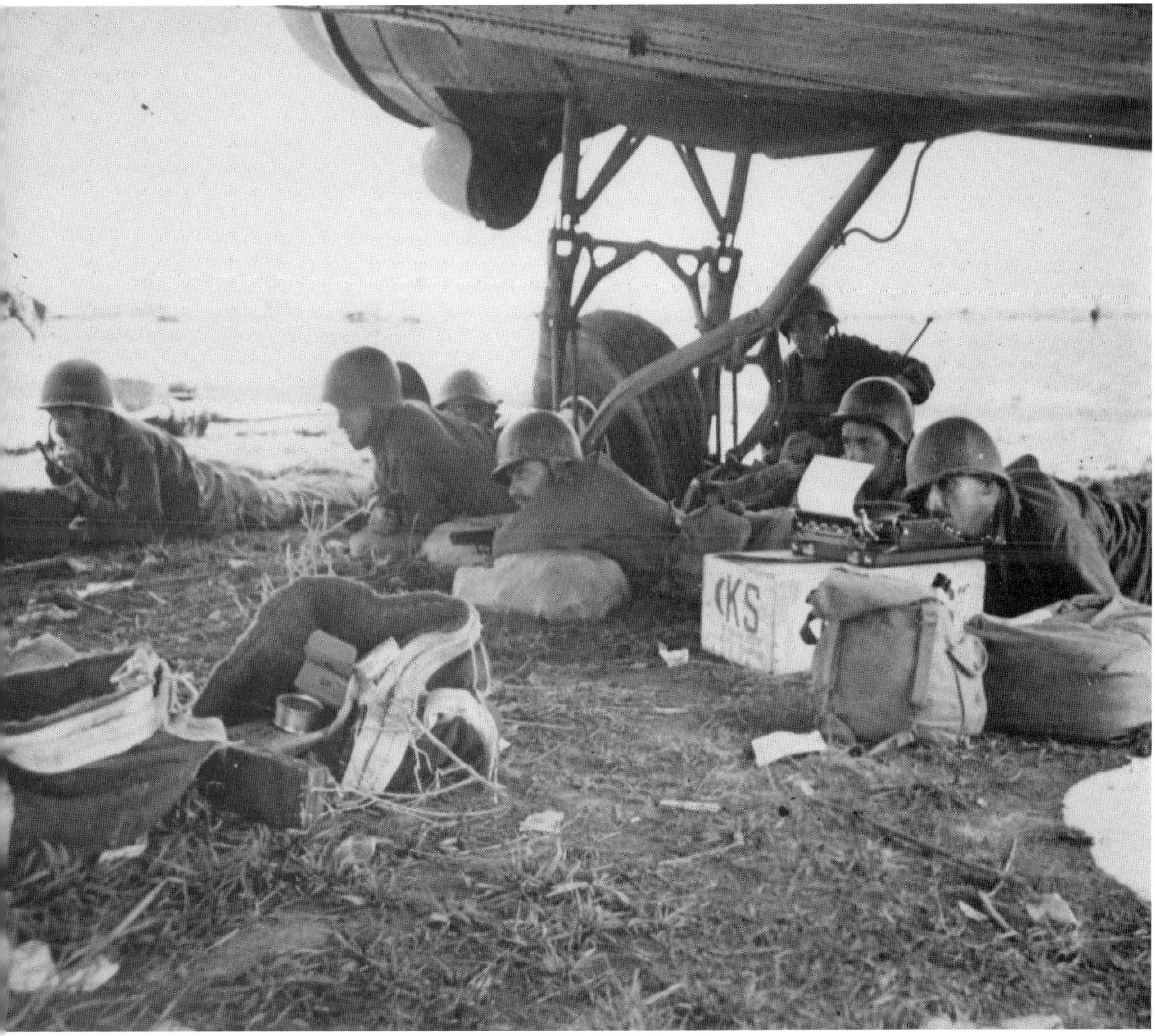

(**Opposite, above**) A 'Galahad' crew fires their M1919A 0.30in-calibre water-cooled MG on Japanese positions in Sitapur, a village north-east of the Myitkyina airfield. Many Burmese villages were attacked by Sino-American forces after the airfield's capture to break up local Japanese counterattacks from Myitkyina town. *(NARA)*

(**Opposite, below**) A British crew at their 40mm Bofors gun scans the skies on 18 July 1944 at the Myitkyina airfield. W and X Troops of the 69th Light AAA Regiment were flown in early to protect the airfield instead of more combat infantry to attack Myitkyina town. Frequent Japanese air attacks attempted to slow reinforcements and supplies to the new Allied airhead. *(NARA)*

(**Above**) Americans take cover under the fuselage of an Allied aircraft from Japanese sniper fire at the Myitkyina airstrip on 19 May 1944. Two of them are war correspondents: Technical Sergeant Dave Richardson for *Yank Magazine* (far left) and Tillman Durdin of the *New York Times* (far right). The press chronicled 'Galahad's (which they nicknamed 'Merrill's Marauders') advance through northern Burma. *(NARA)*

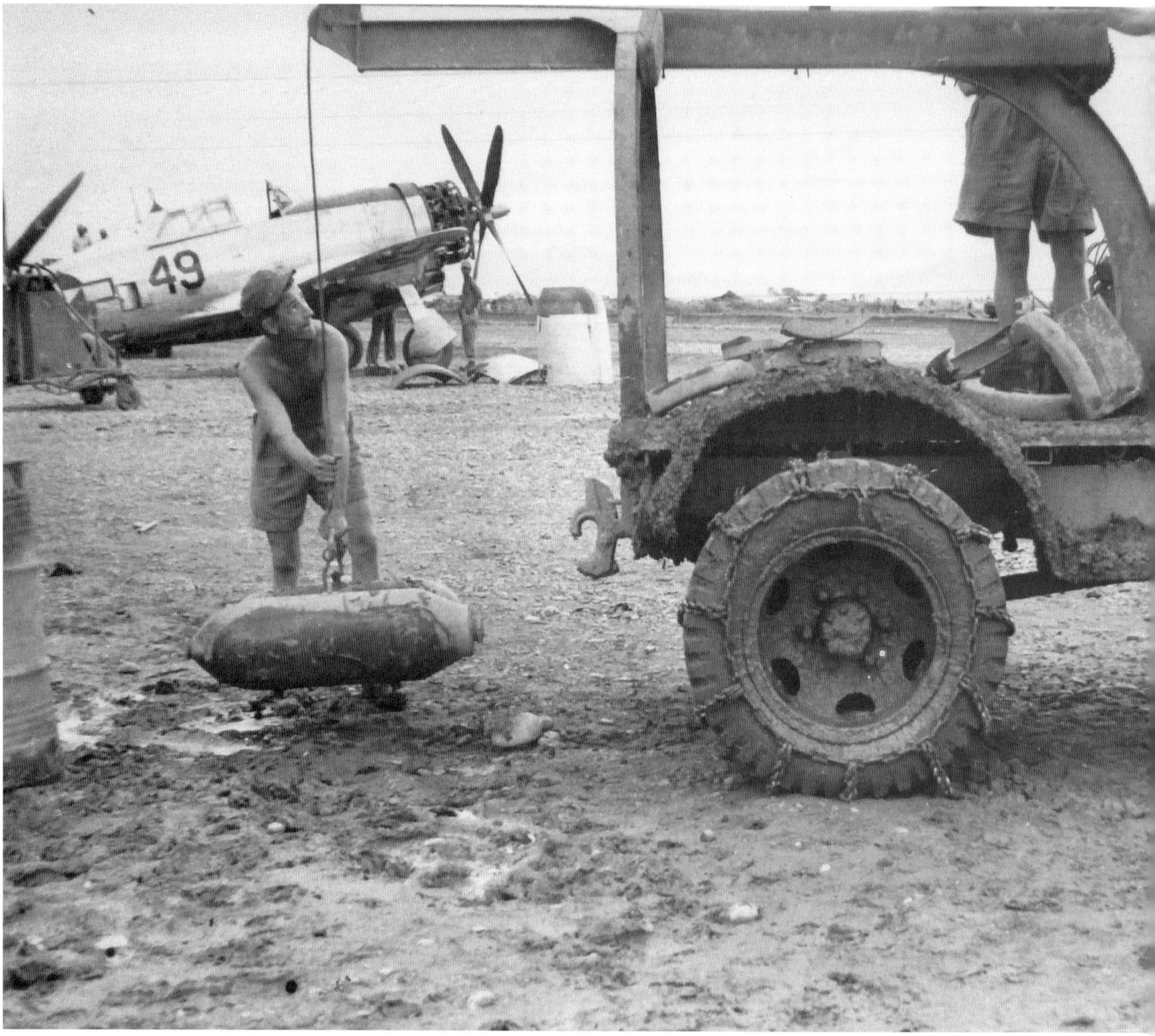
49

(**Above**) A bomb is prepared for loading onto an American Republic P-47 Thunderbolt fighter-bomber at the Myitkyina airfield in support of the Sino-American infantry siege of Myitkyina town. The single-seat P-47 was rugged and able to withstand enemy ground fire as well as providing close air support, with its eight 0.5in-calibre fixed forward-firing MGs in the wings' leading edges. It could carry an external bomb or rocket load of 2,500lb. *(NARA)*

(**Opposite, above**) Operating tables are shown here at the Myitkyina airfield's open-air hospital, supervised by Colonel Gordon Seagrave, to treat the seriously wounded prior to air evacuation to Assam. The Rangoon-born Seagrave, a Johns Hopkins University medical school graduate, practised for almost twenty years in China and Burma before joining the US Army Medical Corps in 1942 and was part of Stilwell's 'Walkout'. *(NARA)*

(**Opposite, below**) Wounded soldiers from the Sino-American force are moved on oxcart-drawn litters from the hospital section of the Myitkyina airfield to nearby C-47 transports for evacuation to India. The C-47s brought in reinforcements and supplies to Allied forces at the airfield and transported the severely wounded on the return trip to Assam. *(NARA)*

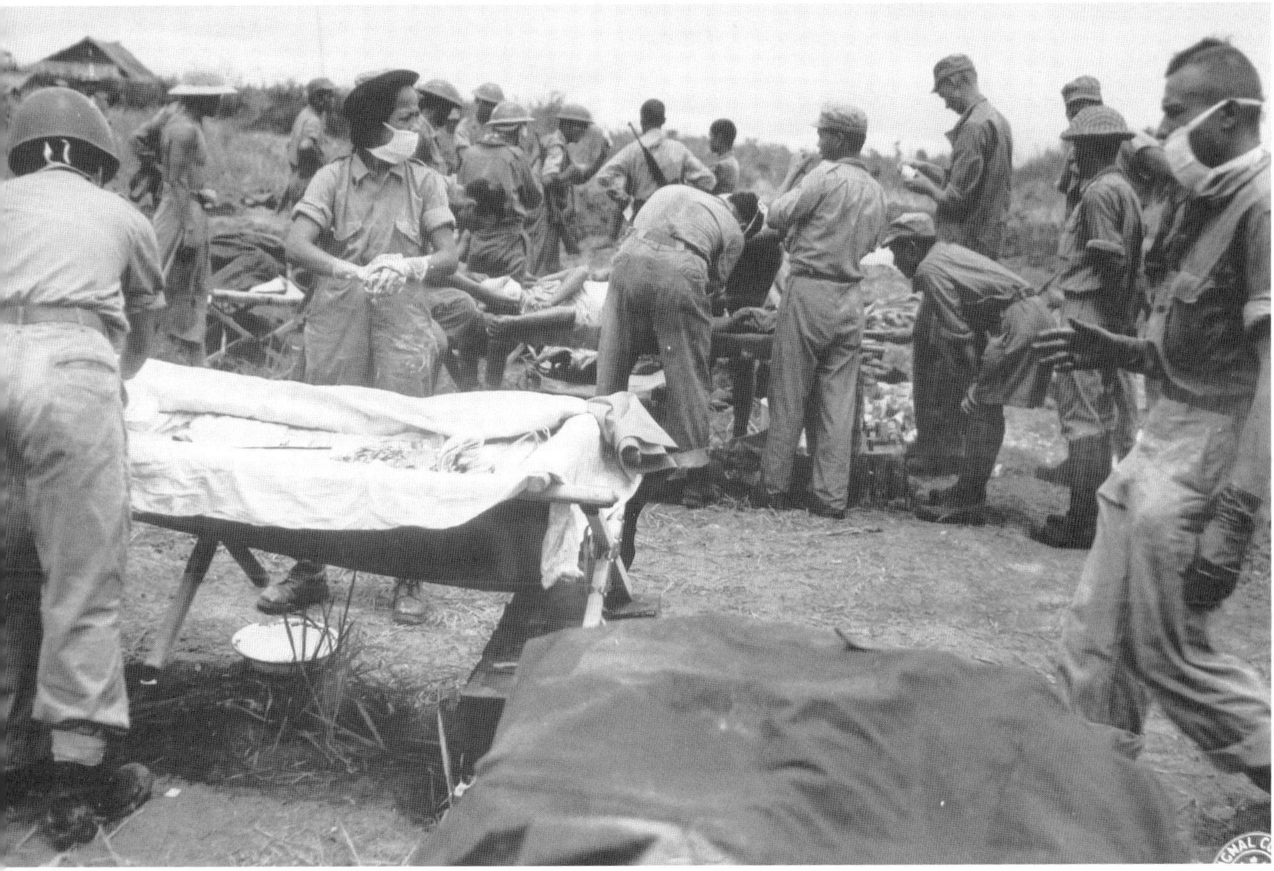

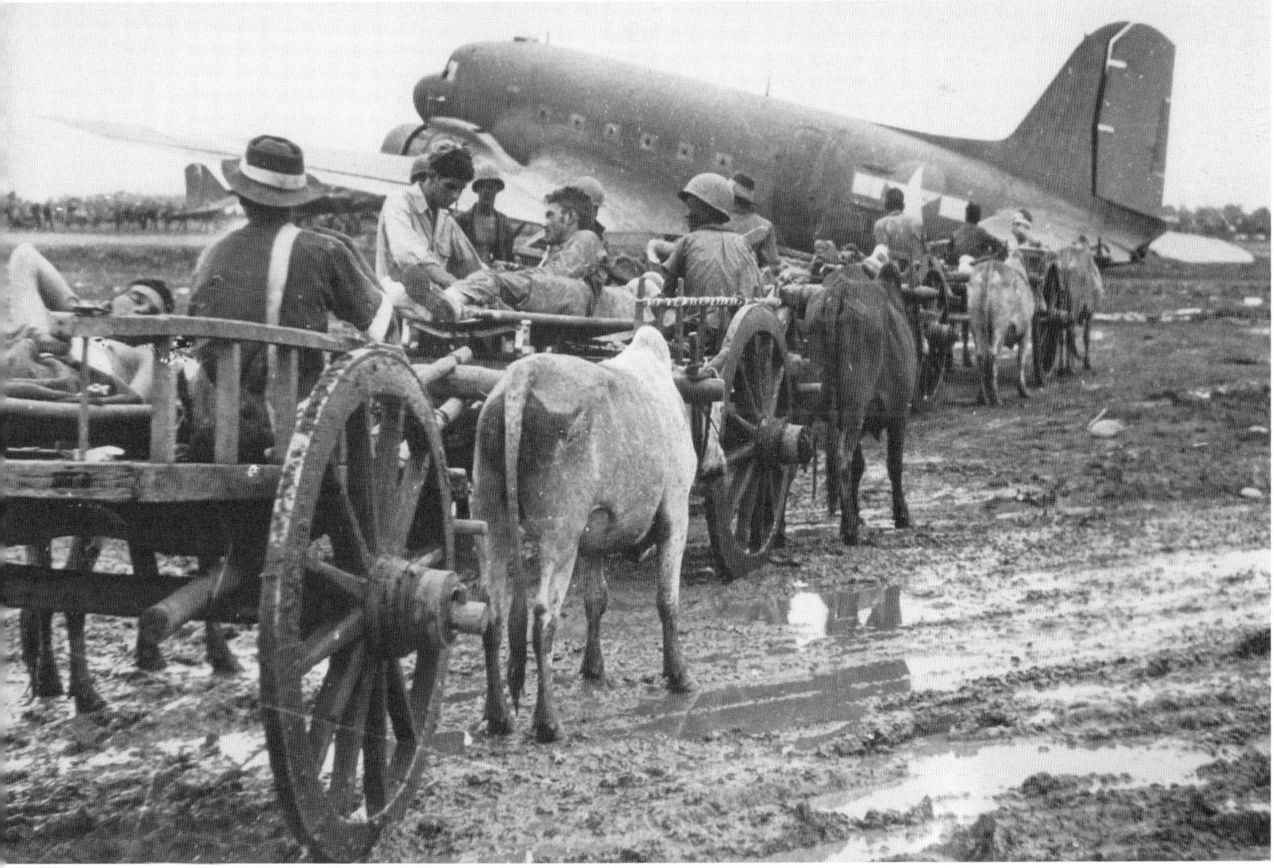

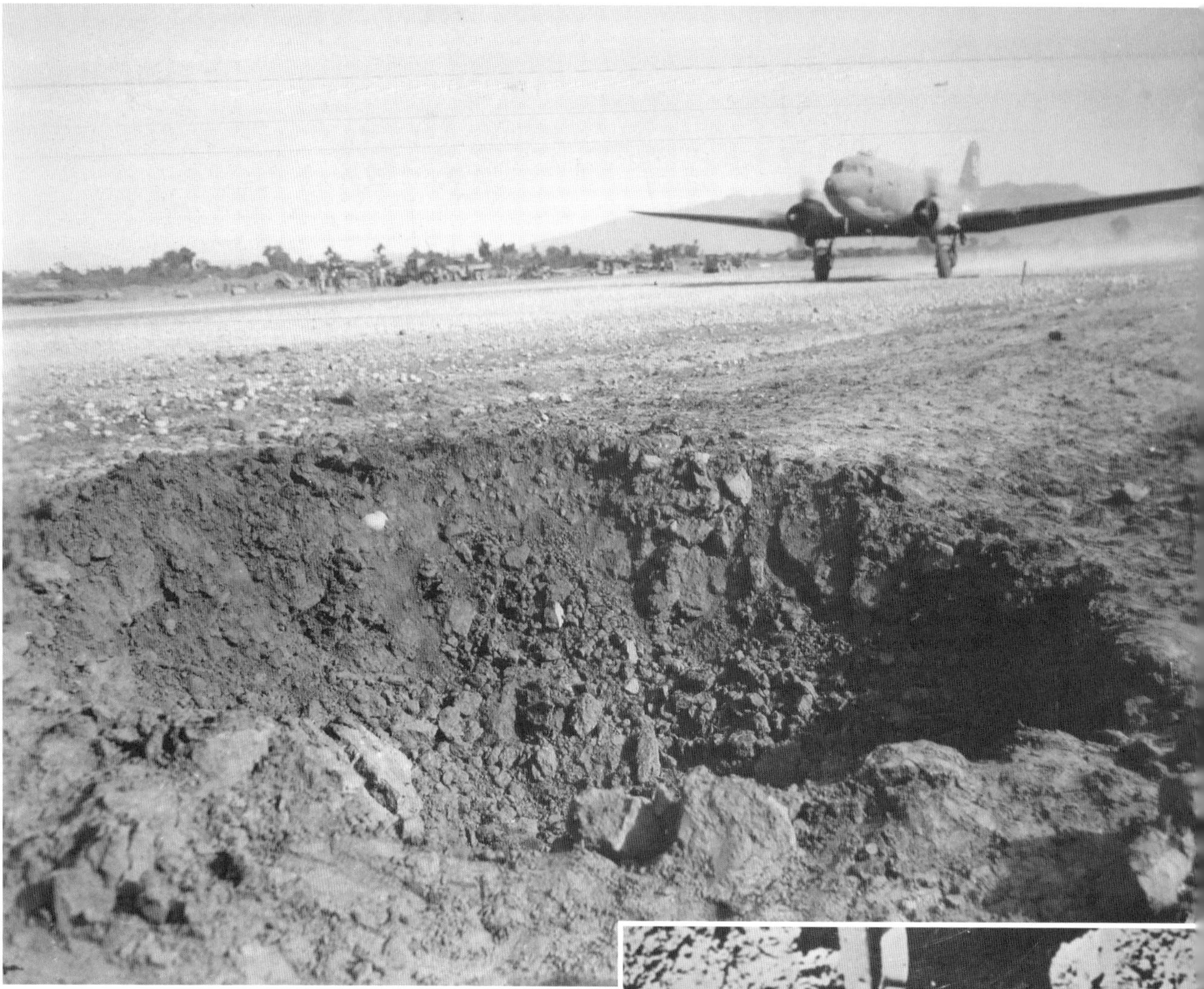

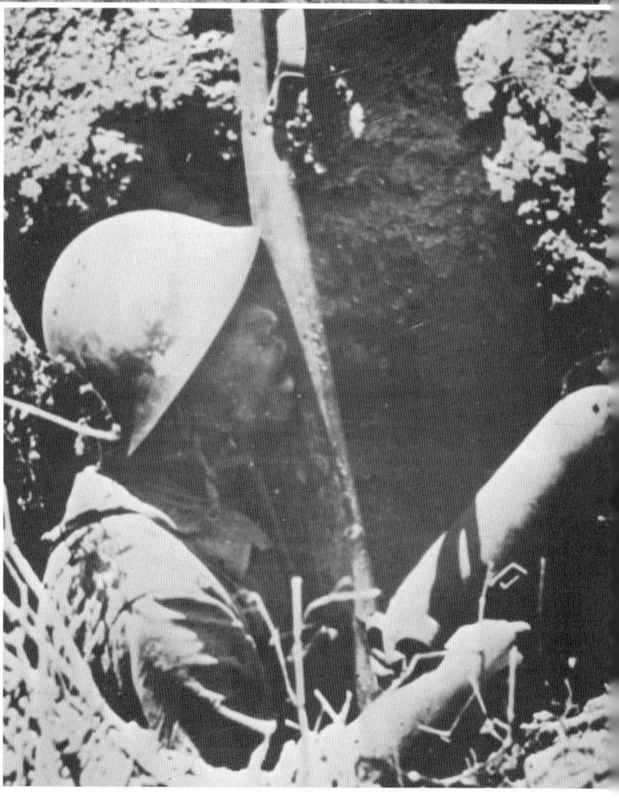

(**Above**) A C-47 transport takes off from the Myitkyina airfield near a 6ft-deep bomb crater at the runway's side. During the siege of Myitkyina, Allied fighters flew up to six missions a day supporting ground troops and defending the airfield from Japanese aerial attack that cratered the runways. *(NARA)*

(**Right**) A dead Japanese soldier in a hole acted as an AT mine with a 100lb bomb between his knees. He was killed by Allied infantry before he could detonate the bomb. *(NARA)*

(**Opposite**) An American infantryman in Myitkyina town gazes at a Japanese soldier who preferred a *bushido* or warrior code death by suicide rather than surrendering. *(USAMHI)*

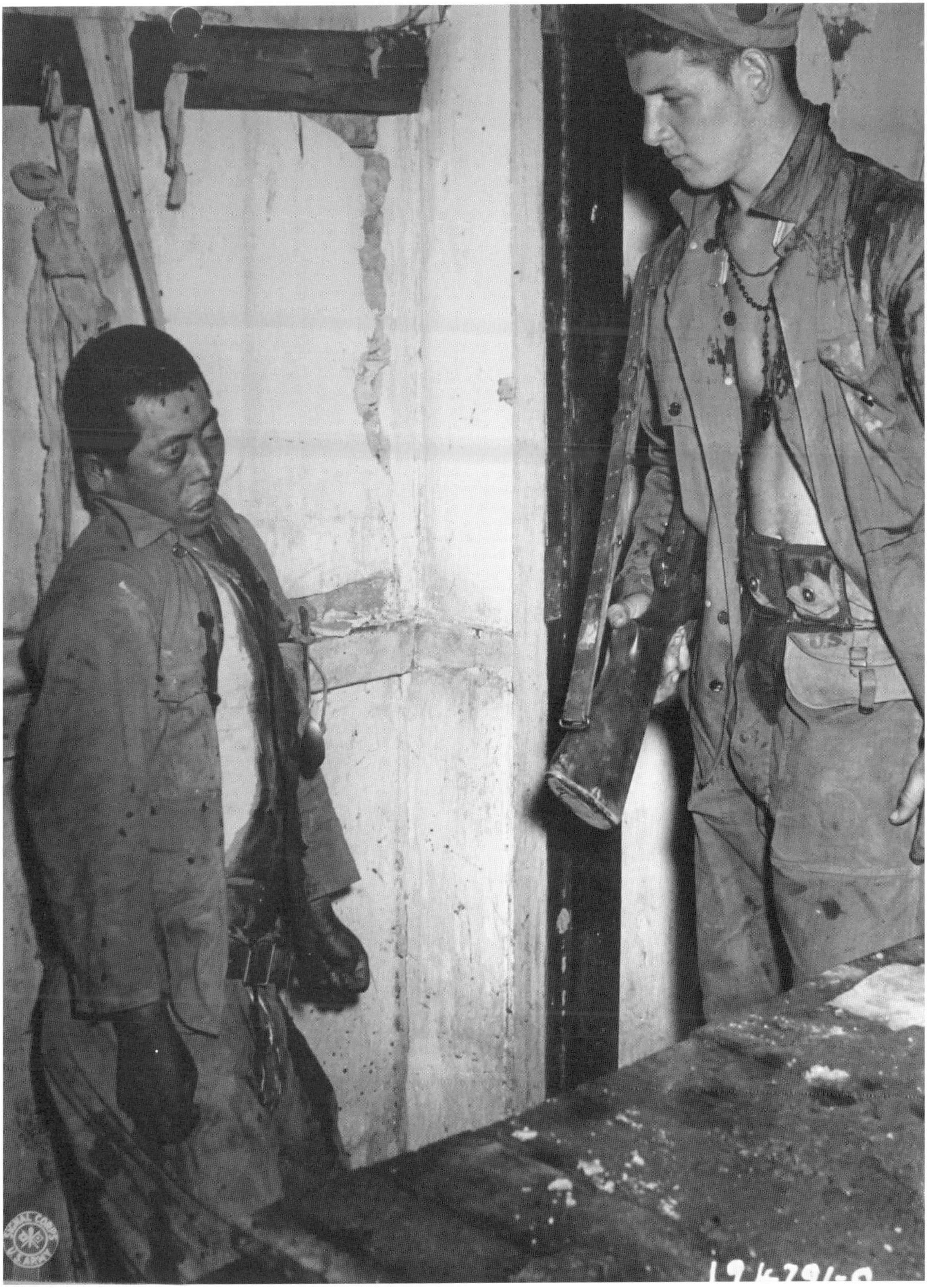
SIGNAL CORPS
U.S. ARMY

(**Right**) Two Japanese soldiers captured at Myitkyina are shown here. In contrast to Japanese prisoners earlier in the north Burma campaign, these two are emaciated from weeks of malnutrition and disease in their trenches at Myitkyina town. *(NARA)*

(**Below**) A 'Galahad' platoon leader speaks to some of the 1st Battalion's 200 survivors at the end of July 1944 at the Myitkyina airfield. Other Chinese and American combat engineer units reinforced the Marauders during their siege of Myitkyina town which lasted until 3 August. *(NARA)*

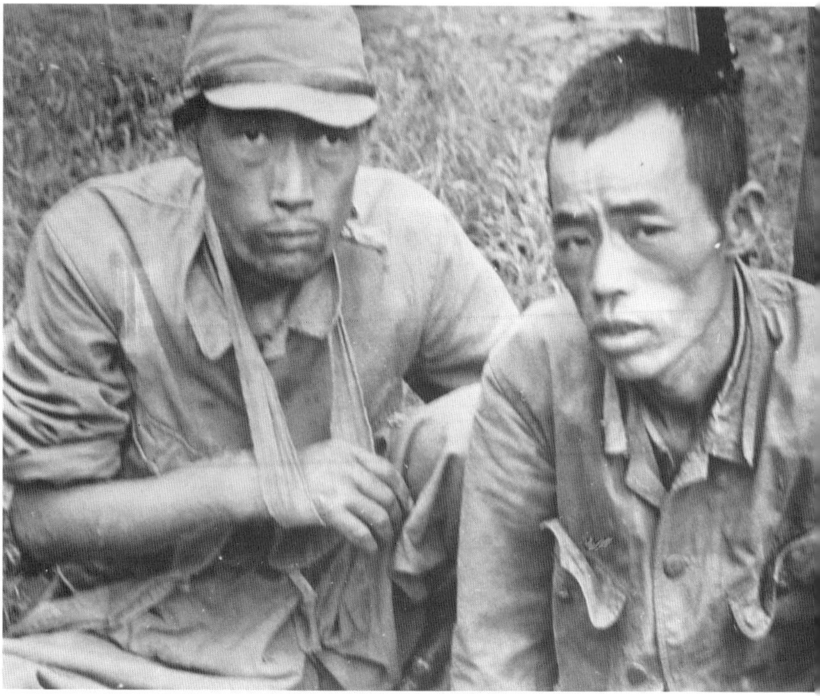

(**Opposite, above**) American troops lead their pack animals laden with supplies and weapons to forward areas from the Myitkyina airfield. A C-47 transport is in the background. *(NARA)*

(**Opposite, below**) An aerial view of the devastated Myitkyina town with destroyed railway cars, buildings and enemy trenches. The Irrawaddy River is in the background. *(NARA)*

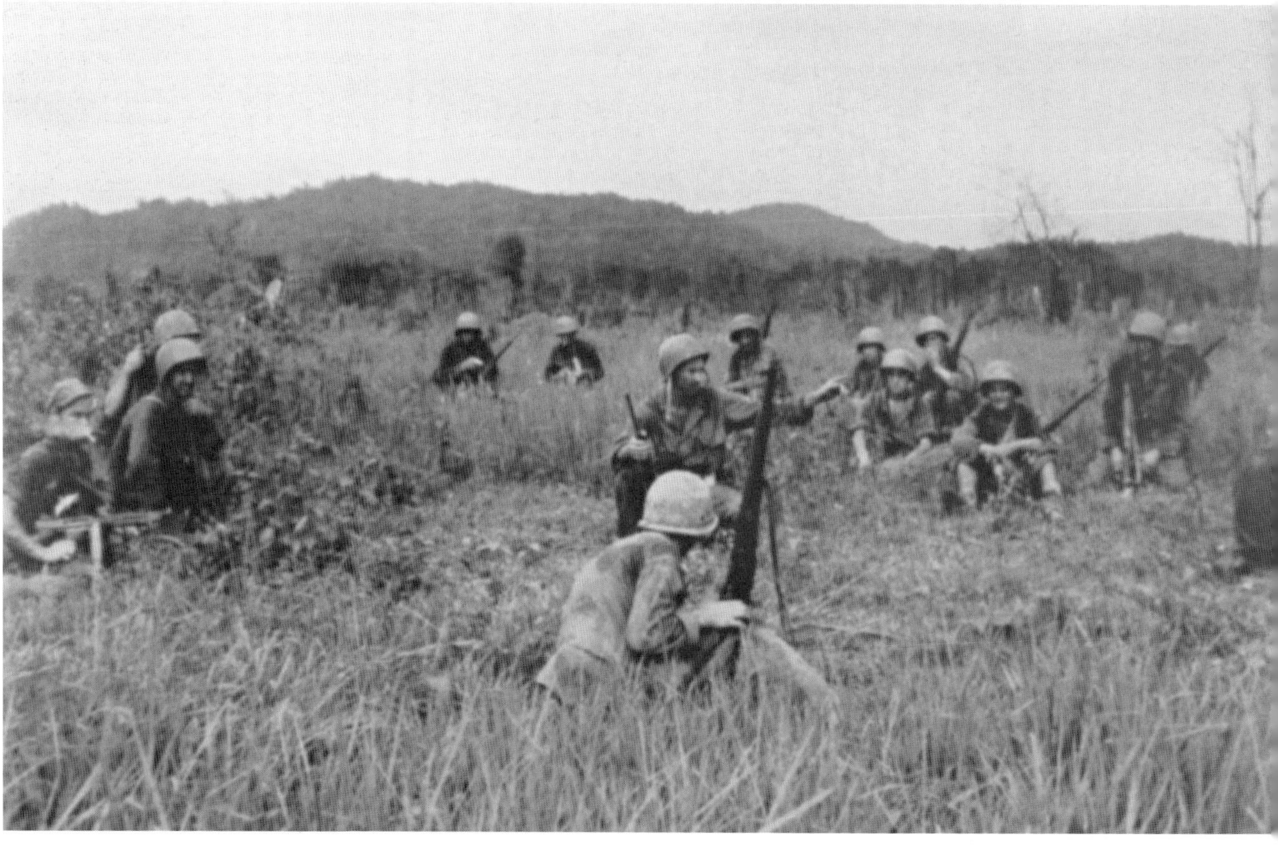

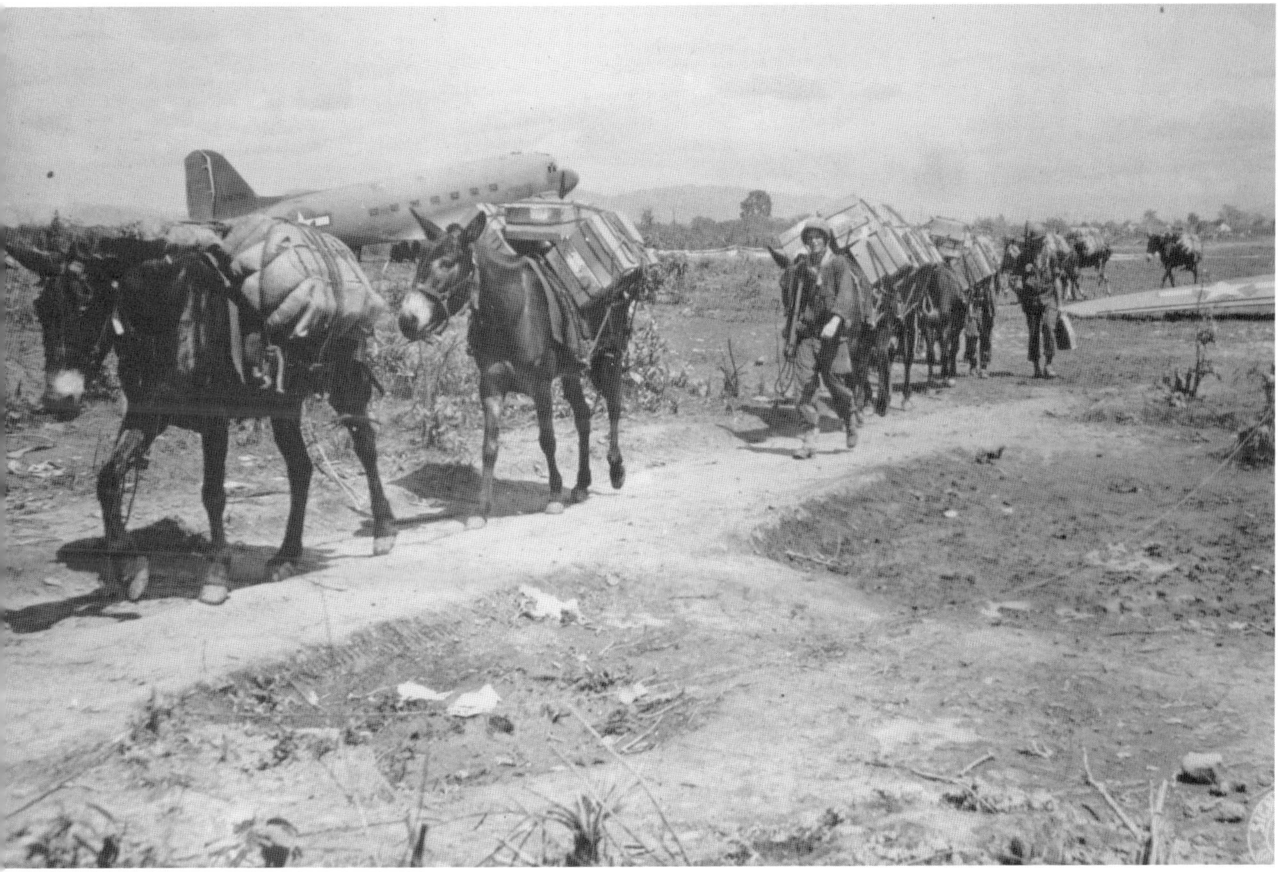

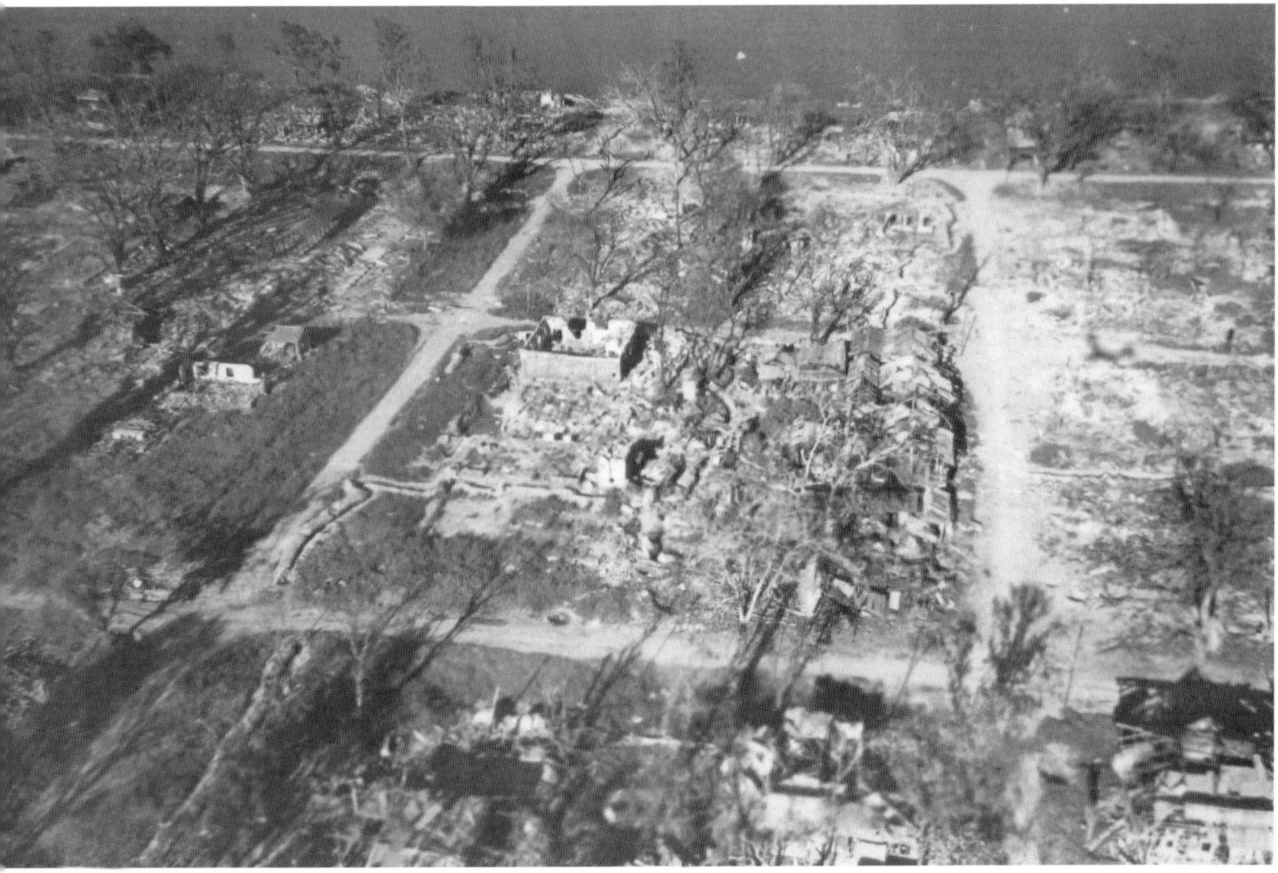

(**Right**) A Chinese soldier surveys destroyed Japanese entrenchments used by the IJA during Myitkyina town's siege in the summer of 1944. The wooden beams and corrugated tin roofs provided some protection from mortar rounds, but not Allied fighter-bomber sorties or heavier artillery such as the 75 and 105mm howitzers. *(NARA)*

(**Opposite**) A Chinese 22nd Division soldier and local Burmese civilians rummage through Japanese equipment and booty in Kamaing after that locale was captured by Ramgarh-trained troops that trekked through the Hukawng and Mogaung valleys to Kamaing. *(NARA)*

(**Below**) An American soldier drinks in front of a fallen building sign in Myitkyina town after this northern Burmese commerce and transportation (terminus of the Mandalay-Myitkyina railway) hub on the Irrawaddy River fell to the Allies on 3 August 1944. *(USAMHI)*

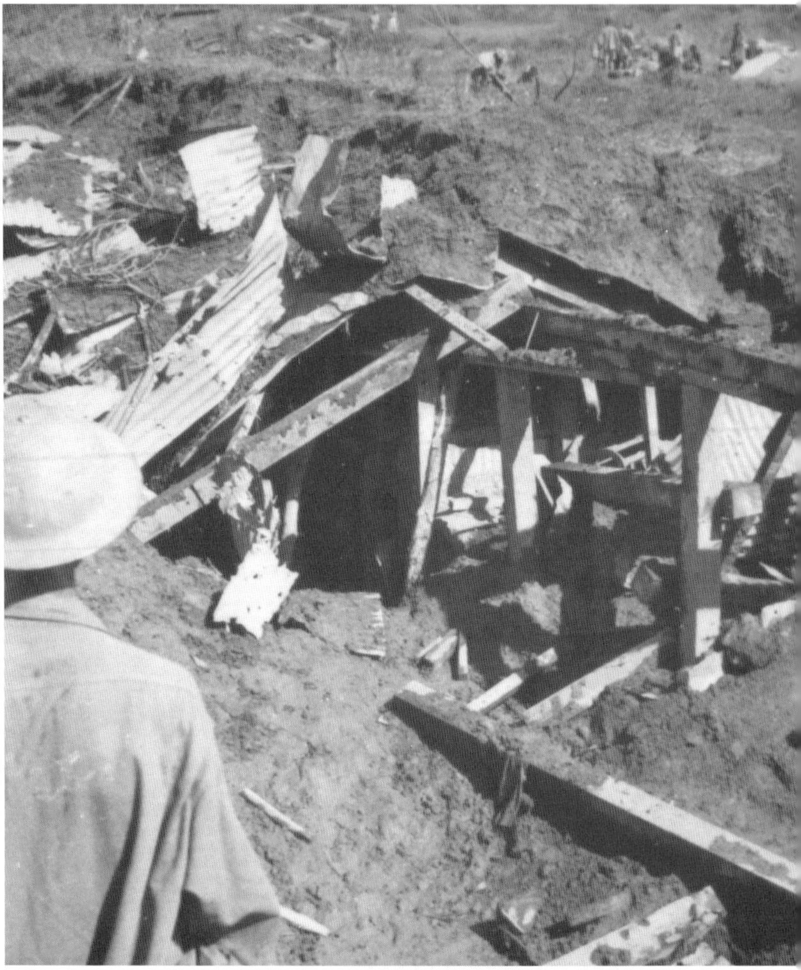

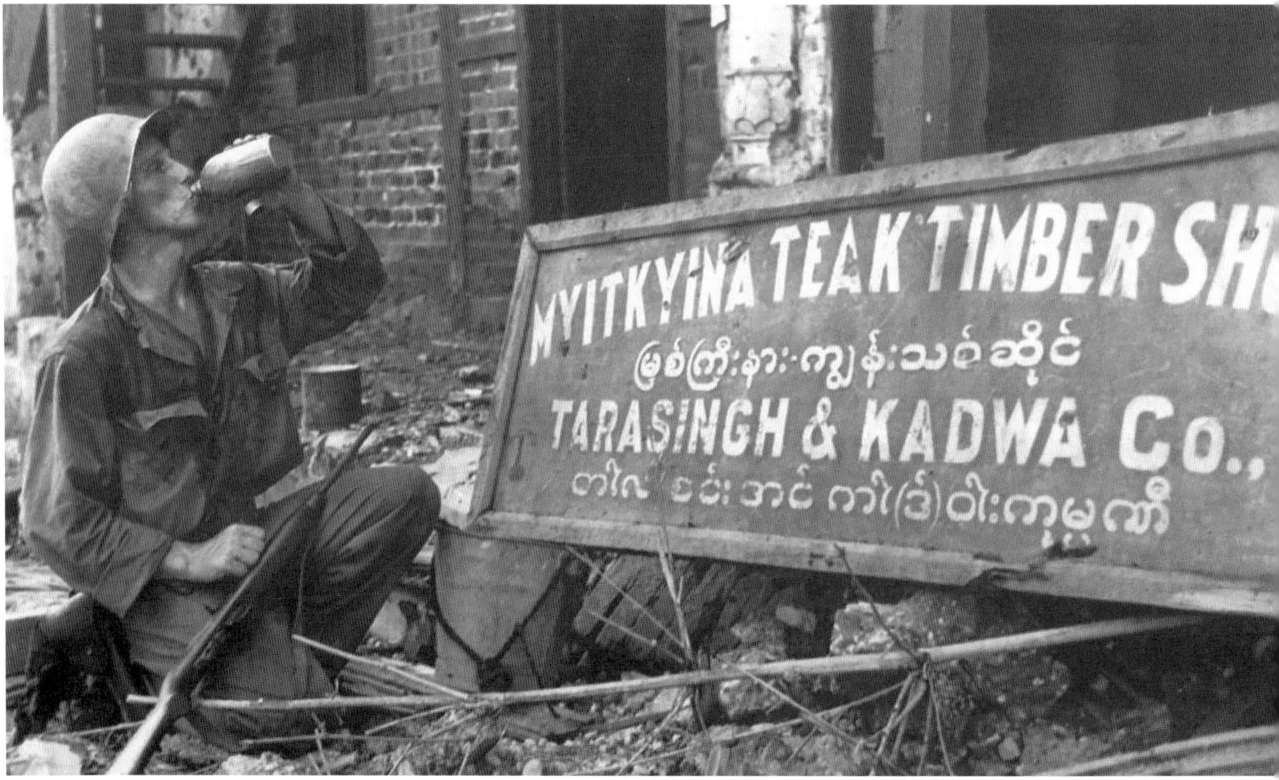
MYITKYINA TEAK TIMBER
TARASINGH & KADWA Co.,

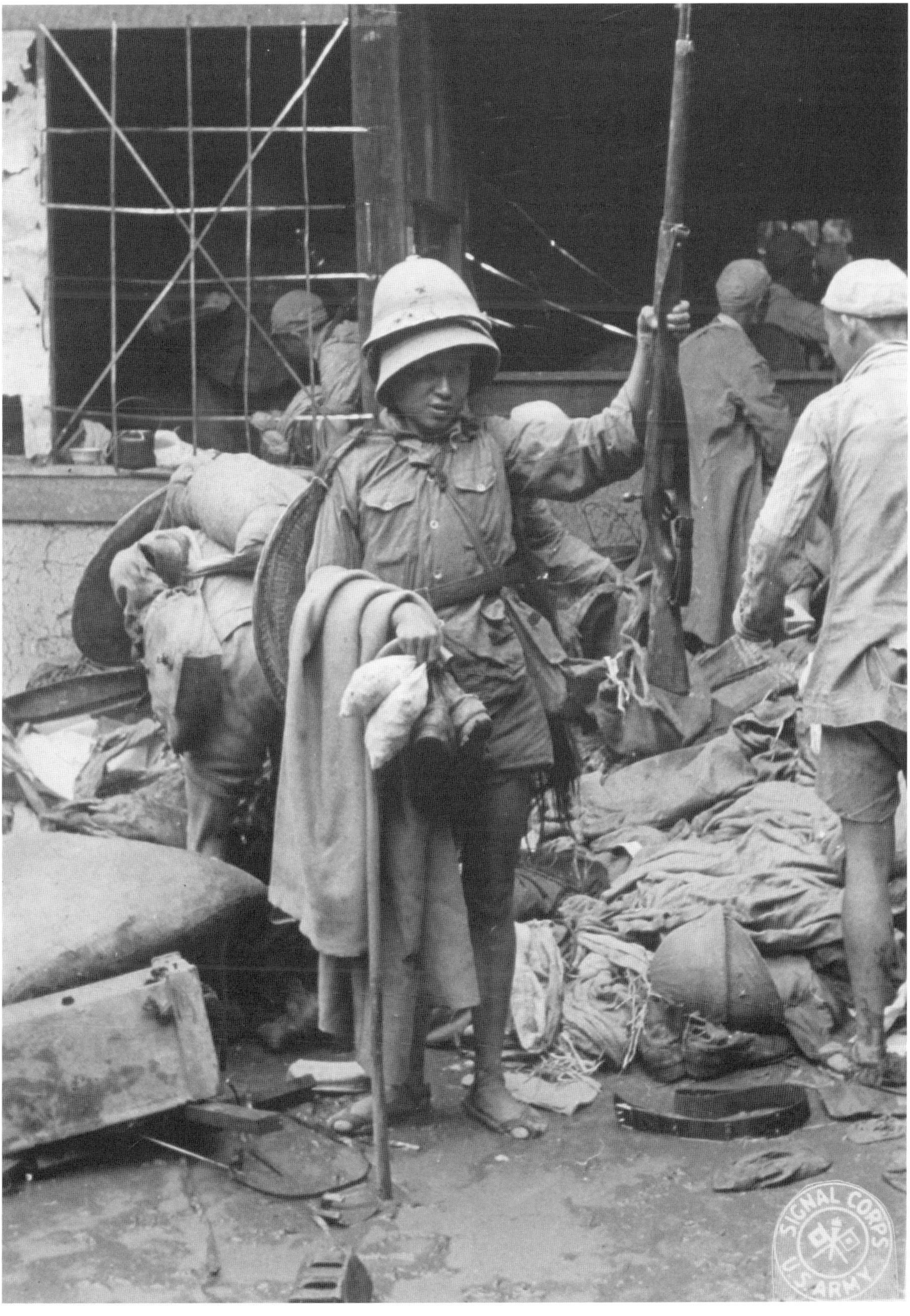
SIGNAL CORPS
U.S. ARMY

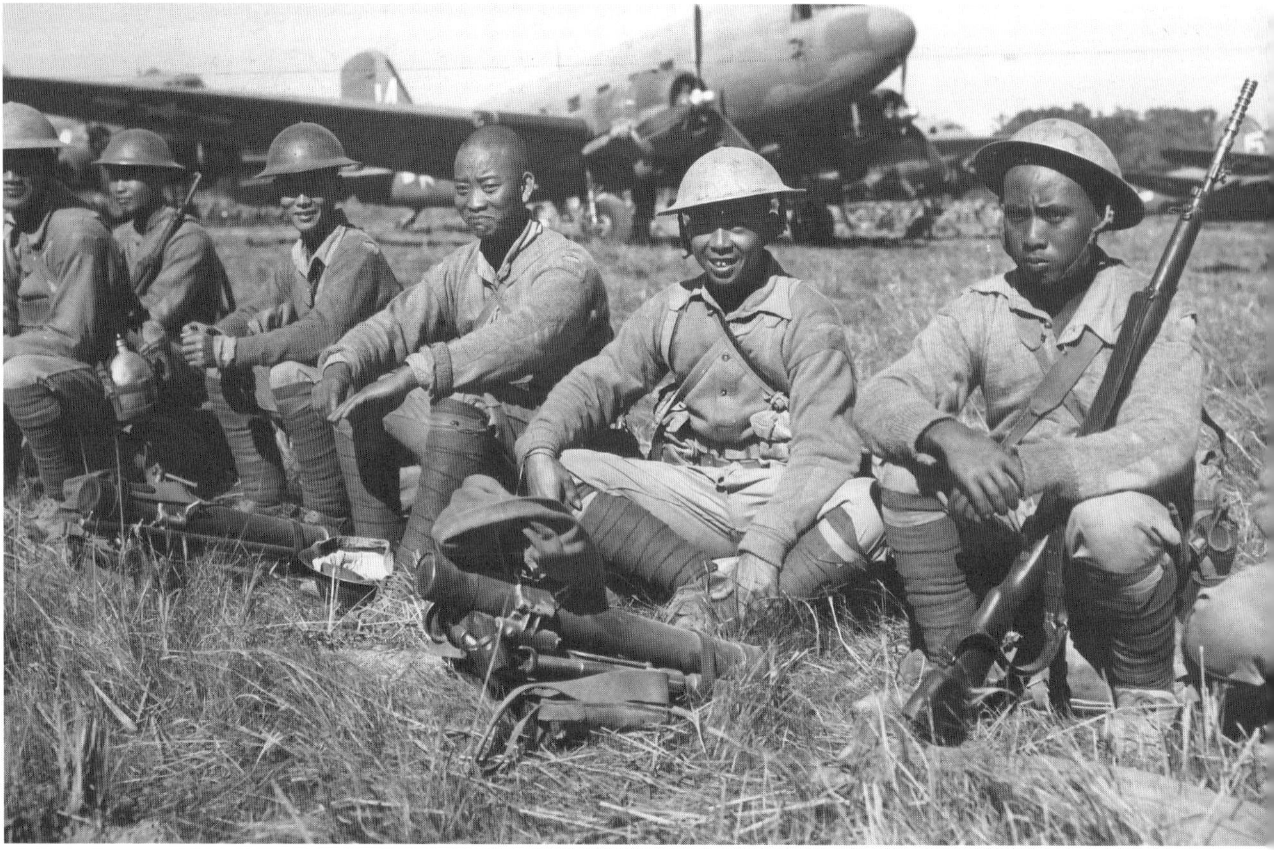

Chinese infantrymen are seated at the Myitkyina airfield after the town's capture in early August 1944. Many of these Ramgarh-trained soldiers were airlifted back to Yunnan in China by C-47 transports to aid Chiang Kai-shek's generals combat the Japanese. *(USAMHI)*

British Lieutenant Colonel Frank O'Neil Ford confers with Kachin Major H'Pan Naw in a jungle clearing in northern Burma in April 1944 prior to a British-led Gurkha and Kachin movement on Nsopzup, a Japanese supply base located on the Irrawaddy River 45 miles north of Myitkyina. These British-led irregular forces had already captured the IJA 2/114th Infantry Regiment's forward base at Sumprabum. *(NARA)*

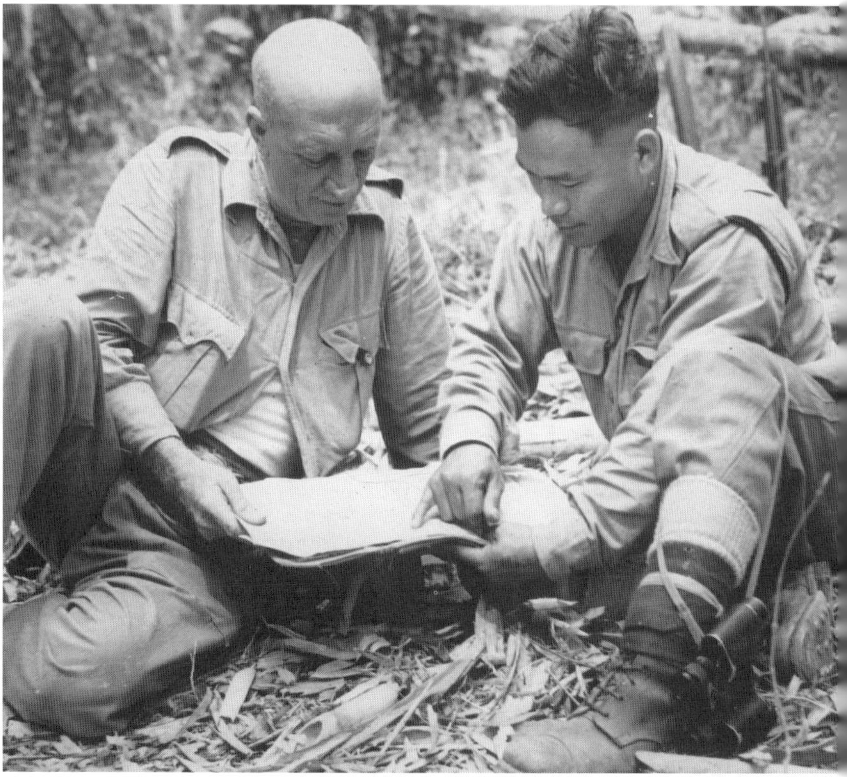

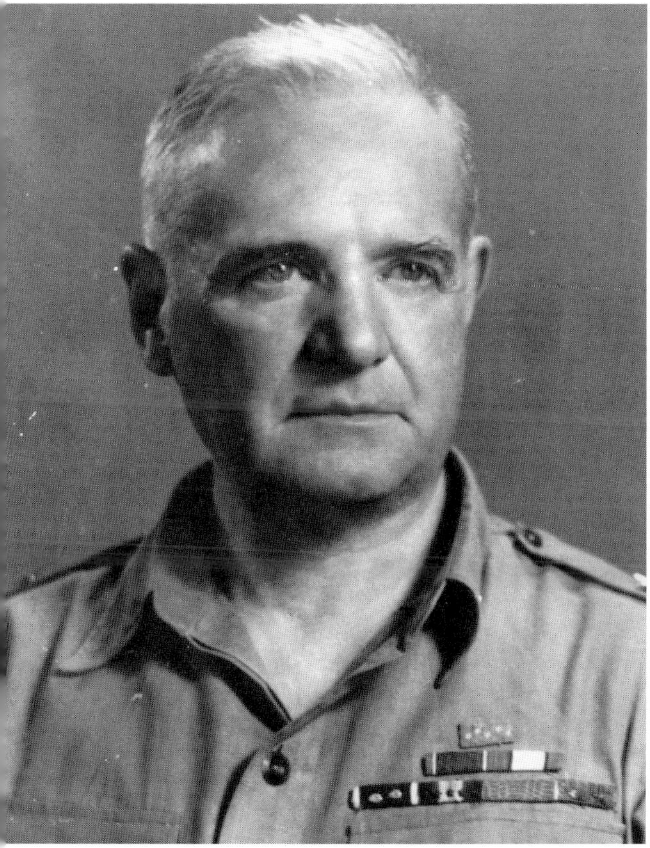

Major General William J. Donovan, the leader of America's OSS is shown here. Donovan had a storied career including a Congressional Medal of Honor as commanding officer of the US 42nd 'Rainbow' Division in the First World War, a successful practice as a Wall Street lawyer, and commander of the OSS, which was the forerunner of the Central Intelligence Agency (CIA) after the Second World War. In June 1942, the OSS was formed under the jurisdiction of the US Joint Chiefs of Staff and played a major role in the CBI theatre. *(NARA)*

An OSS-led Detachment 101 patrol comprising US and British soldiers as well as irregular Kachin tribesmen called Rangers move through a northern Burmese *chaung*. The Kachins were virulently anti-Japanese and were well-suited for reconnaissance, sabotage and guerrilla warfare. The first OSS agents of Detachment 101 infiltrated Burma in January 1943. Kachin loyalty to the Allied cause also stemmed from their pre-war relationship with Christian missionaries and the medical care provided for them. *(NARA)*

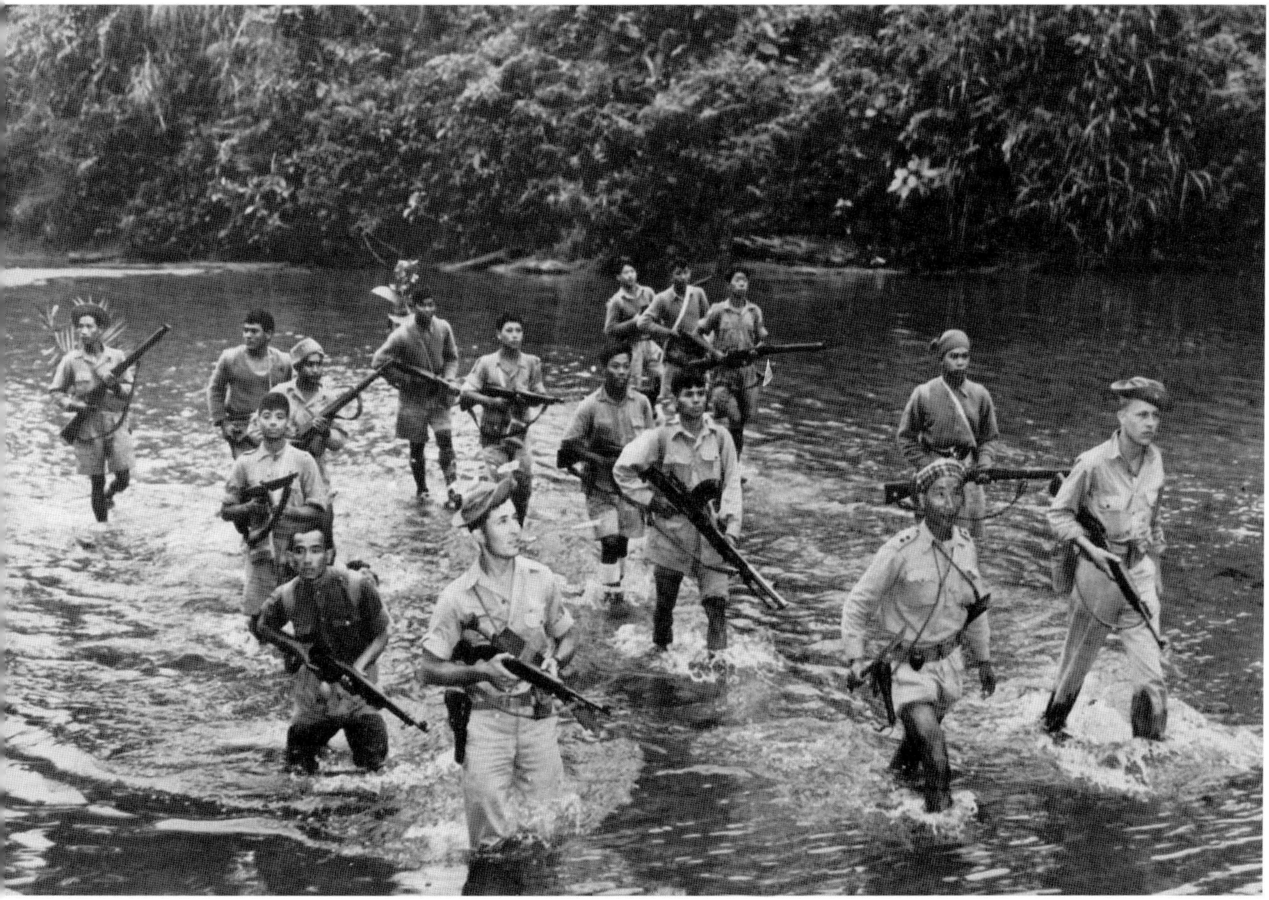

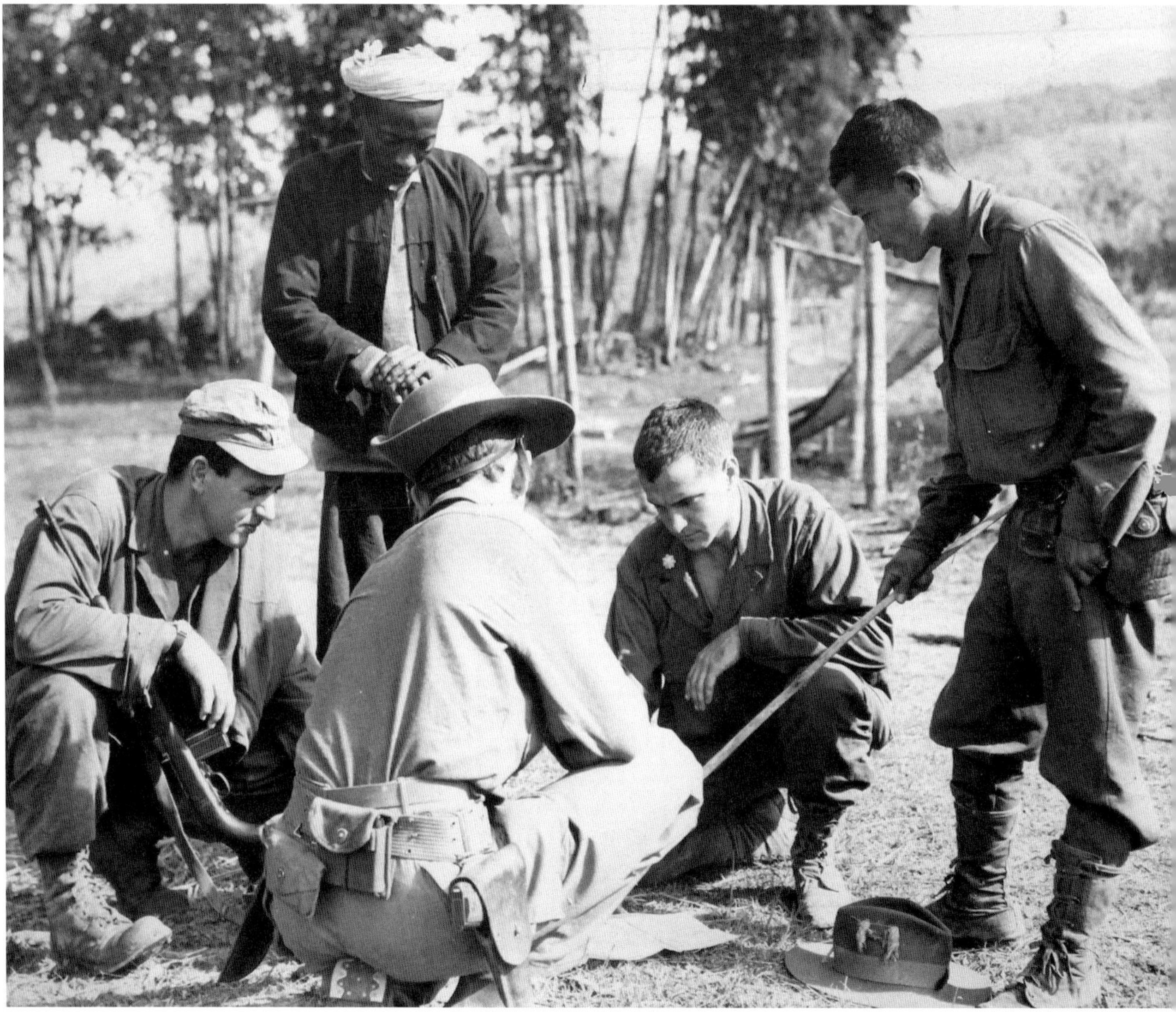

(**Above**) An American OSS Detachment 101 officer reviews a field operation plan with two other Americans and two Kachin Rangers. In the spring of 1944, Detachment 101 supported Allied offensives into Burma with Kachin units scouting ahead of Allied troops, providing flank protection and attacking Japanese LOC. With the Japanese forced out of Burma, Detachment 101 was disbanded in July 1945. *(USAMHI)*

(**Opposite, above**) Young Kachin Rangers are shown here in an ambush position utilizing British-made SMLE rifles and a Bren gun. Many of the Kachin tribesmen were teenagers when they were recruited into the OSS Detachment 101. *(NARA)*

(**Opposite, below**) A pair of Kachin Rangers is shown here operating a Browning 0.30in-calibre LMG along a northern Burmese road. Air supply was the only way to sustain Detachment 101 operations in northern Burma. *(NARA)*

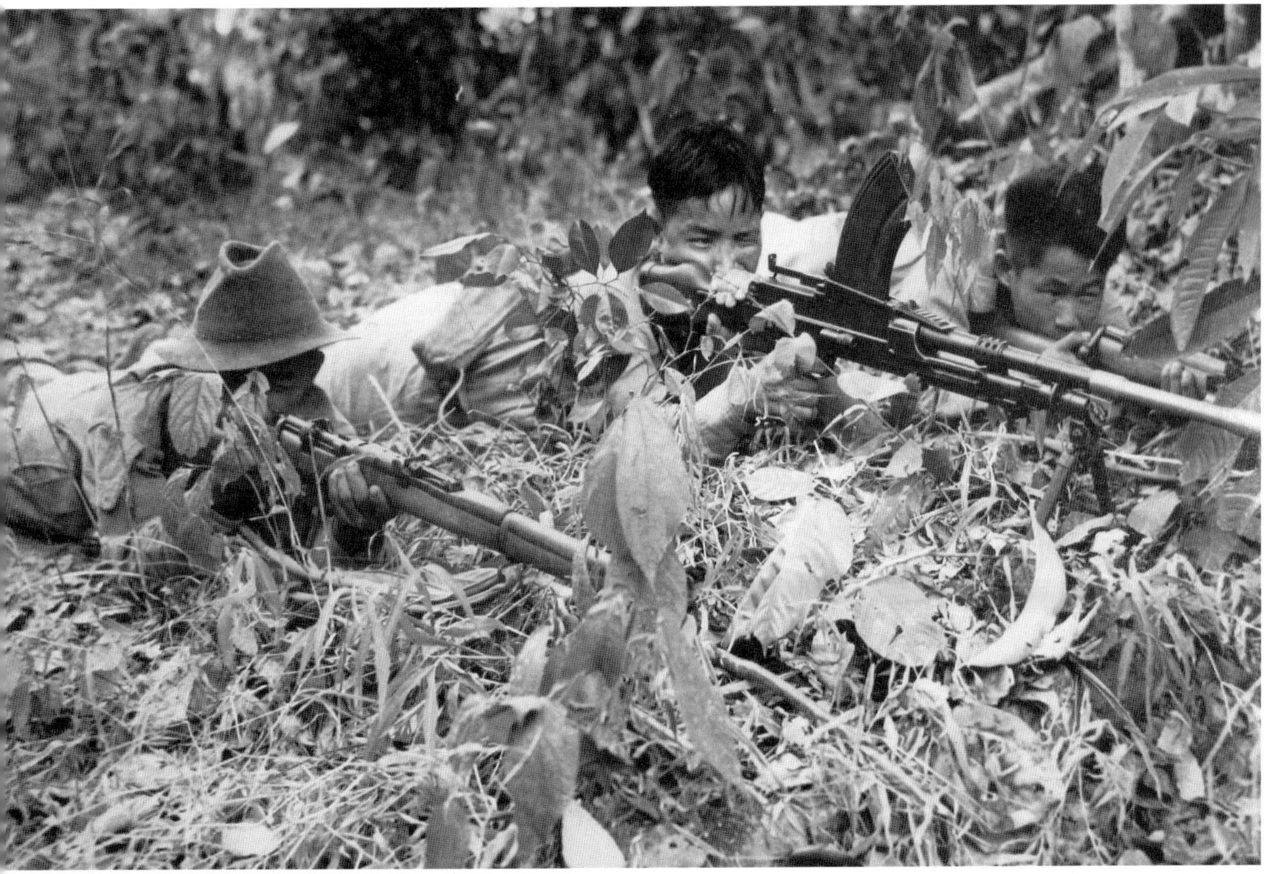

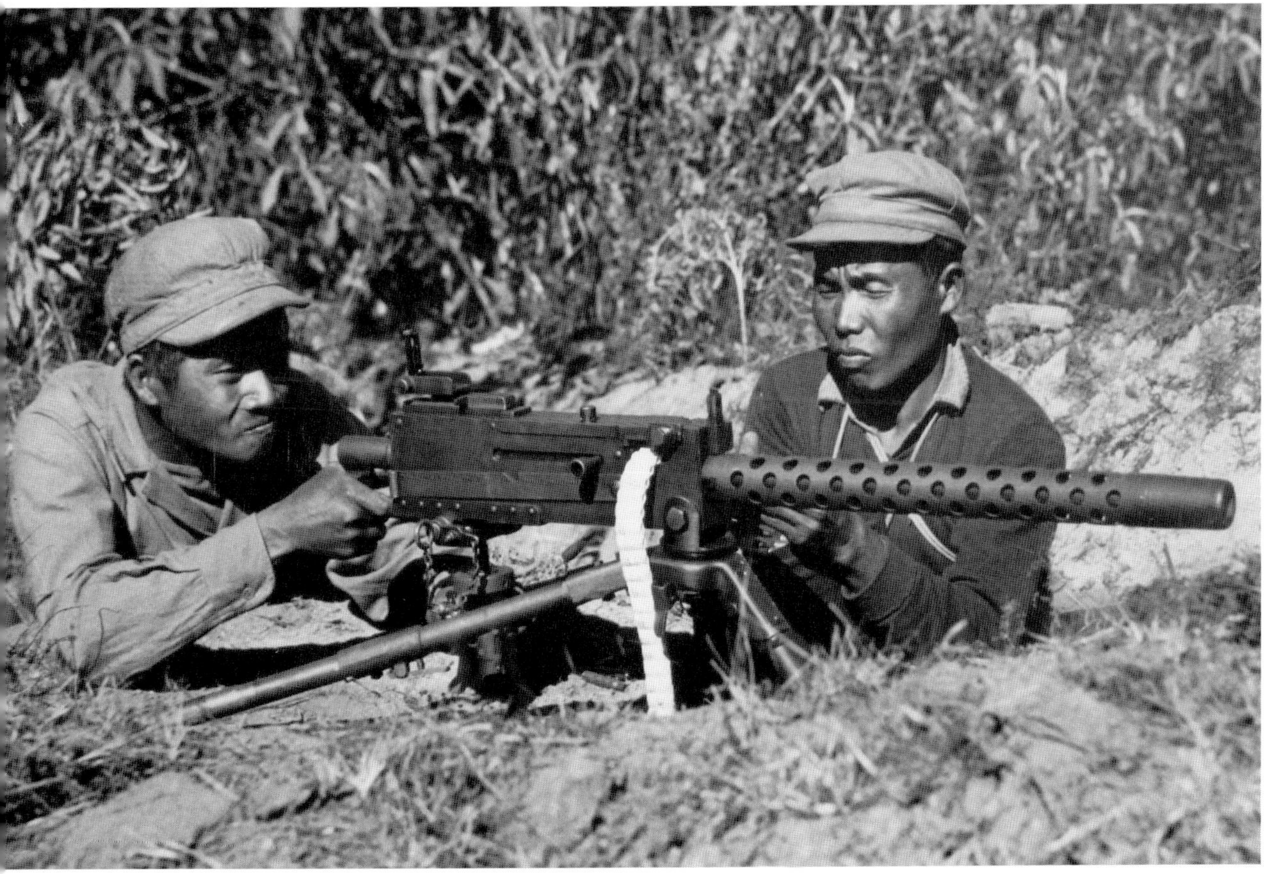

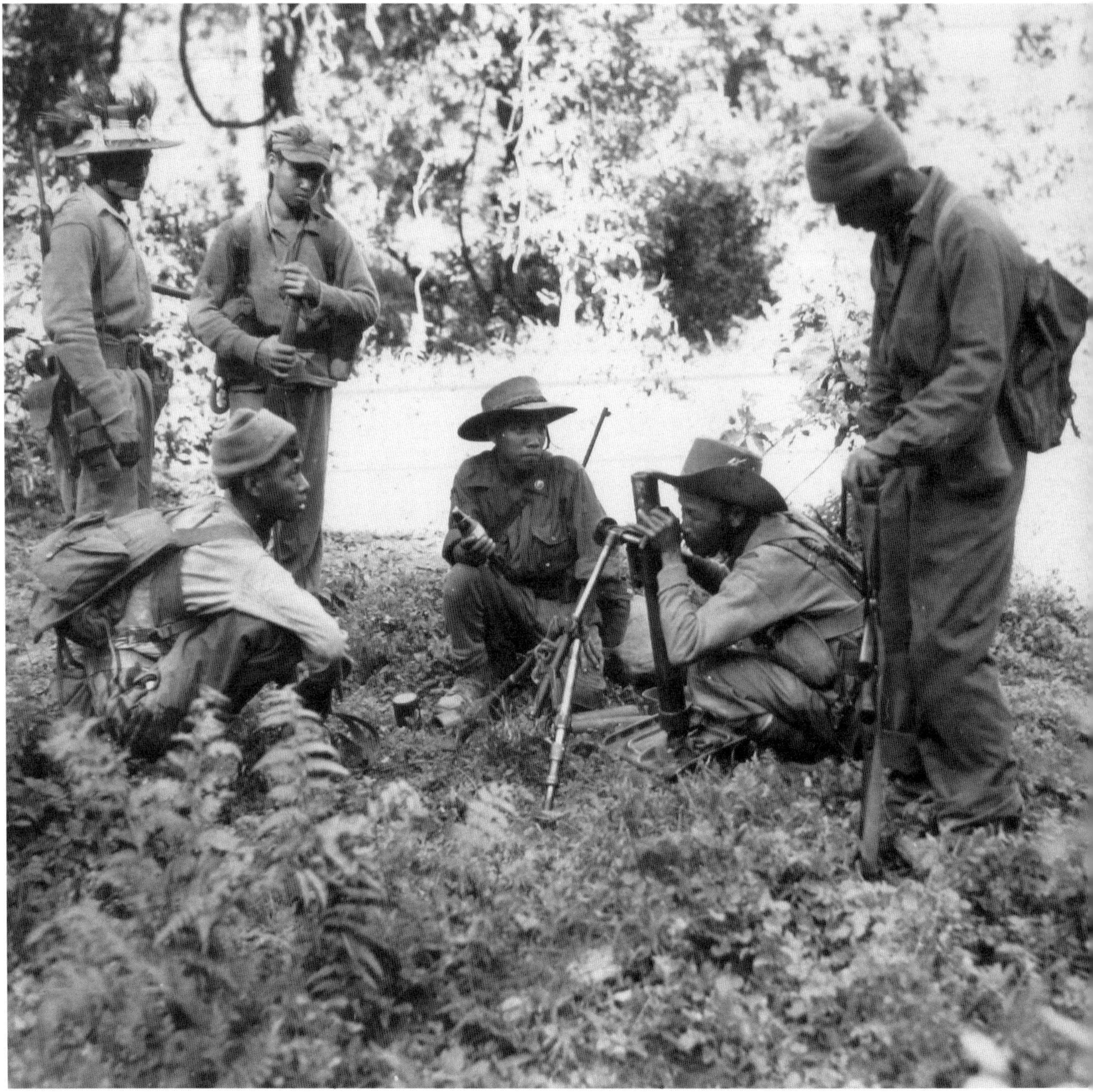

A Kachin Ranger shows his crew how to site in a British-made 3in mortar in northern Burma in December 1944. By that time most Kachin Rangers wore Allied uniforms and jungle boots, although headgear was an individual's preference. The 3in mortar was an invaluable weapon in the CBI theatre as it was portable; re-assembled within minutes, it provided plunging indirect fire that could reach reverse slopes of hills and into ravines concealing enemy troop concentration. *(NARA)*

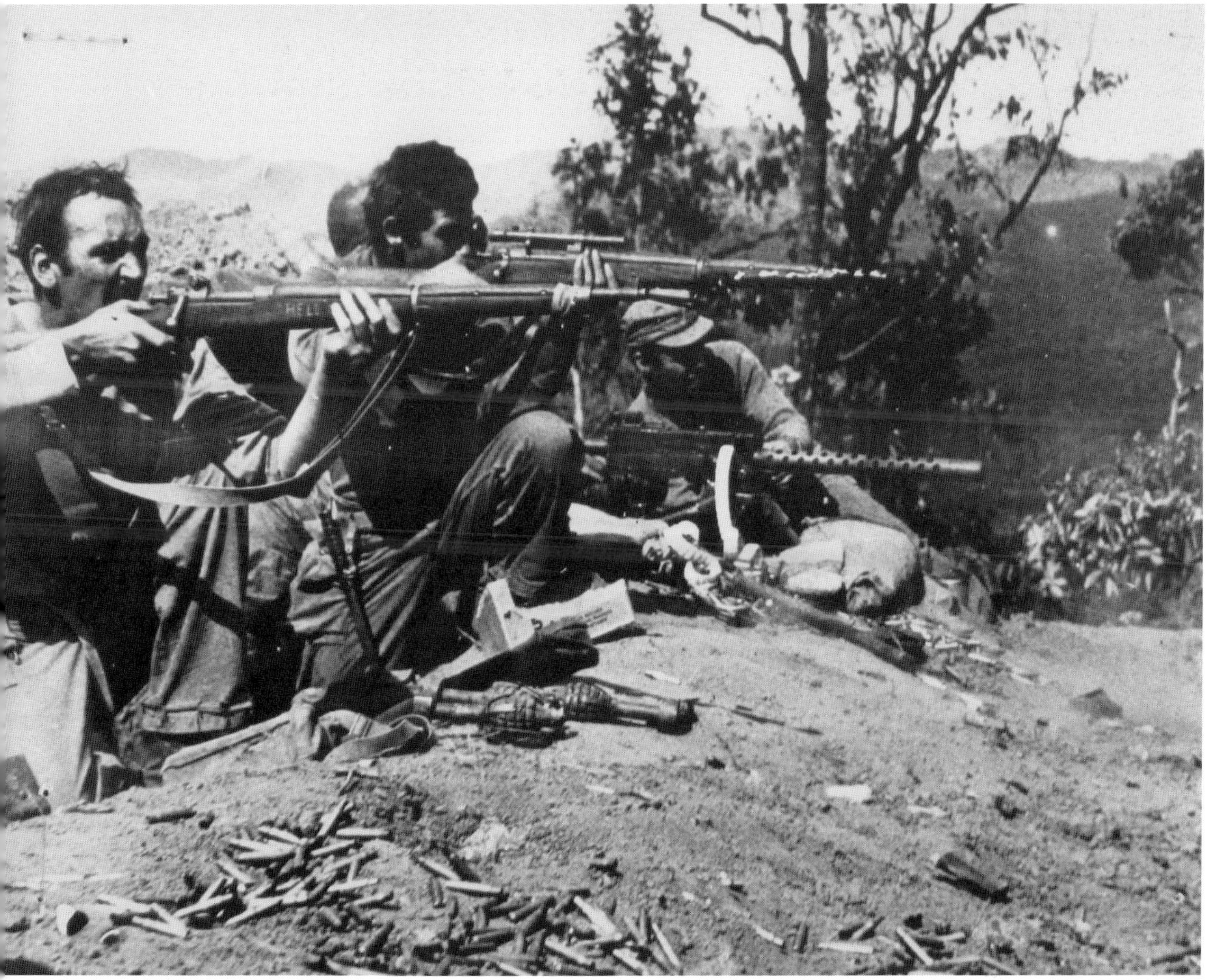

American infantrymen of the 2nd Battalion, 475th Infantry Regiment ('Mars Task Force') are shown here firing an assortment of weaponry at Japanese positions at Loi Kang well to the south of Myitkyina in late January 1945 to eventually link up with the Old Burma Road. Detachment 101 soldiers, both American and Kachin Rangers, acting as a screen for the 'Mars Task Force', saw their bloodiest fighting south of Myitkyina in an effort to clear the area of Japanese troops. *(NARA)*

Chapter Three

Commanders and Combatants

Japanese Commanders

Lieutenant General Renya Mutaguchi led the IJA 18th Division prior to commanding the Fifteenth Army. He overrode the intractable problem of supply and was feared by his subordinate staff officers who presented logistical hurdles to campaigns. Mutaguchi was condescending towards his Chinese opponents as well as to the British that he helped defeat in early 1942 in Malaya and Singapore, leading the IJA 18th Division as part of Yamashita's Twenty-Fifth Army.

After the mid-February 1942 fall of Singapore, elements of his 18th Division took part in the invasion of the Andaman Islands after Rangoon's occupation in early March. His other battalions reached Rangoon via a convoy from Singapore on 25 March and were tasked with severing the Burma Road east of Mandalay. In May 1942, the 18th Division moved on and then cleared the Shan States south of the Burma Road of all Chinese forces. Mutaguchi, among others, was not initially in favour of a Japanese invasion of Assam in 1942–43 for logistical and terrain reasons. The official IJA strategy in Burma for the dry weather of 1942–43 was defensive with the 18th Division garrisoning northern Burma with division HQ at Myitkyina.

In March 1943, Mutaguchi was promoted to command the IJA Fifteenth Army and he changed his strategic focus for an attack on India. After Wingate's 1943 Operation LONGCLOTH, he concluded that the British, having evolved new tactics, might repeat a new Chindit larger-scale offensive in 1944 (Operation THURSDAY) in conjunction with other Allied campaigns to reclaim Burma.

Lieutenant General Shinichi Tanaka was a Military Academy graduate in 1913, who later had extensive military liaison postings abroad including Riga, Moscow and Berlin and also served in Japan's Kwantung Army in Manchuria from 1931 to 1932. From 1936 to 1937, Colonel Tanaka was first the chief of the Military Service Section of the War Ministry and then the chief of the Military Affairs Section. After becoming a major general in 1939, he was COS of the Inner Mongolia Army and participated in the Nomonhan battle in which the Japanese were beaten by a Soviet force under General Georgy Zhukov. The next year he became Chief of the Operations Division of the General Staff. In October 1941, Tanaka was promoted to lieutenant general and thus he was a key figure in the military planning for the Pacific War. He alienated Prime Minister Hideki Tojo with his opinions on the Guadalcanal campaign in late 1942 and was dismissed from the Operations Division's leadership. After Mutaguchi's promotion, Tanaka assumed command of the IJA 18th Division in northern Burma combating Wingate's Chindits and Stilwell's Sino-American troops in the Hukawng and Mogaung valleys in 1943–44. After the fall of Myitkyina and the near destruction of the 18th Division, Tanaka was appointed chief of staff of the Burma Area Army.

Lieutenant General Masakazu Kawabe was COS, Japanese Expeditionary Force in China for a long interval. During 1937's China Incident, Kawabe and Mutaguchi served together in north China. On 27 March 1943, Burma Area Army HQ was established in Rangoon under Kawabe's command, leading the IJA Fifteenth Army and 55th Division to defend central and northern Burma and the Arakan Peninsula respectively. Kawabe reported to Field Marshal Count Terauchi, commander of the Saigon-based Southern Army. Kawabe was also in charge of planning Japanese offensive operations across the Chindwin River frontier into Assam. Kawabe wanted an offensive across the Indo-Burmese frontier to gain the general line of Kohima-Imphal and advance no further; however, Mutaguchi wanted to take his army into the Brahmaputra Valley and eventually his 'March on Delhi', which was beyond the limit of Kawabe's instructions.

Allied Commanders

Lieutenant General Joseph W. Stilwell, a 1904 West Point graduate, served as a lieutenant during the Philippines' Moro insurrection, as an intelligence officer for General Pershing in France, and two years later as the army's initial Intelligence Division's Chinese language officer in Peking. Stilwell was an engineering adviser for a road-building project in a remote area of China where he observed Chinese culture, language and the strong ethic of the Chinese labourer. In 1924, Stilwell was a 15th IR Battalion commander in Tientsin, meeting his mentor, George C. Marshall. In 1926, during Chinese civil war hostilities, Major Stilwell conducted his own reconnaissance of the countryside's unrest. By 1929, he was recognized as an expert on China. After four teaching years at Fort Benning's Infantry School as Marshall's deputy and earning the moniker 'Vinegar Joe' for his acerbic commentary, Colonel Stilwell was appointed military attaché to China in July 1935. After the Pearl Harbor attack, Stilwell expected the command of the North Africa invasion in November 1942. However, US Army Chief of Staff Marshall and Secretary of War Stimson gave him the CBI theatre command and to function as Chiang Kai-shek's deputy among other Lend-Lease supply roles, and to lead Chinese combat troops in Burma. With the Allied military collapse in late April 1942, Stilwell led the 'Walkout' with 114 others in his party westwards towards India. By 13 May, after the 140-mile trek from Indaw to Assam without any losses, a war reporter observed Stilwell exiting the jungle looking 'like the wrath of God and cursing like a fallen angel'.

Brigadier General Frank D. Merrill graduated from West Point in 1929 along with his future 'Galahad' deputy, Charles N. Hunter. Merrill, a Japanese-language officer in the Philippines, was transferred to Burma where he pinpointed the failures of the Allied 1942 campaign to Stilwell as 'no plan, no reconnaissance, no security, no intelligence, no prisoners' and a lack of aggressiveness and mobility. Merrill, who suffered from heart ailments, eventually received the 5307th Composite Unit, Provisional ('Galahad'), being trained by Wingate for the Sino-American invasion of northern Burma for 1943–44.

Brigadier General Lewis Pick, before arriving in the CBI theatre as a colonel, was a civil engineer who planned the Missouri River Division's flood control. On 17 October 1943, he assumed command of the Ledo Road and pipeline project's five Army Engineer battalions and a Quartermaster Regiment at the north-eastern end of the railway line in Assam. The initial work on 'Pick's Pike' started at the end of October 1943 and by the end of November the project had advanced 22 miles. With the road soon to be through the Hukawng Valley's mountain barrier, Pick sent a detachment ahead to Shingbwiyang, 103 miles from Ledo on the Patkai Range's southern end, to establish a supply depot for the first truck convoy. At Shingbwiyang, Pick's construction units were one-third of the way from Ledo to Myitkyina, but now facing the advance units of the IJA 18th Division.

General Sun Li-jen, the Chinese 38th Division commander, was educated at the Virginia Military Institute. British troops under his command in Burma in 1942 respected him, while British officers rated him as an able tactician, alert, aggressive and cool in battle. He was the most competent of the Chinese generals in Burma, earning the respect of both Stilwell and Slim.

Lieutenant General Liao Yao-hsiang graduated from St. Cyr in France. During the March 1942 defeat, Stilwell criticized Liao for his Chinese 22nd Division's tardiness. However, later at the Ramgarh training facility, he complied with all training directives, producing a good combat division during the 1943–44 north Burma campaign. During that campaign, Stilwell fumed that Chiang Kai-shek's orders to Sun and Liao to exercise caution were a greater driving force than his own directives.

Major General Orde C. Wingate graduated from the Royal Military Academy, Woolwich and was posted with the Royal Garrison Artillery in 1923. Learning Arabic and using family connections, Wingate joined the Sudan Defence Force (SDF) leading an infantry company near the Eritrean border in 1928–33. There Wingate developed and drilled military principles of training, fitness and fieldcraft into his soldiers to survive in desolate, inhospitable locales without LOC. Marching his company 500 miles into remote areas of eastern Sudan, Wingate experimented with ground-to-air control with RAF Squadron 47 (B), heralding this tactic for future commands. In September 1936, Wingate was posted as an intelligence officer with the British 5th Division in Palestine. During the Arab Revolt of 1937–38, General Archibald Wavell, GOC Palestine, accepted Wingate's plan to form small units of British soldiers and Jewish paramilitary volunteers, Special Night Squads (SNS), to attack Arab insurgents who were sabotaging the Iraq Petroleum Company's pipeline to Haifa. Wingate received the Distinguished Service Order (DSO) for his nocturnal ambushes that reduced the number of pipeline breaches. In September 1940, Wavell, now C-in-C Middle East, sent Wingate to Ethiopia 'to fan into flame the embers of revolt that had smouldered in parts of the Abyssinian highlands ever since the Italian occupation.' Wingate arrived in Khartoum and developed a force of Ethiopian rebels as well as some Sudanese regular troops to defeat the Italians in Ethiopia's Gojjam Province by May 1941. In Ethiopia, Wingate's Gideon Force became a blueprint for his LRP concept. In early 1942, Field Marshal Archibald Wavell, now C-in-C India, summoned Colonel Wingate to Burma to join his staff to help stop the Japanese advance. In April 1942, Wingate went to Maymyo to command guerrilla operations in Burma. There he met Major (later Brigadier) Michael Calvert at the Bush Warfare School and was impressed by his fighting zeal and willingness to lead Commando-style assaults against the Japanese. Calvert had led a detachment of Royal Engineers during the ill-fated Norwegian campaign. After transferring to the pre-war Pacific, he trained Commandos in demolitions in both Hong Kong and Australia, eventually commanding a unit at the Bush Warfare School. Wingate was unable to direct Calvert's force since the Japanese had overrun that section of Burma. Wingate returned to Delhi at the end of April 1942 and wrote a memorandum to Wavell on LRP, which would 'mushroom' into Operation LONGCLOTH in February 1943 under the field marshal's penchant for unorthodox tactics.

Lieutenant General William J. Slim lacked formal military education, but was commissioned as a temporary second lieutenant into the Royal Warwickshire Regiment in 1914 and fought at Gallipoli, where he was wounded. After rejoining his regiment in Mesopotamia in 1916, he was again wounded in combat and won an MC for his exploits. Most of his life between the wars was spent with the Gurkhas. Earlier in 1940–41, he fought with distinction in Abyssinia, Syria, Iraq and Persia. In March 1942, Alexander gave him command of Burma Corps (Burcorps) as an acting lieutenant general. He led his corps out of Burma to India with distinction. After the failed First Arakan Campaign of 1943, Slim was promoted to command the new Fourteenth Army formed from the various Eastern Army corps in India. The Fourteenth Army decisively destroyed Mutaguchi's Fifteenth Army in its 'March on Delhi' in the Naga Hills and Manipur between March and July 1944.

Lieutenant General Geoffrey Scoones commanded Fourteenth Army's IV Corps at Imphal. He served as the Director of Military Operations at General HQ in Delhi and was considered an excellent analytical officer known for his calm demeanour. However, he was criticized for not having reacted sooner to the enemy advance on Imphal from the south.

Lieutenant General Montagu Stopford, a British army officer, commanded the Fourteenth Army's Indian XXXIII Corps, which opened the road from Kohima south-wards to Imphal with the British 2nd and 5th Indian divisions linking up on 22 June 1944.

Major General D.T. 'Punch' Cowan commanded the 17th Indian Division at Imphal. In 1942, the Japanese had routed the 17th Indian Division, notably at the disastrous Sittang Bridge battle in February 1942, but at Imphal the tables were turned, due in part to Cowan's dedication and inspiration. He was a combat veteran of the First World War and then joined the Indian army.

Major General Frank Messervy, a career Indian army officer, commanded the 7th Indian Division in XXXIII Corps during the Arakan and Assam battles at Imphal and Kohima of 1944. Messervy fought in the Western Desert in 1941 as commander of the 4th Indian Division and the 7th Armoured Division prior to being sent to India in 1943 to command the 43rd Indian Armoured Division and then as Director of Armoured Vehicles prior to his 7th Indian Division command. His reputation was one for always being with his troops at the front and he was credited with utilizing his armour effectively, especially the M3 Lee medium tanks. Messervy was promoted to lieutenant general in command of the Fourteenth Army's IV Corps, which bore the brunt of the 1945 Meiktila battle in the drive on Mandalay in central Burma.

General A.F. Philip Christison was a junior officer on the Western Front in the First World War. In Burma, he commanded XV Corps in Slim's Fourteenth Army. In 1940, he was made commandant of the Staff College, Quetta. In 1941, he returned to England to be GOC of the 15th Scottish Infantry Division as a major general. Promoted to lieutenant general in November 1942, he became GOC to the XXXIII Indian Corps. In November 1943, he took over command of the XV Corps, succeeding Slim, in the new Fourteenth Army. During the Second Arakan Campaign, XV Corps successfully fended off IJA 55th Division attacks and helped Messervy's 7th Indian Division in the surrounded 'Admin Box'. In March 1944, his XV Corps was withdrawn from the Arakan to assist in the defence of Imphal. In May 1945, Christison would lead XV Corps into Rangoon.

Major General T.W. 'Pete' Rees, a Welshman and career Indian army officer, commanded the 19th Indian Division. Like Messervy, Rees led his troops from the front and commanded his division's capture of Mandalay in 1945.

Major General Geoffrey Evans, a British army officer, assumed command of the 7th Indian Division after Messervy's promotion to command the Fourteenth Army's IV Corps. He served in Eritrea and North Africa as a brigade major and battalion commander respectively before being posted to India in 1942 as commandant of the Indian Army Staff College at Quetta. He commanded a brigade in the 5th Indian Division in the First Arakan Campaign and then commanded another brigade in that division as it was airlifted from the Arakan to fight at Imphal. He assumed command of the 5th Indian Division after the Imphal siege was lifted and pursued the retreating IJA 15th Army.

Major General Douglas Gracey commanded the 20th Indian Division since its inception in 1942. He was a combat veteran of the First World War and spent the inter-war years in the Indian army serving with the Gurkhas. The 23rd and 5th Indian divisions respectively were commanded by Major General Ouvry Roberts and Major General Harold Briggs. Two brigades from the 5th Indian Division were flown in from the Arakan in March 1944 to save the situation at both Imphal and Kohima. Both of these men were combat veterans of the First World War and served the Fourteenth Army well at Imphal.

Opposing Forces

Japanese Forces

The IJA prepared late for war in tropical training environments as its major conflicts were in China. At the start of 1941, Lieutenant Colonel Masanobu Tsuji, a highly-regarded staff officer at Twenty-Fifth Army headquarters joined the IJA's jungle warfare school on the island of Formosa as its commander. Practical modes for jungle combat were perfected, including issuing headbands to soldiers to keep the sweat from pouring into their eyes while aiming their rifles, utilizing lighter weapons and loads for the hot, steamy climate, incorporating the terrain as an added dimension such as getting off the trail or jungle track and using the verdant foliage to conceal flanking movements around the enemy. Stilwell, and more convincingly Wingate, tried to imbue these Japanese jungle lessons in their troops at Ramgarh (the CAI training base) and Deogarh (the Chindit and 'Galahad' training base in India) respectively, who would confront the IJA 18th Division.

IJA 18th Division

The 18th IJA Division's three regiments were garrisoned throughout northern Burma and thus fought the Chindits during both the 1943 and 1944 campaigns as well as having contested Stilwell's Sino-American advance down the Hukawng and Mogaung valleys towards Myitkyina, which began in the late autumn of 1943. The vigour of the 18th IJA Division had been shown in the jungle blitzkrieg which had won Malaya for the Japanese in December 1941–February 1942 as well as the rapid advance in Burma from Rangoon to Mandalay and beyond as the campaigning in April to May 1942 progressed.

The Japanese did not just sit back and wait to be attacked. In the Hukawng Valley and the Indaw area, IJA 18th Division battalions were split up into smaller units for active patrolling, since in essence the 55th and 56th IRs were forward outposts in the vastness of the Burmese jungle in the Hukawng Valley. The Japanese 55th IR was responsible for the area west of the Zibyu Range, from Homalin to Mawlaik with the regimental HQ at Katha on the Irrawaddy River. More than 100 miles north of Myitkyina, the 2nd Infantry Battalion of the 114th IR, stationed at Myitkyina, comprised a punitive force directed at the British-led Kachins at Sumprabum. This dispersed nature of the major 18th Division units meant that Japanese commanders would fight the American, Chinese, British and Kachin forces in a piecemeal fashion rather than with an overwhelming concentration of force.

Mutaguchi's IJA Fifteenth Army for Operation U-GO and the Imphal-Kohima Offensive (see also Chapter 4)

From April through the summer of 1943, Mutaguchi planned an eventual three-division attack into Assam, India to disrupt any major Allied offensive utilizing the IJA 33rd, 15th and 31st divisions to capture Imphal and Kohima and advance to Dimapur, the huge supply base 11 miles long and 1 mile wide, which provided for the whole of Slim's Fourteenth Army. Mutaguchi intended that as soon as Kohima and Dimapur were captured, his victorious forces, accompanied by the Indian National Army and its leader, Subhas Chandra Bose, would advance into Bengal where the subjugated Indian populace would mount an internal insurrection against British rule and support his triumphant 'March on Delhi'.

It is seldom mentioned that Mutaguchi almost accomplished his strategic aim. If success had come to Mutaguchi's U-GO campaign of March–June 1944, British, Chinese and American forces operating in Burma would have had all contact severed with the West. An incorrect logistic and supply decision by this otherwise outstanding Japanese commander along with the selfless bravery of Indian and British troops thwarted his U-GO plan. His idea of commencing his offensive with only one month's rations and supplies in anticipation of capturing the stores at Dimapur became a significant factor in their ultimate defeat. The Japanese had no equivalent to the American and British air supply capabilities to troops on the ground in fortified positions (i.e. Wingate's strongholds such as 'Broadway') or on the move in the jungles and hills of Burma.

Allied Forces

Stilwell's Chinese Divisions

Both the Chinese 38th and 22nd divisions fought in Burma during early 1942 prior to their eventual retreat, reformation and retraining by Stilwell at Ramgarh, India. There in August Stilwell built a fighting corps from the 38th and 22nd Chinese divisions' 9,000 survivors of the Burma campaign that had escaped to Imphal in May 1942 as a nucleus. An additional 23,500 Chinese troops were flown in from China. These soldiers received British uniforms, helmets, weapons and eventually training in artillery, Bren carriers and American M3 light tanks under a crash programme using American instructors. Slim noted that Stilwell was ubiquitous as he urged, led and drove the Chinese soldiers. By the end of December 1942, 32,000 Chinese troops were in training at Ramgarh to create a two-division force (the 38th and 22nd Chinese divisions) along with three accompanying artillery regiments and the 1st Provisional Tank Group comprising M3 light tanks, the latter albeit under American commander Colonel Rothwell H. Brown, with many American NCOs serving in the tanks. Colonel (later Brigadier General) Haydon Boatner, who had Chinese language experience and had served in the US 15th Infantry Regiment at Tientsin, became COS of the task force in training and ultimately the deputy commander of the CAI.

5307th Composite Unit, Provisional ('Galahad' or 'Merrill's Marauders')

The 5307th Composite Unit, Provisional left for Burma at the end of January 1944 after nine weeks of training near Deogarh, India, 20 miles south of Lalitpur, the Chindits' training facility. Wingate was to command 'Galahad' in Burma, having indoctrinated them with forced marches and extensive practice with all the weapons that would be carried into Burma.

Originally, 'Galahad' was to furnish three LRP groups to operate under Wingate and enter northern Burma in the 1944 dry season; however, Stilwell pestered Mountbatten for American ground forces and the operational command of 'Galahad' went to the NCAC under Stilwell and Merrill's command, receiving the moniker 'Merrill's Marauders' from American war correspondents. Like their Chindit counterparts, they had no heavy artillery or tanks, but they were effectively organized for Stilwell's particular 'spearheading' role, with pioneer, demolition, intelligence and reconnaissance sections. M1 carbines, sub-machine guns, light and heavy MGs, mortars, rocket-launchers and assorted ammunition were carried by a large number of mules, as with the Chindits. Merrill was fluent in Japanese and used his Nisei interpreters to gain valuable intelligence.

The OSS Detachment 101 and Kachin Rangers

In April 1942, William Donovan, head of the OSS, prepared the activation of Detachment 101 in Burma, which was the brainchild of Lieutenant Colonel Preston Goodfellow, a US army G-2 staff officer. In February 1942, Stilwell approved Goodfellow's choice of Captain Carl Eifler, a former US Treasury agent, to form Detachment 101 to work behind enemy lines gathering intelligence, ambushing Japanese columns, identifying bombing targets, rescuing downed Allied airmen and denying use of the Myitkyina airfield to Japanese fighters. Detachment 101, never more than a few hundred Americans, relied on its manpower from various Burmese tribal groups, in particular the anti-Japanese Kachins. Detachment 101 was one of the earliest American Special Operations units in the Second World War, pre-dating the First Ranger Battalion, the First Special Service Brigade and 'Galahad'. Much of what Detachment 101 did was completely novel and learned via trial and error. At Fort Hertz in the north, British officers commanded a battalion of mountain tribesmen called the Northern Kachin Levies.

American OSS officers infiltrated Burma in January 1943 and recruited the first of 3,000 Kachins of northern Burma under Stilwell's directive. Now renamed Kachin Rangers, they possessed great jungle skills and quickly learned how to use American weapons and radios for effective communication to coordinate their myriad activities.

During Stilwell's Myitkyina offensive across the Kumon Range and ultimately against the airfield at Myitkyina in the spring of 1944, Detachment 101 with their 600 Kachin Rangers scouted ahead of 'Galahad', providing flank protection while also attacking Japanese LOC.

Upon its deactivation in July 1945, Detachment 101 had killed 5,428 Japanese and rescued Allied airmen for a total of approximately 30 Americans and 338 Kachins killed. Thousands of Japanese soldiers were wounded by this group's activities and seventy-eight were taken prisoner. It cannot be emphasized enough that Detachment 101's efforts screened the advances for the three principal larger Allied offensive forces in northern Burma: Stilwell's Chinese forces, Wingate's Chindits and Merrill's 'Galahad' battalions, in addition to their own activities in severing Japanese LOC.

Wingate's 3rd Indian Division or Special Force for Operation THURSDAY in 1944

On 5 March 1944, Major General Orde Wingate launched his second Chindit (3rd Indian Division or Special Force) invasion of northern Burma, Operation THURSDAY. The Allied First Air Commando, headed by USAAF Colonel Philip Cochran and Colonel John Alison, provided troop air-landing, aerial resupply with artillery and ordnance and evacuation of wounded to implement Wingate's new concept of strongholds, which were to serve as defensive bases from which the Chindits would launch their offensive forays to disrupt the Japanese LOC, principally from Indaw to Myitkyina to support Stilwell's Sino-American advance down the Hukawng and Mogaung valleys. After Wingate's death in an air crash on 24 March 1944, the Chindits, now led by Major General W.D.A. 'Joe' Lentaigne, came under the operational control of Stilwell. One Chindit brigade in particular, Calvert's 77th, would play a role in Stilwell's Myitkyina assault by capturing Mogaung in late June to protect the Sino-American left flank.

Slim's Fourteenth Army

In October 1943, after the First Arakan Campaign debacle, Slim returned to India expecting to be sacked by his superior, General Irwin. However, Mountbatten, the SEAC commander, thought Slim was best to raise and lead a revitalized Eastern Army. Both agreed that a number assignation to Slim's new army would aid with morale. Slim, an officer of the Indian army or 'Sepoy General', was confirmed as the first GOC, Fourteenth Army. Slim was aware of the challenges of supply and transport, so he recruited Major General Arthur Snelling, his quartermaster general in Iraq, to his staff. New all-weather roads needed building. Supplying the Fourteenth Army's 500,000 men from different castes, religions, tribes and nationalities was daunting. Slim realized that at the Assam front, only 50,000 tons of foods were stored at Dimapur; however, Auchinleck, the new C-in-C India who replaced Wavell upon the latter's promotion to viceroy, steadily increased the flow of rations there. Ammunition, weapons, lorries and medicine shortages were also problematic for the Fourteenth Army, which Snelling began to tackle. Medical supplies were crucial as disease ravaged the Fourteenth Army, especially malaria, dysentery and 'Naga sores'. As the CBI was at the bottom of the priority list for supplies to Allied fighting forces, Slim chose prevention as a useful tool to combat the sick roster. He attempted to correct the morale problem by being visible and confident among his troops, communicating positive attitudes in English, Urdu or Gurkhali.

Slim imbued two divisions in India with rigorous jungle training to produce battle-worthy reinforcements for the Fourteenth Army. Older divisions, such as the 23rd and 26th that the Japanese had bested in 1942, acquired jungle-fighting methods. The 2nd British Infantry Division acquired new officers that taught fighting and field-craft methods, especially during nighttime. Battle-experienced divisions such as the 70th British and 5th Indian were arriving from the Middle East to the CBI theatre. The non-battle-tested 7th Indian Division received as its GOC Major General Frank Messervy, who had much front-line combat experience in the Western Desert in 1941–42.

Slim's Fourteenth Army was a polyglot formation with its majority from the Indian army, the largest volunteer army in history. There were Sikhs, Dogras, Pathans, Madrassis, Mahrattas, Rajputs, Assamese, Kumaonis, Punjabis, Garhwalis and Gurkhas, as well as native Naga tribesmen. As for the Western forces, there were English, Scottish, Irish and Welsh, while the RAF squadrons had Australians, Canadians, South Africans, New Zealanders and Rhodesians. With regard to indigenous African troops, there were almost 100,000 East and West Africans comprising three divisions and two separate brigades.

Slim's Second Arakan Campaign, 30 November 1943

Lieutenant General Christison's XV Corps commenced the Second Arakan Campaign on 30 November 1943 astride the Mayu Range. Messervy's 7th Indian Division was to the east of the heights and, three weeks later, Briggs' 5th Indian Division on the western side. Slim tactically believed that a repeat of the First Arakan Campaign could be avoided with a narrow front. The Japanese had defended the 16-mile-long east-to-west-running Maungdaw-Buthidaung road, the only one fit for motor transport, with tunnelled defences in jungle-clad hills along the length of the road. Christison also committed the 81st West African Division to advance down the Kaladan Valley. Messervy wanted to use his armour, but first a road over the Ngakyedauk Pass, 6 miles north of the Maungdaw-Buthidaung Road, had to be constructed, which it was by the end of January 1944.

In the second week of January, Briggs' 5th Indian Division took Maungdaw and then Razabil eastward along the road. British M3 Lee medium tanks, superior to any IJA armour, were secretly shipped by landing craft from India to Cox's Bazar. Even in this inhospitable terrain, the 25th Dragoon Guards' armour destroyed the IJA AT weapons pits. Indian infantry brigades followed the tanks across the Ngakyedauk Pass as the 7th Infantry Division advanced on Buthidaung and Letwedet.

As Slim's three divisions were fighting in the Arakan, two IJA offensives were being planned. One was Operation U-GO (starting on 15 March 1944, see Chapter 4) involving Mutaguchi's Fifteenth Army while an IJA Twenty-Eighth Army was formed for the Japanese Arakan offensive, Operation HA-GO (starting on 4 February 1944). In the Arakan the Japanese struck while Christison regrouped his corps for the Buthidaung assault. Messervy's 7th Division's HQ was overrun on 5–6 February. Slim told his Fourteenth Army units that when they were cut off, they were to hold firm and would be supplied by air. As the scale of the Operation HA-GO offensive in the Mayu Range became apparent with the IJA Twenty-Eighth Army's 54th, 55th and 2nd divisions involved, Slim sent in the 26th Indian Division and dispatched the 36th Indian Division as a reserve. Messervy returned to the 7th Indian Division's 'Admin Box', fighting off repeated IJA attacks as they were resupplied by air. Messervy also used 3.7in AA guns sited in the 'Admin Box' in a direct-fire role, which was unusual for British artillery. Tanks of the 25th Dragoons manned the perimeter of the 'Admin Box' to shore up the defences when a breakthrough by the Japanese was threatened. On 27 February, on the twenty-first day of the Battle of the Admin Box, a link-up between Christison's 5th and 7th Indian divisions occurred.

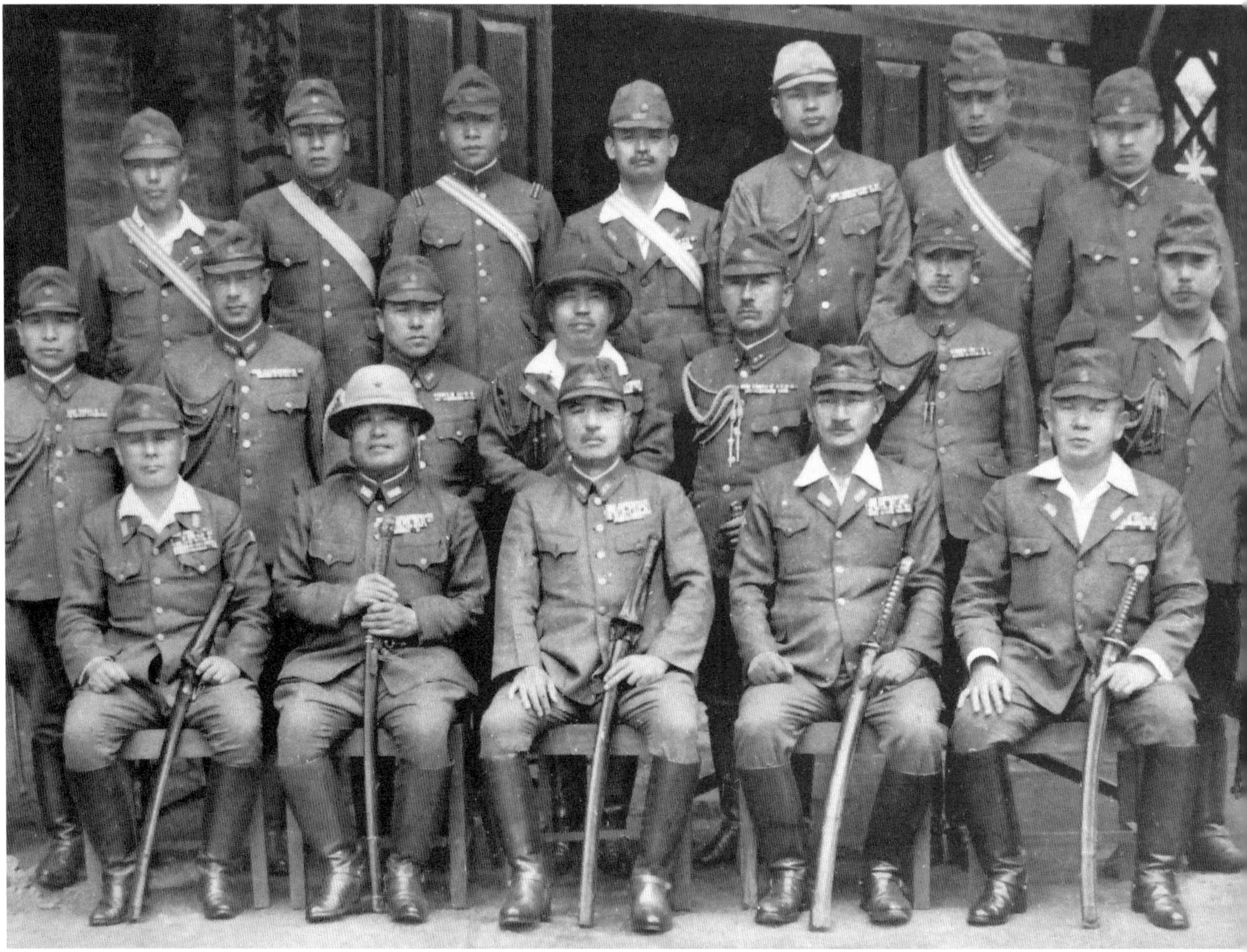

IJA Burma Area Army generals in late 1943 are shown here. Lieutenant General Renya Mutaguchi (front row, middle) commanded the Fifteenth Army for Operation U-GO, while Lieutenant General Shinichi Tanaka, the 18th Division commander in northern Burma (front row, second from left) wore a tropical sun helmet. *(NARA)*

IJA infantrymen are shown here charging in 1942 as the elite of Japanese troops, until Burma's final conquest, were placed on the offensive. In 1943, a shift to an offensive-defensive strategy ensued as logistics precluded a major Indian offensive. Mutaguchi feared an Allied invasion of Burma from India, so he launched Operation U-GO in March 1944 with limited supplies, intending to capture Allied supply depots at Dimapur to Kohima's north-west. *(NARA)*

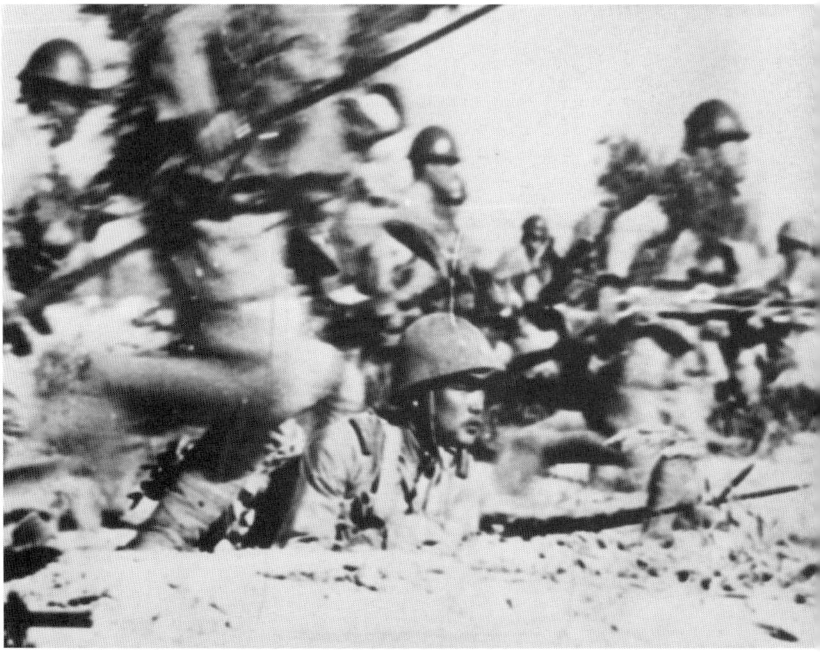

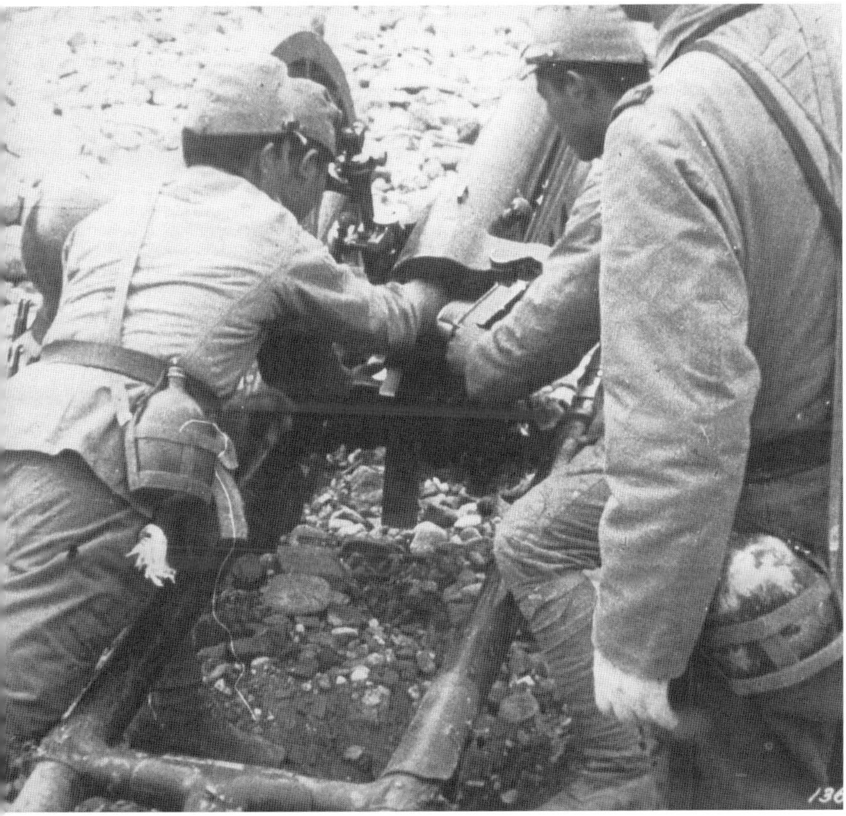

Japanese troops load the breech of a 75mm gun in a mountainous area of Burma during the 1942 invasion. Swift mobility of IJA artillery supporting infantry led to an Allied rout back to India across the Chindwin River. *(NARA)*

A Japanese 7.7mm Type 92 HMG is set up here on a Burmese hilltop during the 1942 advance from Thailand. This weapon was air-cooled with the distinctive barrel cooling rings and was the HMG most often used by IJA troops between 1941 and 1945. *(NARA)*

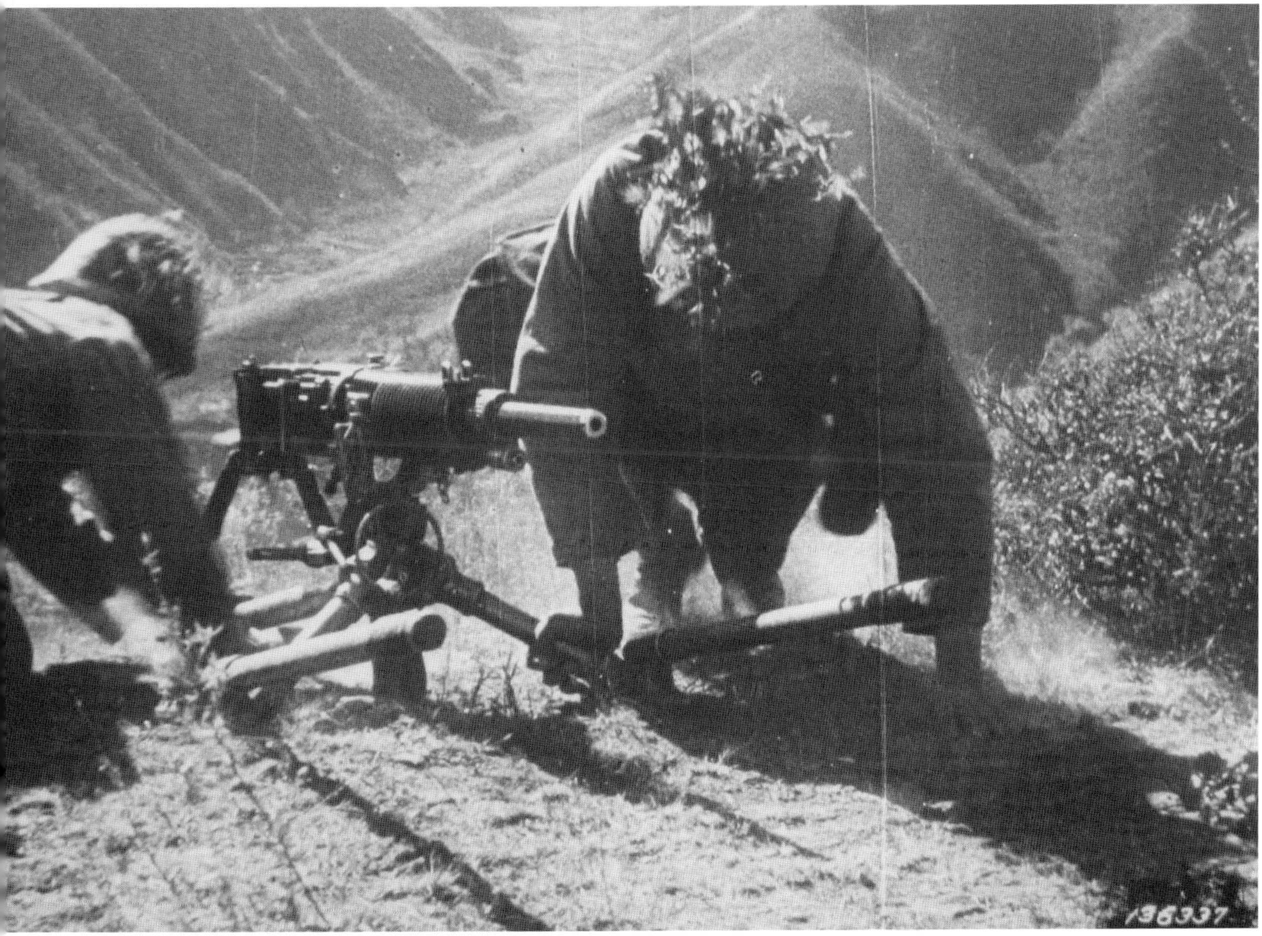

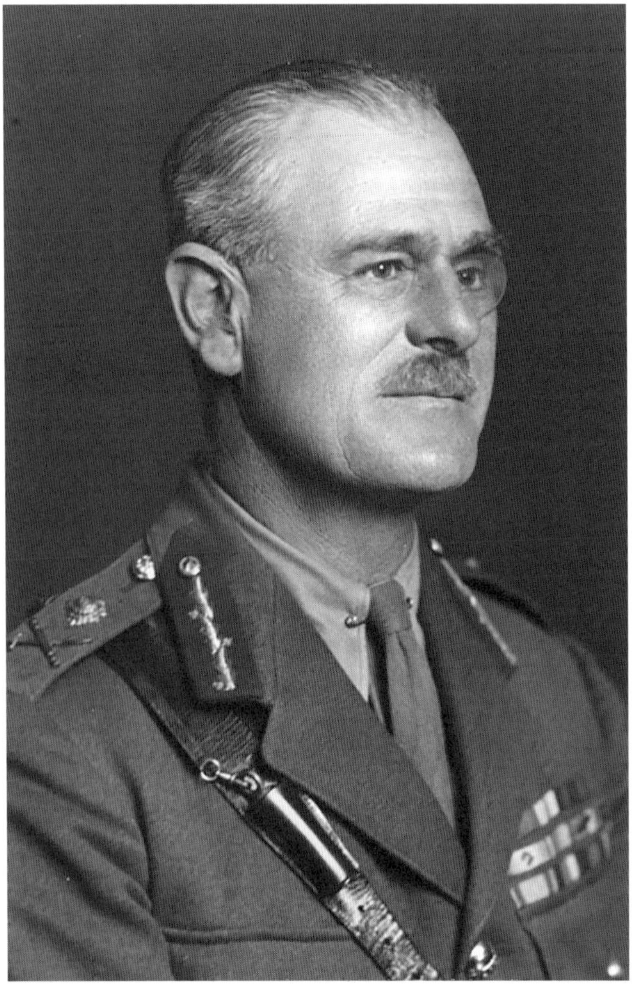

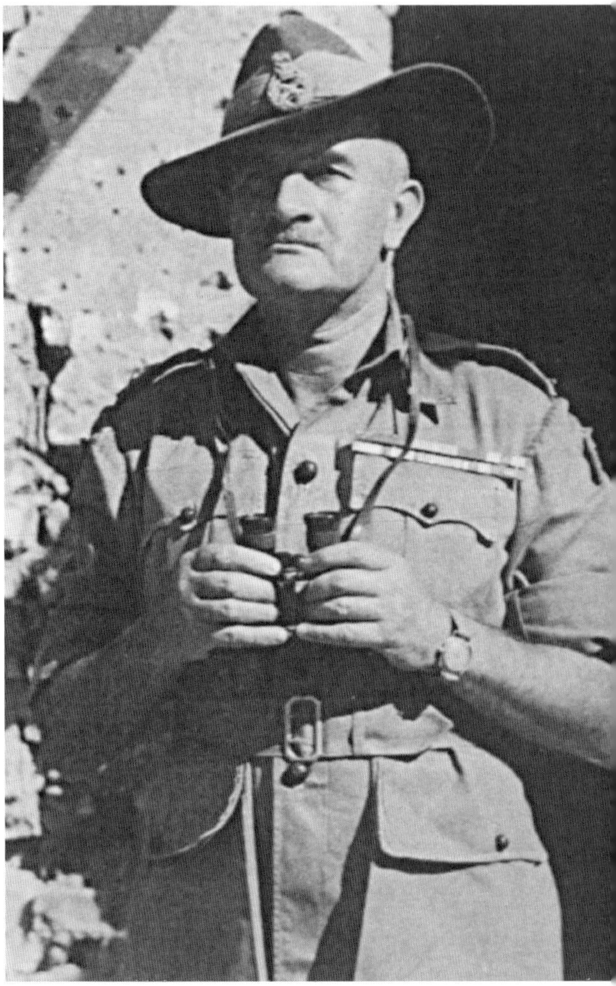

(**Above left**) Lieutenant General Archibald Wavell is shown here as GOC Palestine in 1938, where he was successful at suppressing the Arab Revolt with the aid of the then Major Orde Wingate. Known for his intellect and strategic thinking, he became C-in-C Middle East with initial early 1940 successes against the Italian Tenth Army in Libya, the Vichy French in Syria and a German-inspired Iraqi rebellion, as well as the eviction of Italian forces from Italian Somaliland, Ethiopia and Eritrea. The German entry into the Mediterranean and North Africa led to Wavell's defeats, notably in Greece, Crete and Cyrenaica in 1941. Field Marshal Wavell was transferred to India in June 1941 as C-in-C India. Wavell oversaw the losses of Singapore and Malaya with Percival's surrender to Yamashita's Twenty-Fifth IJA Army on 15 February 1942 as well as the disbanding of his ABDA command one week later with the loss of the NEI. Then the ignominious Allied retreat from Burma occurred during spring 1942. After the lacklustre First Arakan Campaign, December 1942–May 1943, Churchill gave Wavell the viceroyalty of India with General Sir Claude Auchinleck becoming C-in-C India. *(Author's collection)*

(**Above right**) Lieutenant General William Slim is shown here as GOC Fourteenth Army, which he helped form after the failed First Arakan Campaign of 1943. Slim, in the Royal Warwickshire Regiment in 1914, fought and was wounded at Gallipoli. Rejoining his regiment in Mesopotamia in 1916, he was again wounded and won a Military Cross. He spent the interwar years as an Indian army officer in Gurkha units. In 1940–41 he led with distinction in Abyssinia, Syria, Iraq and Persia. In March 1942, Alexander gave him command of Burma Corps (Burcorps) as an acting lieutenant general. Slim's Fourteenth Army decisively defeated Mutaguchi's IJA Fifteenth Army in its 'March on Delhi' at Imphal and Kohima from March–July 1944. *(NARA)*

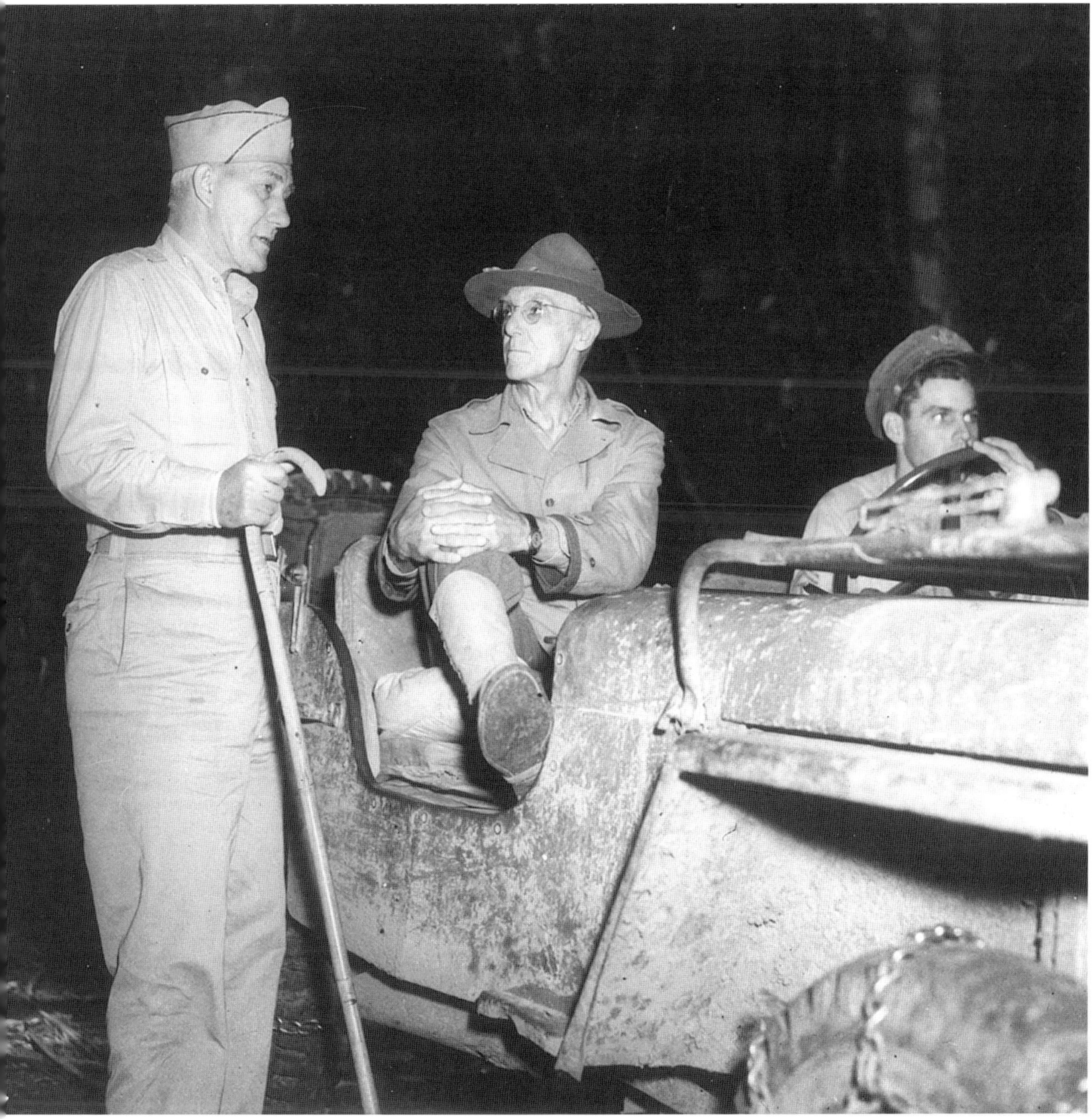

Brigadier General Lewis Pick (left) meets with Lieutenant General Joseph Stilwell (centre) in northern Burma in 1944 during the Ledo Road construction there. As a civilian, he was an engineer of the Missouri River Division creating flood control plans. On 17 October 1943, Pick assumed supervision of the Ledo Road project, commanding five US army engineer battalions and a quartermaster regiment to work on 'Pick's Pike' through the Hukawng and Mogaung valleys until reaching the Old Burma Road south of Myitkyina. The first American truck convoy reached Wanting, China in January 1945. *(USAMHI)*

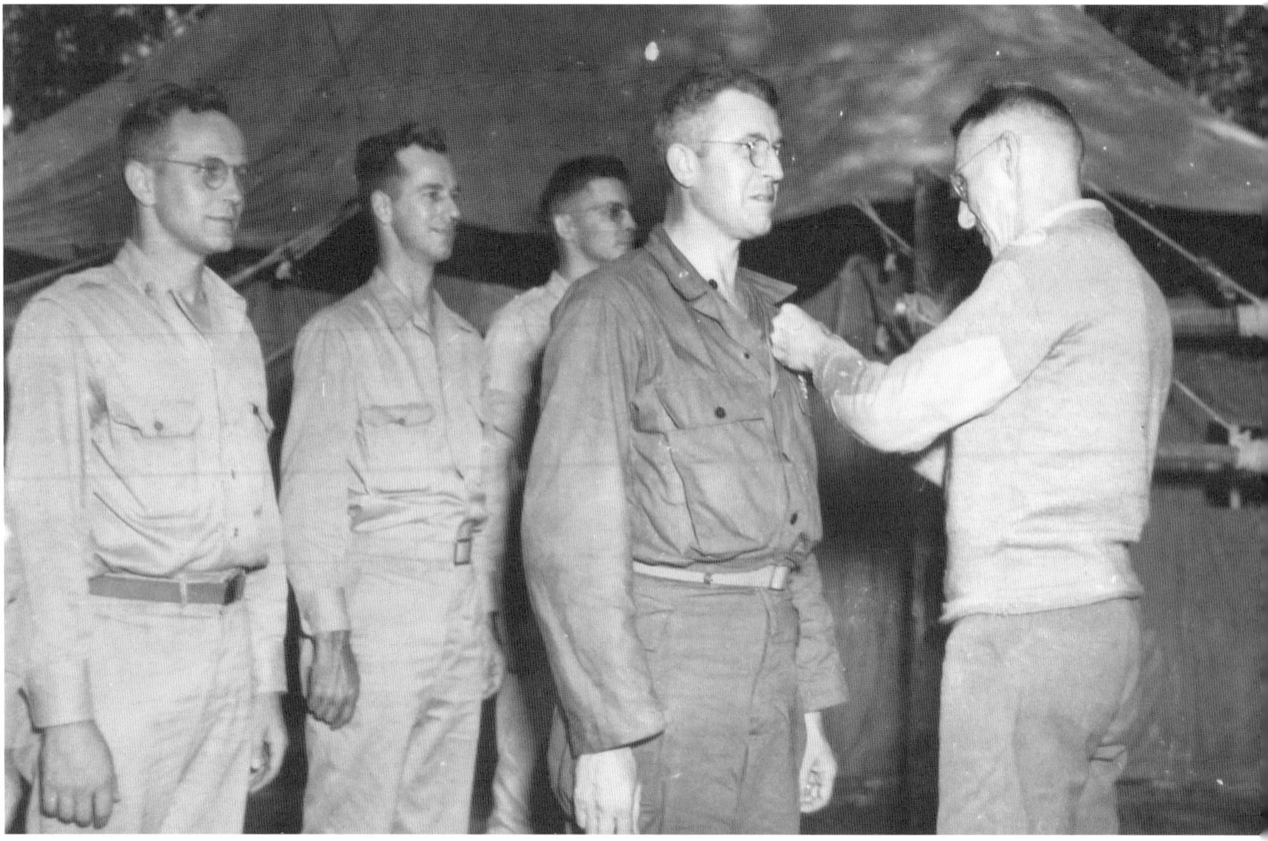

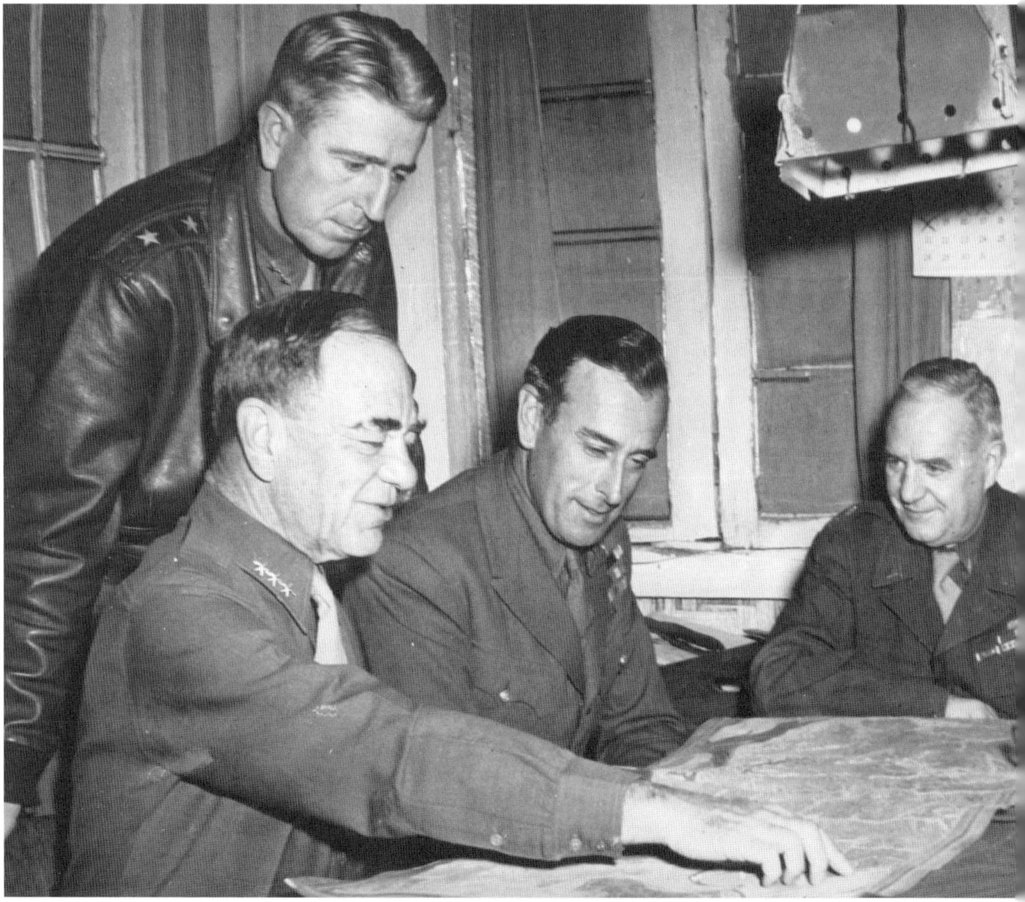

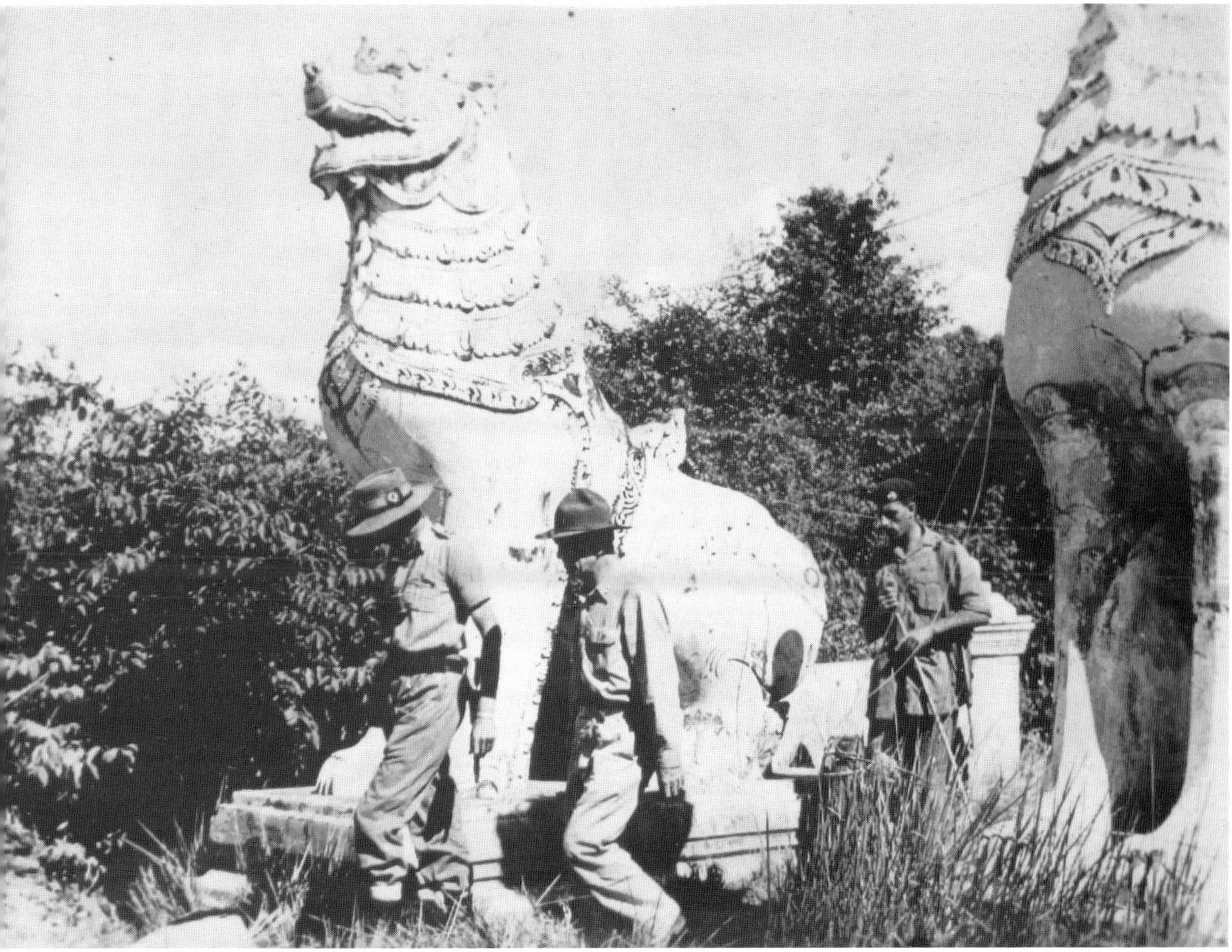

(**Opposite, above**) Lieutenant General Joseph Stilwell decorates Brigadier General Frank Merrill, leader of 'Galahad', on 18 April 1944, a month before Merrill's deputy Colonel Charles Hunter led Marauders, Chinese infantry and Kachins in a *coup de main* capture of the Japanese airfield at Myitkyina on 17 May. Standing behind Merrill are Stilwell's staff officers: Colonels Ernest Easterbrook (middle), Stilwell's son-in-law and Joseph Stilwell, Jr. (right). *(NARA)*

(**Opposite, below**) The CBI commanders after Stilwell's 18 October 1944 recall are from right to left: Lieutenant General Daniel Sultan (American Forces CG India-Burma Theatre); Lieutenant General Albert Wedemeyer (standing, American Forces CG China Theatre); Admiral Lord Louis Mountbatten (SEAC leader); and Major General William Donovan (OSS head). Sultan went to New Delhi in November 1943 as Stilwell's deputy to focus on logistical issues to supply China. Wedemeyer, a Marshall protégé, was Mountbatten's COS at SEAC since 1943 before his promotion. *(NARA)*

(**Above**) Lieutenant General Oliver Leese (left), C-in-C Allied Land Forces, SEAC, leaves a Burmese temple at Mawlu with Lieutenant General Daniel Sultan (centre). In November 1944 Leese, the British Eighth Army commander in Italy, was promoted to direct all Allied ground forces under Mountbatten's SEAC command. The pair of mythical animals standing guard at the Burmese temple are *chinthes* or lions, from which Wingate's force's name of Chindits was derived. The Chindits developed a stronghold ('White City') near Mawlu along the railway south-west of Myitkyina earlier in 1944. *(NARA)*

(**Above**) Air Chief Marshal (ACM) Keith Park, Allied Air C-in-C SEAC, inspects Allied bomb damage to Rangoon's docks in late May 1945. A native New Zealander, Park was an ace in the Royal Flying Corps (RFC) in the First World War. During the dark summer days of 1940, Park assisted Fighter Command's ACM Hugh Dowding to defend Britain's skies as RAF's Number 11 Group leader. In 1942, Park bolstered Malta's air defences from Axis bombing in 1942 and then in the Middle East in 1944. (*NARA*)

(**Opposite, above**) On 31 March 1945, Lieutenant General William Slim (right) with his corps and divisional commanders wave their slouch hats on a makeshift review stand to cheer the Union Jack flag-raising after Mandalay's recapture. After narrow victories at Imphal and Kohima, Slim's Fourteenth Army relentlessly drove the Japanese out of central and southern Burma. (*NARA*)

(**Opposite, below left**) Lieutenant General Geoffrey Scoones, Indian IV Corps' commander at Imphal is shown here. Prior to his combat command, Scoones was the Director of Military Operations at Indian Army HQ in Delhi. A sound military thinker, he was criticized for a slow response to the IJA Fifteenth Army's Imphal attack in March 1944. (*Author's collection*)

(**Opposite, below right**) Lieutenant General Montagu Stopford led the Indian XXXIII Corps with the Fourteenth Army's British 2nd Infantry and Indian 7th divisions' reserve group to relieve the Kohima garrison from IJA Lieutenant General Kōtoku Satō's 31st Division's assault. Stopford also employed the 5th Indian Division's 161st Infantry Brigade in the Kohima defence. (*Author's collection*)

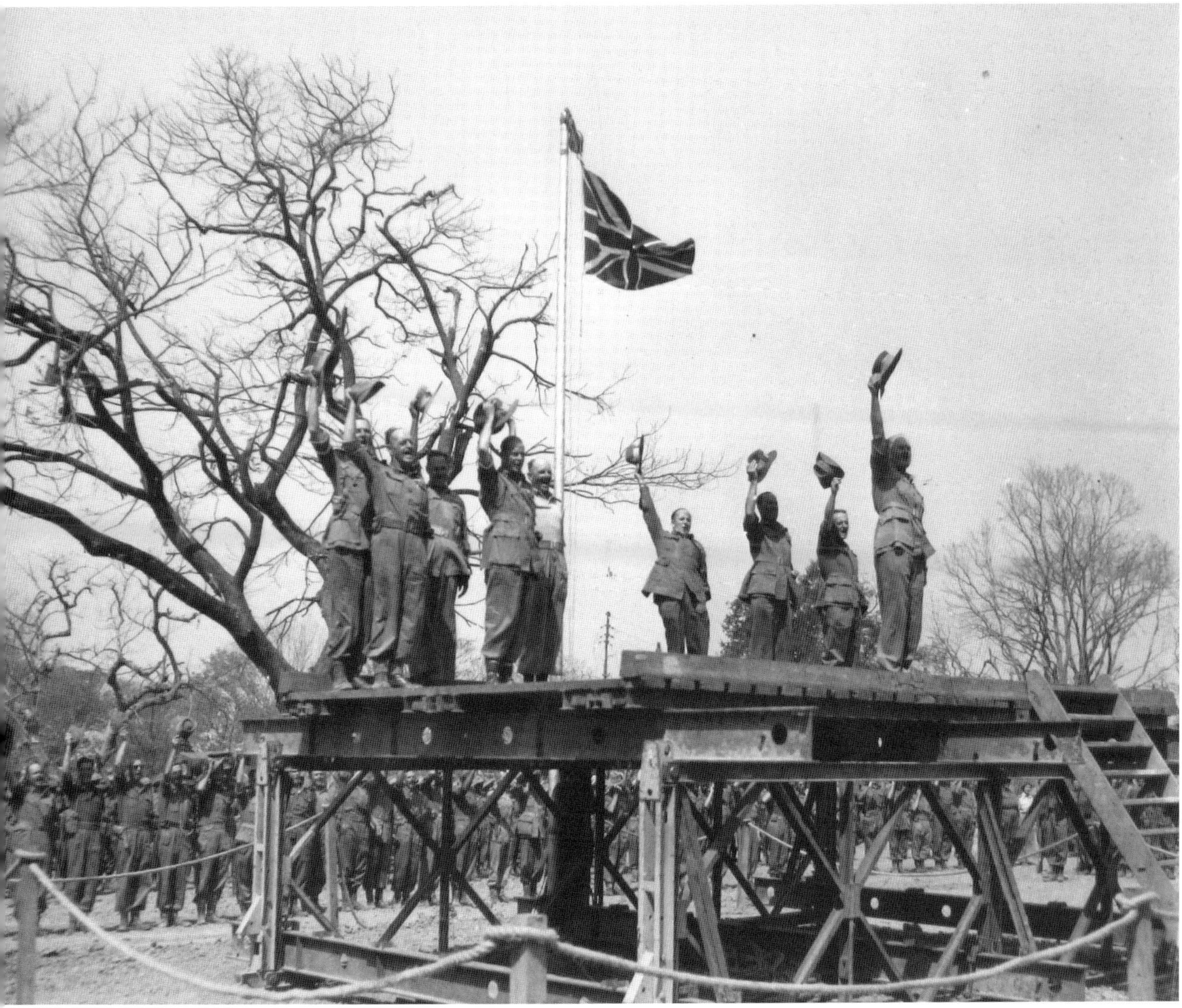

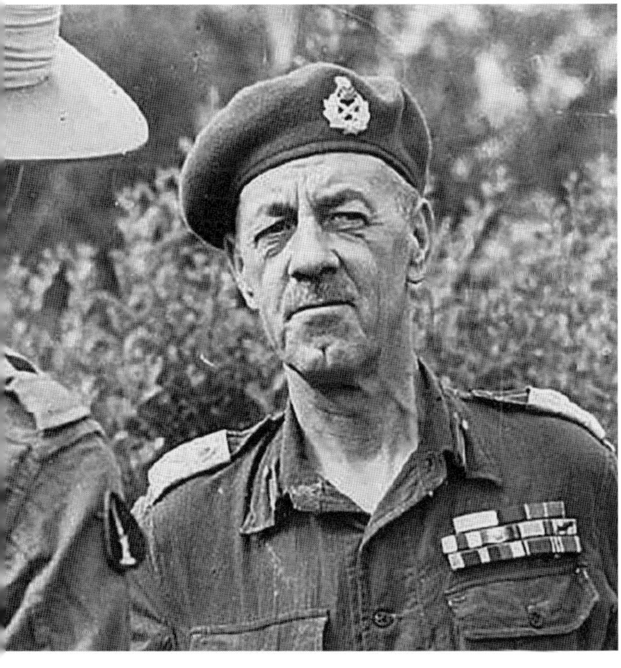

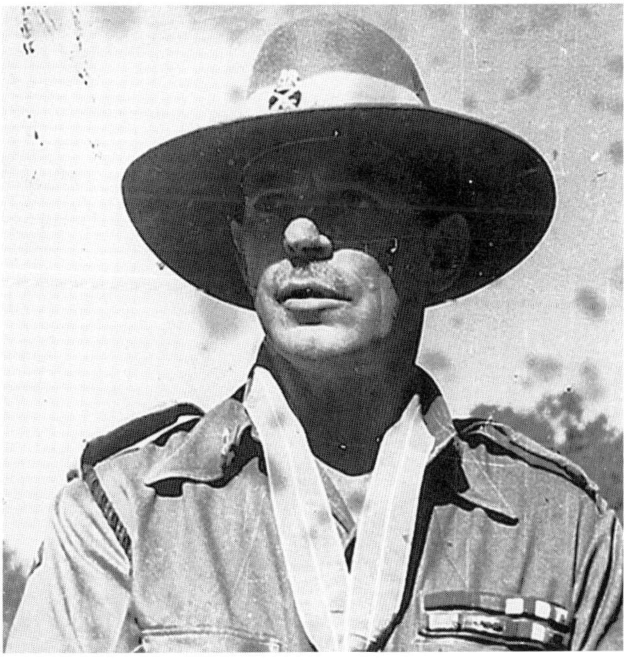

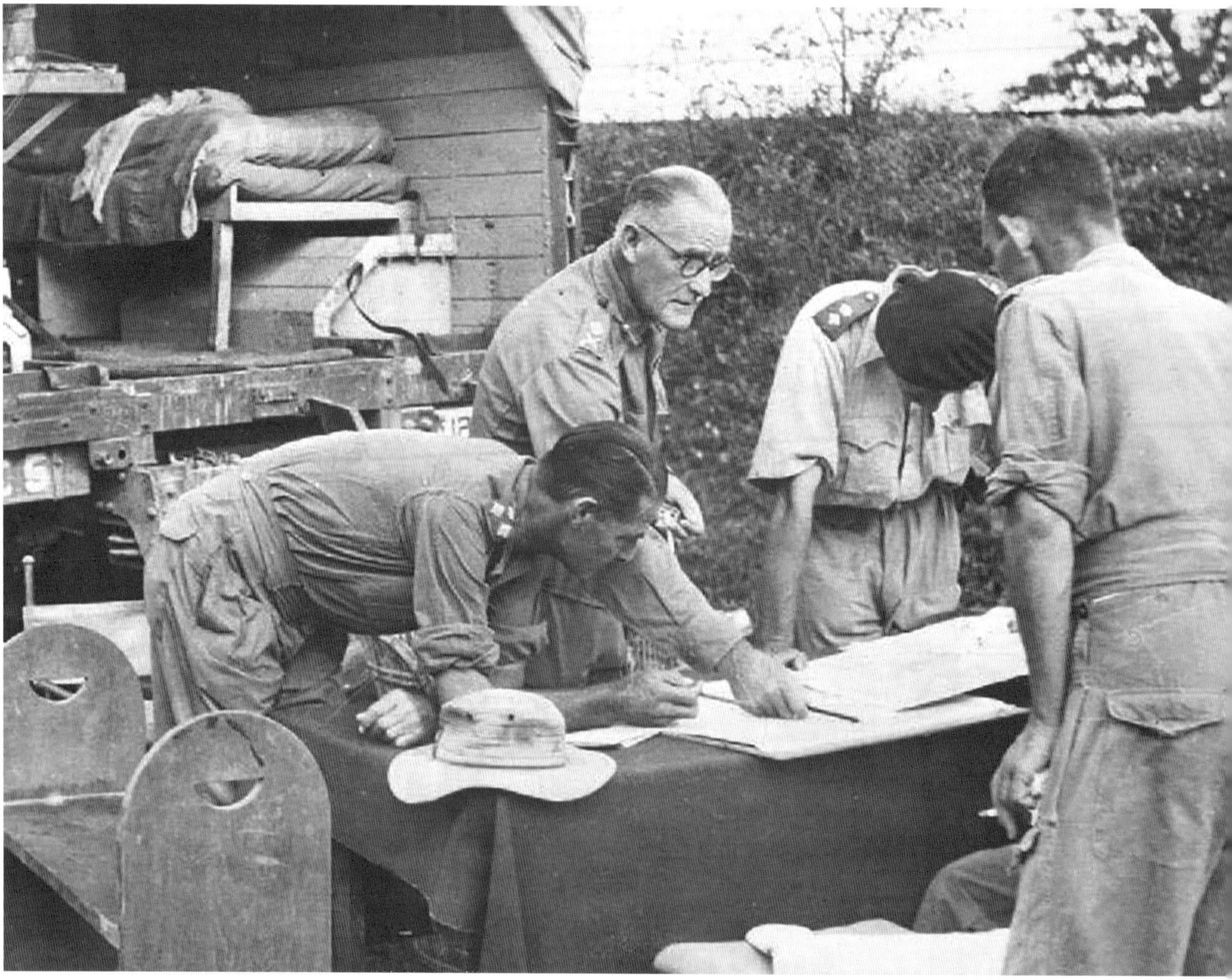

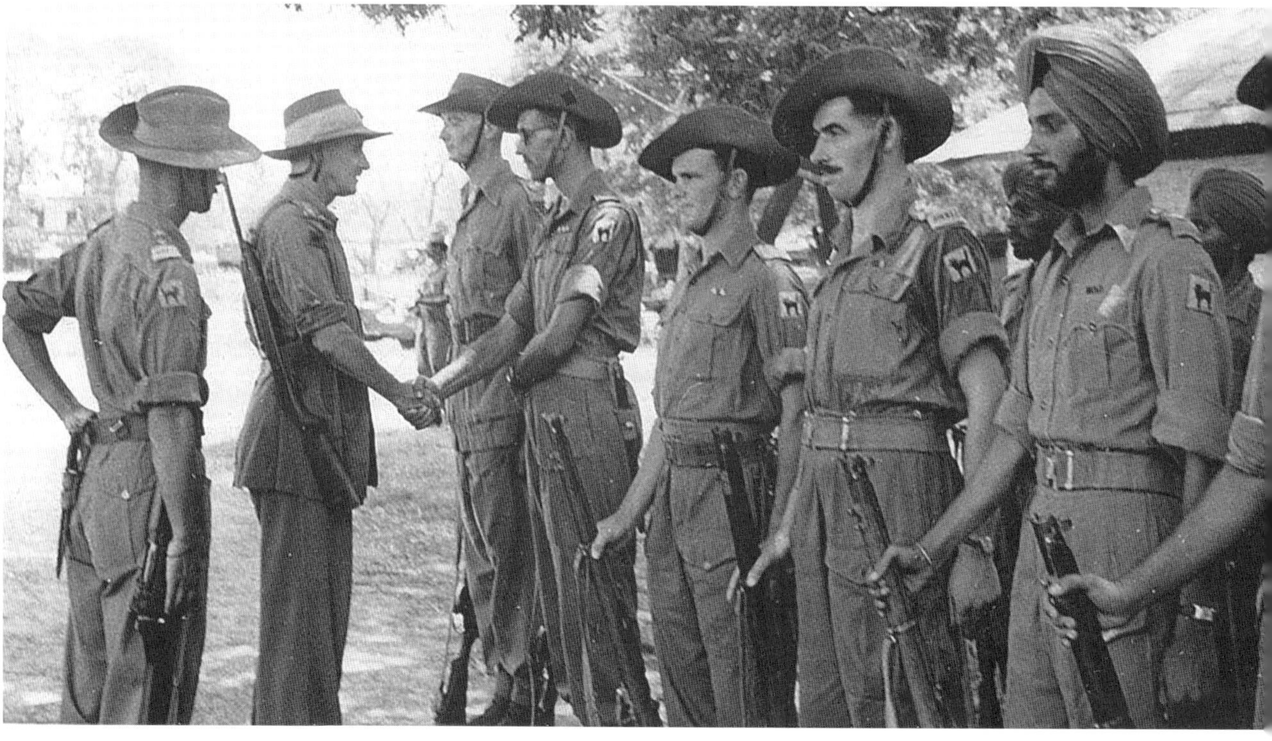

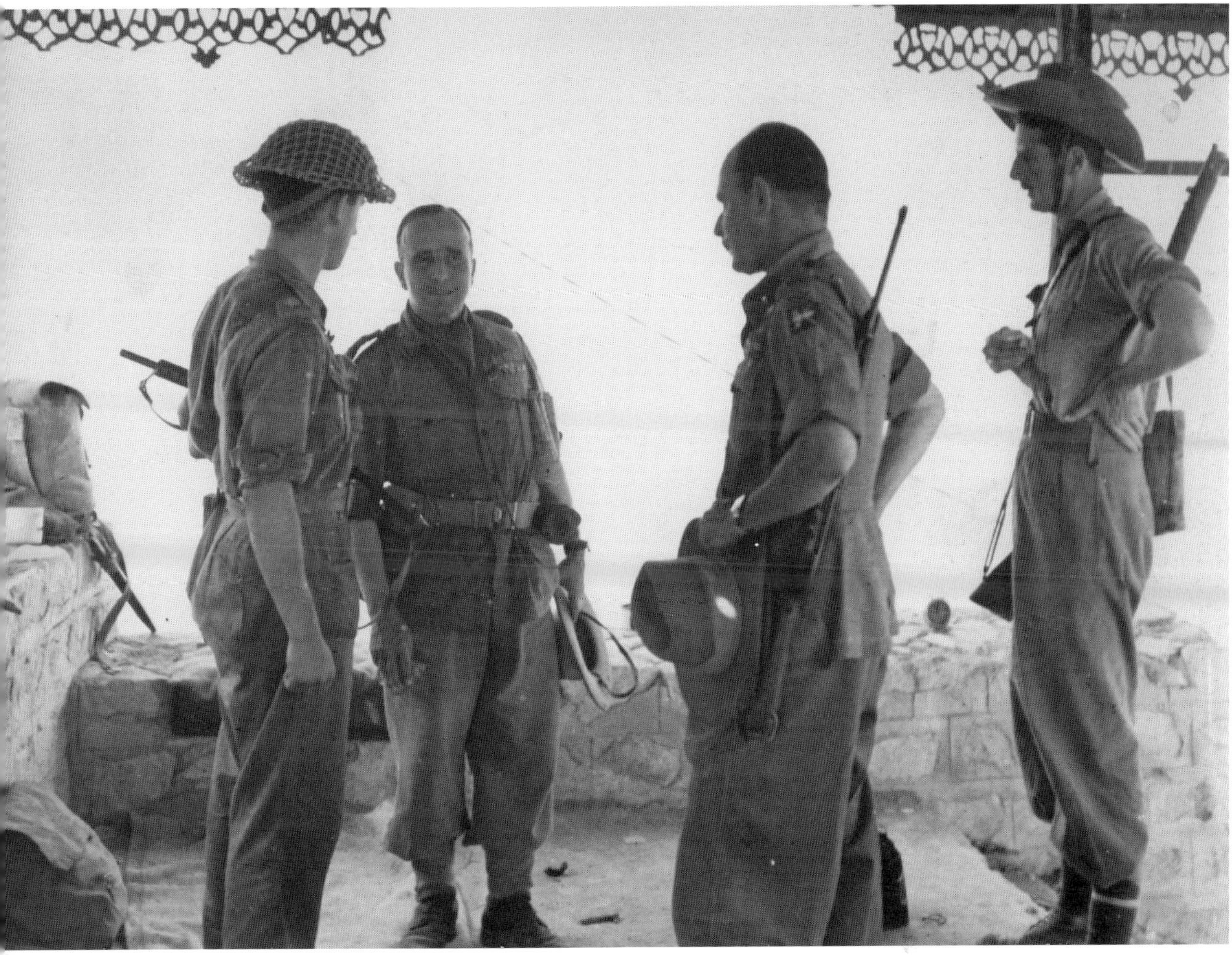

(**Opposite, above**) Major General David Cowan (centre), commander of the 17th Indian Division, reviews maps with staff officers during the Imphal combat against IJA Lieutenant General Motoso Yanagida's 33rd Division and a separate force under Major General Tsunoru Yamamoto comprising detached units from the IJA 33rd and Lieutenant General Masafumi Yamauchi's 15th divisions. In 1942, Cowan's 17th Indian Division was bested by the Japanese along the Sittang River after the waterway's bridge was prematurely detonated, stranding many of his troops on the eastern bank. Victory over the IJA 33rd Division at Imphal in the summer of 1944 avenged that debacle. *(Author's collection)*

(**Opposite, below**) Lieutenant General Frank Messervy, Indian IV Corps CG, greets his Corps' 17th Indian Division troops. A career Indian army officer, Messervy led the 4th Indian and then the 7th Armoured divisions in the Western Desert before returning to India in 1943. After fighting from the front at the 'Admin Box' during the Second Arakan Campaign and at Kohima, he was given command of the Indian IV Corps in October 1944 for the duration of the Burma campaign. *(Author's collection)*

(**Above**) Slim's commanders for his 1944–45 offensive include career Indian army officer Major General Thomas 'Pete' Rees (second from left), 19th Indian Division CG and Lieutenant General Montagu Stopford, XXXIII Indian Corps CG (second from right). They discussed attack plans against the Japanese on the heavily-defended Mandalay Hill in the middle of March 1945. The 19th Indian Division also had to reduce IJA defences at Fort Dufferin before the Japanese abandoned Mandalay on 20 March. *(NARA)*

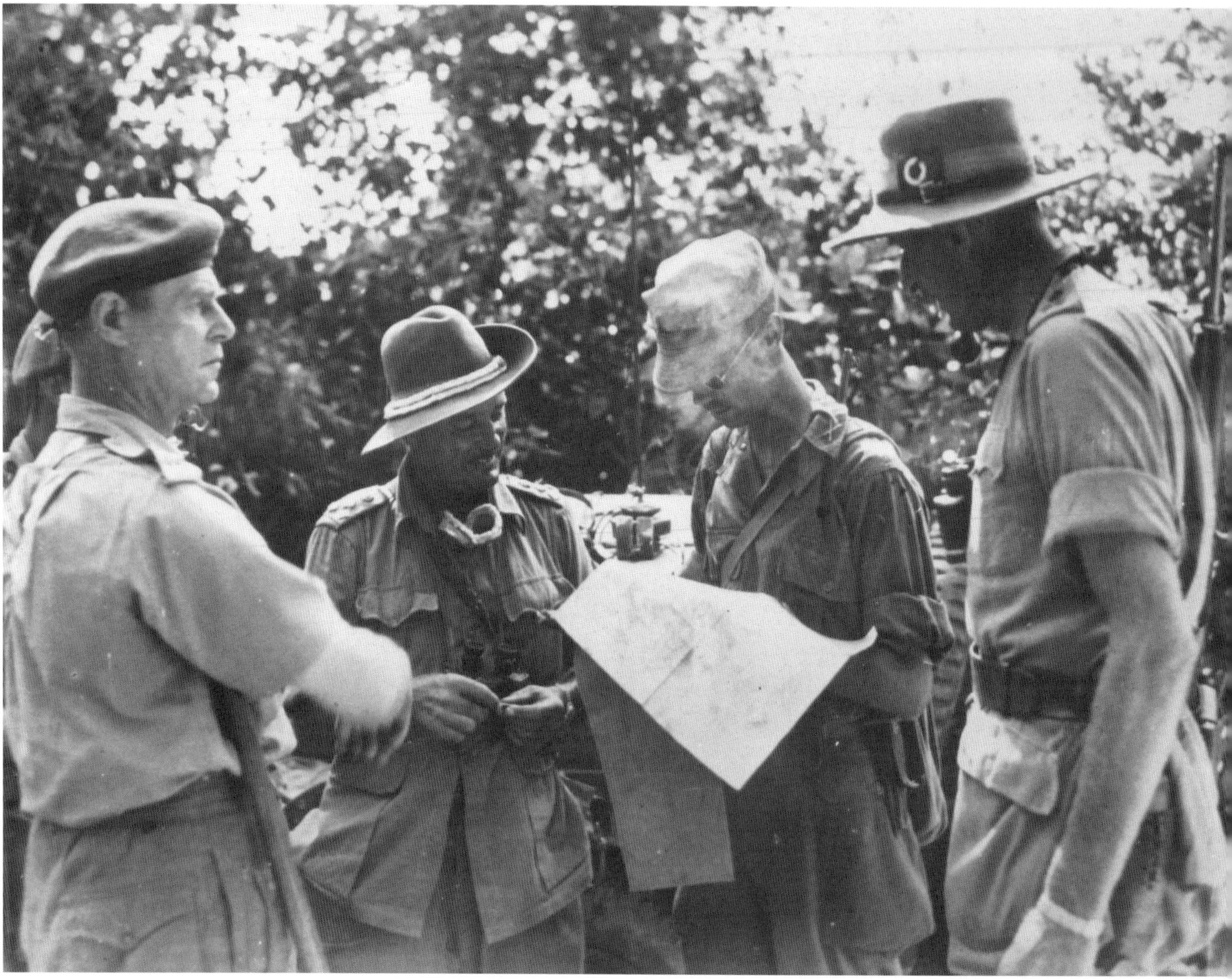

(**Above**) Major General Colin Jardine (far left), Brigadier A.R. Aslett, 36th British Division's 72nd Indian Brigade commander, Lieutenant Colonel Trevor Dupuy, American liaison officer with Chinese artillery, and Major General Francis Festing, 36th British Division CG (far right) review plans for the 36th British Division's southward advance down the 'Railway Corridor' towards Mandalay in December 1944. In September 1944, the division was redesignated from the 36th Indian Division to the 36th British Division until the war's end. Dupuy graduated from West Point in 1938. In Burma, he commanded a Chinese artillery group and an artillery detachment from the British 36th Infantry Division and is reported to have spent more combat time in Burma than any other American. *(NARA)*

(**Opposite, above**) Major Generals Francis Festing, CG 36th British Division (left) and Colin Jardine (right) during a break on the 'Railway Corridor's southward advance towards Mandalay. Festing was known as 'Front-Line Frankie', typified by his leading the advance into Mawlu on 21 October 1944 when one of his subordinate officers was killed after being tasked with that mission. He served during the Norwegian and Madagascar campaigns before being given command of the 36th Indian Division in January 1943. Jardine, a decorated First World War artilleryman, served as military commander of Gibraltar in May 1942 when Lord Gort was sent to Malta. *(NARA)*

(**Opposite, below**) From left to right are Havildar (or Sergeant) Mahdo Singh reporting to British Majors P.W. Wheeler and M.H.S. Hogh as well as Captain M.B. Flatau. All were from the 11th Sikh Regiment in Rees' 19th Indian Division in March 1945 after the victory at Mandalay. *(NARA)*

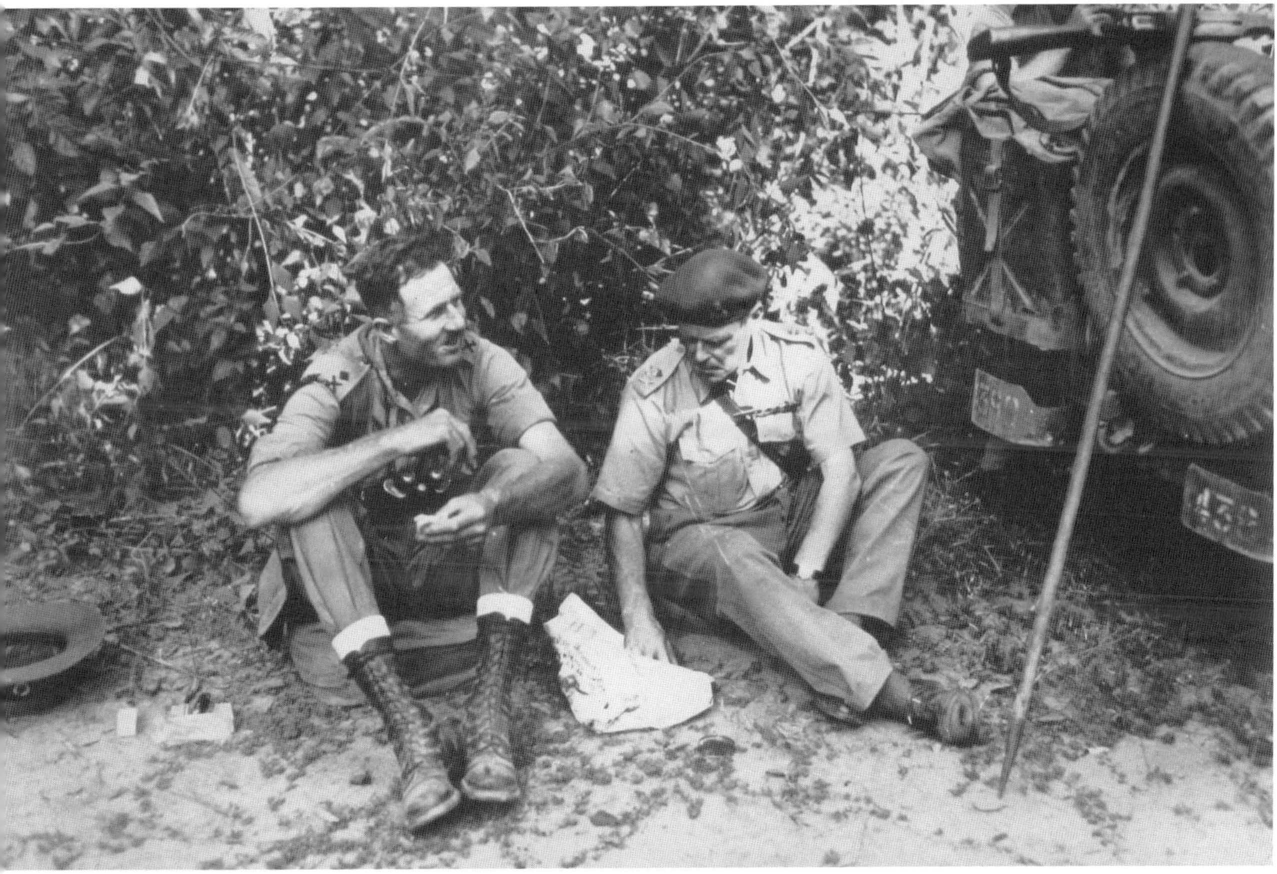

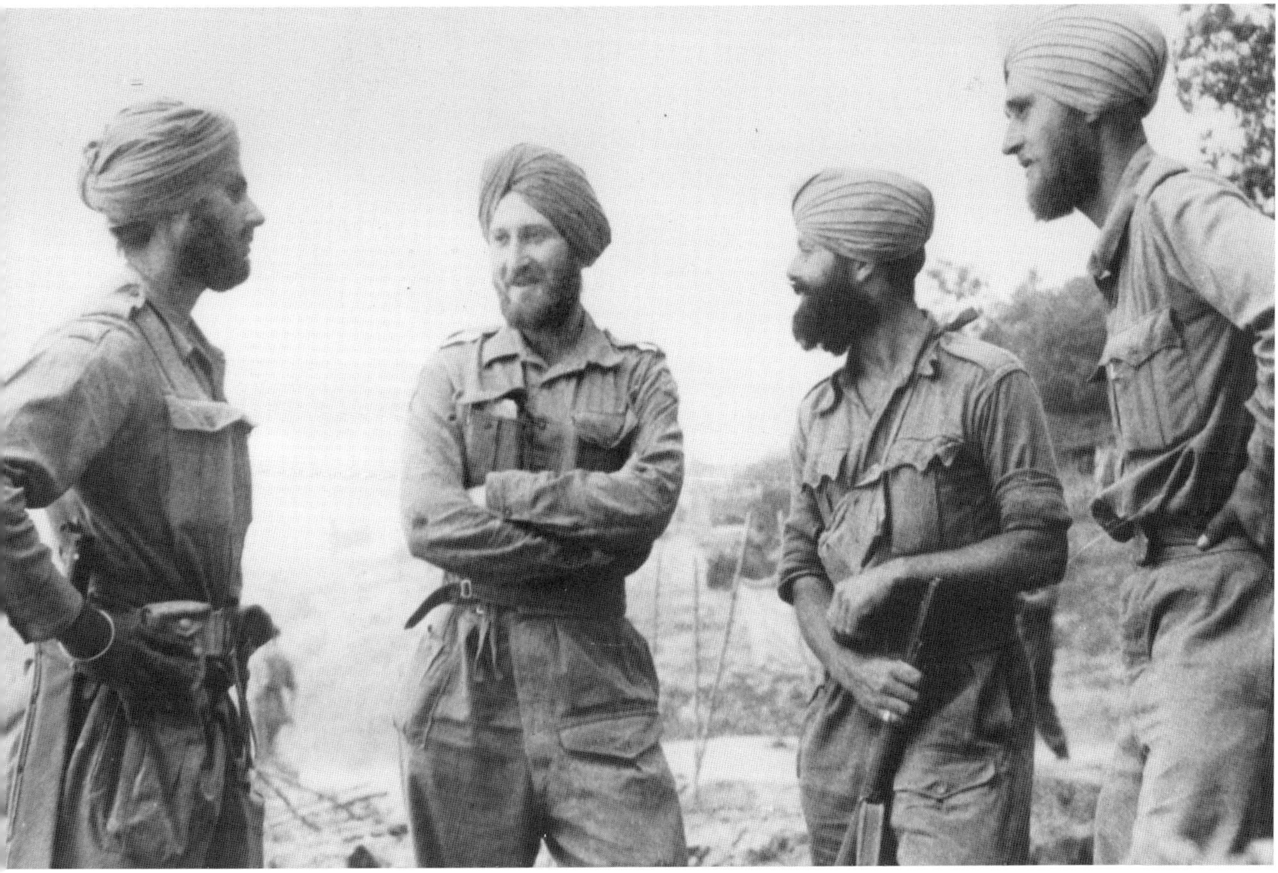

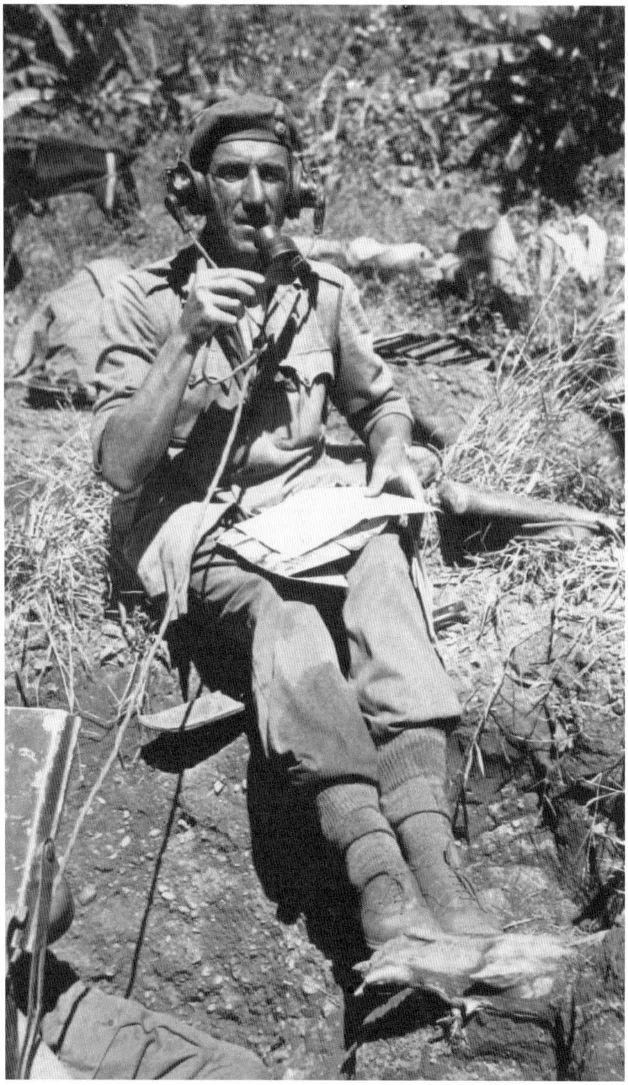

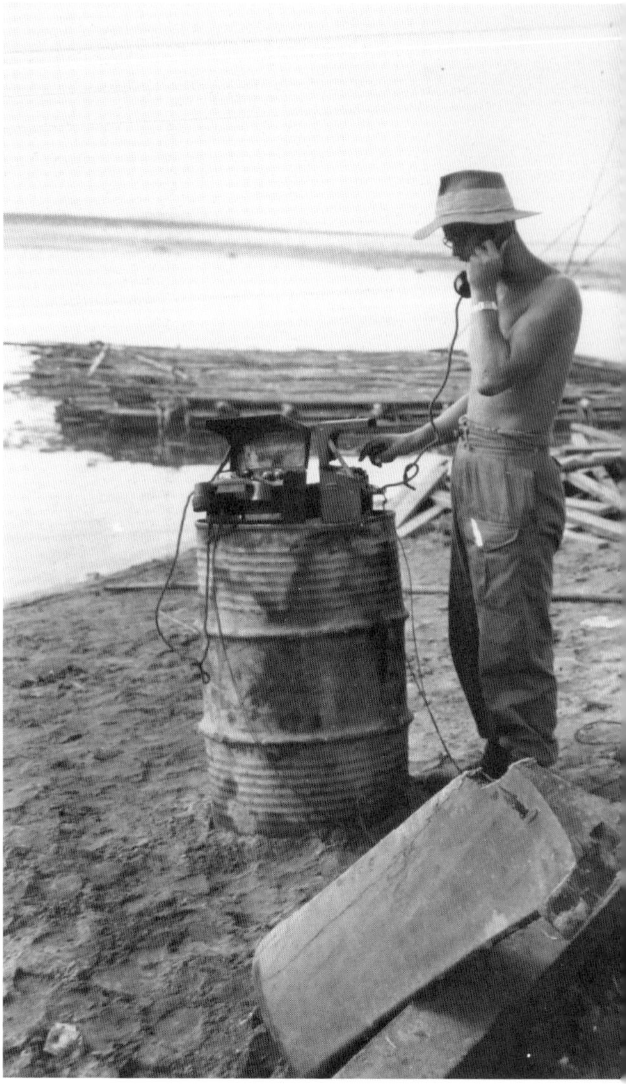

(**Above, left**) Lieutenant Colonel Gwyden Jones, CO Royal Welsh Fusiliers, 36th British Division, directs troops via a wireless set at Pinthe in October 1944 during action along the 'Railway Corridor'. The 36th British Division was part of the NCAC first led by Stilwell and then after his recall by Sultan. *(NARA)*

(**Above, right**) Captain J. Hayne RE uses a wireless set while attached to the 36th British Division at Tigyaing. He was reporting on loading operations for the crossing of the Irrawaddy River at the end of December 1944 after elements of the 36th British Division entered Tigyaing on 22 December. *(NARA)*

(**Opposite, below**) A detachment of the British 36th Division's Royal Scots Fusiliers of the 29th Indian Infantry Brigade under the NCAC is piped across a Burmese *chaung* on its southward advance from Myitkyina down the 'Railway Corridor' towards Myitsone, which is situated south of Mabein and north of Mogok on the Shweli River. After Indaw's capture in December 1944 and having made contact with Rees' 19th Indian Division moving east after crossing the Chindwin River, Sultan ordered Festing to advance astride the Irrawaddy River as far south as Tigyaing. From there, the 36th British Division was to operate east of the Irrawaddy River to clear the Shweli River crossings south of Mabein and then take Mogok. *(NARA)*

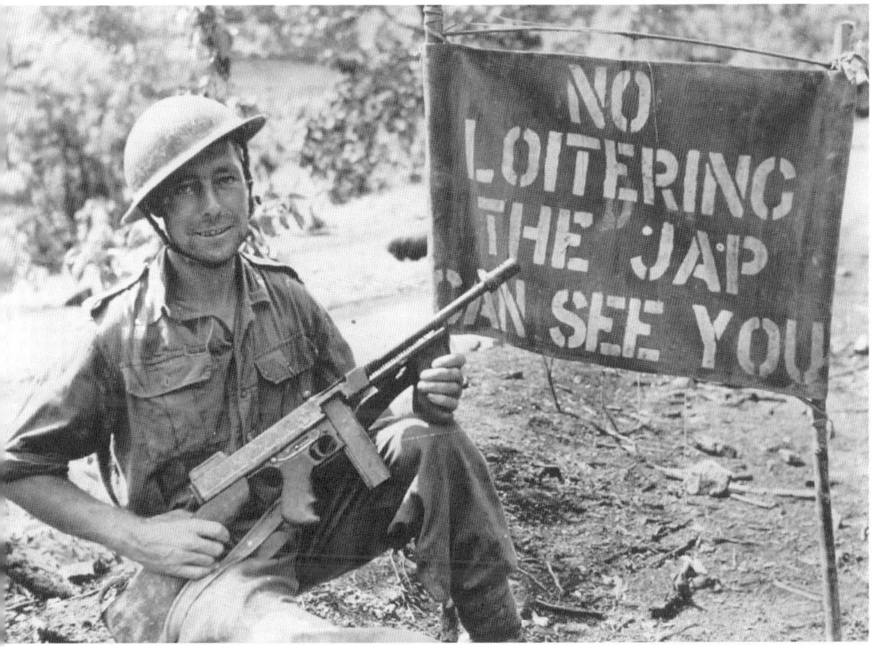
NO
LOITERING
THE JAP
AN SEE YOU

A British lance corporal poses on sentry duty in front of a warning sign: 'No Loitering: The Jap Can See You'. He is holding his American-made 0.45in-calibre Thompson SMG, a weapon renowned for its stopping power. This SMG had a range of approximately 400ft and utilized an eighteen-, twenty- or thirty-round detachable magazine. *(NARA)*

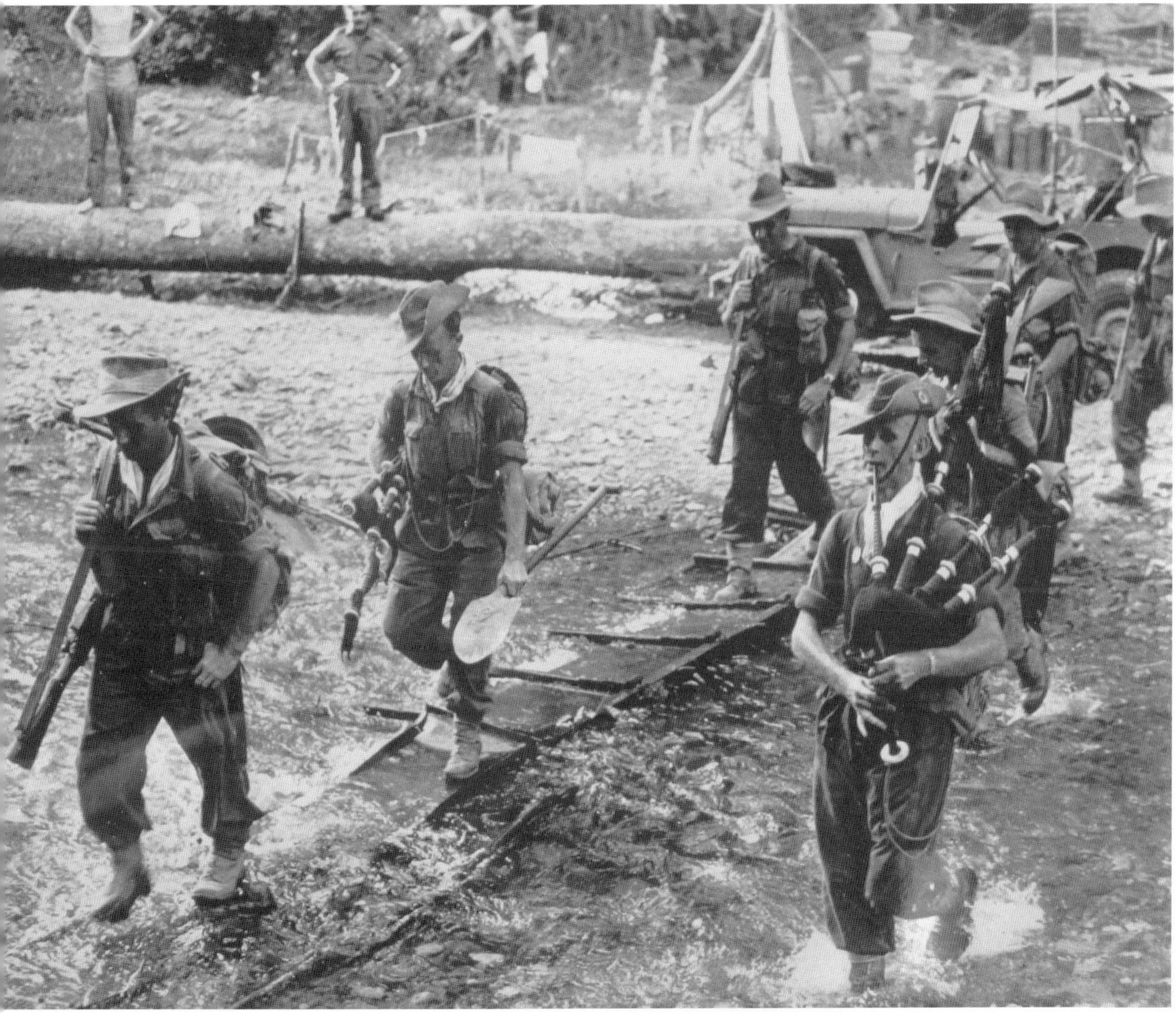

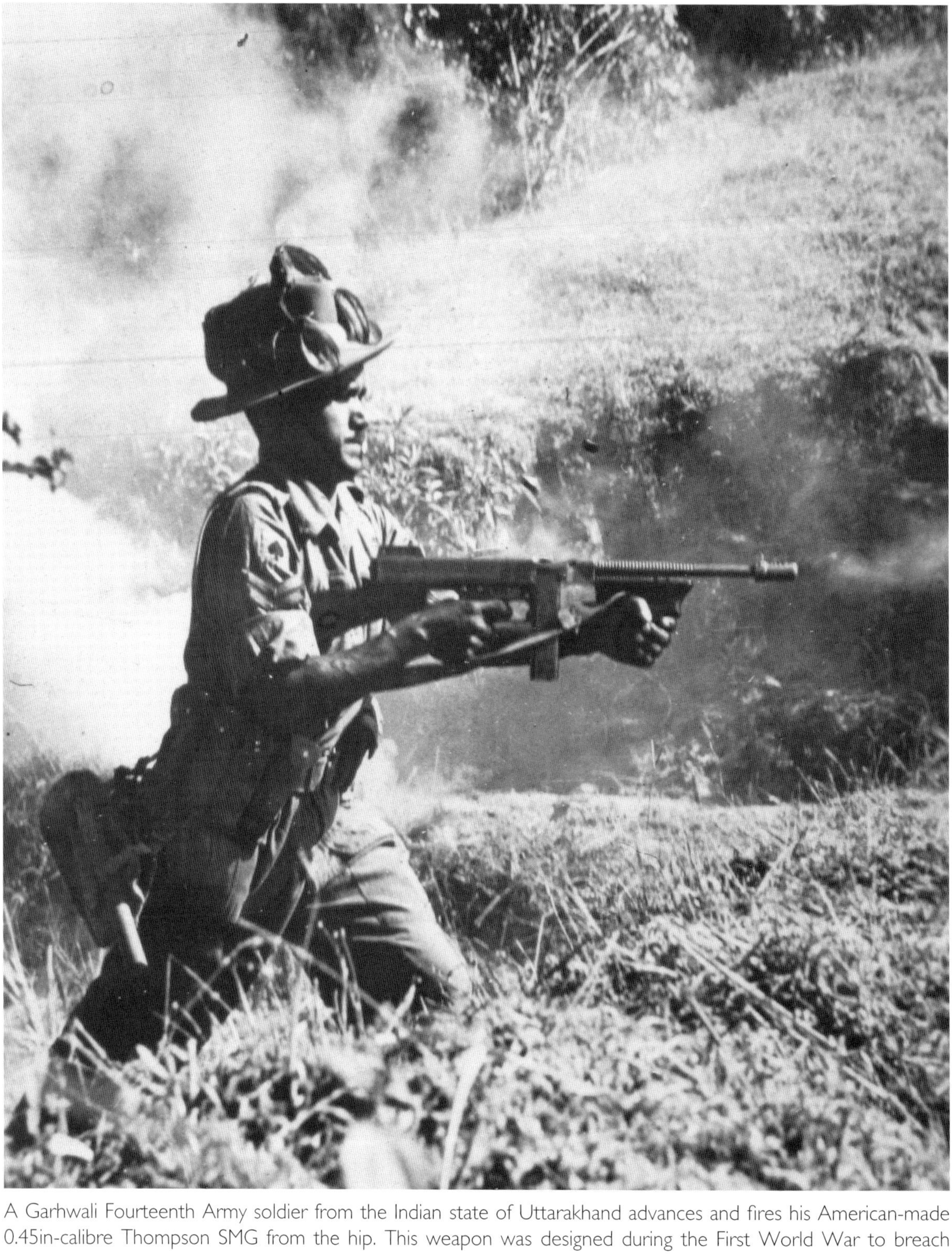

A Garhwali Fourteenth Army soldier from the Indian state of Uttarakhand advances and fires his American-made 0.45in-calibre Thompson SMG from the hip. This weapon was designed during the First World War to breach enemy trenches with heavy, sustained mobile gunfire. *(NARA)*

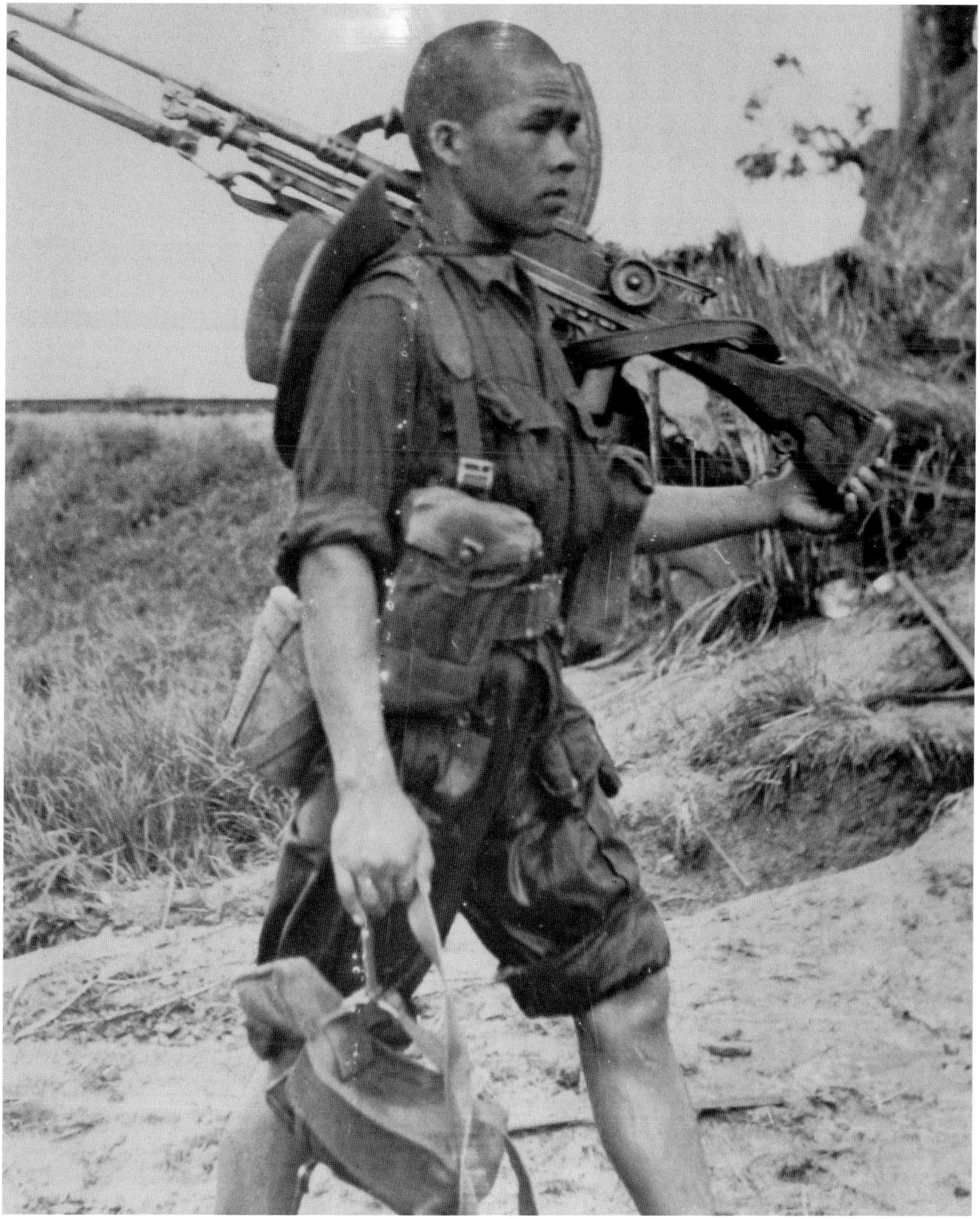

A 4/8th Gurkha infantryman carries his Bren SMG on his shoulder after a recent combat engagement with the Japanese at Laya Station in the vicinity of the Sittang River in early July 1945. (*NARA*)

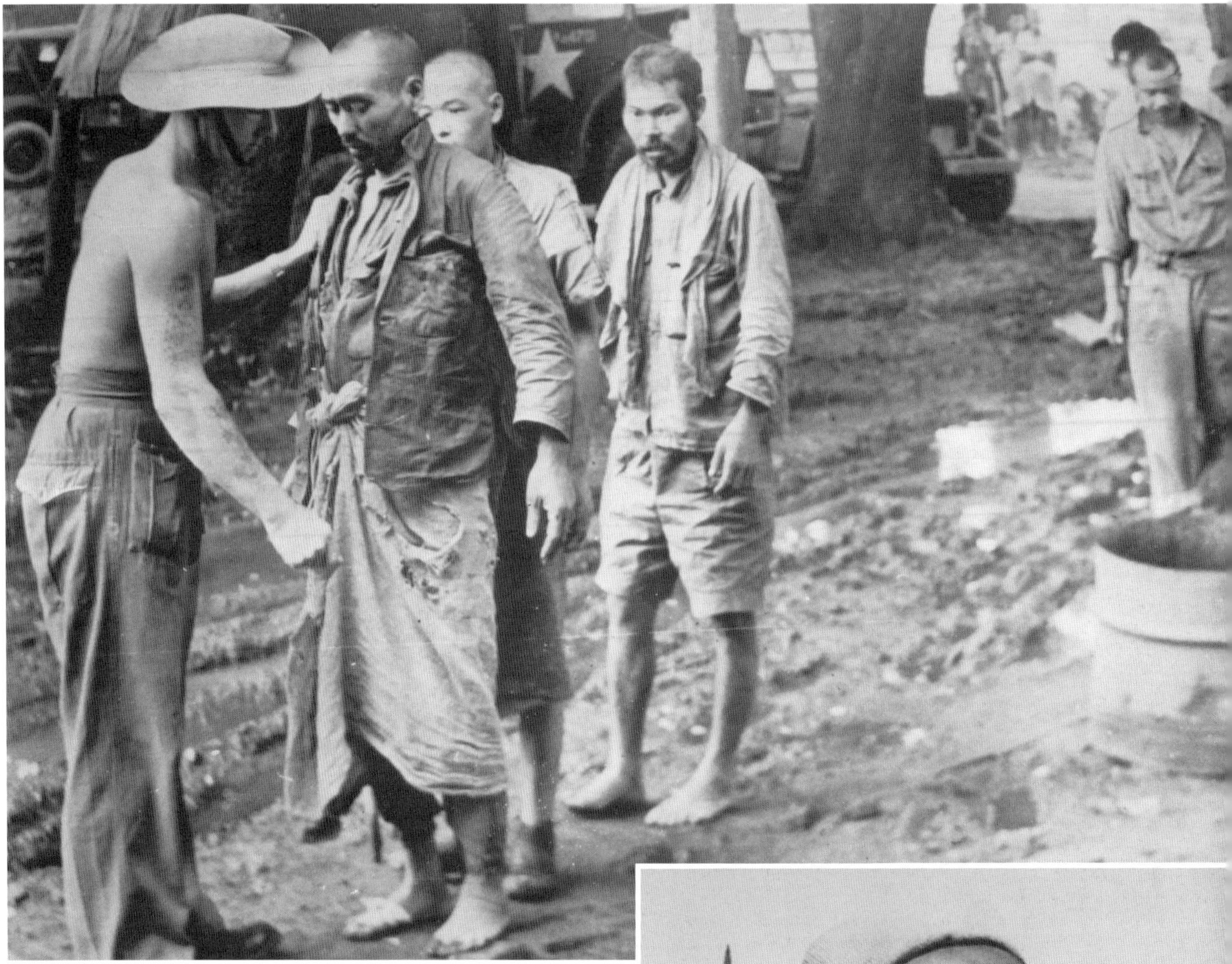

A Fourteenth Army British soldier searches Japanese survivors of the Battle of the Sittang Bend in late July to early August 1945 for weapons hidden in their dishevelled uniforms. The IJA Twenty-Eighth Army tried moving eastward across the Pegu Yomas and then to the Sittang River's eastern bank, but Messervy's IV Indian Corps with intelligence beforehand awaited them. *(NARA)*

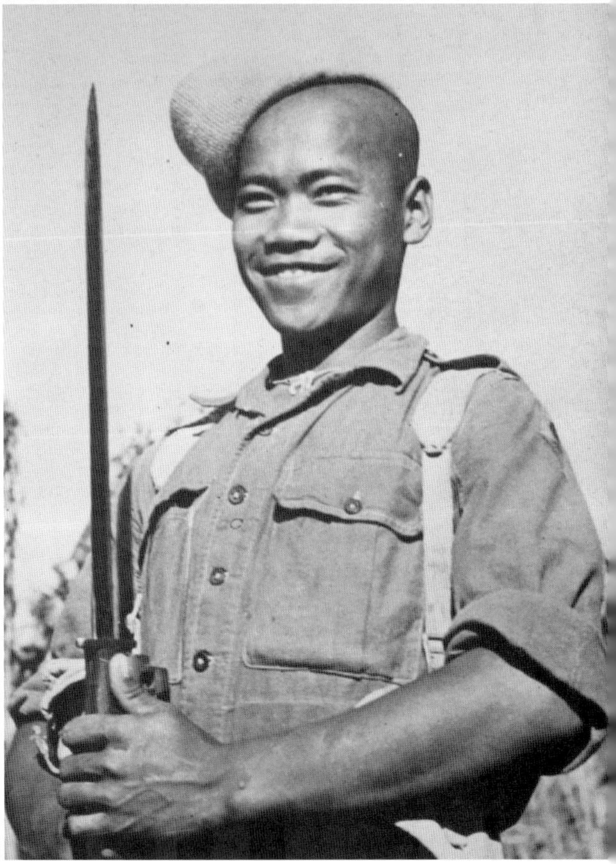

Manprasad Pun, a Gurkha rifleman from Nepal, is shown here standing with his sword bayonet attached to his SMLE rifle. Pun was with the 25th Indian Division during the Third Arakan Campaign of Slim's general counteroffensive of 1944–45. *(NARA)*

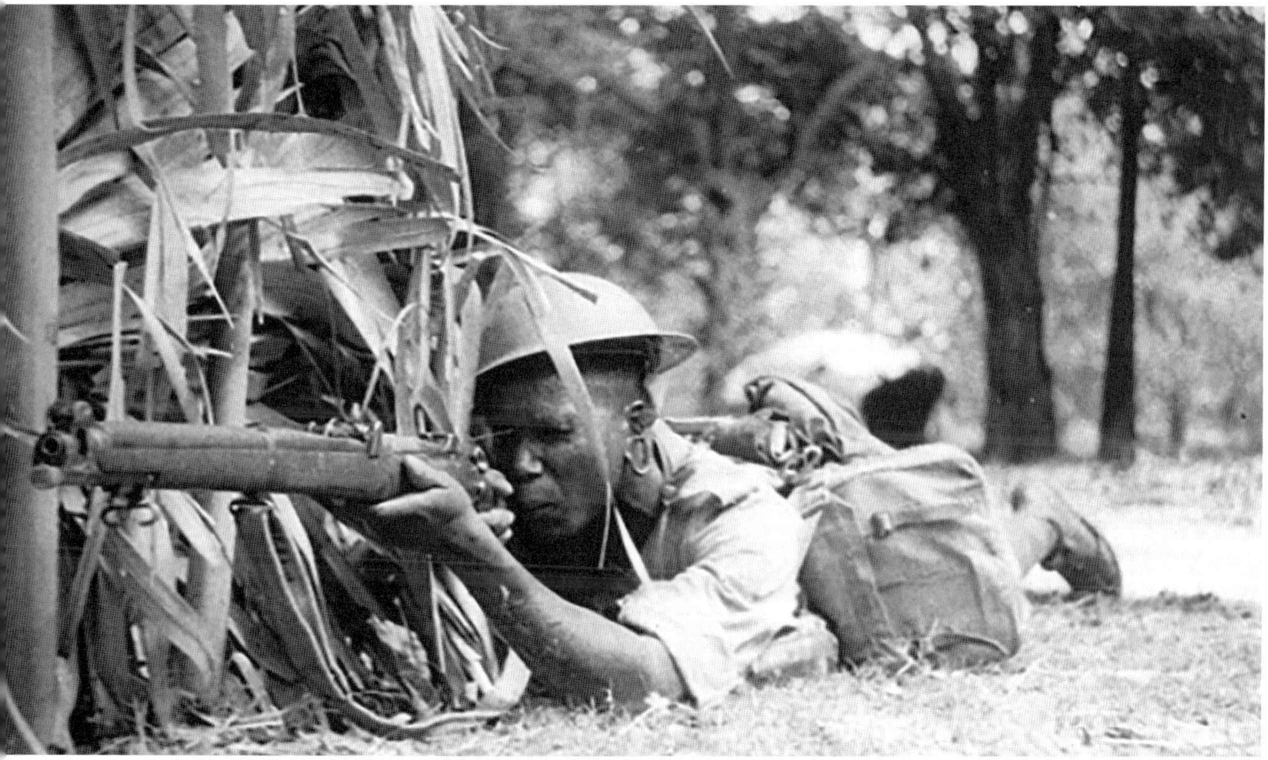

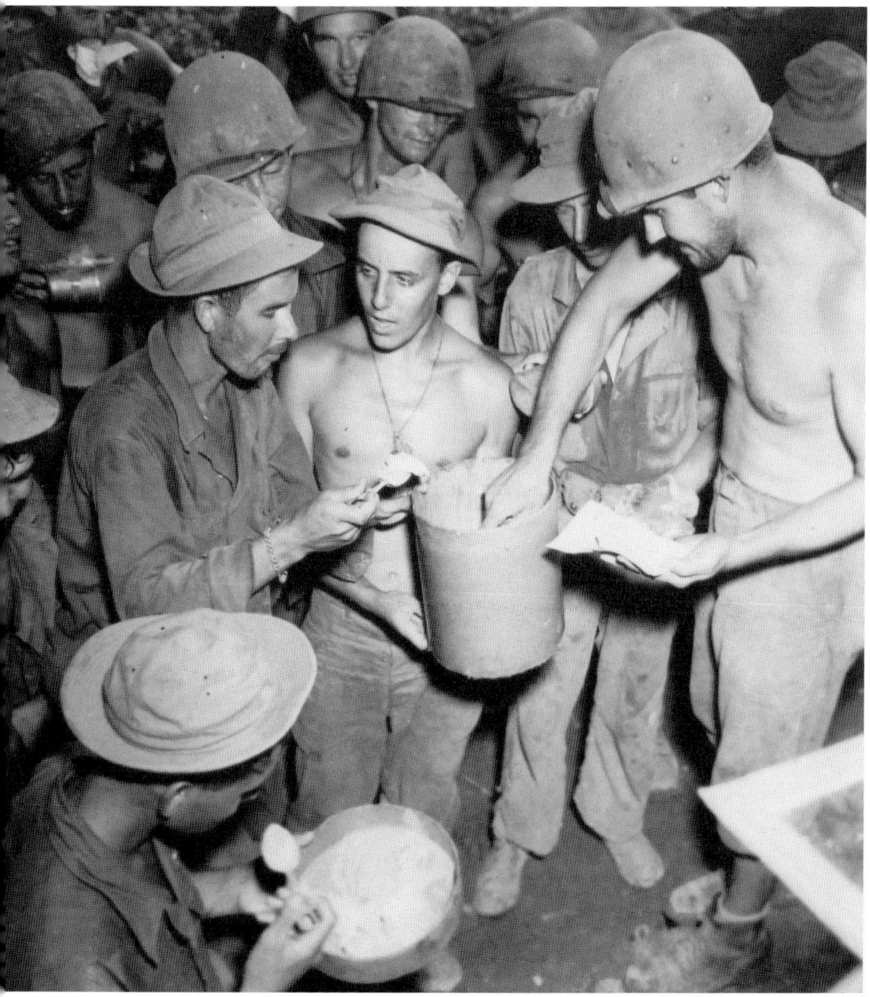

A King's African rifleman covers a road during the First Arakan Campaign during the attempt to seize Akyab Island and its airfields there from December 1942 to May 1943. However, it ended in a disastrous Indian army retreat after several battalions failed to overwhelm the Japanese defenders. *(Author's collection)*

American members of the 209th Combat Engineers, reassigned from their Ledo Road construction work to Stilwell's force at Myitkyina airfield after its capture, line up for ice cream. The non-front-line troops were needed to augment 'Galahad' and Chinese units laying siege to the town of Myitkyina during the summer of 1944. *(NARA)*

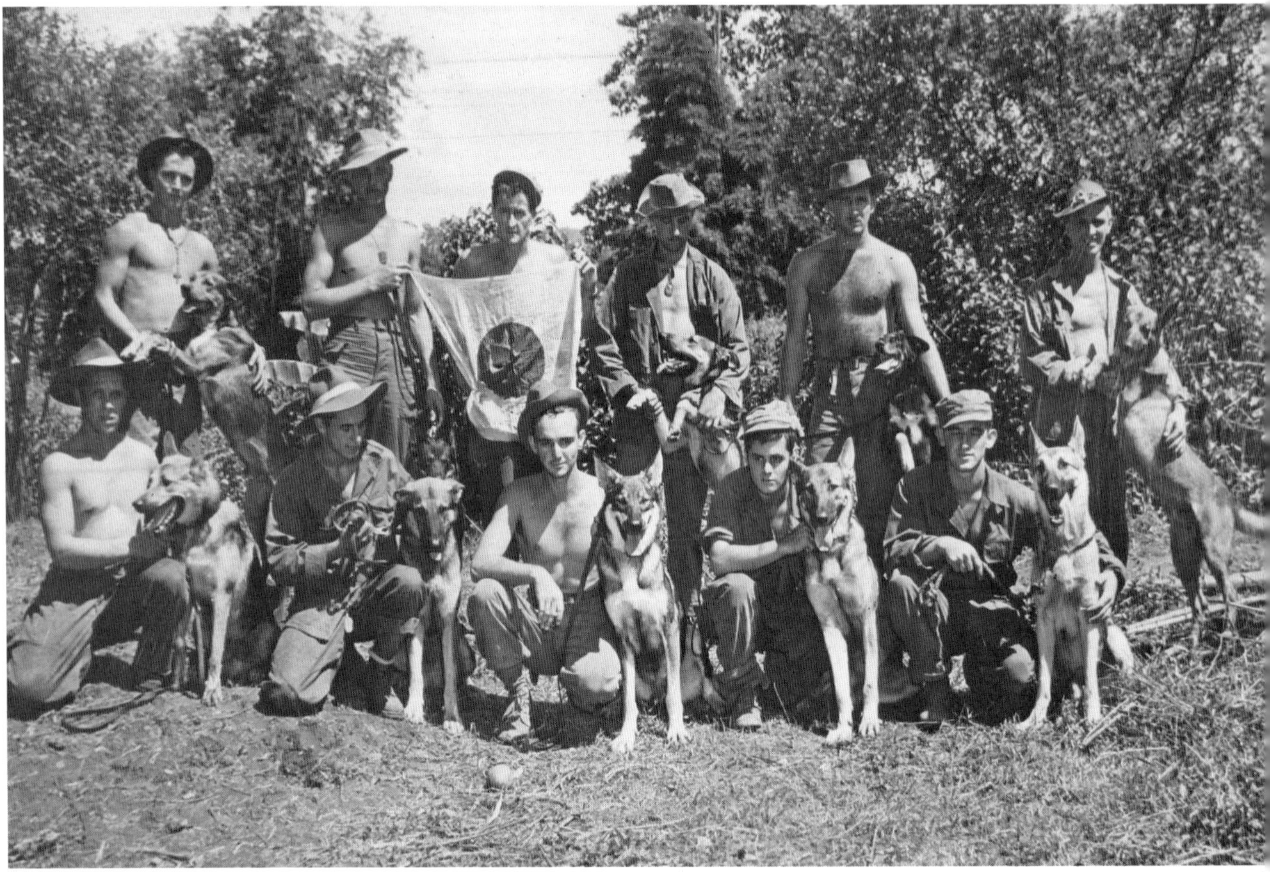

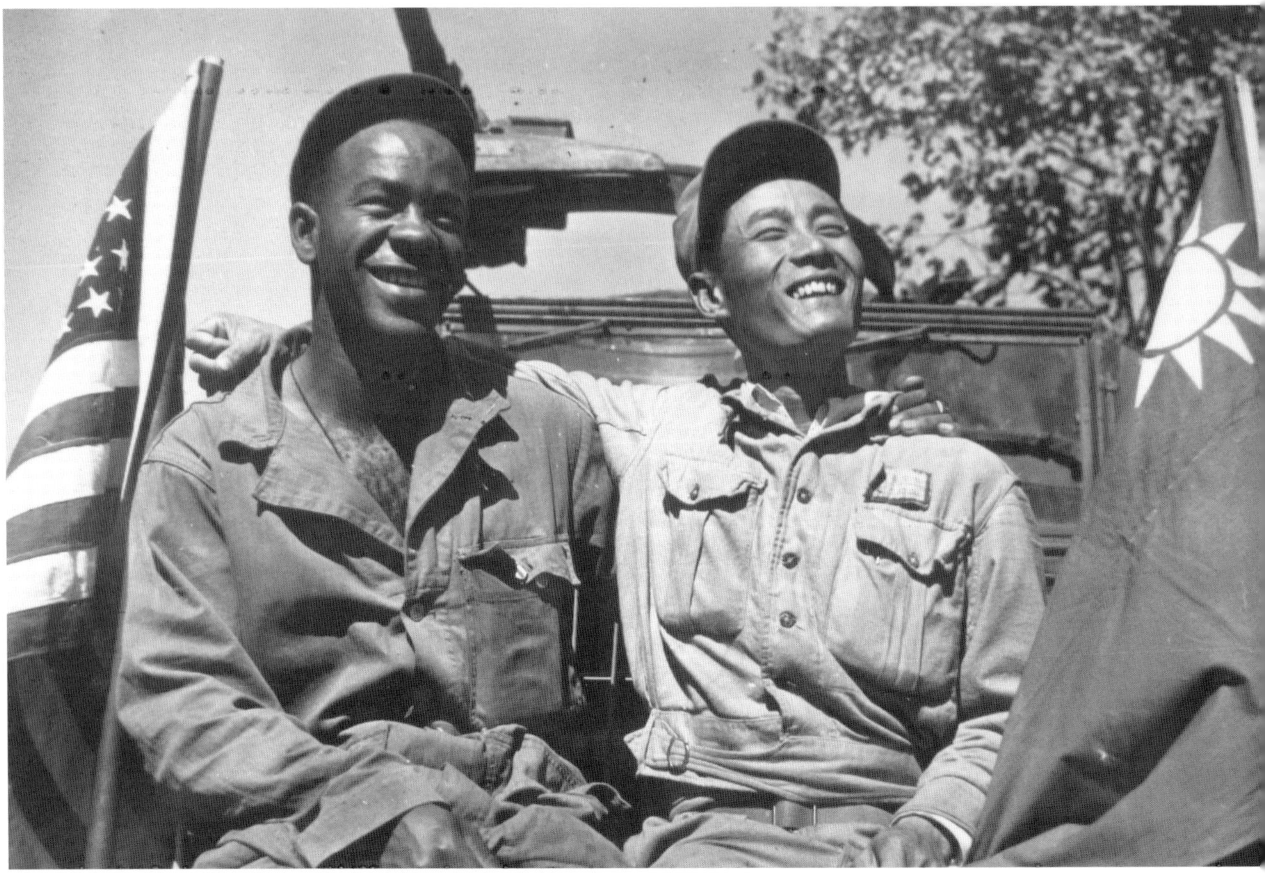

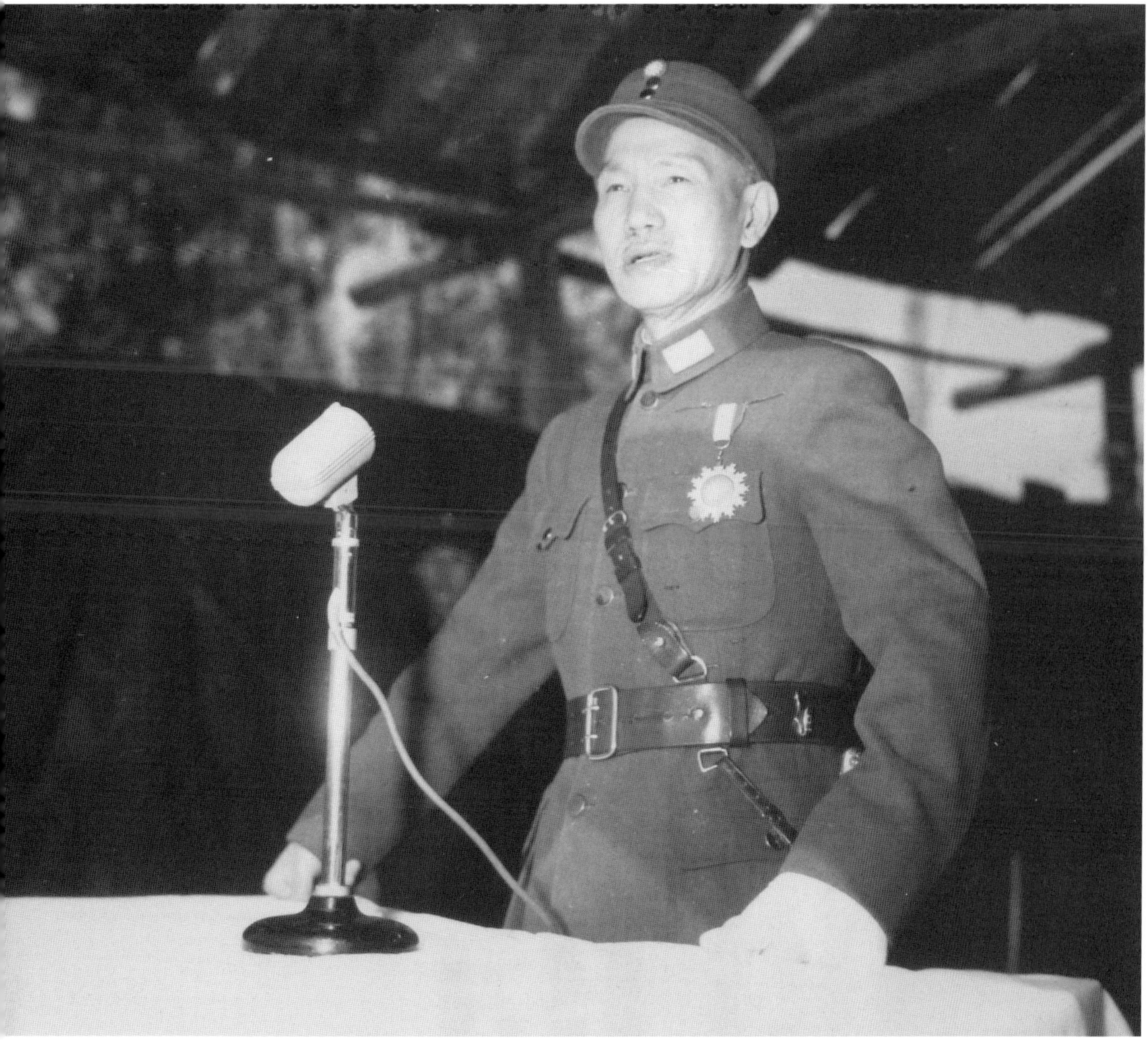

(**Opposite, above**) Allied servicemen with their 'war dogs' pose with some battle trophies in Burma. The dogs were excellent at smelling concealed Japanese spider holes and dugouts, as well as serving as sentry animals against enemy infiltration. *(NARA)*

(**Opposite, below**) An African-American combat engineer and a Chinese solder from Yunnan Province pose on an American M5 light tank. The Ledo Road extended south from Myitkyina and eventually wound its way into this Chinese province with the initial American truck convoy arriving at Wanting in January 1945. *(NARA)*

(**Above**) *Generalissimo* Chiang Kai-shek addresses his troops and students of the Nationalist Party. Chiang had long been involved in overthrowing several Chinese warlords in the 1930s to consolidate his power for the upcoming war with Japan. With America's involvement, Chiang feuded with Stilwell, the CBI commander, about troop dispositions and the flow of Lend-Lease funds to China which peaked in October 1944, necessitating Roosevelt to recall Stilwell. *(NARA)*

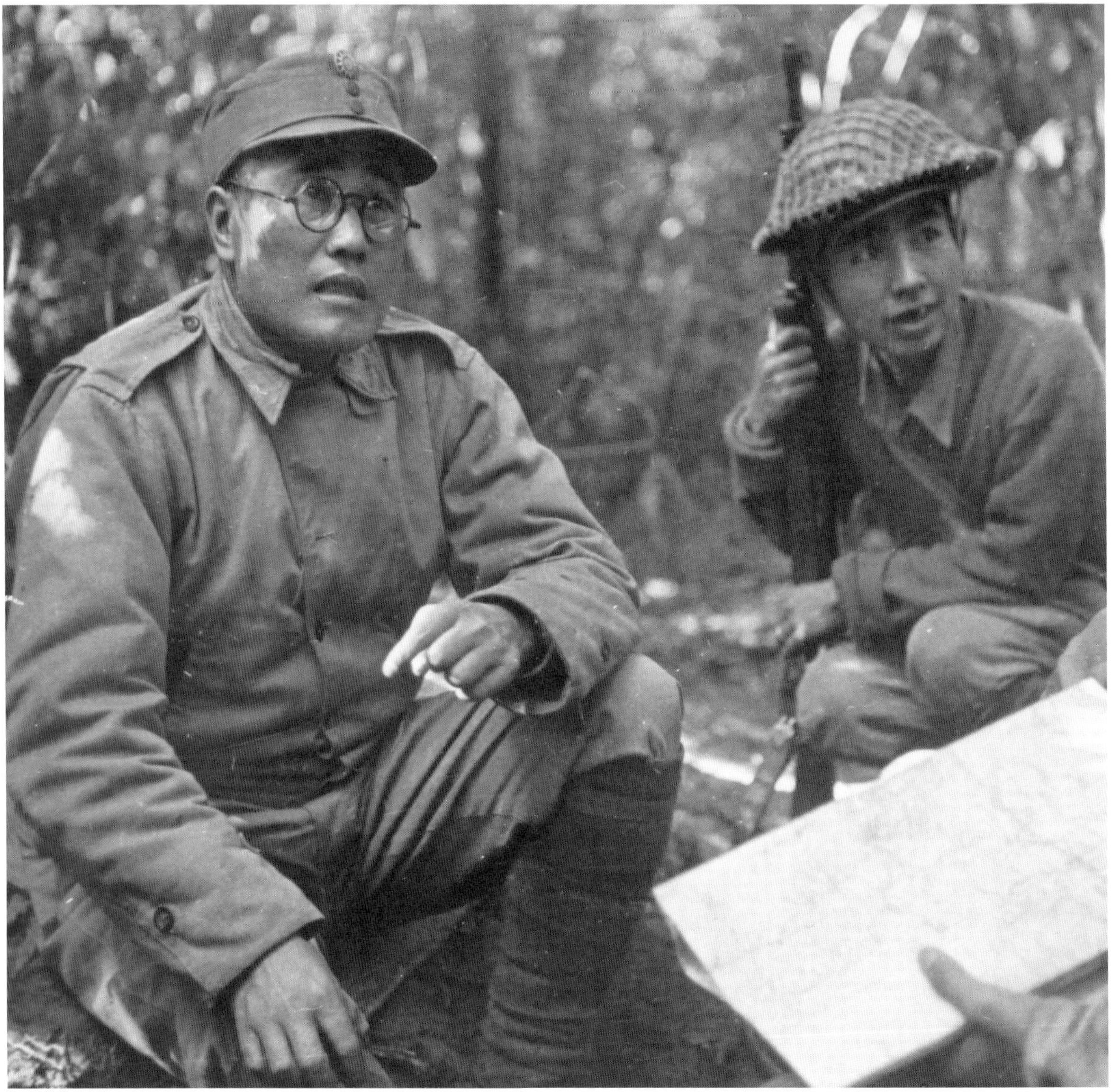

(**Above**) Major General Liao Yao-hsiang, the Ramgarh-trained 22nd Chinese Division commander who was also a graduate of France's St. Cyr military academy, poses with one of his infantrymen in British kit and uniform, customary for a Ramgarh trainee schooled by Stilwell and his subordinate American infantry and artillery instructors. *(NARA)*

(**Opposite, above**) Ramgarh-trained Chinese infantrymen in their British uniforms and kit meet with a Nationalist Army soldier in Yunnan Province. After the successful capture of Myitkyina airfield and town, many of these American-trained troops were airlifted into Yunnan Province to combat the Japanese in another of their offensives against Chiang's forces. *(NARA)*

(**Opposite, below**) A British NCO leads a Madrassi 3.7in-calibre AA gun crew as a shell is breech-loaded for firing. Major General Frank Messervy of the 7th Indian Division employed these AA guns in an additional role as direct fire ordnance against Japanese bunkers and concentration areas in the vicinity of the 'Admin Box' during the Second Arakan Campaign of 1944. *(NARA)*

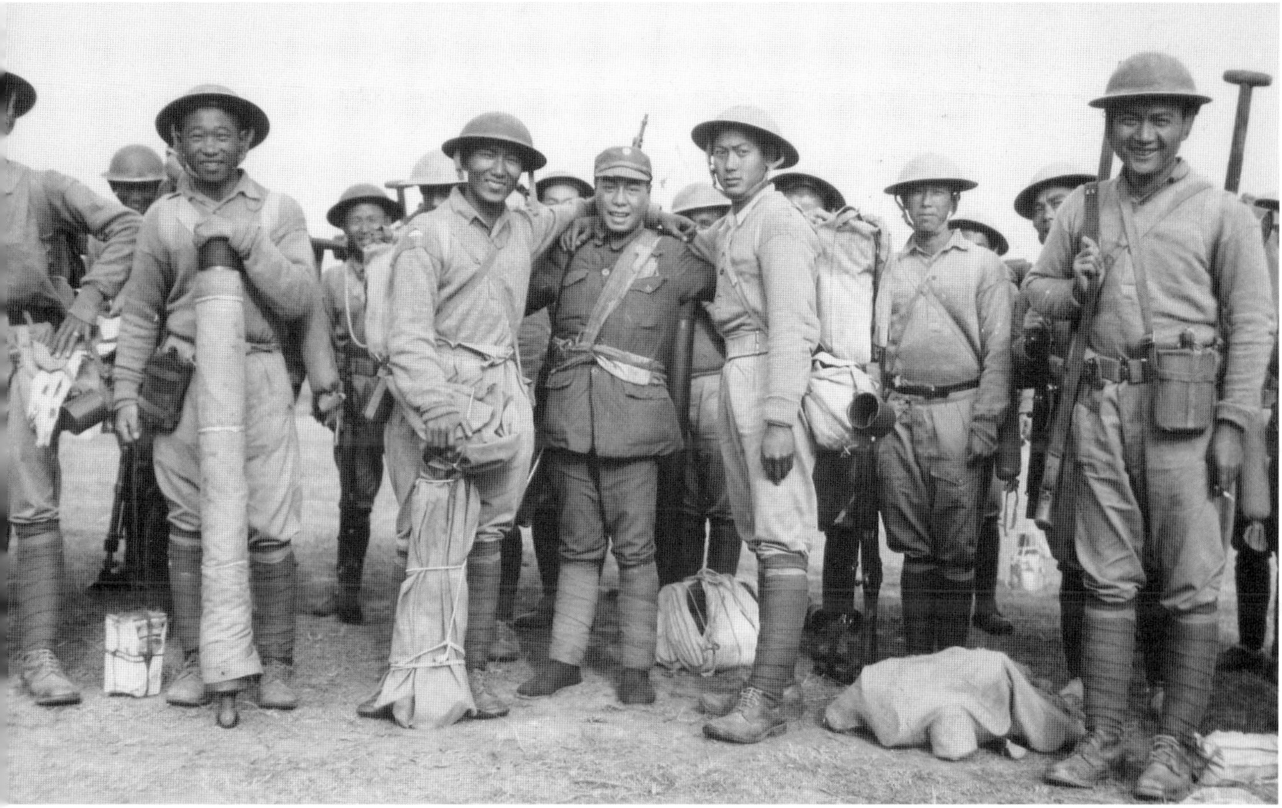

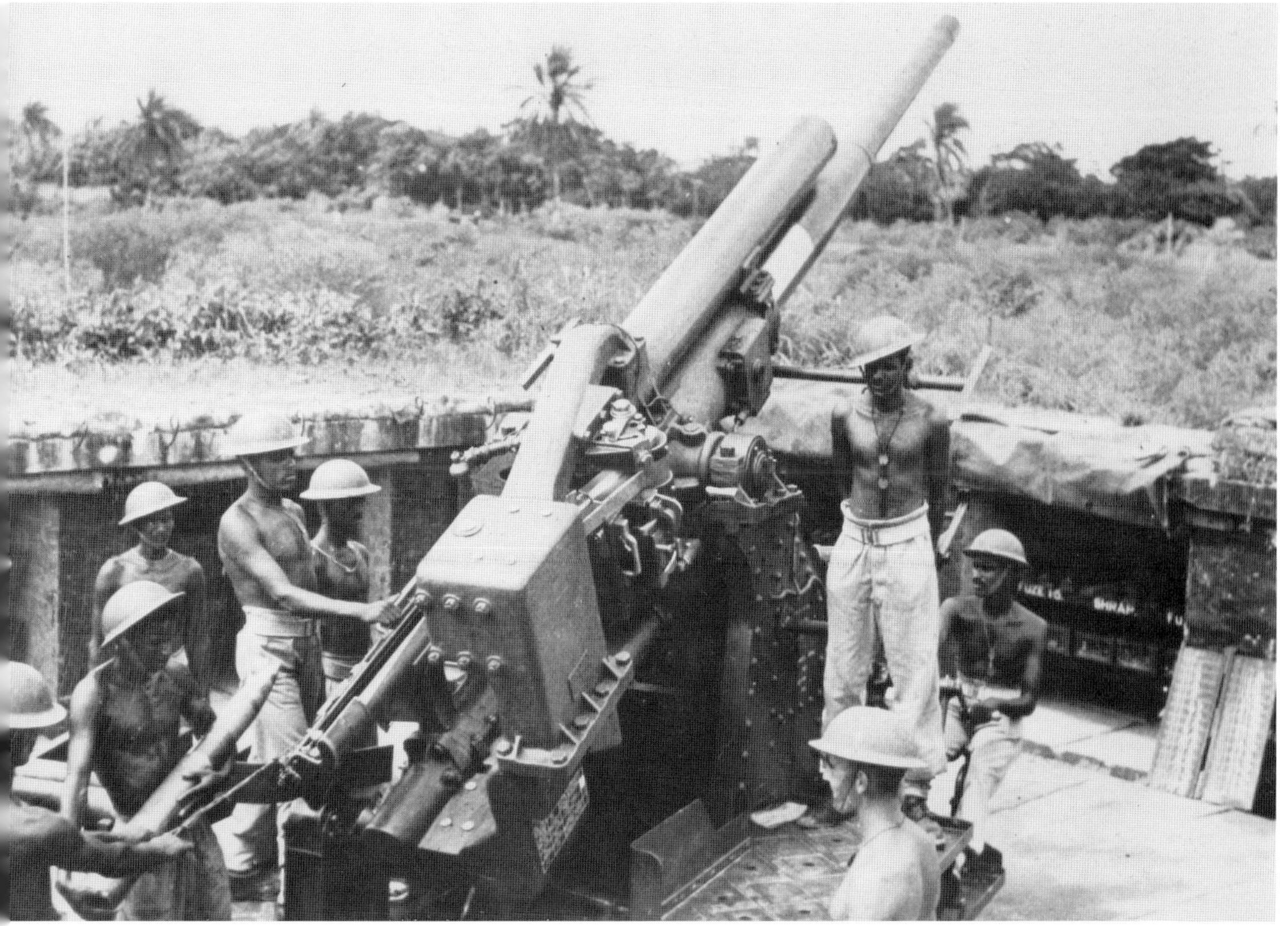

Chapter Four

British and Indian Defence of Imphal and Kohima, 1944

Operation U-GO and the Battle for Imphal

Manipur, the Indian state with its capital at Imphal, borders on Assam and lies between the Naga Hills to the north and the Chin Hills to the south. The Imphal plain, surrounded by jungle-covered mountains, had three entrances. One, a motor road, began north of Dimapur and passed through Kohima. A second, a track suitable for pack animals, ran through mountain passes before reaching Bishenpur to Imphal's south. A third route to the Imphal plain was a narrow path through the mountains from Tamu on the Indo-Burmese frontier border and on the edge of the disease-plagued Kabaw Valley beyond which flowed the wide Chindwin River, a tributary of the Irrawaddy River to the east. By the autumn of 1943, roads were improved leading to the Imphal Plain to accommodate troops, trucks and the American-made M3 Lee medium tanks.

Before the start of Operation U-GO, Scoones' IV Corps (17th, 20th and 23rd Indian divisions) covered a 200-mile front from Homalin on the Chindwin River south-west to Tiddim in the Chin Hills, where Cowan's 17th Indian Division was situated. Gracey's 20th Indian Division at Tamu was midway between Homalin and Tiddim, while Roberts' 23rd Indian Division was situated in the Imphal area.

The Japanese were concerned about Imphal as a base for an Allied offensive given the road-building out from the plain and the improvement of airfields. In September 1943, Mutaguchi was instructed to plan for Imphal's capture with his Fifteenth Army's 15th, 31st and 33rd divisions, plus the I Indian National Army Division made up of Indian army officers and troops taken prisoner in Malaya and other theatres. In January 1944, Kawabe's Burma Area Army HQ issued orders to Mutaguchi to start Operation U-GO at the beginning of March. A Japanese Arakan offensive, Operation HA-GO against the XV Indian Corps was to precede Mutaguchi's Imphal attack by one month in order to draw Slim's attention and reserves away from U-GO's thrust.

The Imphal plain's loss, with its airfields and supply dumps, would prevent an Allied reconquest of Burma and Mutaguchi would capture the matériel there. Despite Scoones' IV Corps armour, artillery and air superiority, the Japanese could

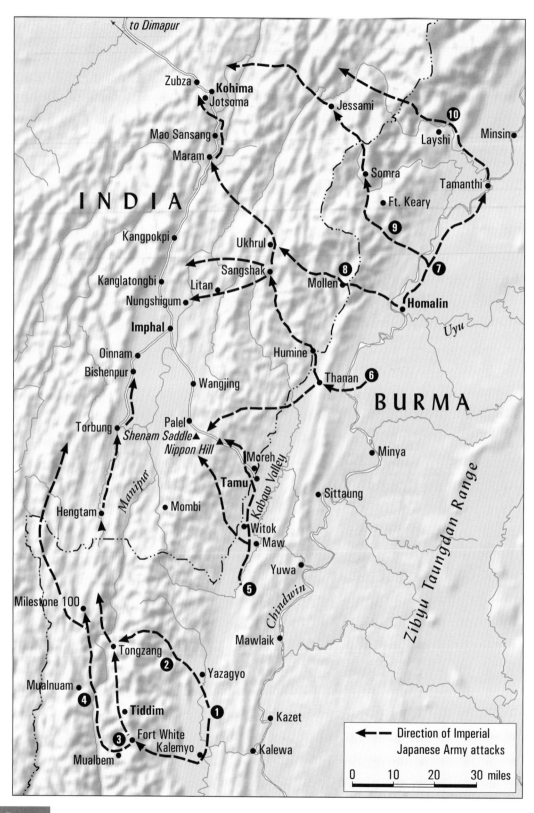

to Dimapur

INDIA

Zubza • • **Kohima**
• Jotsoma
Mao Sansang •
Maram •

Kangpokpi •

Kanglatongbi •
Litan •
Nungshigum •

Imphal •

Oinnam •
Bishenpur •

Torbung •
Shenam Saddle ▲
Nippon Hill

Hengtam •

Milestone 100 •

Mualnuam •
Tongzang •
②
Yazagyo •

④

Tiddim
Fort White
③ Kalemyo
Mualbem •

Ukhrul •
Sangshak •

Mollen •
⑧
Homine •
Homalin

Wangjing •

Palel •

IMoreh •
Tamu
Witok •
Maw •
Yuwa •
⑤

Manipur

Chindwin

Mawlaik •

Jessami •
⑩
Layshi • Minsin •

Somra •
Tamanthi •
• Ft. Keary
⑨
⑦

Uyu

Thanan • **⑥**

BURMA

• Minya

• Sittaung

Kabaw Valley

• Mombi

• Kazet
• Kalewa

Zibyu Taungdan Range

←--- Direction of Imperial
Japanese Army attacks

0   10   20   30 miles

concentrate superior forces at vital locales. Scoones could not safeguard the 130-mile-long Dimapur-Imphal Road without withdrawing his outlying divisions from Tamu in the Kabaw Valley and Tiddim within Burmese territory well to the south of Imphal. A series of self-sustaining defensive points ('boxes') with sufficient food, water and ammunition for ten days were formed on the Imphal plain.

The IJA 33rd Division was to advance towards Imphal from the south; the 15th IJA Division, together with units of the Indian National Army (led by Subhas Chandra Bose) was to attack Imphal from the east; and the 31st Division was to advance to Kohima first and then north-west on to Dimapur, the huge supply base which provided for Slim's Fourteenth Army. Once Kohima and Dimapur were captured,

---

Map 3. Operation U-GO, the IJA Fifteenth Army's Invasion of India, March 1944.

❶ On 7–8 March 1944, the IJA 33rd Division advances across the Chindwin River near Kalewa towards Tiddim a week earlier than expected. ❷ A northern pincer arm by the IJA 33rd Division's 214th IR advances northward from Kalemyo to Tonzang, enveloping Tiddim. ❸ Other IJA 33rd Division troops move on axis Kalemyo-Fort White-Tiddim-Tonzang. On 13 March, the 17th Indian Division begins withdrawing northward from Tiddim towards Imphal. By 14 March, the IJA 214th and 215th IRs cut the Tiddim Road near Milestone 100. On 15 March, the 23rd Indian Division's 37th Infantry Brigade rushes south from Imphal to attack the first Japanese roadblock near Milestone 100 and rendezvous with the 17th Indian Division's retreating 48th Infantry Brigade on the Tiddim Road on 28 March. On 4 April, the 17th Indian Division arrives in Imphal Valley, entering IV Corps' reserve. ❹ The IJA 33rd Division's 215th IR passes through Mualbem on 9 March, then north-east to Mualnuam on 12 March and then on to Milestone 100. ❺ The IJA 33rd Division's 'Yamamoto' Force crosses the Chindwin River near Mawlaik on 7–8 March into the Kabaw Valley to attack the 20th Indian Division near Maw and then Witok on 11 March. ❻ The IJA 15th Division crosses the Chindwin River towards Thanan on 15–16 March as predicted by British Intelligence. An IJA 15th Division detachment moves south-west to converge with the 'Yamamoto' Force exiting the Kabaw Valley to confront the retreating 20th Indian Division at Shenam Saddle and Nippon Hill on the Tamu-Palel Road. Both locales are initially captured by the Japanese on 26 March. The 20th Indian Division completes withdrawal from Moreh on 4 April. Another IJA 15th Division detachment attacks Sangshak, south of Ukhrul, on 22 March and moves west to Kanglatongbi, to Imphal's north, reaching it on 29 March to cut the Imphal-Kohima Road and begin Imphal's siege. Another IJA 15th Division detachment advances south-west from Sangshak, arriving at Nungshigum on 6 April. Between 18 and 27 March, two 5th Indian Division brigades, the 9th and 123rd, are air-lifted from the Arakan to Imphal and evict the Japanese from Nungshigum on 13 April. ❼ On the night of 15/16 March, the IJA 31st Division crosses the Chindwin River near Homalin and advances along several north-west axes. ❽ The IJA 31st Division's 138th IR moves on an axis of Homalin-Mol-Len to attack the 23rd Indian Division's 49th Infantry Brigade at Ukhrul on 21 March prior to advancing north-west to Maram and then northward via Mao Songsang to Jotsoma to begin encircling Kohima from the south to Zubza on the Dimapur Road on 4–5 April. ❾ The IJA 31st Division's 58th IR crosses the Chindwin River to Homalin's north to advance north-westward on a Fort Keary-Somra-Jessami axis, arriving at Jessami on 1 April and then encircling Kohima from the north, reaching Zubza on 5 April to converge with the 138th IR on the Dimapur Road. ❿ The IJA 31st Division's 124th IR, after crossing the Chindwin River near Tamanthi, moves to the north of Lay Shi to remain north of Jessami.

Mutaguchi's forces, now resupplied, would advance into Bengal to mount an insurrection against British rule.

Mutaguchi's troops depended largely on bullocks to move stores and munitions across terrible terrain, making the supply line for the IJA Fifteenth Army into Assam tenuous. Operation U-GO did not have an air component for resupply, reinforcement, evacuation of wounded or 'aerial artillery' support, which would become catastrophic for the IJA. Also the IJA Fifteenth Army well-armoured tanks or effective anti-tank guns had had their supplies and ammunition rationed.

Part of the IJA 33rd Division (under Lieutenant General Yamamoto) began its offensive on the night of 7/8 March 1944 advancing north up the Kabaw Valley towards the Indian 20th Division based in Tamu. Also at that time two remaining regiments of the IJA 33rd Division (the 214th and 215th IRs) began a pincer movement around the Indian 17th Division at Tiddim. By 13 March, the 17th Indian Division's LOC were in jeopardy and Scoones gave Cowan permission to withdraw his division north to the Imphal plain and also ordered Gracey's 20th Indian Division to evacuate on the Tamu Road north-west to Shenam Saddle to Palel's south. However, it took more than a day for the 17th Indian Division with its 16,000 troops, 2,500 vehicles and 3,500 mules to implement Scoones' order to evacuate Tiddim towards Imphal. Roberts also had to deploy two of his 23rd Indian Division brigades south to assist the 17th Indian Division as IJA 33rd Division troops were attempting to cut the Tiddim Road at several places, including a large Allied supply depot at Milestone 109, which was eventually lost to the enemy. By 17 March, the 17th Indian Division crossed the Manipur River bridge after receiving aerial resupply along the way.

On 15–16 March, the IJA 31st and 15th divisions began their offensives across the Chindwin River at Homalin and opposite Thanan in the Kabaw Valley respectively. The 15th Division faced small-sized Allied detachments which withdrew. The IJA 31st Division's 138th IR that crossed the Chindwin River at Homalin moved north-west, first towards Ukhrul then further north-west against Kohima. The other two 31st Division IRs, the 58th and 124th, crossed the Chindwin River further north to assault Kohima in a pincer movement.

Slim rapidly airlifted the 5th Indian Division to reinforce Imphal from the Arakan front beginning on 19 March through to 29 March. Elements of the reinforcing 5th Indian Division arrived with some IJA units only 30 miles away with the airlifted troops sent immediately into combat. On 29 March, the Japanese had cut the Imphal-Kohima Road with the former locale now to be supplied only by air.

Combat at Ukhrul and Sangshak between the Indian 50th Parachute Brigade from Kohima and elements from both the IJA 31st and 15th divisions slowed up Mutaguchi's timetable and inflicted irreplaceable enemy casualties. However, the

50th Parachute Brigade's remnants had to retreat west through the jungle to Imphal, leaving their wounded behind.

On 28 March the retreating 17th Indian Division linked up with the 23rd Indian Division's 37th Brigade at Milestone 100 on the Imphal-Tiddim Road. On 4 April, the 17th Indian Division marched into the Imphal plain, bringing 1,200 casualties for eventual evacuation to the rear echelon. On 4 April, the Indian IV Corps was concentrated for Imphal's all-out defence. The 5th Indian Division covered the Japanese attack from the north and north-east while the 20th Indian Division was situated at Shenam in the vicinity of Palel and covered the enemy's approach from Tamu and the east. The 23rd Indian Division held off the Japanese to the south on the Imphal-Tiddim Road south of Bishenpur. The 17th Indian Division refitted at Imphal as the IV Indian Corps reserve. Nungshigum, a 1,000ft-high hill just to the north-east above the Imphal plain was the closest the Japanese came to conquering Imphal as an IJA 15th Division IR arrived on 6 April. Combat raged there for a week until the Japanese were driven away on 13 April. After that, the 5th and 23rd Indian divisions went onto the offensive against the IJA 15th Division's defensive works to the north-east of Imphal.

The Shenam position comprised a series of terrain features including Scraggy, Gibraltar, Malta, Crete East and West, Nippon Hill and Sita. For ten weeks, Yamamoto's columns, part of the IJA 33rd Division, repeatedly attacked the troops of the 20th Indian and later the 23rd Indian divisions, the latter relieving the former in the middle of May. The Indian divisions held their positions while the IJA assaults became more hellacious.

The other 214th and 215th IRs from the IJA 33rd Division fought on the Tiddim Road near Bishenpur and along the track that headed west to Silchar, against the 17th Indian Division and the 20th Indian Division's 32nd Brigade in May. The siege operations occurred day after day. Of the five VC awards acquired during the Imphal battle, four were won on this part of the front.

As the battle wore on into late June, the 7th Indian Division's 89th Brigade was flown in to replace the 5th Indian Division brigade that was flown into Kohima in March. The whole of the 5th Indian Division was deployed onto the Kohima Road to break the Japanese block at Kanglatongbi, while the 20th Indian Division, relieved from Shenam, moved on towards Ukhrul to the north-east of Imphal.

Slim ordered Stopford's XXXIII Corps to exert pressure on Satō's IJA 31st Division to prevent his troops from reinforcing Yamauchi's IJA 15th Division's attack on Imphal from the north. By 3 June, the Battle of Kohima (see below) ended and Stopford's XXXIII Corps moved south down the Kohima-Imphal Road to Imphal. The IJA Fifteenth Army was rapidly dissolving and Mutaguchi dismissed all three of his divisional commanders. On 22 June, the advancing British 2nd and 5th Indian divisions moved south on the Kohima Road to lift Imphal's siege.

The Battle of Kohima

On 15 March 1944, Lieutenant General Kōtoku Satō's IJA 31st Division comprising the 58th, 124th and 138th IRs crossed the Chindwin River north of Homalin, rapidly heading for Kohima, despite rear-echelon troops moving 5,000 oxen for three months' supply of meat. However, many animals perished due to bad terrain and weather. On 18 March, Assam Regiment soldiers on the Indo-Burmese frontier detected Japanese troop movement. Slim ordered the British 2nd Division's 5th Brigade to Assam by road and rail. Colonel Hugh Richards was appointed the Kohima garrison commander on 20 March as Stopford's XXXIII Corps HQ would not arrive there until 30 March. Separate companies of the Assam Regiment formed defensive boxes at Jessami with combat commencing there on 28 March. Also on that day the 5th Indian Division's 161st Brigade was airlifted from the Arakan into Kohima. The Allied Jessami defenders received word to retreat during the night of 31 March, leaving the path to Kohima open.

Brigadier Warren, GOC of the 5th Indian Division's 161st Brigade ordered a defensive box with mountain artillery to be situated at Jotsoma, 2 miles west of Kohima, known as 'Garrison Hill'. A number of other hillocks (e.g. 'Jail Hill') were also within the 'box'.

The IJA 31st Division's 58th IR arrived at Kohima early on 5 April and attacked 'Jail Hill', which the enemy captured with other hillocks in that 'box'. The next day, the Royal West Kents of the 5th Indian Division's 161st Brigade killed all the Japanese troops that had infiltrated the defensive perimeter. The 1,500-man Kohima garrison was facing 12,000 troops of the IJA 31st Division.

On 11 April, the British 2nd Division's 5th Brigade moved towards Zubza, a few miles to the north-west of Kohima, encountering a strong Japanese position there. An attack was not mounted on that IJA position until 14 April. Intense hand-to-hand combat occurred at both ends of the Garrison Hill defensive perimeter on the night of 13 April. The 5th Indian Division's 161st Brigade's mountain guns at Jotsoma helped defeat the Japanese advance at Garrison Hill. The next day elements of the British 2nd Division's 5th Brigade wiped out a company of Japanese near Zubza.

On 17 April, the Japanese attacked Garrison Hill in strength and Richards' perimeter was weakened with many Allied dead. The next day, Punjabi infantry and RAC tanks began moving down the road to relieve the position. Despite repeated Japanese attacks on Garrison Hill, on 20 April the Royal Berkshire Regiment relieved the hotly-contested perimeter. At this time, Mutaguchi also ordered Satō to send one of his regimental groups south to Imphal. Slim ordered renewed pressure on Satō's troops and the Japanese general disobeyed Mutaguchi's order.

On the night of 22/23 April, Satō launched a massive and final attack on Garrison Hill. The IJA attack was rebuffed by the Royal Berkshire and 2nd Durham Light Infantry (DLI) regiments. Four companies of IJA troops had been killed and wounded, with the DLI losing more than 100 men, of whom 15 were officers. Satō's officers reverted to the defensive to avoid any more futile attacks.

During the last days of April, the 2nd British Division's 4th and 5th brigades pressed on towards Kohima from the east and west with battles at the deputy commissioner's bungalow and the 'Tennis Courts'. On 3 May, the British 2nd Division's 5th Brigade moved into Naga Village, north of Garrison Hill, and held it despite a counterattack. The division's 4th Brigade continued its advance northward towards Garrison Hill and captured another nearby hillock. The 6th Brigade attacked in the centre from the west at other hillocks, including 'Jail Hill' from 4–7 May, but the bunkered enemy repelled them. On 11 May, elements of the 7th Indian Division's 33rd Brigade renewed the attack on 'Jail Hill'. In less than two hours, the hill's summit was reached and enemy bunkers reduced one at a time. The RAC 149th Brigade's M3 Lee tanks' gunfire aided the 33rd Brigade infantrymen attacking the IJA bunkers on the reverse slopes of 'Jail Hill'. Soon other hillocks were taken painstakingly. By 13 May, the entire central sector of Kohima had fallen to the Allies except the deputy commissioner's bungalow and the 'Tennis Courts', which were still strongly defended by Satō's infantry.

At the 'Tennis Courts', a lone M3 Lee tank destroyed the Japanese bunkers with its 75mm gun and eventually all the enemy were killed either inside the bunkers or fleeing from them. Hunter's Hill and Church Hill were still to be assaulted against dug-in Japanese by elements of both the British 2nd and 7th Indian divisions throughout the second and third weeks of May. On 25 May, the 4/1st Gurkhas outflanked the Japanese on Hunter's Hill, securing it without heavy casualties. On 1 June other M3 Lee tanks advanced to meet the infantry. On 31 May, Satō formed a rearguard of 700 troops under his infantry group commander General Miyazaki and ordered the withdrawal from Kohima. Miyazaki pulled back on 6–7 June and the Battle of Kohima was over after sixty-four days of ferocious combat. Stopford's XXXIII Corps prepared its advance towards Imphal.

By 18 July 1944, Kawabe and Mutaguchi ordered a general withdrawal to the Chindwin River. On 22 July, troops of the British 2nd and 5th Indian divisions reached the defenders of Imphal south on the Kohima Road.

Of 85,000 Japanese soldiers invading Assam, 53,000 became casualties (30,000 fatalities) along with 17,000 pack animals lost. Mutaguchi was sacked a few months later, detested and scorned by his officers and men. Kawabe was relieved of his command. The IJA in Burma was crippled at Imphal and Kohima before Slim's Fourteenth Army left Assam for Burma. The defence of Imphal and Kohima by British and Indian forces made it the turning-point of the war in Burma.

The IV Corps' 17th and 23rd Indian divisions, after two years of fighting, were sent back to India for rest and refitting. Stopford's XXXIII Corps was reinforced with the 11th East African Division and took over the pursuit of the retreating IJA forces to the Chindwin River via the Kabaw Valley and Tiddim Road.

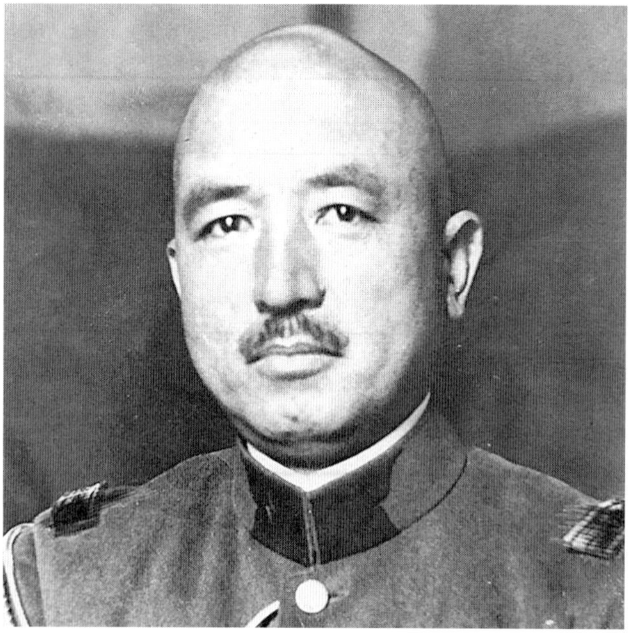

Lieutenant General Renya Mutaguchi, the IJA Fifteenth Army CG is shown here. He planned Operation U-GO with his superior Lieutenant General Kawabe and then launched his three-division attack at the Allied strongholds of Imphal and Kohima in March–July 1944 with a poor logistical plan to support his troops once committed to the attack. *(Author's collection)*

Lieutenant General Kōkuku Satō, 31st Division CG who attacked Kohima, is shown here. An intelligent commander, he quarrelled with Mutaguchi over an order to send an IR to Imphal, as well as food and ammunition shortages at Kohima. Replaced as division CG on 5 July, Satō was ordered back to Fifteenth Army HQ. *(Author's collection)*

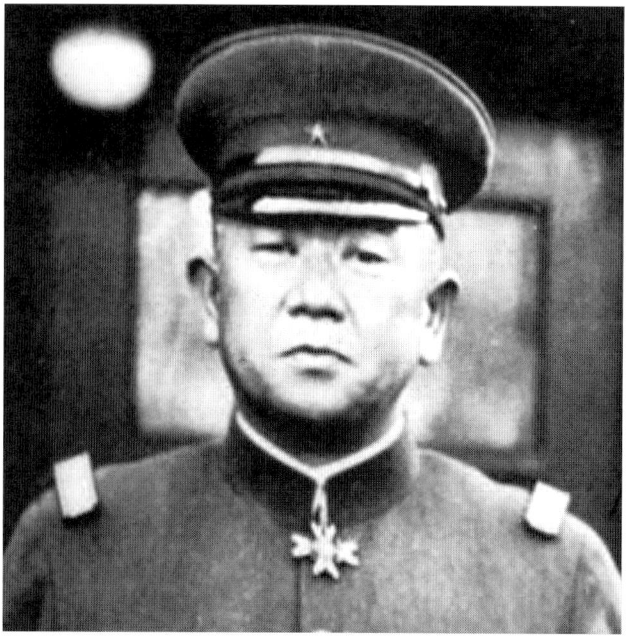

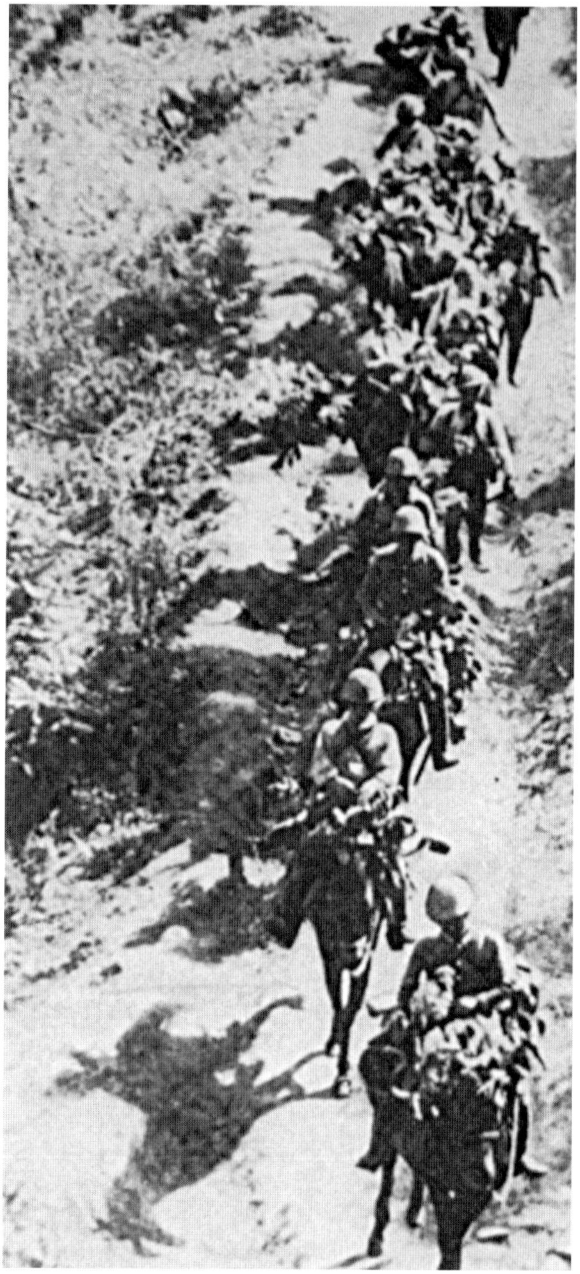

A Japanese mounted column begins its crossing of the Chindwin River at Homalin in March 1944. The mountainous terrain and narrow trails exacted a steep toll on pack animals with their heavy loads and on oxen that were to provide meat for the troops. Some of Satō's 31st Division units crossed at Homalin on 15–16 March and then moved north-west to Ukhrul to engage the 23rd Indian Division's 49th Brigade and the Indian 50th Parachute Brigade prior to moving on to Kohima. *(Author's collection)*

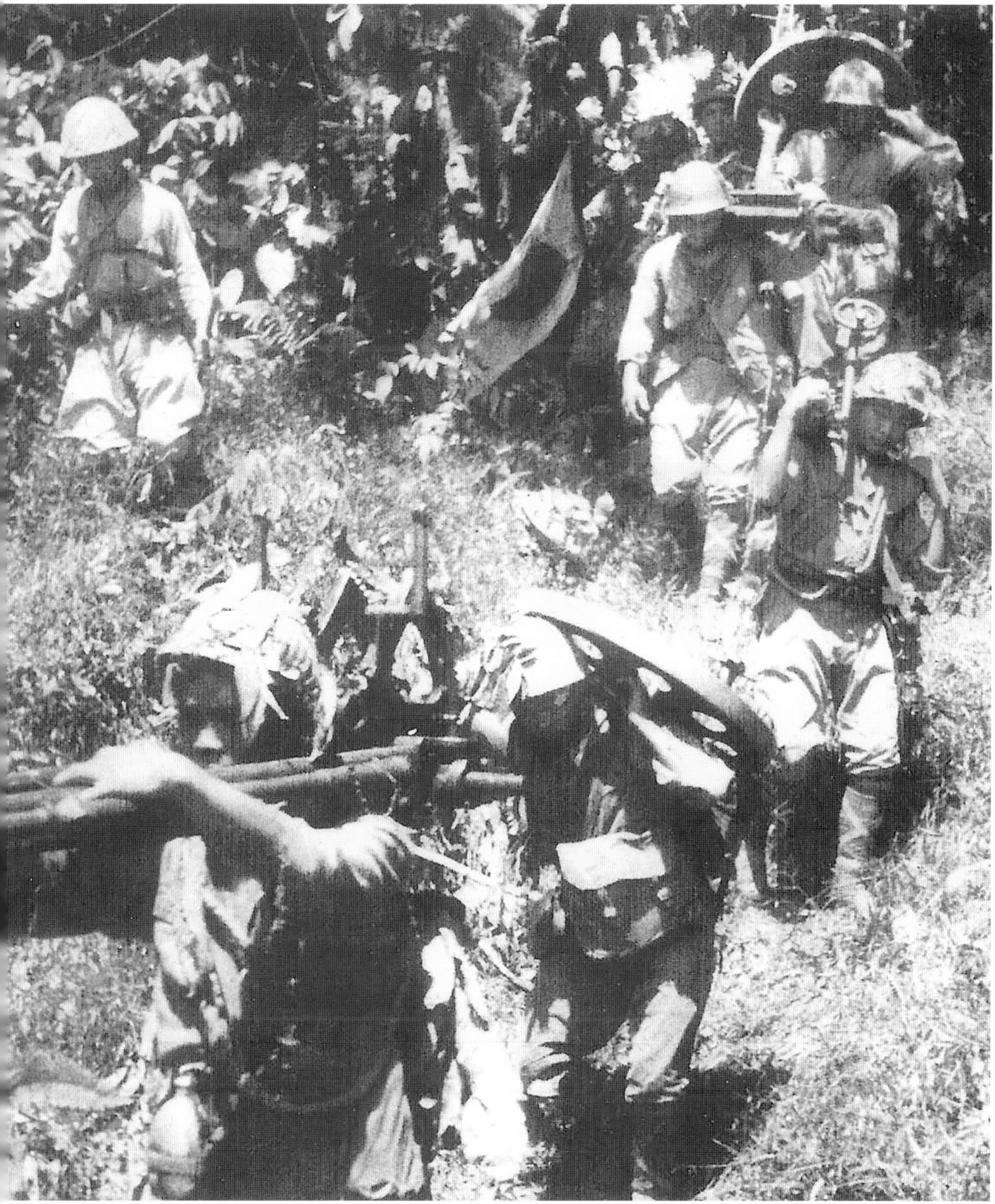

Japanese infantrymen emerge from the jungle with each carrying disassembled field artillery pieces to get behind an Allied position for an attack. Note the infantryman soldier (rear centre) holding the *Hinomaru* or 'flag of the rising sun' which his family gave him to keep his spirits high. (*Author's collection*)

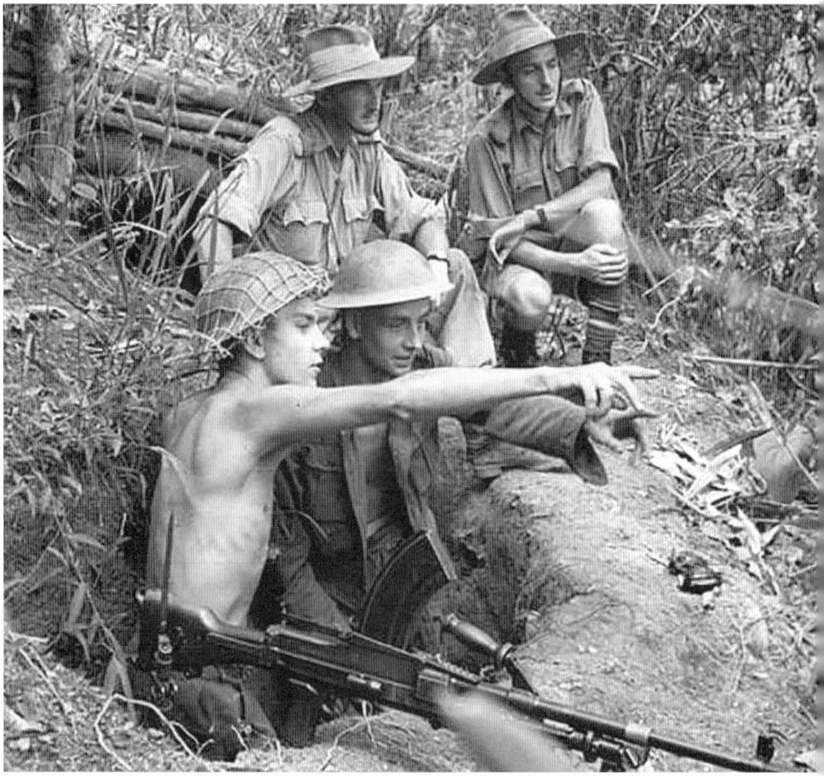

A Bren gun position situated on high ground and manned by RAF personnel guards the approaches to an Imphal plain airfield. Slim and the Delhi high command prepared this area with road-building, airstrips and reinforcements before Operation U-GO was unleashed in March 1944. *(Author's collection)*

Bren gun carriers transport the British 2nd Division's 5th Brigade soldiers from XXXIII Corps as reinforcements from Zubza for the Indian 5th Division's 161st Brigade combating IJA 31st Division troops at Jotsoma in mid-April 1944. *(Author's collection)*

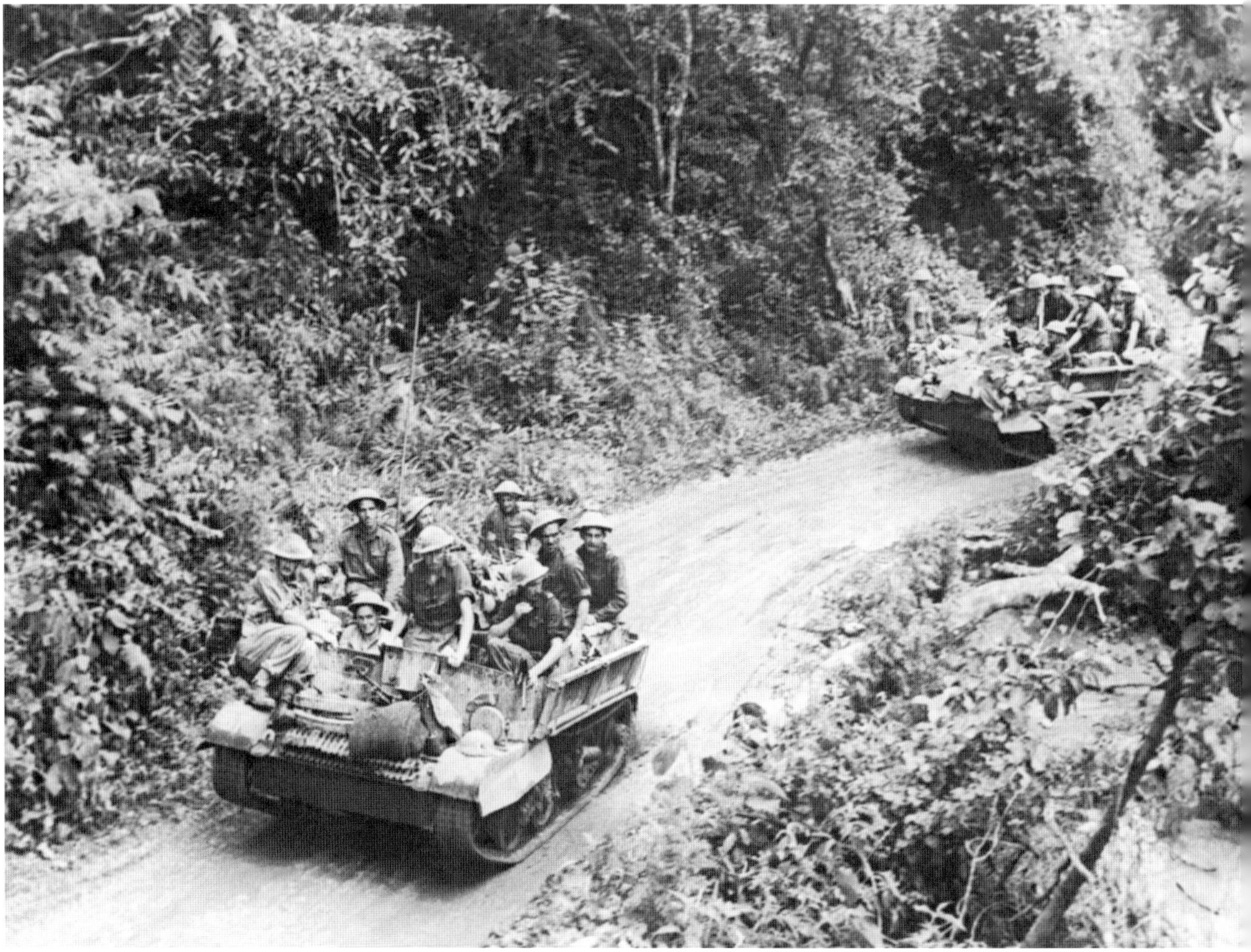

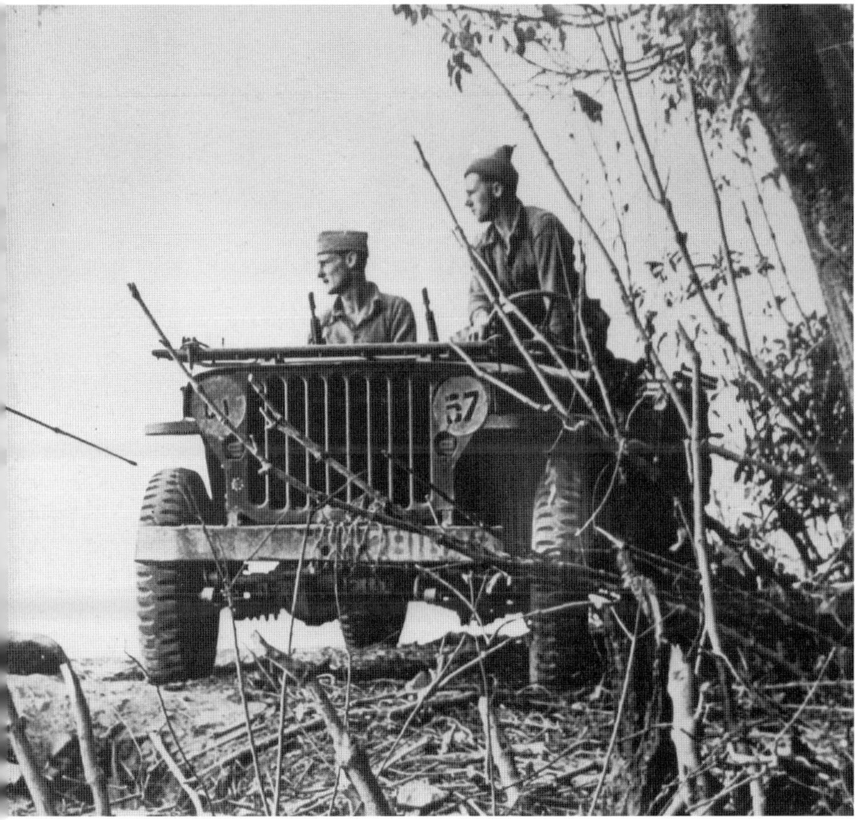

Two infantrymen from the 17th Indian Division's 1st West Yorkshire Regiment reconnoitre a motor track in the Chin Hills along the Tiddim-Imphal Road. The 17th Indian Division retreated with its casualties and vehicles back from Tiddim into the Imphal plain during the 7–8 March IJA 33rd Division attack across the Chindwin River. *(NARA)*

An Allied C-47 transport plane parachutes supplies to Allied troops at Kohima as Slim urged forming defensive 'boxes' rather than retreat. During the first week of May 1944, when aerial resupply was vital to Kohima's defence, Slim's HQ was informed by the RAF that the transports, on loan from the Middle East, were to be withdrawn by 8 May. Mountbatten, with Churchill's support, took personal responsibility for keeping the transports supplying Kohima. *(NARA)*

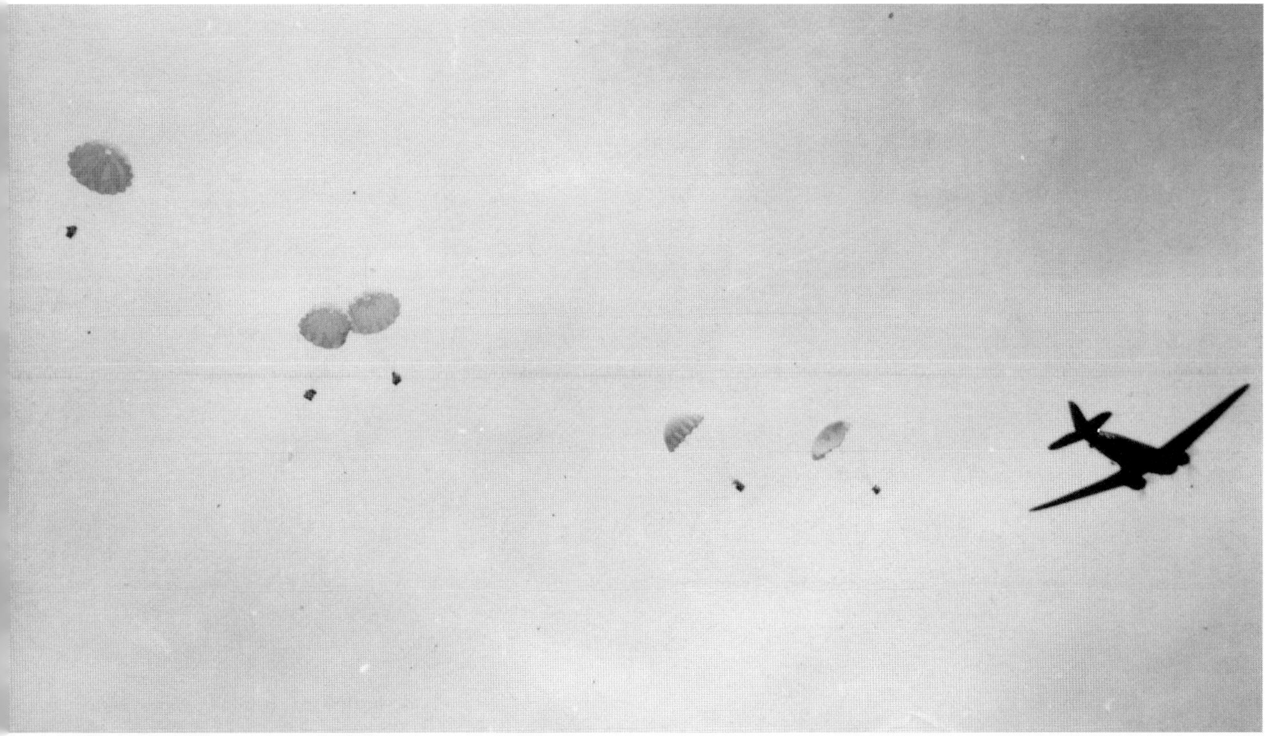

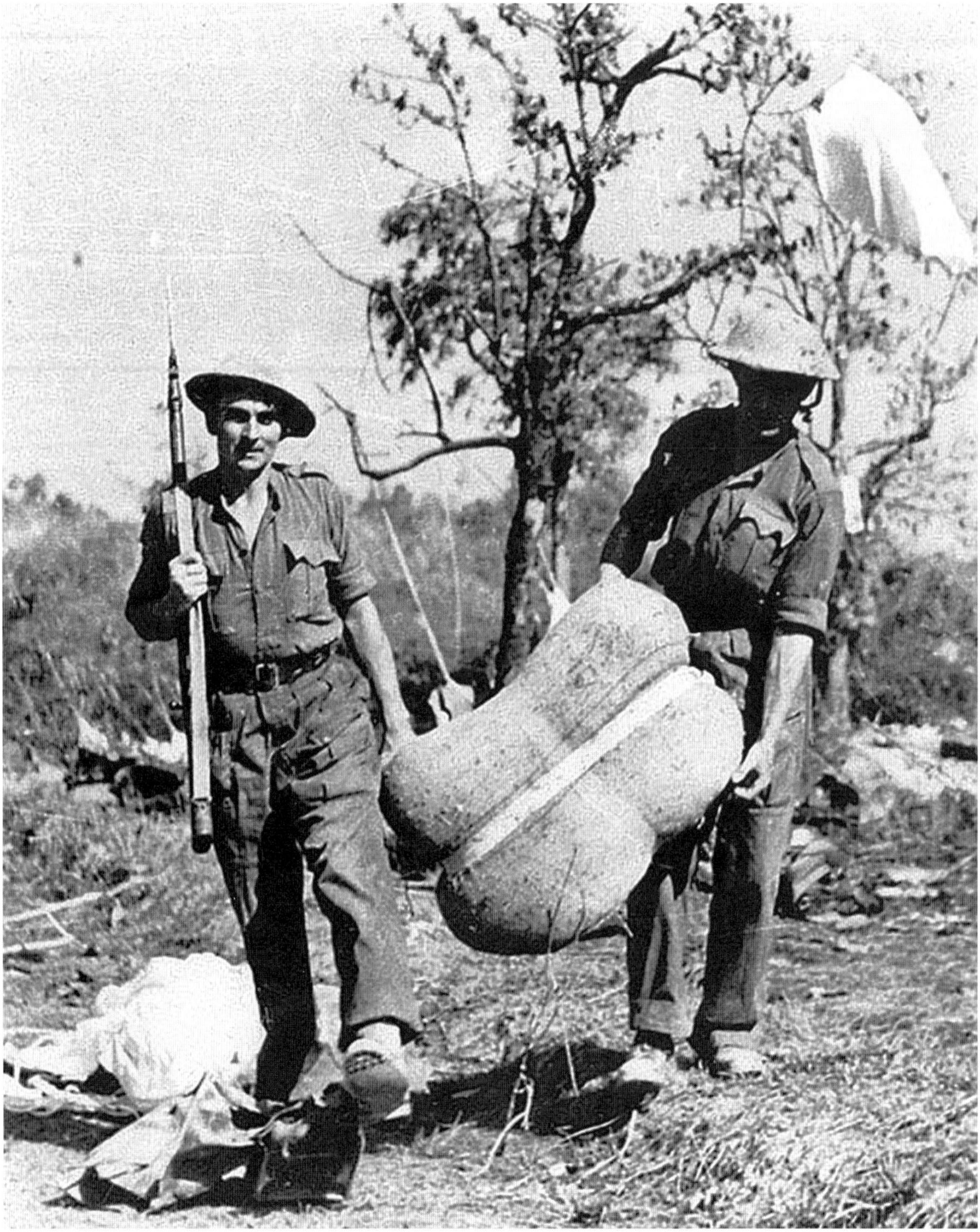

Two 7th Indian Division infantrymen from Yorkshire carry a 180lb bale of parachuted supplies into their 'Administrative Box' in February 1944 during the Second Arakan Campaign. The colour of the parachute indicated the type of supplies air-dropped in the load. *(Author's collection)*

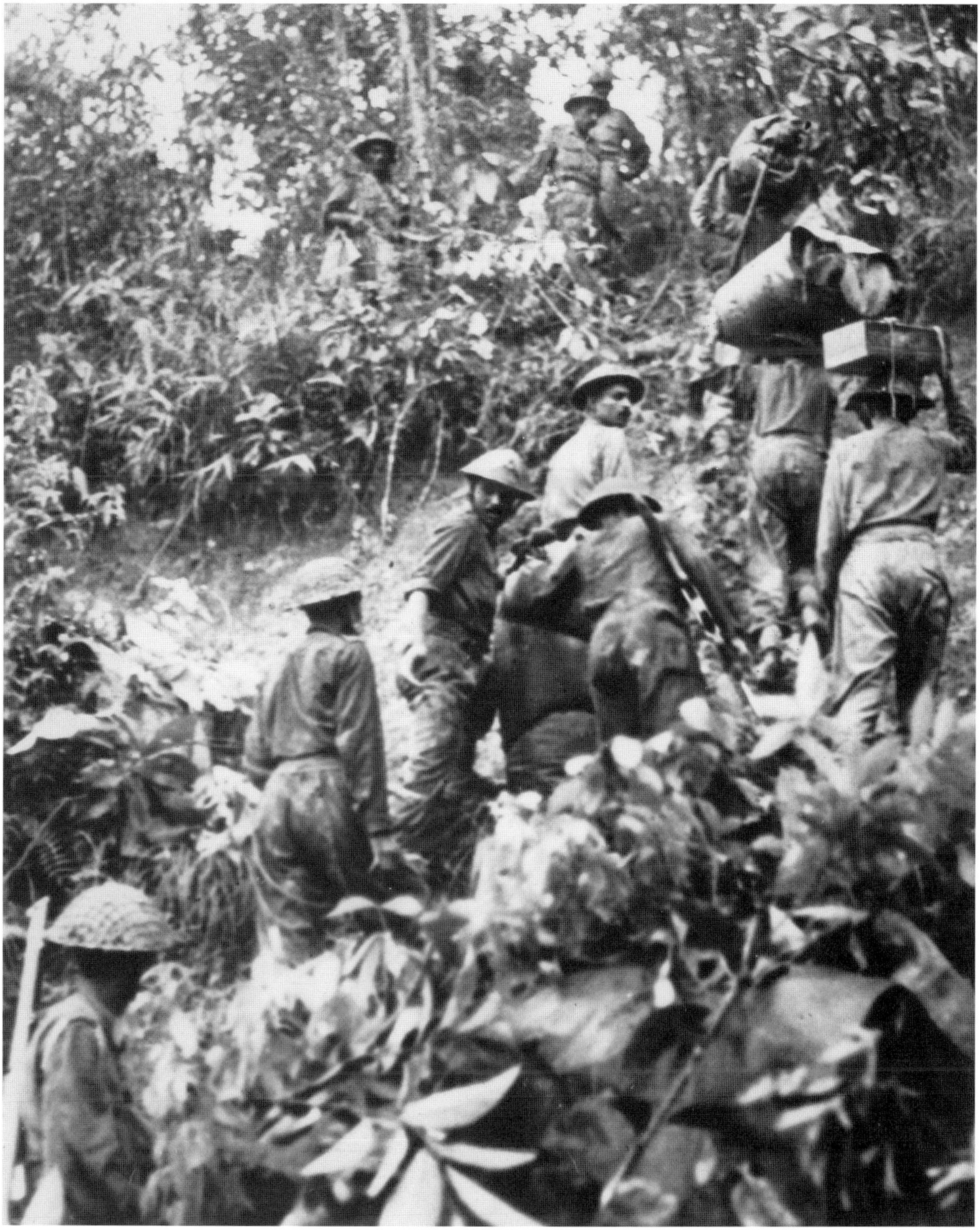

At Kohima, 1st Punjab Regiment soldiers of the 5th Indian Division's 161st Brigade carry ammunition and food up a steep slope. The 5th Division's 161st Brigade was airlifted from the Arakan to Dimapur on 20 March to provide infantry reinforcements for Kohima's defensive 'boxes'. *(NARA)*

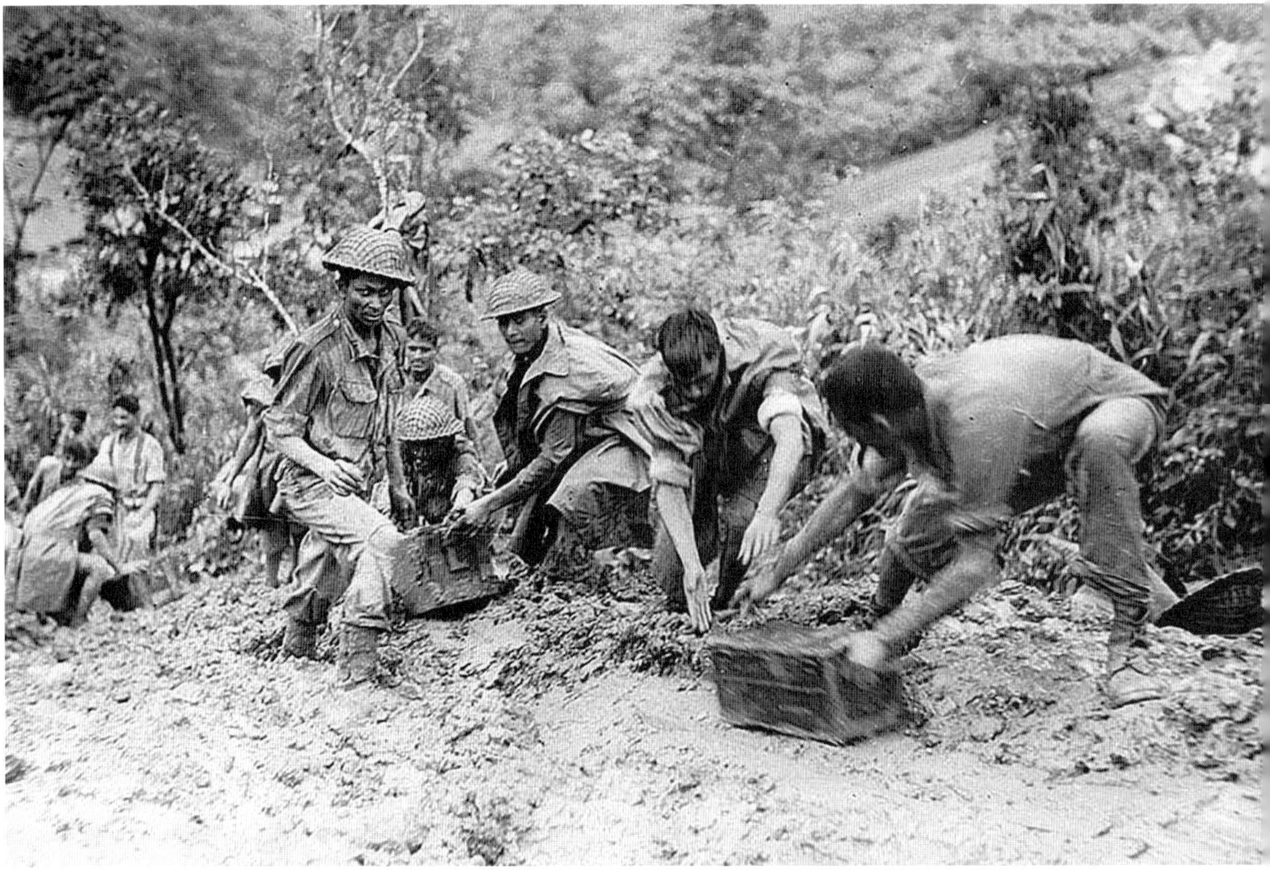

Here 20th Indian Division soldiers, manning a defensive 'box' situated on the Shenam Saddle terrain during the Imphal battle, manhandle ammunition boxes on the Tamu-to-Palel Road. Part of the IJA 33rd Division ('Yamamoto's Column') attacked the 20th Indian Division from Tamu, forcing a withdrawal across the Kabaw Valley in mid-March 1944. The 33rd Division, reinforced by a detachment from the IJA 15th Division, moved south from their Chindwin River crossing. *(Author's collection)*

British SBs carry a wounded soldier along a track in the vicinity of the Imphal plain while other infantrymen move to the front lines. Scoones' IV Corps comprised the 17th and 23rd Indian divisions and was later reinforced by elements of the 5th Indian Division airlifted from the Arakan on 19–20 March. *(NARA)*

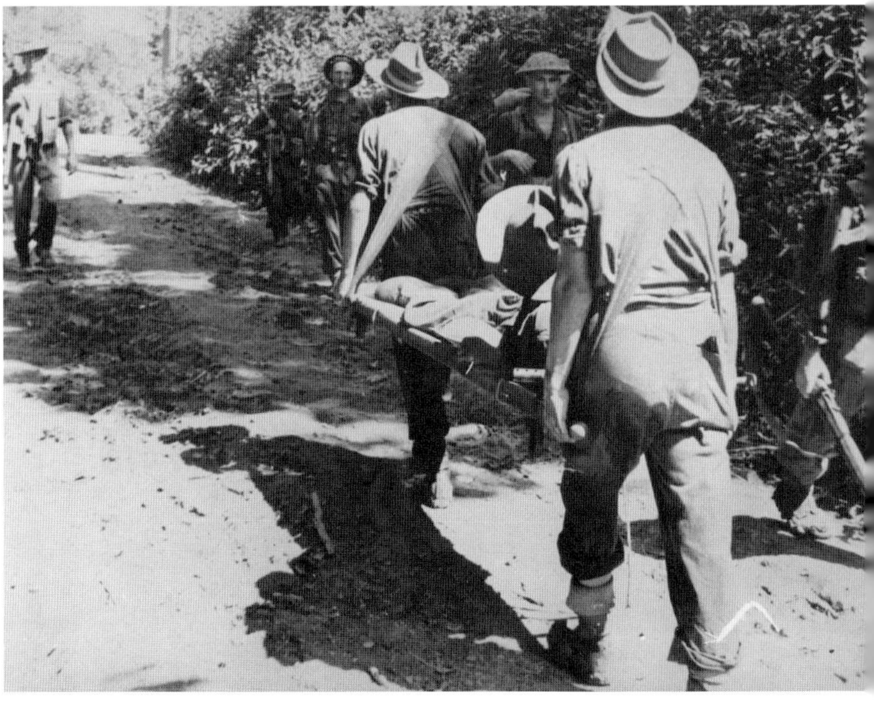

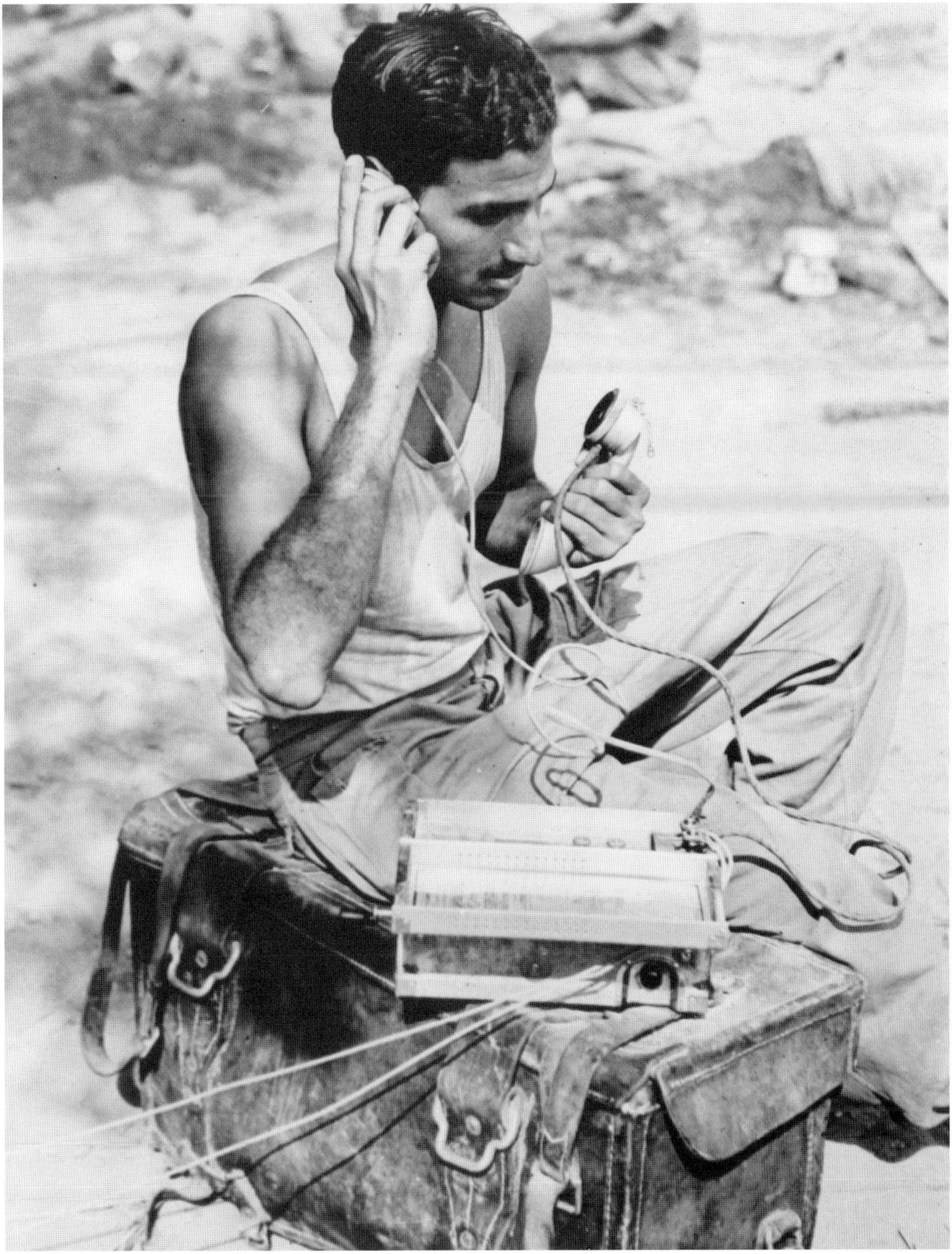

A Punjabi signal officer, Lieutenant Mohammed Zafarullah Khan, tests a captured Japanese field telephone near Kohima. The 7th Indian Division fielded the 7/2nd Punjab Reconnaissance and the 4/15th Punjab battalions. The 5th Indian Division's 161st Brigade, attached to the XXXIII Corps on 5 April, fielded the 1/1st Punjab Battalion within its ranks. *(NARA)*

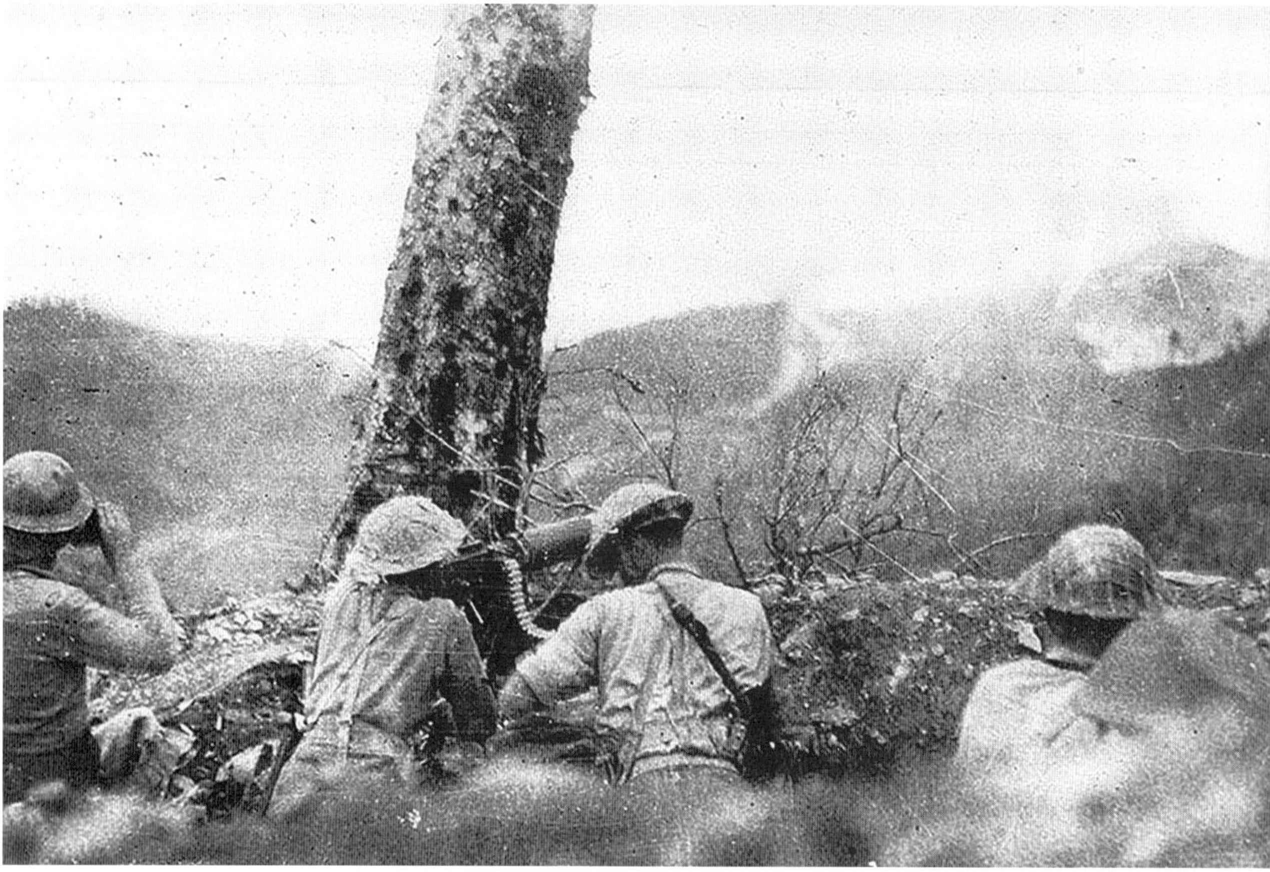

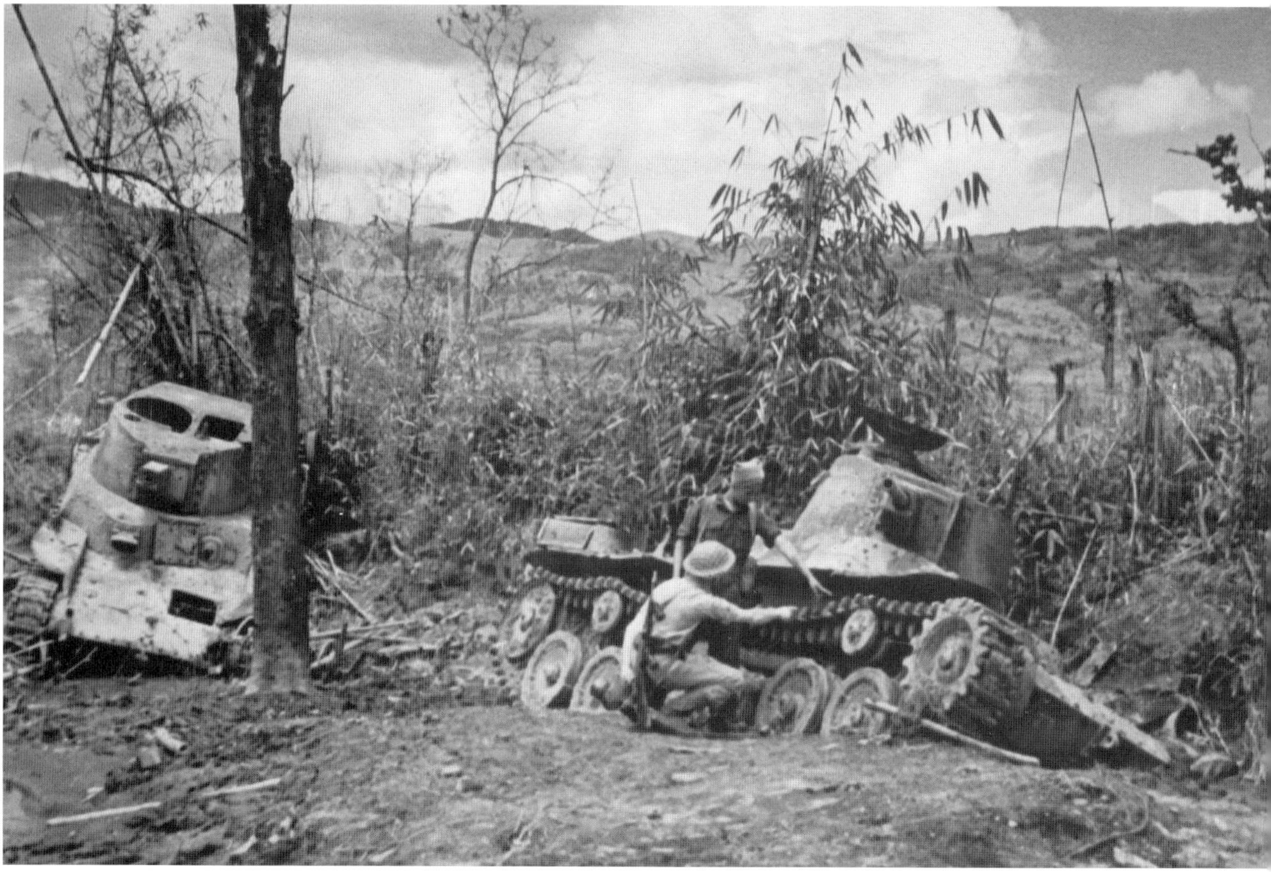

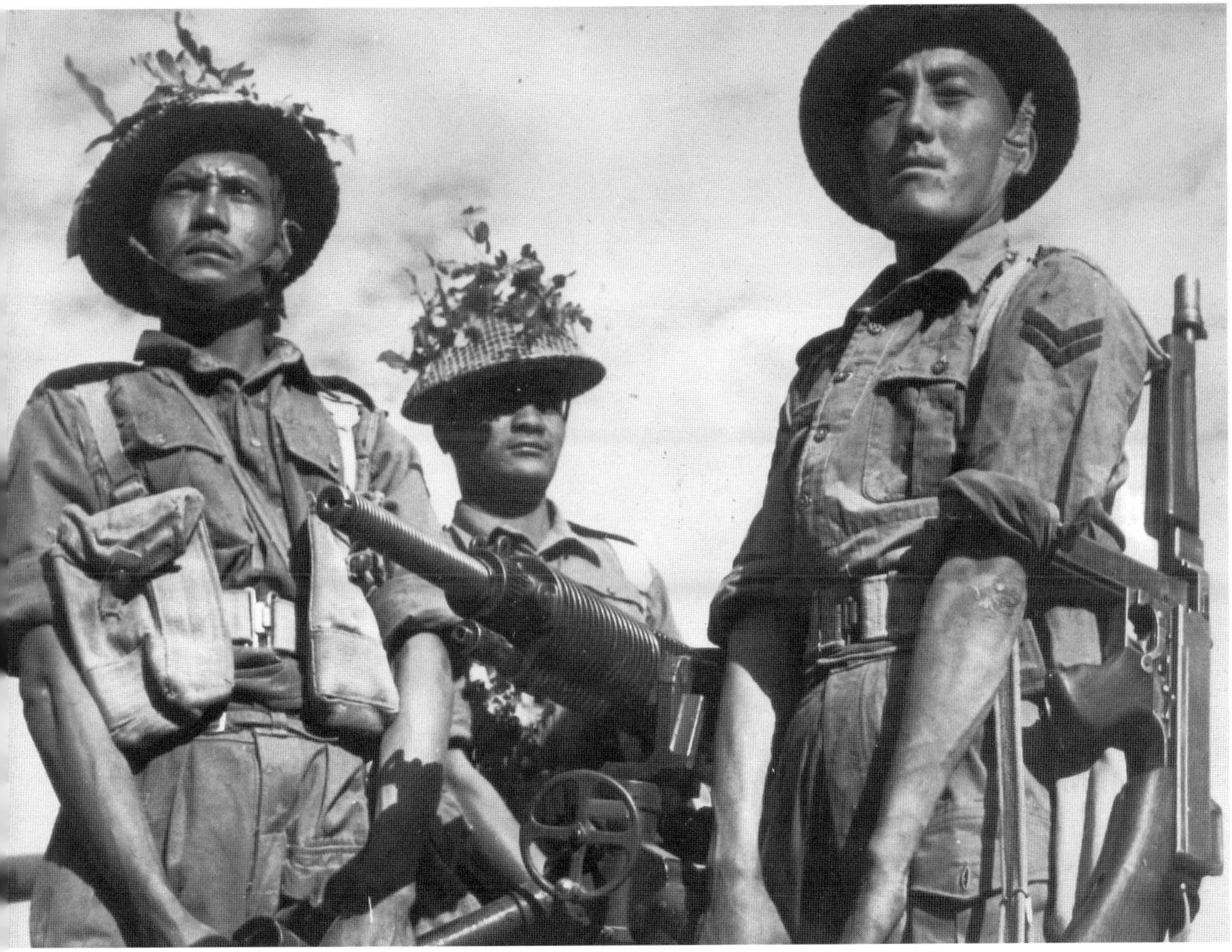

(**Opposite, above**) A Gurkha Vickers MG position is shown here providing indirect fire support while the RAF bombs Japanese positions in Palel in April 1944. Near the end of the battle in July, Mutaguchi considered a final combined attack on the Palel area by the IJA 15th Division, the remnants of the 31st Division and some elements of the 33rd Division; however, by this time Burma Area Army HQ had ordered the IJA Fifteenth Army to withdraw. *(NARA)*

(**Opposite, below**) On 12 June, Rifleman Ganju Lama of the 1/7th Gurkha Rifles won a VC at Ningthoukhong, a village on the Tiddim Road, by single-handedly knocking out the above two enemy tanks with a PIAT weapon. Lama then proceeded to kill the IJA tank crewmen. The IJA 33rd Division made its last major effort to break through to Imphal on this route. *(NARA)*

(**Above**) At the end of June 1944, Indian Army Naik (Corporal) Agan Sing Rai (right) and two other surviving Gurkha members of his C Company section of the 2/5th Royal Gurkha Rifles in the 17th Indian Division's 48th Infantry Brigade pose with a captured IJA MMG after action against Japanese bunkers on Mortar Bluff near Bishenpur to Imphal's south-west. After C Company was pinned down by MG fire and a bunkered 37mm gun, Rai led his section in a charge on the MG position, killing three of the four-man crew. Rai then led another attack on the 37mm gun position during which all but three of Rai's men were killed or wounded before reaching the target. Rai then charged the enemy bunker, killing the Japanese gun crew with a Bren LMG. *(NARA)*

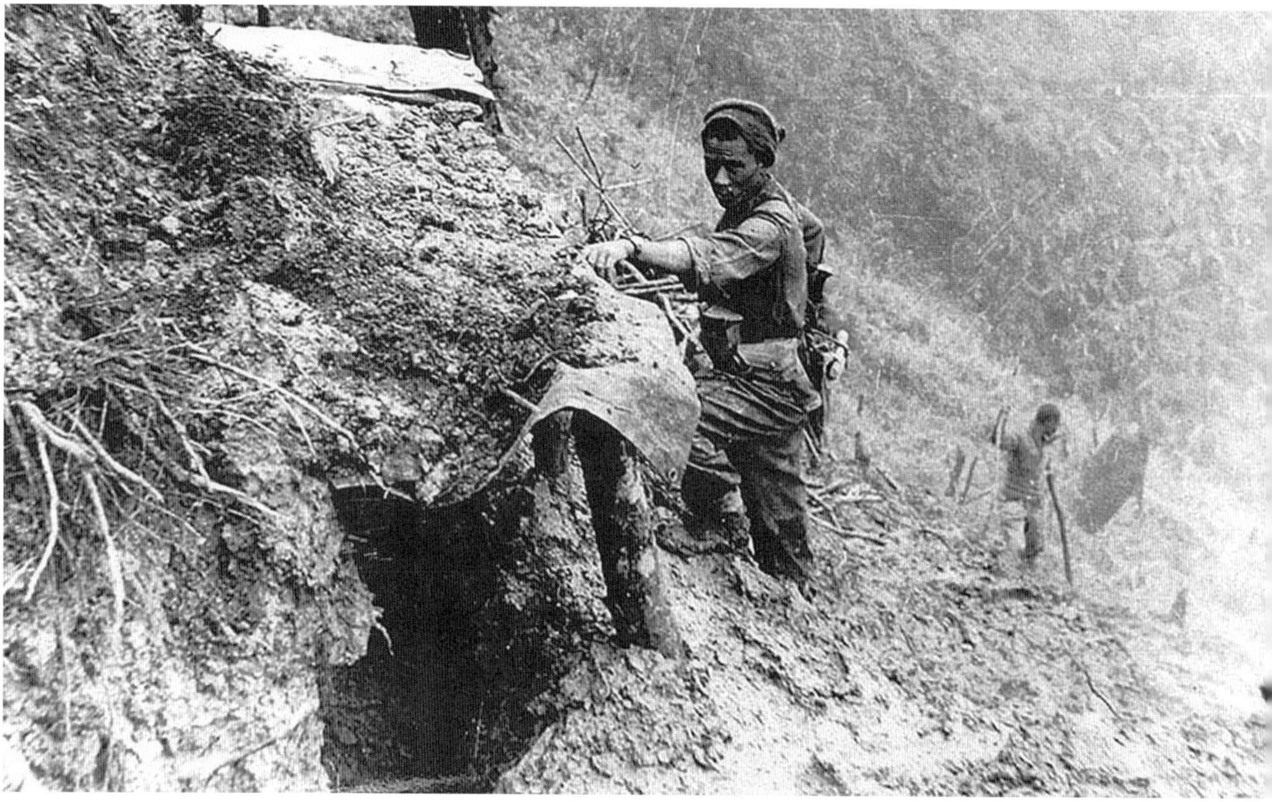

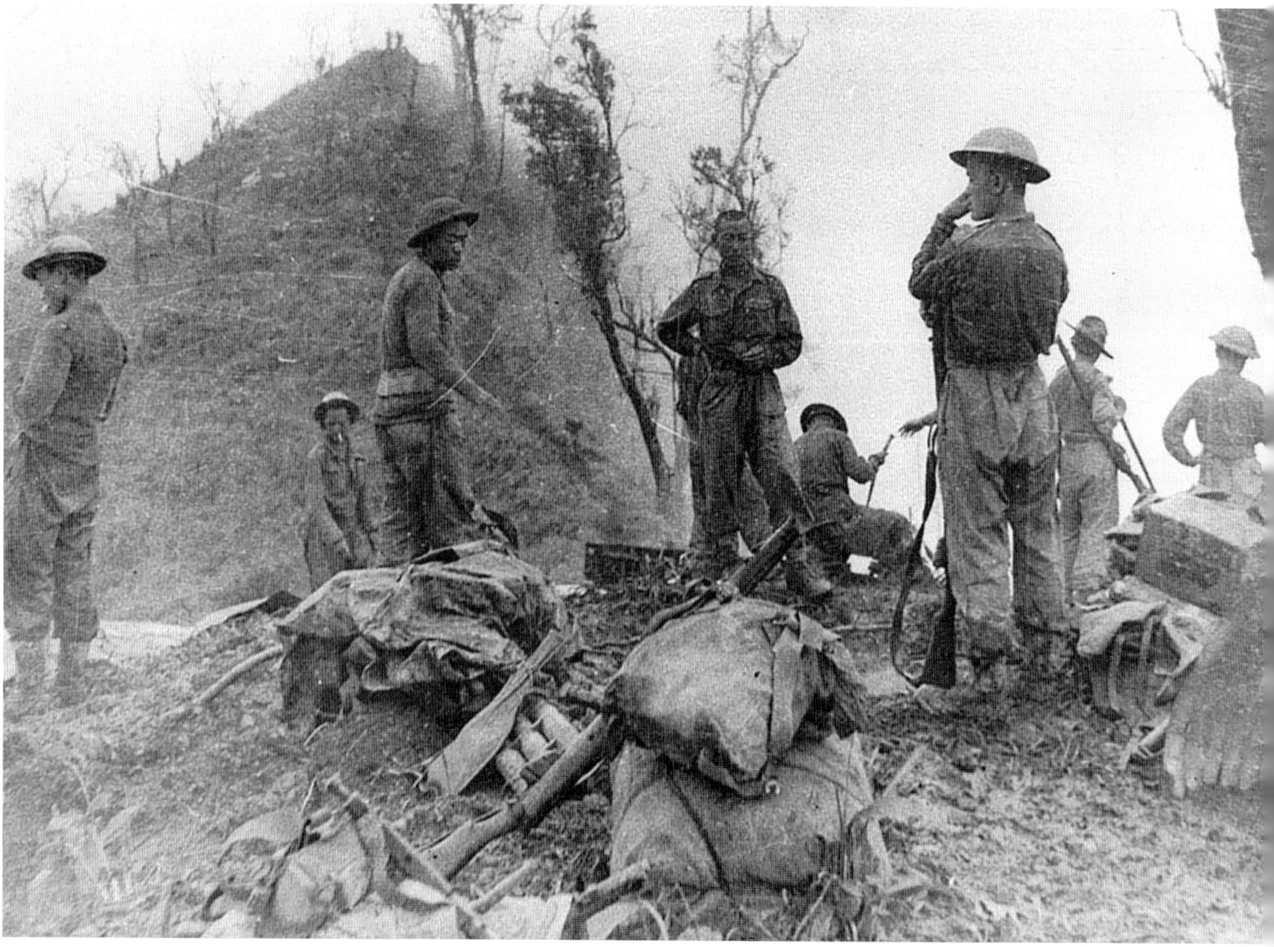

(**Opposite, above**) A 10th Gurkha Rifles infantryman from one of the regiment's battalions serving in the 17th, 20th and 23rd Indian divisions during the Imphal combat examines a small reinforced earthen Japanese bunker on 'Scraggy' Hill after the battle was won at the end of July 1944. 'Scraggy' was the easternmost Allied position on the Shenam Saddle, a hilly terrain feature that included sites such as 'Malta' and 'Gibraltar', was first attacked on the night of 10 May and was captured by elements of the IJA 33rd Division's 'Yamamoto' Force. 'Scraggy' remained under enemy control until the Battle of Imphal ended. (*Author's collection*)

(**Opposite, below**) After combat at Shenam Saddle to Imphal's south-east ended, Gurkha soldiers rest at a topographical feature called 'Gibraltar' (background). On the night of 20/21 May 1944, two battalions of the IJA 15th Division which had moved south to reinforce the 33rd Division's 'Yamamoto' Force renewed attacks on Shenam Saddle. On the night of 23 May, the IJA units captured the crest of 'Gibraltar'. The next day this crest was recaptured in a counterattack by the 5/6th Rajputana Rifles and the 3/10th Gurkha Rifles of the 23rd Indian Division's 37th Infantry Brigade. 'Gibraltar' was the furthest west the IJA would advance on the Shenam Saddle. (*Author's collection*)

(**Above**) A British lance corporal examines an IJA Model 92 105mm field gun on the Tamu front during the enemy withdrawal from Imphal and Kohima that commenced during the final days of July 1944. In addition to the above ordnance, the IJA had Model 94 75mm mountain, 70mm battalion and 75mm regimental guns along with Model 96 150mm howitzers. (*NARA*)

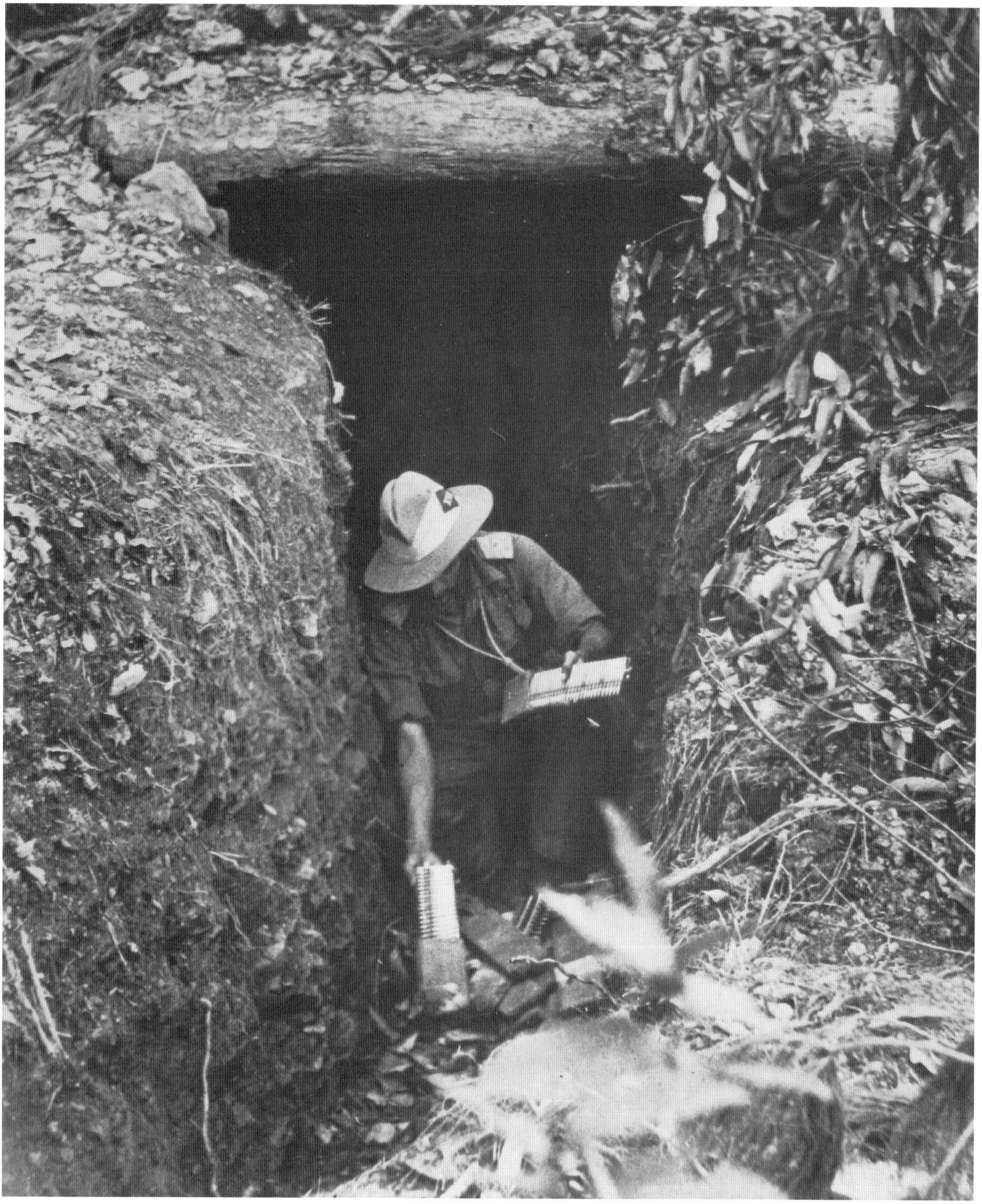

A 5th Indian Division soldier collects Japanese MG ammunition from a deserted IJA bunker near Tiddim. Allied artillery and RAF Hurricane fighter-bombers destroyed many before advancing Fourteenth Army infantry arrived after the Japanese withdrawal at the end of July 1944. The RAF 221 Group had numerous squadrons of Hurricanes, Spitfires, Vultee Vengeances and Beaufighters stationed at fair-weather airfields on the Imphal plain. *(NARA)*

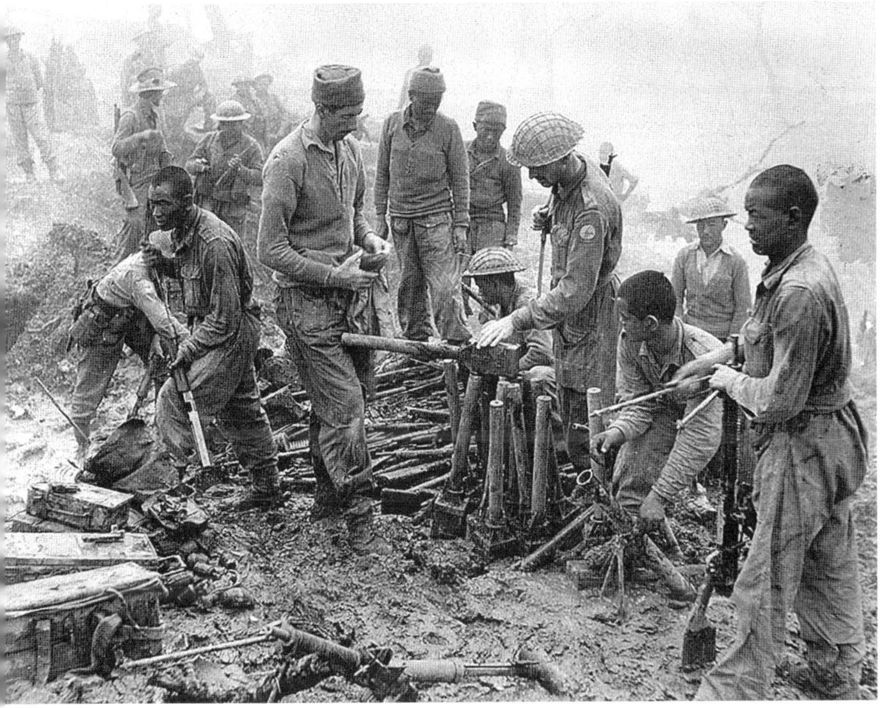

British soldiers and infantrymen of the 3/10th Gurkha Rifles, part of the Indian 23rd Division's 37th Infantry Brigade, inspect IJA ordnance captured on 'Scraggy' at the eastern end of Shenam Saddle after combat ceased there at the end of July 1944. *(Author's collection)*

Infantrymen from the 2nd West Yorkshire Regiment, part of the 5th Indian Division's 9th Infantry Brigade and Gurkhas from a 10th Gurkha Rifles Battalion, are seen here advancing northwards from Imphal towards Kohima at the end of July 1944. The rear of an M3 Lee medium tank from IV Corps' 254th Indian Tank Brigade is seen on the right. This armoured brigade also fielded M3 Stuart light tanks with 37mm turret guns. *(NARA)*

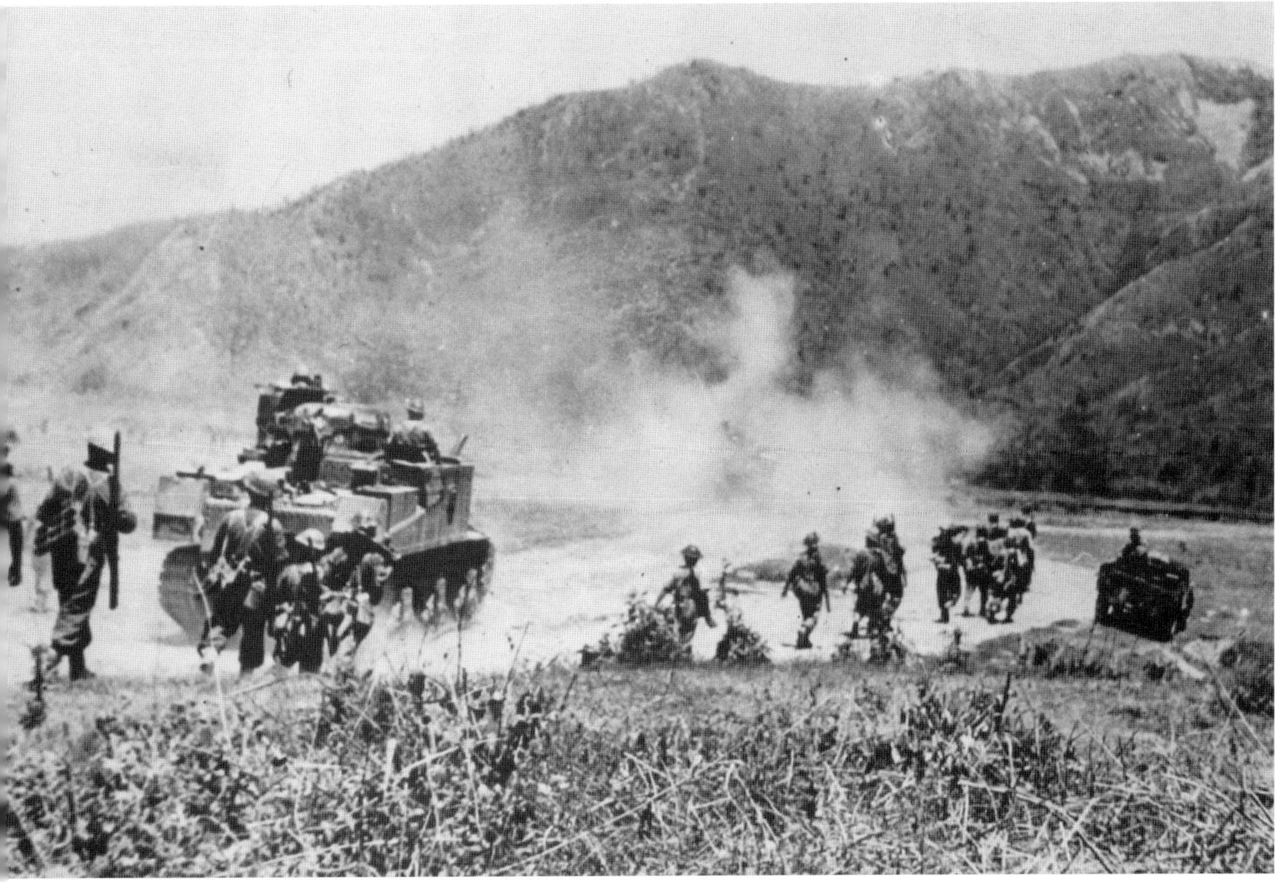

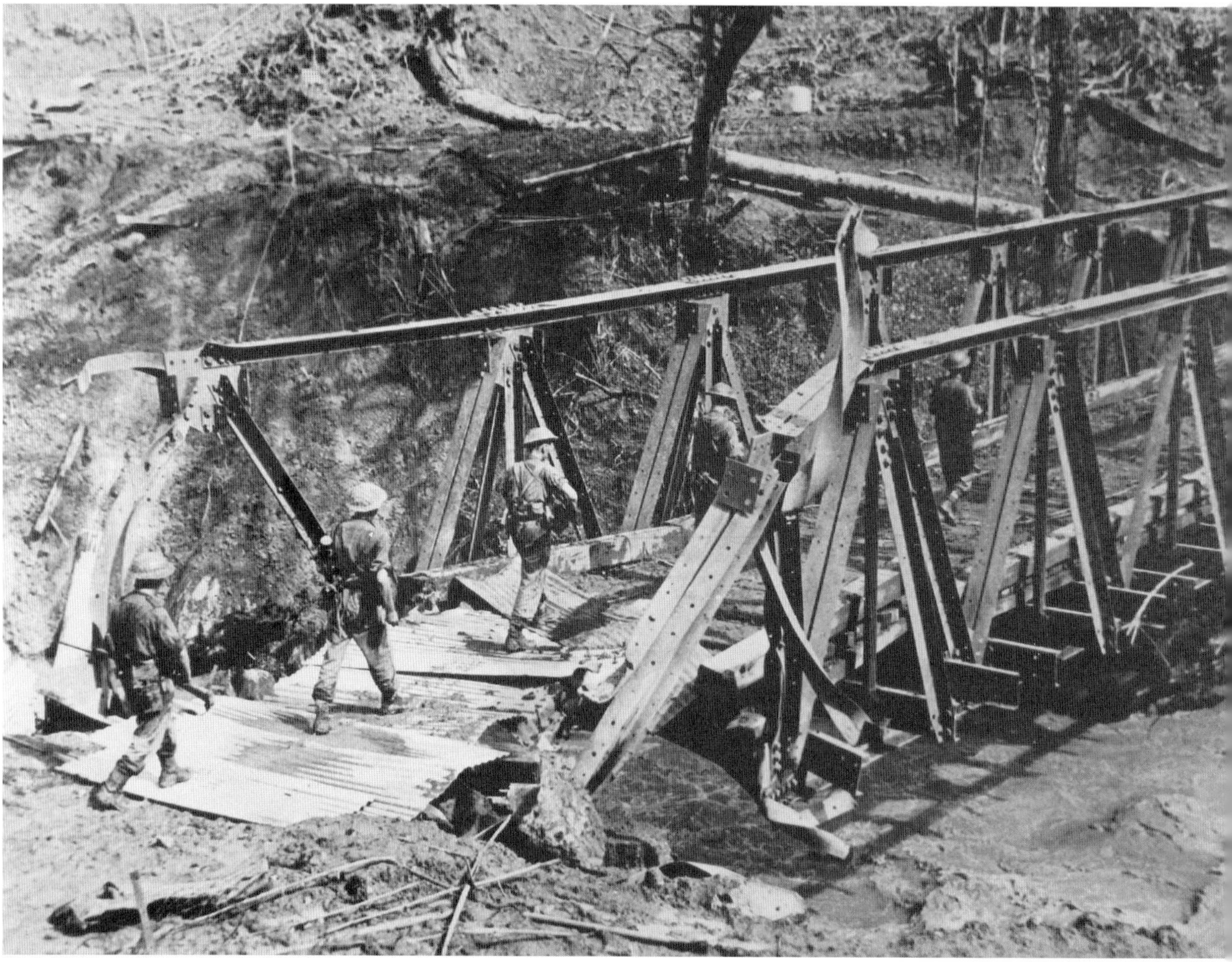

British infantrymen from the 23rd Indian Division walk over a bridge that the retreating Japanese tried to destroy along the Palel-to-Tamu Road as the Allies returned to the offensive to reclaim the Kabaw Valley after the hard-fought victories at Imphal and Kohima. *(NARA)*

Chapter Five

Allied Advances across Burma from India

By the end of August 1944, the Japanese Fifteenth Army was in full retreat with the IJA 15th and 31st divisions recrossing the Chindwin River as the 33rd Division resisted Stopford's XXXIII Corps' 11th East African Division advance towards Tamu and the Kabaw Valley and the 5th Indian Division on the Tiddim Road. A full-blown monsoon brought Allied motor transport and artillery movement to a near halt as bridges had to be constructed over the Burmese *chaungs* from the raging Manipur River running south to Kalemyo. Bridgeheads on the Chindwin River were constructed at Mawlaik and Sittaung to the Kabaw Valley's east and north of Kalewa. Finally, on 13 November the 11th East African and 5th Indian divisions linked up at Kalewa with that locale's capture on 2 December by the East Africans. One week later, an 1,100ft-long Bailey bridge spanned the Chindwin River there. Slim's Fourteenth Army was ready for its advance across central Burma.

General Kimura assumed command of the Burma Area Army after the disasters at Imphal and Kohima. Kimura had ten IJA divisions in three Japanese armies to hold a line from Mandalay south-west through the Yenangyaung oilfields to Ramree Island off the Arakan's coast. Kimura placed General Honda's Thirty-Third Army, comprising two IJA divisions and a regiment, in the north to hold the Lashio-Mandalay line. In the centre, General Katamura's 20,000-man Fifteenth Army, with the remnants of the 15th, 31st and 33rd IJA divisions along with the combat-rested 53rd Division was to defend a line from Mandalay to Meiktila. In the south, General Sakurai's Twenty-Eighth Army with two IJA divisions and an attached regiment was to cover the Yenangyaung oilfields, the Arakan coast and the rice paddy-rich Irrawaddy delta.

Slim's Central Burma Offensive to Capture Mandalay and Meiktila

The Shwebo Plain, situated between the Chindwin and Irrawaddy Rivers, was initially the best area for Slim's Fourteenth Army's superiority in tanks and air power to destroy the Burmese Area Army. On 3 December 1944, Slim's IV and XXXIII Corps were launched approximately 25 miles east of the Chindwin River to defeat the Japanese and cross the Zibyu Taungdan Range running 120 miles north to south with

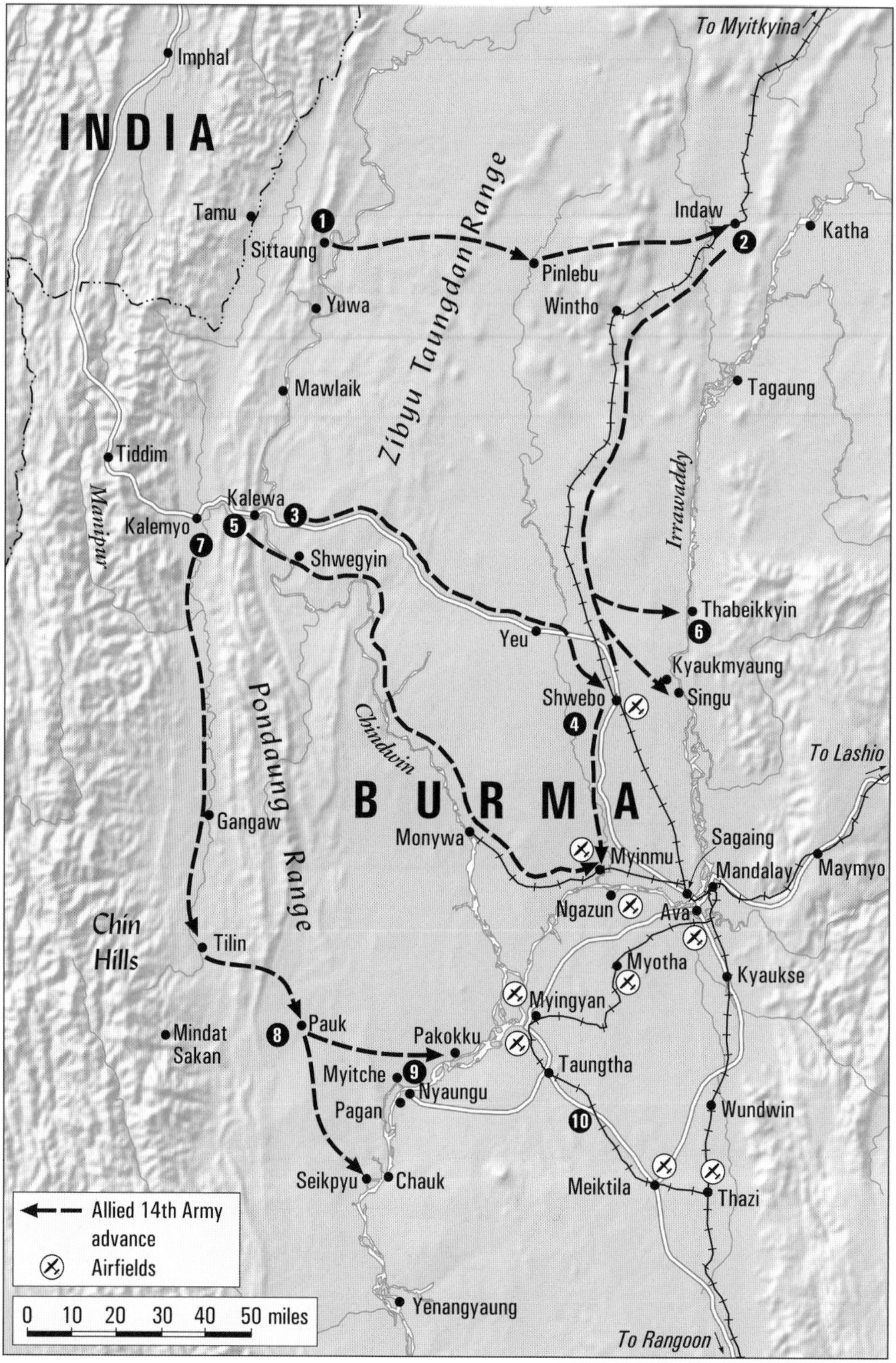
INDIA
BURMA
Imphal
Tamu
Sittaung
Yuwa
Mawlaik
Tiddim
Kalemyo
Kalewa
Shwegyin
Zibyu Taungdan Range
Pondaung Range
Chin Hills
Manipur
Chindwin
Irrawaddy
To Myitkyina
Indaw
Katha
Pinlebu
Wintho
Tagaung
Thabeikkyin
Yeu
Kyaukmyaung
Singu
Shwebo
To Lashio
Gangaw
Monywa
Myinmu
Sagaing
Mandalay
Maymyo
Ngazun
Ava
Tilin
Myotha
Kyaukse
Myingyan
Mindat Sakan
Pauk
Pakokku
Taungtha
Myitche
Nyaungu
Pagan
Wundwin
Seikpyu
Chauk
Meiktila
Thazi
Yenangyaung
To Rangoon
1
2
3
4
5
6
7
8
9
10
Allied 14th Army advance
Airfields
0 10 20 30 40 50 miles

hills up to 2,000ft and to 'capture IJA airfields at Ye-U and Shwebo. Rees' 19th Indian Division crossed the Sittaung River and headed east towards Pinlebu and then Indaw, the latter on the Myitkyina-Shwebo-Mandalay railway corridor. The 19th Indian Division crossed the Zibyu Taungdan Range in eight days and by 15 December its patrols made contact at Indaw with the 36th British Division (part of Sultan's NCAC) moving south down the railway corridor from Myitkyina. Other elements of the 36th British Division moved south along the east bank of the Irrawaddy River, which the Burma Area Army had already crossed, compelling Slim's Fourteenth Army to now cross the wide river to engage the Japanese on a Meiktila-Thazi west-to-east axis, the former locale 70 miles south of Mandalay. This corridor was the main rail and road LOC for the IJA Fifteenth and Thirty-Third armies from Rangoon to the south. Slim's planners found a jungle path from Kalemyo, on the Tiddim-to-Kalewa Road, south-eastward through Gangaw-Tiln-Pauk and then on to Pakokku on the Irrawaddy River with roads on the river's east bank leading to Meiktila. Allied engineers improved the jungle track for the passage of armour and other vehicles.

Map 4. Slim's Central Burma Offensive, 1944–45. ❶ On 4 December 1944, the 19th Indian Division (now part of Indian XXXIII Corps) advances from Sittaung, east of the Kabaw Valley opposite Tamu, across the Zibyu Taungdan Range towards Pinlebu and east to Indaw, the latter on the 'Railroad Corridor'. On 15 December, the 19th Indian Division meets the British 36th Division, which marched south along the 'Railroad Corridor' on a Myitkyina-Katha-Indaw axis. ❷ In mid-December 1944, the 19th Indian Division moves south from Indaw to the west of the Irrawaddy River towards Shwebo to Mandalay's north-west, which is reached on 24 December. The British 36th Division moves south-east to clear the Japanese from a large area east of the Irrawaddy River in an advance towards Lashio. ❸ On 24 December 1944, the British 2nd Division (Indian XXXIII Corps) crosses the Chindwin River near Kalewa to advance on Shwebo, reaching it on 5 January 1945. ❹ The British 2nd Division moves south to the west of the Irrawaddy River, arriving near the Ngazun area on the river's north bank to Mandalay's west. ❺ In late December 1944, the 20th Indian Division (Indian XXXIII Corps) crosses the Chindwin River to Kalewa's east and moves south-eastward through Shwegyin, reaching Monywa on 14 January 1945 on the east-to-west railway towards Mandalay to then converge at the Ngazun bridgehead on the north bank of the Irrawaddy on 13 February 1945. ❻ The 19th Indian Division crosses to the east side of the Irrawaddy, first at Thabeikkyin on 11 January 1945 and later further south at Singu on 21 February as a prelude to the advance on to Mandalay. ❼ The Indian IV Corps' 7th Indian Division, the 28th East African Brigade and the 255th Indian Tank Brigade move south from Kalemyo paralleling the Pondaung Range from 18 to 30 December 1944 through Gangaw (10 January 1945) and on to Tiln and then Pauk (by 26 January). A 7th Indian Division detachment feigns an Irrawaddy River crossing by attacking Pakokku and later moves on to Myitche on the river's western bank where the bulk of the division makes the main river assault to the eastern bank at Nyaung U. ❽ In early 1945, to cover for the 7th Indian Division's river crossing at Nyaung-U, the 28th East African Brigade moves 45 miles south of Pauk to Seikphyu opposite Chauk with oilfields to the south at Yenangyaung, feigning Chauk as the main Irrawaddy crossing site. ❾ At 0400 hours on 14 February 1945, the 7th Indian Division begins the Irrawaddy crossing at Nyaung-U one day ahead of the scheduled target date. ❿ Three days after Nyaung-U was taken by the 7th Indian Division, the 17th Indian Division and attached tank brigade begins the Irrawaddy crossing on 21 February. The Division's armour and motorized vehicles stream northwards towards Taungtha and on to Meiktila.

Slim issued the new axis of advance to his corps commanders on 16 December. The XXXIII Corps, comprising the 19th and 20th Indian and British 2nd divisions, were to continue to the Shwebo-Monywa area between the Chindwin and Irrawaddy Rivers to eventually cross the Irrawaddy and advance on Mandalay. Slim's revised strategy was to now send Messervy's IV Corps, comprising the 7th and 17th Indian divisions along with an East African infantry and the 255th Tank brigades, to establish an Irrawaddy bridgehead at Nyaung-U as it was a shorter crossing and was a minimally-defended boundary between the IJA Fifteenth and Twenty-Eighth armies. A IV Corps' surprise attack on Meiktila at the end of February 1945 was to force the Burma Area Army to shift reserves from Mandalay, weakening IJA defences there. On 14 February IV Corps successfully crossed the Irrawaddy River after artillery and RAF aerial bombardment destroyed an IJA battalion sent to Nyaung-U. A week after the crossing, the 17th Indian Division was on the road to Meiktila ahead of schedule.

On 24 December, XXXIII Corps' 20th Indian Division advanced from the Kalewa bridgehead on to Monywa while the British 2nd Division marched towards Shwebo for an Irrawaddy River crossing at Thabeikkyin well to the north of Mandalay. The 20th Indian Division approached Monywa on 14 January 1945, whereas the British 2nd Division and the southerly advancing 19th Indian Division took Shwebo on 5 January. On 11 January, the 19th Indian Division reinforced the Thabeikkyin bridgehead and to the east at Kyaukmyaung, which were attacked by the IJA Fifteenth Army. On 12 February, the 20th Indian Division crossed the Irrawaddy River at Myinmu, 30 miles east of Monywa and directly due west of Mandalay. The IJA counterattacked the 20th Indian Division's bridgehead repeatedly with units from different divisions until 5 March. On 21 February, the British 2nd Division crossed the river at Ngazun to the west of Mandalay. The Japanese reacted fiercely and by 5 March, the British 2nd Division was across the Irrawaddy and was set to advance east on Mandalay. However, Mandalay's siege was preceded by the seizure of the road and rail centre of Meiktila which supplied the enemy via Rangoon.

The 17th Indian Division with the 255th Indian Tank Brigade advanced from the Irrawaddy bridgehead on 21 February 1945 and the RAF resupplied them before an airstrip was completed to airlift another infantry brigade and an Indian mountain artillery unit. The 17th Indian Division's 63rd Infantry Brigade encountered and reduced IJA defensive positions at a *chaung* 9 miles before Meiktila. Once Meiktila's airfield, along with the rail and road network, fell to the 17th Indian Division and attached M4 medium tanks, the IJA counterattacked with 3,500 troops, lasting from 28 February through to 3 March.

Burma Area Army HQ diverted reinforcements under Lieutenant General Honda from the Mandalay area to Meiktila as Allied control of this transportation hub was disastrous for the IJA in central Burma. On 4 March 1945, Japanese troops recaptured Taungtha to Meiktila's north-west, severing Cowan's LOC and necessitating

Allied infantry and armour resupply by RAF C-47s landing at the Meiktila airstrip. The 17th Indian Division infantry and attached 9th Royal Deccan Horse armour attacked other IJA columns moving on Meiktila during the second week of March. A crisis occurred when the 17th Indian Division's main airfield was assaulted, so Slim airlifted the 5th Indian Division's 9th Infantry Brigade from Jorhat, India into the Meiktila cauldron on 15 March. Fighting for the airfields was intense on 22 March, forcing the RAF to air-drop rather than land supplies onto the main airstrip. Wounded were evacuated from a shorter airstrip west of Meiktila by L-5 Sentinel aircraft. On 24 March, IJA tanks briefly penetrated the Allied perimeter as Japanese artillery, situated 5 miles north of Meiktila, peppered the airstrip and the 17th Indian Division's defensive positions. After two weeks of fighting around the main airfield's runways, the Japanese retreated to Meiktila's south and east on 29 March.

The advance towards Mandalay was made by the 19th and 20th Indian as well as the British 2nd divisions. On 26 February, the 19th Indian Division's three brigades of 15,000 troops and motor transport broke out of their Singu bridgehead on the east bank of the Irrawaddy. On 2 March, the 19th Indian Division's 98th Infantry Brigade continued south along the Irrawaddy's eastern bank, reaching Madaya, a small railway terminus town, five days later. On 6 March, the 19th Indian Division's 62nd Infantry Brigade was dispatched to Maymyo, surprising the enemy garrison. Lashio, to the east on the old Burma Road, was in the American-led NCAC zone. The 19th Indian Division's 64th Infantry Brigade moved south down the Irrawaddy River corridor towards Mandalay. On 7 March a 19th Indian Division ad hoc motorized column called 'Stiletto Force' quickly moved along the river's mud flats through the village of Kabaing unopposed, 4 miles from Mandalay. The next day, 'Stiletto Force' and the 98th Infantry Brigade entered the city's northern outskirts where Mandalay Hill with its 3,000 IJA 15th Division defenders were situated with artillery. To the south of Mandalay Hill were the rectangular-shaped Fort Dufferin and the city proper.

The assault on Mandalay Hill began on the night of 8/9 March by the 19th Indian Division's 98th Infantry Brigade's 4/4th Gurkha Rifles followed by the 2nd Berkshire Regiment. Tenacious combat ensued among the pagodas above and below ground. Next, the remainder of the 19th Indian Division's 98th Infantry Brigade assaulted the mostly-bombed Mandalay city. Rees had to deploy his 62nd Infantry Brigade from the city's eastern approaches to attack the well-defended Fort Dufferin.

For several days, British medium artillery failed to make a serious dent in Fort Dufferin's thick walls. When howitzers arrived, the results of the bombardment improved; however, the IJA defenders within the fortress held out. On 20 March, a coordinated aerial bombardment of Fort Dufferin commenced using a variety of bombers and fighter-bombers. However, the Japanese fortress defenders escaped through drains leading under the fortress walls late at night on 19 March before the aerial assault began.

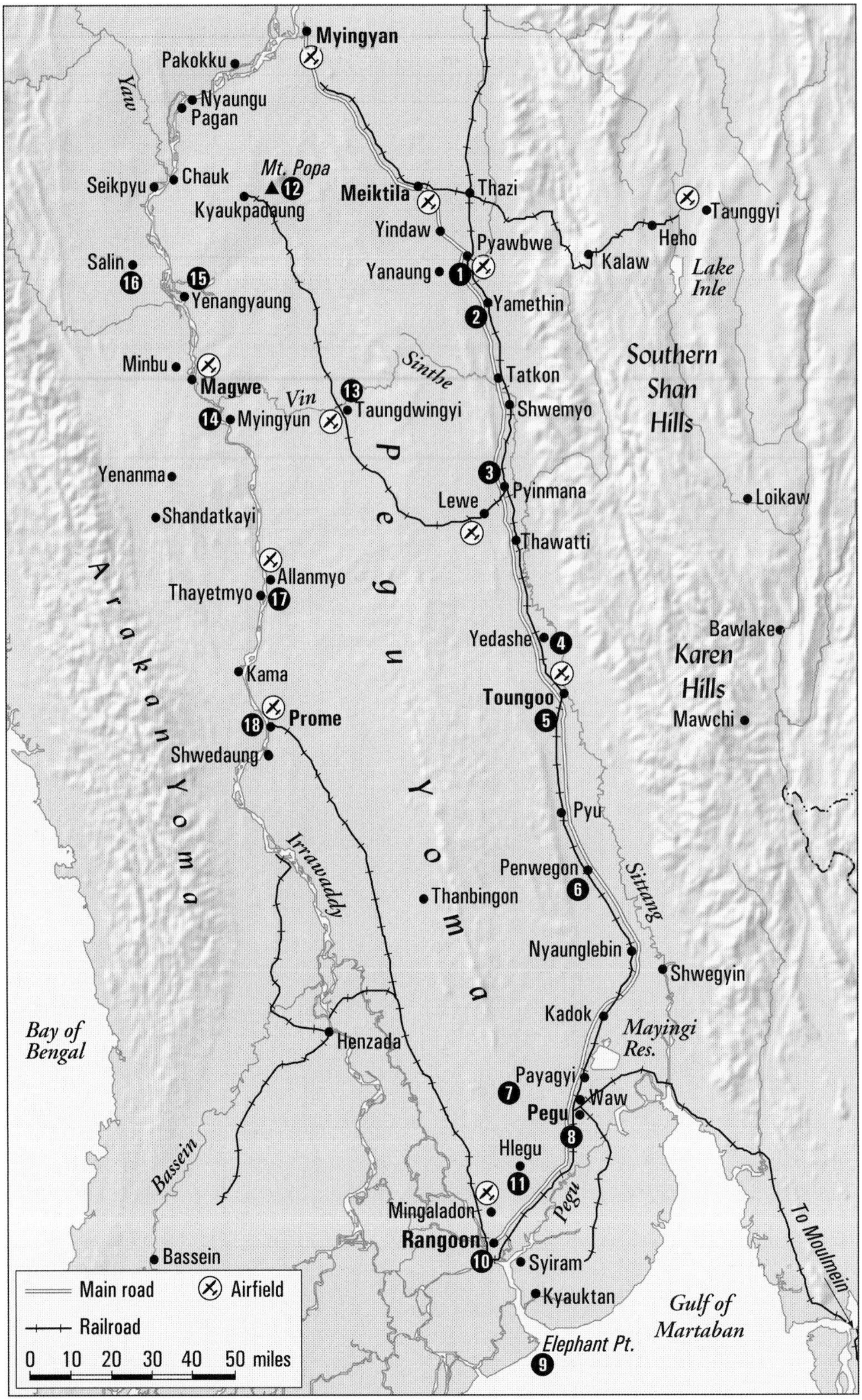
Myingyan
Pakokku
Yaw
Nyaungu
Pagan
Mt. Popa
12
Chauk
Seikpyu
Kyaukpadaung
Meiktila
Thazi
Taunggyi
Yindaw
Heho
Pyawbwe
Kalaw
Yanaung
1
Lake Inle
Salin
16
15
Yenangyaung
Yamethin
2
Minbu
Magwe
Sinthe
Tatkon
Southern Shan Hills
Vin
13
Taungdwingyi
Shwemyo
14
Myingyun
Yenanma
3
Pyinmana
Lewe
Loikaw
Shandatkayi
Thawatti
Pegu Yoma
Arakan Yoma
Allanmyo
Thayetmyo
17
Yedashe
4
Bawlake
Karen Hills
Kama
Toungoo
Prome
18
5
Mawchi
Shwedaung
Pyu
Irrawaddy
Penwegon
6
Sittang
Thanbingon
Nyaunglebin
Shwegyin
Kadok
Mayingi Res.
Bay of Bengal
Henzada
Payagyi
7
Waw
Pegu
8
Hlegu
Bassein
11
Mingaladon
Pegu
Rangoon
10
Syiram
To Moulmein
Bassein
Kyauktan
Gulf of Martaban
Elephant Pt.
9
Main road
Airfield
Railroad
0 10 20 30 40 50 miles

Map 5. On to Rangoon, Spring 1945. ❶ Slim selected the shorter railway axis from Meiktila-Toungoo-Pegu-Rangoon as the main Irrawaddy Valley advance route since the monsoon was soon to arrive and the IJA might form a strong defensive line north of Rangoon. The 17th Indian Division moved towards Pyawbwe, 30 miles south of Meiktila, on 30 March 1945 with first Yindaw captured on 6 April. On 10 April, the 17th Indian Division drives the Japanese from Pyawbwe with more than 1,000 IJA soldiers killed. ❷ With Pyawbwe captured, the 5th Indian Division passes through the 17th Indian Division to secure Toungoo's airfields by 25 April. First Yamethin is captured on 14 April after the 5th Indian Division's 123rd Infantry Brigade with the 7th Indian Cavalry's and Royal Armoured Corps' tanks reaching the town early on 11 April. ❸ Pyinmana, IJA General Honda's HQ, is captured by the 5th Indian Division's 161st Indian Brigade and attached armour on 20 April as preliminary rains of the monsoon begin. ❹ Yedashe, 184 miles from Rangoon, is entered on 21 April by the 5th Indian Division's 123rd Infantry Brigade and attached armour against light opposition. ❺ Tanks of the Indian IV Corps arrive in Toungoo on 23 April, two days ahead of schedule, causing General Honda to flee again. Toungoo had two of Burma's best airfields and RAF fighters began to arrive, with Rangoon now within fighter range. Elements of the 19th Indian Division and the RAF Regiment assumed responsibility for defending the airfields, which were starting to flood with an earlier-than-expected monsoon onset. The 5th Indian Division advanced 200 miles in two weeks. ❻ The 5th Indian Division passes through Pyu and advances to Penwegon on 25 April. Thereafter, the 17th Indian Division resumes its southward advance, and on 26 April elements of this division almost reach Nyaunglebin. ❼ On 27 April, the 17th Indian Division advanced towards Payagyi, where the IJA defended roadblocks against Allied tanks with poles with picric charges on their ends. Other IJA soldiers were crouched in holes with aerial mines, waiting to detonate them in suicidal fashion on Allied tanks. ❽ Pegu was attacked from three sides simultaneously by the 17th Indian Division. Although Pegu's residential area was easily occupied, attempts to enter the city from the east were unsuccessful on 29 and 30 April. After repelling IJA counter-attacks and hidden sniper nests, 17th Indian Division troops controlled the entire Pegu locale by 2 May. A Bailey bridge was erected by sappers over the Pegu River to replace the bridge destroyed by the retreating Japanese. ❾ On 1 May, the 2/3rd Gurkha Parachute Battalion of the Indian 50th Parachute Brigade lands against minimal opposition from the Japanese at Elephant Point to neutralize enemy defences that could hamper an upcoming amphibious landing. On 2 May, the 26th Indian Division makes seaborne landings at Elephant Point. ❿ Syriam, an oil refinery town across the Pegu River from Rangoon, is attacked by elements of the 26th Indian Division's 71st Infantry Brigade after Kyauktan was taken without any Japanese opposition. ⓫ An RAF pilot observes Rangoon unoccupied on 1 May. Frontier Force and Gurkha Rifles units arrive at the Rangoon docks via landing craft on 3 May and the port-city is retaken after three years of Japanese occupation. The 17th and 26th Indian divisions meet at Hlegu on 6 May, 28 miles north-east of Rangoon. ⓬ Early in April, the 268th Infantry Brigade and British 2nd Division's 5th Brigade move south-west from Myingyan into the Irrawaddy Valley and encounter no stiff opposition until reaching Mount Popa on 10 April. The IJA defenders hold until 19 April. The 7th Indian Division progresses from Nyaung-U down both sides of the Irrawaddy River and captures Kyaukpadaung, an important rail and road junction on 12 April. ⓭ On 13 April, the 20th Indian Division moves along a railway paralleling the Irrawaddy River to the west to capture Taungdwingyi, a point on the IJA Twenty-Eighth Army's escape route. ⓮ The 20th Indian Division turns west and on 19 April captures Magwe and Myingyan on the Irrawaddy River with 600 Indian National Army members surrendering. ⓯ The 7th Indian Division's 33rd Infantry Brigade attacks the oilfields at Yenangyaung on the eastern side of the Irrawaddy on 21 April against fierce IJA resistance and captures the site on 25 April. ⓰ Salin, west of the Irrawaddy River, is attacked by the 7th Indian Division's 89th Infantry Brigade from Chauk and the 114th Infantry Brigade from Seikphyu. ⓱ Elements of the 20th Indian Division move on Allanmyo, which is captured on 28 April after fanatical IJA resistance. ⓲ By losing the river port of Prome on 2 May to the 20th Indian Division, the IJA's last escape route from the Arakan is blocked.

To the Irrawaddy River's south, three other Allied divisions – the 11th East African and the 7th and 20th Indian – moved on the oilfields at Chauk and towards the volcanic 5,000ft Mount Popa. Elements of the 7th Indian Division fought their way into the outskirts of Myingyan on 18 March and four days later eliminated the last of the suicidal IJA defenders. Work immediately commenced to restore bridges and the railway to Meiktila's north-west.

On 8 March, the 20th Indian Division moved south of Mandalay along a tangent past Ngazun, Myotha, Pyinzi and then to Wundwin on the rail line to Meiktila's north-east. During the first two weeks of March, the British 2nd Division advanced south along the Irrawaddy River on a two-brigade front. That division's 5th and 6th Infantry brigades fought on a course paralleling the river as the IJA forces retreated east-wards. Late on 17 March, the 1st Queen's Own Cameron Highlanders captured Ava with its moat-surrounded fortress. Ava had once been the capital of Burma situated to the south-west of Mandalay at a westward bend of the Irrawaddy River. The 7th Worcestershires secured the southern end of the Ava Bridge across the Irrawaddy, 1,300 yards wide at this site.

On to Rangoon (see Map 5)

In mid-April 1945, the IV Indian Corps' 5th and 17th Indian divisions advanced south of Meiktila capturing Toungoo on 23 April and Pegu, further to the south along the road and railway line west of the Sittang River on 25 April. By 2 May, IV Corps moved rapidly south-west towards Rangoon to prevent the IJA from forming a new front and to capture the port-city before the monsoon. In fourteen days, the 5th Indian Division advanced more than 210 miles.

On 2 May, the 26th Indian Division landed from the sea close to Rangoon at Elephant Point following an inland parachute drop by the 2/3rd Gurkha Parachute Battalion on 1 May. These forces captured Rangoon on 3 May, with IV Corps 25 miles away. A key Allied objective was the seizure of Prome on the Irrawaddy on 2 May, closing the last IJA escape route from the Arakan. The Fourteenth Army rounded up scattered IJA units trying to escape eastward, first across the Irrawaddy and then the Sittang River. The monsoon flooded the Burmese countryside as rivers became torrents and paddy fields and villages were surrounded by water.

(**Opposite, above**) A section from the Royal Welsh Fusiliers' 2nd Battalion of the British 36th Division's 29th Infantry Brigade fords a Burmese *chaung* towards a village hut (background) on the way to Pinwe in October 1944. This former Indian army division, under Major General Francis Festing, redesignated as a British army division in September 1944, was allocated to the NCAC first under Stilwell and then Sultan. When Festing first met Stilwell in the late summer of 1944, he enquired about orders and Stilwell told him to advance down the 'Railway Corridor' and capture Indaw, which his division did ahead of schedule on 15 December 1944. The 'Railway Corridor' ran from Wuntho in the south and extended north past Indaw, Mawlu and Taungni for 160 miles before opening up into the Mogaung River Valley and on to Myitkyina. (*NARA*)

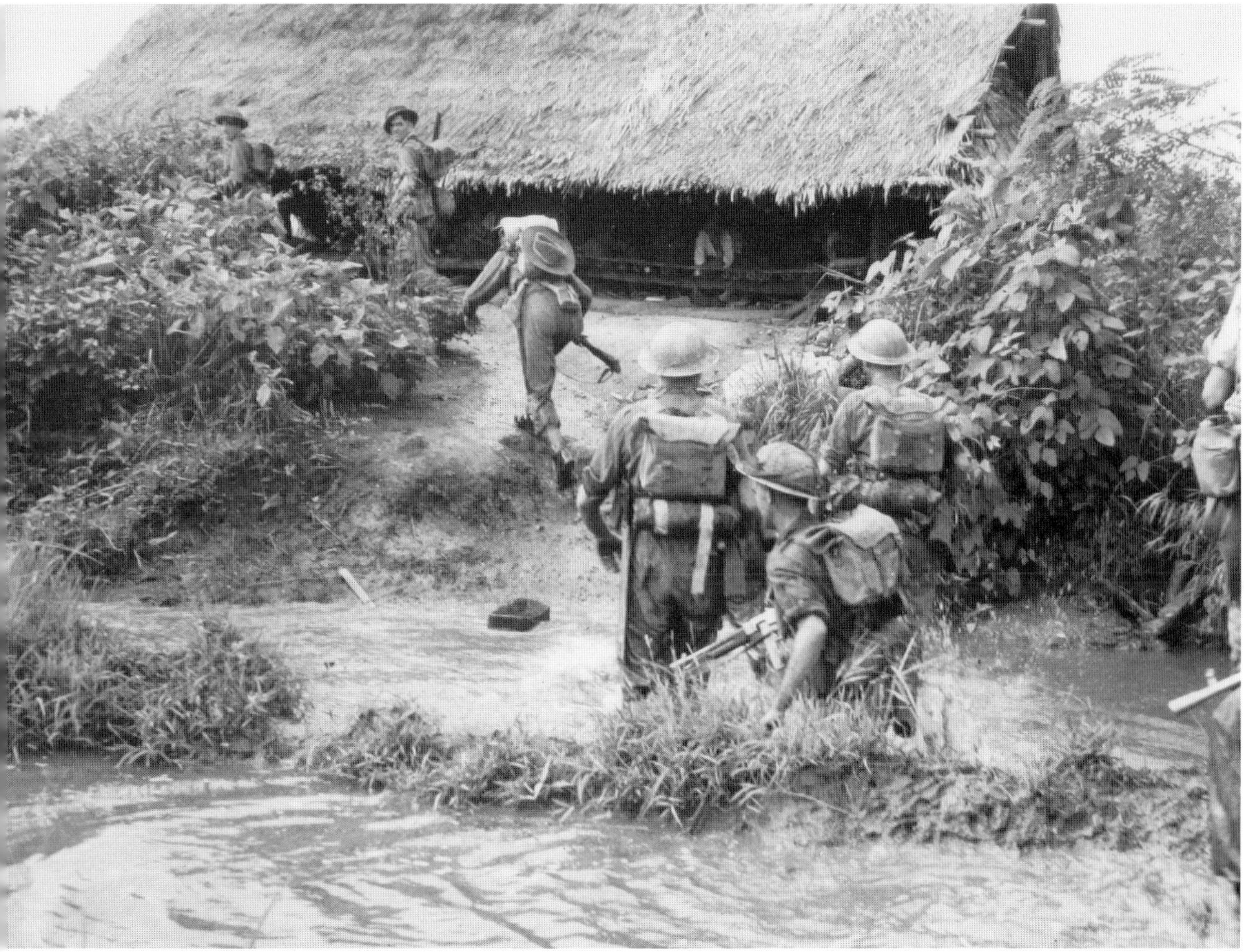

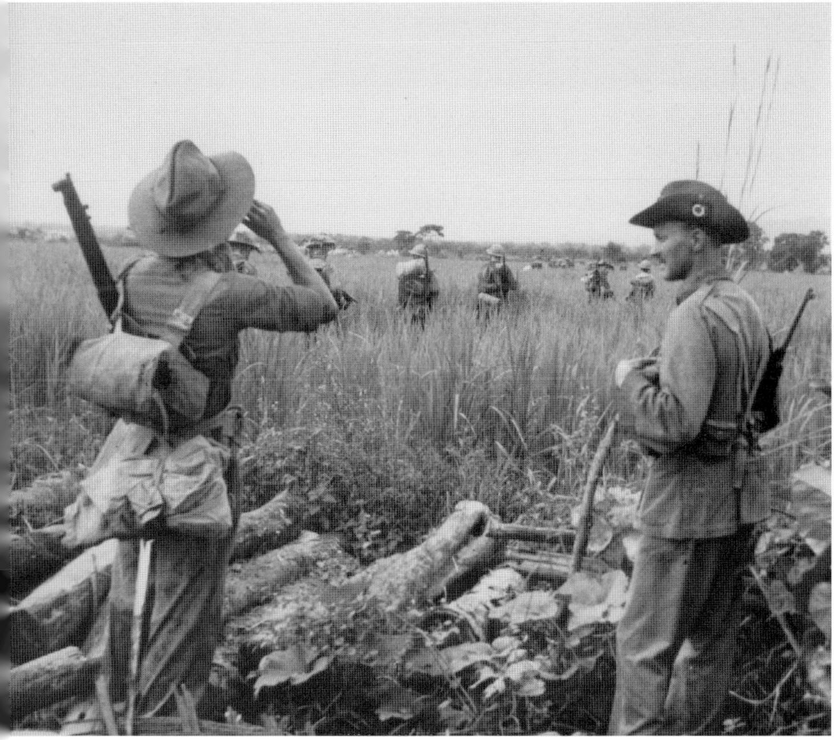

A Burmese scout (left) looks through binoculars, while an officer from the British 36th Division's 29th Infantry Brigade's 1st Battalion, Royal Welsh Fusiliers (right) awaits information as infantrymen advance on the movement to Pinwe in late October 1944. On 1 April 1945 the division transferred back from the NCAC to Slim's Fourteenth Army. *(NARA)*

(**Above**) Infantrymen from the 36th British Division's 1st Battalion Royal Scots Fusiliers move through waist-high water in November 1944 on the way to Mohnyin, situated between Namma and Mawhun in the 'Railway Corridor'. On 25 October, the 36th British Division broke through IJA defensive blocks along the railway near Mawhun. Mawlu, to the south of Mawhun and north of Pinwe, was occupied on 31 October. The 36th Division waited there until the Chinese 50th Division arrived to protect Festing's rear LOC before resuming its advance on to Pinwe on 9 November. (*NARA*)

(**Opposite, above**) A 36th British Division infantryman views glider wreckage and a destroyed jeep in the 'Railway Corridor' in late 1944. The crashed glider, part of Wingate's Operation THURSDAY, was prematurely released by its C-47 towing transport far from the 77th Brigade's stronghold airfield at 'Broadway'. (*NARA*)

(**Opposite, below**) Infantrymen from the 36th British Division are seen here climbing over destroyed Japanese rolling stock as these Allied forces campaigned down the 'Railway Corridor'. Scenes like this were not uncommon as Wingate's Chindit forces had combated the Japanese in these areas during the earlier Operations LONGCLOTH (1943) and THURSDAY (1944). (*NARA*)

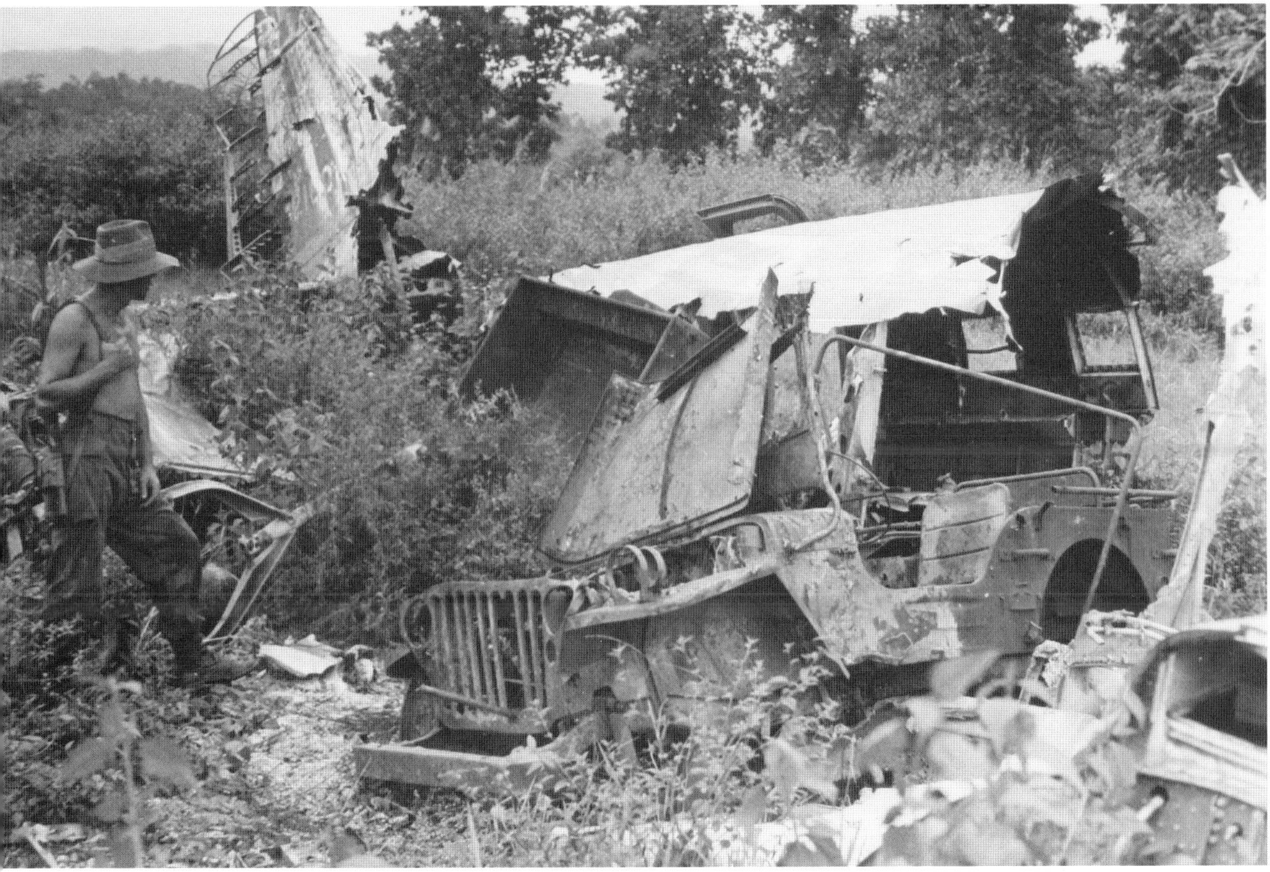

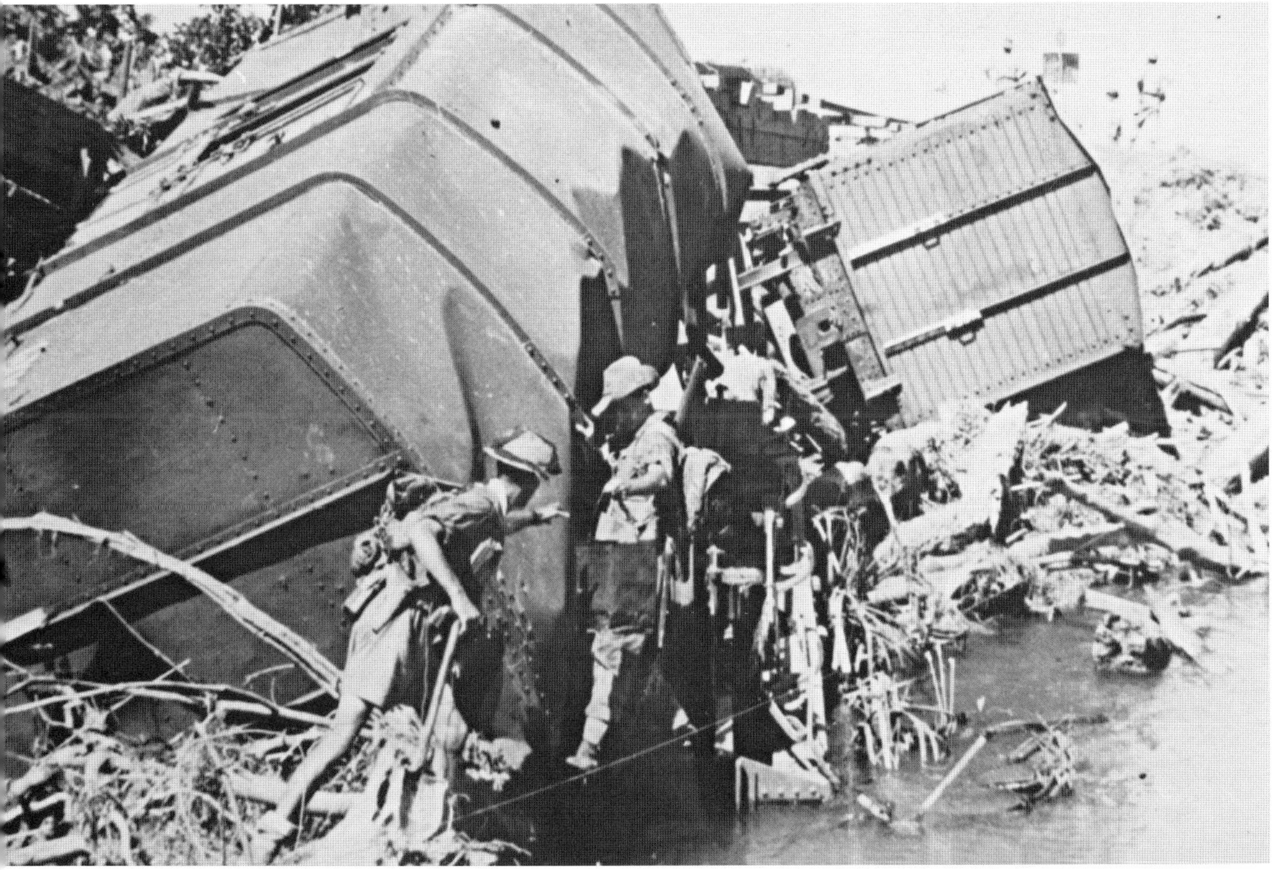

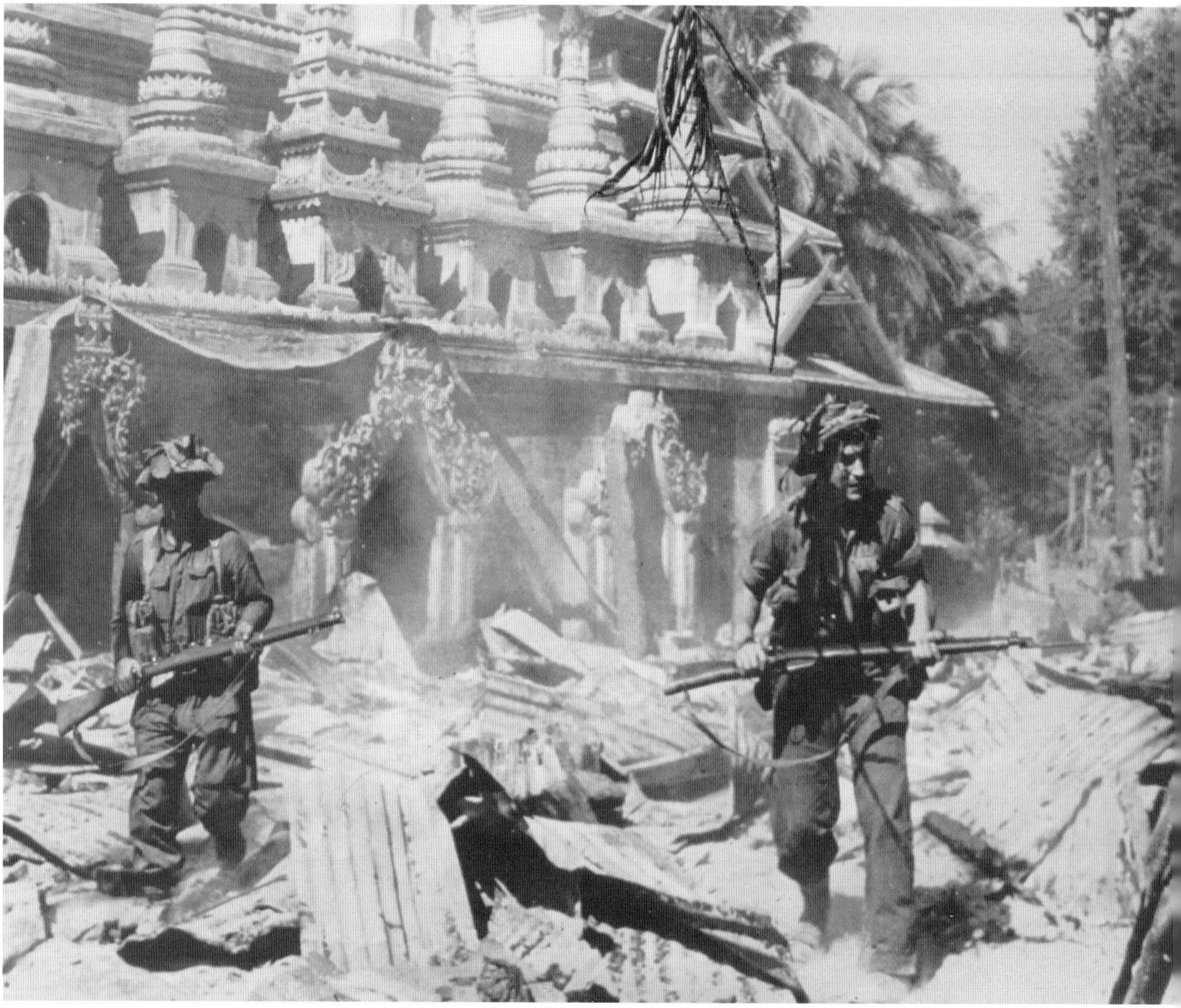

(**Above**) Two 6th South Wales Borderers of the British 36th Division's 72nd Infantry Brigade patrol in front of the Bahe Village's Pagoda wreckage between Myitsone and Mabein after its capture on 26 January 1945. Myitsone, situated on the Shweli River, was defended by remnants of the IJA 18th and 56th divisions to prevent the Allies from reaching Mongmit, south of the Shweli River, to attack Mandalay from the north-east. *(NARA)*

(**Opposite, above**) A 36th British Division jeep convoy passes a village temple south of Inywa and Katha along the Irrawaddy River. Naba, Indaw and Katha were occupied by the 36th British Division between 9 and 13 December 1944. On 16 December, contact was made with the 19th Indian Division, heading east from its Chindwin River crossing. Sultan, Stilwell's replacement as NCAC commander, then ordered Festing's Division to advance south along the Irrawaddy River to Tigyaing and then to operate to the river's east to clear the Shweli River crossings south of Mabein and take Mogok. *(NARA)*

(**Opposite, below**) British 2nd Division sappers cross the Mu River after rigging their universal carrier with empty oil drums for buoyancy while the tracks paddled the vehicle. The Mu River, a tributary of the Irrawaddy, runs north-to-south to the west of Ava and Mandalay. Elements of the British 2nd Division crossed the Mu near its mouth in late February 1945. *(NARA)*

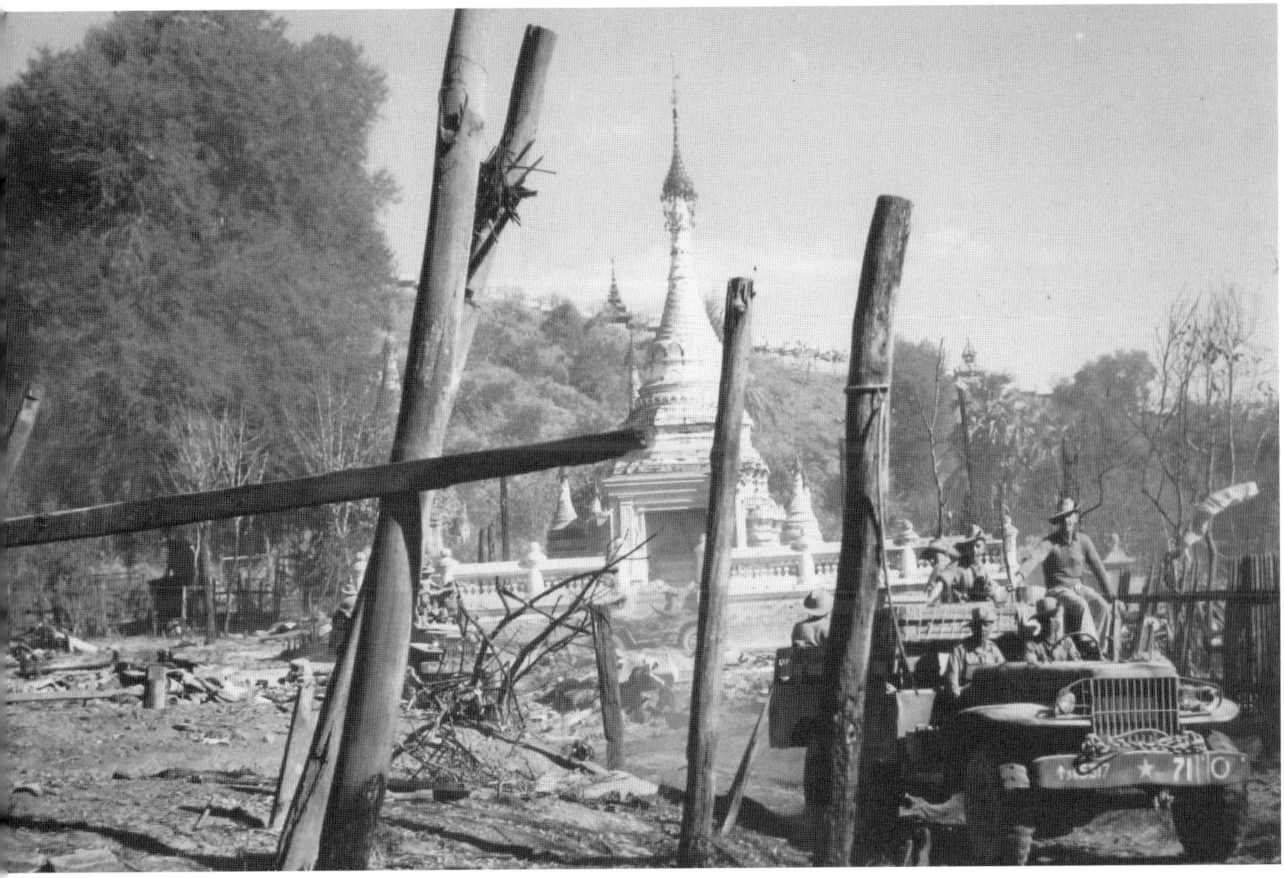

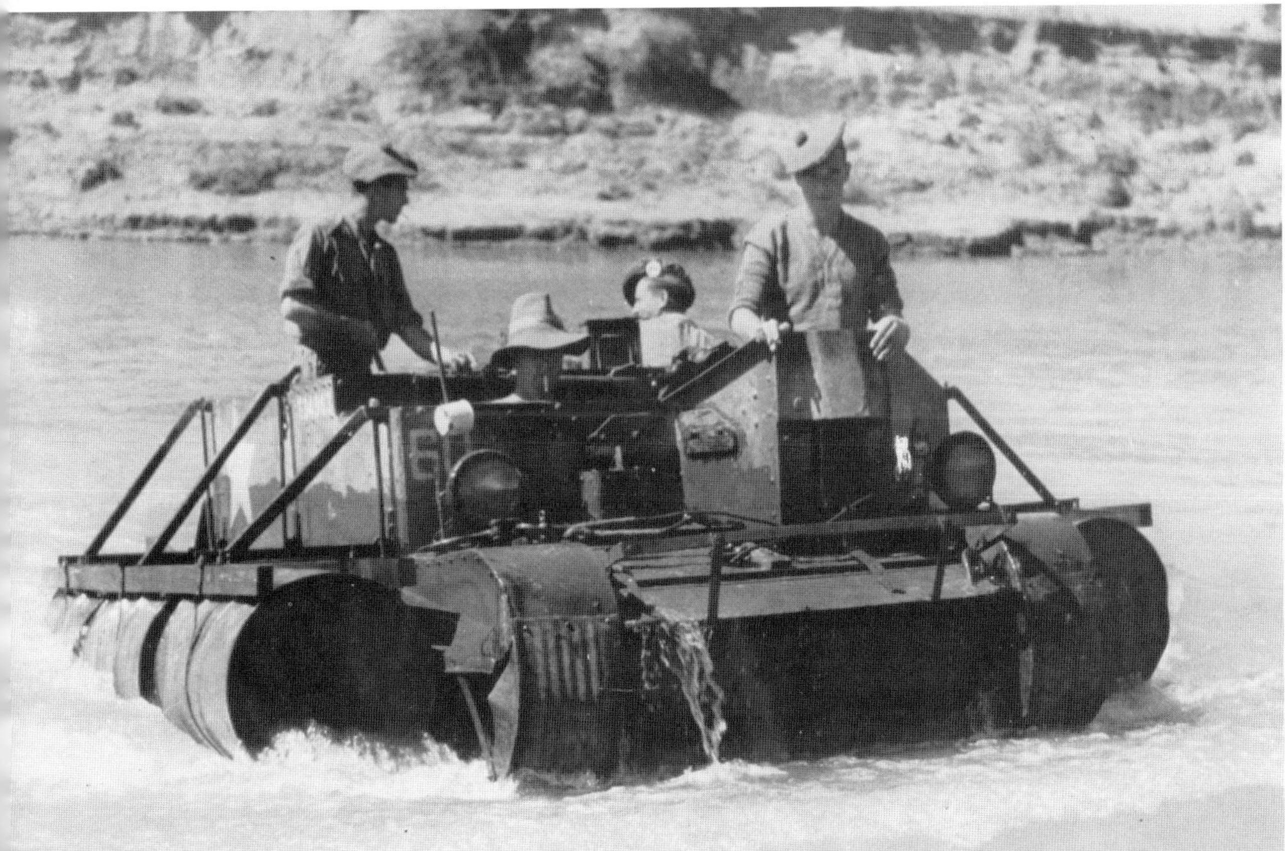

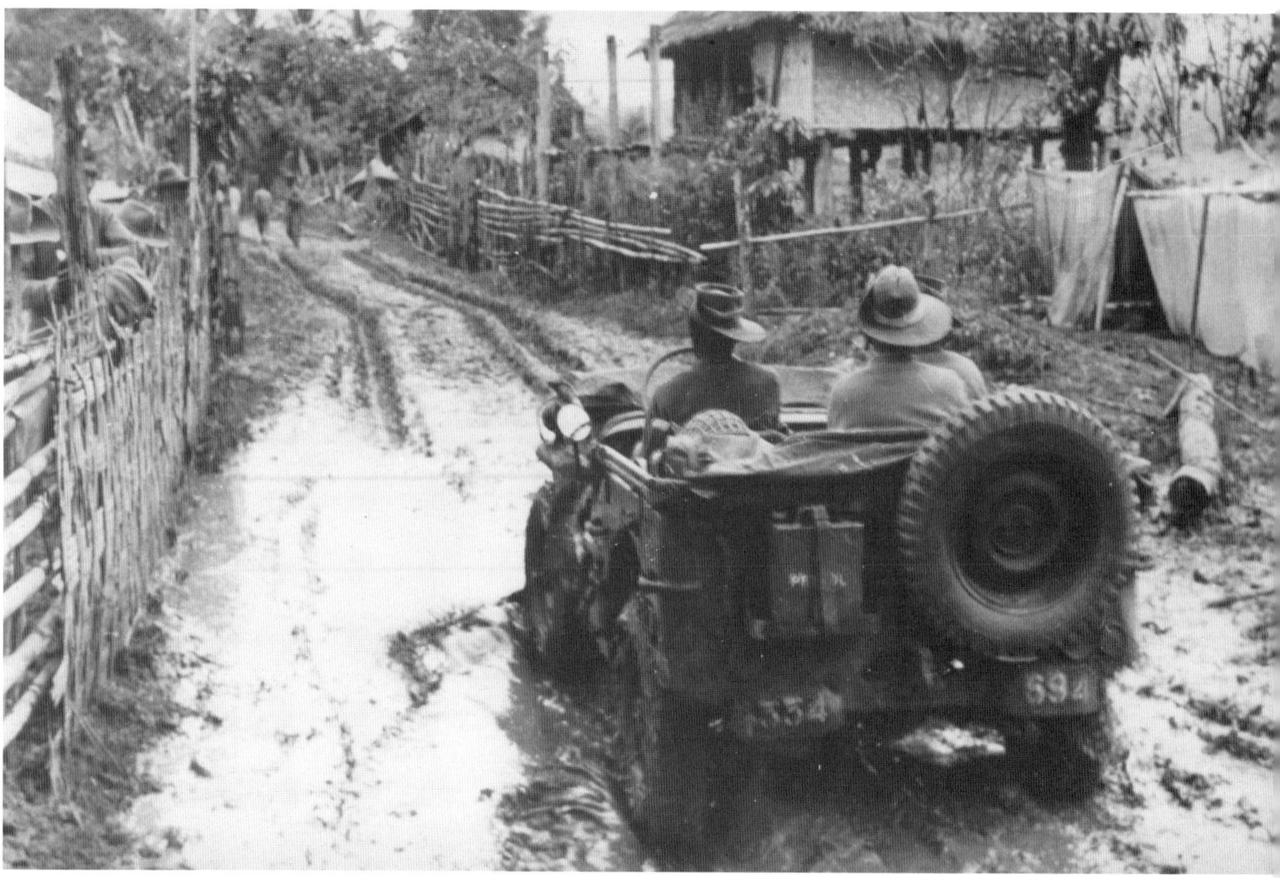
694

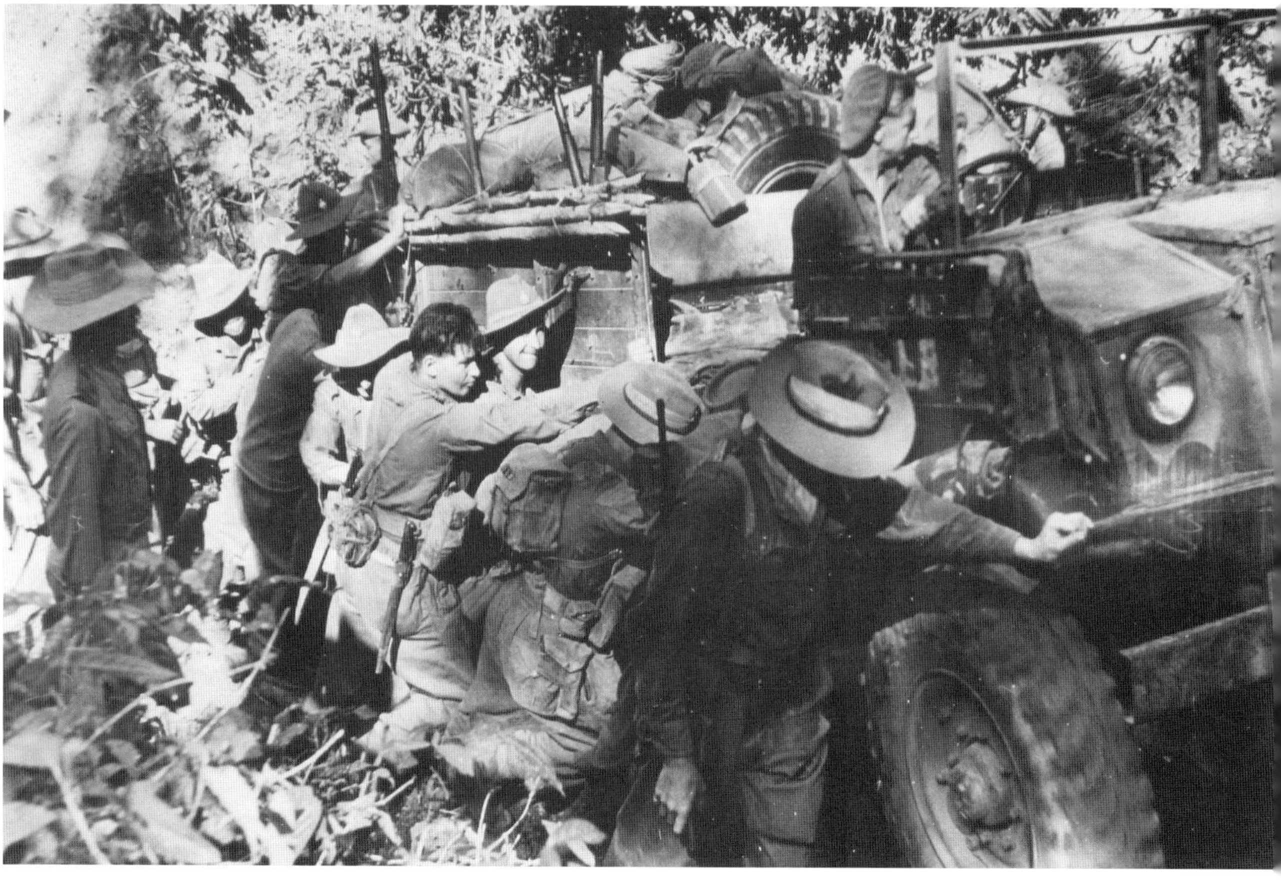

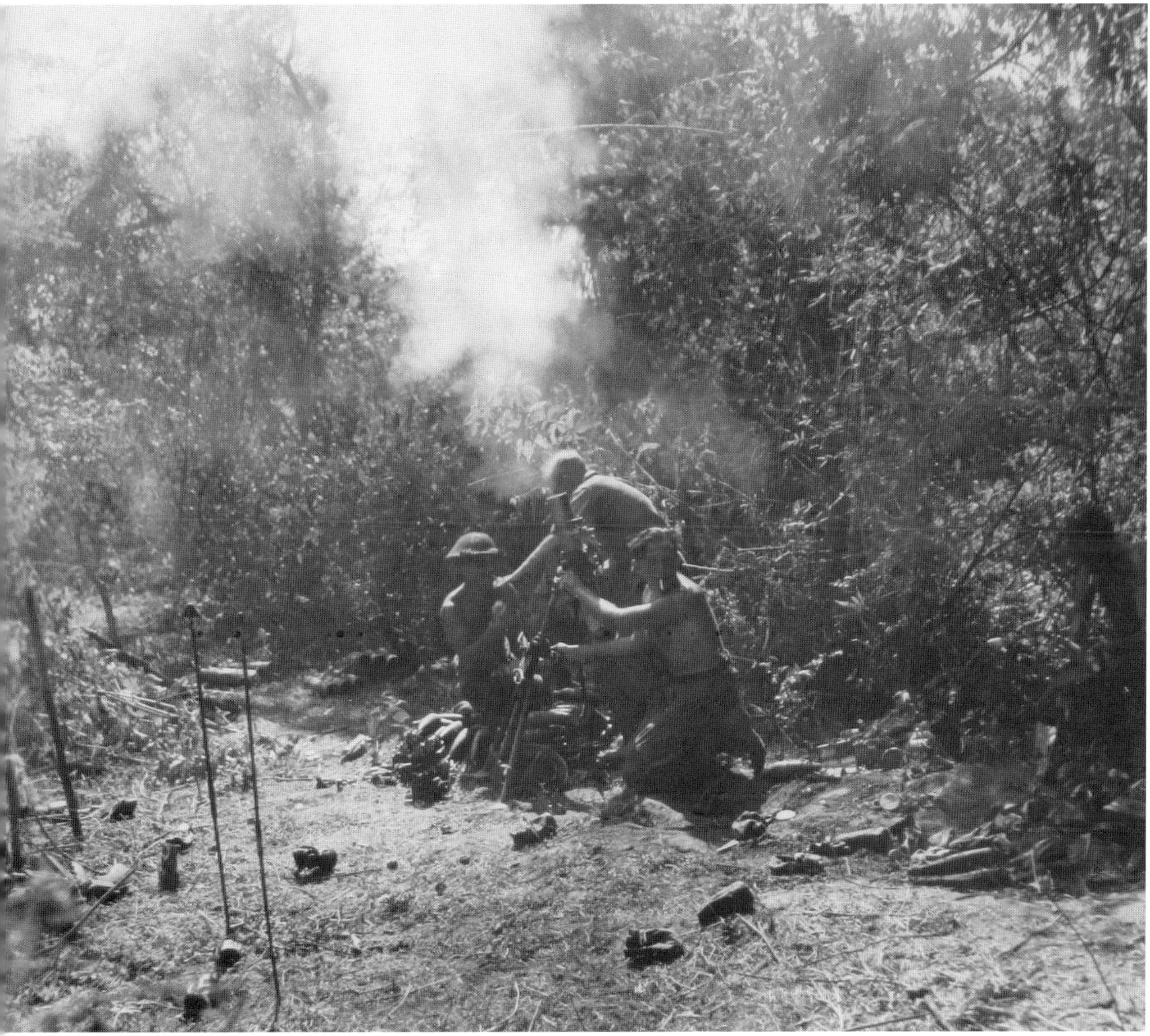

(**Opposite, above**) A British 36th Division jeep moves over a Burmese village mud track on the road to Yanbe during an advance amid a short monsoon. The 36th British Division, part of the NCAC, moved towards Myitsone and the lower Shweli River area during the early winter of 1945. The division attacked Mongmit south of the river before its Mandalay advance from the north-east. *(NARA)*

(**Opposite, below**) British 36th Division troops manhandle a supply truck uphill through jungle mud during a short monsoon south-east of Katha during the advance to the Shweli River in the winter of 1945. Two years earlier, Wingate's Chindits used LRP methods to fight the Japanese in this same area before a withdrawal was ordered because aerial resupply ended for Operation LONGCLOTH's troops. *(NARA)*

(**Above**) A 3in mortar crew from the 36th British Division's 26th Infantry Brigade lays down a barrage for the Shweli River crossing on 1 February 1945. It was initially unsuccessful due to elements of the IJA 18th and 56th divisions defending the far banks. *(NARA)*

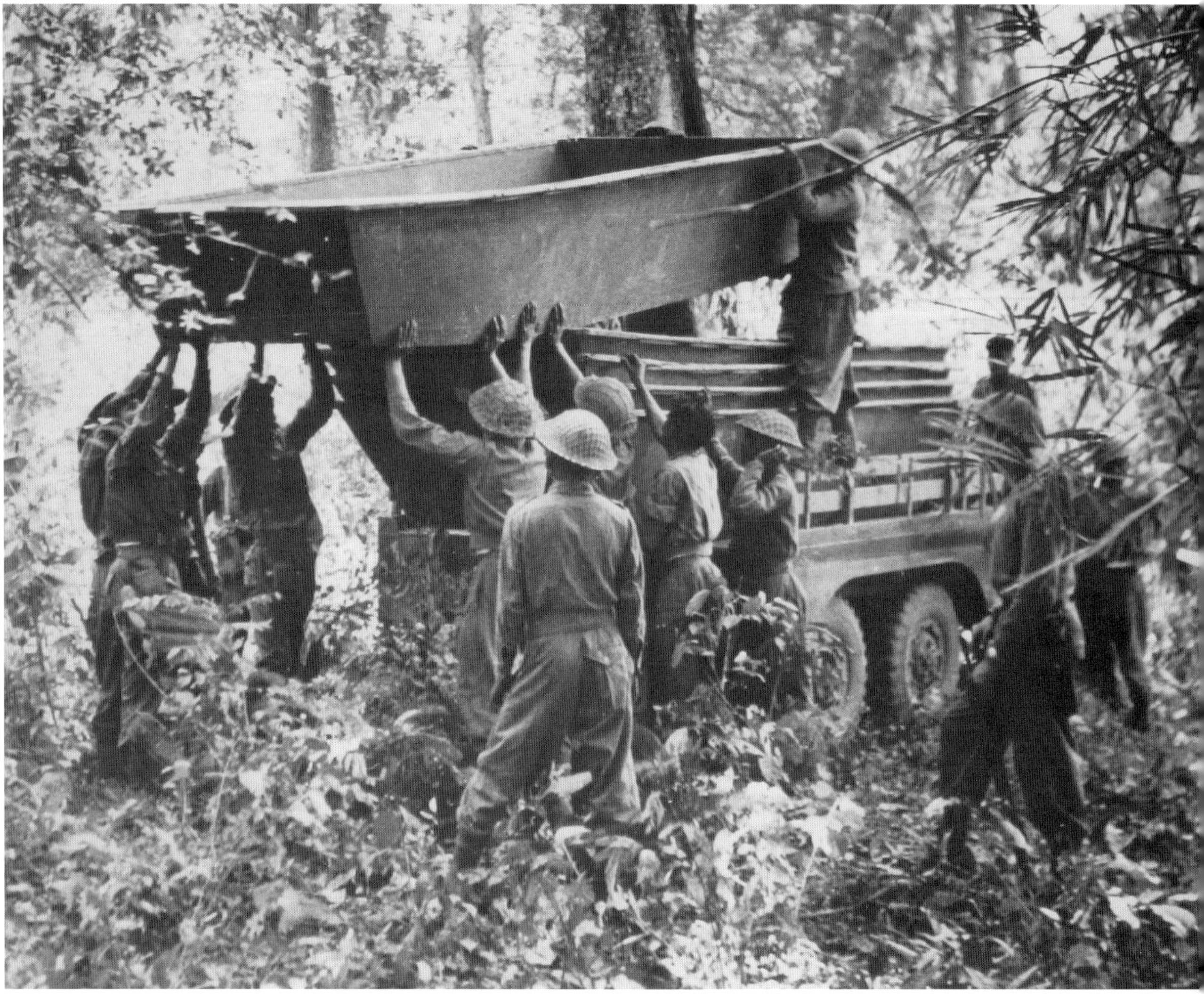

(**Above**) Metal assault boats are unloaded by the 36th British Division's 26th Infantry Brigade's Indian troops for the contested Shweli River crossing near Myitsone in late February 1945. The 26th Infantry Brigade fielded the 1/9th Hyderabad Regiment and the 2/8th Punjabi Regiment. The Japanese contested the river crossing, fearing that the 36th British Division once across would be able to move south-west to Mandalay and threaten the LOC of the IJA 15th and 53rd divisions situated there along the Irrawaddy River. *(NARA)*

(**Opposite, above**) Troops of the 25th Indian Division march on Akyab Island off the Arakan coast uncontested on 3 January 1945. A day earlier, an artillery air observation officer landed on the island and was informed that the Japanese had left. Orders were immediately issued for the 25th Indian Division and the 3 Commando Brigade to land without any prior bombardment. Akyab town was occupied on 4 January and the anchorages were clear. Airfield repair commenced and a squadron of Spitfires operated from it a few days later in time to repel the first Japanese air attack on the recaptured Allied airstrip. *(NARA)*

(**Opposite, below**) Troops of XV Corps' 26th Indian Division prod Japanese corpses during the Third Arakan Campaign of mid-October 1944 on a line of Godusara-Ngakyedauk-Taung and Goppe Bazars. When the bulk of the IJA 55th Division withdrew, XV Corps prepared to clear the Japanese out of north Arakan, including Akyab Island, by the end of January 1945. *(NARA)*

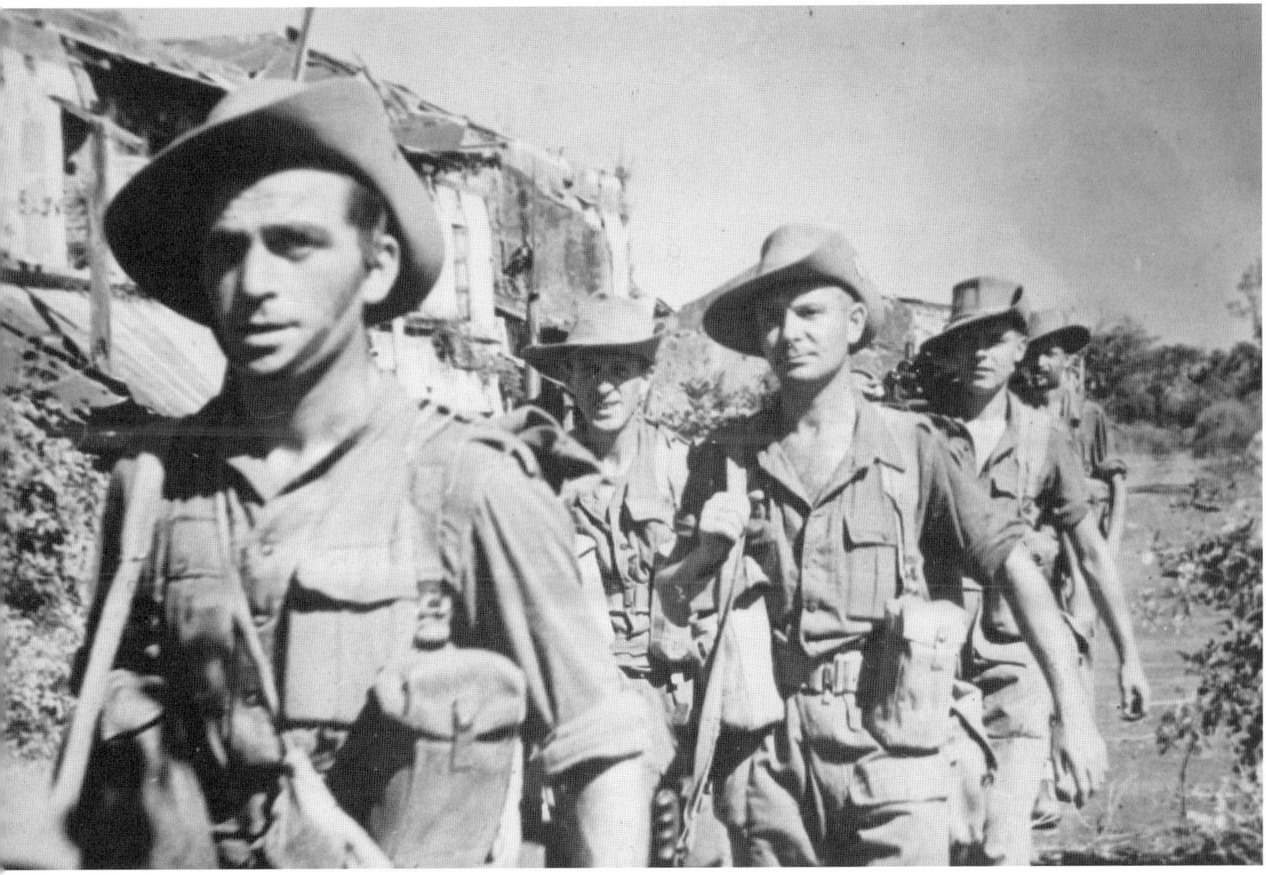

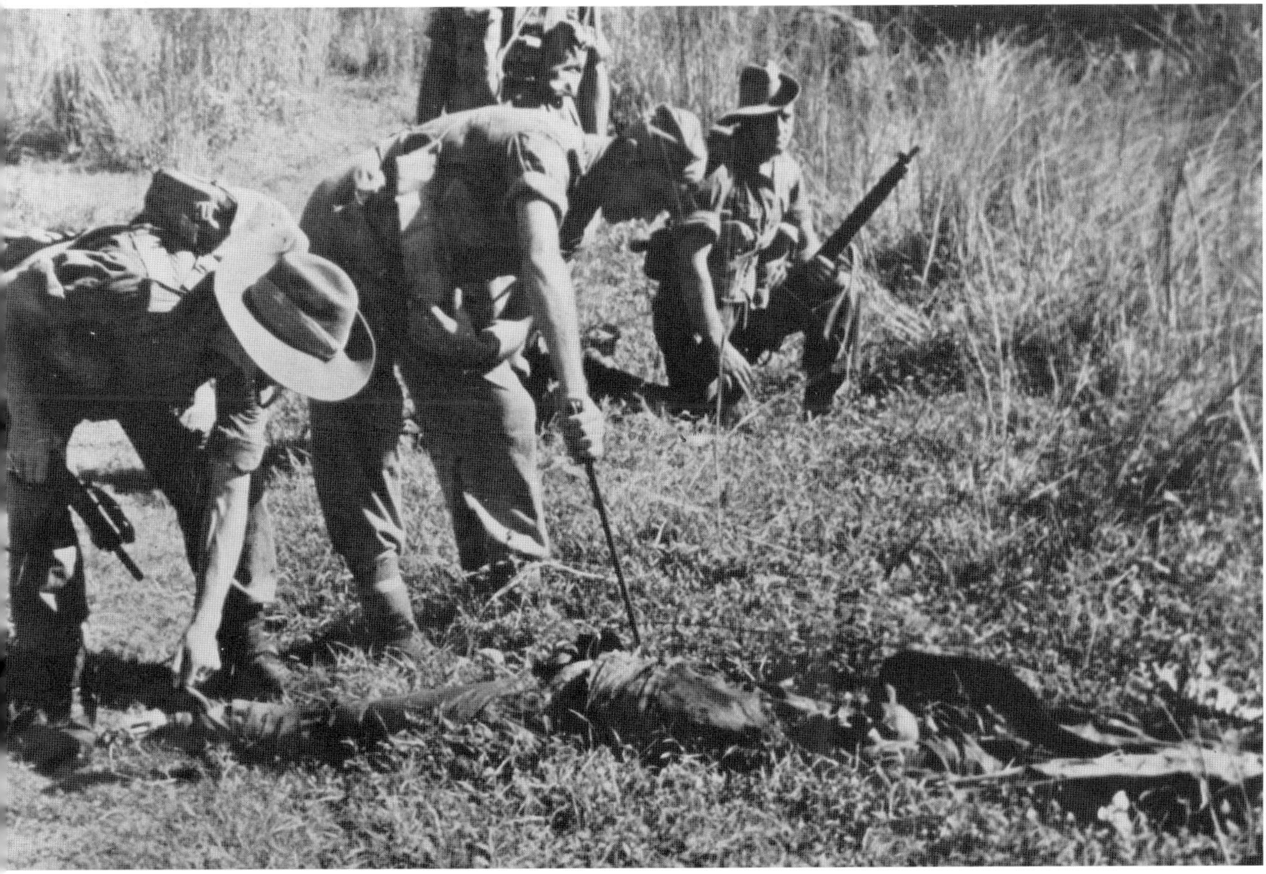

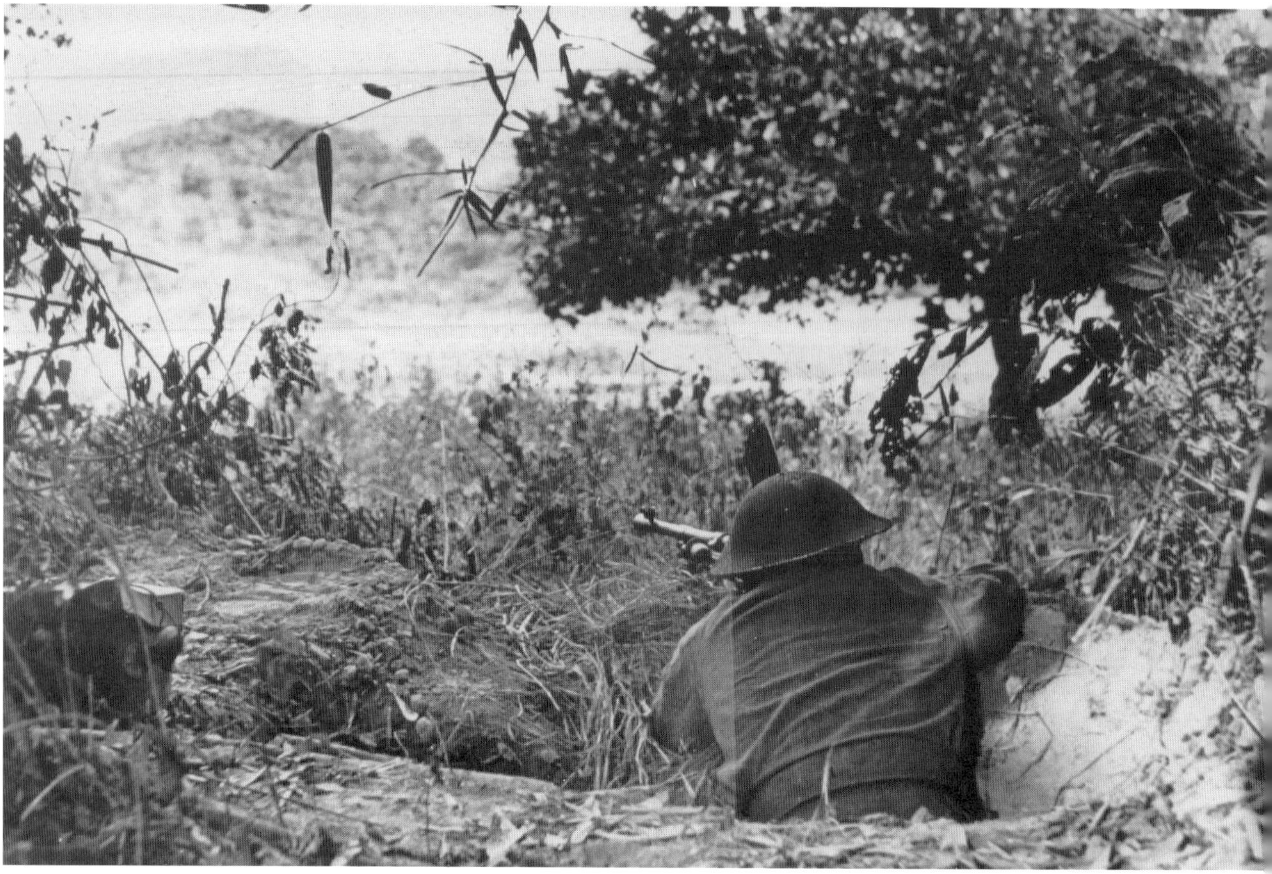

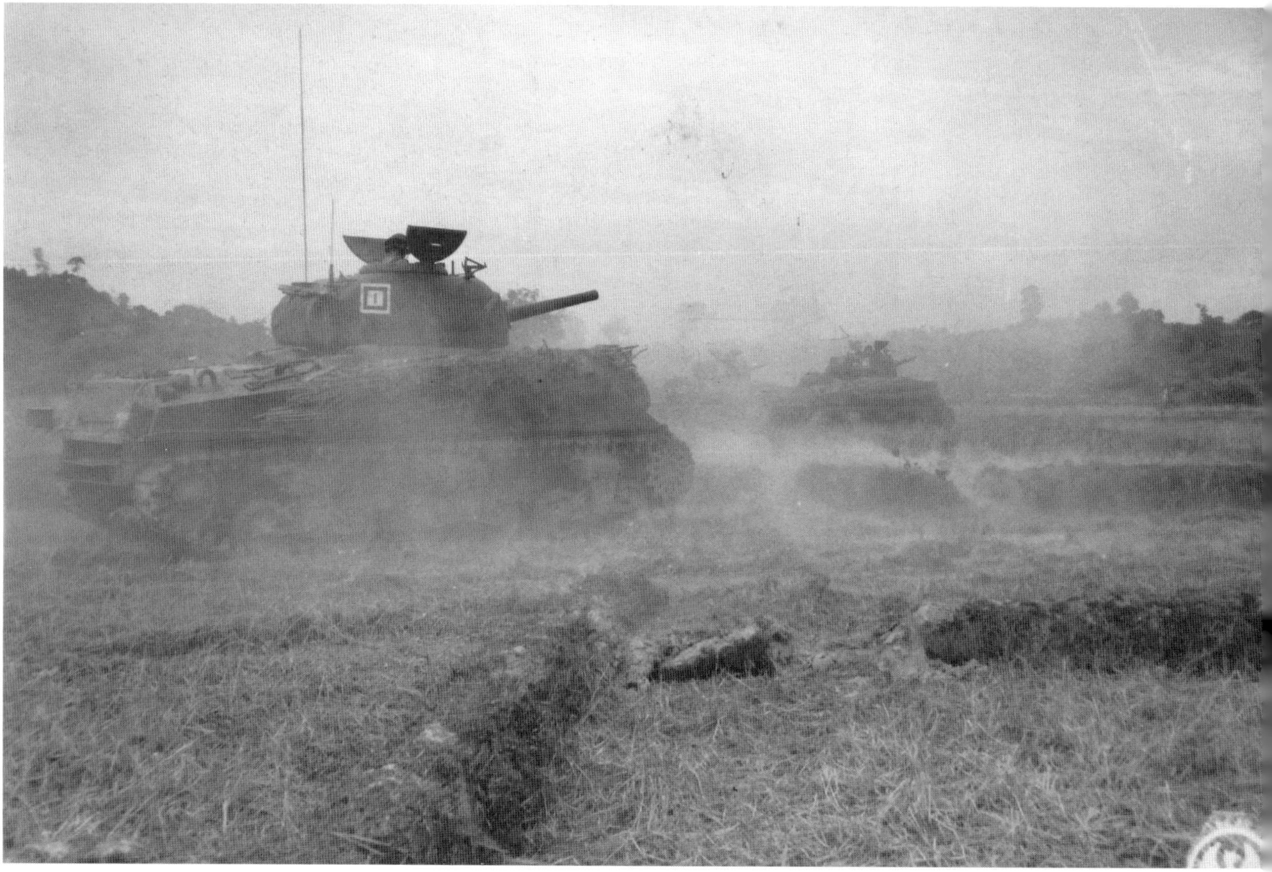

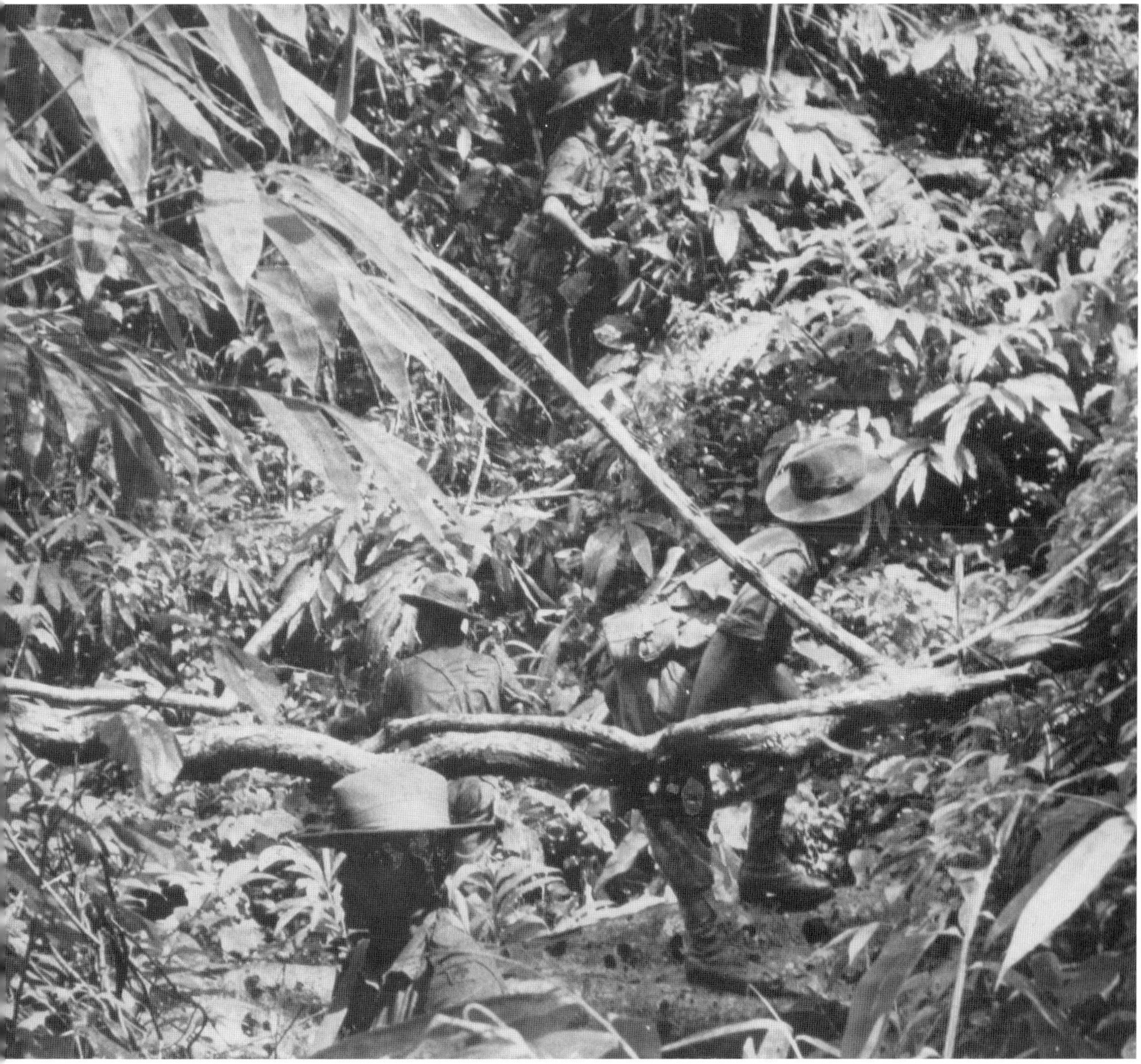

(**Opposite, above**) A XV Corps 25th Indian Division Bren-gunner fires his LMG near Maungdaw on the north Arakan coast's Mayu Range in December 1944. This division moved down the west bank of the Mayu River starting on 11 December and then closed in on 'Foul Point', north of Akyab Island, to eliminate Japanese forces on the Mayu Peninsula. *(NARA)*

(**Above**) A Royal 1/18th Garhwal Rifles' section of the 25th Indian Division's 53rd Infantry Brigade patrols the Arakan jungle in December 1944. On 31 December, this XV Corps Brigade crossed the Mayu River and without opposition occupied Rathedaung on the eastern bank and Kudaung Island to the south. *(NARA)*

(**Opposite, below**) B Squadron's M4 medium tanks of King George V's Own 19th Lancers, a XV Corps armoured reconnaissance regiment attached to the 25th Indian Division shells Japanese positions in the hills on the approach to Kangaw on 28 January 1945. The tanks were supporting troops from the 51st Infantry Brigade's assault. *(NARA)*

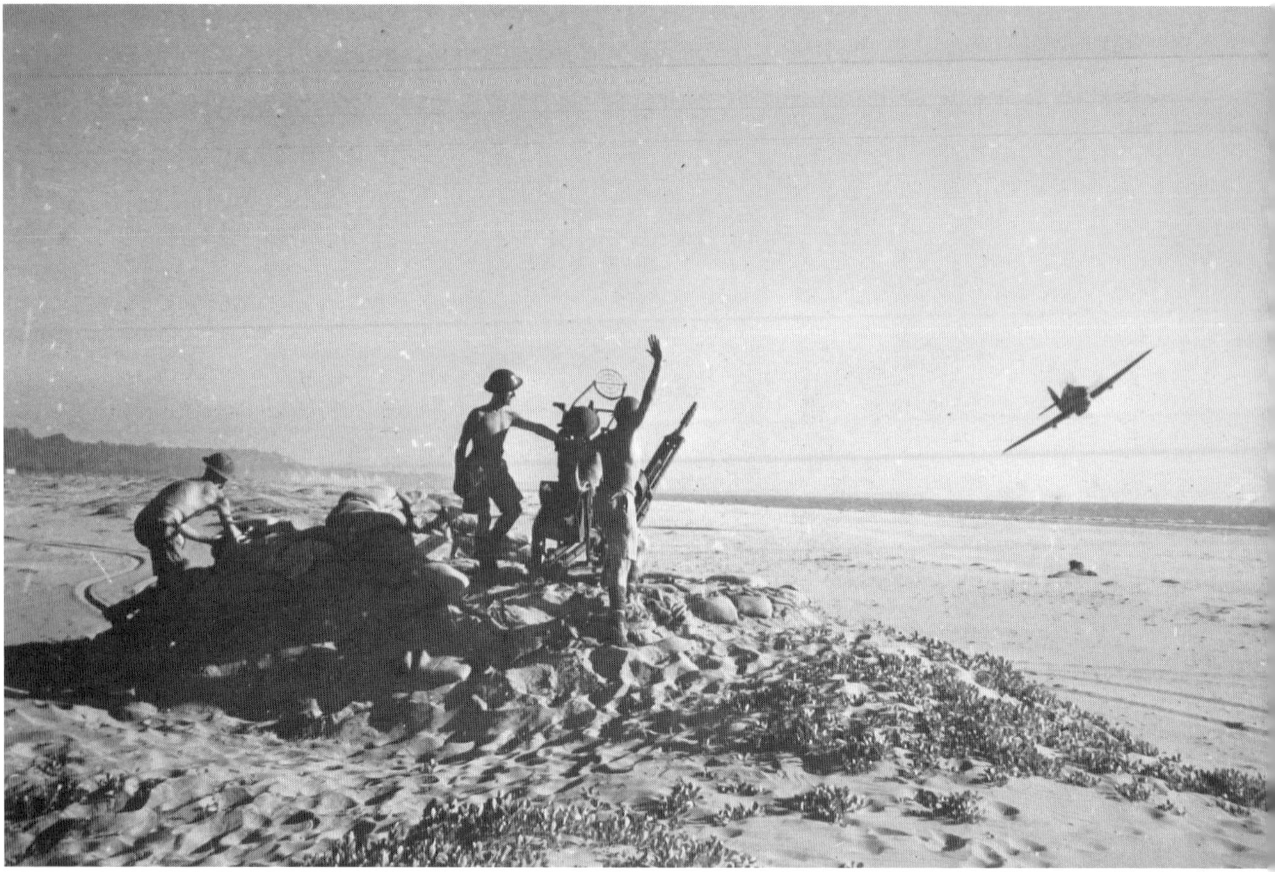

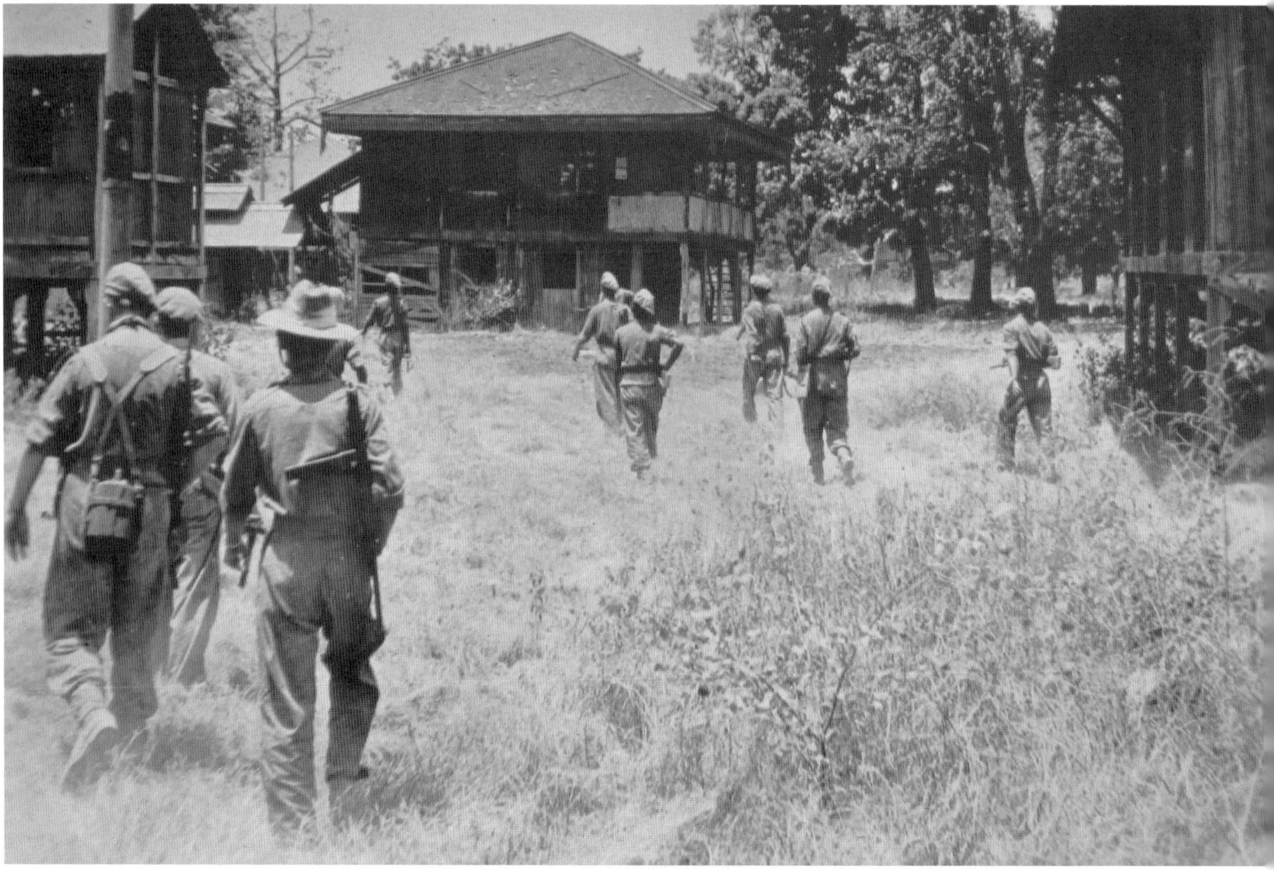

(**Opposite, above**) An RAF Regiment Light AA Squadron's gun crew waves to an RAF Hurricane on arid terrain in the Arakan in January 1945. Following its formation in early 1942, the RAF Regiment provided a specialist ground force for the active defence of airfields which were essential for the provision of fighter and bomber support as well as air supply supporting Slim's Fourteenth Army amid Burma's remote jungles and swamps. The defence of RAF airfields was pivotal during the crucial battle at Imphal and the nighttime defence and daytime clearance from the prolonged Japanese counterattacks at Meiktila Airfield as well as across the dry plains of Burma. (*NARA*)

(**Opposite, below**) A 7th Rajput Regiment patrol of the 26th Indian Division's 4th Infantry Brigade enters Taungup to the south-east of Ramree Island in the Bay of Bengal, a major enemy position on the south Arakan coast. On 9 March 1945, the 26th Division was to cut the coastal north-to-south-running Tamandu-Taungup road to prevent an eastward withdrawal of IJA troops from Taungup to the Irrawaddy River. By the end of March, the 4th Infantry Brigade was 4 miles from the Taungup *chaung* to the village's east. (*NARA*)

(**Above**) A Fourteenth Army seaborne raiding party is ferried in a coastal vessel off the Arakan in early winter 1945. On 14 January, British HQ ordered the 26th Indian Division to assault Ramree Island on 21 January and a Royal Marine detachment to occupy Cheduba Island, just to the south-west in the Bay of Bengal. A separate assault on Kangaw on the Arakan coast by elements of the 25th Indian Division and 3 Commando Brigade, after the capture of Akyab Island, was to prevent IJA 28th Army units from withdrawing east towards the Irrawaddy River from the Arakan. (*NARA*)

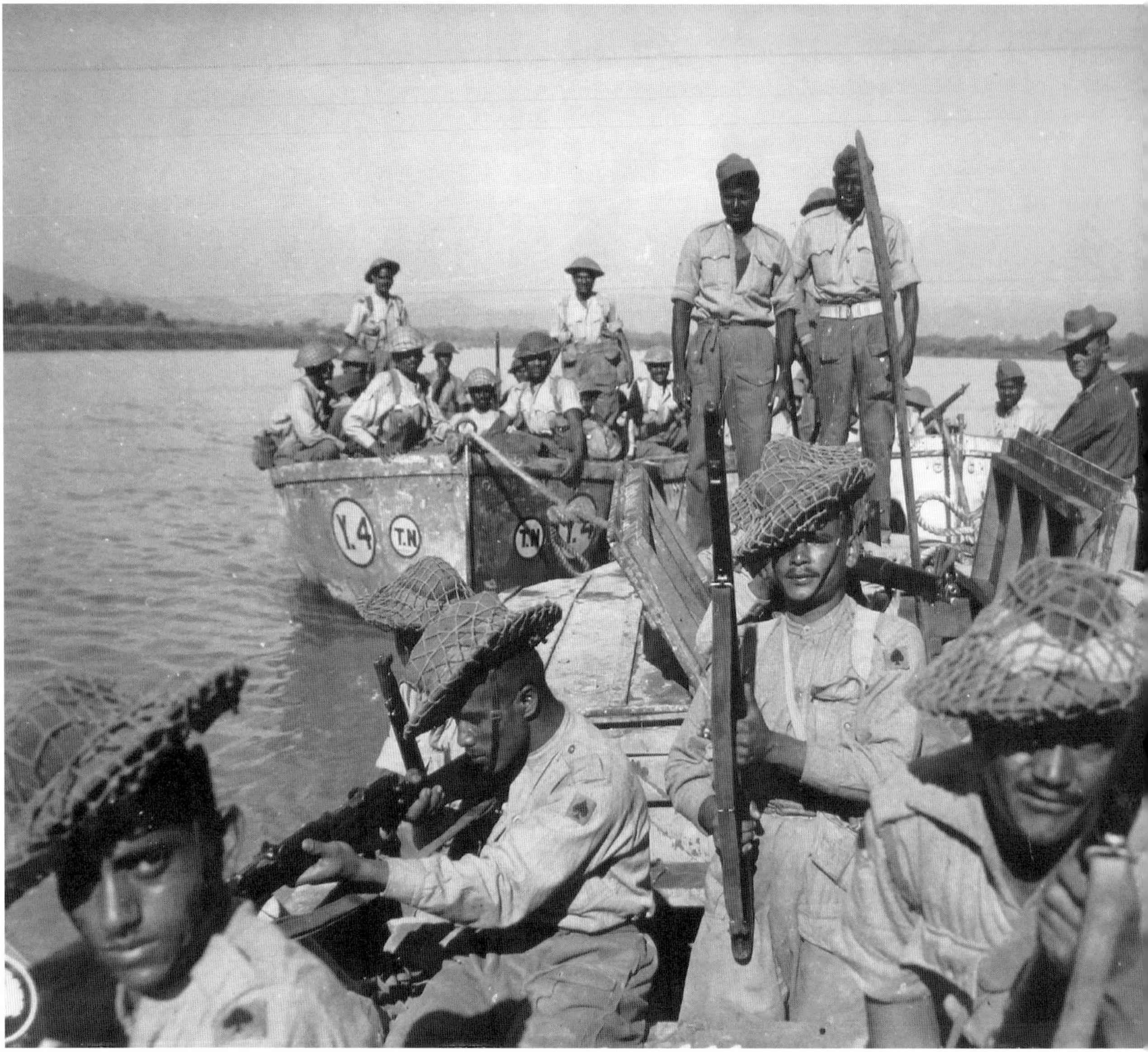

(**Above**) Troops of the 1/18th Royal Garhwal Rifles from the 26th Indian Division's 71st Infantry Brigade are transported southwards down the Kalapanzin River, which flows through Goppe Bazar and Taung Bazar on the eastern side of the Mayu Range in the northern Arakan, in assault boats on 24 December 1944. *(NARA)*

(**Opposite, above**) Troops from the 26th Indian Division's 71st Infantry Brigade march onto Cheduba Island to relieve Royal Marines sitting nearby after having assaulted Cheduba Island, south of Ramree Island in the Bay of Bengal, on 26 January 1945. The enemy had deserted Cheduba Island and the 71st Infantry Brigade moved to Ramree Island to join other 26th Indian Division units in sharper conflict with IJA troops. *(NARA)*

(**Opposite, below**) Two 25th Indian Division infantrymen search a deserted Japanese bunker on Akyab Island in January 1945. After the island's capture, the airfield was restored for RAF Spitfires to sortie over the Arakan. *(NARA)*

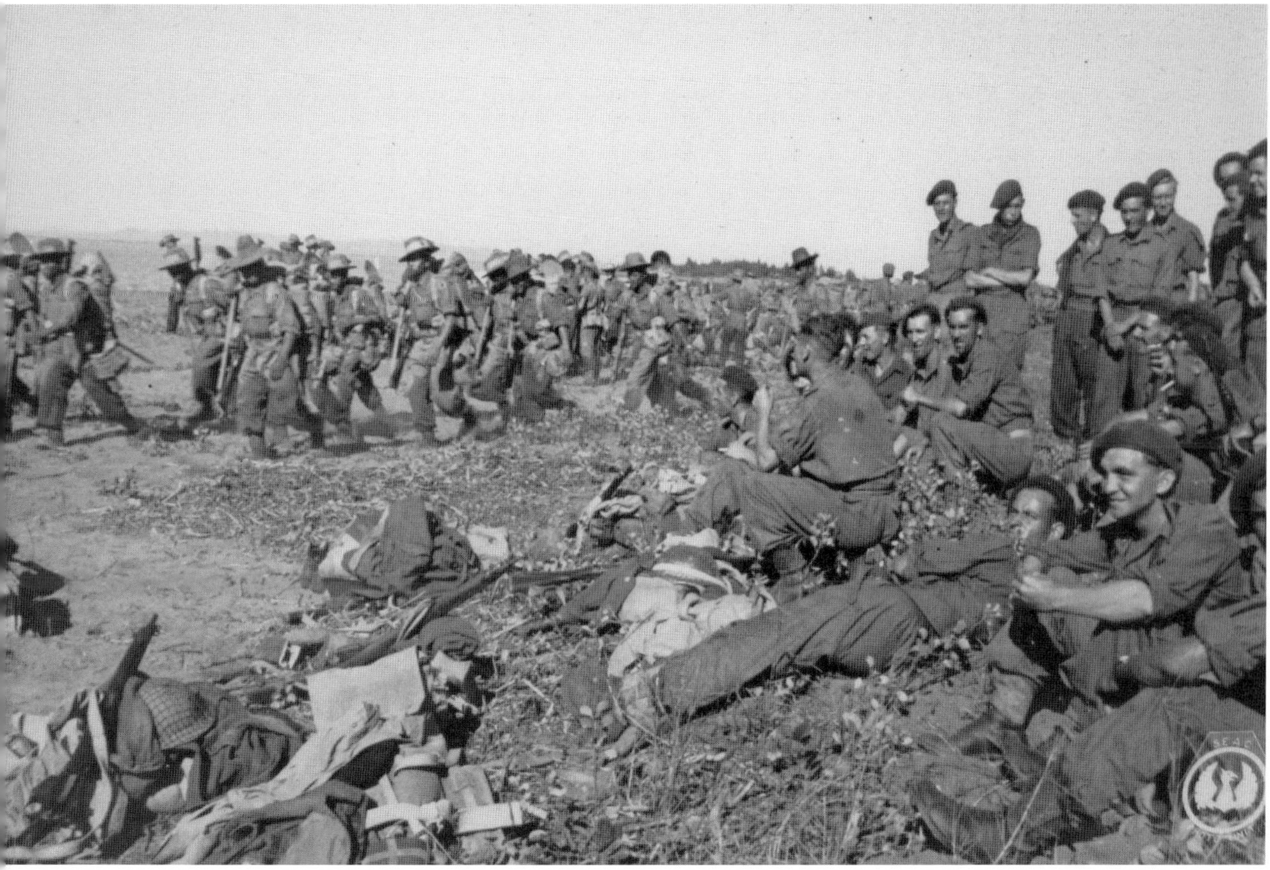

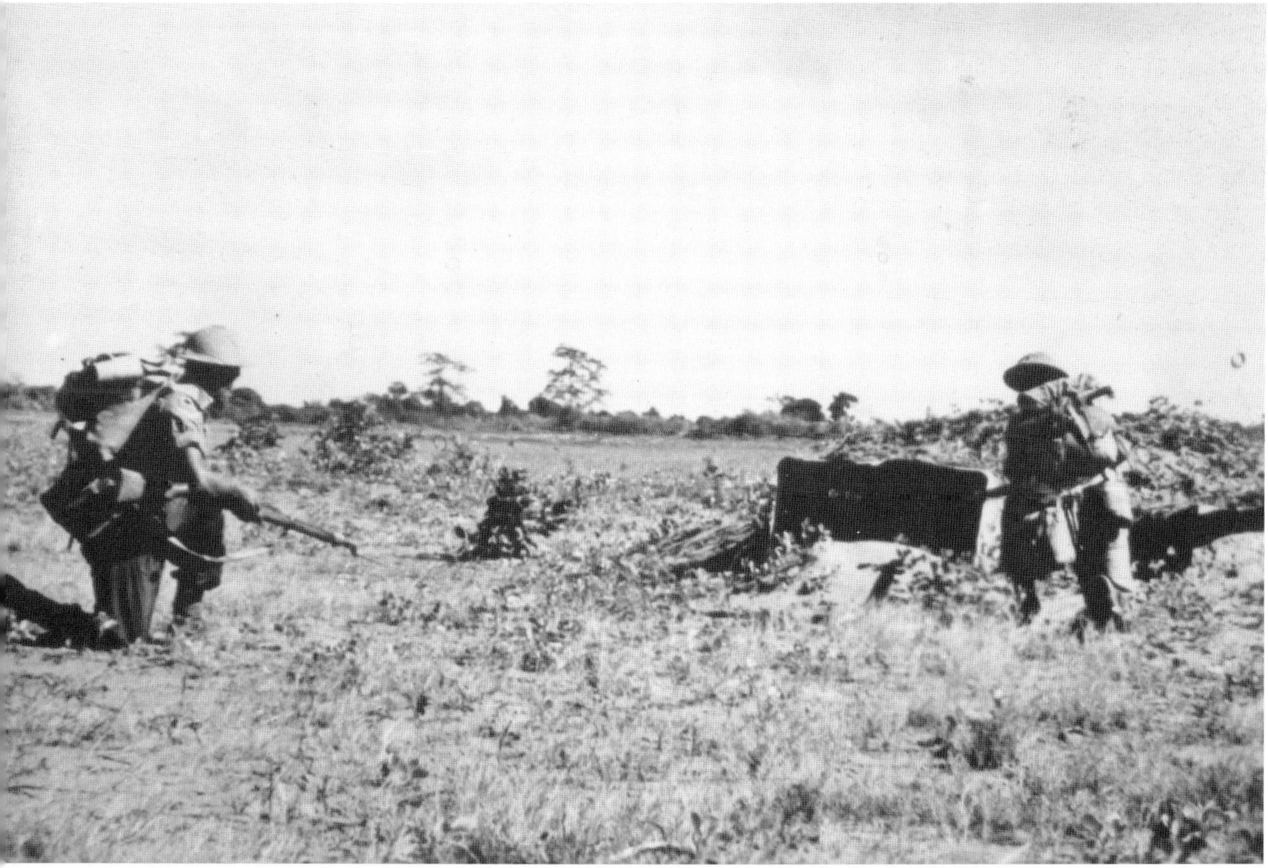

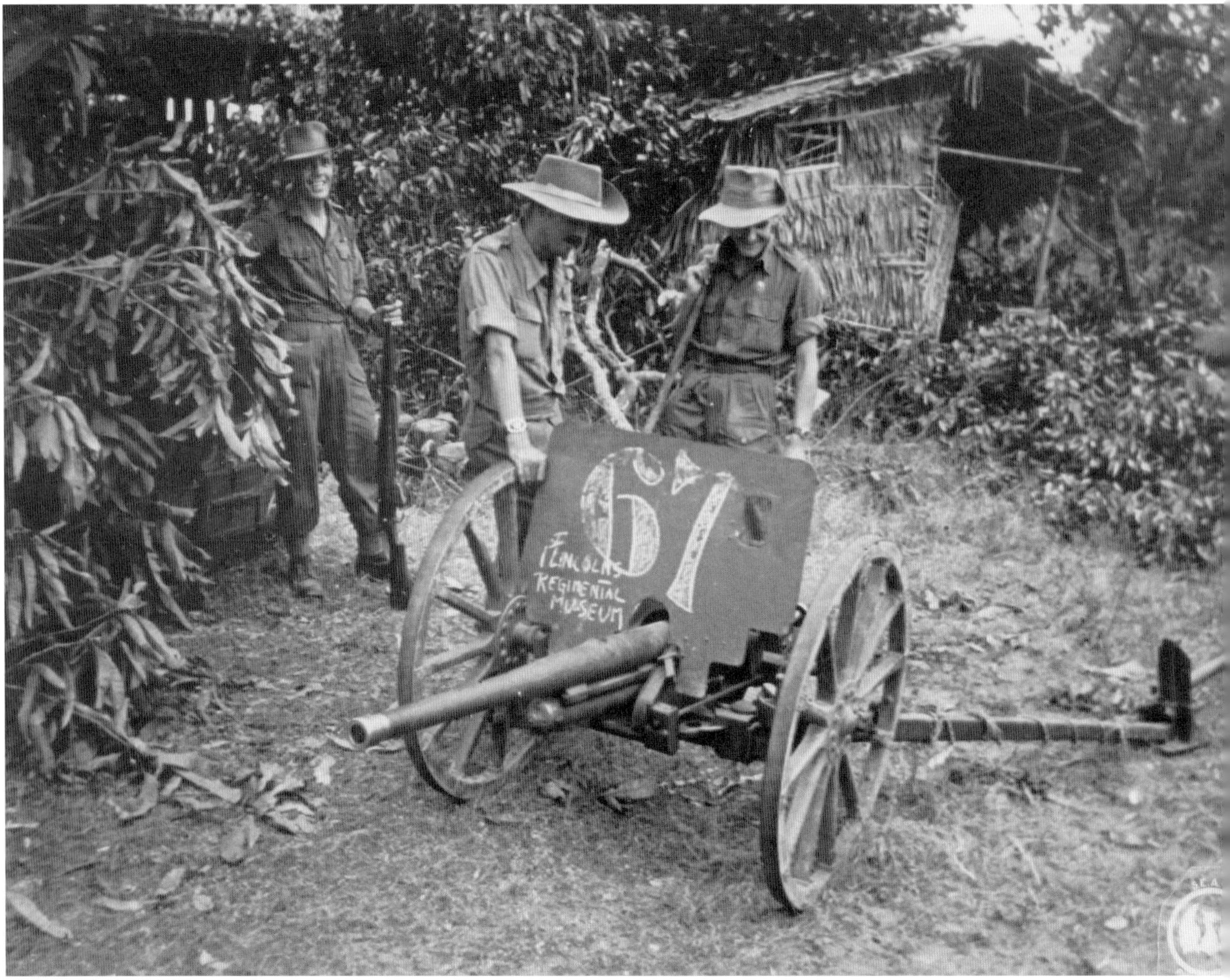
67
LINCOLNS
REGIMENTAL
MUSEUM

(**Above**) Three Lincolnshire Regiment infantrymen from the 26th Indian Division's 71st Infantry Brigade inspect an abandoned Japanese 37mm gun on Ramree Island's west side off the southern Arakan coast on 25 February 1945. On 14 January, the 26th Division was ordered to assault Ramree Island a week later. On 23 January, the 71st Infantry Brigade moved south along the island's west coast. By 31 January, the 71st Infantry Brigade encountered strong IJA resistance and moved north-east to Sane and then southwards to Ramree Town, which it reached on 7 February. IJA resistance on the island ceased on 17 February. *(NARA)*

(**Opposite, above**) An East African Division motor column manoeuvres slowly down the Kabaw Valley through post-monsoon muck en route to Kalemyo on the Indo-Burmese border. The East Africans joined the 5th Indian Division beyond Tiddim for the seizure of Kalemyo and Kalewa, the latter further east on the Chindwin River, in the autumn of 1944. An undamaged IJA airfield was captured at Taukkyan near Kalemyo on 13 November enabling C-47 air-landed supply of the 5th Indian Division. *(NARA)*

(**Opposite, below**) Infantrymen from the 11th East African Division's 21st, 25th and 26th Infantry brigades are ferried across the Chindwin River in late November 1944 to capture Kalewa. This division furnished the bridging equipment to construct a Bailey pontoon bridge across the Chindwin River in early December. In order to get the bridging materials to the forward areas, roads in the rear had to be repaired and demolished bridges fixed to carry the trucks forward. *(NARA)*

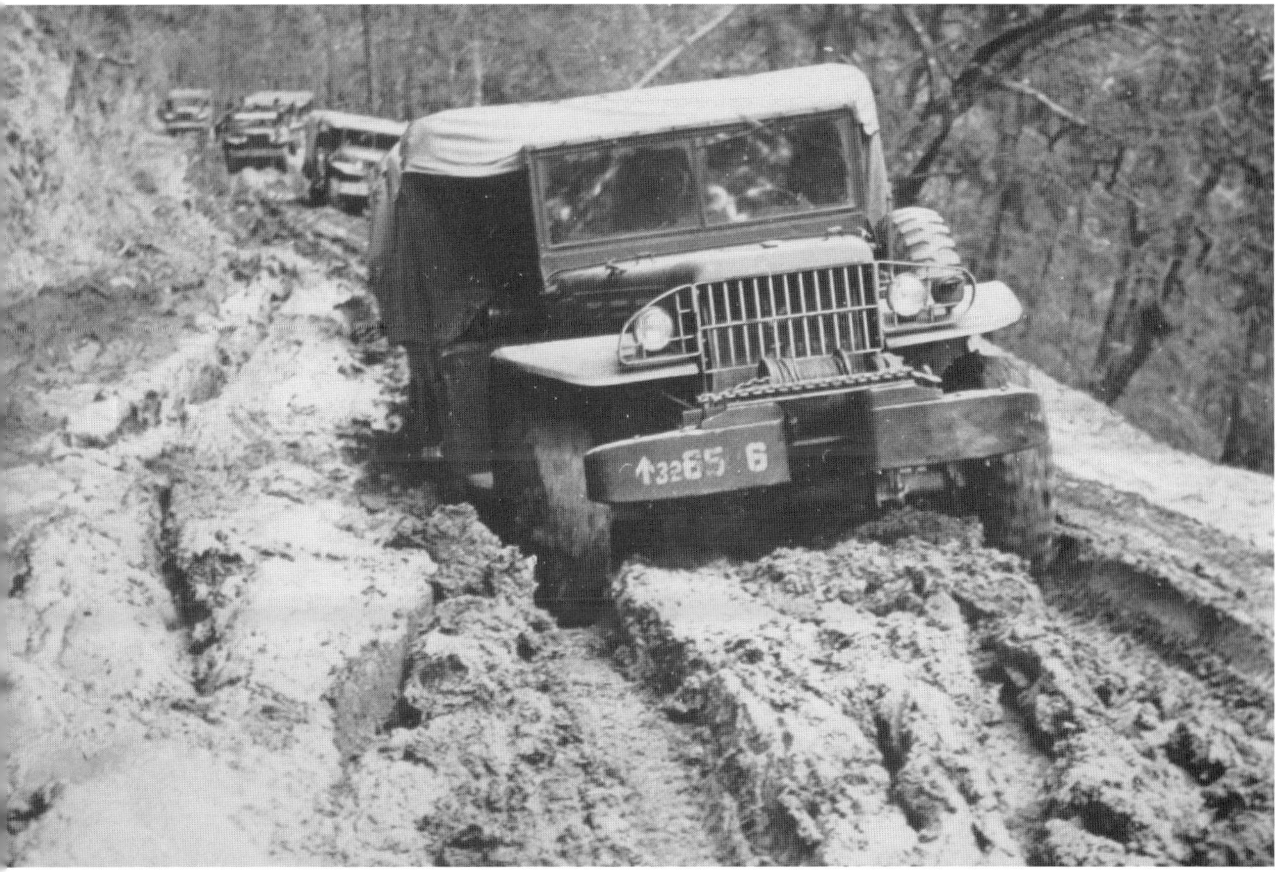
↑3265 6

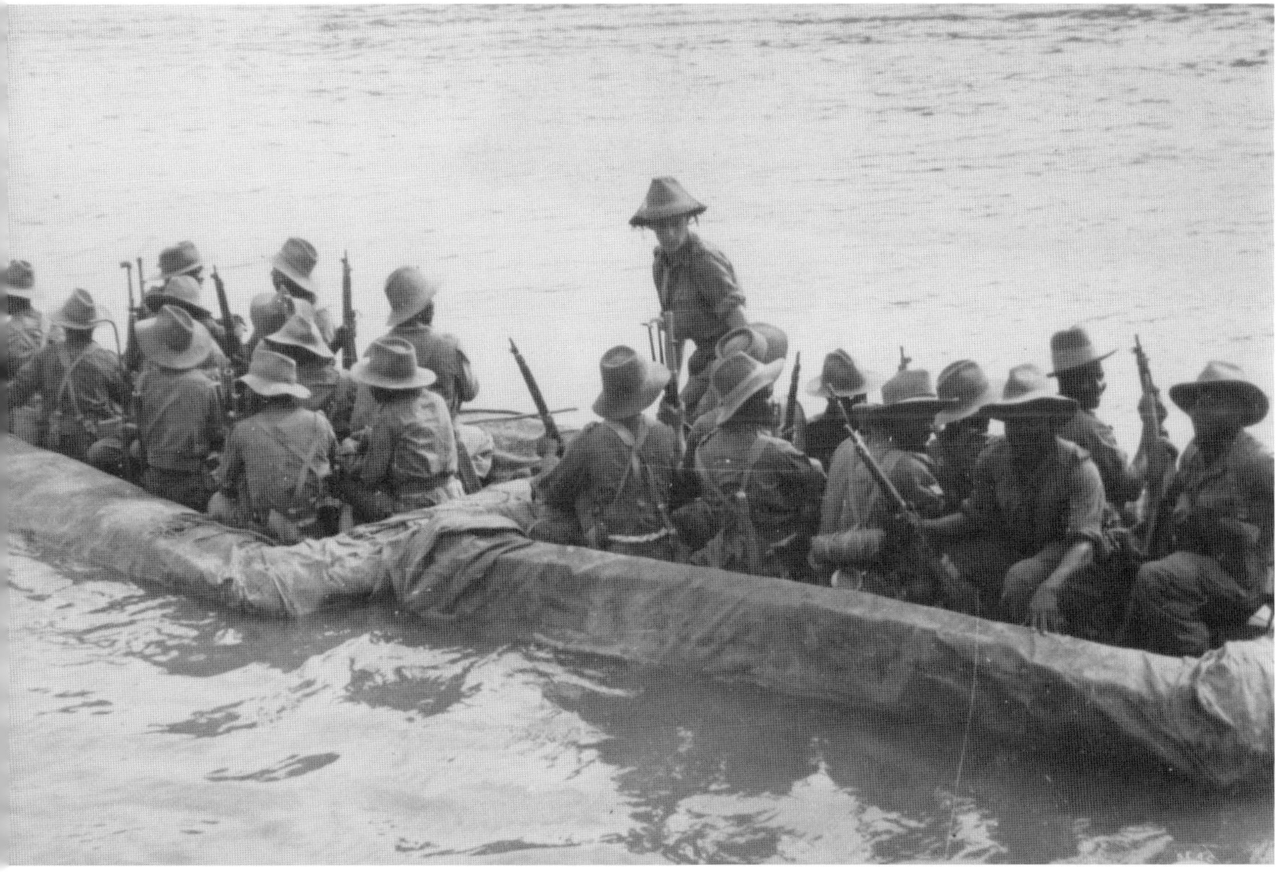

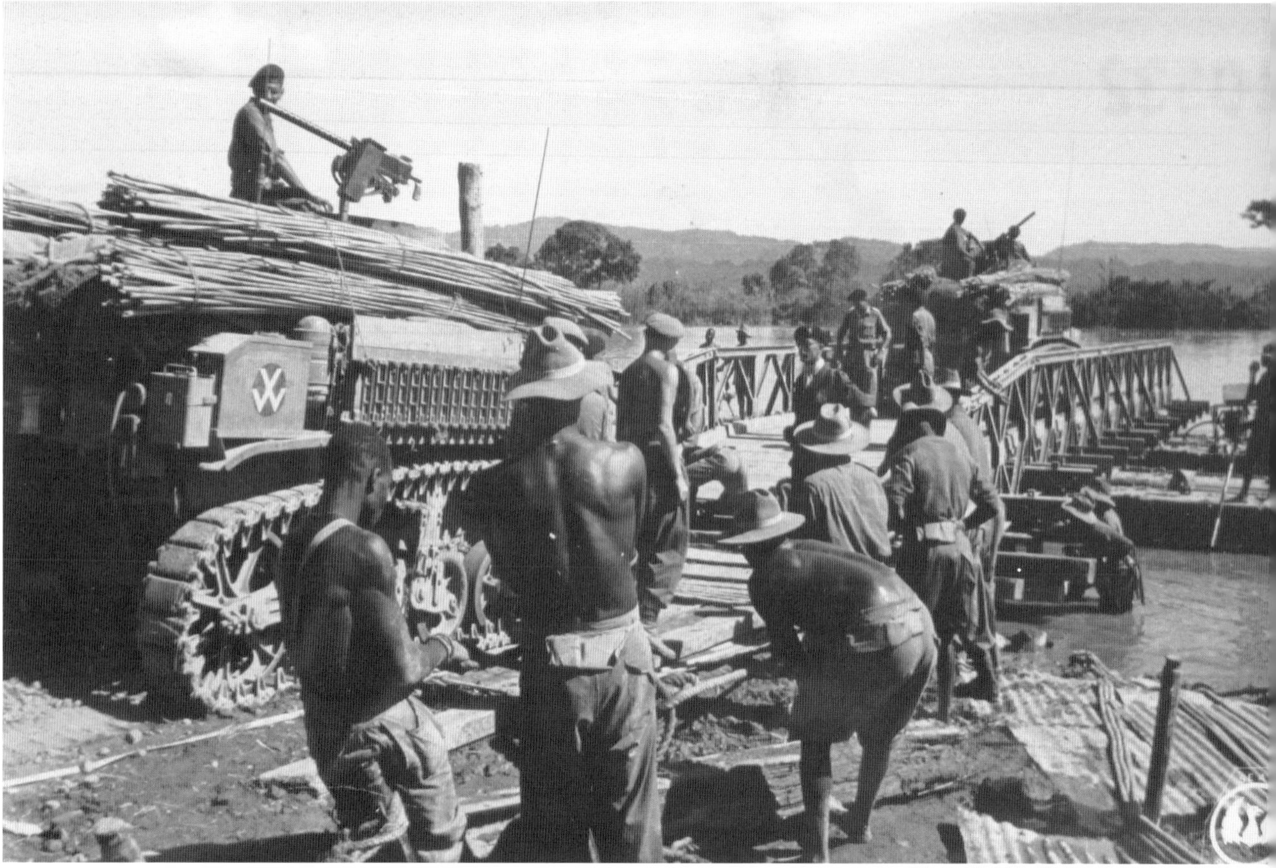

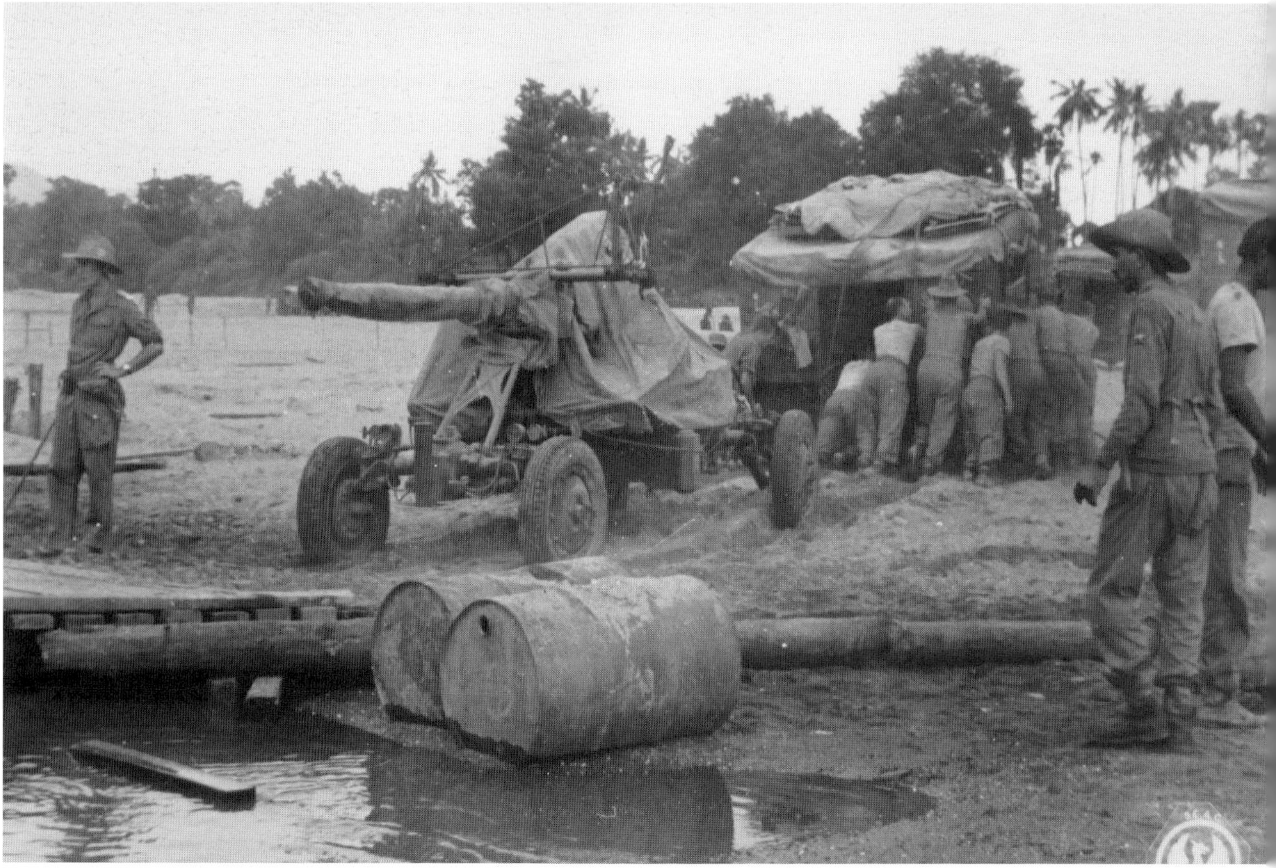

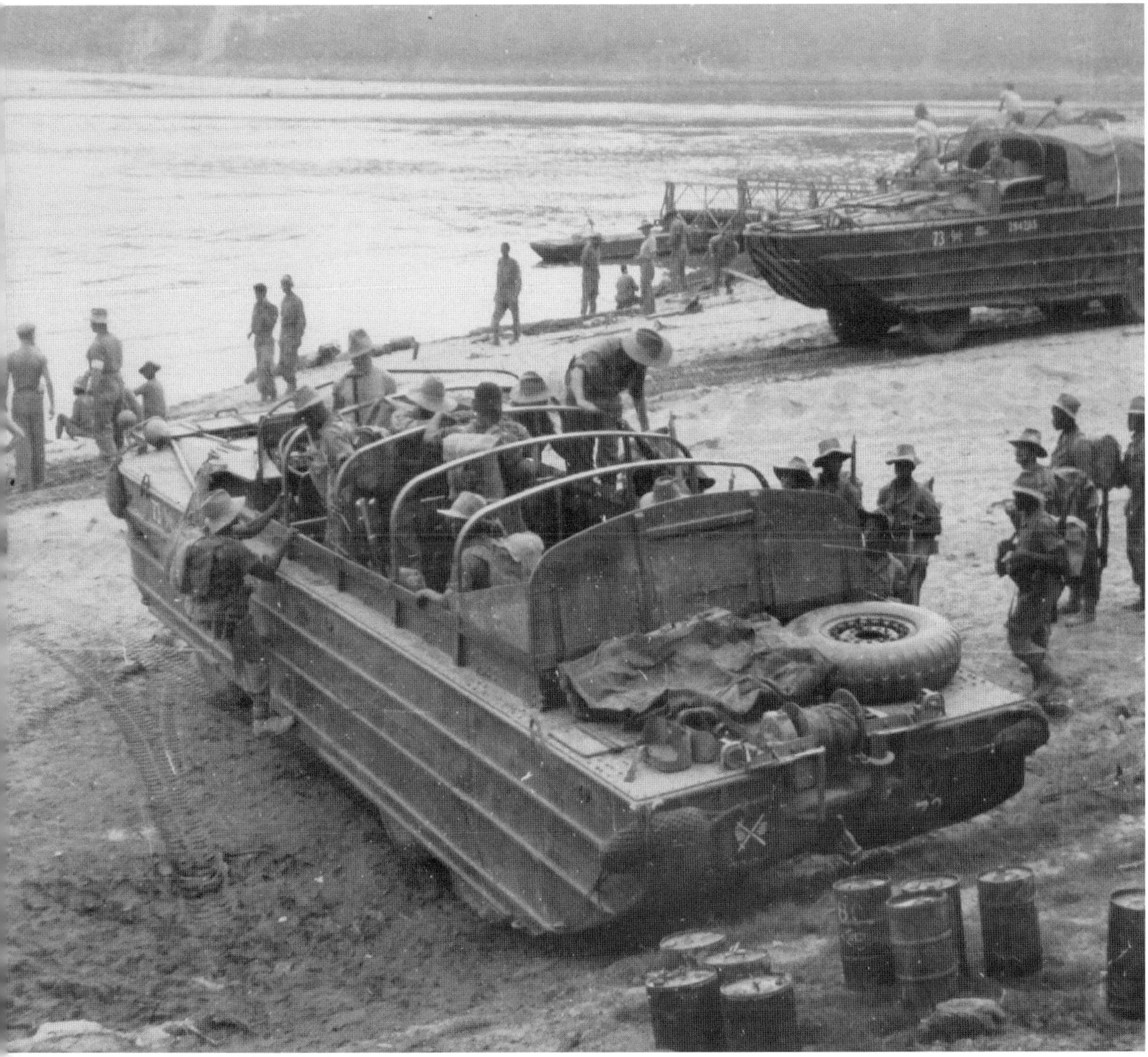

(**Opposite, above**) Two XV Corps armoured vehicles carrying fascines board a Bailey pontoon bridge ferry to cross the An River in February 1945 as the 82nd West African Division's 2nd Brigade moved south to prevent the Japanese from escaping across the Arakan's Myebon Peninsula eastward towards Kangaw. These pontoon bridge ferries were useful until sturdier Bailey bridges were erected. *(NARA)*

(**Above**) DUKWs transport infantrymen of the XV Corps' 11th East African Division across the Chindwin River towards Kalewa situated to the east of Tiddim and Kalemyo at the Indo-Burmese border. The DUKW entered service in 1942 as an amphibious modification of the American-made 2.5 ton truck carrying 5,000lb or twenty-four troops in water, across beaches and over inland terrain. *(NARA)*

(**Opposite, below**) XV Corps' troops push a Morris tractor towing a 40mm Bofors AA gun through soft sand on the eastern bank of the Chindwin River during the offensive on Kalewa in the autumn of 1944. *(NARA)*

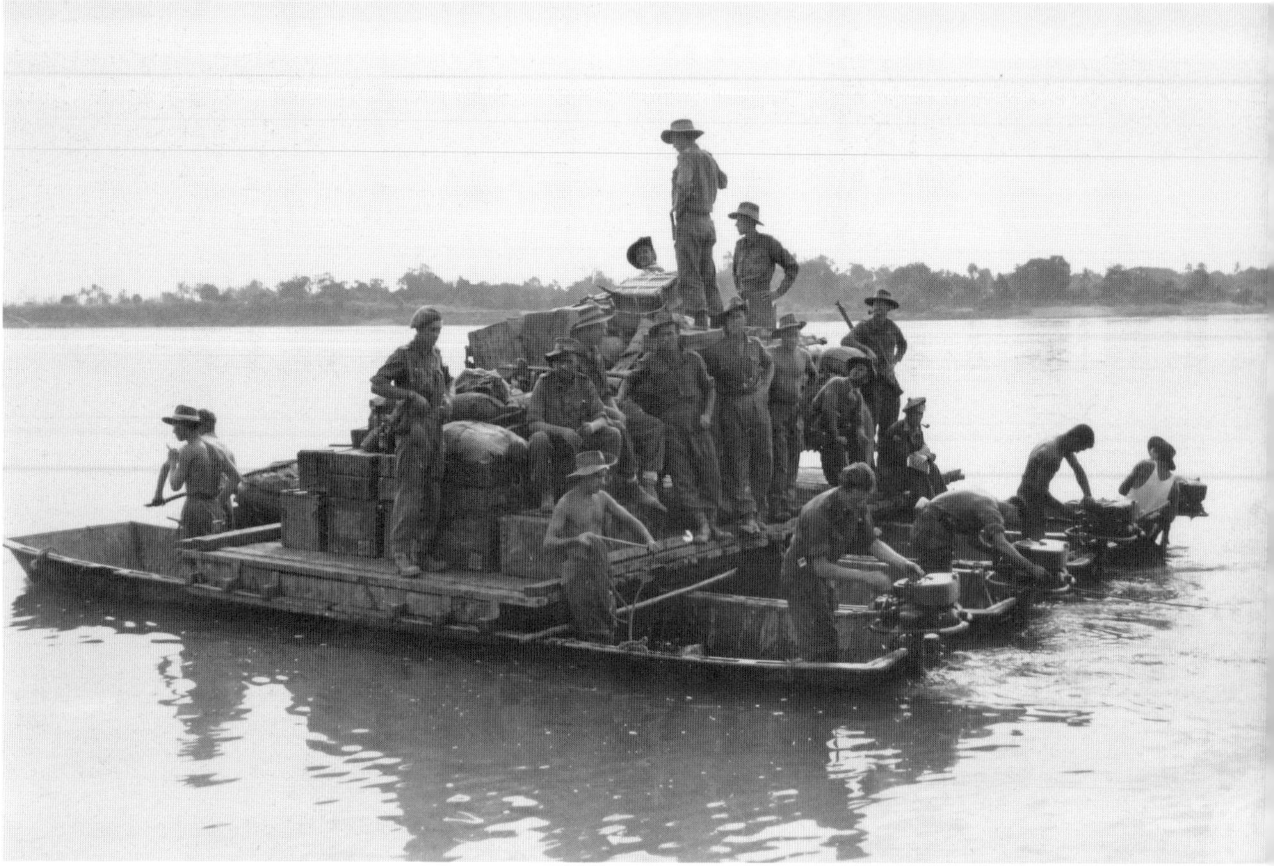

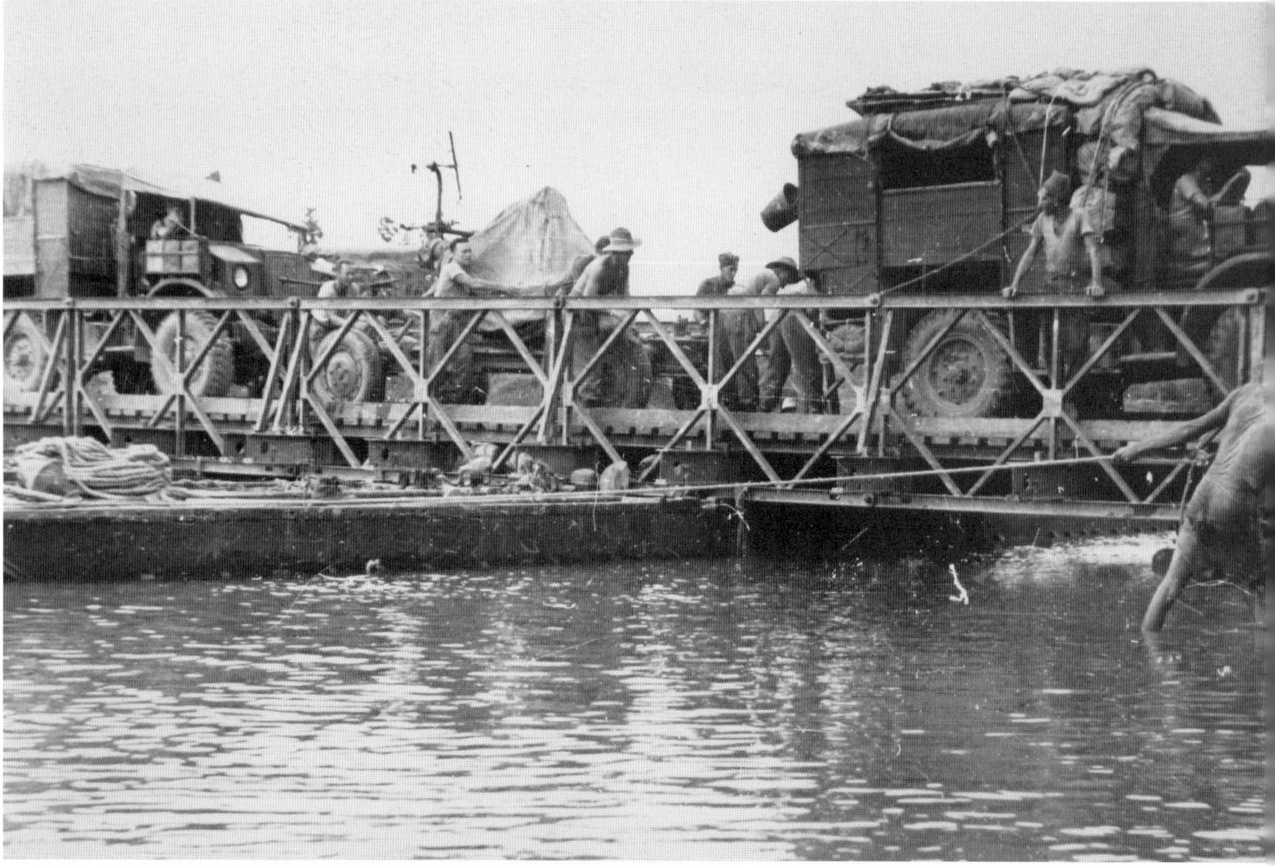

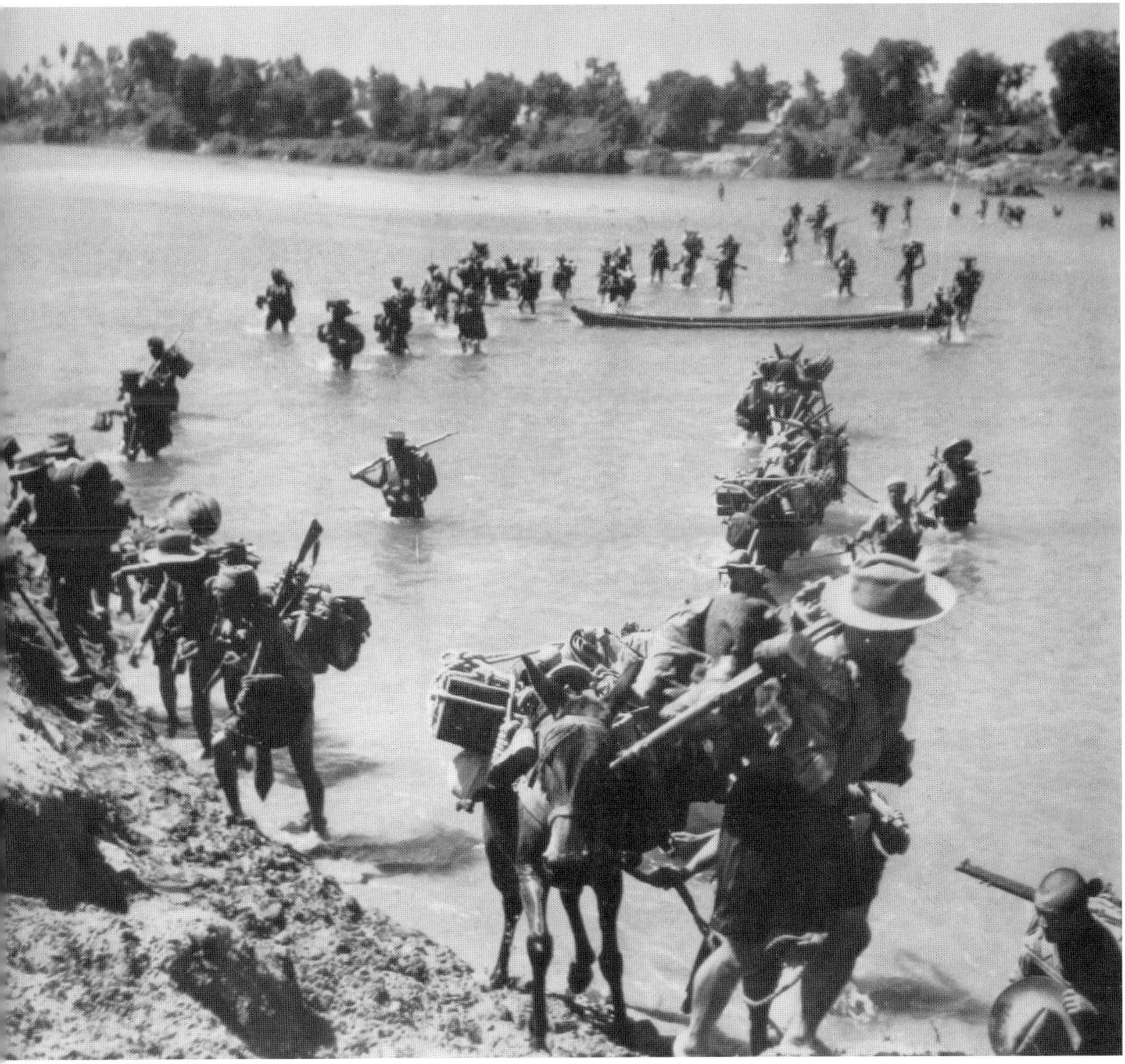

(**Opposite, above**) Soldiers of the 7th Indian Division's 33rd Infantry Brigade cross the Irrawaddy River on a pontoon raft with outboard motors (right) between Myitche and Pakokku in mid-February 1945. Battalions of the 15th Punjab, 1st Gurkha Rifles and the 1st Burma regiments comprised the 33rd Brigade. *(NARA)*

(**Opposite, below**) A Bailey pontoon bridge ferry is hauled in after the Irrawaddy River crossing. Lorries, jeeps and artillery pieces are seen as part of Slim's corps commanders' movements to capture Meiktila and Mandalay before a southward move on Rangoon. *(NARA)*

(**Above**) Gurkha soldiers of XXXIII Corps' 19th Division cross a shallow Irrawaddy River ford in the southward drive on Mandalay in March 1945. Each of the three 19th Division's infantry brigades contained a Gurkha Rifles battalion from either the 4th or 6th Gurkha Rifles. *(NARA)*

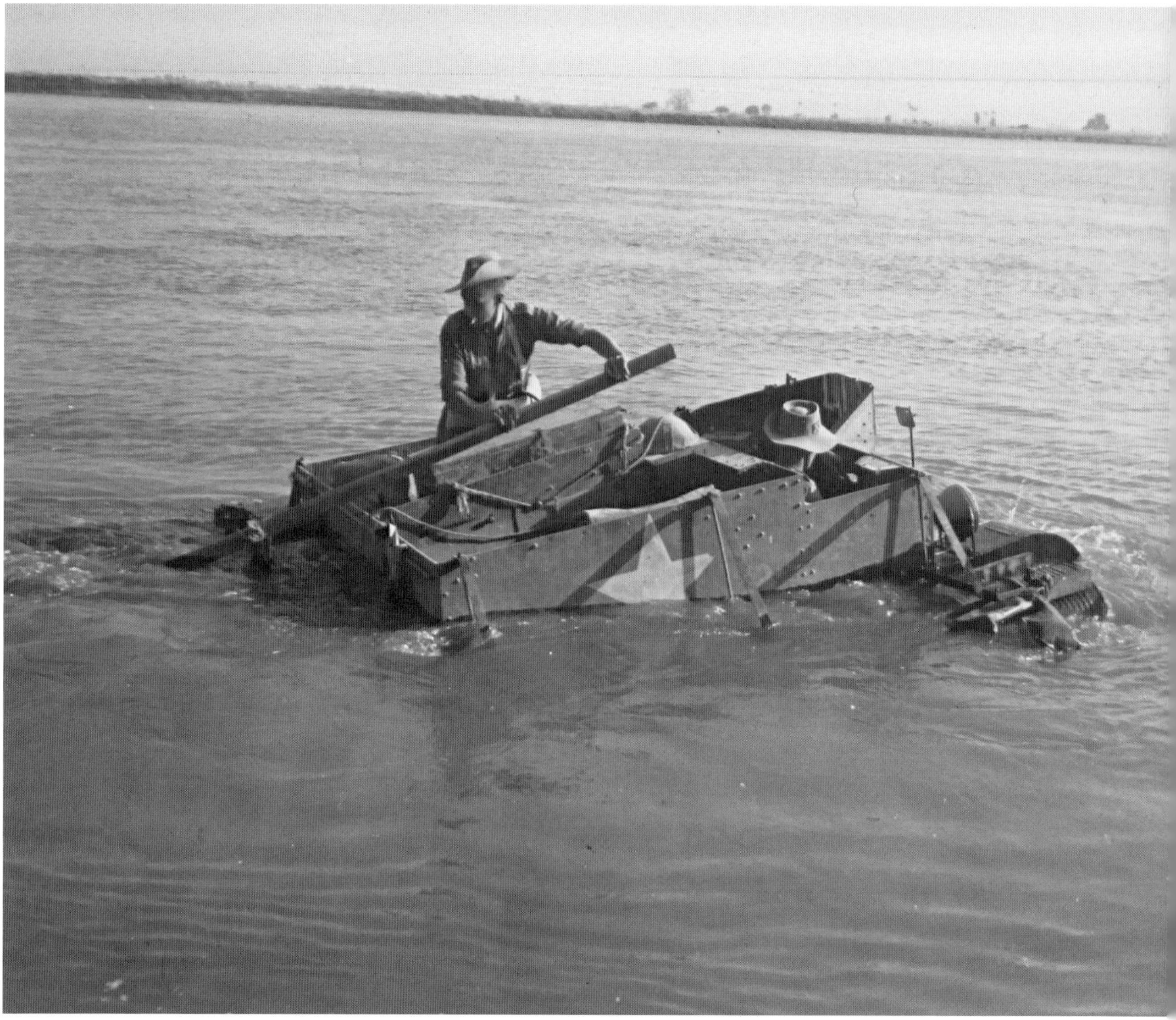

(**Above**) A Bren gun carrier crewman using an improvised rudder steers his amphibious universal carrier across the Irrawaddy River at the end of February 1945. The carrier's treads served as 'mobile paddles' to propel the vehicle through the water. *(NARA)*

(**Opposite, above**) Troops from the 17th Indian Division's 48th Infantry Brigade cross a dry river bed en route to Taungtha, a village east of the Irrawaddy River with a nearby airfield. The 48th Brigade's combat-hardened battalions of the 12th Frontier Force and 10th Gurkha regiments captured Taungtha in late February 1945 after crossing the Irrawaddy River at Nyaung-U to the south. Taungtha was retaken by the Japanese on 4 March putting an enemy force in the 17th Division's rear. *(NARA)*

(**Opposite, below**) A British 2nd Division Bren gun carrier and an accompanying infantryman approach a village along the Irrawaddy's northern bank near Sagaing situated between Ava and Mandalay. In late January 1945, the Japanese had prepared extensive positions covering the Sagaing area to counterattack XXXIII Corps' advance on Mandalay with the British 2nd and Indian 19th divisions. The British 2nd Division attacked the IJA defences at Sagaing and threatened an Irrawaddy crossing in late February/early March. *(NARA)*

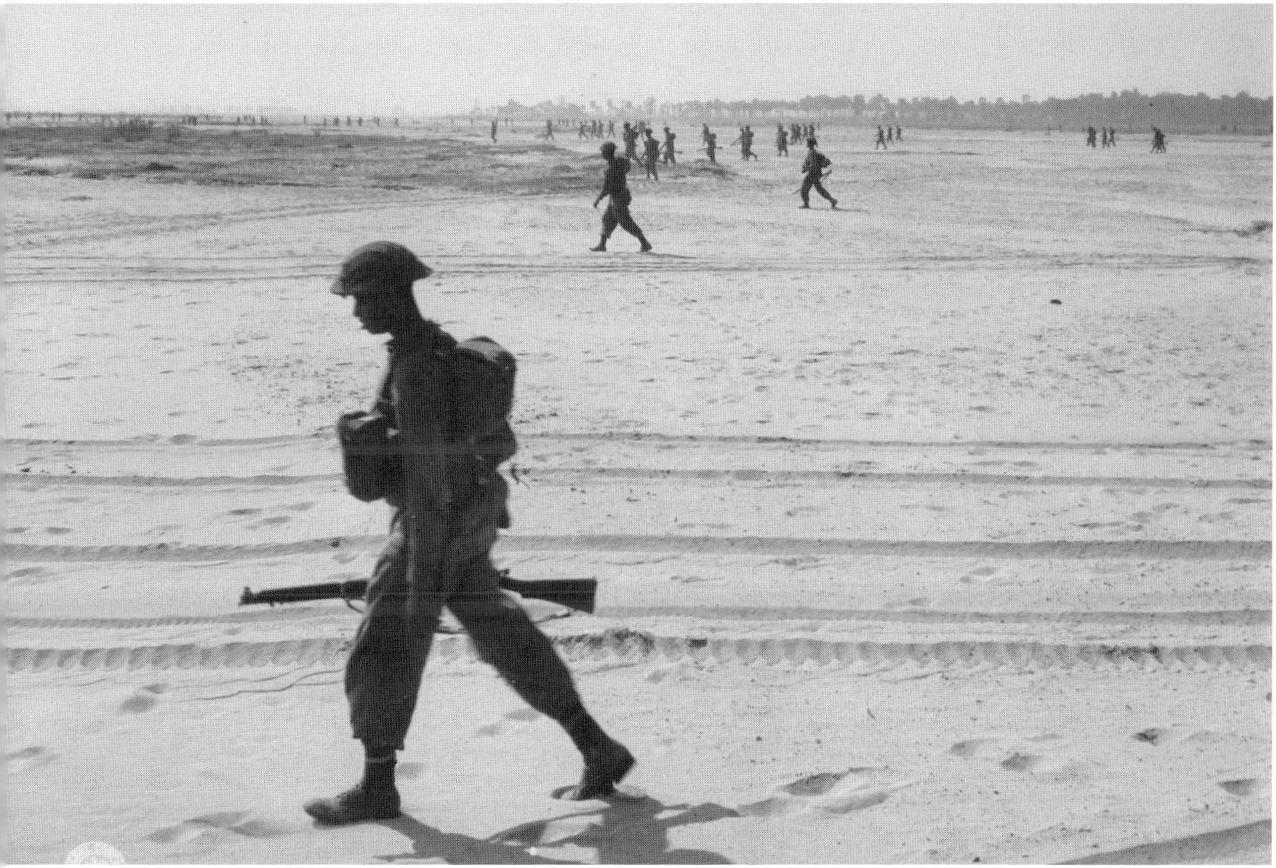

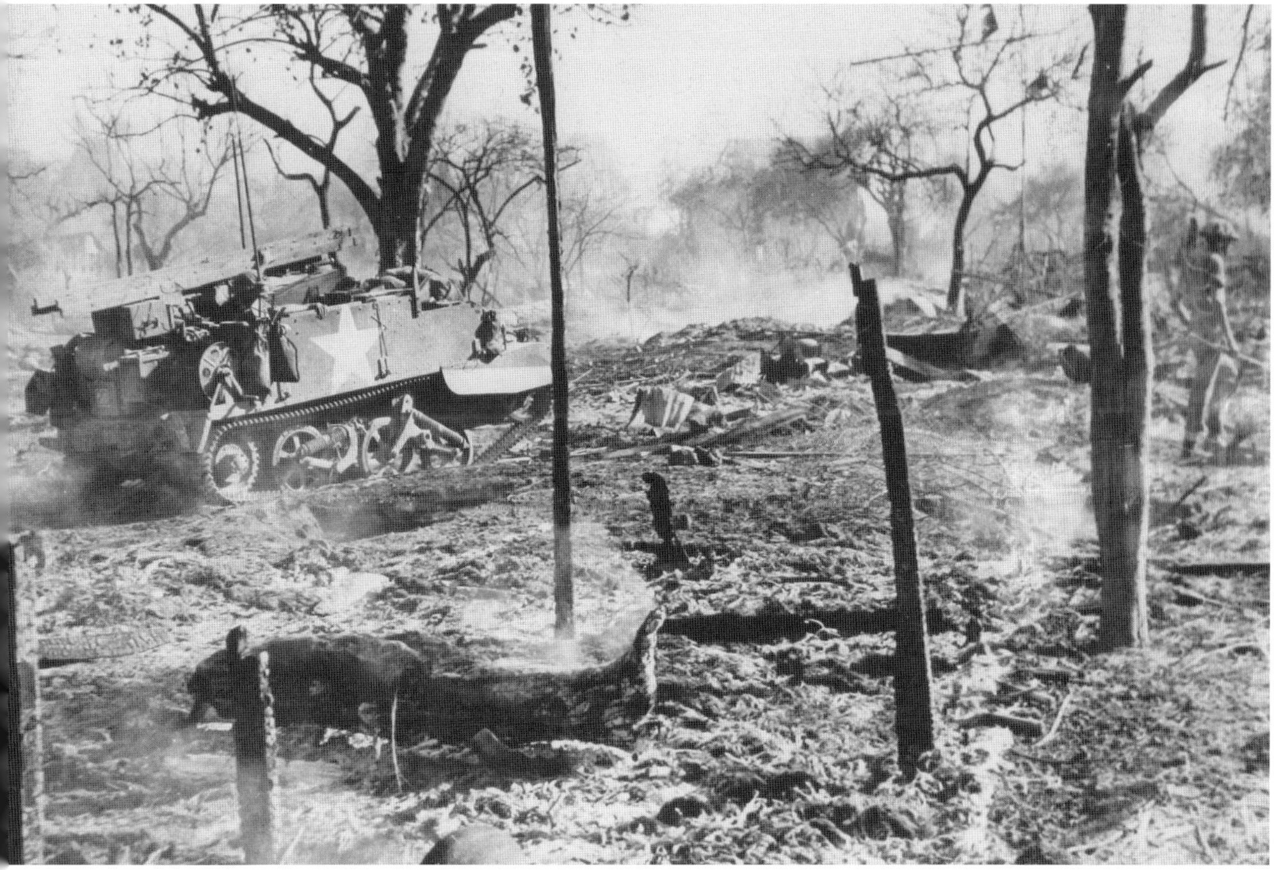

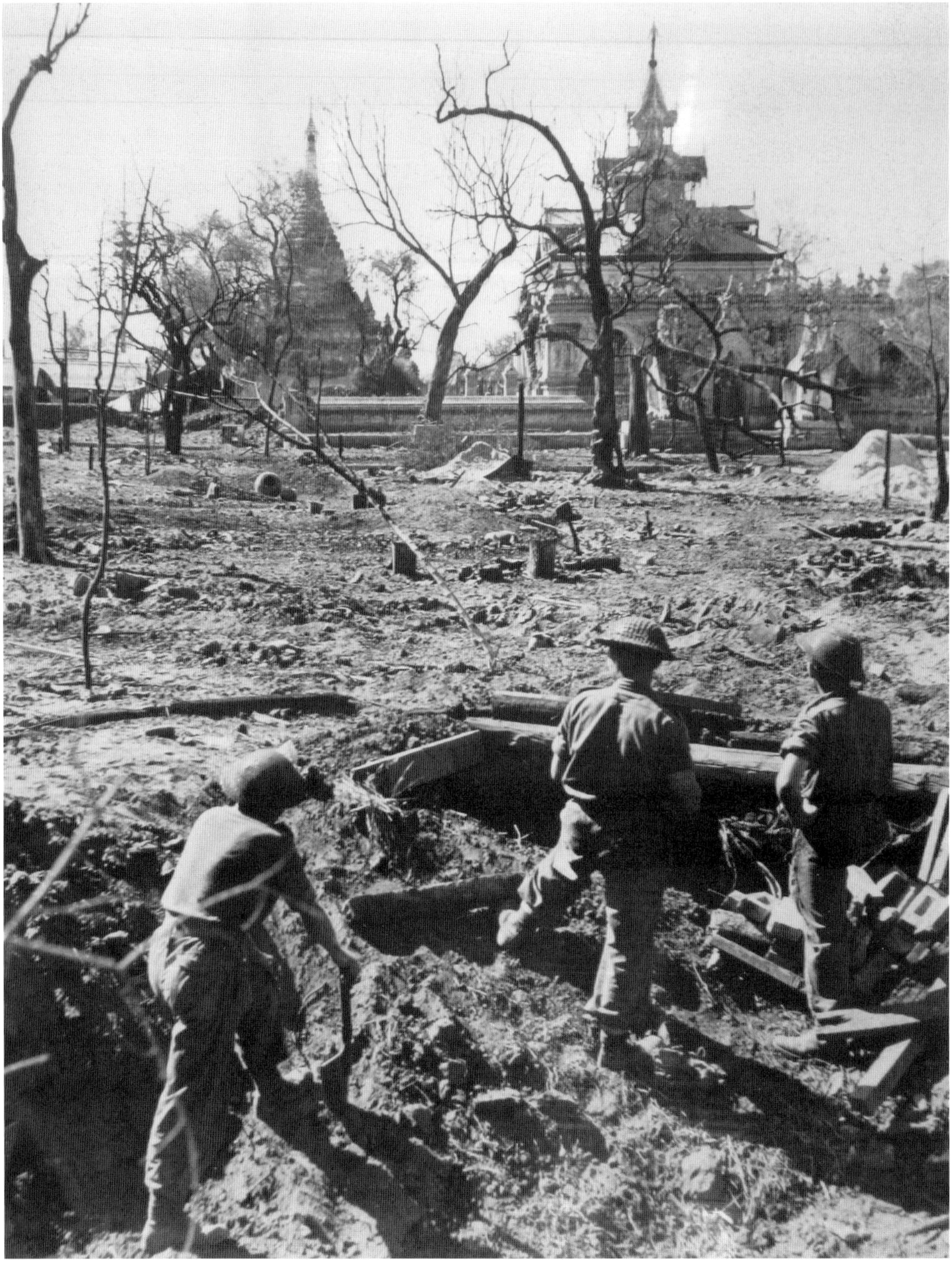

British 2nd Division soldiers advance through the ruins of the Japanese defences at Ywathitgyi, an IJA stronghold near Sagaing along the Irrawaddy's northern bank between Ava and Mandalay in late February/early March 1945. Burmese spiritual pagodas (background) were often included into the Japanese defensive works. *(NARA)*

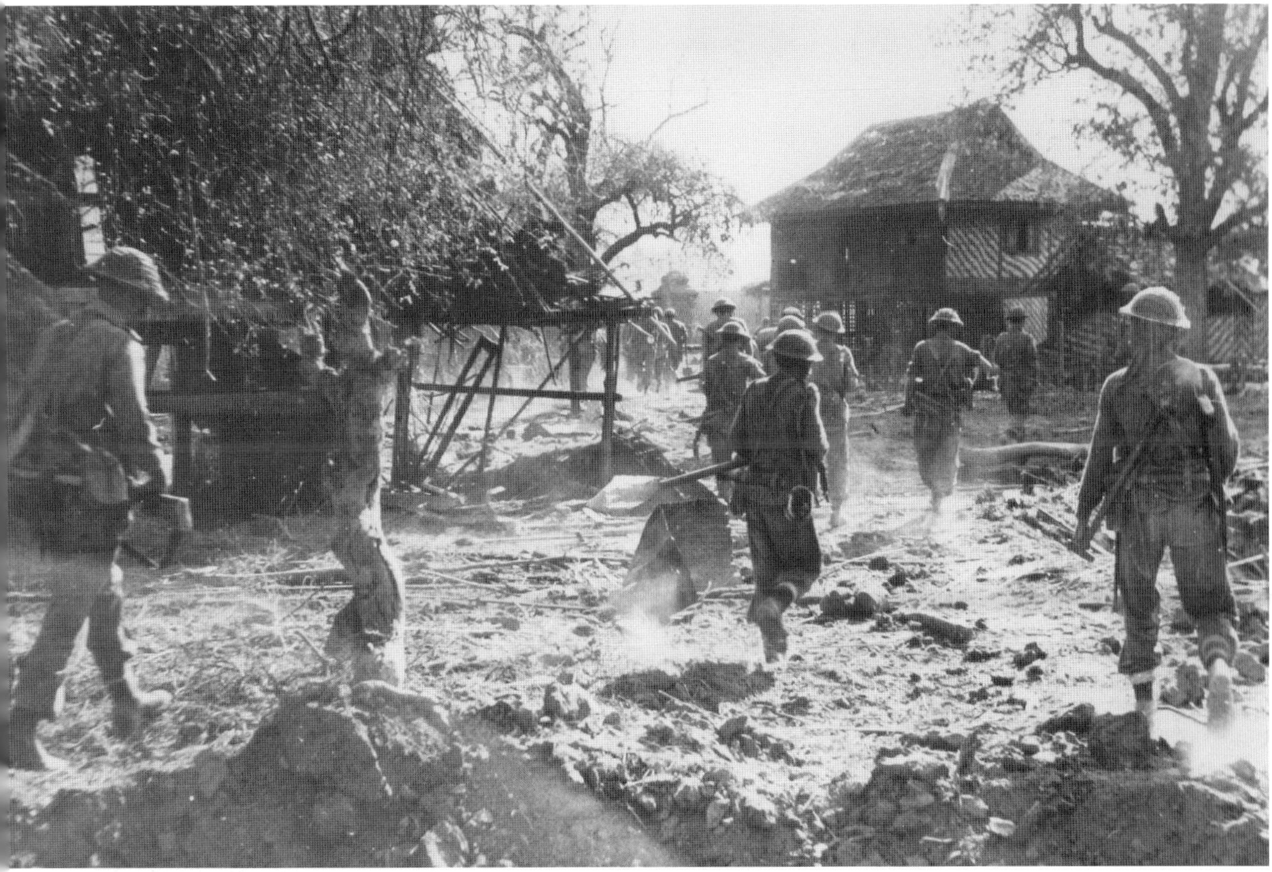

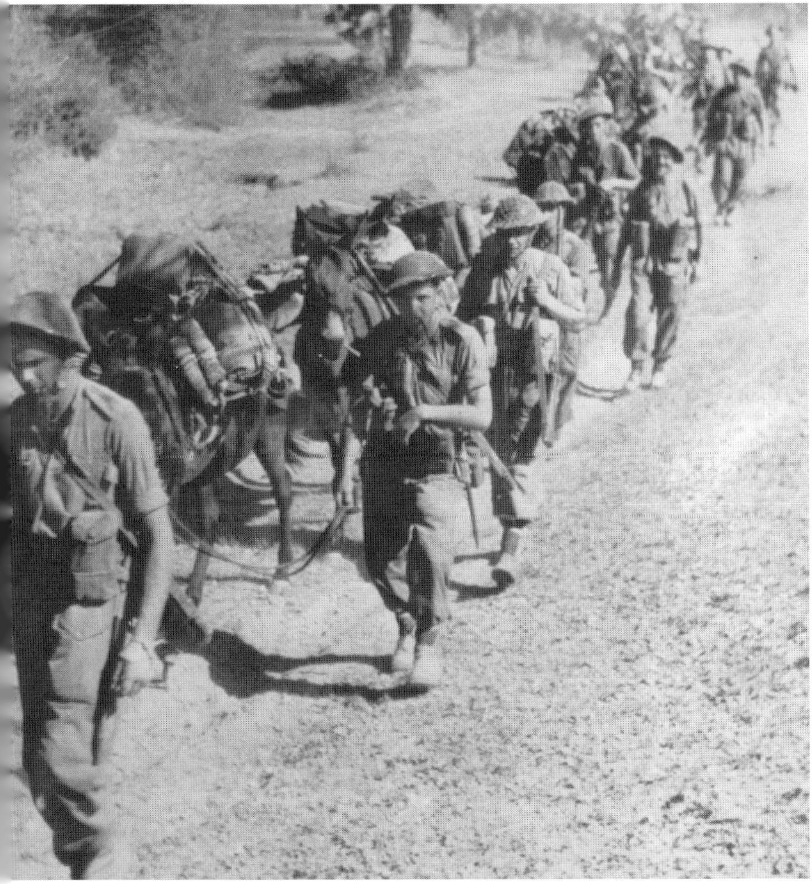

British 2nd Division troops advance through Ywathitgyi on the northern bank of the Irrawaddy River in the vicinity of Sagaing to Mandalay's west in late February 1945. After its capture, XXXIII Corps' British 2nd and 20th Indian divisions moved east to attack Mandalay from the south. *(NARA)*

A British 2nd Division pack mule train, led by British muleteers, moves on a dry dirt track towards Ywathitgyi to relieve XXXIII Corps' troops that captured the village in late February/ early March 1945. The Division's 4th, 5th and 6th Infantry brigades had troops from the Royal Scots, Royal Norfolk, Lancashire Fusilier, Worcestershire, Dorsetshire, Royal Welch, Royal Berkshire and Durham Light Infantry regiments. *(NARA)*

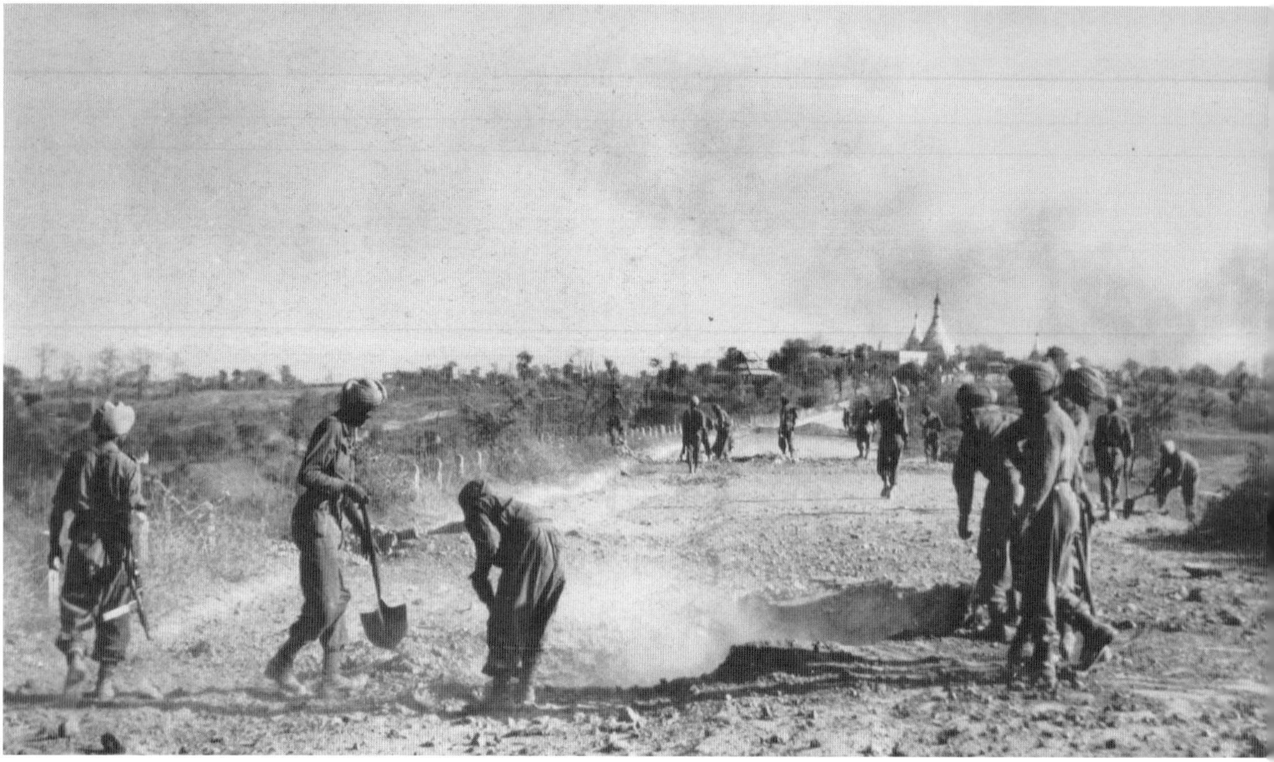

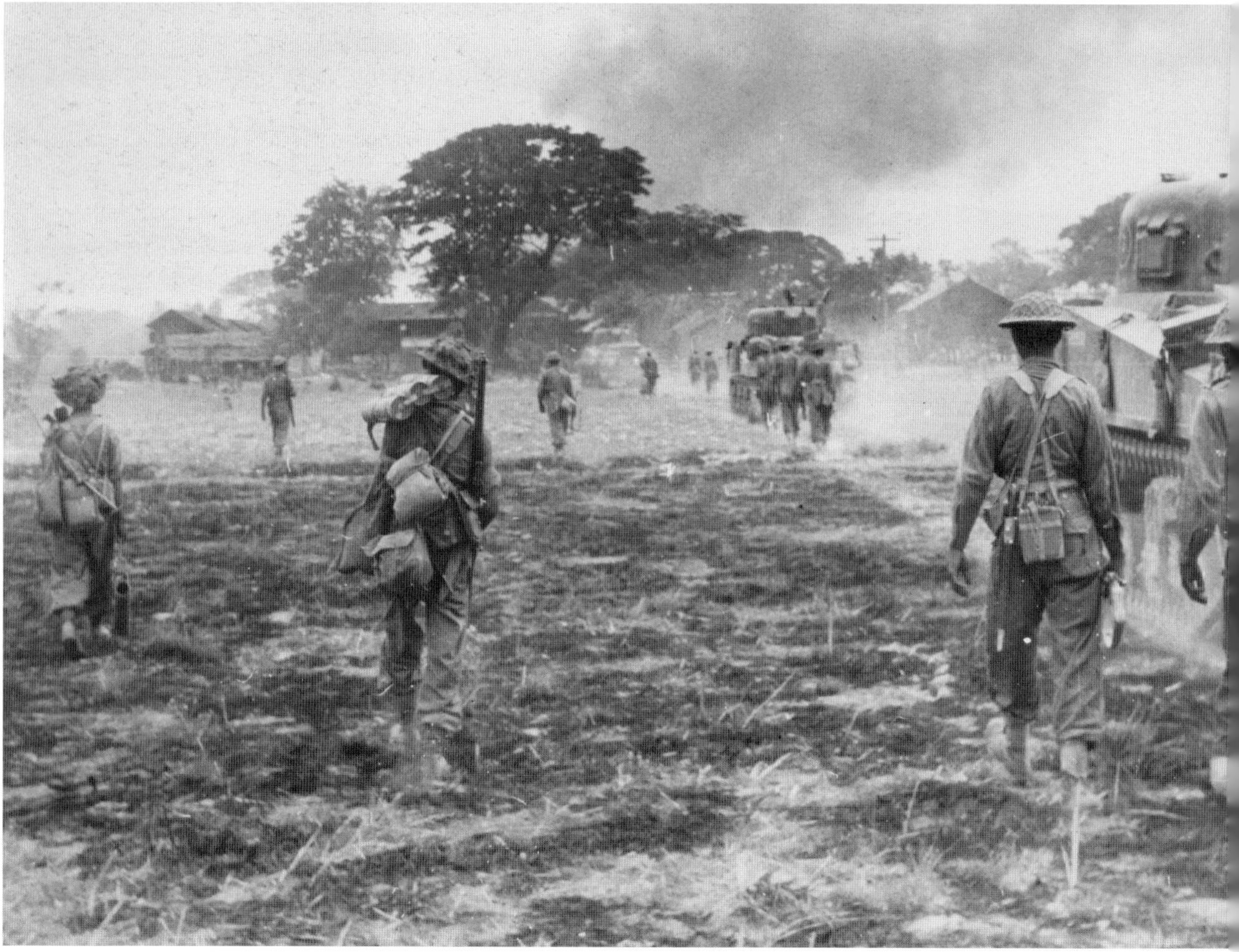

(**Opposite, above**) Sappers of the 17th Indian Division's 1st Sikh Light Infantry Regiment fill a crater on the road to Meiktila in March 1945 with visible Burmese pagodas (background). Slim's deployment of Messervy's IV Corps' 7th Indian Division crossing of the Irrawaddy (2,000 yards) at Nyaung-U in the early morning hours of 14 February was the longest amphibious operation of the war and deceived the IJA's attention that was focused on XXXIII Corps' river crossings made to the north and south-west of Mandalay. *(NARA)*

(**Opposite, below**) M4 medium tanks of the 255th Indian Tank Brigade's 5th (Probyn's) Horse attached to the 6/15th Punjab Rifles of the IV Corps' 17th Indian Division's 99th Infantry Brigade move across the perfect armour terrain on the way north of Meiktila towards Wundon to block any Japanese counterattack south from Mandalay in early March 1945. Previously at nightfall on 27 February, elements of the 17th Division's 63rd Infantry Brigade were within 6 miles of Meiktila with a general attack ordered for 1 March. By 4 March, the 17th Indian Division's possession of Meiktila was consolidated and its IJA garrison was dispersed at a cost of 6 tanks and 200 Allied soldiers killed or wounded. Defensive plans for Meiktila's airfield were implemented by the 17th Indian Division as IJA forces recaptured Taungtha on 4 March in the Allied rear echelon. *(NARA)*

(**Above**) A patrol of M4 medium tanks of the 255th Indian Tank Brigade with Indian infantrymen climbing atop them readies itself to engage IJA forces counterattacking 17th Indian Division units defending Meiktila after its capture on 4 March 1945. The next day these Allied patrols were mopping up the area to Meiktila's west and moving east to the railway line there. *(NARA)*

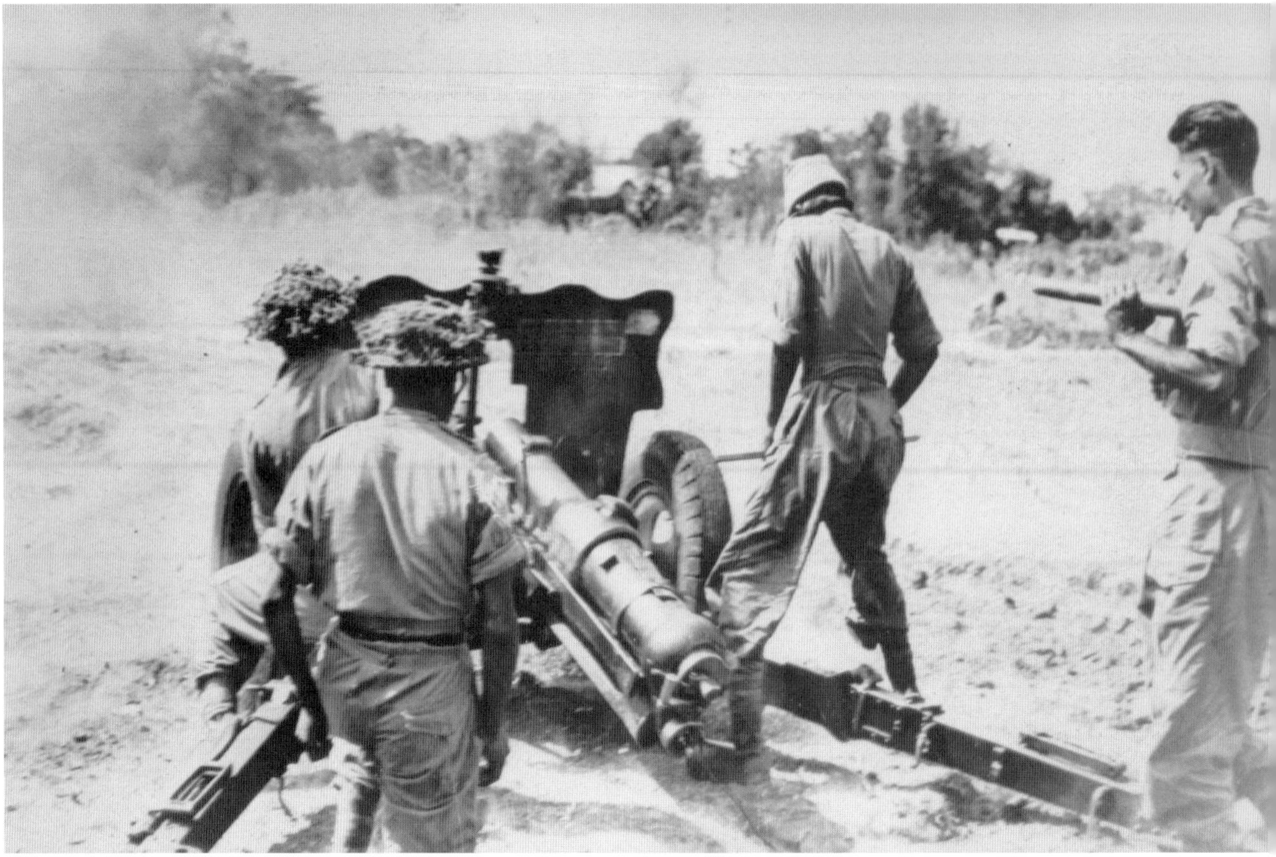

A 17th Indian Division's QF 3.7in howitzer of the 24th Indian Mountain Regiment's 6th Jacob's Battery fires on IJA positions at Meiktila in March 1945 with its characteristic split trail shown. The split trail allowed the gun to be fired at very high angles which was very useful in mountainous terrain. This weapon was designed to be broken down into eight mule loads for transport over difficult terrain and for reassembly within minutes. *(NARA)*

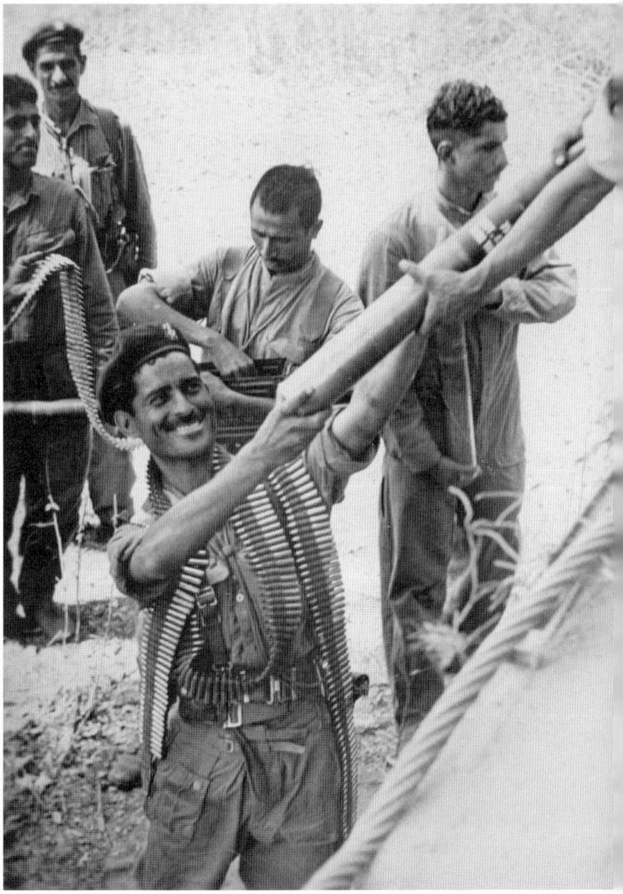

Indian 255th Tank Brigade crewmen from 5th (Probyn's) Horse are shown here rearming their M4 medium tank with 75mm shells for the main turret gun and 0.30in-calibre ammunition for the armoured vehicle's MGs. The reloading occurred during a lull in the fighting south of Meiktila in mid-March 1945 as elements of the tank brigade moved from Meiktila towards Pyawbwe. On 1 April, IJA Lieutenant General Honda ordered his 18th Division to withdraw to Pyawbwe while the IJA 49th Division was to retreat to Yamethin as by 31 March, the Japanese had abandoned all hopes of recapturing Meiktila. Cowan's 17th Indian Division was regrouping to attack Pyawbwe. *(NARA)*

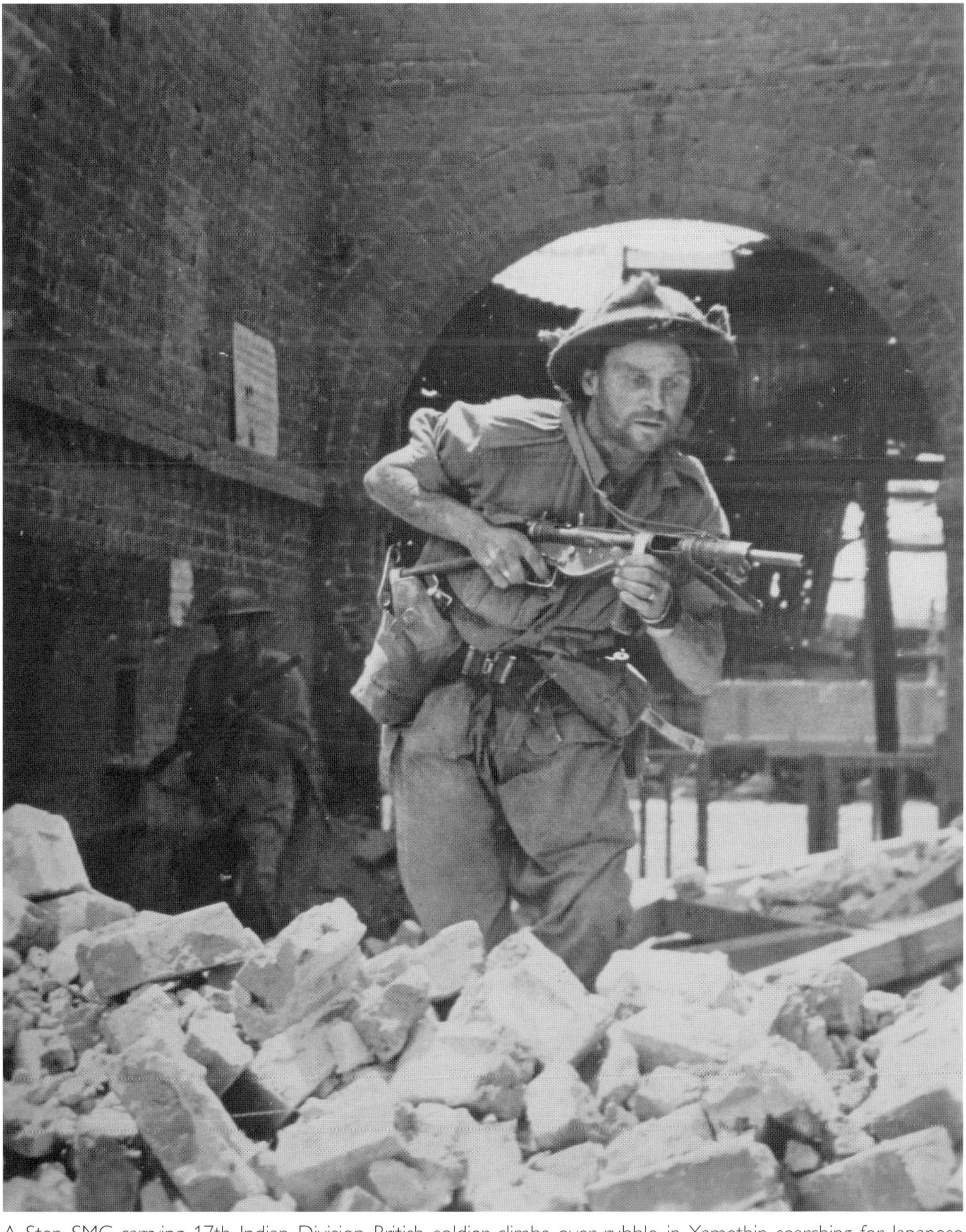

A Sten SMG-carrying 17th Indian Division British soldier climbs over rubble in Yamethin searching for Japanese snipers in April 1945. After the Japanese defeat at Meiktila, the IJA 49th Division's remnants withdrew into Yamethin, south of Pyawbwe along the Meiktila-Rangoon road. *(NARA)*

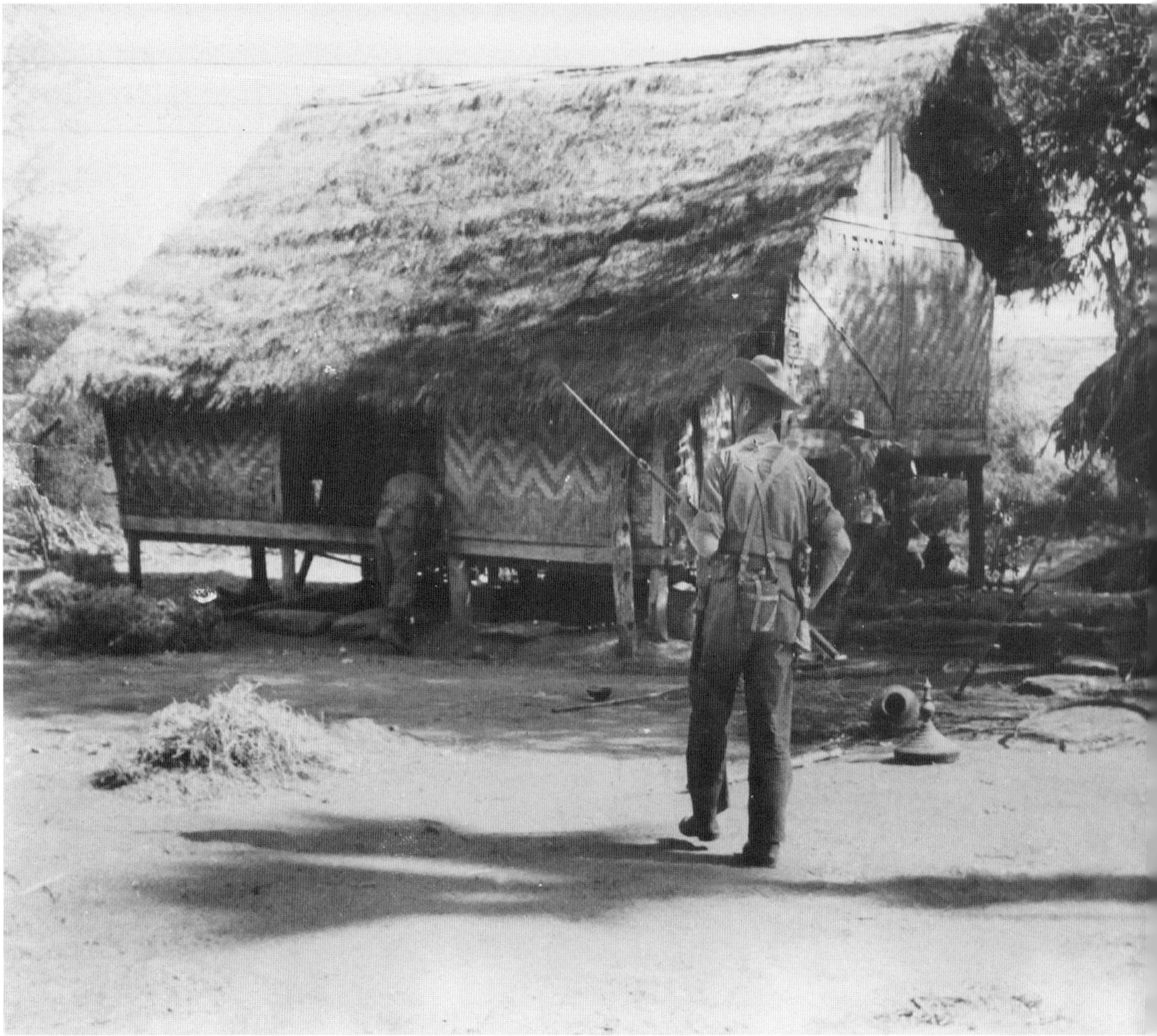

(**Above**) British infantrymen from the 17th Indian Division advance with fixed bayonets through a Burmese village near Meiktila in March 1945. The soldiers reconnoitred native huts for Japanese snipers or wounded left behind. After the Japanese isolated the 17th Indian Division at the Meiktila airfield, vigorous patrolling of the perimeter was the routine with both infantry and armour. *(NARA)*

(**Opposite, above**) Troops of 1st Sikh Light Infantry in the 17th Indian Division's 99th Infantry Brigade wait behind a smokescreen before pushing back Japanese soldiers 3 miles to the east of Pyawbwe and 22 miles south-east of Meiktila. More than 100 Japanese soldiers were killed in that engagement. The remnants of the IJA 18th Division retreated to Pyawbwe on 1 April 1945. *(NARA)*

(**Opposite, below**) Sikh infantrymen from the 99th Infantry Brigade's 1st Sikh Light Infantry Regiment climb a *nullah* or ravine with bayonets fixed to their SMLE rifles 4 miles to the south of Pyawbwe. At the ravine's top, the Sikhs routed an IJA 18th Division outpost. After Pyawbwe, the 17th Indian Division moved south on Yamethin on the Rangoon road. *(NARA)*

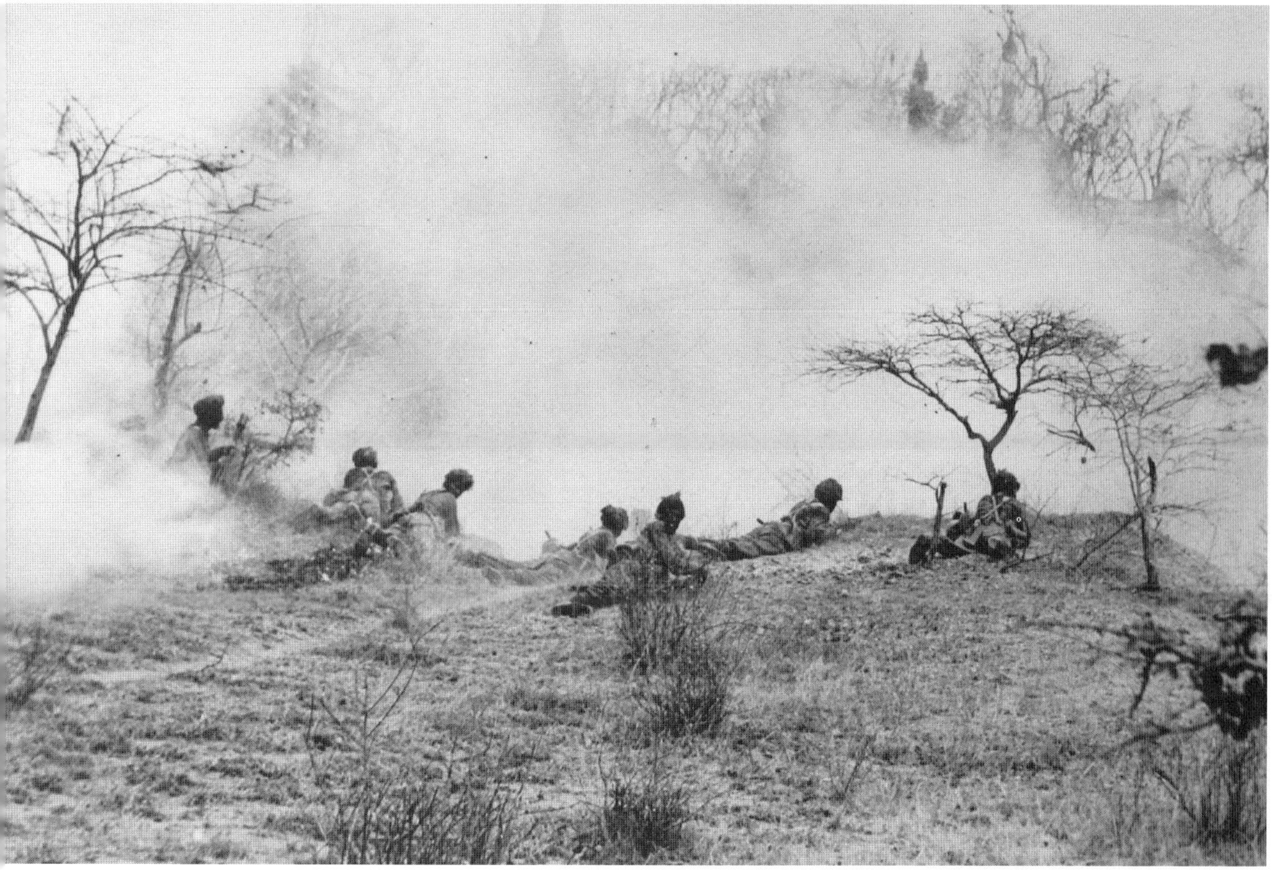

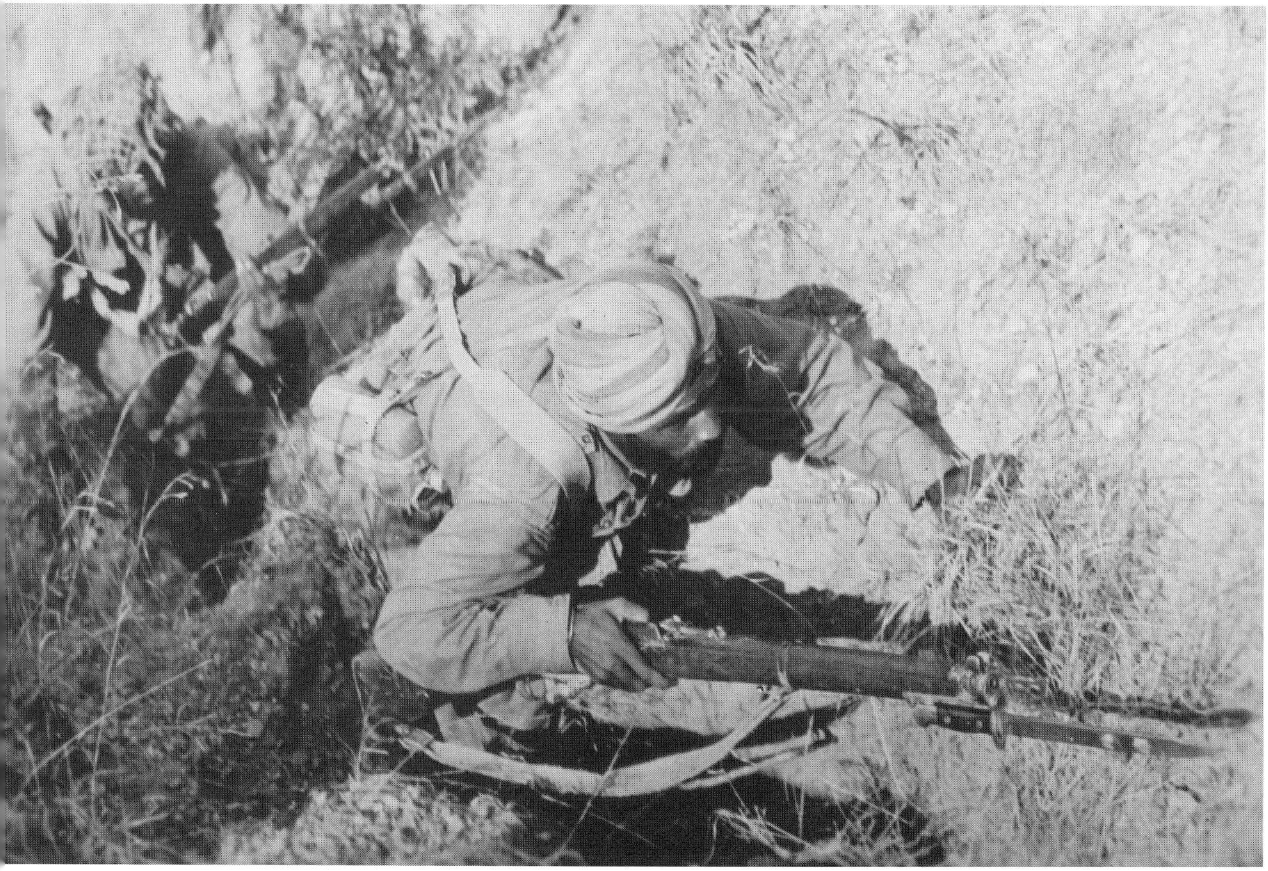

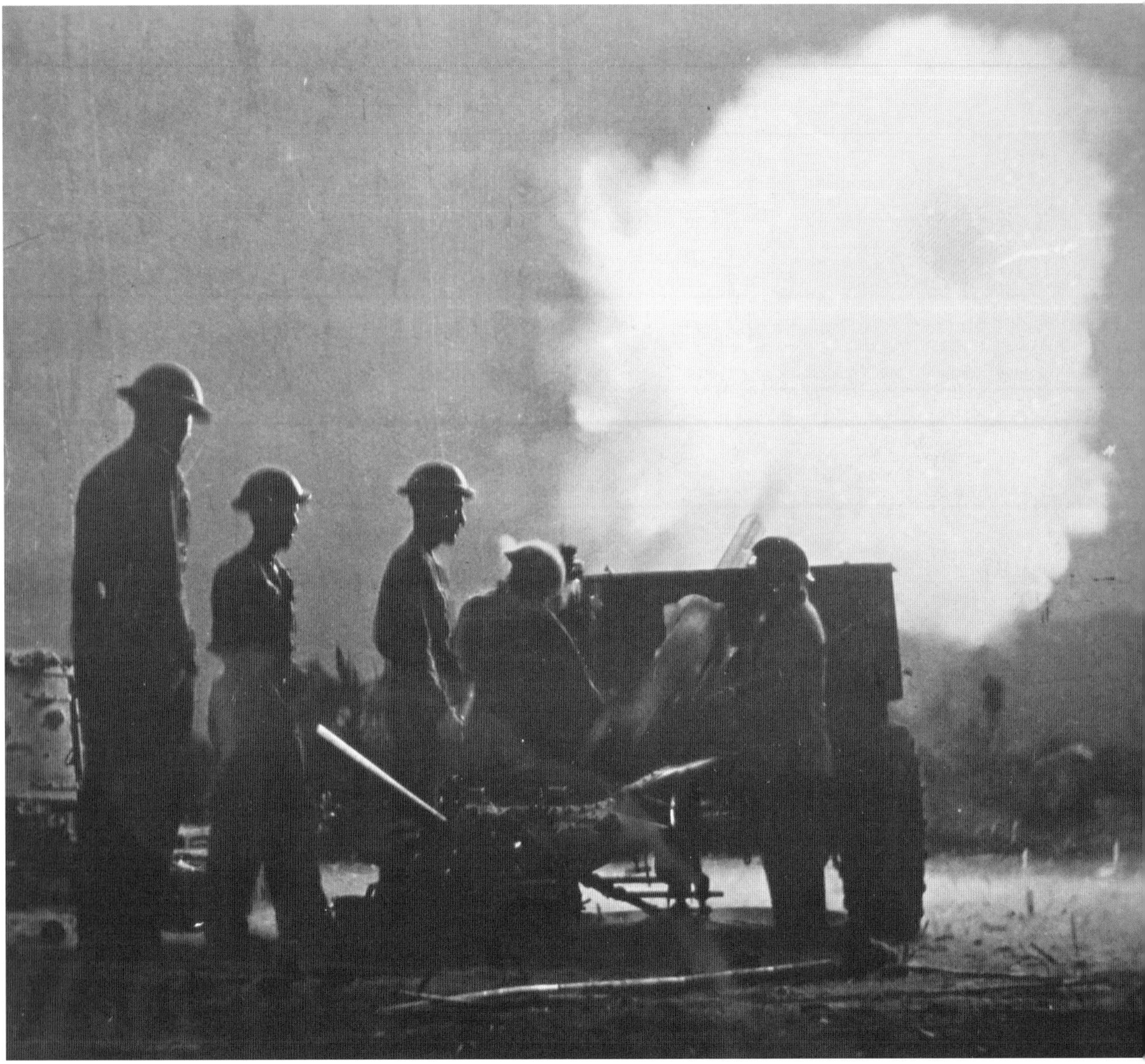

(**Above**) A 7th Infantry Division 25-pounder field gun fires at night against Japanese troops retreating from the Mount Popa vicinity east of the Irrawaddy and south of the confluence with the Chindwin River. During the struggle for Meiktila, elements of the IJA 154th and 112th IRs held Mount Popa and also counterattacked the flank of the IV Corps' 5th Indian Division near Taungtha, which the IJA recaptured on 4 March. *(NARA)*

(**Opposite, above**) A 1/11th Sikh regimental patrol of the 7th Indian Division in a Bren LMG outpost is seen here near the derricks of the Yenangyaung oilfields, 70 miles to the south-west of Meiktila and to the south of Chauk. Elements of the 7th Indian Division crossed the Irrawaddy River at Seikphyu with Chauk on the eastern bank of the river before heading south to the Yenangyaung oilfields, which had previously been captured by the Japanese in April 1942. *(NARA)*

(**Opposite, below**) Troops of the 19th Indian Division's Gurkha Rifles emerge from the Singu bridgehead to the south of Mabein with accompanying armour over arid terrain on the way south to Mandalay in March 1945. *(NARA)*

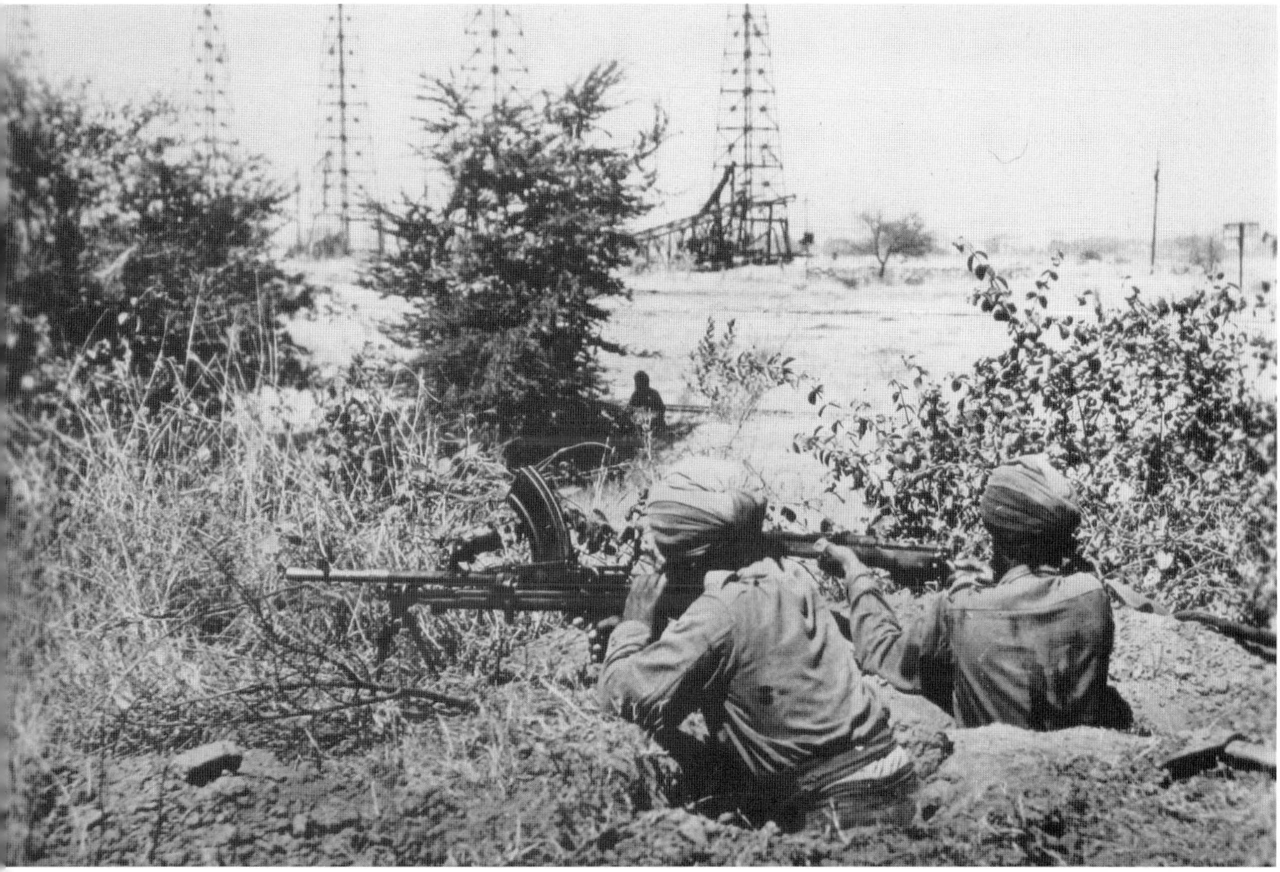

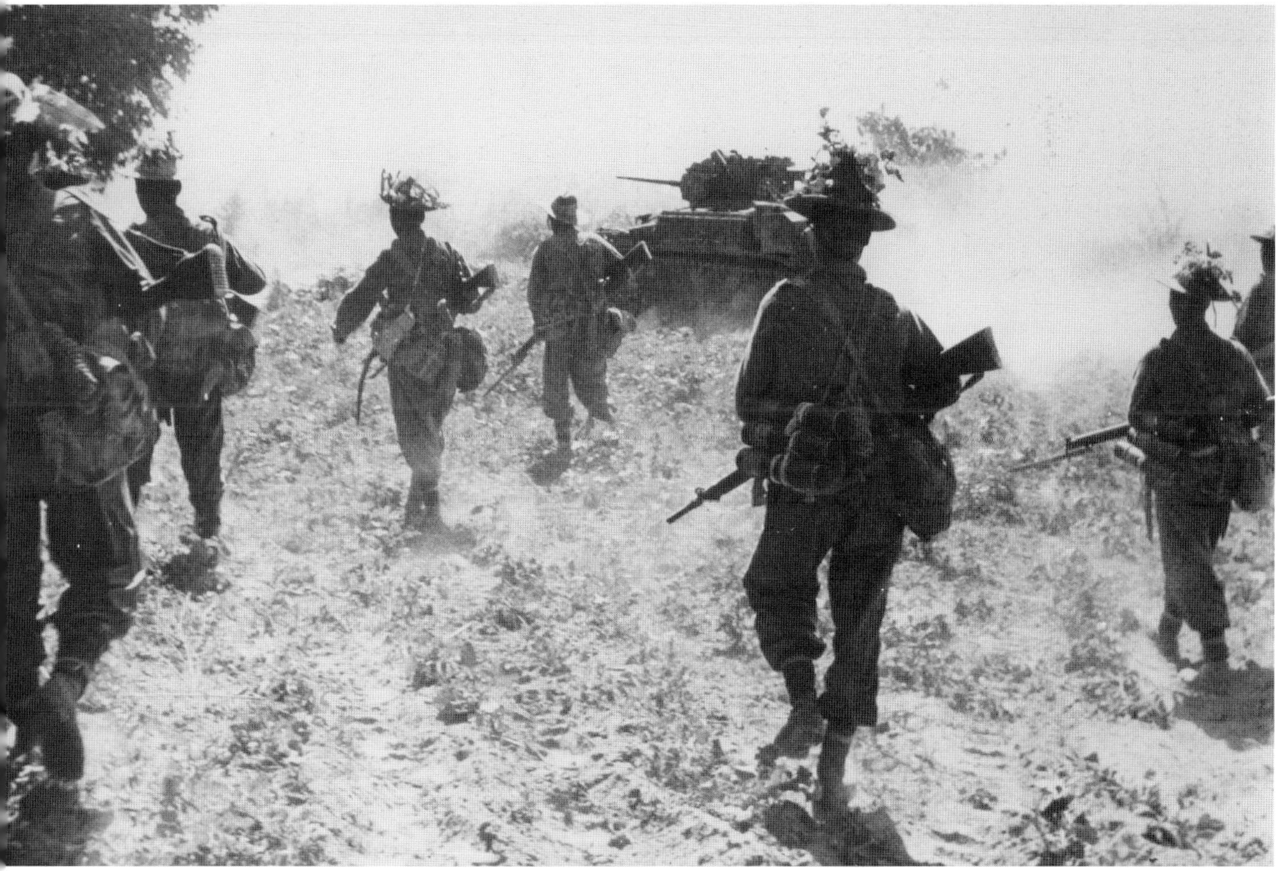

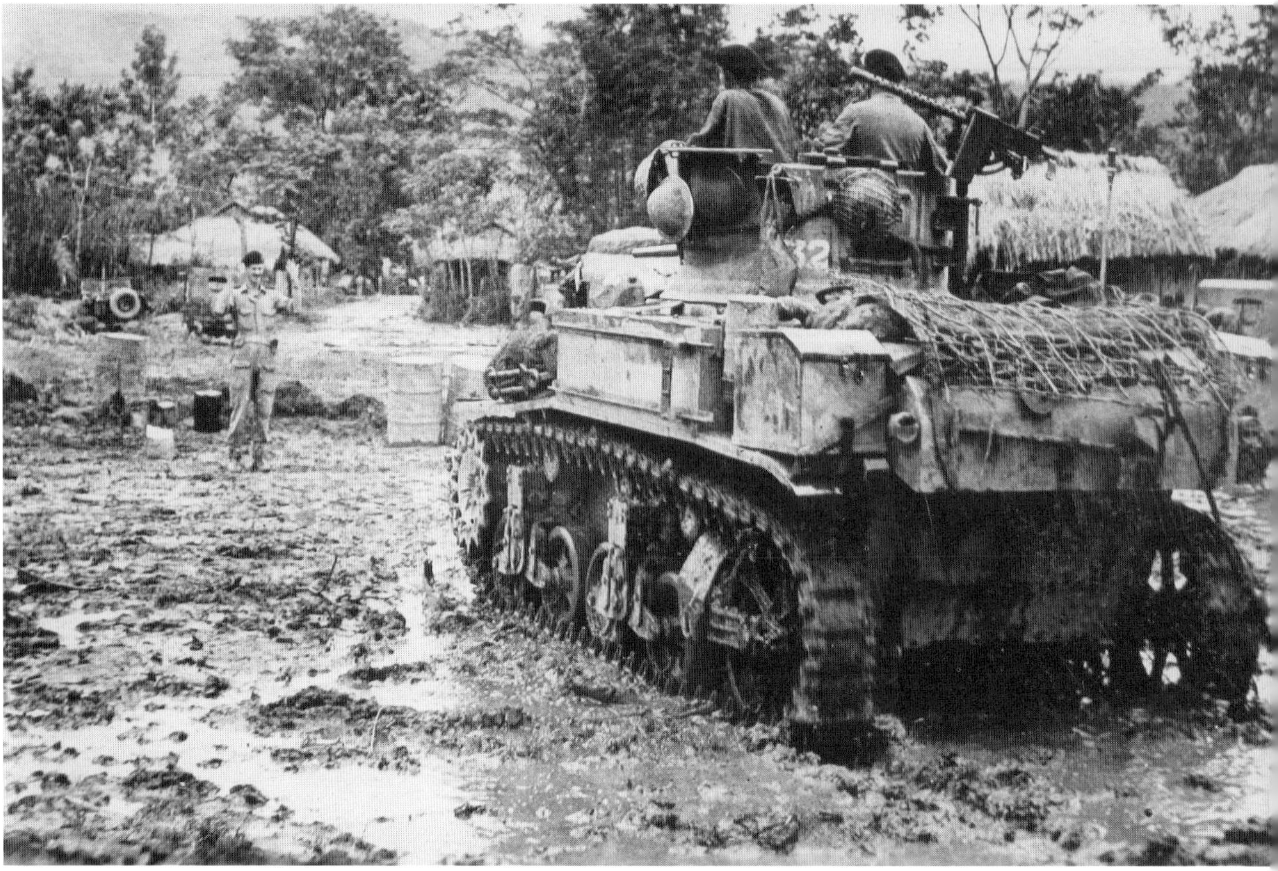

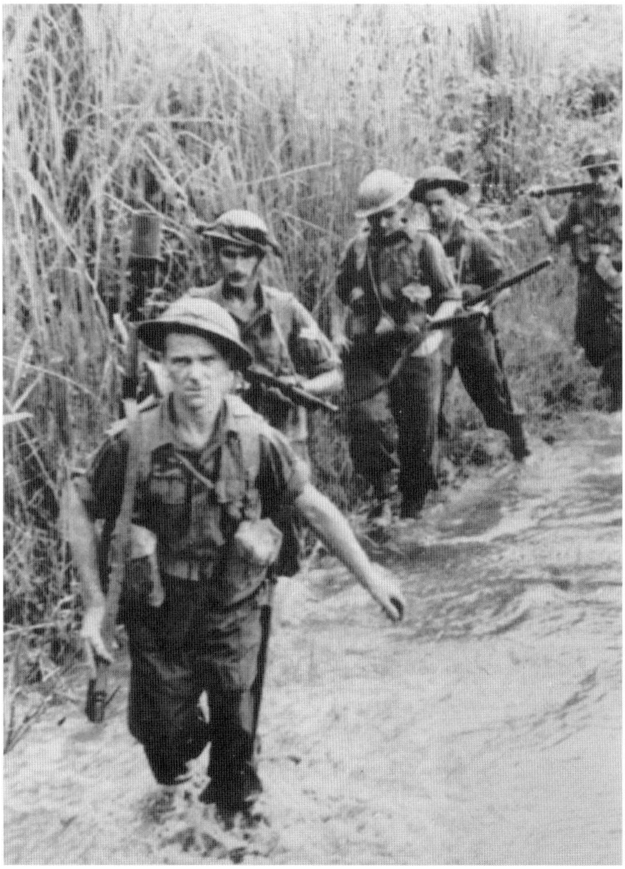

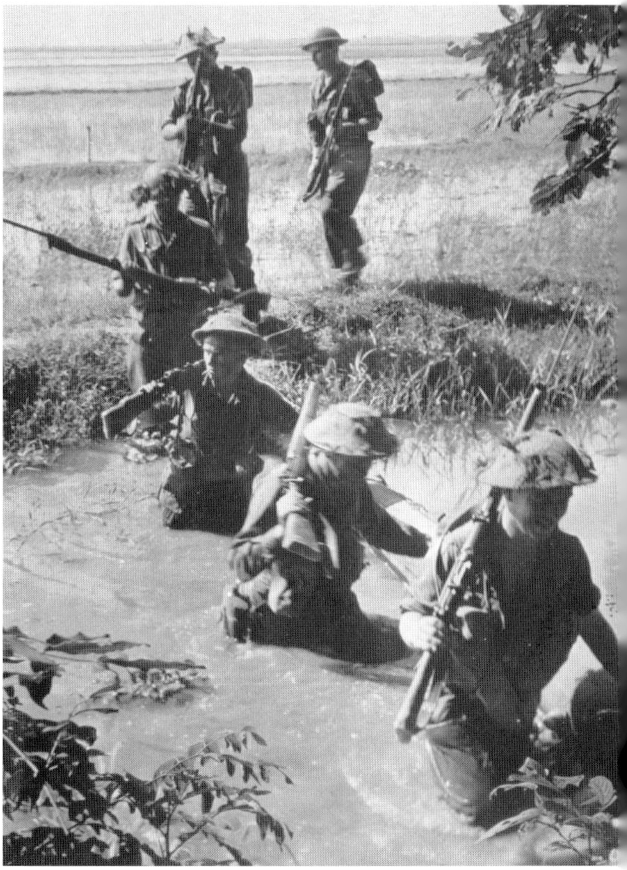

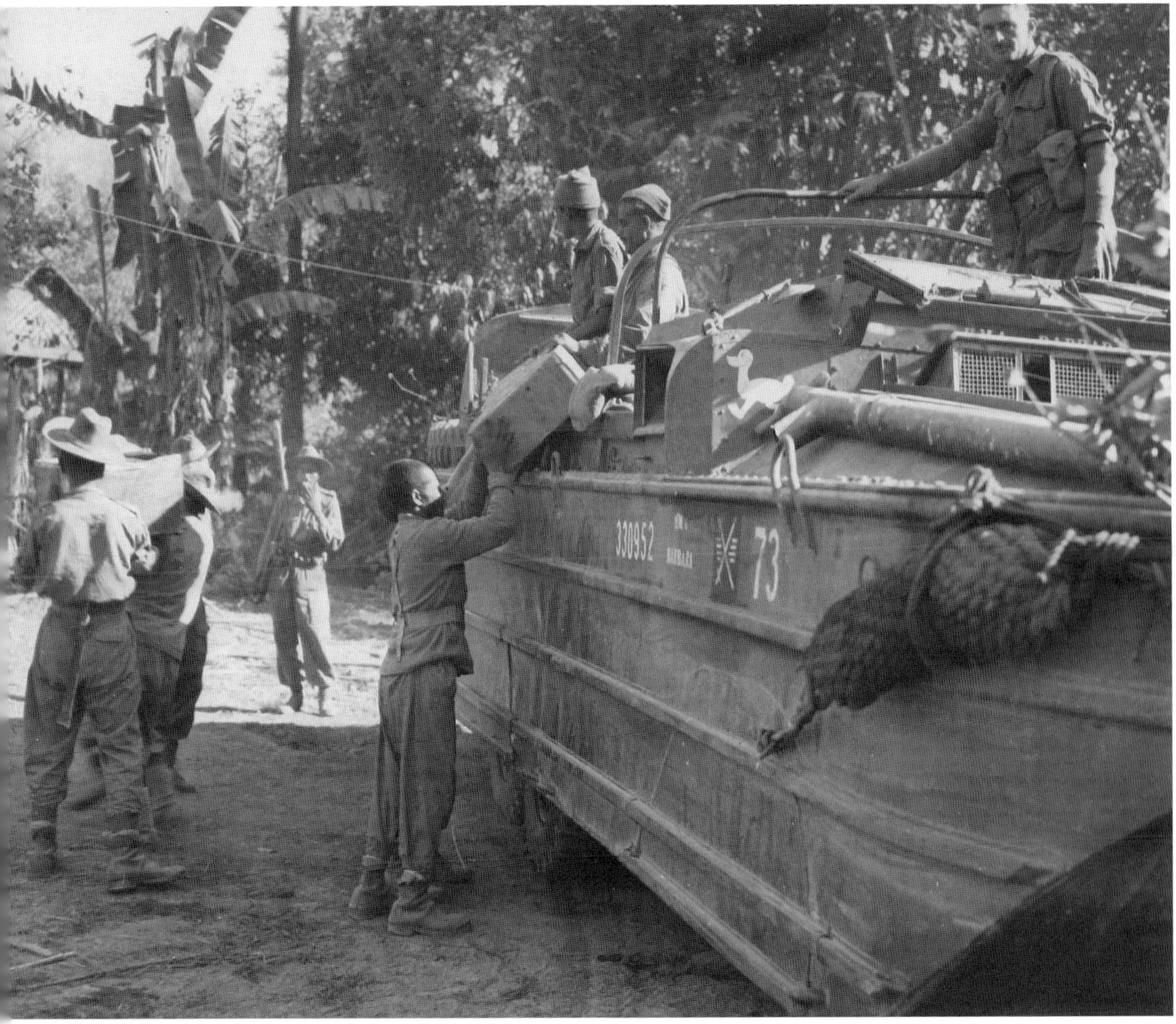
330952
73

(**Opposite, above**) An M5 light tank of the XXXIII Corps' 254th Indian Tank Brigade is stuck in the mud in a village on the way to Mandalay in March 1945. The M5 light tank was primarily used in a reconnaissance role as it was lightly-armoured and had only a 37mm turret gun. Nonetheless, it was reliable with a maximum speed of 35 mph. *(NARA)*

(**Opposite, below left**) A British infantry section on patrol skirts one of the innumerable Burmese *chaungs*, which could be formidable waterways during the monsoon season's torrential rains. The dense vegetation on either side of this *chaung* afforded the Japanese excellent cover for MGs, snipers and even light artillery pieces. *(NARA)*

(**Opposite, below right**) A British infantry section moves through another water obstacle, a flooded rice paddy to the soldiers' waists during the Meiktila-Mandalay campaign of February–March 1945. The terrain in the background was typical of the advance through the Irrawaddy River valley. *(NARA)*

(**Above**) During the 19th Indian Division's advance towards Mandalay, Gurkha soldiers unload supplies from an amphibious DUKW that was built on a truck chassis, enabling it to transport a great quantity of supplies or troops. Each 19th Indian Division brigade had a Gurkha Rifles battalion. *(NARA)*

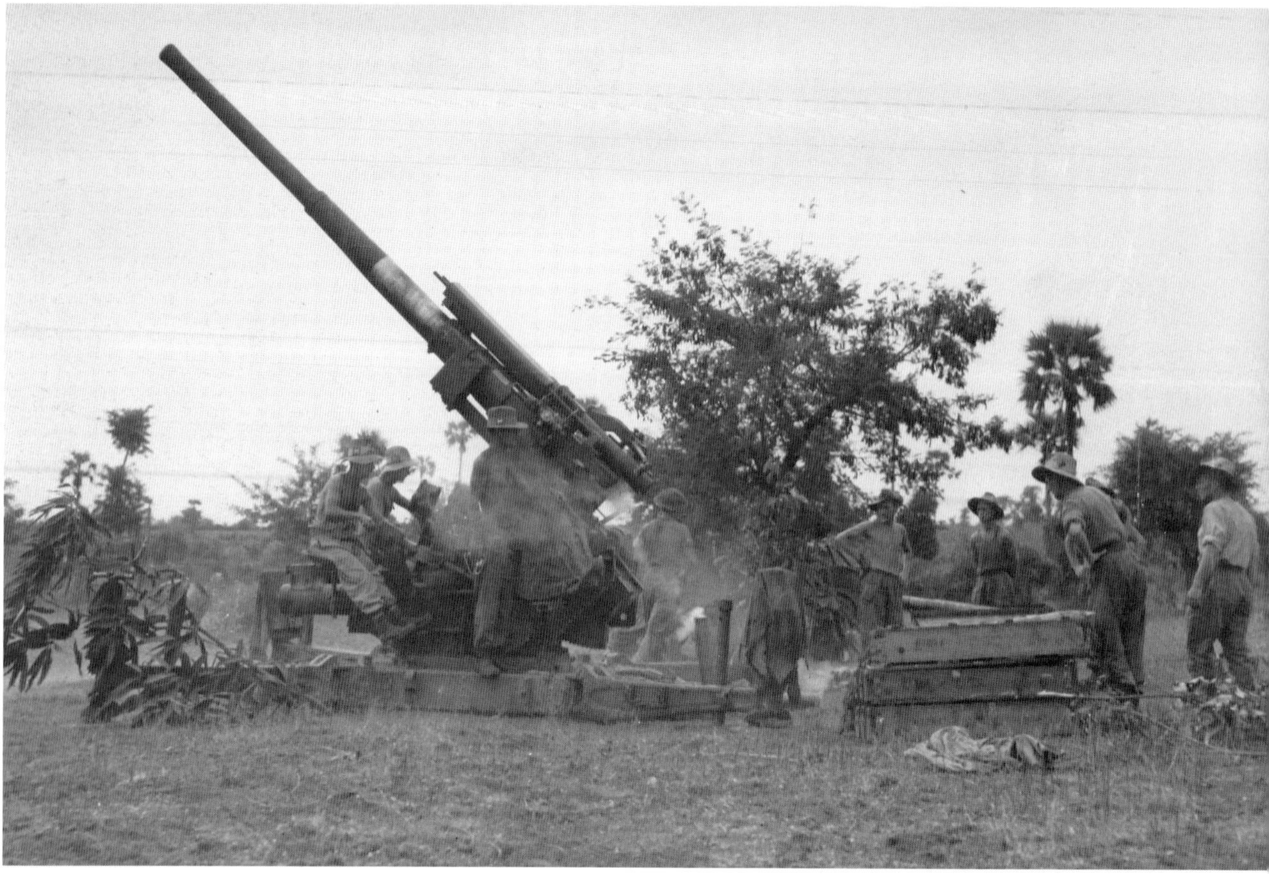

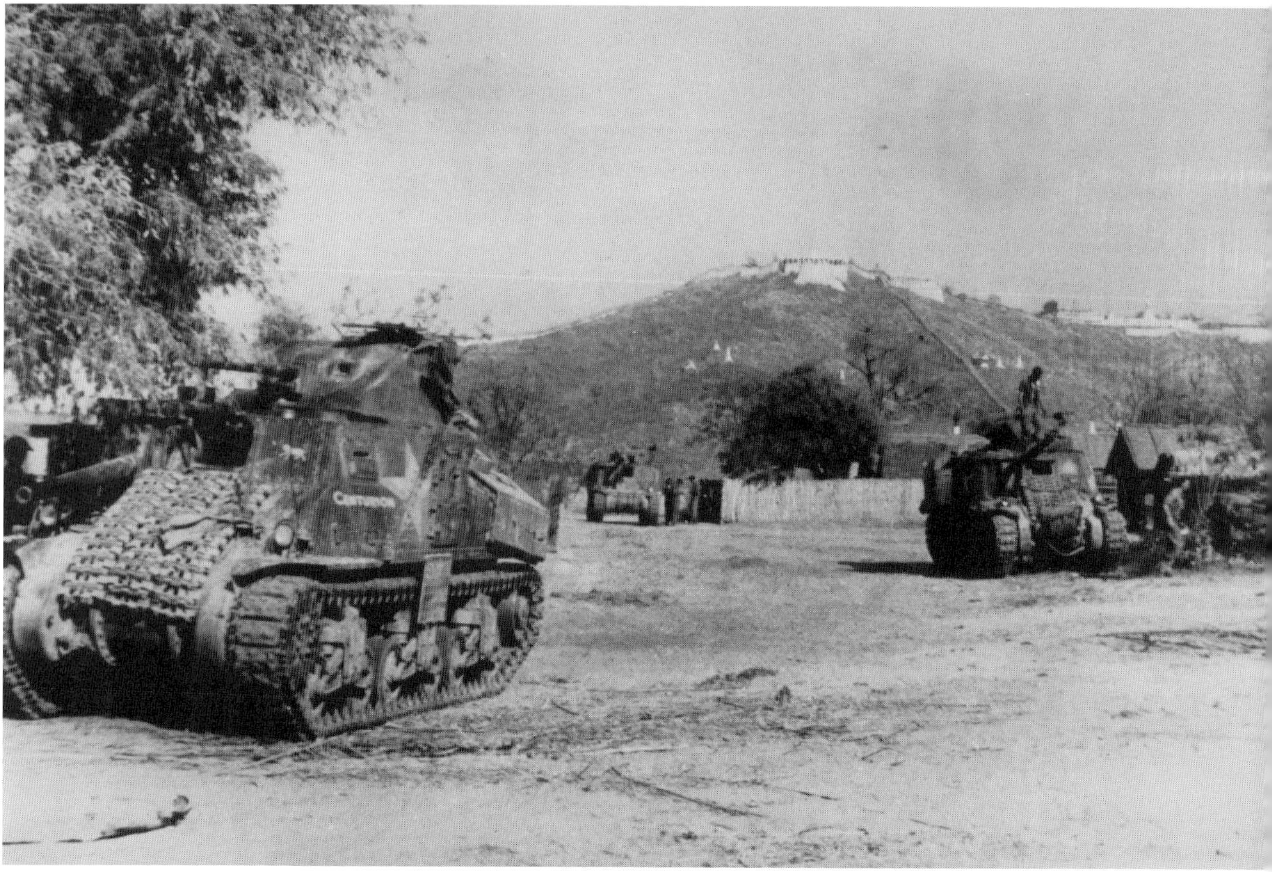

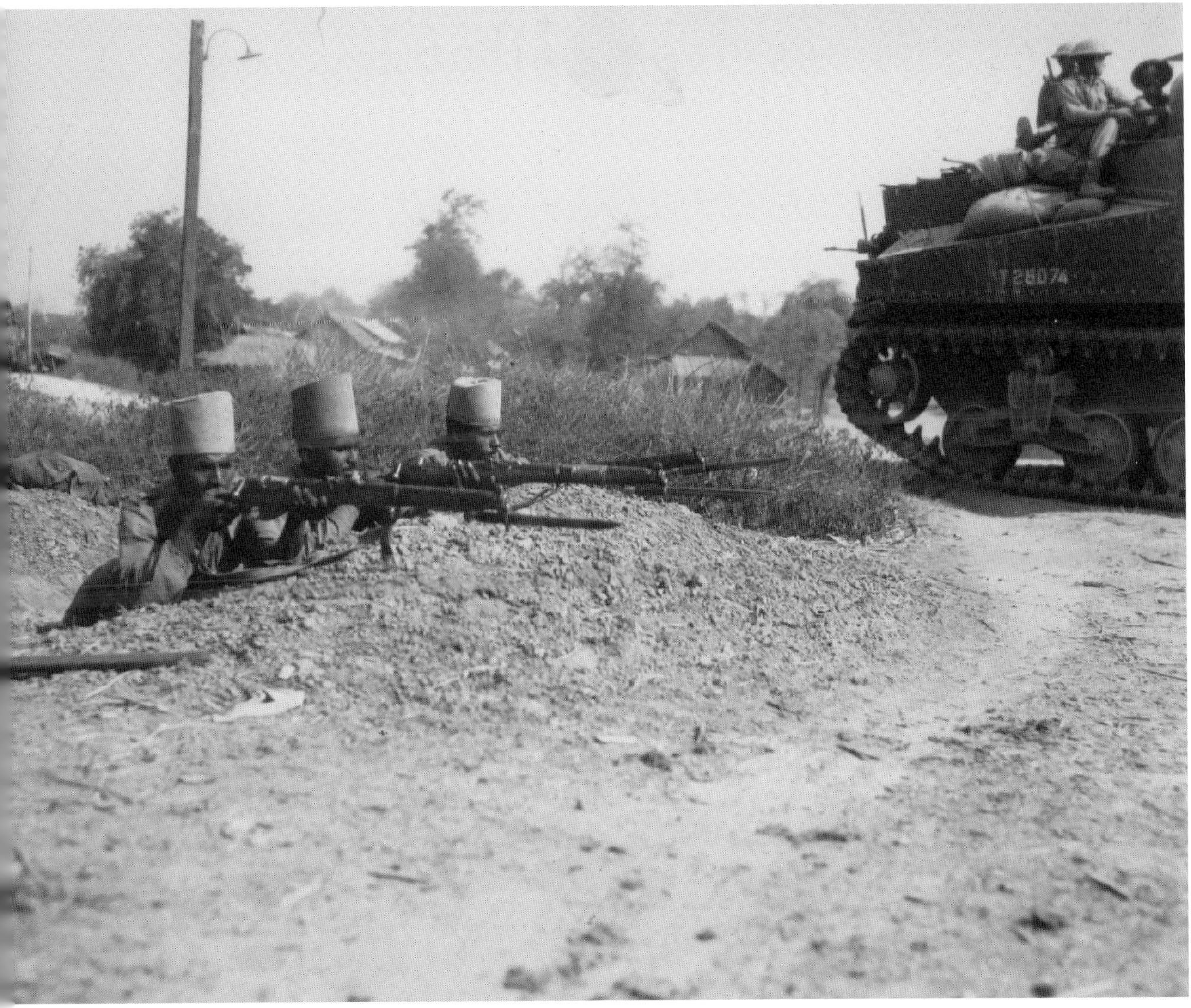

(**Opposite, above**) An Ordnance QF 3.7in AA gun of the RA's Field Regiment of the British 2nd Division is seen here used in a dual bombardment role to shell Mandalay in March 1945. This gun and the howitzers that were brought in later were needed to reduce the walls of Fort Dufferin for the Battle of Mandalay. The British 2nd Division had the 10th, 16th and 99th Field regiments in its order of battle. Earlier in February 1944, during the Second Arakan Campaign's Battle of the Admin Box at Ngakyedouk Pass, Messervy, then CG of the Indian 7th Division in XV Corps, had his 8th Belfast Heavy AA Regiment use the 3.7in AA gun in a direct fire role in February 1944 against repeated Japanese attacks. *(NARA)*

(**Above**) Soldiers of the 19th Indian Division's 3/6th Rajputana Rifles move closer to Mandalay's Fort Dufferin on 9 March 1945 as an M4 medium tank with infantrymen on board passes them (right background). *(NARA)*

(**Opposite, below**) M3 medium tanks of the 254th Indian Tank Brigade attached to the 19th Indian Division prepare to engage the Japanese for Mandalay Hill in March 1945. Obsolete by ETO standards, these tanks were effectively used in Burma where they combated lightly-armoured IJA tanks. In addition to the turret 37mm gun, the sponson on the hull's left side housed a 75mm gun with a limited traverse. *(NARA)*

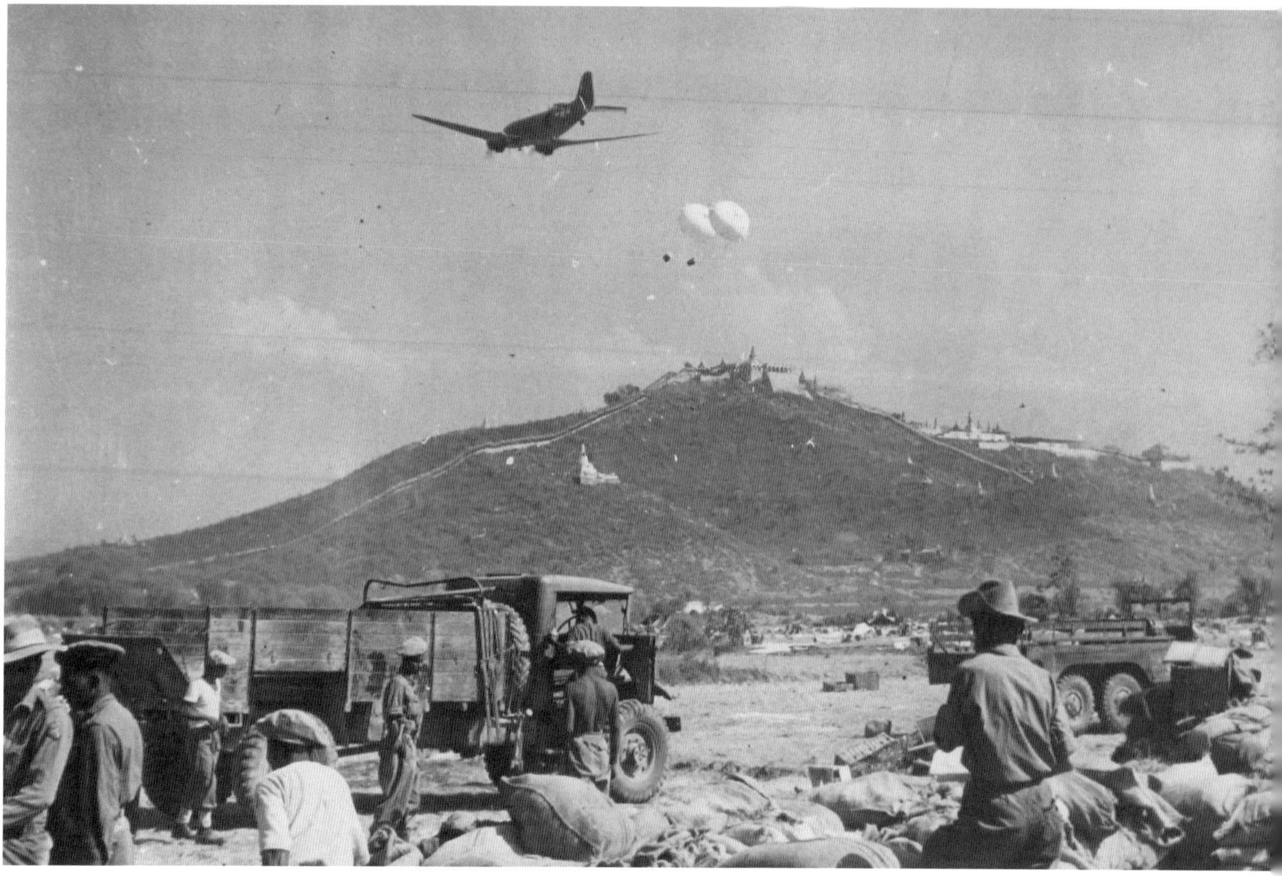

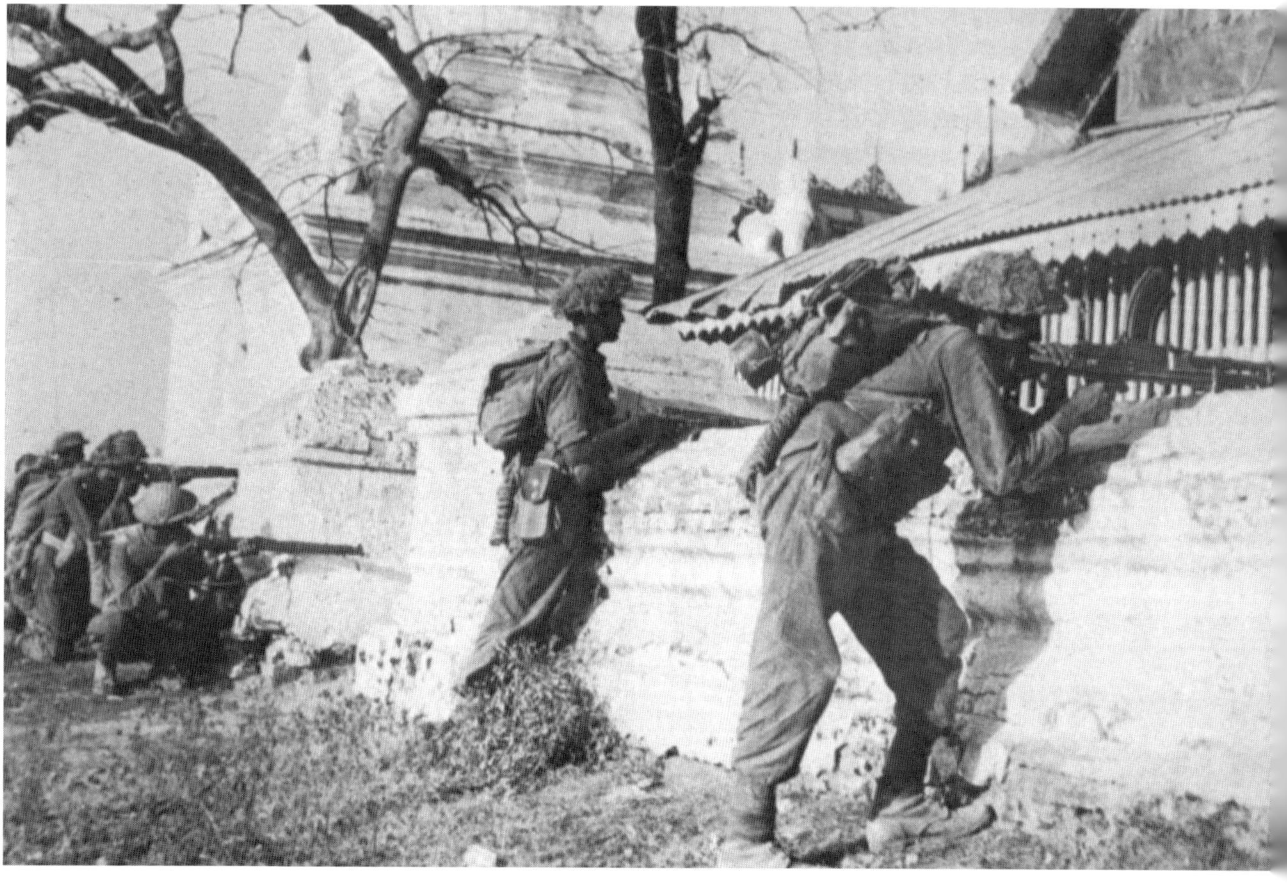

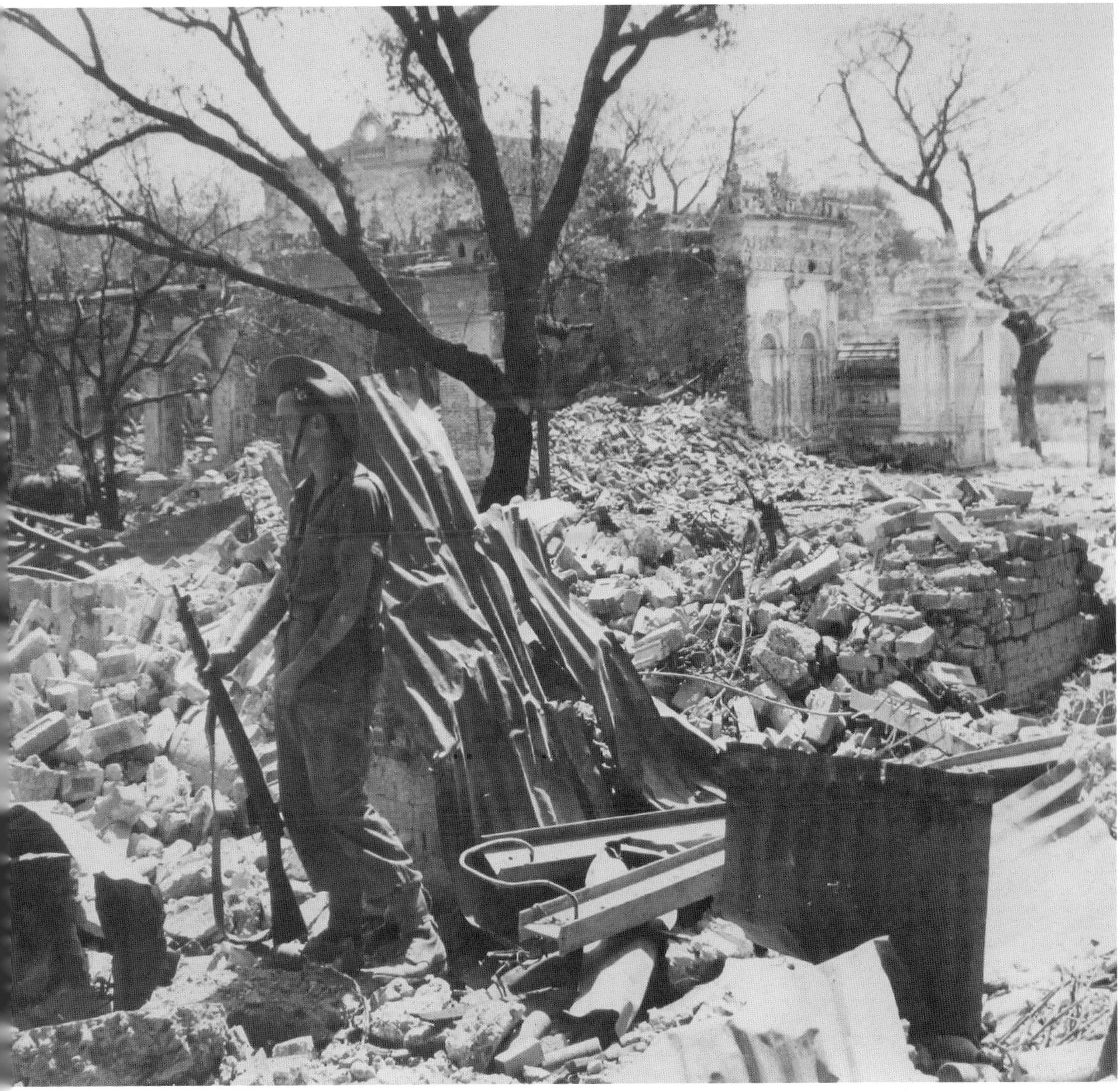

(**Opposite, above**) An American C-47 transport parachutes supplies to 19th Indian Division troops near Mandalay Hill in March 1945. The expansive Burmese theatre that lacked many road or rail networks necessitated airlifting or parachuting supplies and men vital to the Allied Central Burma offensive of 1944–45. *(NARA)*

(**Opposite, below**) A 19th Indian Division infantry section takes cover behind a pagoda wall near Mandalay Hill in March 1945. Often the Japanese would set up MG or sniper positions around temple locations, necessitating their elimination in order for Allied advances to continue. *(NARA)*

(**Above**) A British infantryman stands amid the ruins of Mandalay Hill and Fort Dufferin as XXXIII Corps' 19th Indian, 20th Indian and British 2nd divisions converged on the city from different axes in March 1945. *(NARA)*

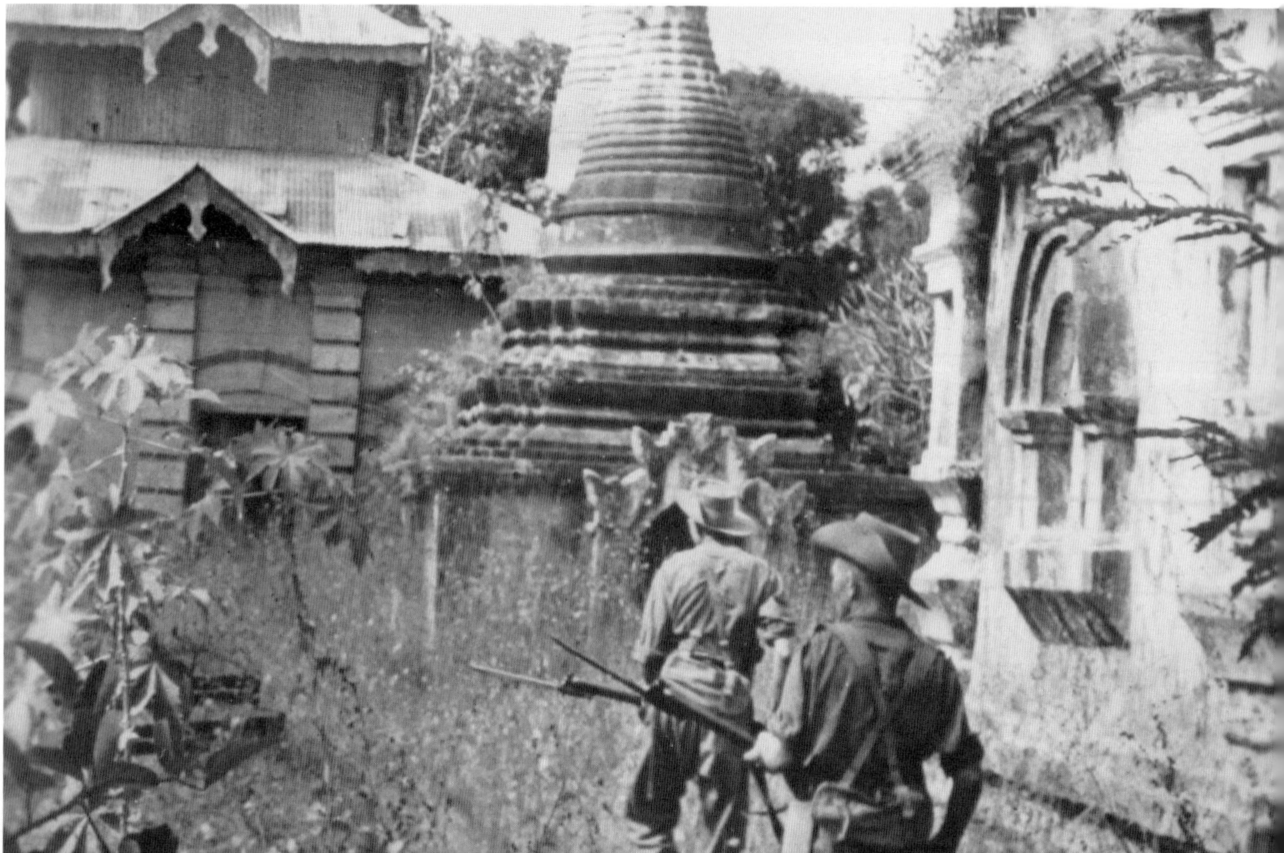

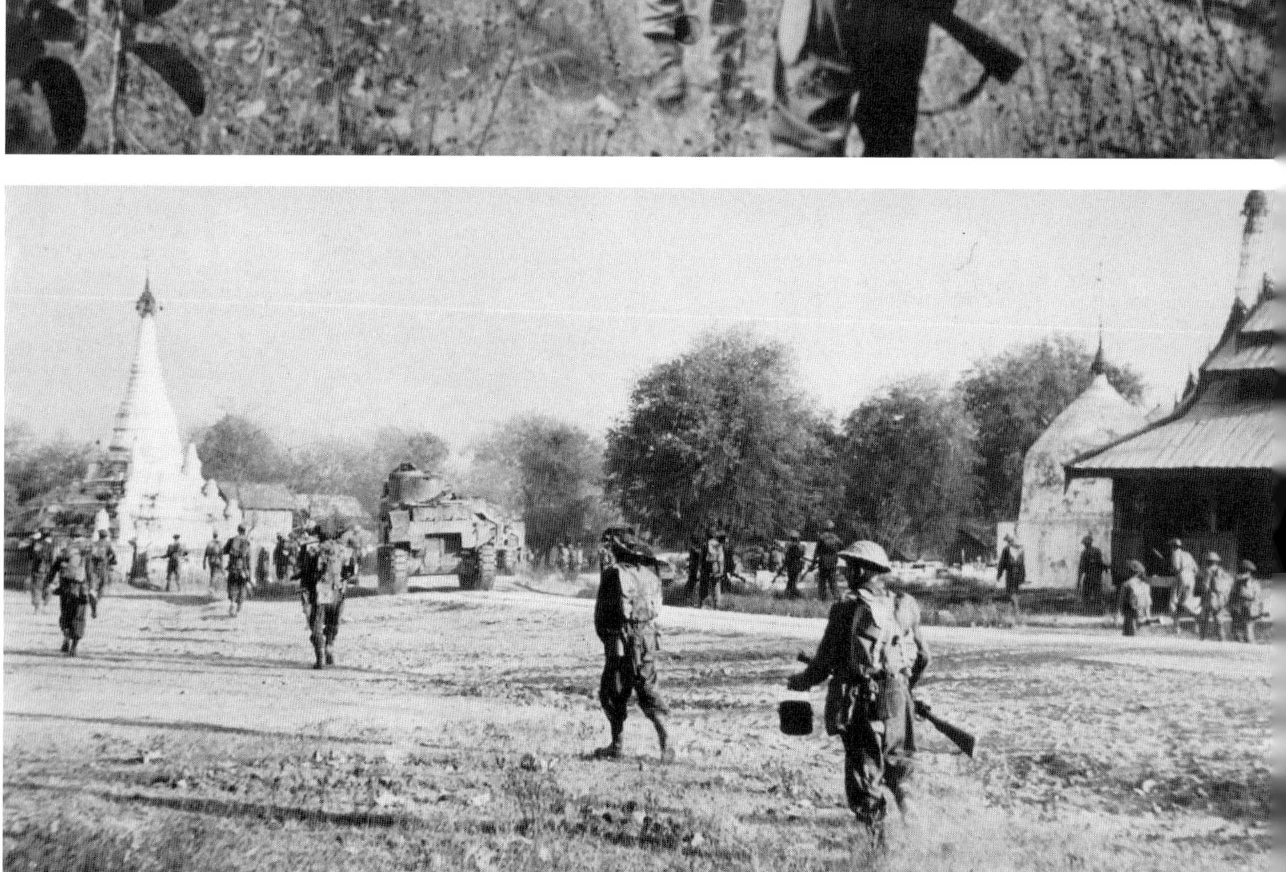

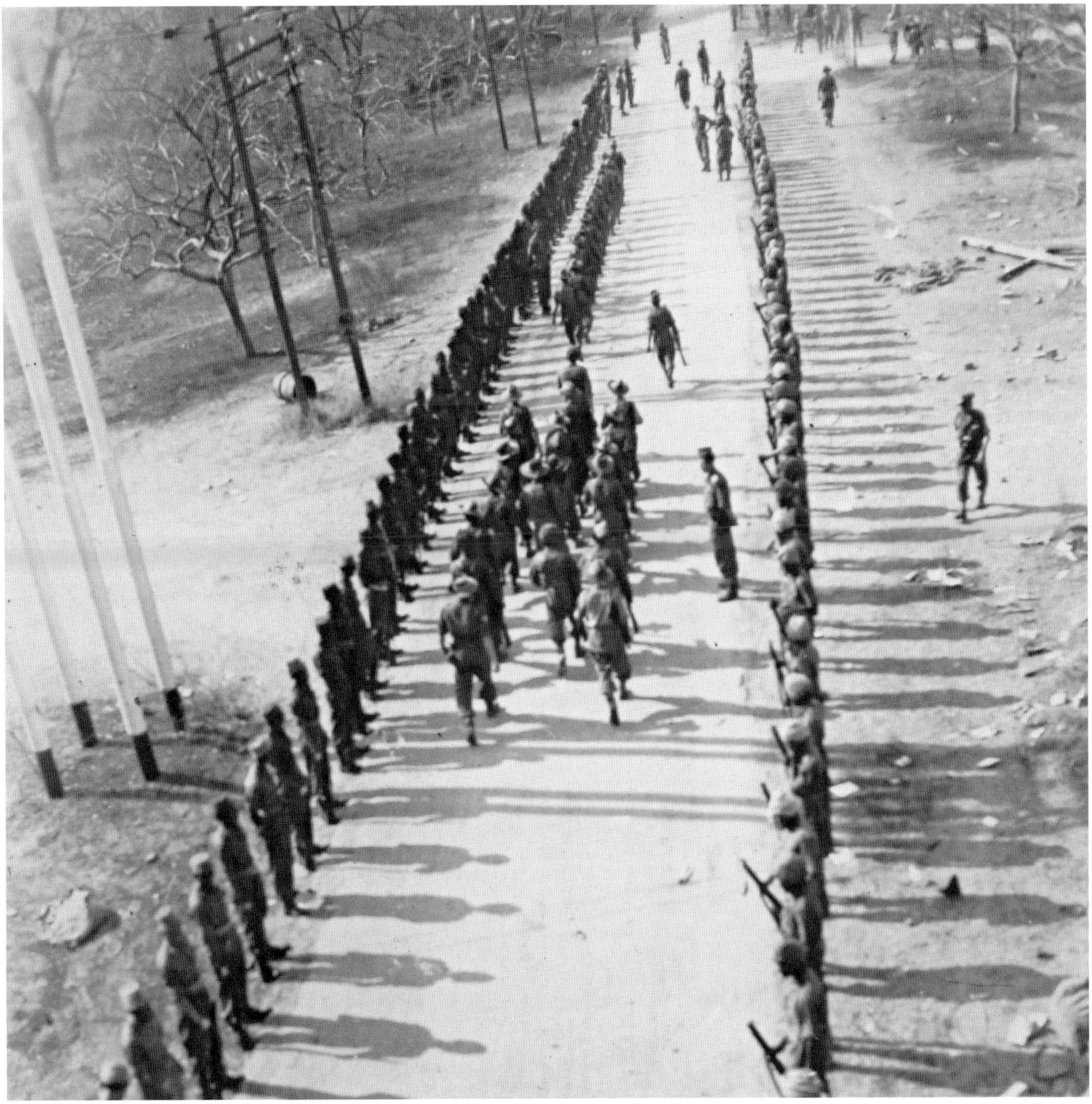

(**Opposite, above**) British infantrymen of the 19th Indian Division advance with fixed bayonets upon entering a Burmese pagoda near Mandalay's city centre in March 1945. British battalions in the 19th Indian Division were from the 2nd Welch, the 2nd Worcestershire and 2nd Royal Berkshire regiments. *(NARA)*

(**Opposite, below**) M3 medium tanks and 19th Indian Division infantrymen move through Mandalay's outskirts after the Battle of Mandalay Hill. These troops then contested the Japanese redoubt within Fort Dufferin in March 1945. *(NARA)*

(**Above**) An honour guard of 19th Indian Division infantrymen lines both sides of a road leading to Fort Dufferin after it and Mandalay were captured. Lieutenant General Slim and Major General Rees, among other Indian army generals, move towards a reviewing stand for the flag-raising ceremony at the fort on 21 March 1945. *(NARA)*

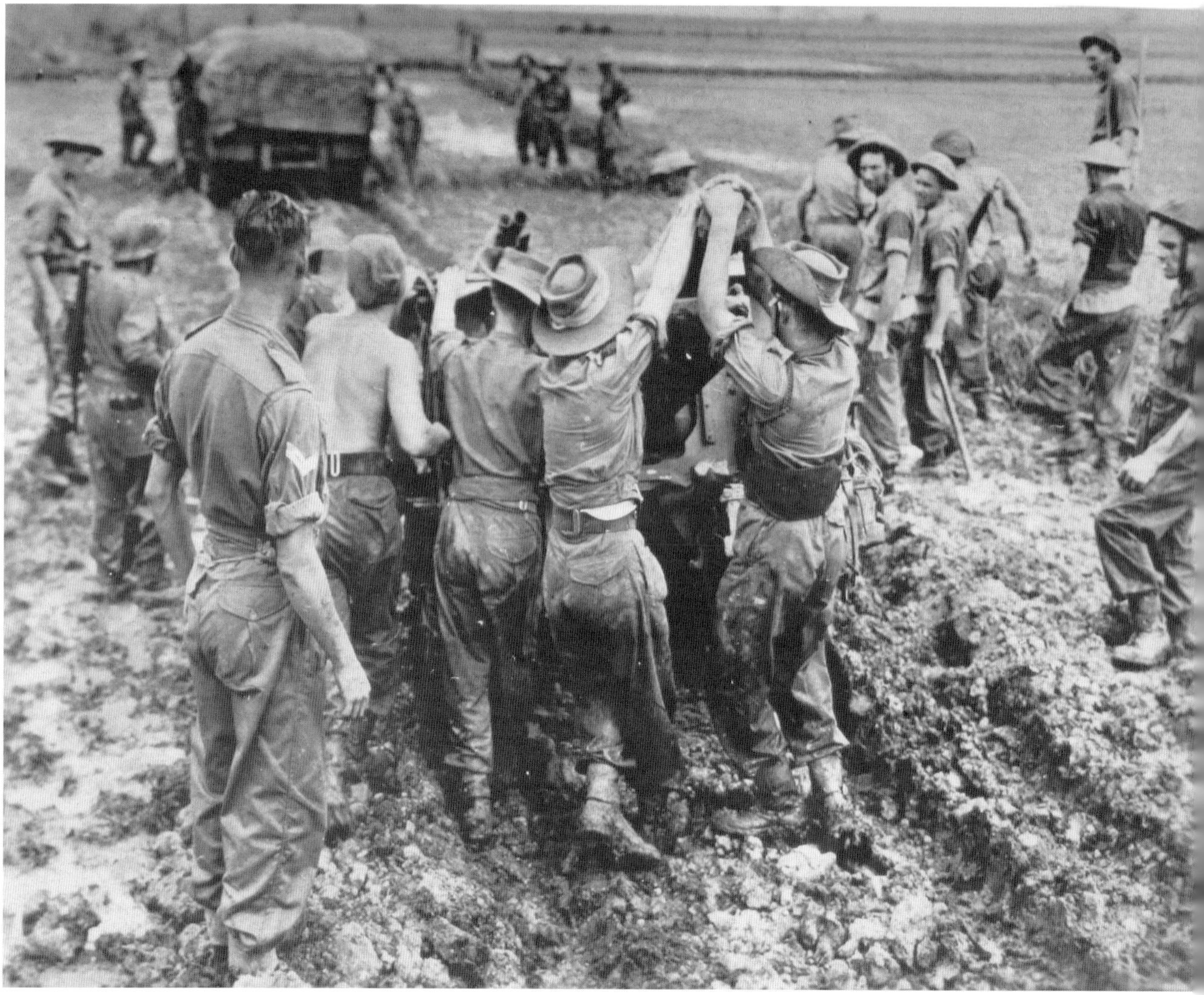

(**Above**) British gunners and infantrymen manhandle a 25-pounder field gun stuck in mud after monsoon rains on the road to Rangoon. Weather and terrain were constant concerns for Allied logistics throughout the central Burma offensive now heading south to Rangoon after Mandalay's capture. *(NARA)*

(**Opposite, above**) Fourteenth Army trucks of the 161st Infantry Brigade carrying troops and supplies cross a temporary wooden bridge across the Pyu *Chaung* on 23 April 1945 on the 5th Indian Division's advance to Pyu, situated between Toungoo and Pegu on the main road axis of advance southwards towards Rangoon. The offensive commenced south of Meiktila and ran on a line through Yamethin-Shwemyo-Pyinmana-Toungoo-Pyu. After Pyu's capture on 25 April, the 17th Indian Division resumed the southerly advance to Pegu, which was captured on 1 May. The line of advance from Meiktila to Pegu paralleled the Sittang River to the east and the Pegu Yomas to the west with Rangoon situated south of the mountain range. *(NARA)*

(**Opposite, below**) Here 17th Indian Division infantrymen are seen taking cover on a grassy plain with a disabled enemy tank (background) en route to Rangoon in late April 1945. The 17th Indian Division attacked Pegu on 29 April, but an attempted ford of the Pegu River north-east of Rangoon met with difficulties. An IJA/IJN independent mixed brigade, the 'Rangoon Defence Force' numbering 7,000 troops held Pegu. This enemy force possessed the remnants of the IJA 14th Tank Regiment. *(NARA)*

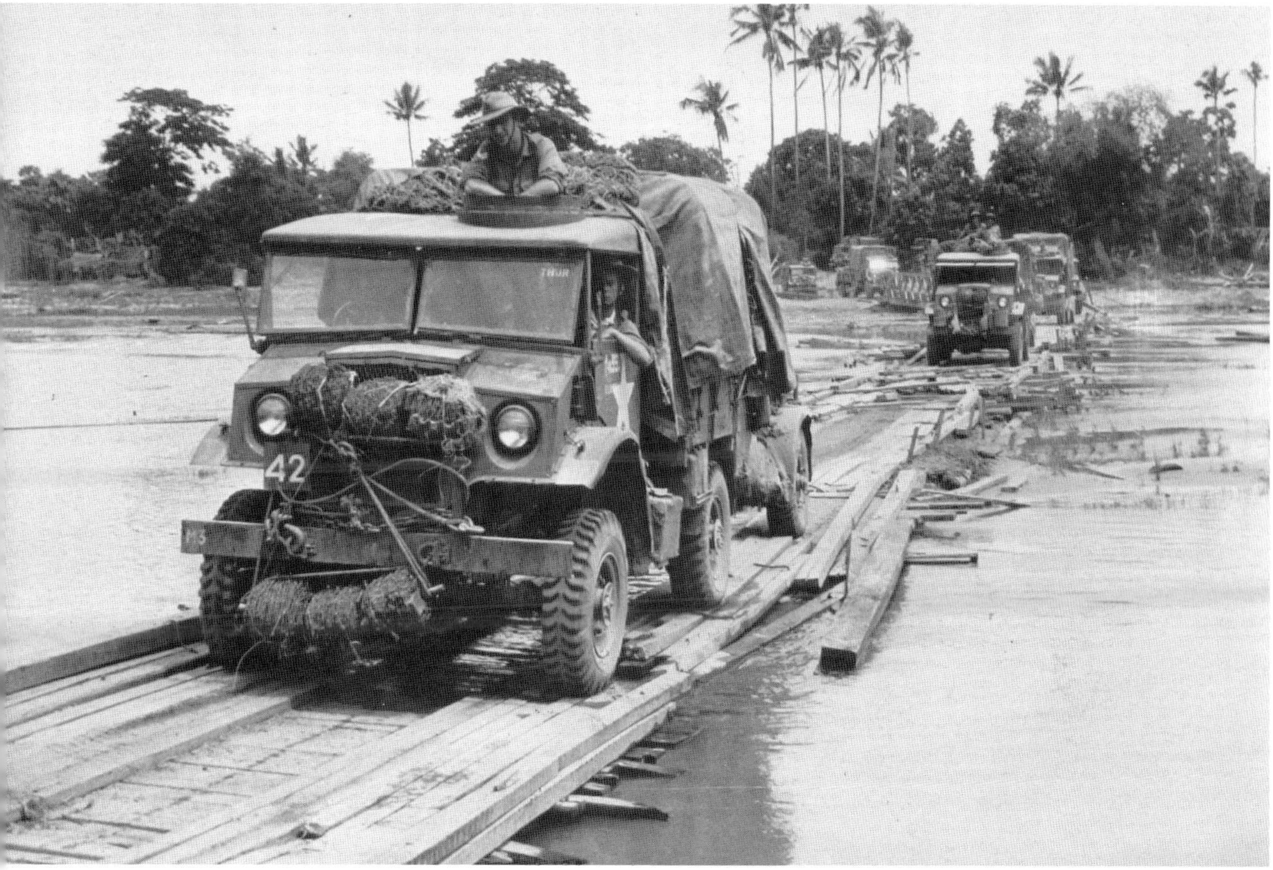
42

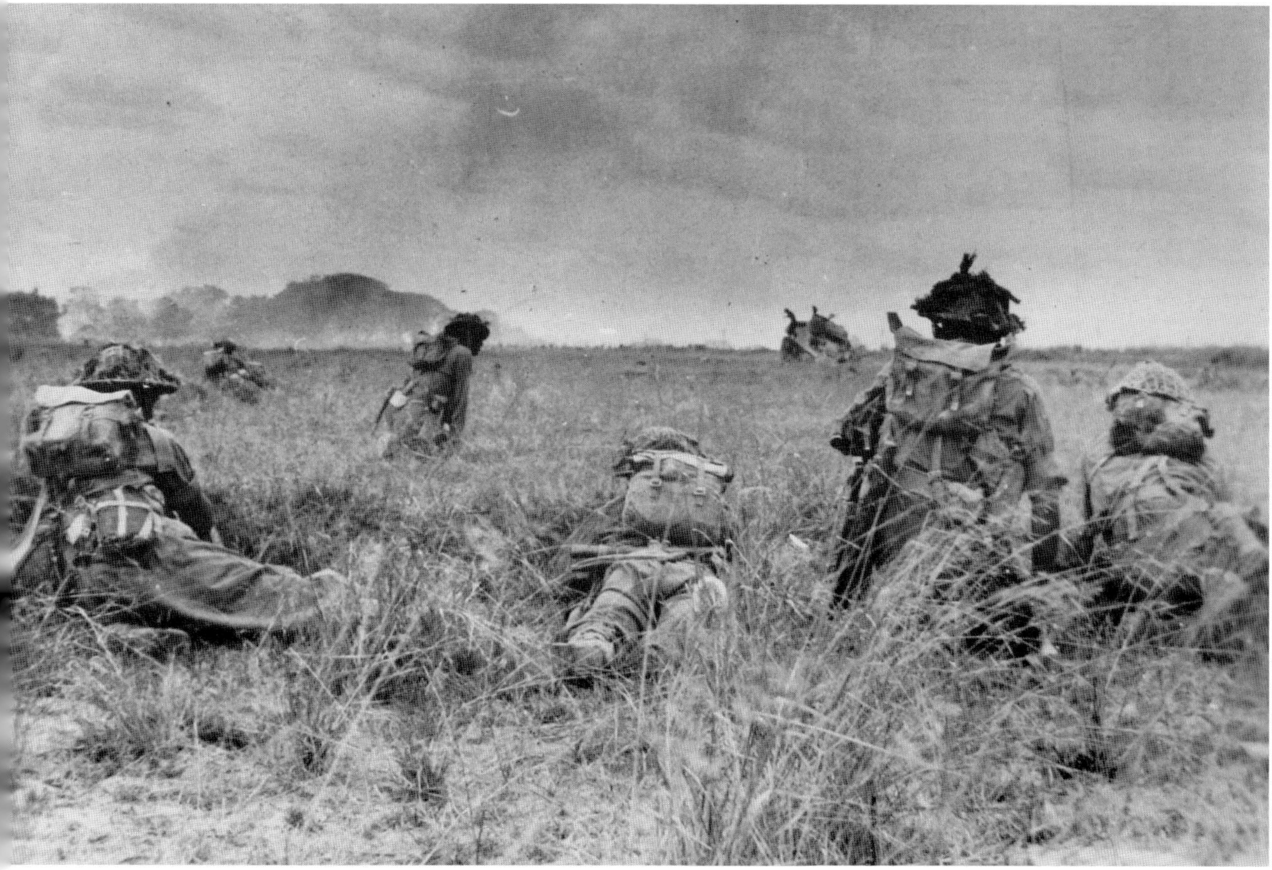

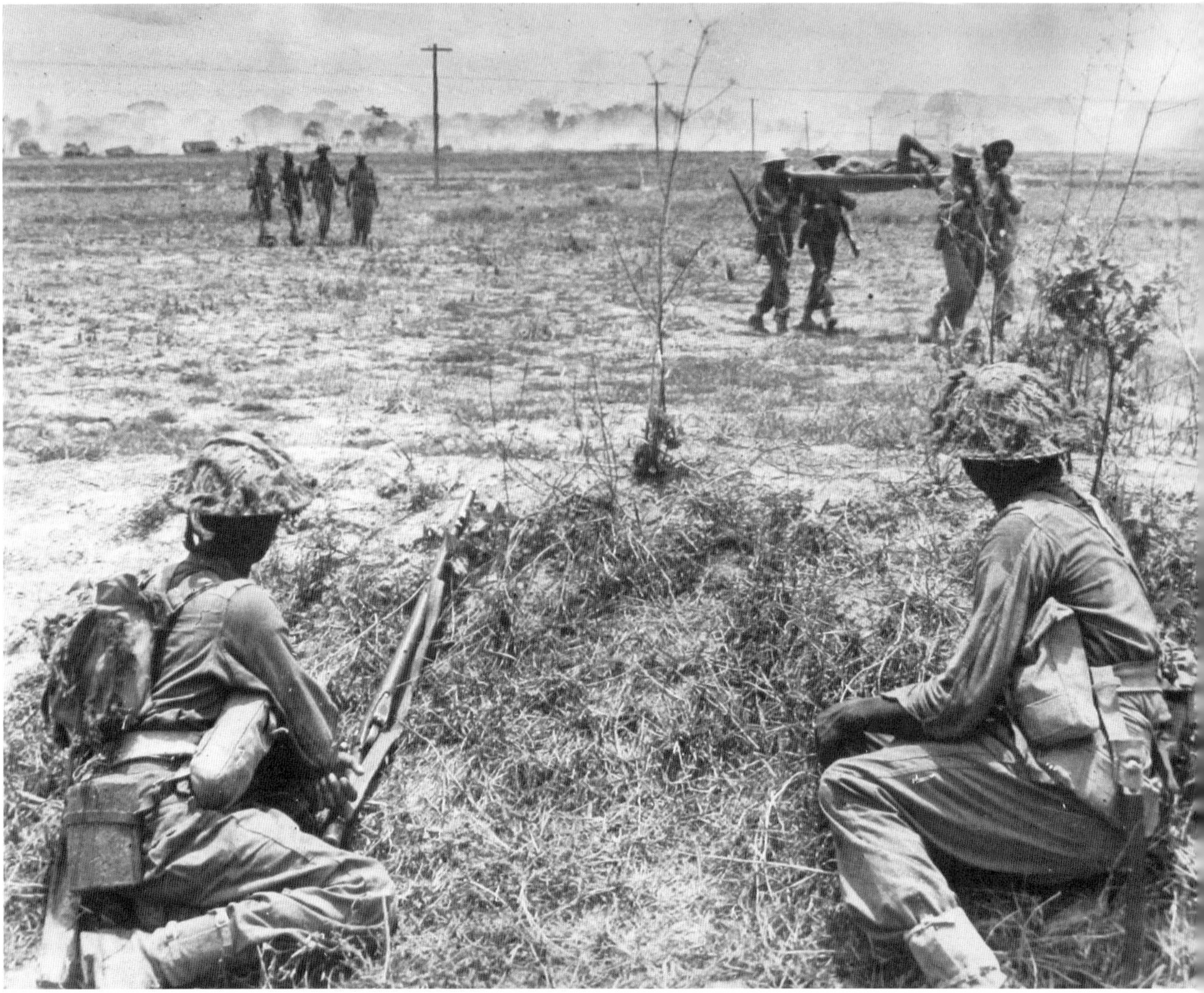

Some 17th Indian Division SBs carry their wounded across an open plain during the Rangoon advance in late April 1945. Armoured cars of the 16th Light Cavalry and tanks of 5th (Probyn's) Horse supported the infantry. *(NARA)*

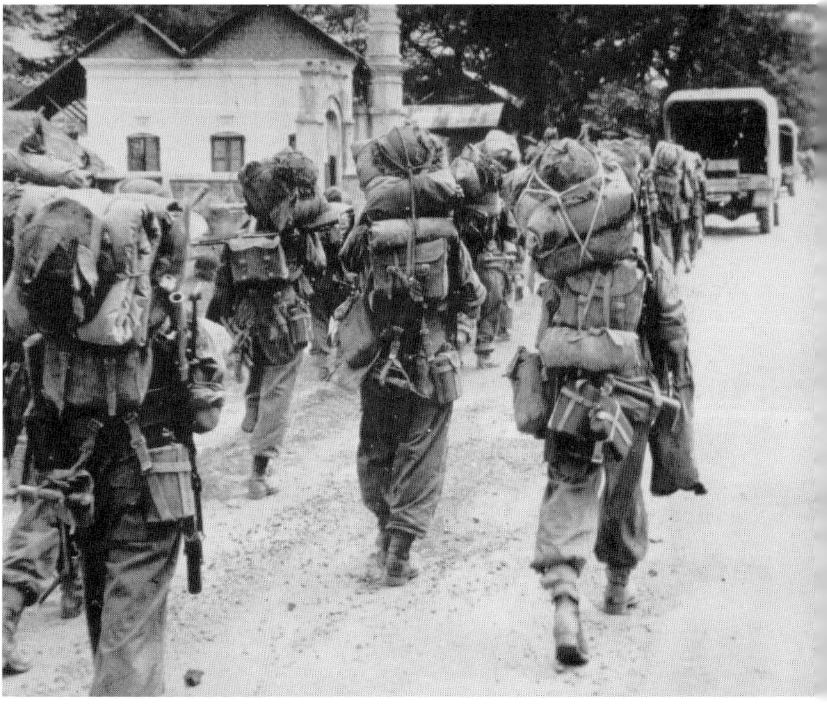

Infantrymen from the 17th Indian Division's 1st West Yorkshire Regiment (48th Infantry Brigade) march towards Rangoon at the end of April 1945. The troops are carrying their full packs and kit with supply trucks ahead of them (background). *(NARA)*

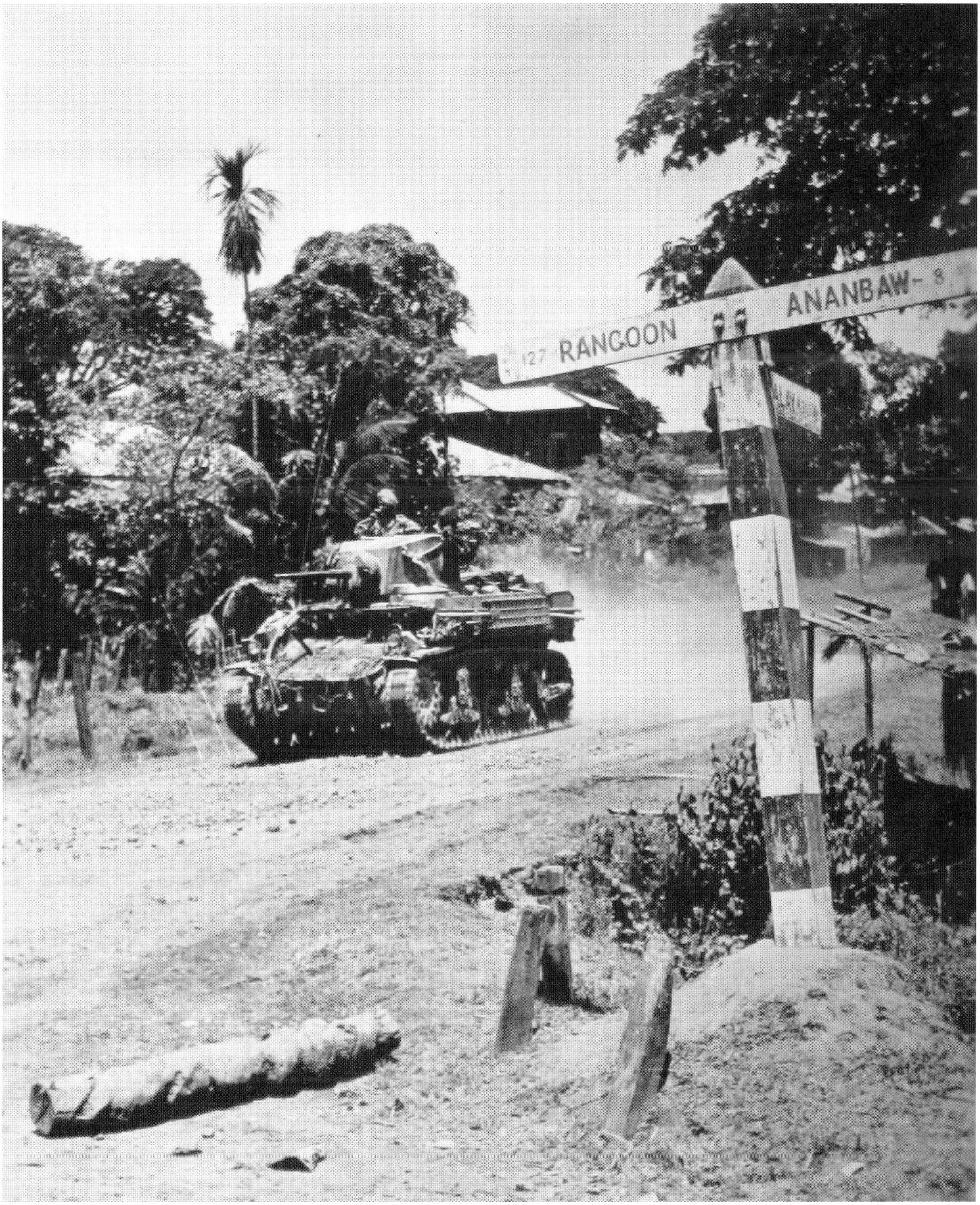
127 RANGOON
ANANBAW- 8

A 255th Indian Tank Brigade's M5 light tank attached to IV Corps supports the 17th Indian Division advancing to Rangoon through a Burmese village in late April 1945. After dark on 30 April, the 63rd Infantry Brigade entered Pegu to find the Japanese withdrawing. The next day a 17th Indian Division armoured advanced guard left Pegu and the race for Rangoon was resumed. *(NARA)*

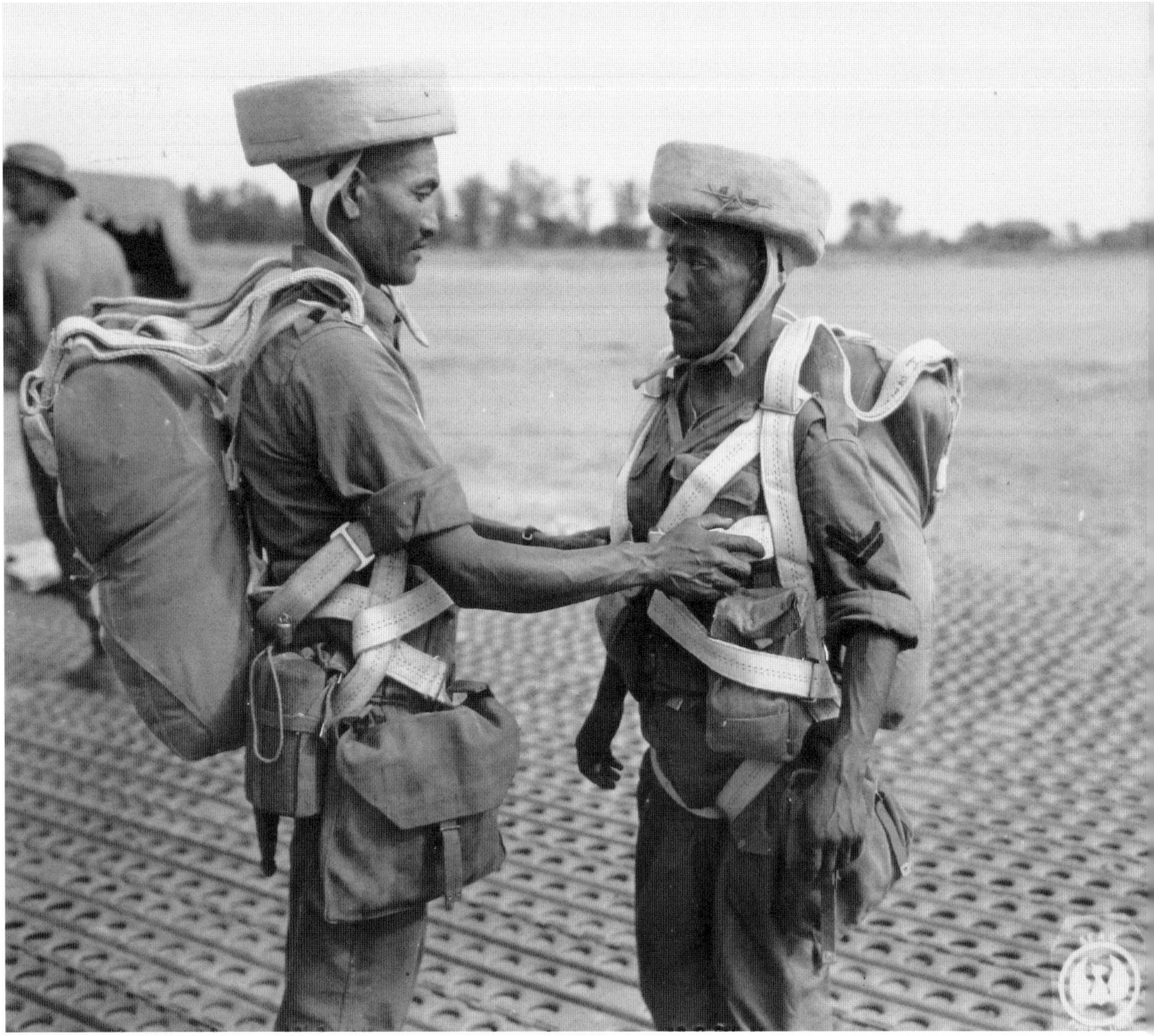

(**Above**) Two 50th Gurkha Parachute Regiment members check equipment before jumping near Elephant Point for the airborne part of Operation DRACULA's Rangoon assault in early May 1945. Marston matting was used as the forward airfield's runway surface. This pierced steel planking was developed by the US Waterways Experiment Station in Marston, North Carolina where Camp McNeill's airfield first utilized the matting. *(NARA)*

(**Opposite**) Gurkha paratroopers descend during the airborne stage of Operation DRACULA to capture Rangoon in early May 1945. The 50th Gurkha Parachute Regiment, part of the 44th Indian Airborne Division, consisted of the 151st, 152nd and 153rd Gurkha Parachute battalions. A Gurkha Parachute Battalion landed behind Japanese coastal defences at the mouth of the Rangoon River on 1 May, clearing an enemy artillery battery and supporting bunkers at Elephant Point to enable the 26th Indian Division's passage up the Rangoon River as Operation DRACULA's amphibious portion after the waterway was cleared of mines. About forty IJA soldiers and artillerymen were killed during the airborne assault in which close-quarter fighting with flame-throwers occurred against Japanese bunkers supporting the battery that guarded the Rangoon River. By dawn of 2 May, the paratroopers watched minesweepers clearing the Rangoon River. *(NARA)*

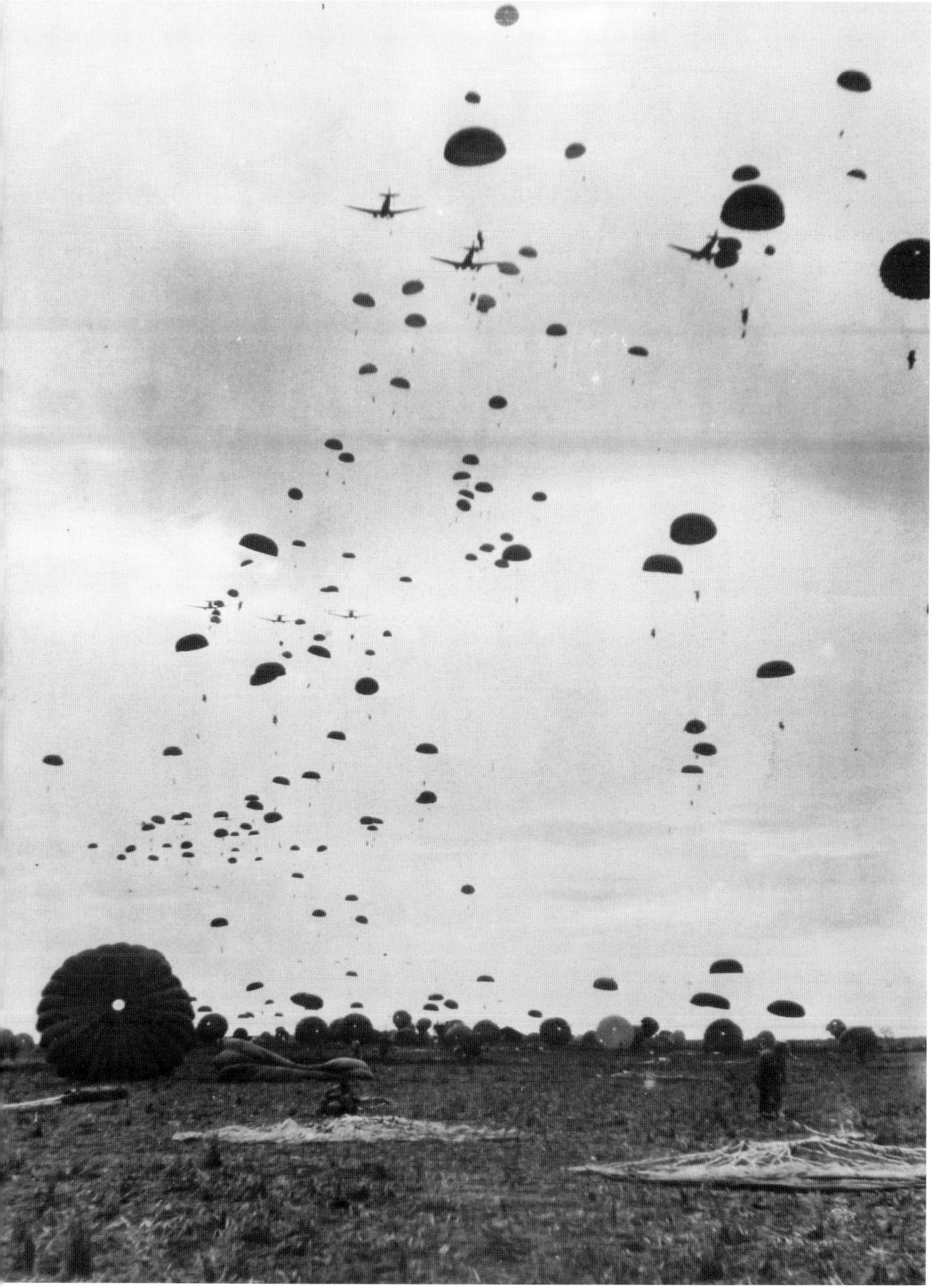

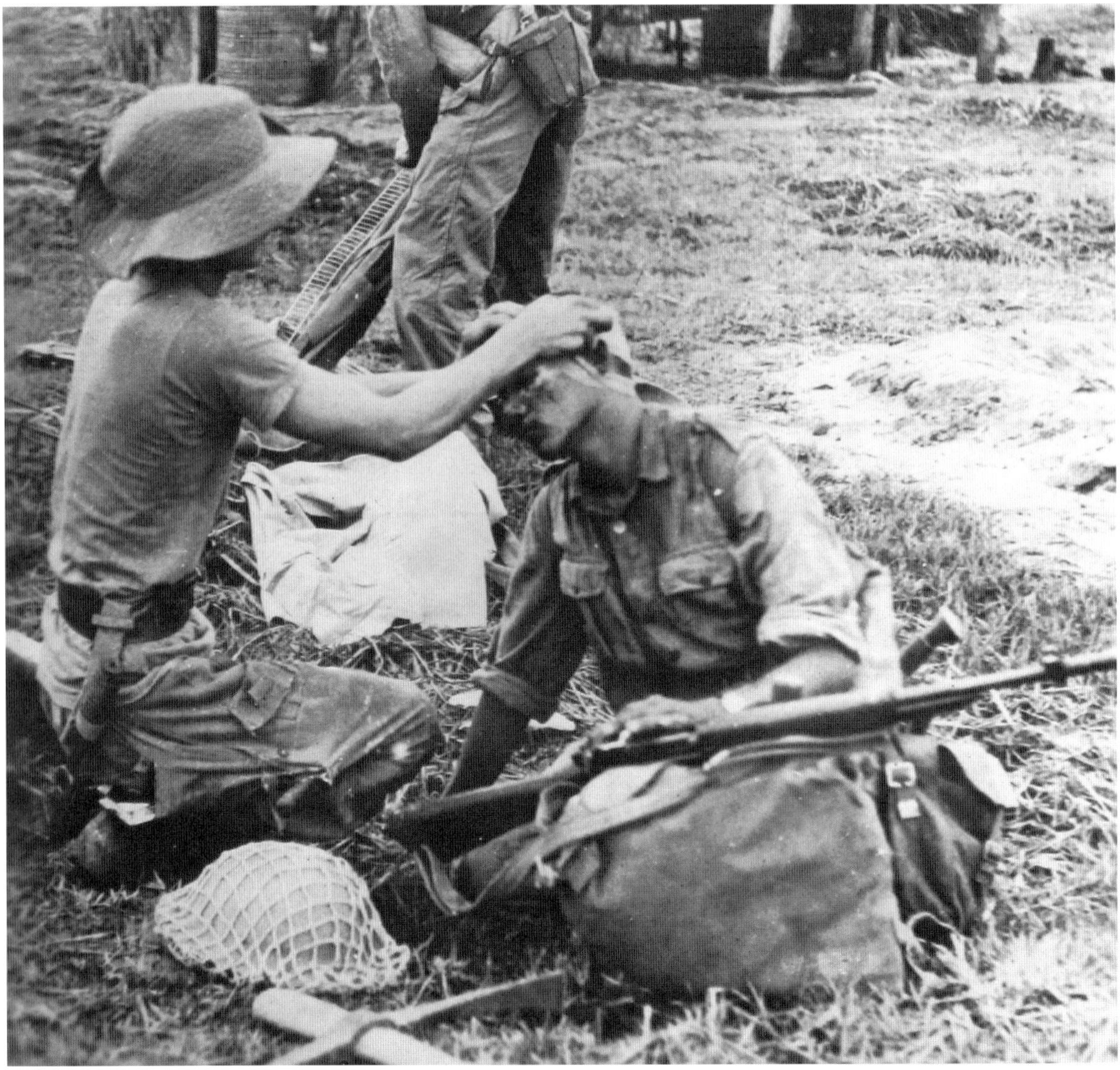

(**Above**) A Gurkha paratrooper receives medical attention at Elephant Point after Operation DRACULA's airdrop to seize an artillery battery at the Rangoon River's mouth. The Gurkhas incurred some air-landing casualties but several more to USAAF aerial 'friendly fire' bombing of the enemy battery by B-24 bombers. Additional casualties occurred in the storming of the Japanese bunkers guarding the battery to rout the defenders. *(NARA)*

(**Opposite, above**) Indian infantrymen descend the forward ramps of their LCIs south of Rangoon on 2 May 1945 during Operation DRACULA's amphibious portion. After the Rangoon River had been cleared of mines, XV Corps' 26th Indian Division landed on both banks of the river. The IJA had abandoned Rangoon several days earlier and elements of the 26th Division occupied the city and its important docks without opposition. *(NARA)*

(**Opposite, below**) British infantrymen of the 26th Indian Division descending from their LCI on 2 May 1945 in order to amphibiously seize Rangoon from the south. The Rangoon River's bank was flooded as the monsoon started that day. The British units in the 26th Indian Division included the 2nd Green Howards and the 1st Lincolnshire Regiment of the 4th and 71st Infantry brigades respectively. *(NARA)*

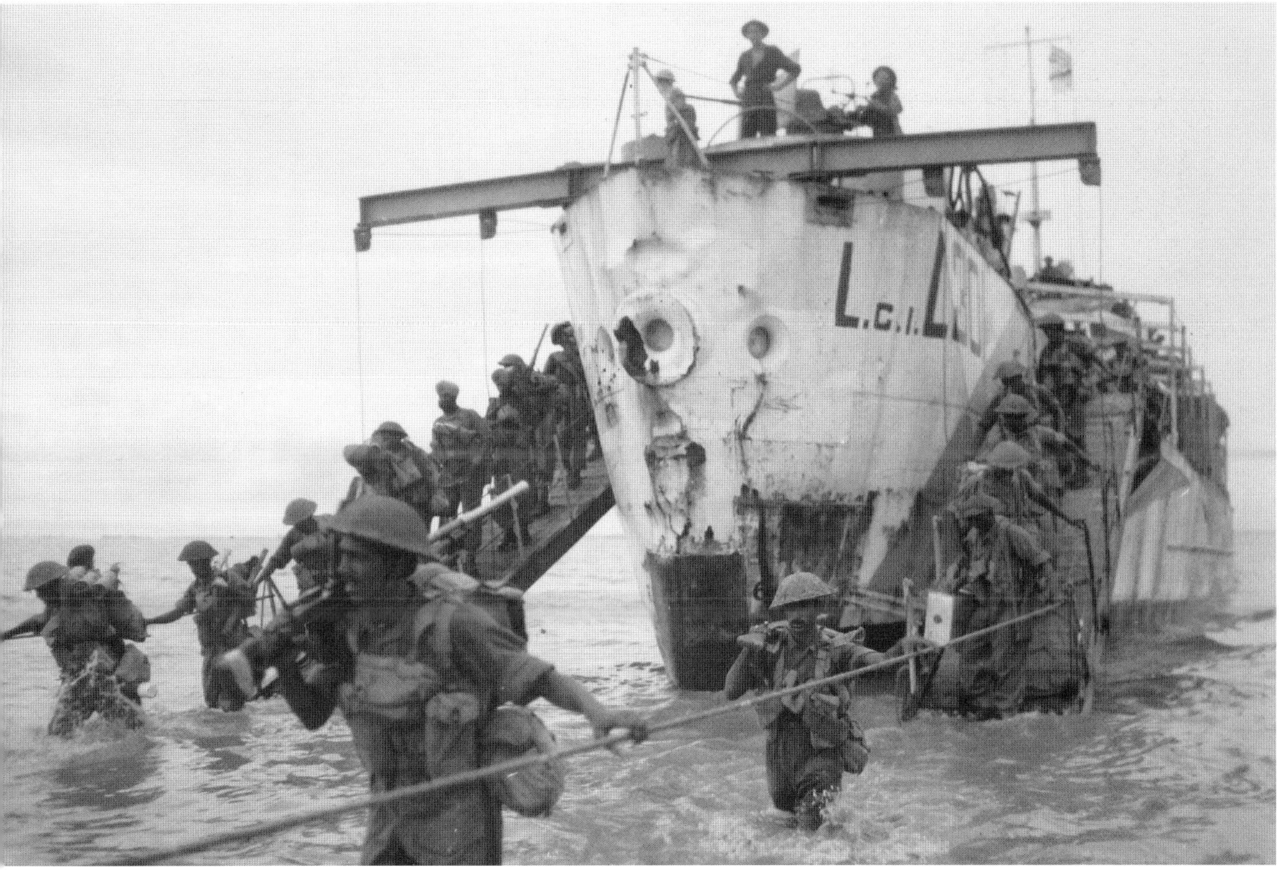
L.C.I.

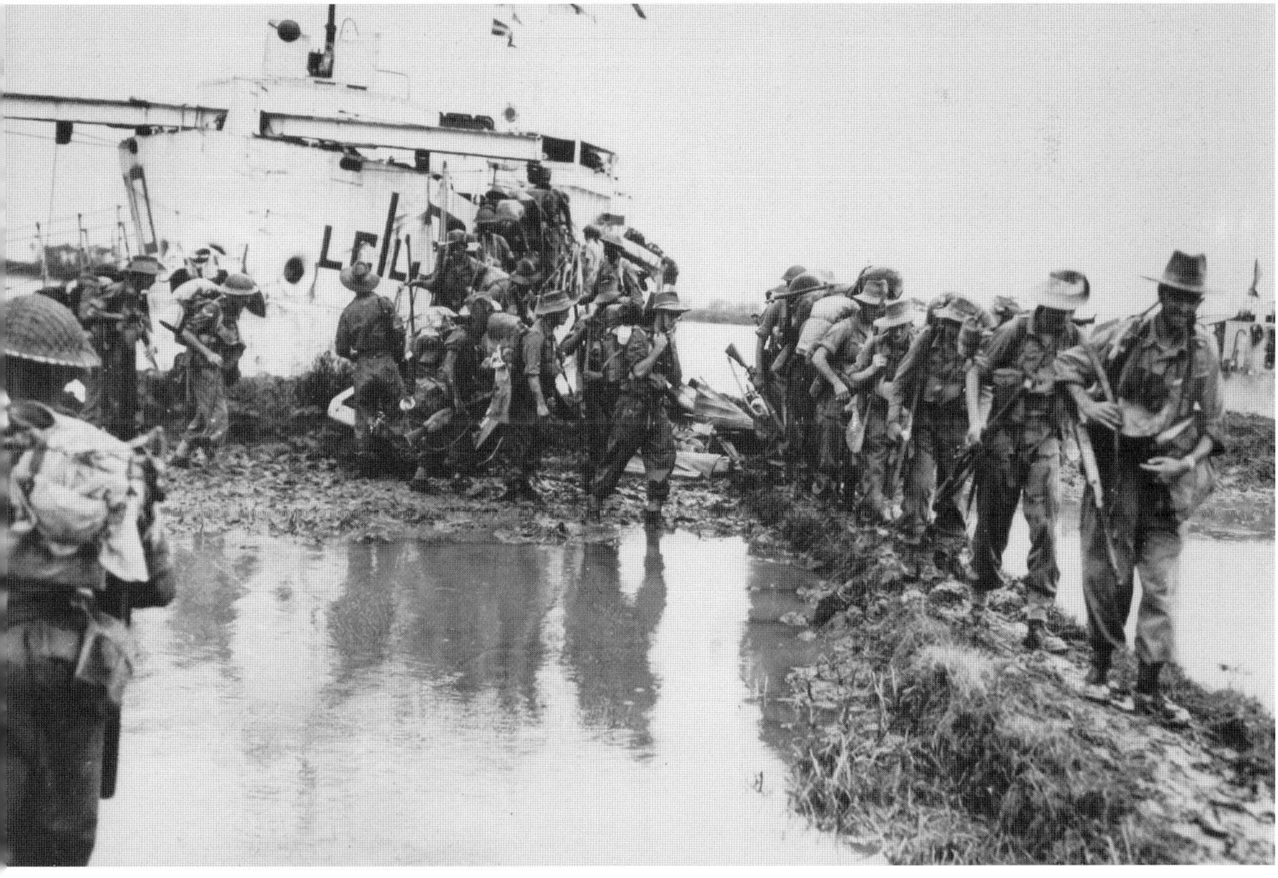

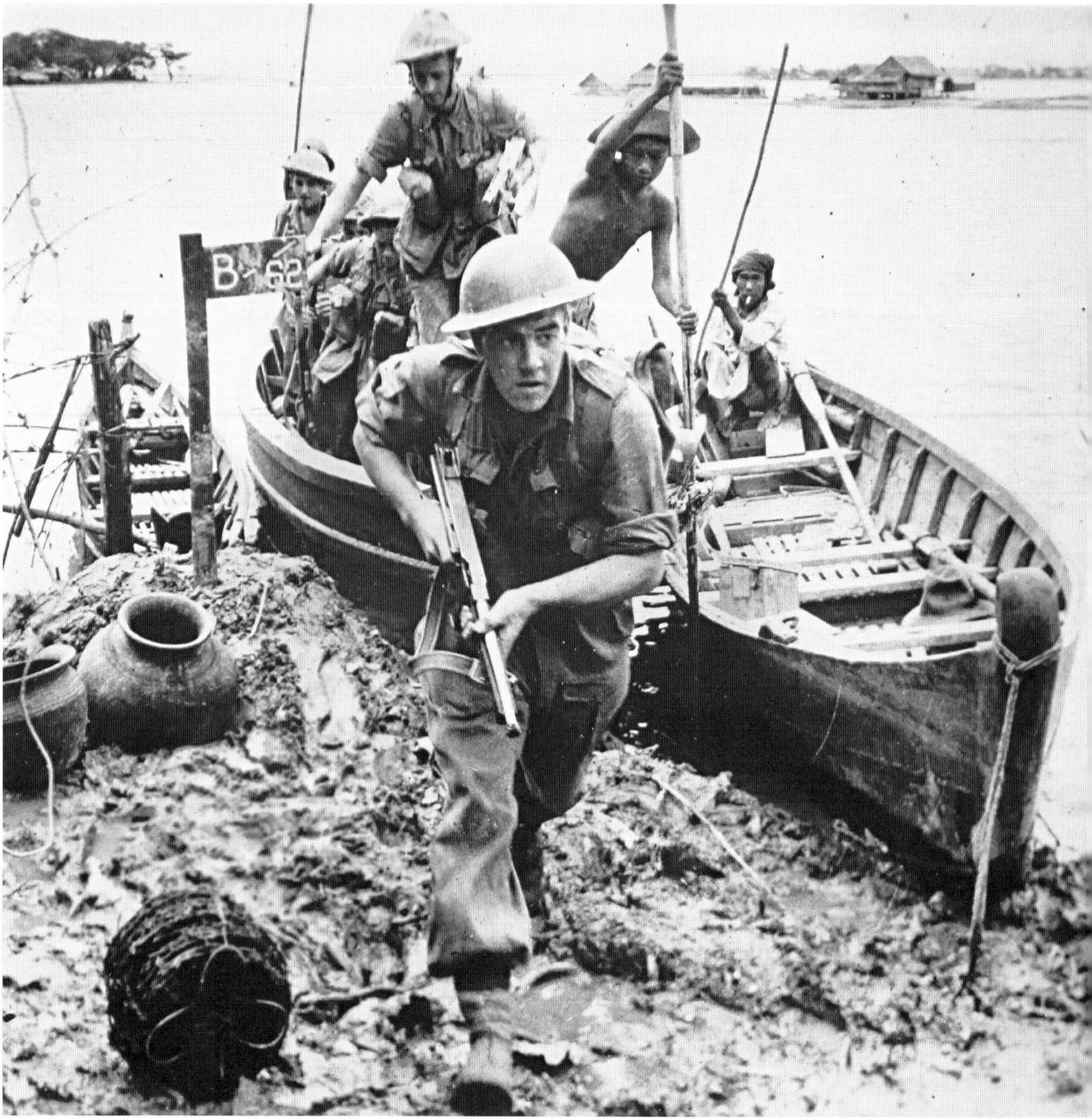
B-62

A British patrol disembarks from local boats manned by Burmese civilians across flooded fields searching for any signs of Japanese resistance in the advance to Rangoon in late April to early May 1945. *(NARA)*

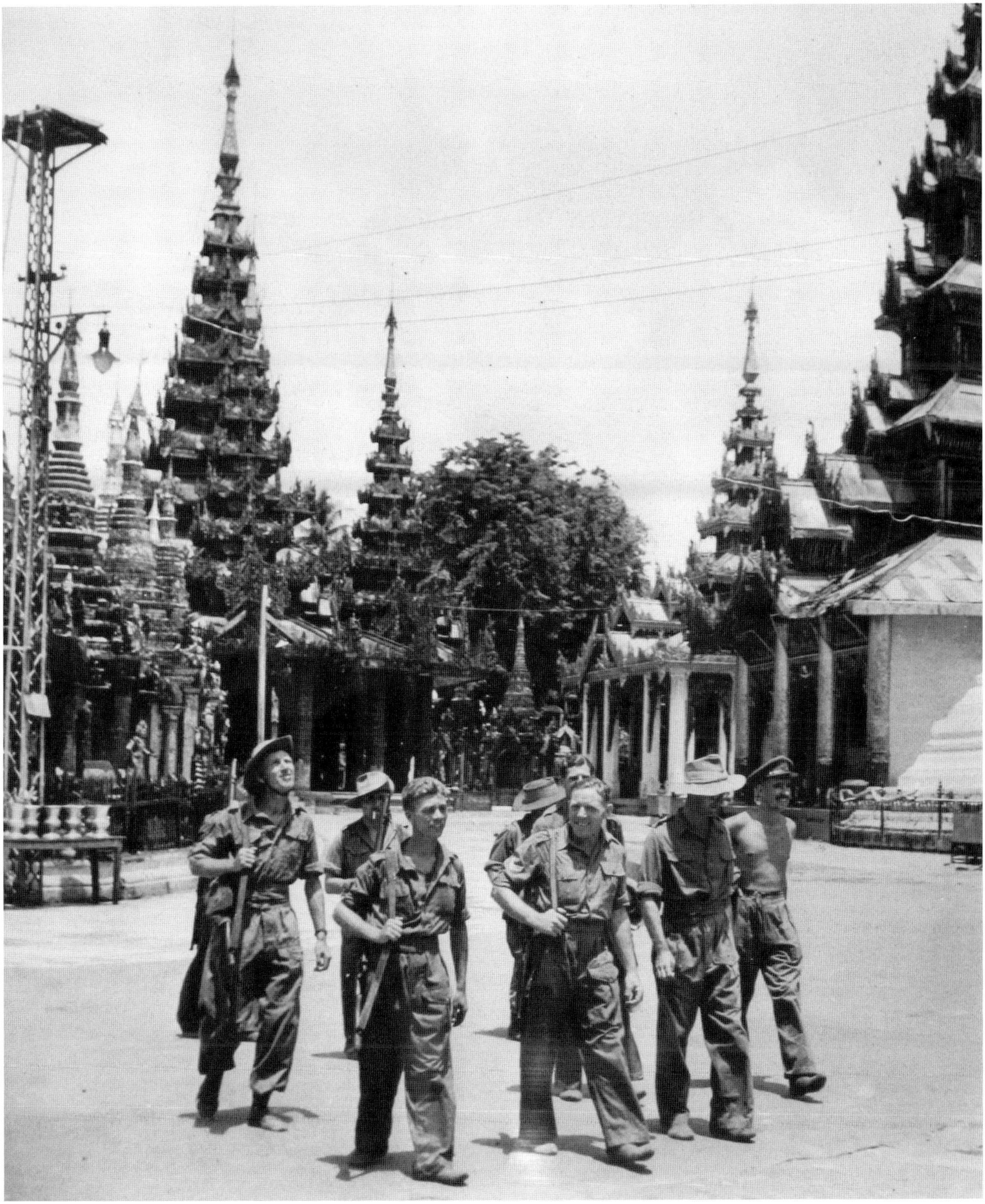

In May 1945, British troops visit Rangoon's most sacred Shwedagon pagoda as it is reported to contain strands of Buddha's hair. This Buddhist pagoda was constructed more than 2,600 years ago, surviving many wars and conflicts. *(NARA)*

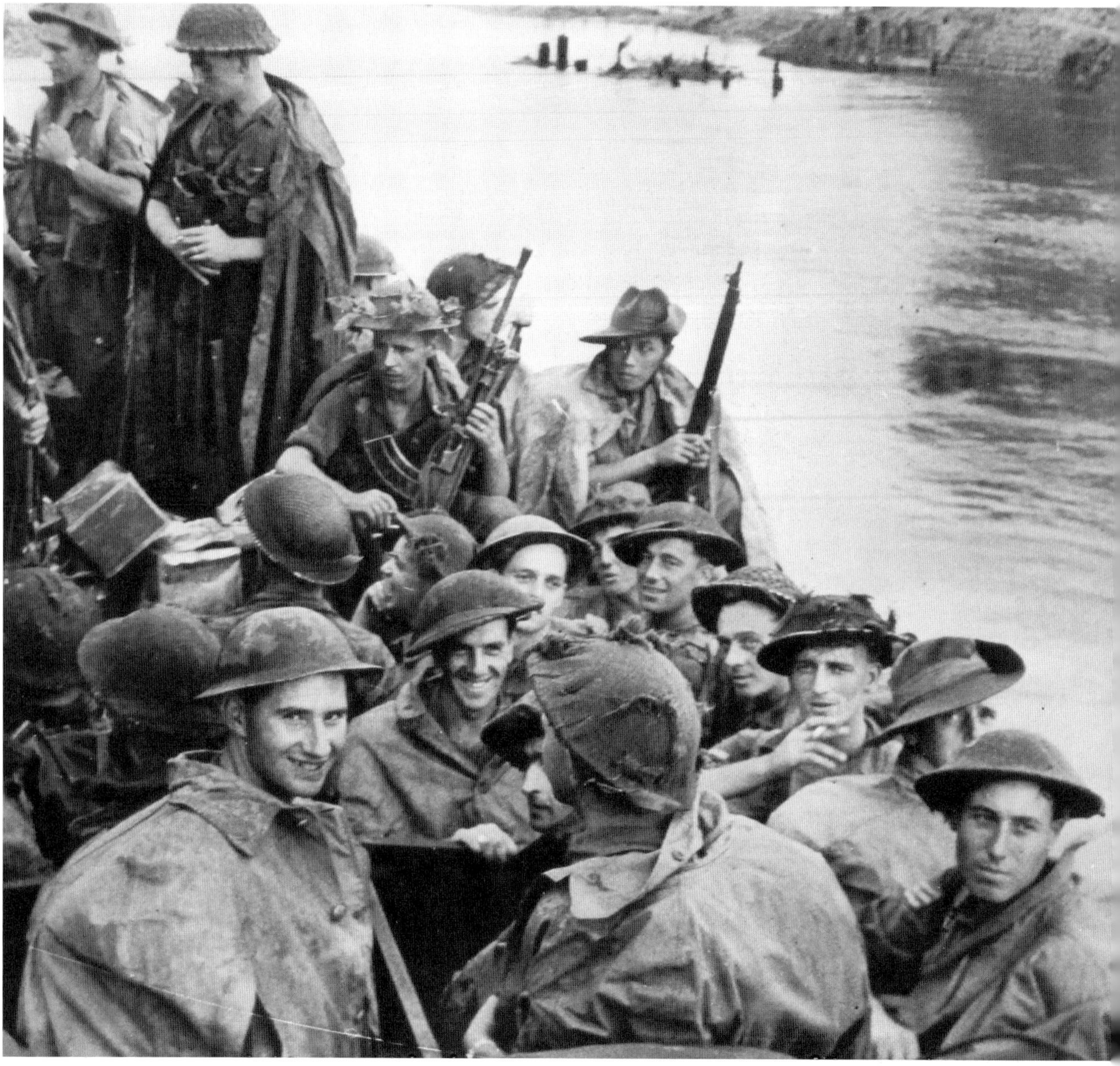

(**Above**) British troops in the 17th Indian Division are aboard assault craft on the Pegu Canal near Waw, 50 miles north-east of Rangoon on 1 May 1945. The soldiers wear raingear as the monsoon had recently started. On 29 April a small column of infantry and armoured cars cut the Payagyi-Waw road, which was the last escape route east to the Sittang River for the Japanese fleeing Pegu and Rangoon. *(NARA)*

(**Opposite, above**) A British patrol in a local craft steered by Burmese at the Sittang River's mouth during a monsoon accompanying the Battle of the Sittang Bend in July 1945. The retreating IJA Twenty-Eighth Army attempted an eastward movement across the Pegu Yomas to the eastern bank of the Sittang River. Elements of IV Indian Corps arrived beforehand to halt the Japanese exodus. The IJA Thirty-Third Army attacked the Sittang Bend on 3 July to assist the eastward break-out of the IJA Twenty-Eighth Army across the Pegu Yomas; however, after incurring heavy casualties, the IJA Thirty-Third Army withdrew on 7 July. On 21 July, the retreating IJA Twenty-Eighth Army began its last attempt to cross the Sittang River to the east bank and suffered heavy casualties. *(NARA)*

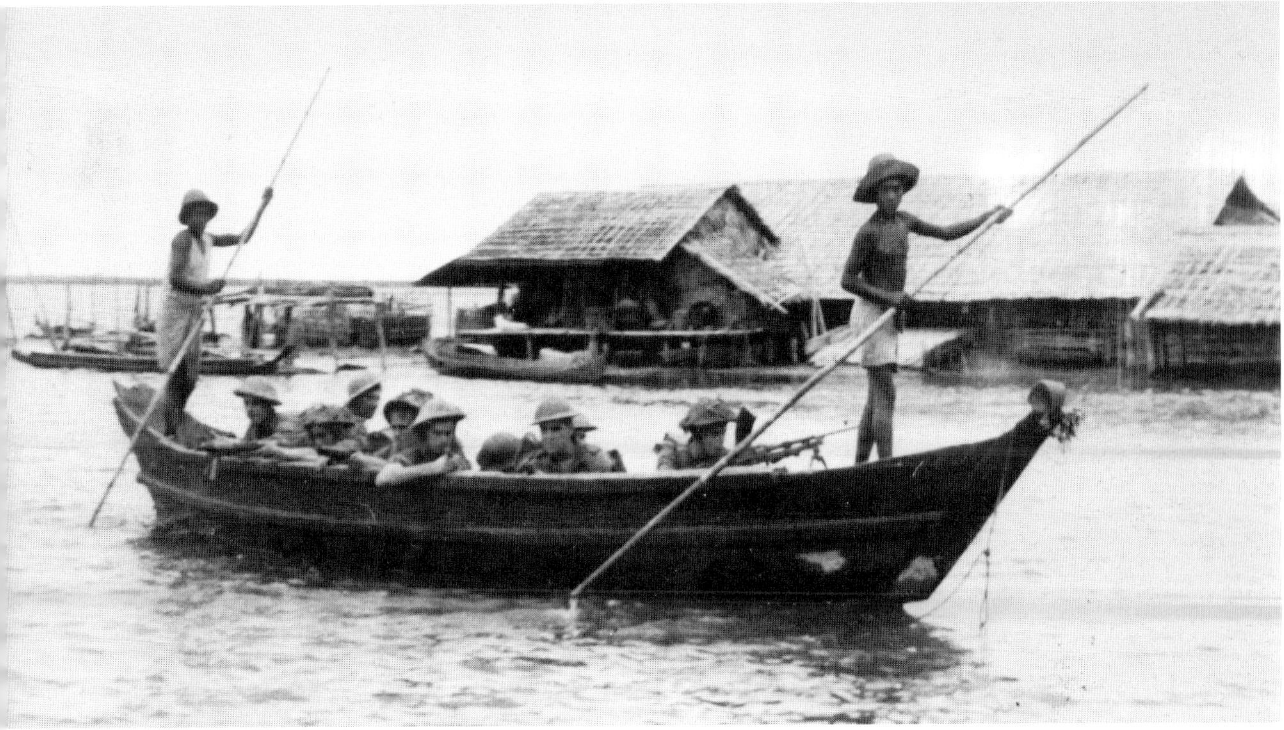

(**Below**) An RA 5.5in medium gun battery fires on Satthinagyon during the Battle of the Sittang Bend in early August 1945 near the war's end. Coupled with air sorties, RA 4.5in, 5.5in and 25-pounders shelled the routes of the Japanese retreat, slaughtering hundreds throughout July into early August. *(NARA)*

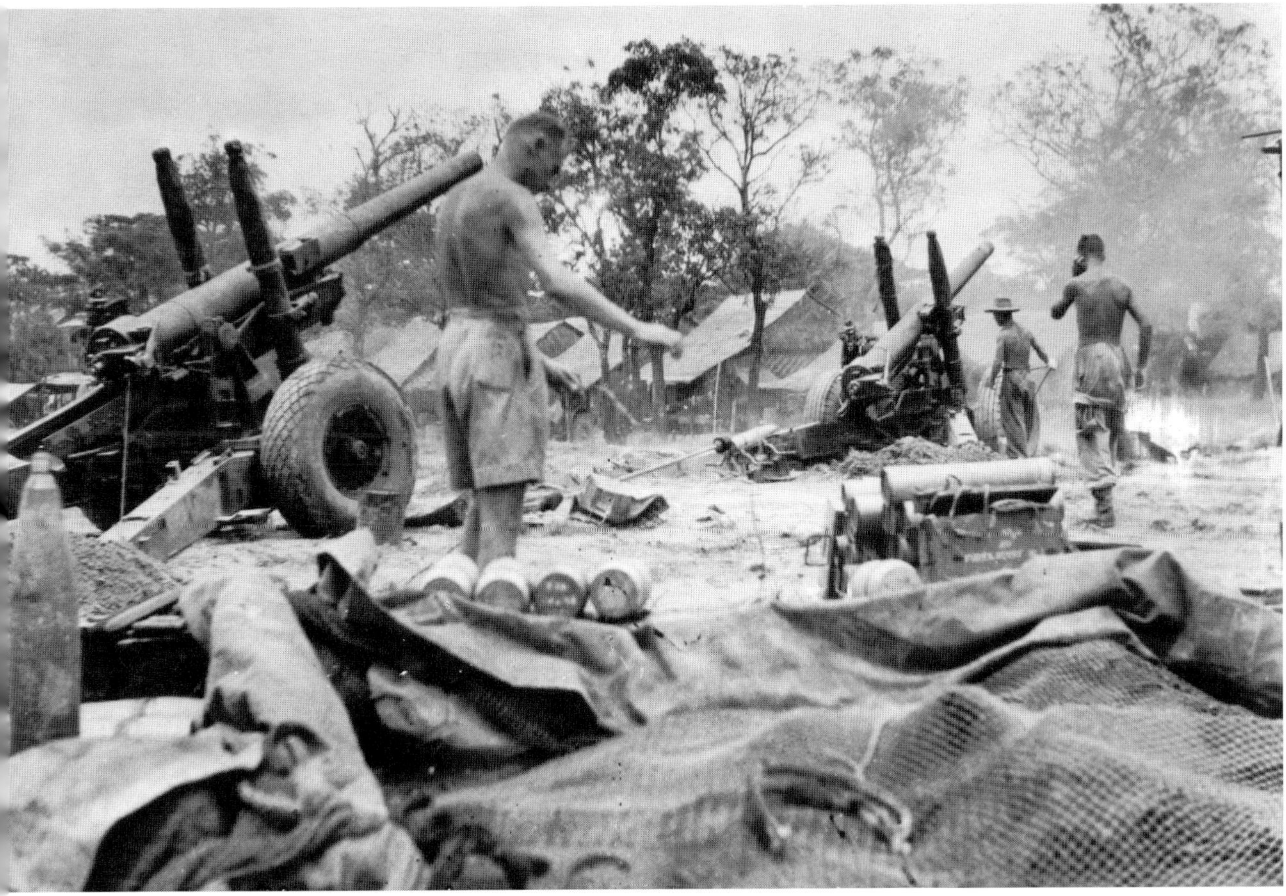

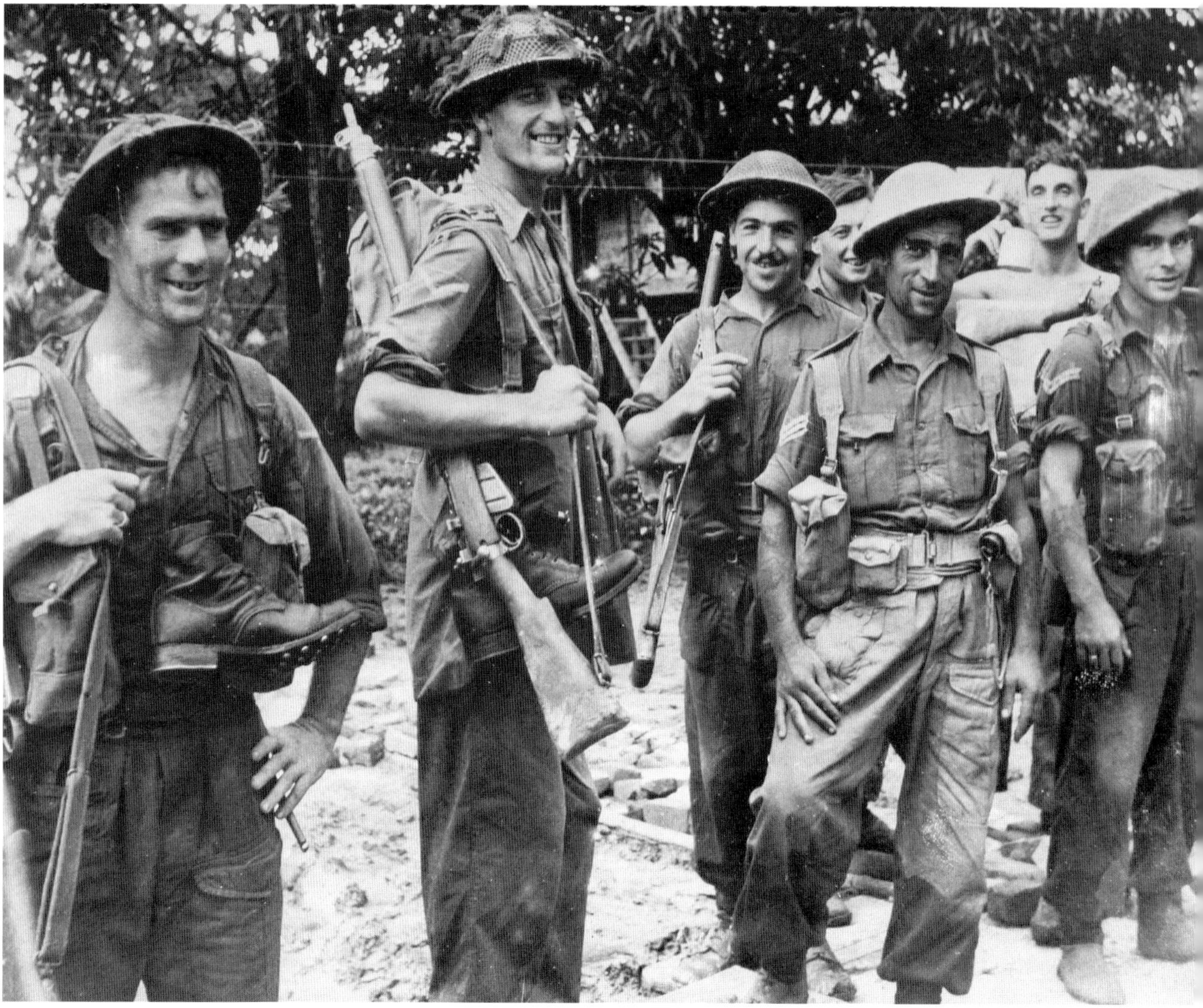

British infantrymen are seen here in the Sittang River area at the war's end. These IV Corps troops were instrumental in fighting off the IJA Thirty-Third Army in early July 1945 and then decimating the retreating remnants of the IJA Twenty-Eighth Army as they attempted to cross to the eastern side of the Pegu Yomas and then cross to the eastern bank of the Sittang River. *(NARA)*

Chapter Six

Allied Drive South of Myitkyina with the Construction of the Ledo/Stilwell Road

After Myitkyina town's capture in August 1944, Stilwell reorganized his forces with the Chinese 38th and 30th divisions forming the New 1st Army commanded by Sun Li-jen, the former general of the 38th Division since 1942. The Chinese 22nd, 50th and 14th divisions formed the New 6th Army under Liao Yao-hsiang, who had previously commanded the 22nd Division since 1942. Stilwell merged his surviving older 'Galahad' unit with 'New Galahad' US reinforcements to form the 475th Infantry Regiment. He also added the newly-arrived 124th Cavalry Regiment, in October and with a supporting US 612th FA Battalion and a newly-raised 1st Chinese Regiment formed the 5332nd Brigade (Provisional) ('Mars Force').

Stilwell planned a sweep through northern Burma towards Lashio to destroy the IJA Thirty-Third Army. Also the NCAC's southern offensive from Myitkyina was to have the Ledo Road and oil pipeline beside it join up with the old Burma Road north of Lashio. With the Myitkyina town's capture in early August, the Allied armies prepared to recapture the previous terminus of the Burma Road at Lashio.

The British 36th Division was to continue down the 'Railroad Corridor' to protect Stilwell's NCAC's right flank and first seize Mohnyin and then the Indaw-Katha region (see below). The New 1st Army was to advance from Myitkyina to Bhamo, east of the Irrawaddy River. The New 6th Army's 22nd Division, followed by the 'Mars Force' and the Chinese 14th Division, was to advance through a mountainous region crossing the Irrawaddy on 6 November and seizing Shwegu the next day. A few days later, the New 6th Army's 50th Division was to cross the Irrawaddy further east. From May through to November, Chinese Y Force divisions were fighting the IJA 56th and 2nd divisions on the Salween front, attempting to take Longling in Yunnan Province which was captured on 1 November. Then Y Force divisions in Yunnan were to move from Longling down the Burma Road to aid in crushing the Japanese in north-east Burma in Stilwell's grand Allied pincer envelopment. However, on 3 January 1945, Y Force was stopped by the Japanese at Wanting on the

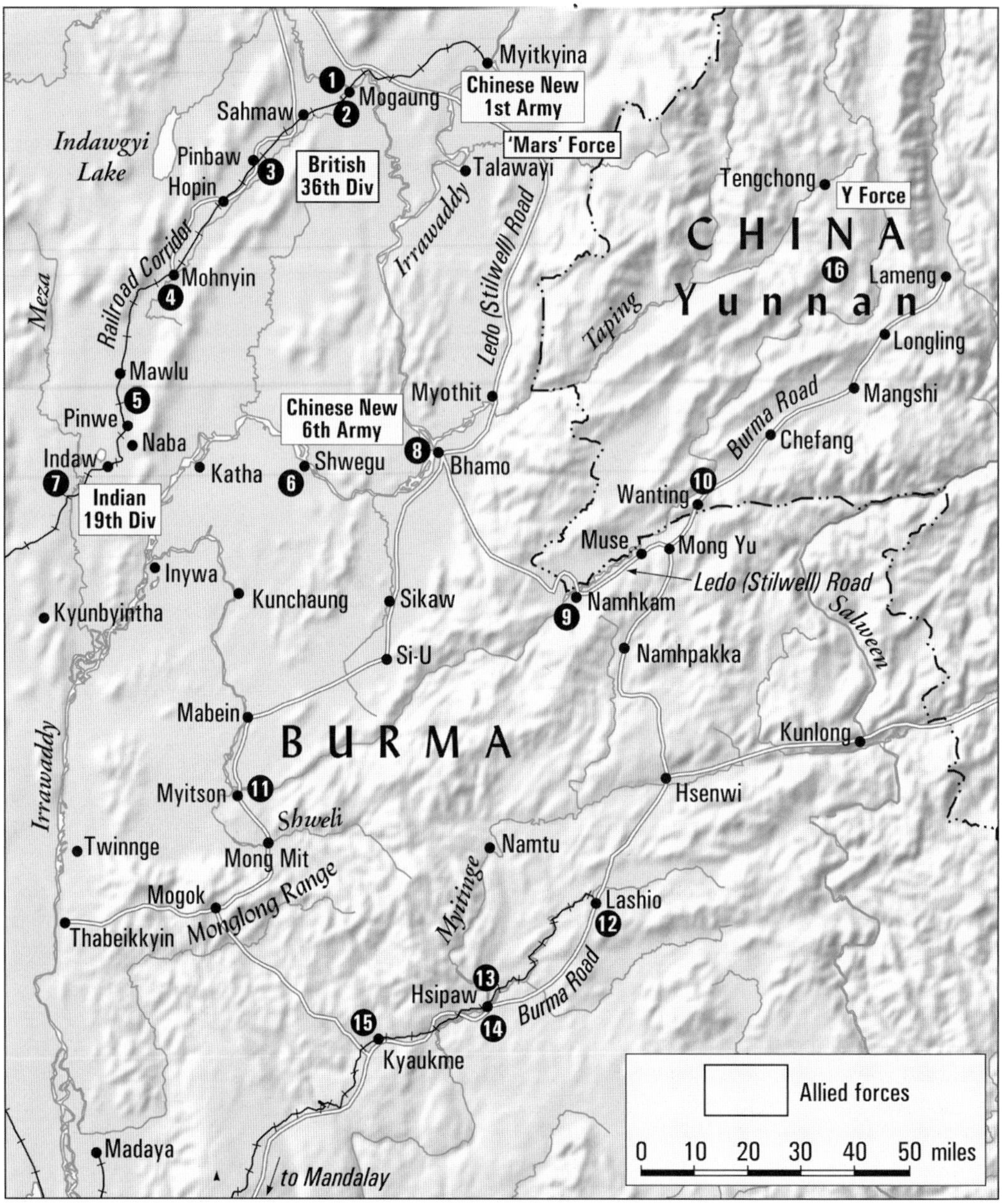
Myitkyina
Mogaung
Chinese New 1st Army
Sahmaw
Indawgyi Lake
Pinbaw
Hopin
British 36th Div
'Mars' Force
Talawayi
Irrawaddy
Ledo (Stilwell) Road
Tengchong
Y Force
CHINA
Yunnan
Lameng
Railroad Corridor
Mohnyin
Meza
Taping
Longling
Mawlu
Myothit
Mangshi
Burma Road
Chefang
Pinwe
Naba
Chinese New 6th Army
Bhamo
Indaw
Katha
Shwegu
Indian 19th Div
Wanting
Muse
Mong Yu
Ledo (Stilwell) Road
Inywa
Kunchaung
Sikaw
Namhkam
Salween
Kyunbyintha
Namhpakka
Si-U
Mabein
BURMA
Kunlong
Myitson
Hsenwi
Irrawaddy
Shweli
Twinnge
Mong Mit
Namtu
Monglong Range
Myitinge
Mogok
Lashio
Thabeikkyin
Hsipaw
Burma Road
Kyaukme
Allied forces
0 10 20 30 40 50 miles
Madaya
to Mandalay

Map 6. NCAC Campaign after Myitkyina's Capture, August 1944–January 1945.
❶ In late June 1944, after Mogaung's fall to the Chindit 77th Brigade and reinforcing Chinese troops, the West African 3rd Brigade was ordered by Stilwell to occupy Pinbaw at the northern end of the 'Railroad Corridor', a 160-mile-long area through which the Burma Railway ran from the Mu River Valley in the south and extending north past Wuntho, Mawlu, Indaw and Katha where it opened up into the Mogaung Valley and on to Myitkyina. ❷ The West African 3rd Brigade with attached Chinese artillery are held up by a strong Japanese position on high ground overlooking the road and railroad to the north of Sahmaw. ❸ The leading units of the British 36th Division, which arrived at the Myitkyina

airfield in mid-July 1944, are ordered by Stilwell to relieve the stalled West Africans on 4 August. Despite numerous IJA defensive positions and monsoon conditions, the British 36th Division captures Pinbaw on 27 August and continues along the 'Railroad Corridor' past Hopin. ❹ On 13 October 1944, the British 36th Division secretly envelops Japanese positions around Mohnyin, launching a surprise attack two days later and capturing the locale on 17 October. ❺ Continuing the advance south down the 'Railroad Corridor', the British 36th Division overcomes stiffening IJA resistance in front of Mawlu (previously the Chindit 77th Brigade's 'White City') and captures the town on 31 October. ❻ In late October-early November, a reorganized Chinese New 6th Army comprising the 22nd, 50th and 14th divisions moves through the mountains between the 'Railroad Corridor' and the upper Irrawaddy River towards the river's bend at Shwegu. The Chinese New 1st Army is followed by 'Mars Force' comprising the US 475th IR (the remnants of 'Galahad' and new replacements ('New Galahad'), the 124th Cavalry Regiment (dismounted) and a new Chinese regiment). 'Mars Force' is officially called the 5332nd Brigade (Provisional). On 6 November, the Chinese 22nd Division crosses the Irrawaddy River and seizes Shwegu against minor IJA resistance. ❼ The 19th Indian Division (XXXIII Indian Corps), after crossing the Chindwin River and moving east, arrives at Indaw in mid-December 1944, meeting elements of the British 36th Division. The 19th Indian Division moves south along the western side of the Irrawaddy River towards Mandalay, while units of the British 36th Division move down the eastern side of the river towards Twinnge and then move directly due east towards Mong Mit. Other British 36th Division forces move inland on a south-eastern axis of Katha-Kunchaung-Mabein. ❽ The Chinese New 1st Army comprising the Chinese 38th and 30th divisions advances from Myitkyina towards Bhamo east of the Irrawaddy River on 15 October 1944. On 10 November, the Chinese set up a siege against Bhamo's Japanese bunkers and entrenchments reminiscent of Myitkyina town. Approximately 800 IJA 56th Division's Bhamo defenders break through the encirclement on 14–15 December to rejoin other IJA 56th Division troops at Namhkam. ❾ In early January 1945 Sultan, who replaced Stilwell as American commander of the India and Burma theatres and NCAC troops, directs the Chinese New 1st Army to advance towards Namhkam and the junction with the Burma Road and 'Mars Force' to continue east to cut the Burma Road south of Mong Yu, preventing Japanese reinforcements to Namhkam from Lashio. Namhkam falls to Chinese troops on 16 January. ❿ Wanting, in China's Yunnan Province, falls to the Chinese Y Force comprising the Chinese 11th Army Group's 16 divisions on 20 January 1945. Two days later, Sultan announces that the Ledo (Stilwell) Road joined with the Burma Road is open for truck convoy traffic. ⓫ The British 36th Division fights its last major battle in NCAC at Myitsone, crossing the Shweli River on 31 January 1945, which the IJA reinforced to defend the northern approaches to the Mandalay plain. British troops advanced through the IJA defensive positions by 21 February and then continued their southward advance towards Mogok. ⓬ Lashio, situated on the Burma Road and its nearby airfield are captured on 7 March 1945 by the Chinese 30th Division heading south-west from Hsenwi. ⓭ The Chinese New 6th Army's 50th Division encounters strong IJA resistance at Namtu, which they eventually capture in late February 1945. This Chinese force reaches the Burma Road at Hsipaw on 15 March, repelling strong Japanese counterattacks from 17 to 20 March. ⓮ The Chinese New 1st Army's 30th Division moves south-west on the Burma Road from Lashio to join the Chinese New 6th Army's 50th Division near Hsipaw on 24 March 1945. ⓯ The British 36th Division, advancing south-eastward, reaches Kyaukme on the Burma Road on 31 March, completing an eight-month campaign in the NCAC. ⓰ After engagements between the Chinese Y Force and the IJA 56th Division, the latter holding north-east Burma and part of China's Yunnan Province west of the Salween River, the Y Force occupies Longling on 1 November 1944 and advances south-westward along the Burma Road to Mangshi on 20 November and Chefang on 1 December. Wanting is occupied by the Chinese in late January 1945.

China-Burma border. With the Chinese 38th Division approaching from Bhamo and threatening encirclement of the Japanese troops in Wanting, the IJA abandoned Wanting and the Chinese Y Force linked up with New 1st Army troops at Mong-Yu on 27 January.

The West African 3rd Brigade, which had been airlifted into Burma to reinforce the Chindits late in their Kamaing-Mogaung campaign in June 1944, was ordered by Stilwell with attached Chinese artillery to occupy Pinbaw, 20 miles south-west of Mogaung at the northern end of the 'Railroad Corridor'. The corridor continued south-westward to Indaw and then towards Mandalay. Allied capture of Indaw would block a Japanese thrust northward to recapture Mogaung and Myitkyina. The West African advance faltered against IJA 53rd Division resistance near Sahmaw between Mogaung and Pinbaw, necessitating Stilwell dispatching the British 36th Division's lead brigade, which flew into the Myitkyina airhead in mid-July and on 4 August passed through the West African 3rd Brigade, breaking the stalemate and capturing Pinbaw on 27 August after three days of combat.

Despite monsoon rains, the British 36th Division attacked Mohnyin, between Pinbaw and Mawlu, on 15 October 1944 and captured it after two days of fighting with the assistance of attached Chinese artillery. Mawlu was attacked next and fell to the Allies on 31 October with British infantry and Chinese artillery continuing its advance on to Indaw and Katha, the latter on the Irrawaddy River on 10 December.

On 14 October 1944, Roosevelt recalled Stilwell as CBI commander upon Chiang Kai-shek's demand. This followed a long-running feud which escalated over control of Lend-Lease supplies and Washington's desire to have Stilwell appointed field commander of all Chinese forces in China following a major Japanese ground offensive threatened advance airfields of Major General Claire Chennault's Fourteenth Air Force. Chiang refused Stilwell as China's field commander and along with Stilwell's non-diplomatic style and hubris, the *generalissimo* forced his recall. Ironically, Stilwell received his 'fourth star' on 1 August, two days before Myitkyina town fell to the Allies. The American CBI theatre was divided into a China theatre led by Lieutenant General Albert Wedemeyer and the Burma-India theatre commanded by Lieutenant General Daniel Sultan, who now took over the NCAC command from the recalled Stilwell.

The Chinese 38th Division's siege of Bhamo began on 10 November 1944 and was resisted by 1,200 IJA defenders in bunkers and trenches eerily similar to Myitkyina. The Chinese 30th Division took the mountainous terrain between Bhamo and Namhkam; however, on 9 December the IJA 56th Division counterattacked, enabling 1,000 Japanese Bhamo defenders to escape the Chinese 38th Division siege lines. Sultan now ordered the New 1st Army to move on Namhkam and the Burma Road. 'Mars Force' was to cut the Burma Road south of Mong Yu to trap the IJA 56th Division between the New 1st Army and Y Force.

The British 36th Division, still under Sultan's command, advanced southward on a broad front in the Irrawaddy and lower Shweli valleys towards Mogok and Mandalay, maintaining contact on its right with the left flank of Slim's Fourteenth Army, namely the 19th Indian Division. On the left flank of the British 36th Division was the Chinese 50th Division, advancing south of Bhamo across the Shweli River towards Namtu and Lashio.

Namhkam fell to the New 1st Army on 16 January 1945 with Wanting captured by Y force on 20 January. On 27 January, Sultan proclaimed the Ledo (Stilwell)-Burma Road open for truck traffic into China after Muse and Mong-Yu were captured by New 1st Army troops. The initial convoy entered Wanting on 28 January and arrived in Kunming on 4 February.

Elsewhere, the 'Mars Force's' US 475th Infantry and 124th Cavalry regiments approached the Burma Road at Namhpakka on 18 January 1945 to block it from the IJA 56th Division, the latter withdrawing east from the Wanting-Muse area so it could participate in the fight for Mandalay to the south.

The British 36th Division fought its last major battle in northern Burma as it attempted to cross the Shweli River on 31 January 1945, its target being Myitsone. Allied possession of Myitsone, which lasted from 31 January to 21 February, prevented IJA forces from reaching the Mandalay Plain from the north. After Mogok was captured by the 36th British Division, this battle-hardened force reached the Burma Road on 31 March, eight gruelling months after arriving at the Myitkyina airfield in July 1944.

To the east, the New 6th Army's Chinese 50th Division encountered enemy resistance at Namtu in late February 1945. After capturing the town, they reached the Burma Road at Hsipaw on 15 March and repelled IJA counterattacks from 17–20 March. New 1st Army units captured Lashio after a two-day battle on 6–7 March, linking up with the Chinese 50th Division troops near Hsipaw on 24 March, essentially ending the campaign in northern Burma.

American 'Mars Force' troops, part of Stilwell's NCAC, march near Washaing at the end of the first day's reconnaissance, the 'Thrailkill Expedition' (see below), into China's Yunnan Province from Myitkyina on 28 August 1944. This force returned to Myitkyina on 14 September, establishing that a passable trail to China for infantry with pack animals existed with numerous potential air-drop and camp sites. *(NARA)*

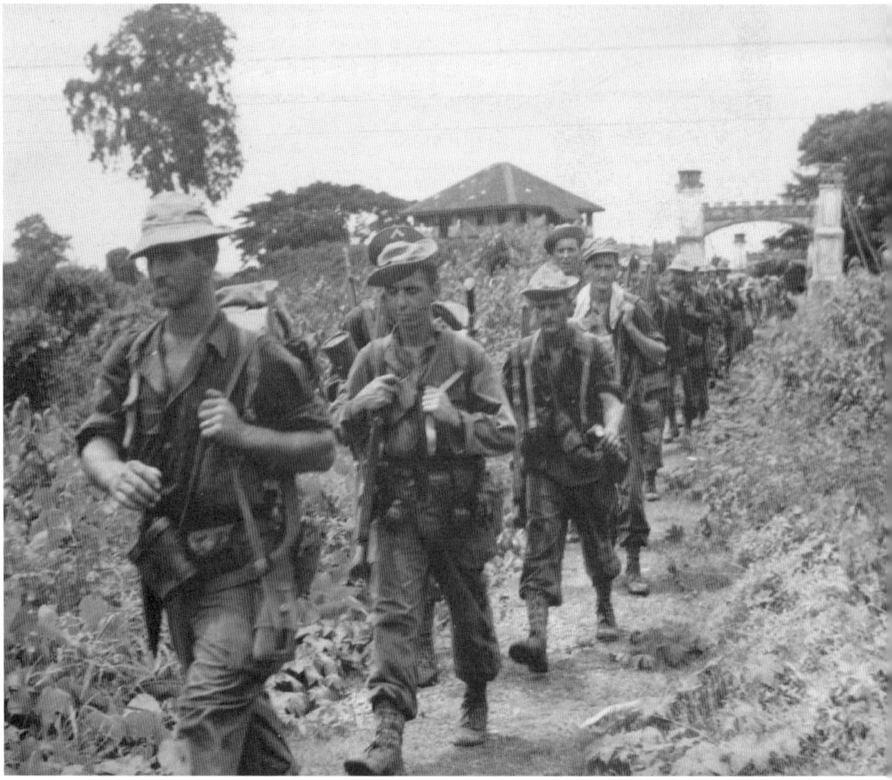

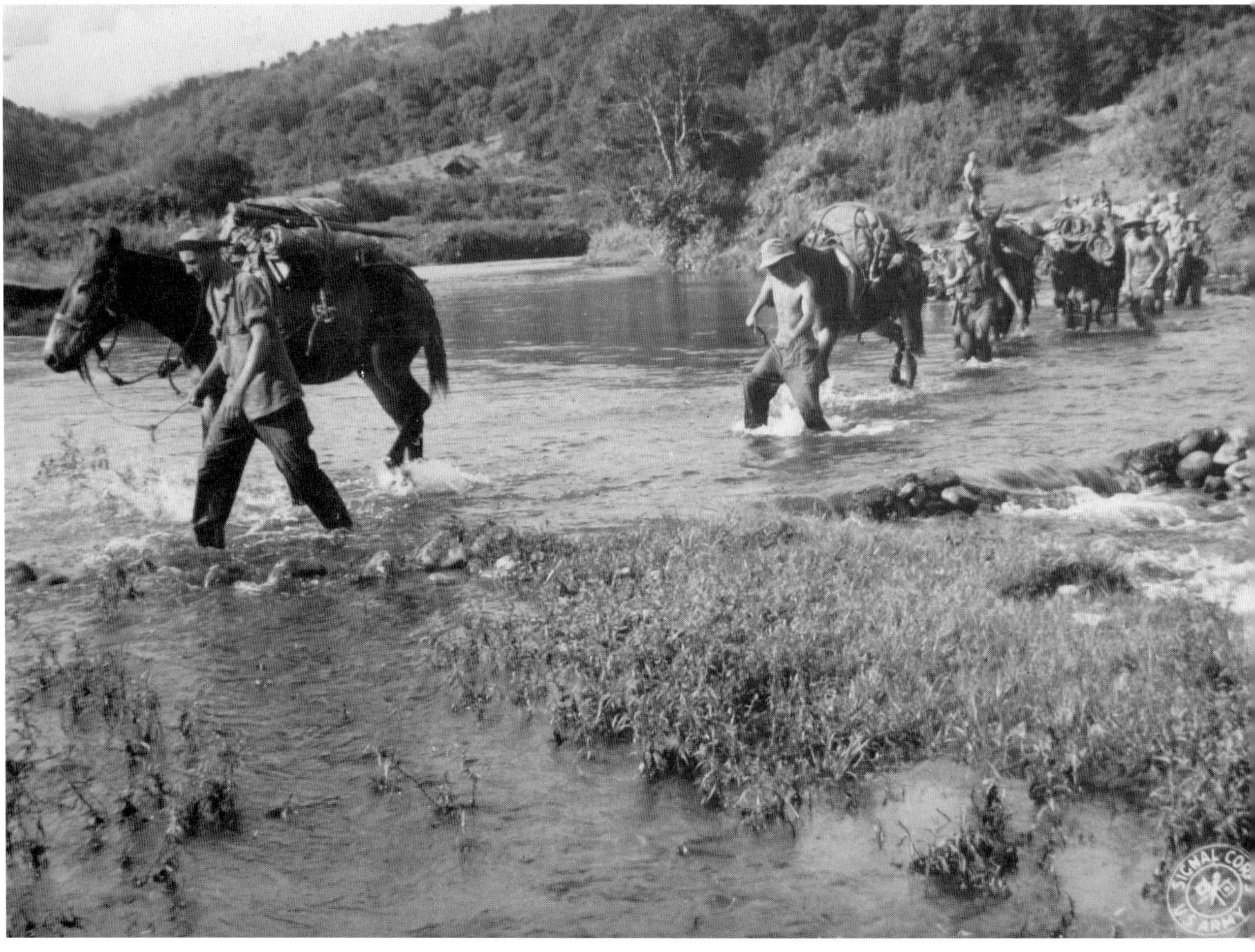

(**Opposite, below**) Major Benjamin Thrailkill's reconnaissance force crosses a stream in early September 1944 between Sadon and Lahpal in their trek into China's Yunnan Province to establish contact with Chinese Y Force, which he met on 6 September in the Kambaiti Pass. Thrailkill previously commanded the 475th IR's 2nd Battalion. The 475th IR consisted of surviving 'Galahad' troops reinforced with American replacements. Thrailkill left Myitkyina on 29 August with a Chinese company, a 475th IR platoon and assorted engineers, signallers, medical personnel and OSS officers. (*NARA*)

(**Above**) 'Mars Force's' US 475th IR crosses a Burmese *chaung* over a wooden bamboo tree-trunk bridge moving south from Myitkyina to Nalong, the latter to Bhamo's north in November 1944. 'Mars Force', also known as the 5332nd Brigade (Provisional), comprised three regiments: the US 475th IR; the US 124th Cavalry Regiment, a dismounted former Texas National Guard unit functioning as an IR; and a US-trained and equipped elite Chinese 1st Regiment (Separate). (*NARA*)

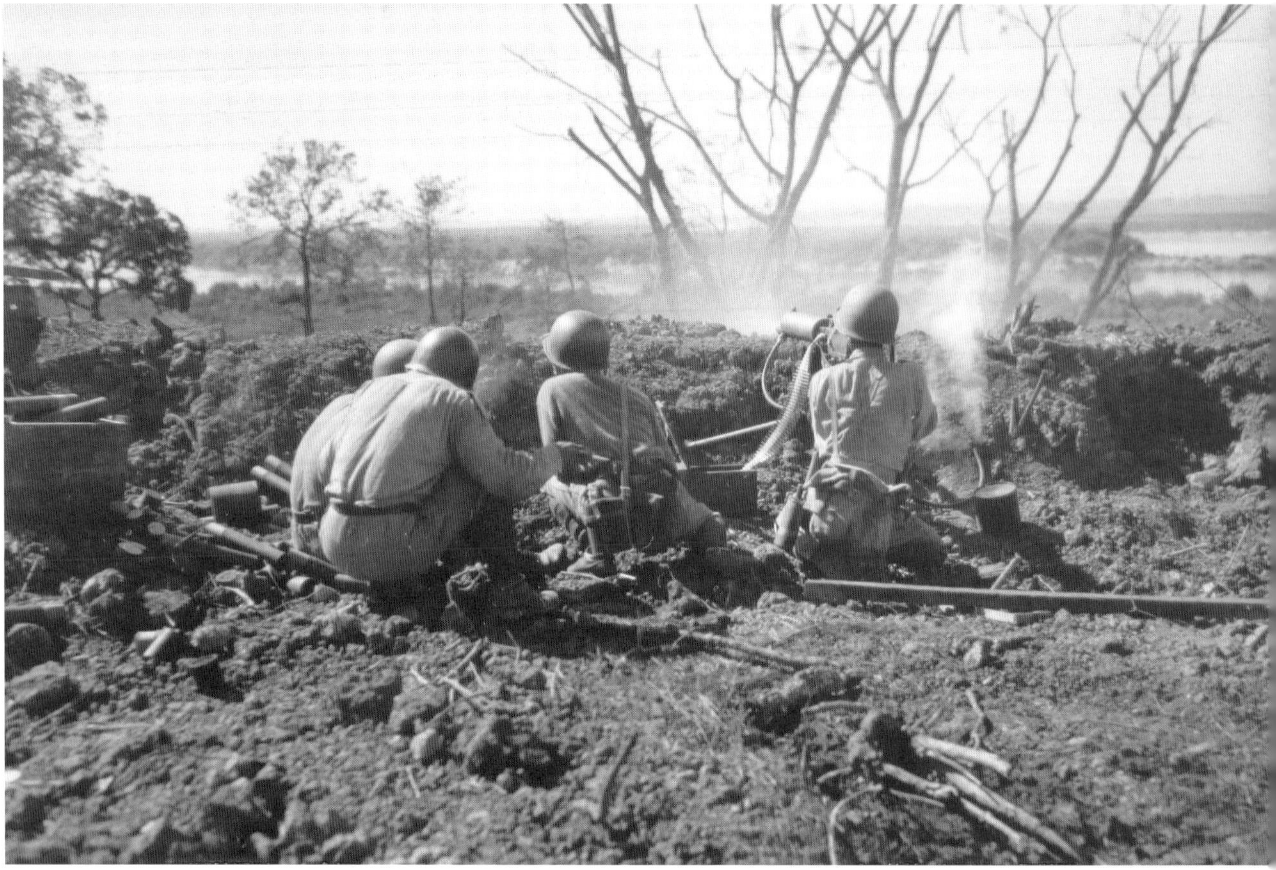

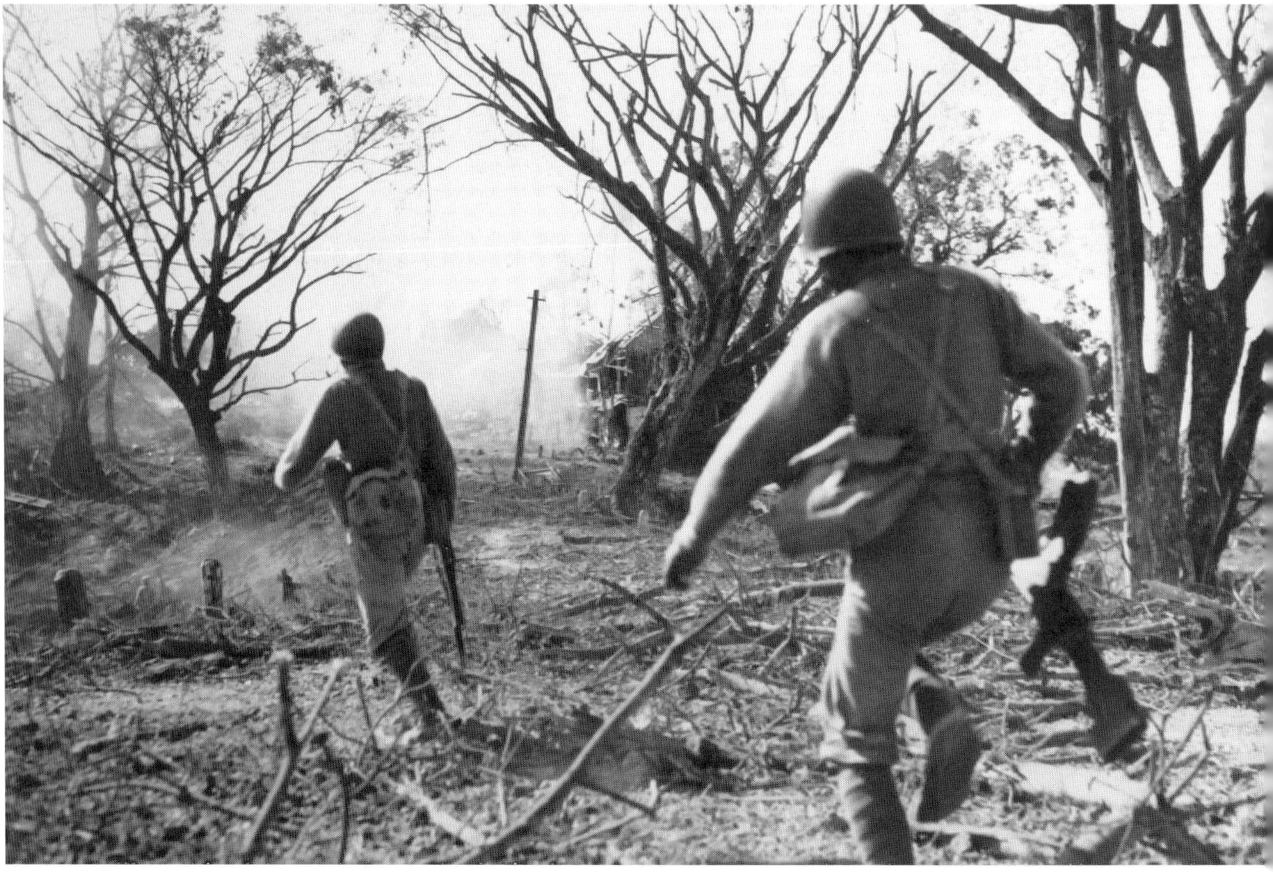

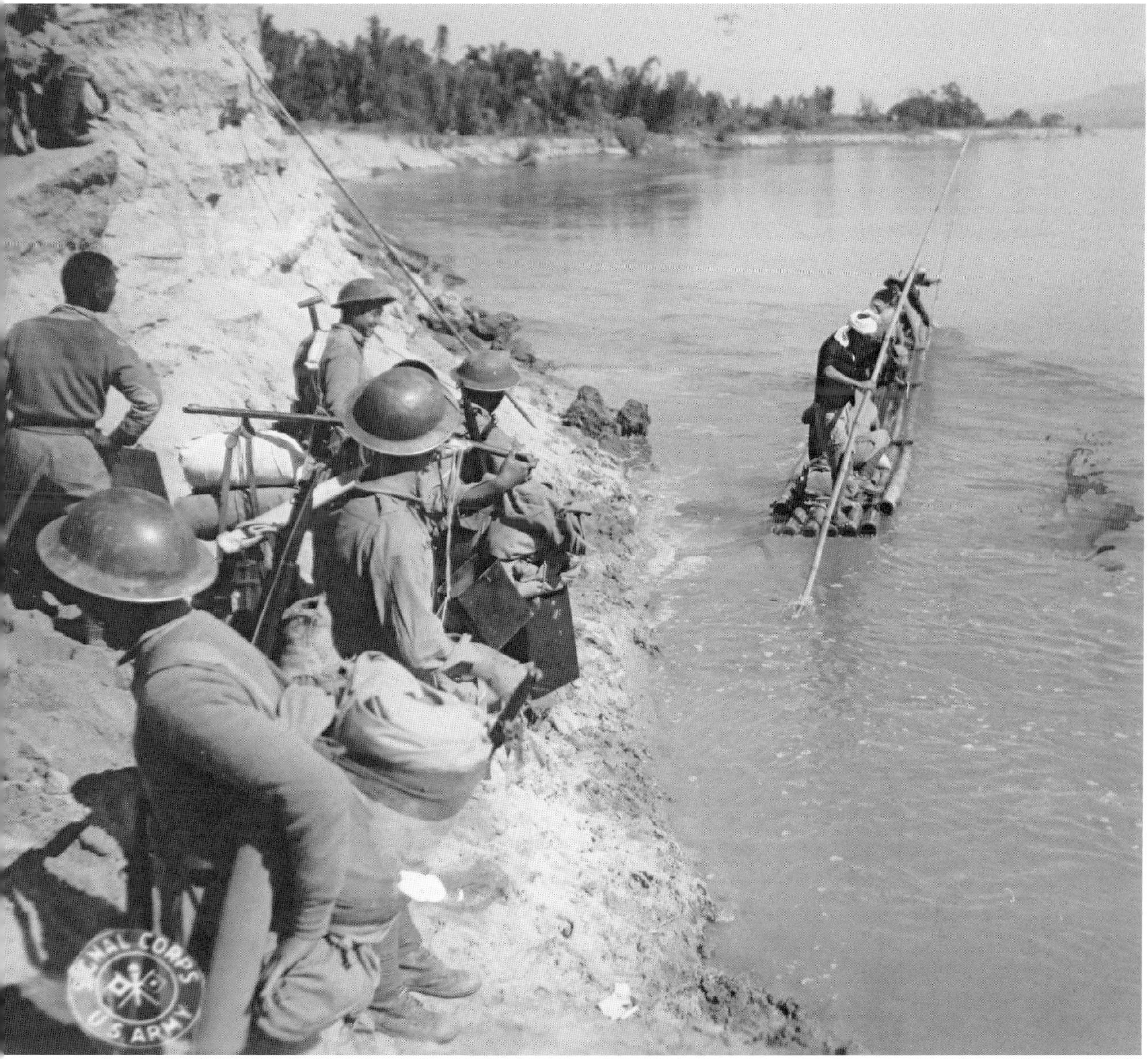

(**Opposite, above**) A Chinese 38th Division crew fires its M1917 water-cooled Browning MMG during the siege of Bhamo, which began on 10 November 1944 and met with stiff resistance from 1,200 Japanese defenders in bunkers and trenches similar to Myitkyina. On 9 December, the IJA 56th Division counterattacked, enabling most of the IJA defenders to escape the Chinese siege lines. *(NARA)*

(**Opposite, below**) Chinese 38th Division infantrymen attack Japanese trench works at Bhamo's siege lines in November 1944. The majority of IJA defenders that escaped Bhamo joined the IJA 56th Division for the later defence of the Mandalay Plain against Slim's Fourteenth Army divisions. *(USAMHI)*

(**Above**) Chinese New 1st Army troops are seen here being ferried across the Shweli River near Namhkam to attack that locale from the west in mid-January 1945. After capturing Namhkam, New 1st Army units moved on Muse on the Burma Road to link up with the Chinese Y Force at Wanting at the end of January. *(NARA)*

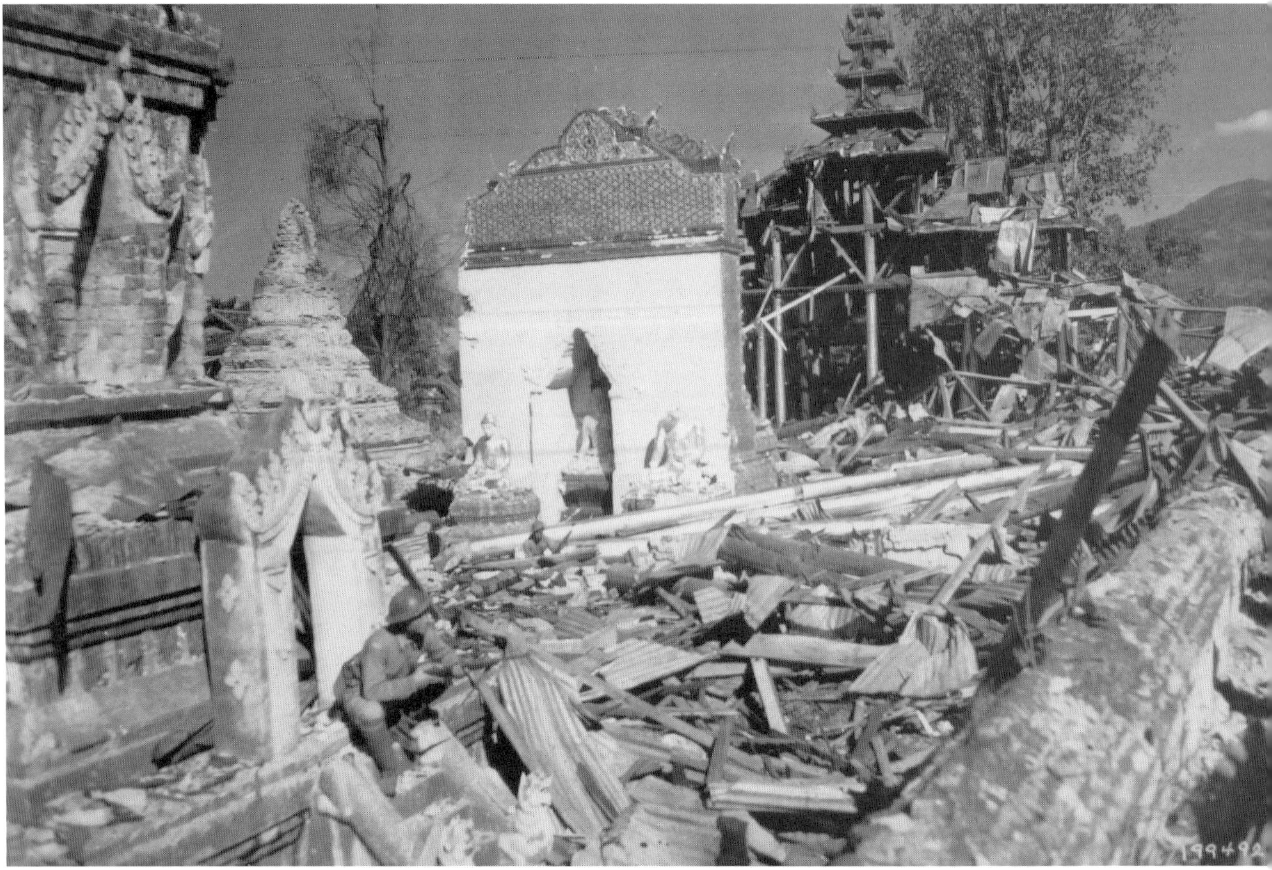

A Chinese New 1st Army's 30th Division infantryman in British kit (left foreground) sits amid Namhkam's ruins after it fell to that division's 29th IR on 16 January 1945. Namhkam, situated south-east of Bhamo and south-west of Muse, was captured by the New 1st Army as it moved south after Bhamo's siege and then north-east into China's Yunnan Province. *(NARA)*

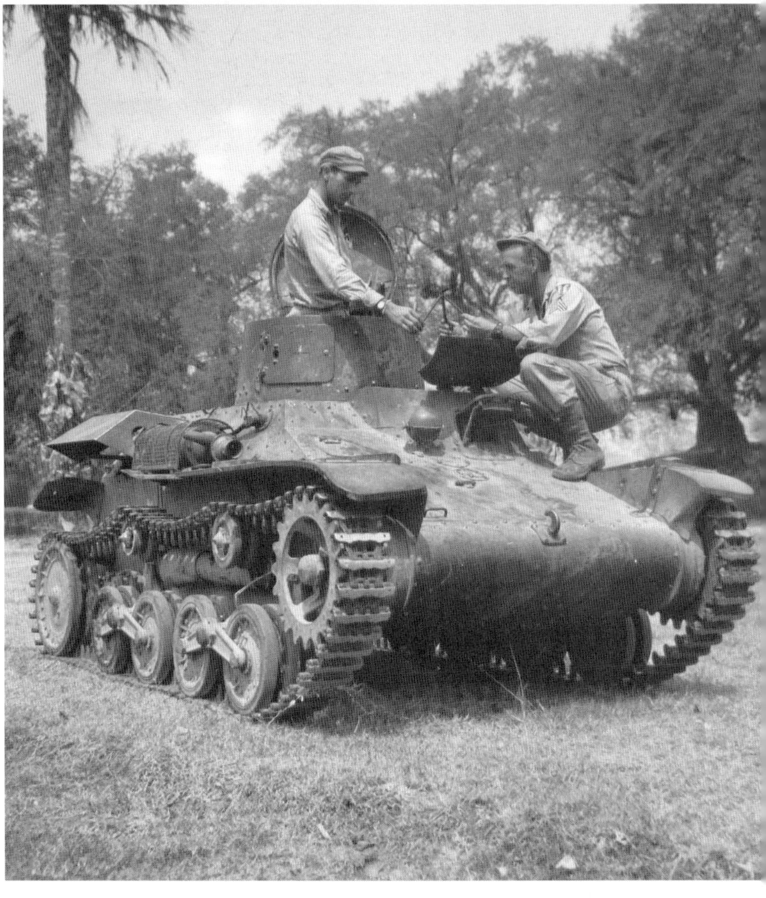

An American captain and sergeant examine a captured IJA Type 95 *Ke-Go* light tank in Hsipaw on the Burma Road to Lashio's south-east on 21 March 1945. The *Ke-Go* had thin armour and lacked firepower, making it wholly inadequate against the American M5 light and M4 medium tanks. *(NARA)*

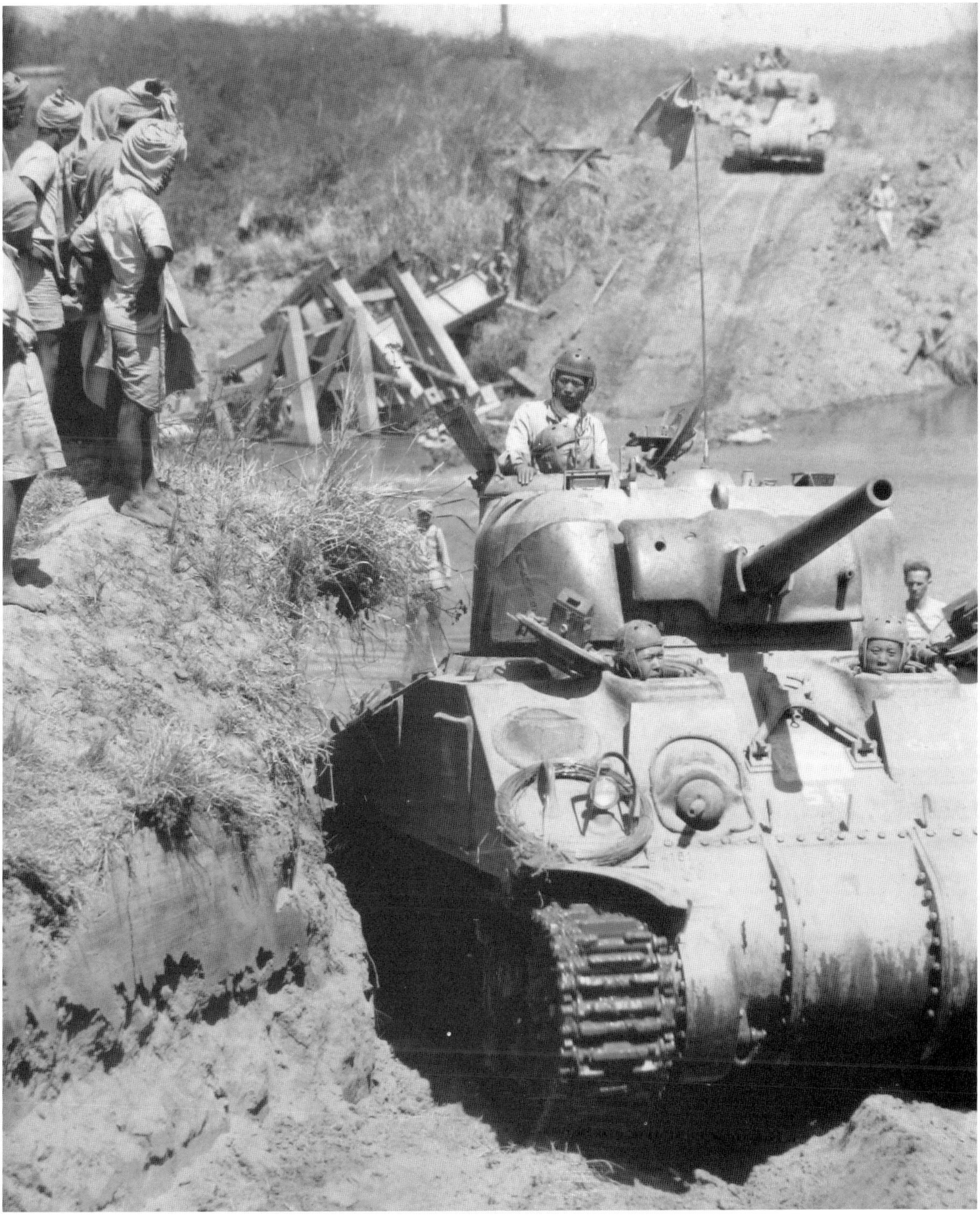

M4 medium tanks of the Chinese 1st Provisional Tank Group cross the Nam Yoo River in their drive towards Lashio on the Burma Road in early March 1945. Burmese natives (left) watch the tank's movement. *(NARA)*

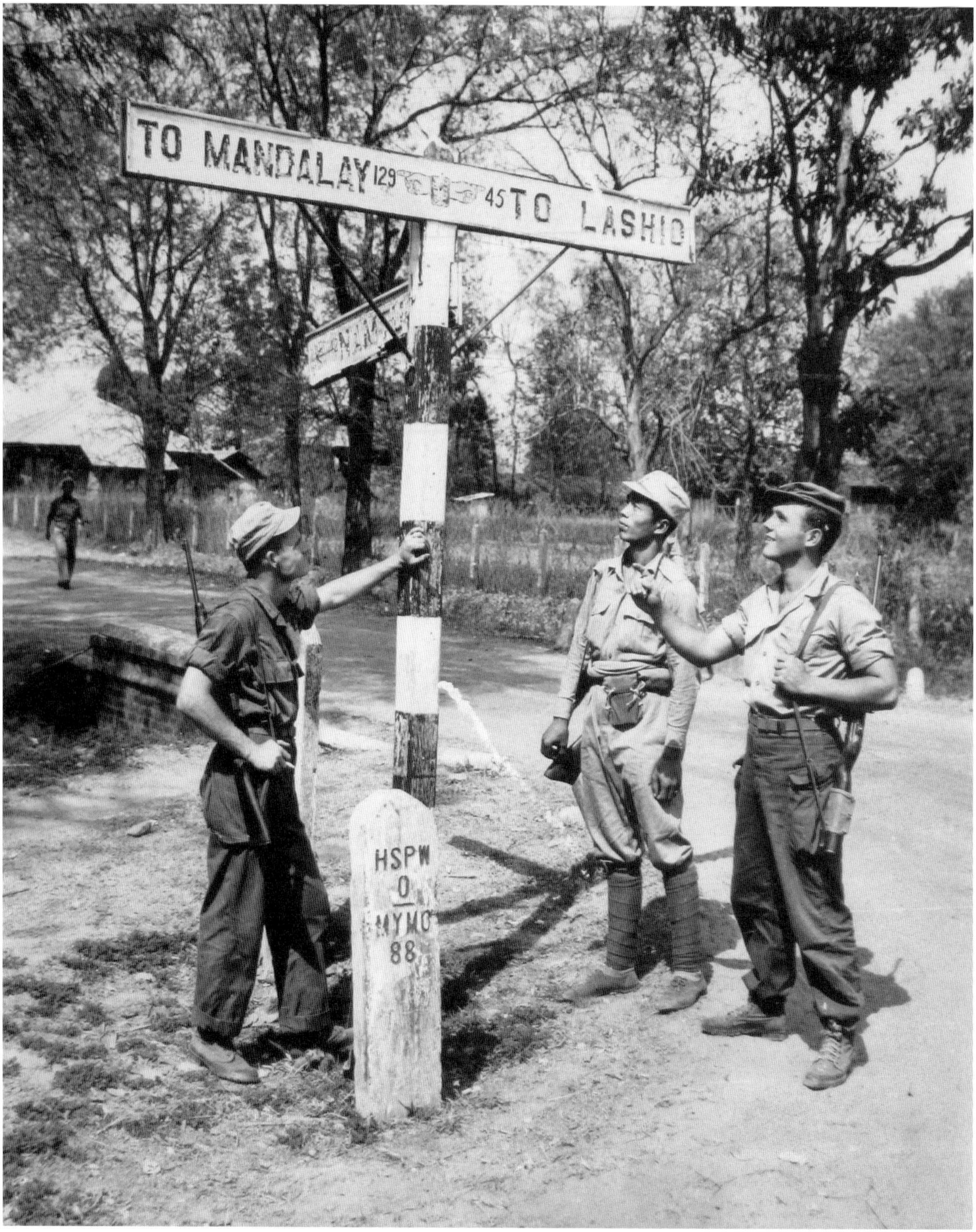
TO MANDALAY 129
45 TO LASHIO
HSPW
0
MYMO
88

A 50th Division Chinese infantryman from the 149th IR stands alongside two American soldiers by the Hsipaw signpost on 21 March 1945, which indicated Lashio 45 miles to the north-east on the Burma Road and Mandalay 129 miles to the south. *(NARA)*

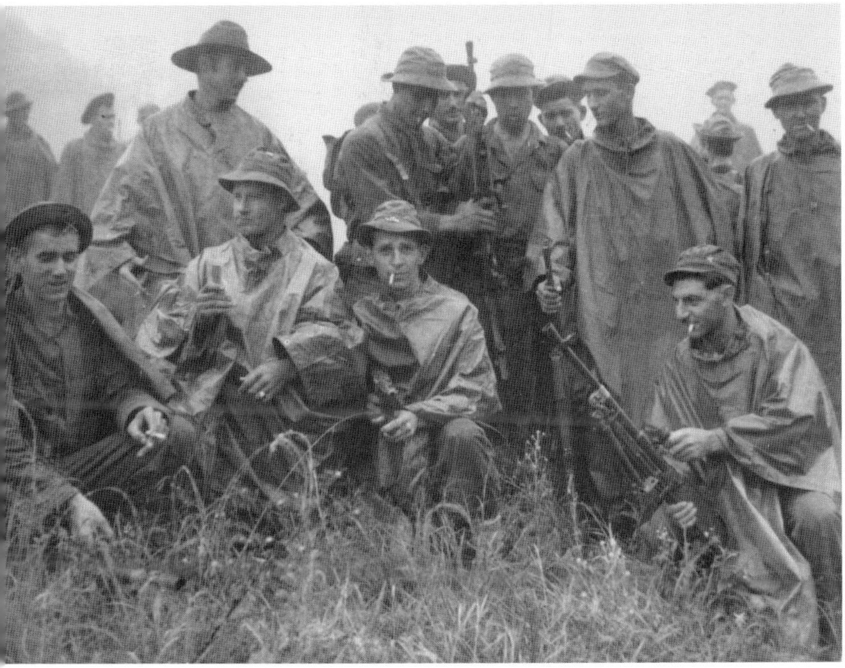

The US 'Mars Force' troops, part of Sultan's NCAC, pose after rendezvousing with the Chinese Y Force on the Sino-Burma border in January 1945. 'Mars Force' moved east from Si-U towards Namhpakka on the Burma Road south of Namhkam. On 18 January 'Mars Force' cut the Burma Road to Japanese movement between Hosi and Namhpakka and fought the IJA 56th Division before the latter escaped south for the Mandalay Plain battle. *(NARA)*

American OSS officers and Chinese guides sit by a campfire at an Advanced Echelon HQ 200 miles north of Kunming on the way to Chunking to assist Chennault's Fourteenth Air Force. There were fewer than 2,000 OSS personnel in China in 1945, but this small force was credited with direct responsibility for killing more than 12,000 Japanese troops. *(NARA)*

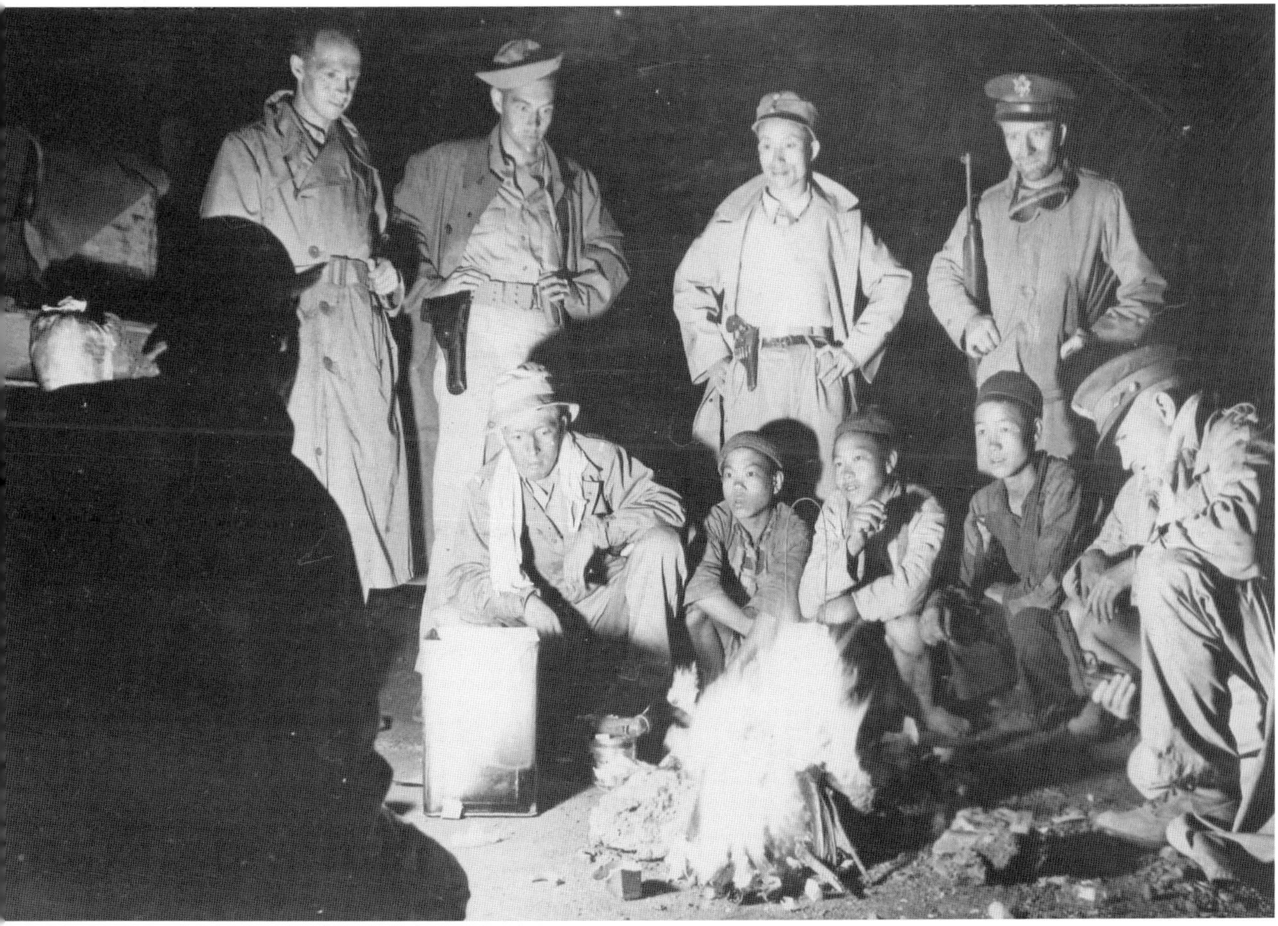

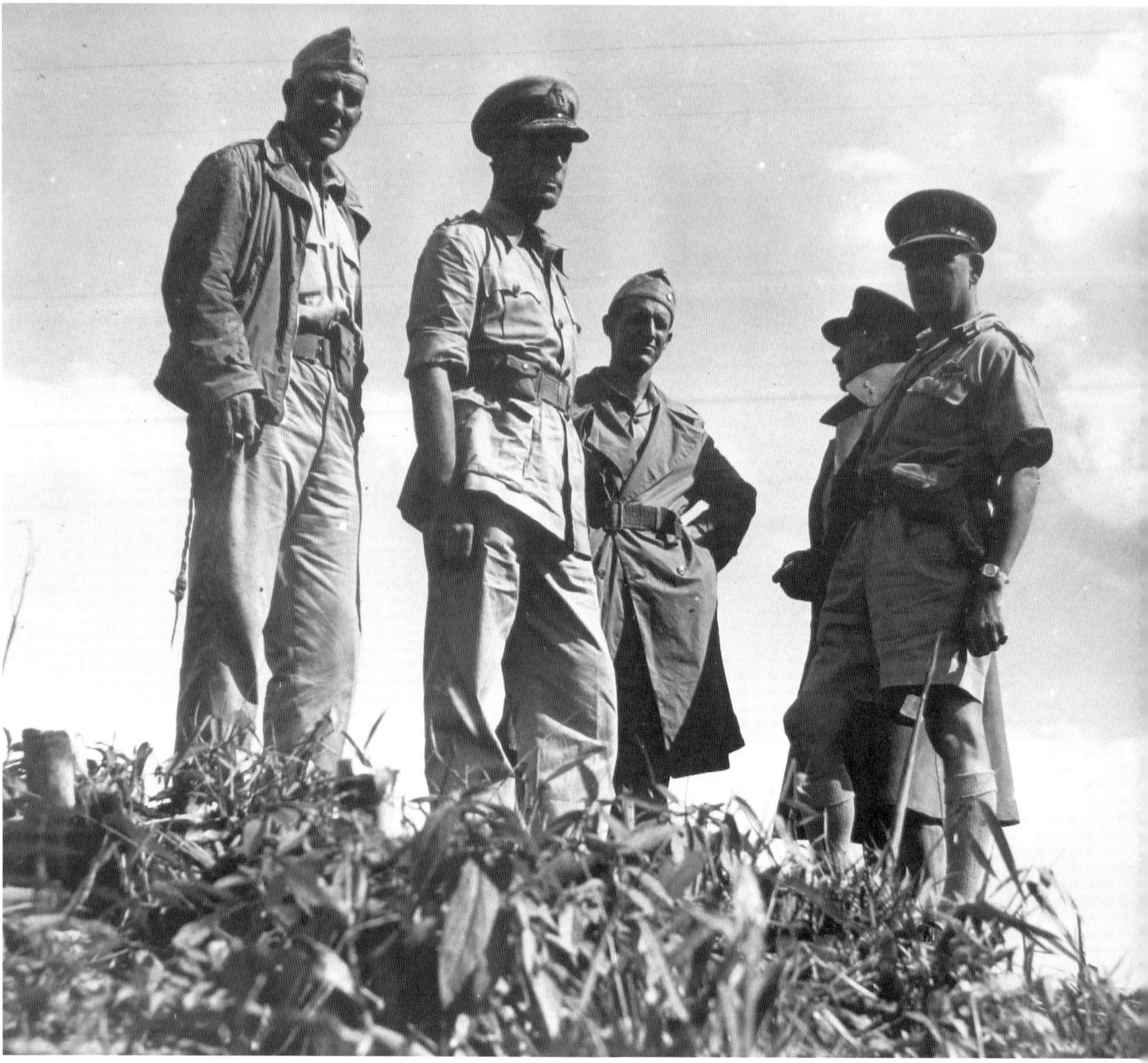

(**Above**) In Burma, Brigadier General Lewis Pick, Admiral Lord Louis Mountbatten and other British officers observe construction of the Ledo (Stilwell) Road in April 1944, which joined with the Burma Road at Mong Yu as it entered China's Yunnan Province at the town of Wanting. *(NARA)*

(**Opposite, above**) US Combat Engineers of a Light Pontoon Company build a pontoon bridge across the Irrawaddy River connecting the Ledo (Stilwell) Road to Bhamo in mid-December 1944. The company comprised an HQ platoon, two bridge platoons and a light equipment platoon. M2 assault boats served as the pontoons. *(NARA)*

(**Opposite, below**) American engineers build a Bailey bridge to traverse a Burmese *chaung* during the construction of the Ledo (Stilwell) Road. This bridge was a portable, pre-fabricated, truss structure developed by British civil servant Donald Bailey in 1940–41. It required only simple hand tools to connect the pre-fabricated sections. The Bailey bridges solved the problem of retreating enemy troops destroying bridges or to traverse waterways as the Ledo (Stilwell) Road was under construction. *(NARA)*

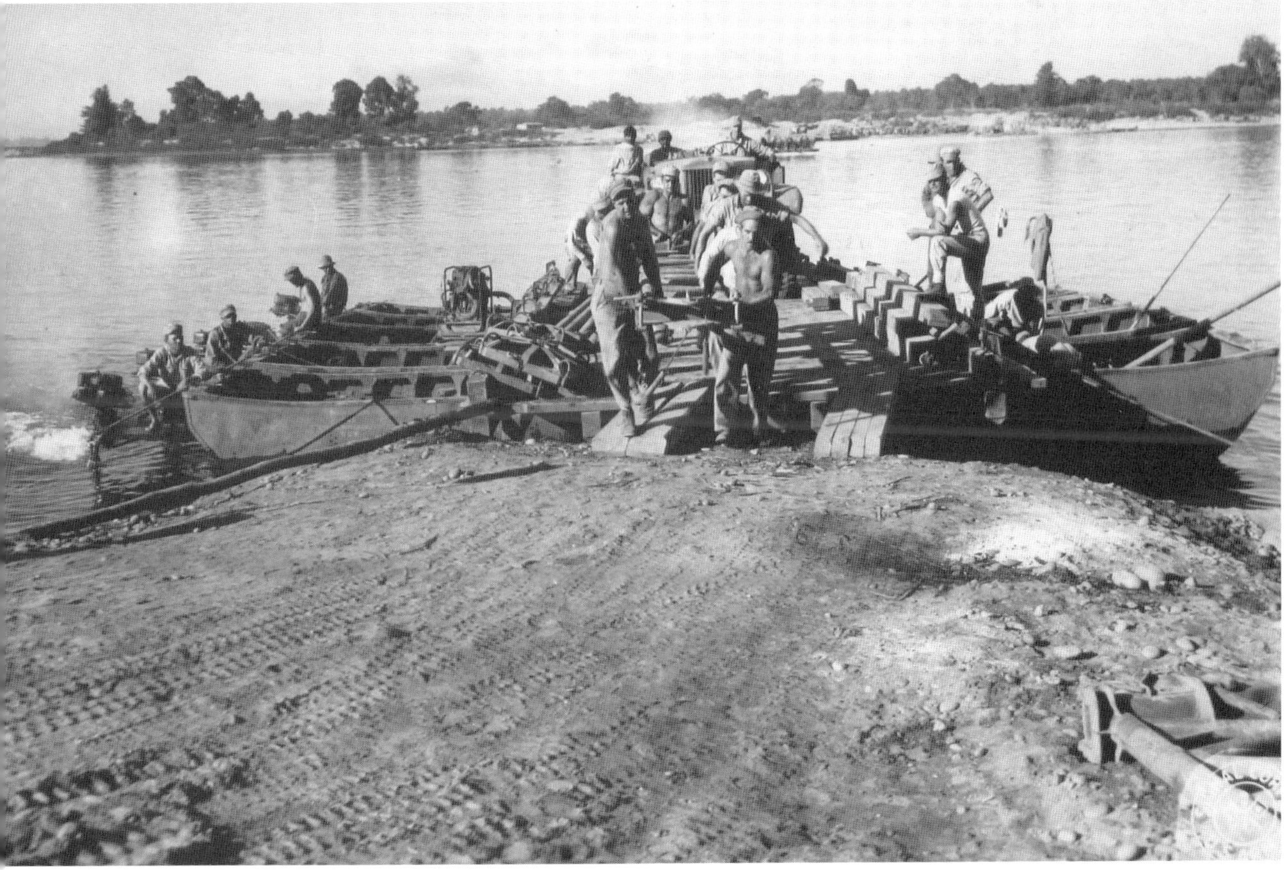

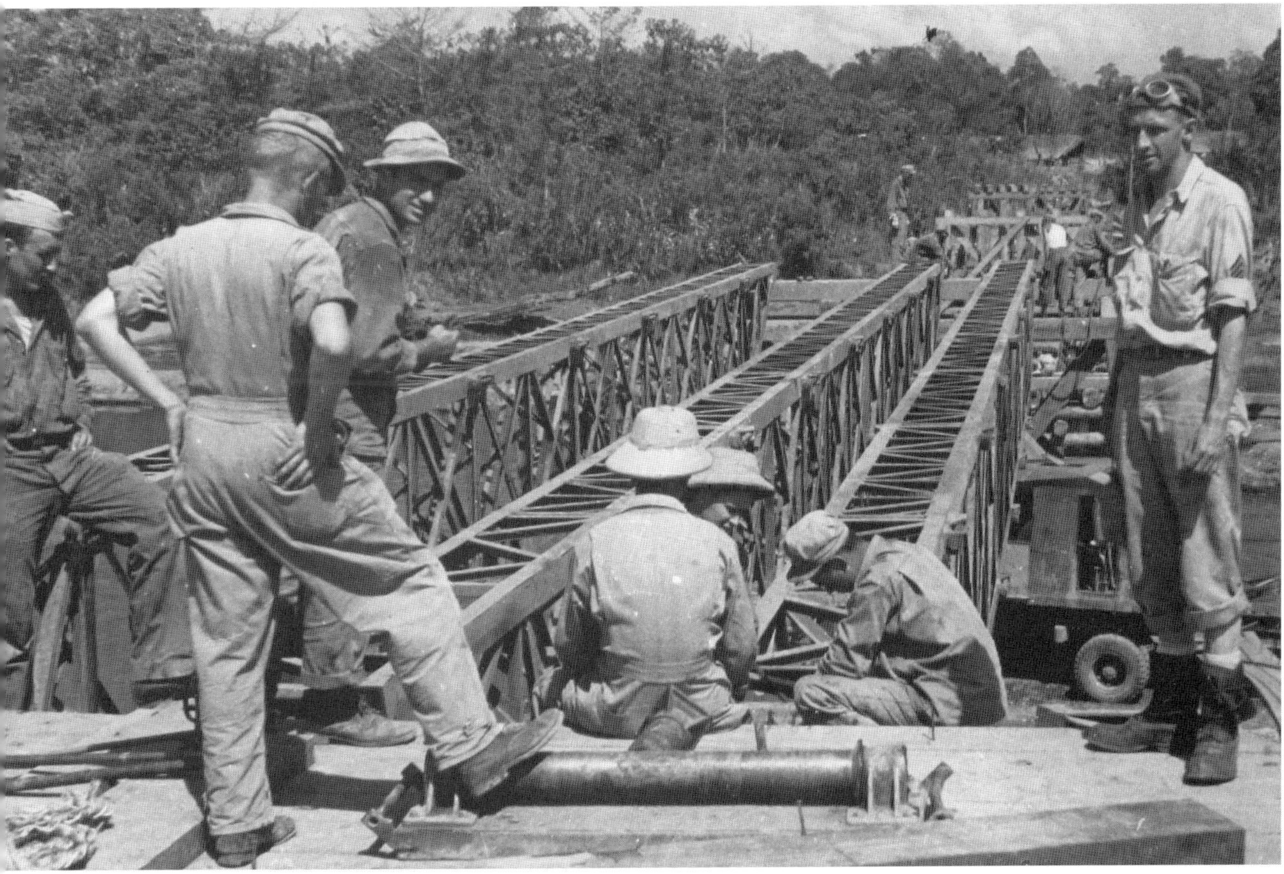

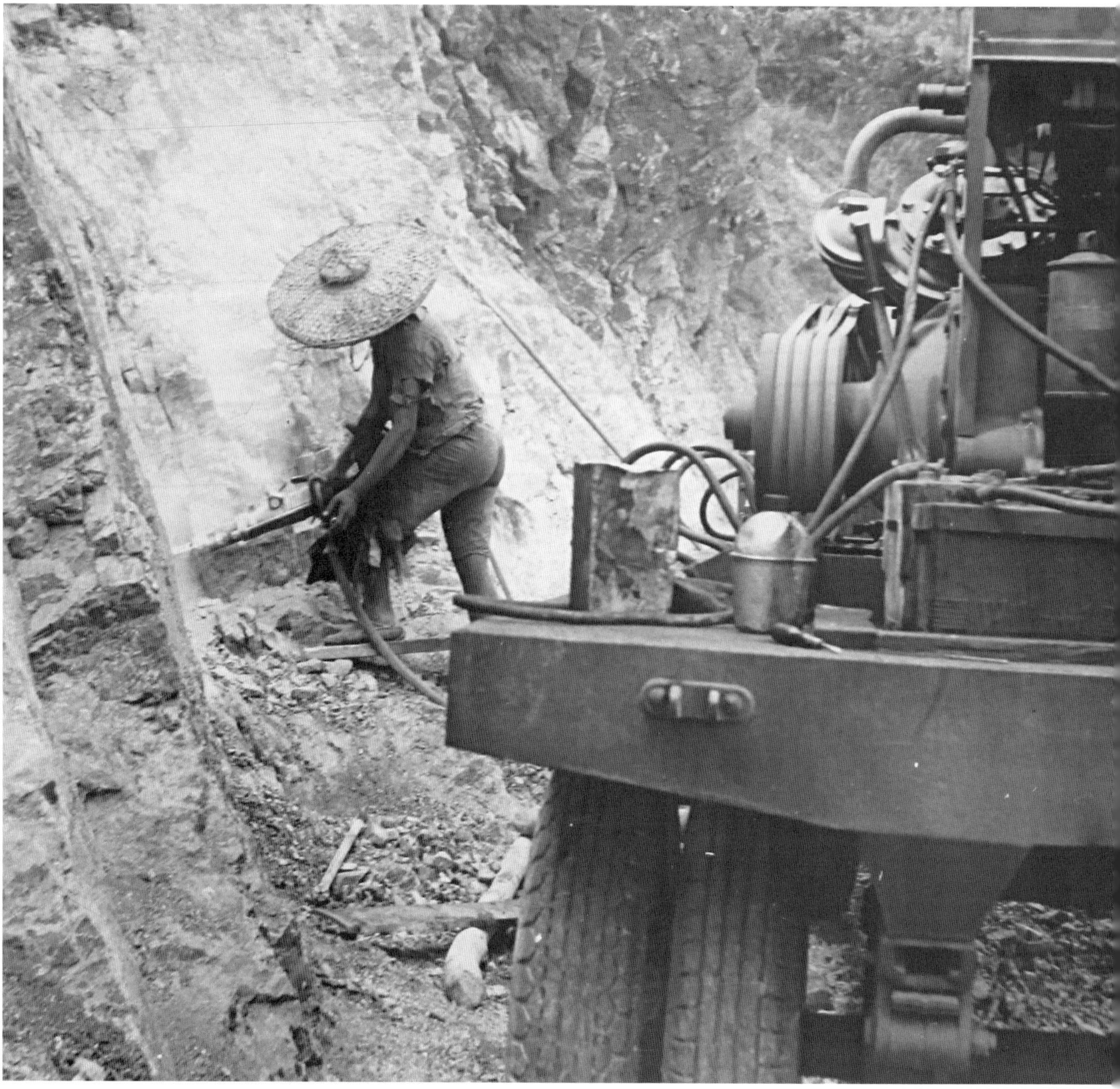

(**Above**) A Chinese worker uses a pneumatic drill to carve away Burmese hillside during the construction of the Ledo (Stilwell) Road. An American engineer operates a bulldozer (foreground). *(NARA)*

(**Opposite, above**) Chinese and Burmese civilians aid an American bulldozer engineer amid the painstaking construction of a stretch of the Ledo (Stilwell) Road. The extent of manual labour, single-operator drilling, explosives and clearing of rock debris was under the overall command of Brigadier General Lewis Pick, who in 1942 was an engineer in the Missouri River Division controlling the water resources of the Missouri River basin. *(NARA)*

(**Opposite, below**) American soldiers wheel tyres to a truck convoy starting along the Ledo (Stilwell) Road towards Wanting and a rendezvous with the Chinese Y Force in Yunnan Province during the early winter of 1945. *(NARA)*

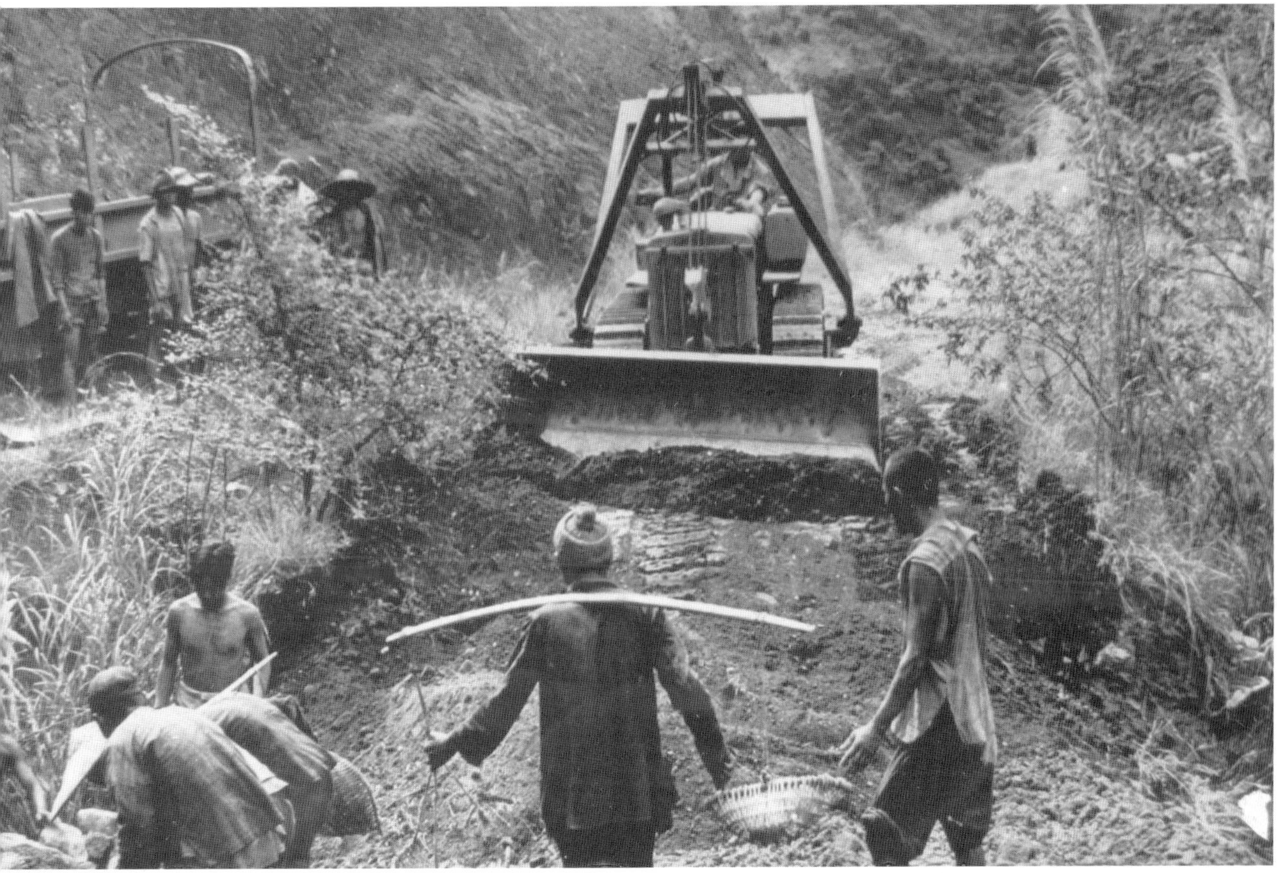

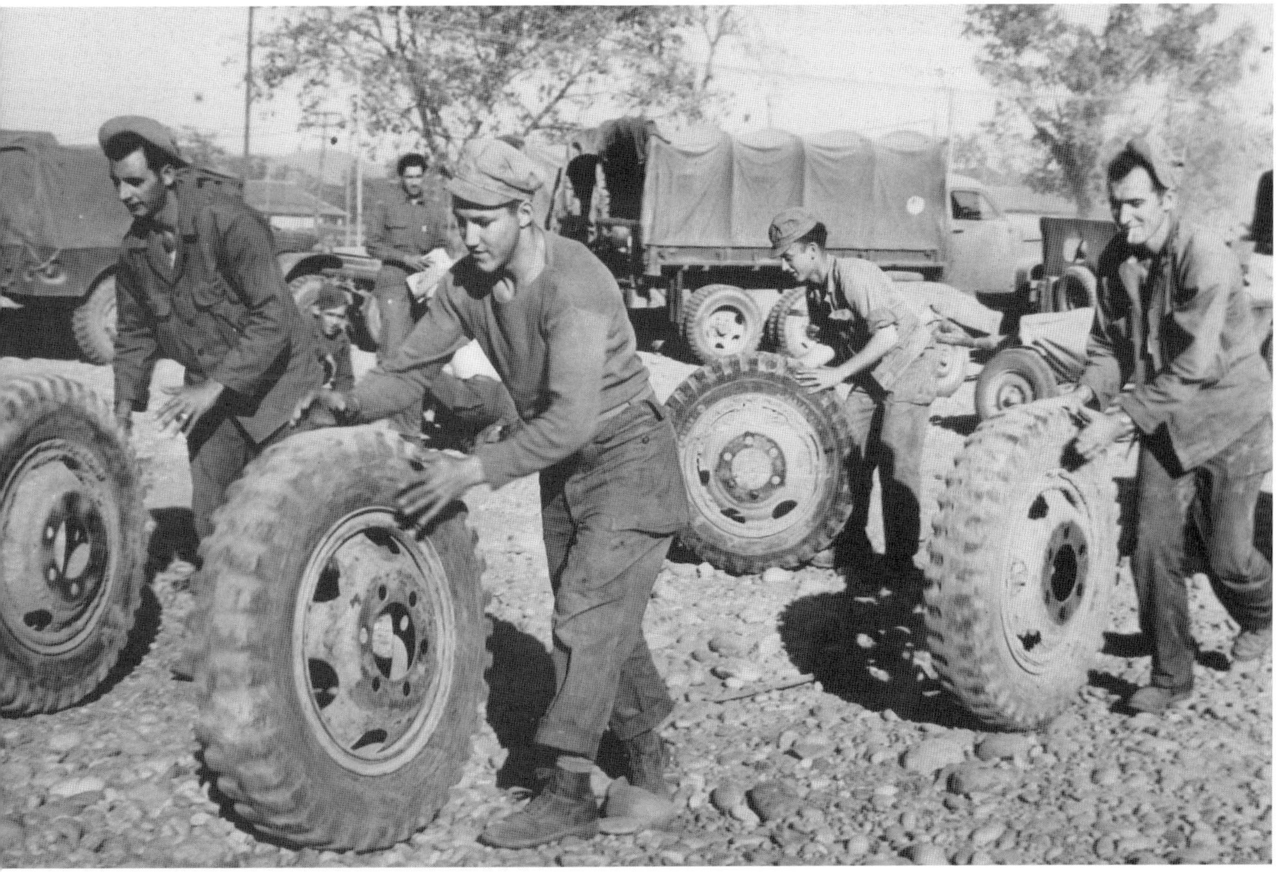

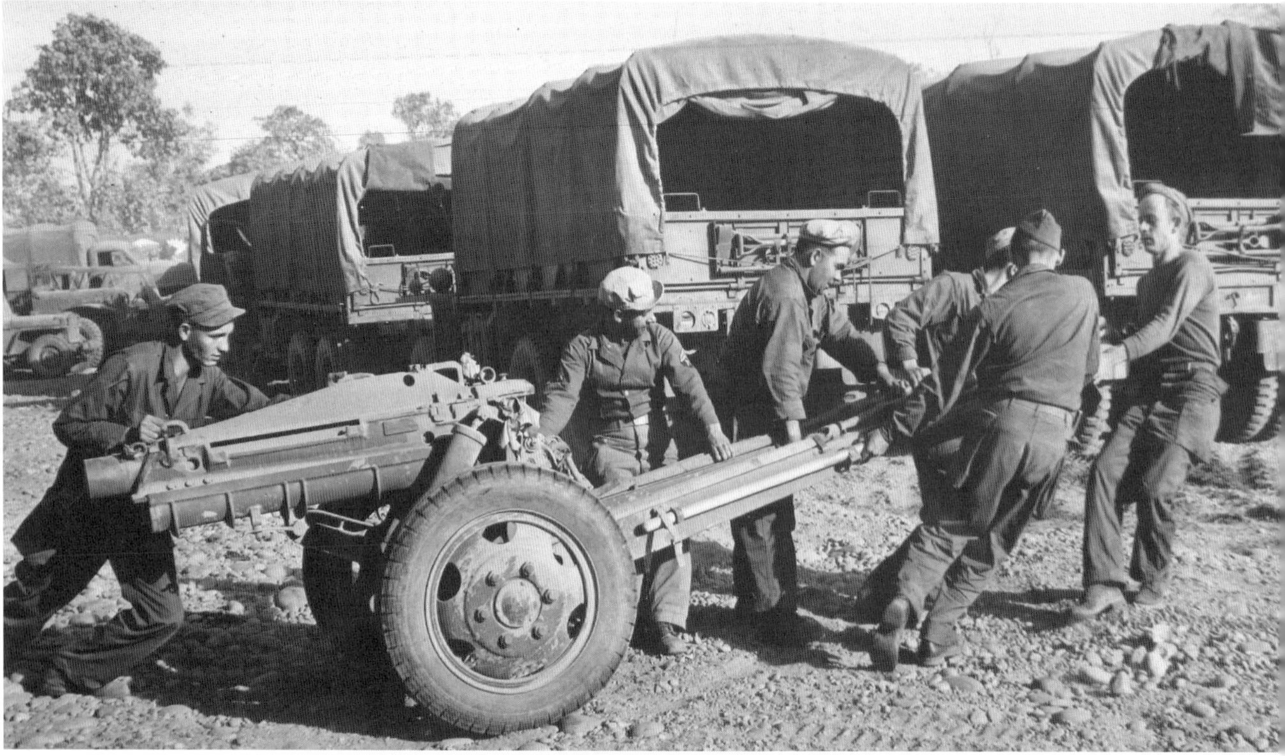

American soldiers drag an assembled 75mm pack howitzer towards a truck hitch for towing along the Ledo (Stilwell) Road towards China's Yunnan Province. *(NARA)*

A section of the Ledo (Stilwell) Road demonstrates the narrow roadway excavated from the side of a Burmese hill. The truck's height is shown just making it under a rocky overhang on the hillside. *(NARA)*

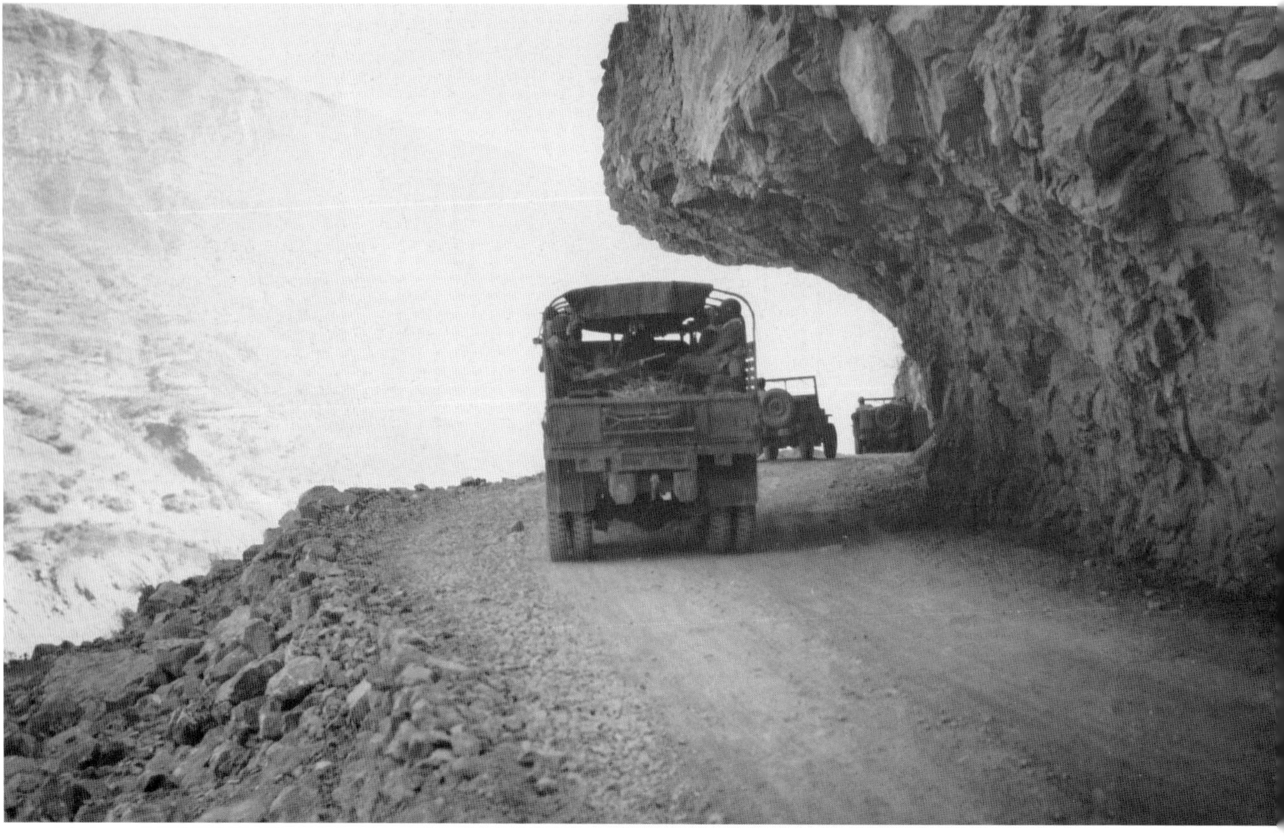

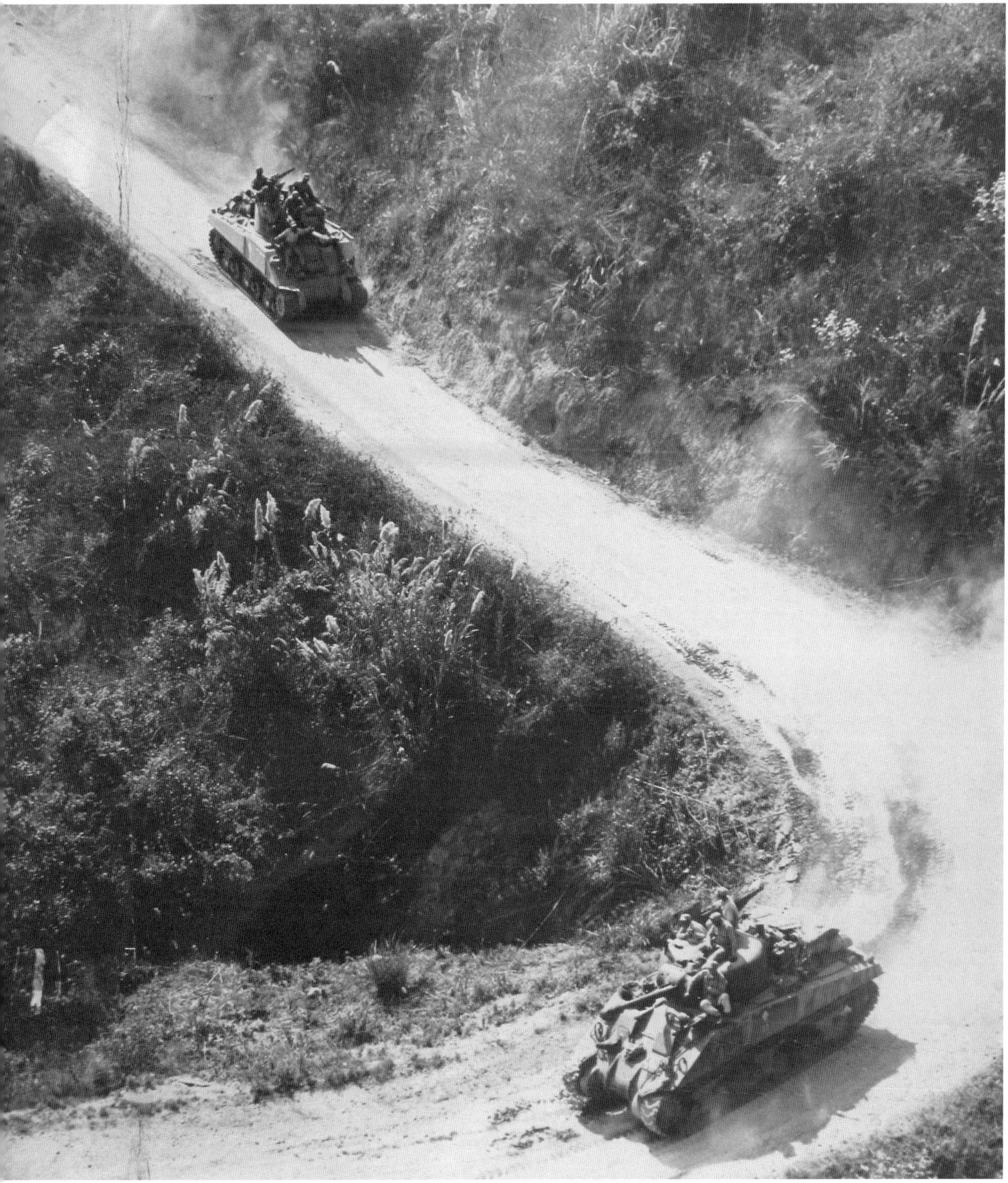

Two M4 medium tanks of the Chinese 1st Provisional Tank Group wind around a curve of the Ledo (Stilwell) Road on the way south of Myitkyina to Bhamo for an ultimate passage to merge with the Old Burma Road at Mong Yu and then on to Wanting in Yunnan Province. *(NARA)*

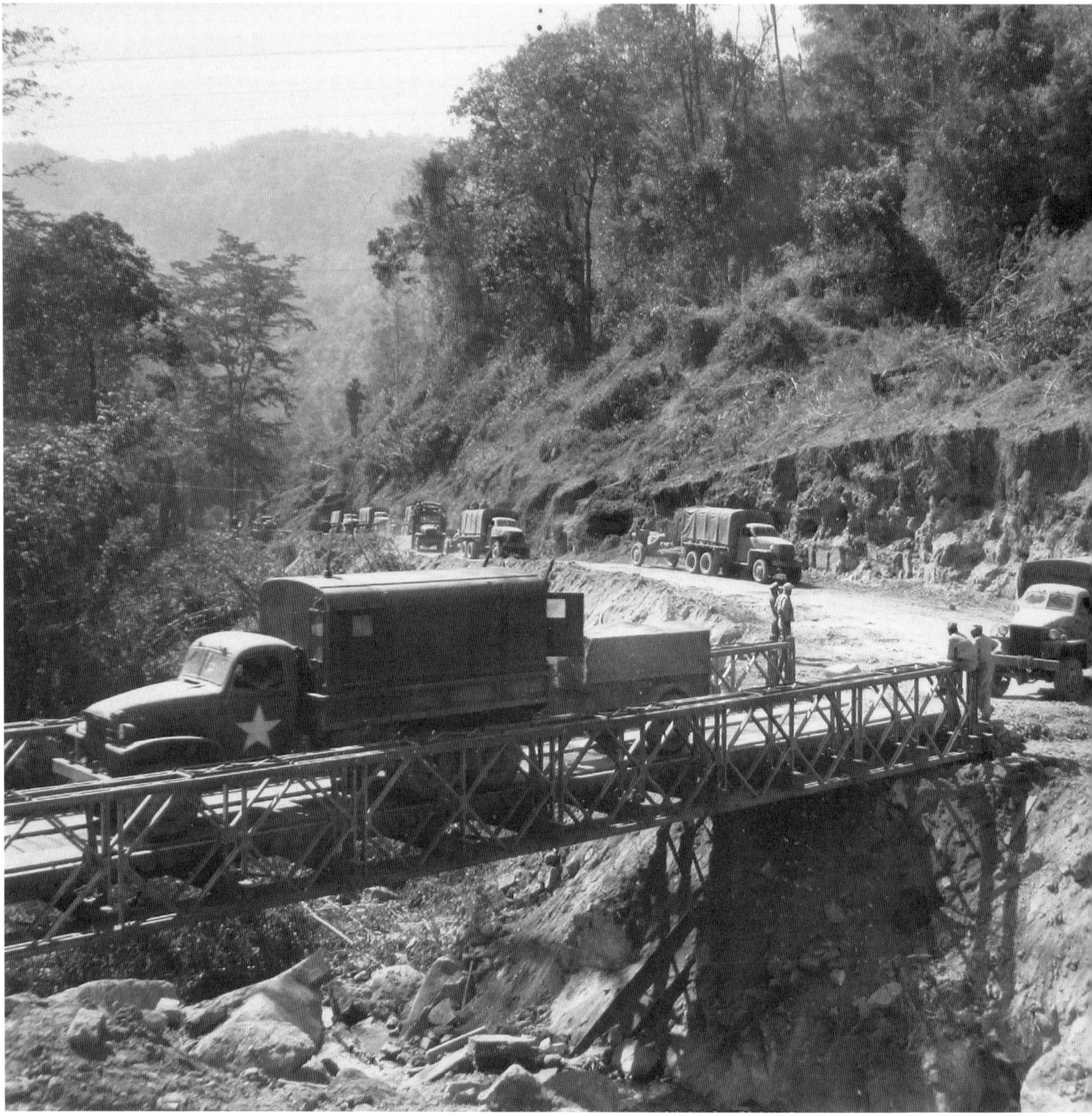

(**Above**) American trucks pass over a Bailey bridge across a gorge on the Ledo (Stilwell) Road south of Bhamo towards Namhkam and then the north-east turn to the Old Burma Road and Yunnan Province at Wanting. *(NARA)*

(**Opposite**) A portion of a road in China called 'Twenty-Four Curves or Bends' situated in Qinglong County in China's Guizhou Province: a civil engineering feat with the road descending along a mountainside as vehicles wind around the hairpin curves. During the Second Sino-Japanese War, Western supplies were carried over the Burma Road from Rangoon north though Mandalay and first arrived at Kunming, the capital of Yunnan Province, before travelling over mountain roads (above) to cities such as Guiyang, the capital of Guizhou Province, until the Burma Road was captured by the Japanese in April 1942. *(NARA)*

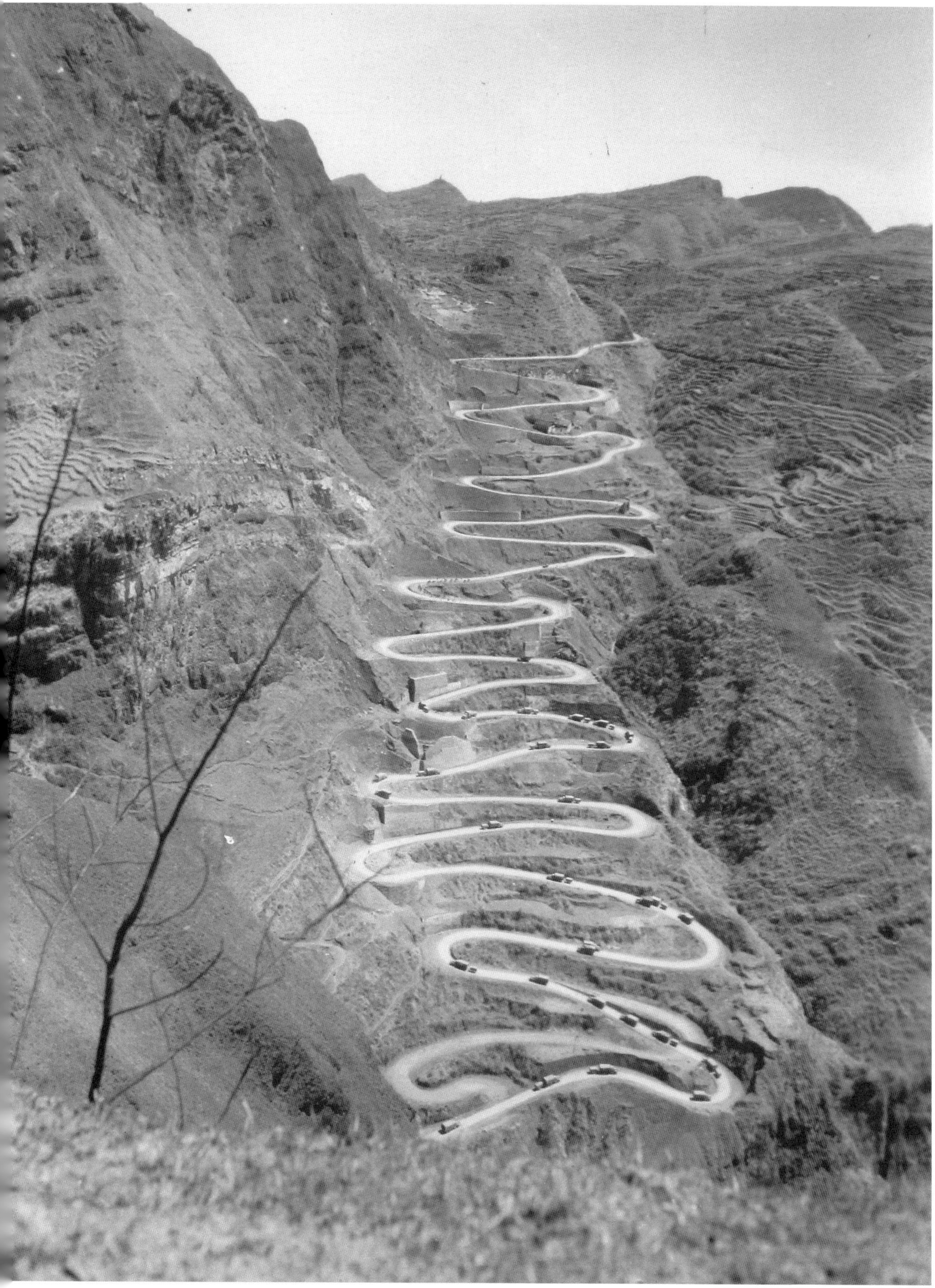

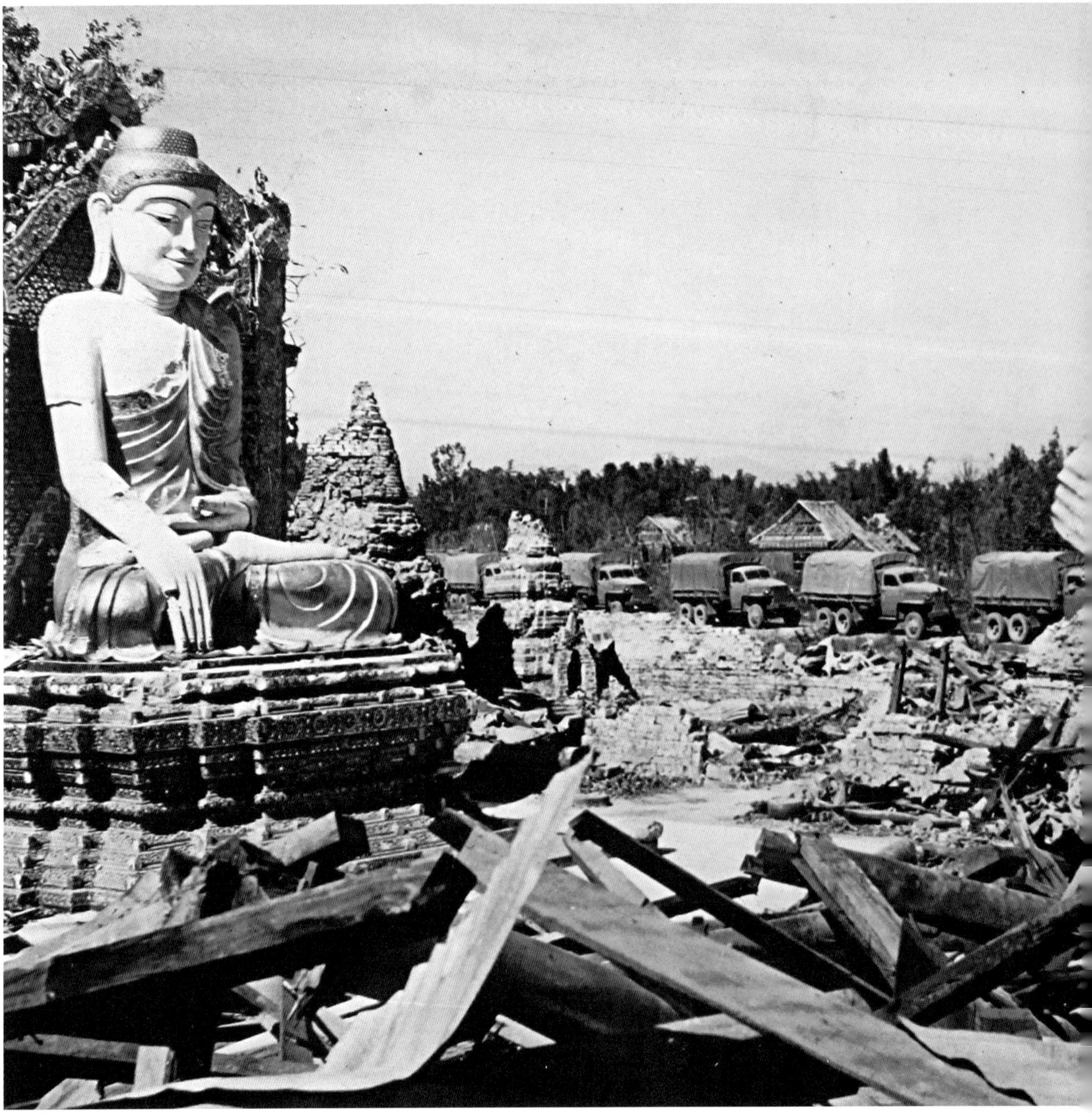

(**Above**) An American truck convoy passes Burmese temple ruins with intact Buddha statues in Namhkam located at a bend on the Ledo (Stilwell) Road that continued north-east to join the Burma Road at Mong Yu just south of Wanting in China's Yunnan Province. *(NARA)*

(**Opposite**) A portion of an American truck convoy crosses a Chinese suspension bridge into Yunnan Province in January 1945. A Chinese infantryman guards the bridge's tower (foreground). *(NARA)*

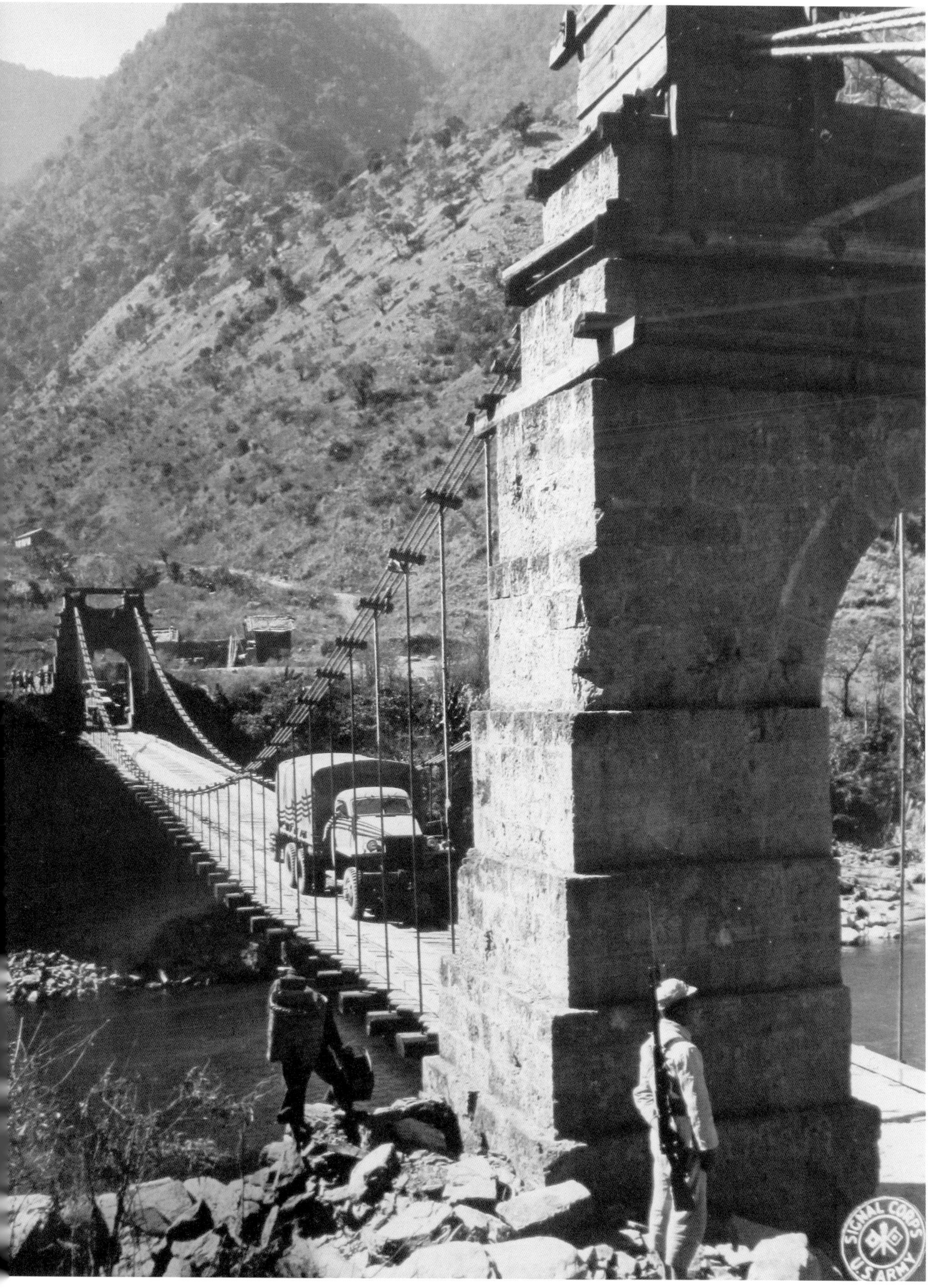
SIGNAL CORPS
U.S. ARMY

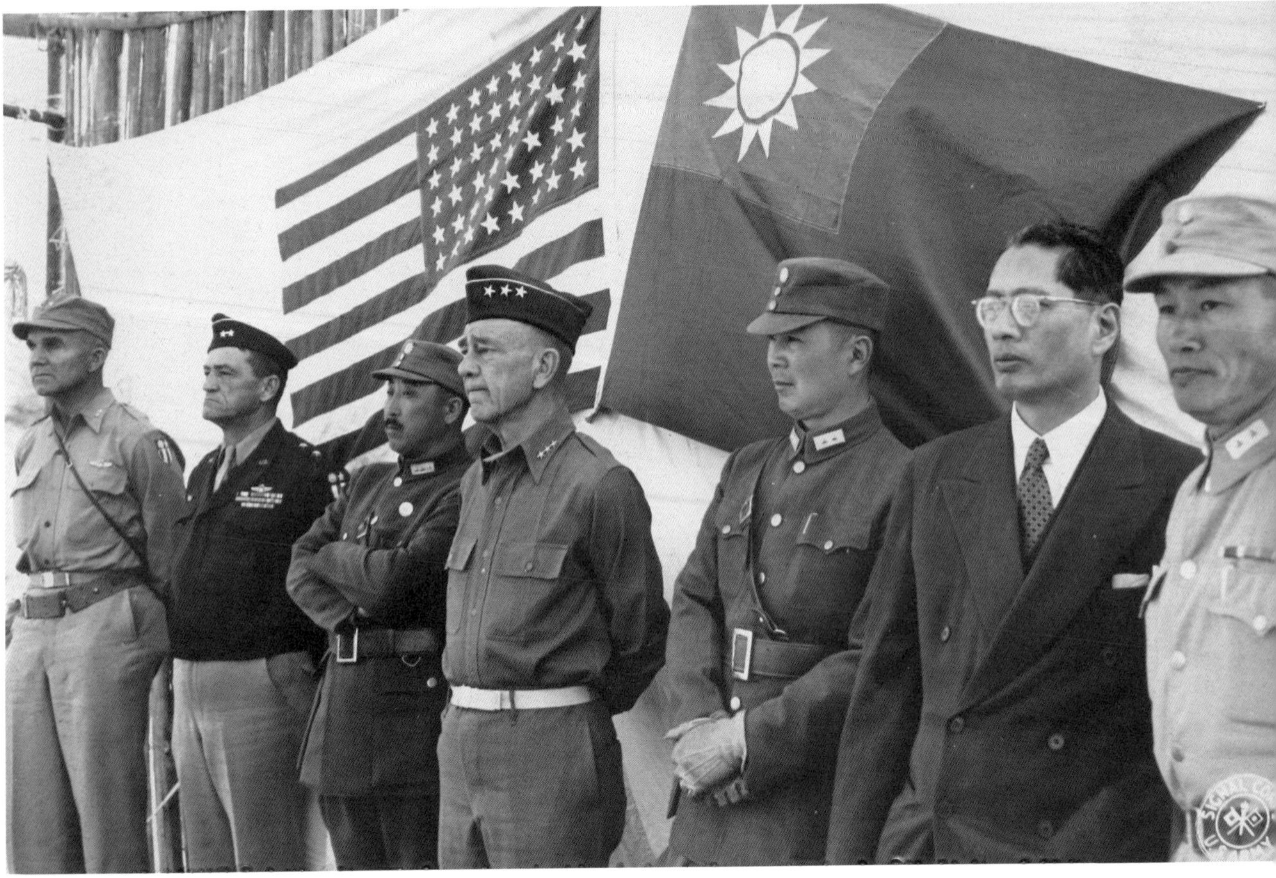

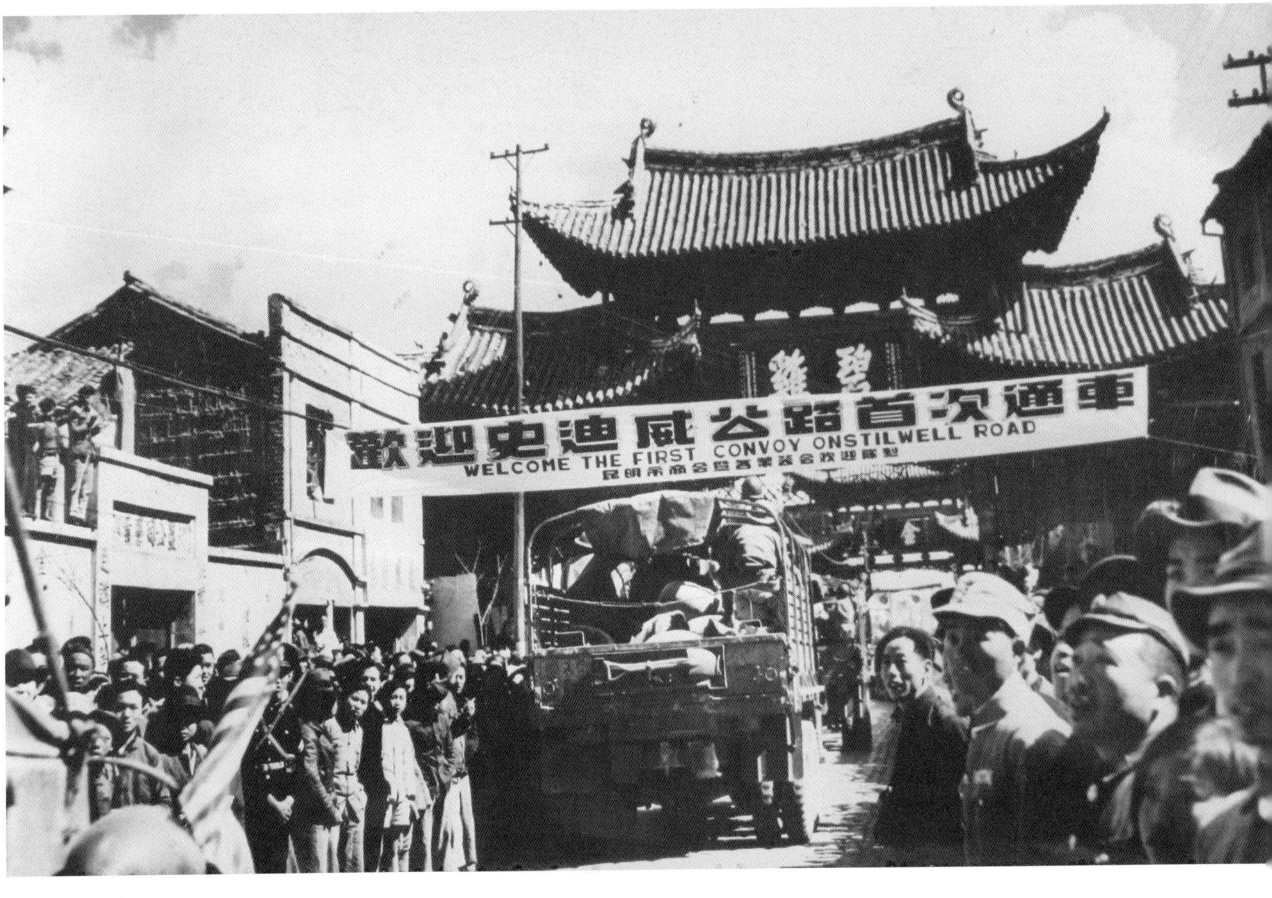
碧雞
歡迎史迪威公路首次通車
WELCOME THE FIRST CONVOY ONSTILWELL ROAD

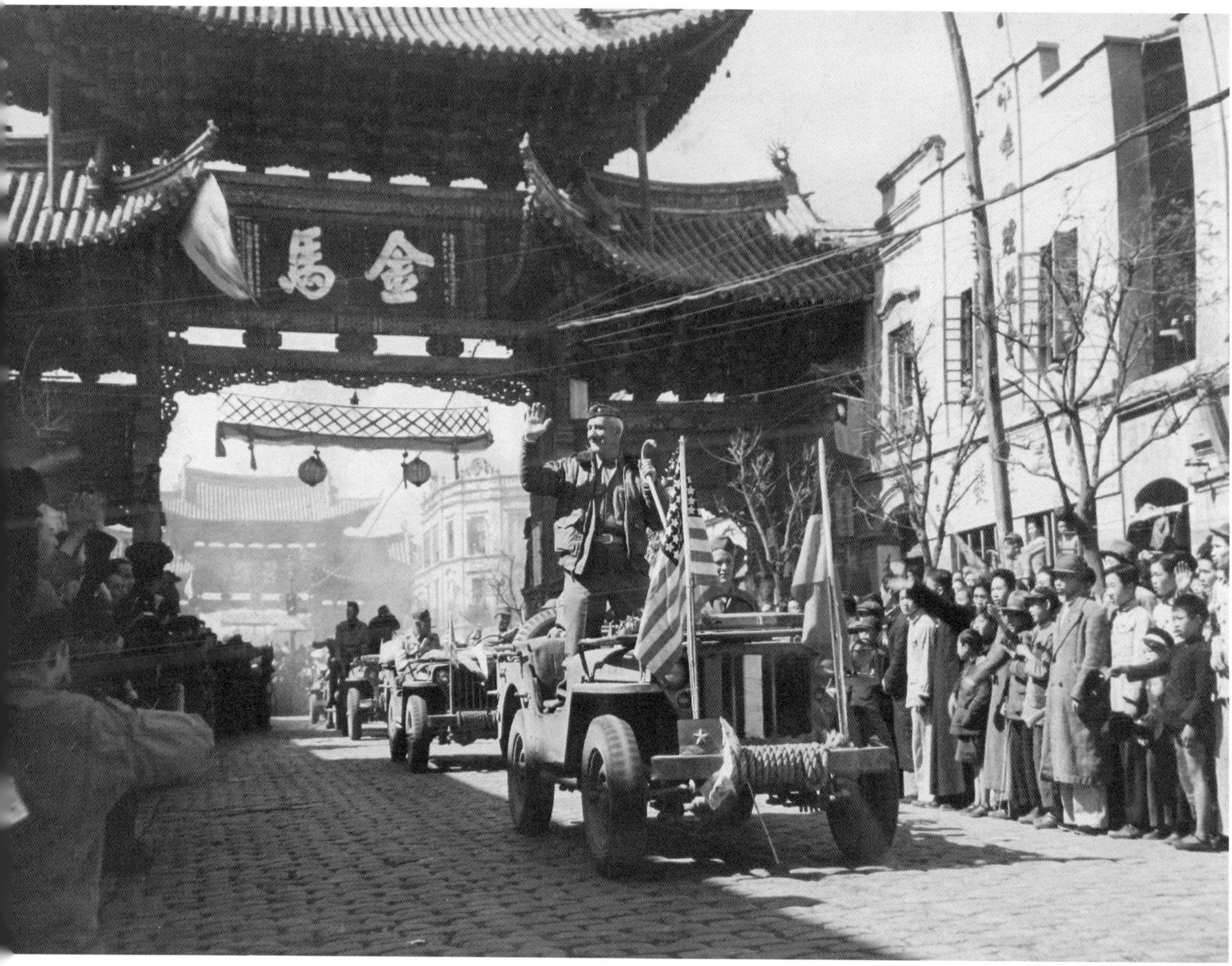
金馬

(**Opposite, above**) Major General Claire Chennault, commander US Fourteenth Air Force in China (second from left), waits with Lieutenant General Daniel Sultan, CG of the India-Burma theatre and the NCAC (fourth from left), with other American and Chinese officers and officials for the first truck convoy to traverse the Ledo (Stilwell) Road and join the Burma Road prior to entering Wanting in Yunnan Province in January 1945. *(NARA)*

(**Opposite, below**) American trucks enter Wanting in China's Yunnan Province. Although Chiang demanded the recall of Stilwell in October 1944, the *generalissimo* exhibited political correctness by renaming the Ledo Road the 'Stilwell Road' on the stretched banner across Wanting's main street. *(NARA)*

(**Above**) Brigadier General Lewis Pick, the overseer of the Ledo or Stilwell Road construction project, stands in the lead jeep proceeding along Wanting's main street in Yunnan Province. During construction the Ledo Road was nicknamed 'Pick's Pike'. *(NARA)*

Epilogue

With the recapture of Rangoon, British and Indian formations were withdrawn in preparation for the invasion of Malaya, forming a regrouped Fourteenth Army in India and Ceylon. Troops remaining in Burma were redesignated the Twelfth Army under Lieutenant General Montagu Stopford, who had led the Indian XXXIII Corps. Both armies remained under Slim's overall command. The fall of Rangoon did not indicate the end of the fighting. Pitched battles with remaining Japanese troops in Burma took place from the latter part of May to July 1945. The principal Allied formation was IV Corps, now under the command of Lieutenant General Francis Tuker with the 7th, 17th and 19th Indian divisions that were combating the IJA Twenty-Eighth Army's remnants in the Pegu Yomas trying to cross the Rangoon-Mandalay road to get further east, which lasted until mid-July. As the IJA troops were running the gauntlet of the Sittang River, the 'Battle of the Breakout' was disastrous for the enemy. By 4 August, the attempted break-out at the banks of the Sittang River cost the Japanese 17,000 casualties, of which 11,000 were killed and 4,000 missing.

In Burma, the fighting went on until the last minute as the atomic weapons were unleashed on Hiroshima and Nagasaki on 6 and 9 August 1945 respectively. Of the 330,000 Japanese soldiers who went to Burma more than 200,000 never returned, which was thirteen times the number of British and Commonwealth troops that died. It was the greatest land defeat in the history of Japan. By 14 August, Emperor Hirohito personally intervened in order that the Japanese government should accept the Allies' unconditional surrender terms.

The Allied effort was truly multinational with around 350,000 Indians, 100,000 British, 90,000 Africans and 65,000 Chinese troops. About 10,000 Americans took part as a few infantry regiments, OSS officers and almost 50 USAAF squadrons. This Allied force won the battles in Burma at unpronounceable locales and amid some of the world's harshest terrain in which to wage warfare.

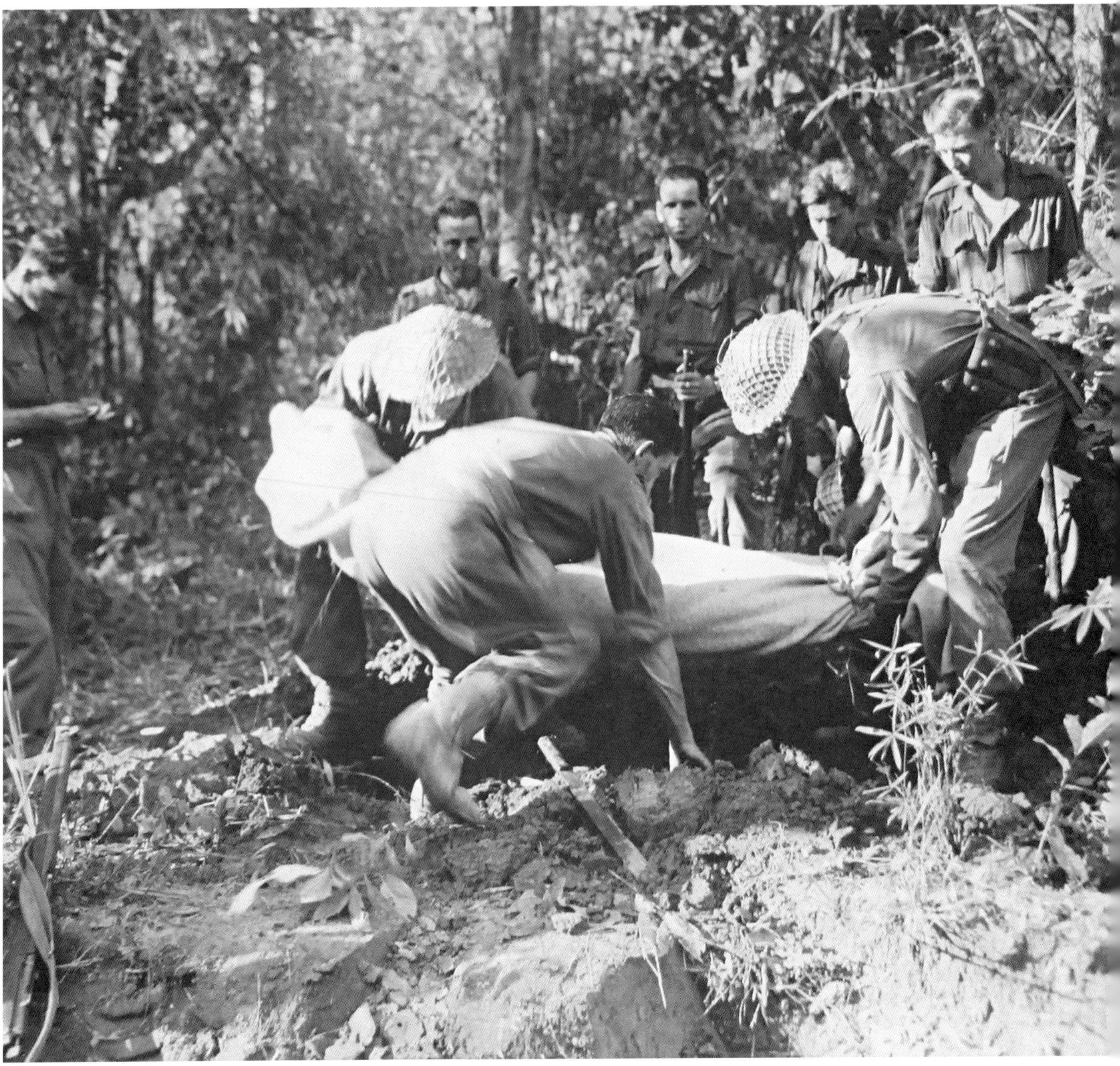

(**Above**) A group of British 36th Division soldiers bury a mate in November 1944 during that unit's 'Railroad Corridor' march from Mawlu through Pinwe, ultimately seizing Katha and Indaw. The photograph animates Rupert Brooke's poetic stanza from his 1915 poem *The Soldier*: 'If I should die, think only this of me. That there's some corner of a foreign field that is for ever England. There shall be in that rich earth a richer dust concealed …' *(NARA)*

(**Opposite**) An American from the 'Mars' Task Force stands by his recently-interred comrades somewhere between Myitkyina and the Burma Road near a Burmese temple's pagoda (background) in the NCAC theatre of battle from mid-October1944 to January 1945. *(NARA)*

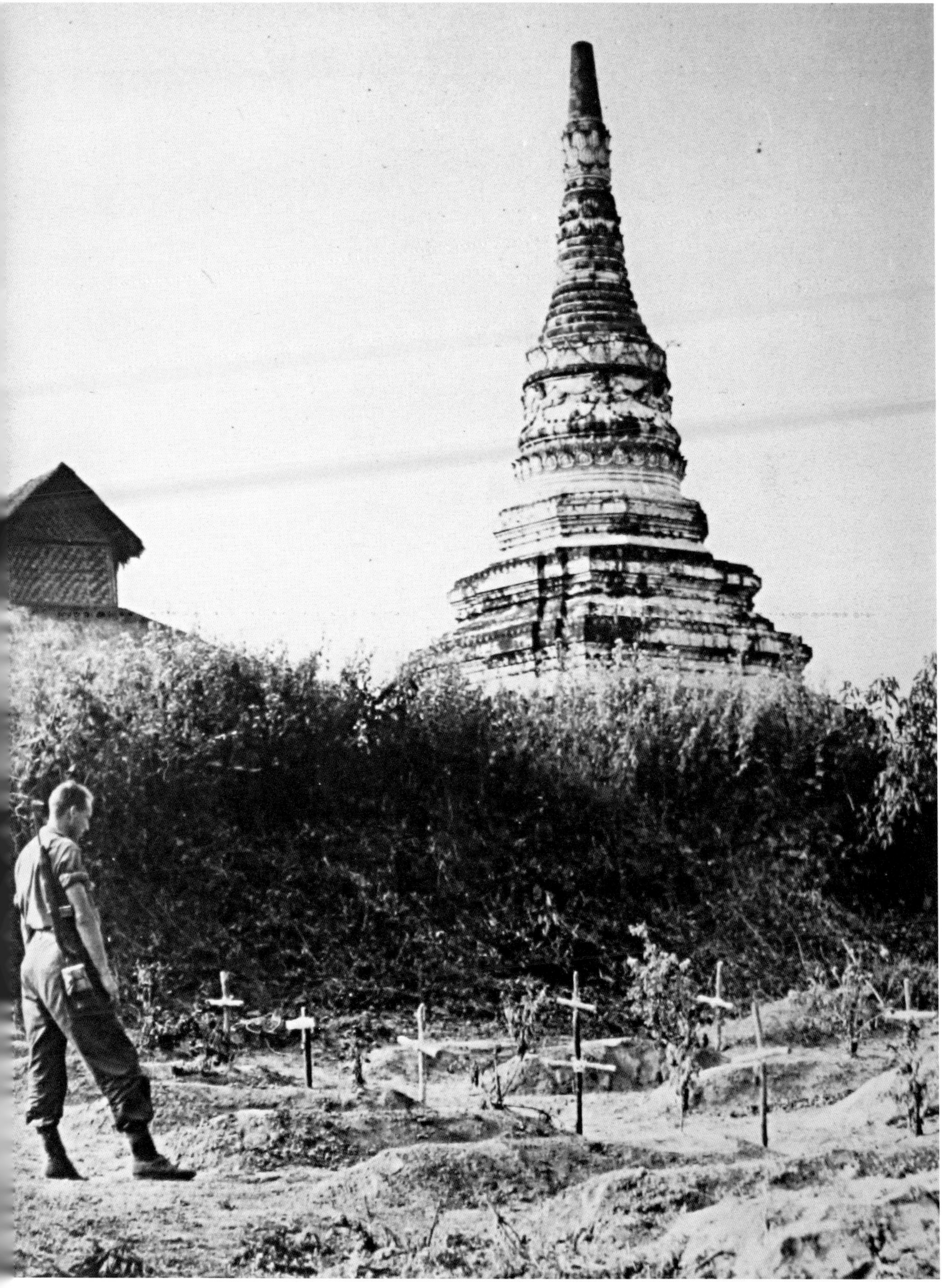

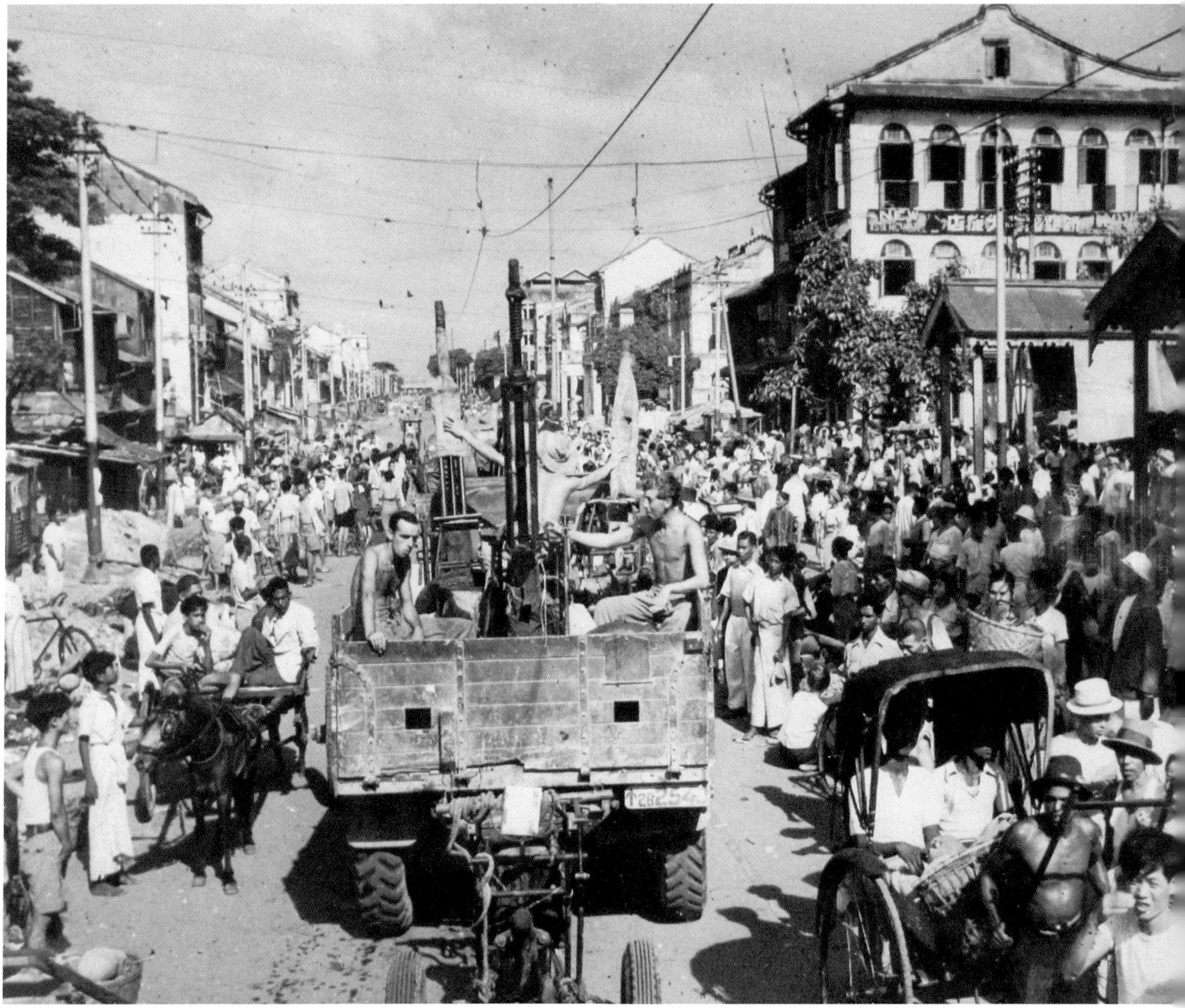

(**Above**) A truck of the RAF Regiment's light AA unit from Mingaladon airfield, 9 miles north of Rangoon centre, tows a small ordnance piece through crowded Dalhousie Street after the Allies recaptured the port city from the Japanese in early May 1945, ending more than three years of enemy occupation. *(NARA)*

(**Opposite, above**) Admiral Lord Louis Mountbatten, SEAC theatre commander (front row, centre) sits with the upper echelon of Allied officers at Rangoon's Government House soon after that port-city's reoccupation by Allied forces in May 1945. Some notable Allied officers seated in the front row (left to right) to the left of Mountbatten include Lieutenant General Frank Messervy, CG Indian IV Corps; Lieutenant General Daniel Sultan, American CG of the India-Burma theatre and leader of the NCAC force; Lieutenant General Sir Oliver Leese, Allied Land Forces CG, SEAC; and American Lieutenant General Raymond Wheeler, principal administrative SEAC staff officer and director of construction of the Ledo (Stilwell) Road. ACW Keith Park, RAF Commander SEAC sits third from the right. *(NARA)*

(**Opposite, below**) Lieutenant General William Slim, the CG Fourteenth Army and architect of the Burma reconquest after the heroic defence of Imphal and Kohima in 1944, sits on the far left of Mountbatten and other high-ranking Allied officers as they draw up surrender terms for the Japanese forces in Burma. *(Author's collection)*

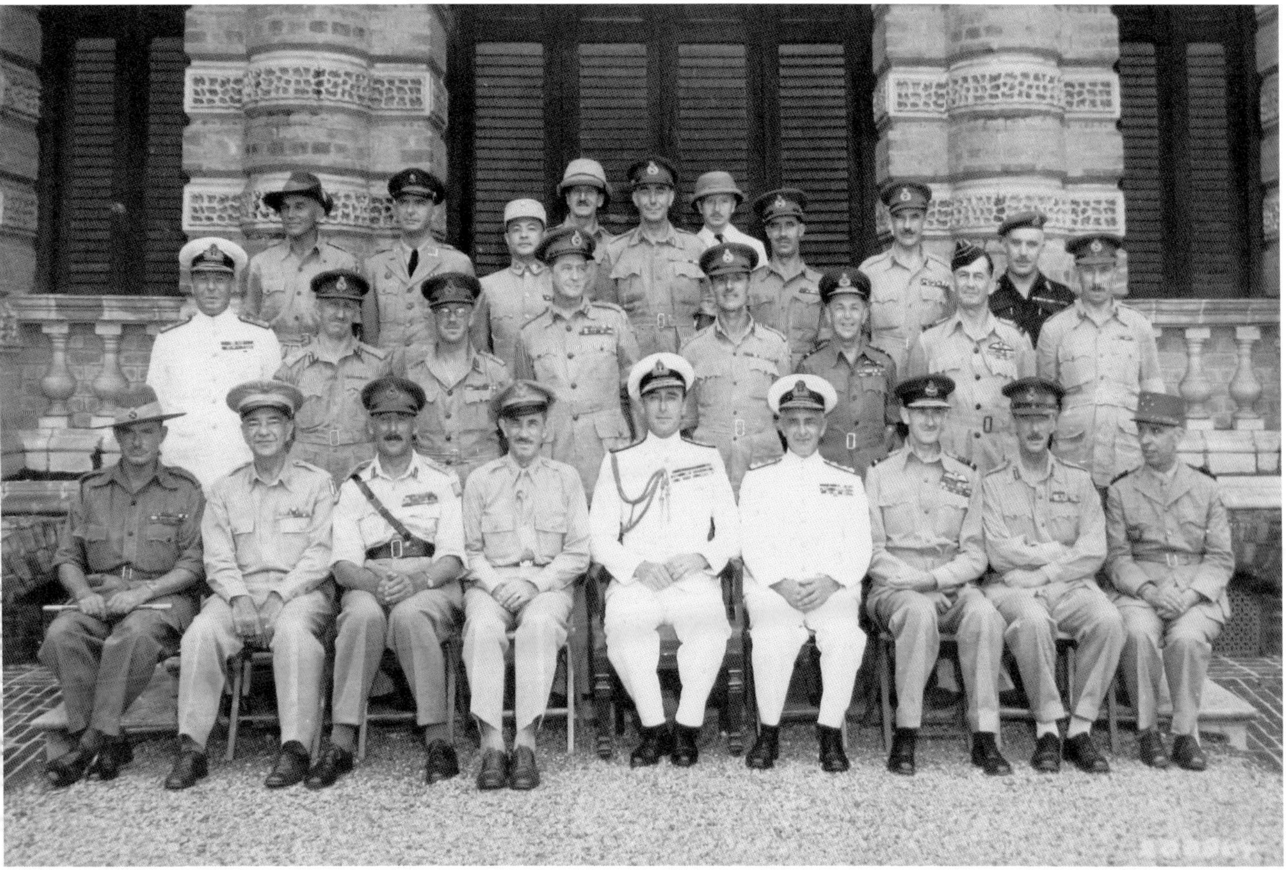

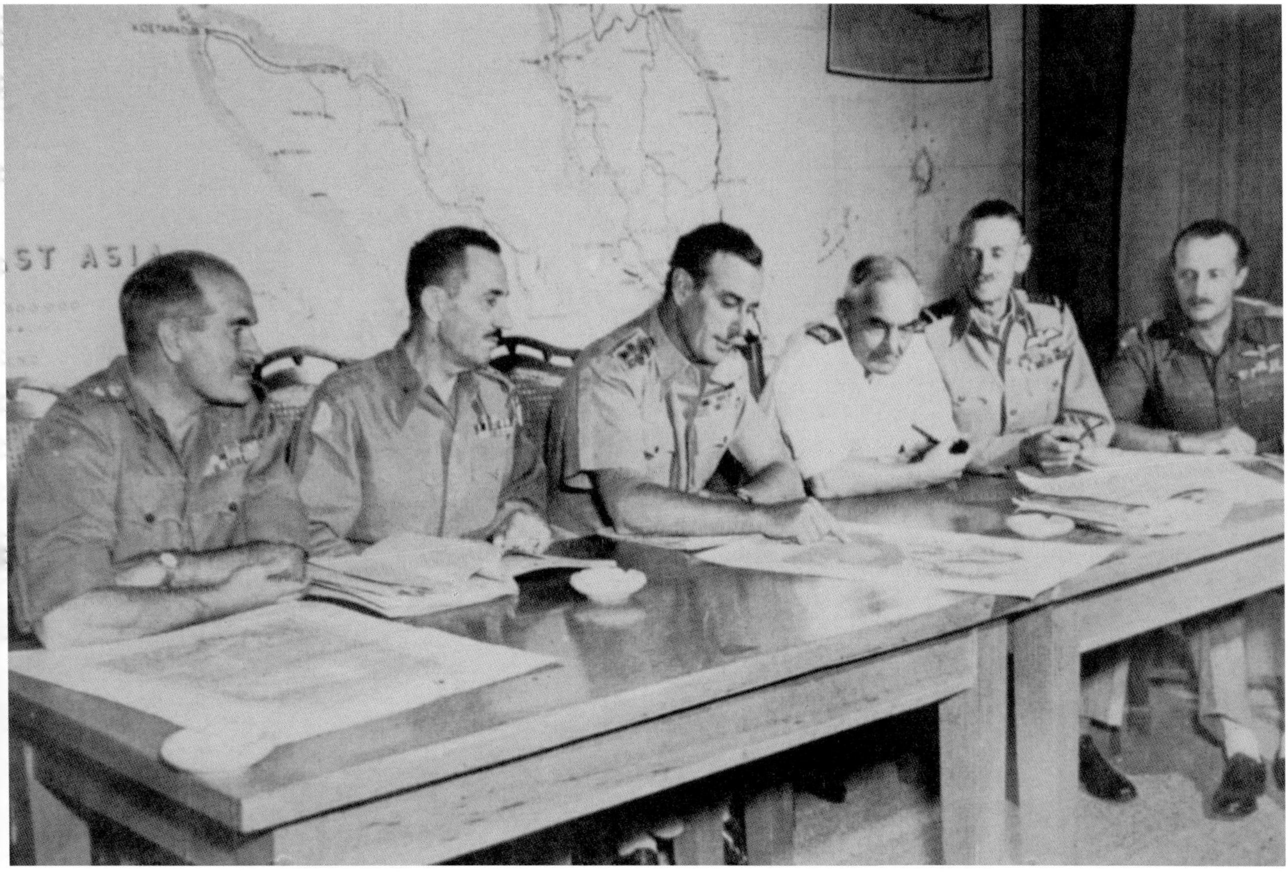

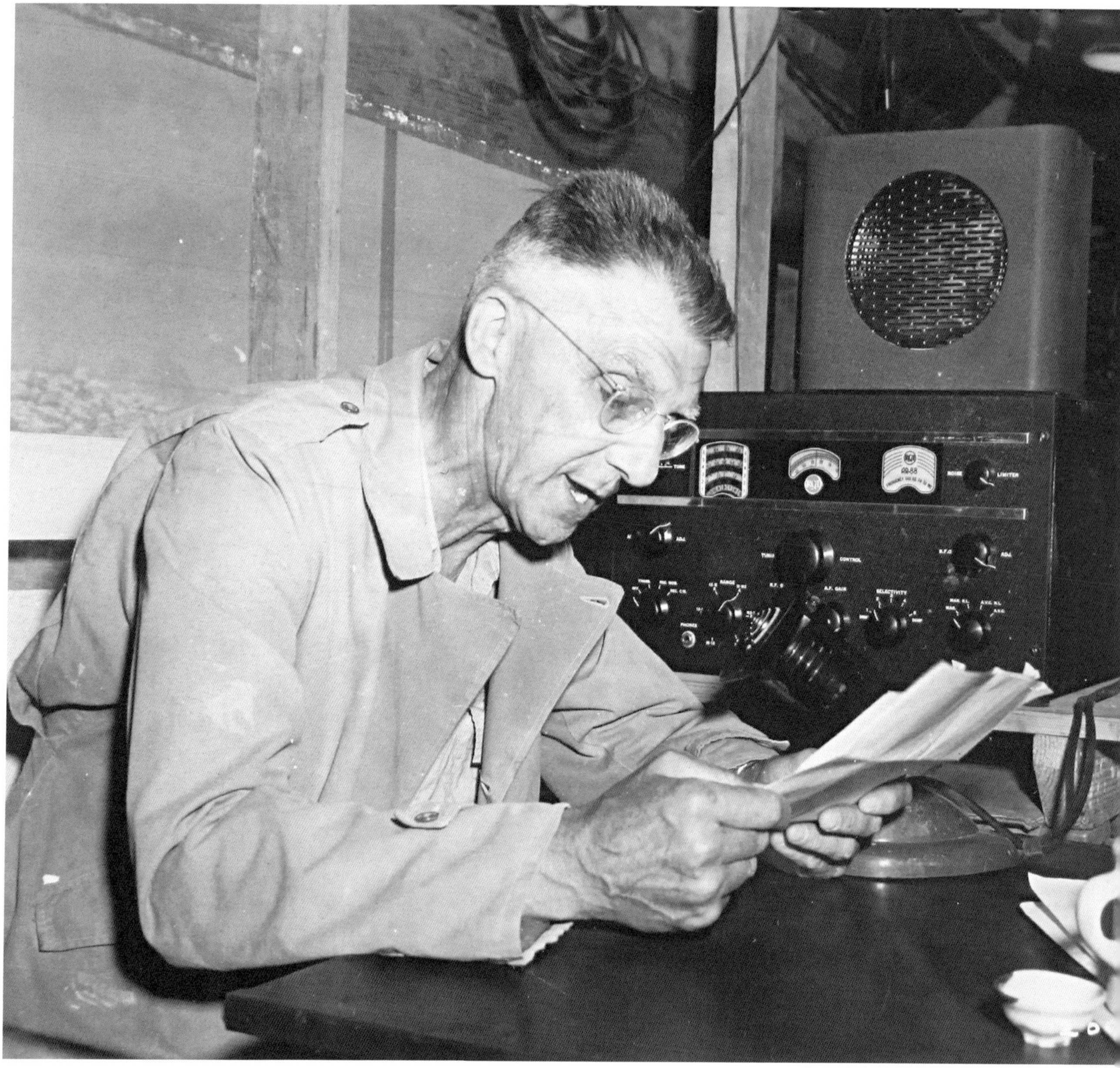

Lieutenant General Joseph Stilwell is seen here giving a 4 July 1945 Independence Day address to troops on Okinawa. Stilwell, who walked out of Burma in 1942, led his Ramgarh-trained Chinese divisions and 'Galahad' troops through the Hukawng and Mogaung valleys in 1943–44, directed the capture of the western airfield at Myitkyina in May 1944 and captured Myitkyina town after a protracted siege in August 1944. He had his final posting as the US Tenth Army commanding general during the last days of the Okinawa campaign in June 1945. After the end of hostilities on Okinawa, Stilwell was to ready the US Tenth Army for the Japanese Home Islands' invasion. *(NARA)*

The devastation of Nagasaki, one of the largest seaports in southern Japan and a major producer of ordnance, is shown here after the atomic detonation of 9 August 1945. A few days later, Emperor Hirohito sued for peace and Japan surrendered to the Allies on 15 August. More than 225,000 Japanese, mostly civilians, died in Nagasaki, half during the first day, while for months afterwards large numbers died from burns, radiation sickness, illness and malnutrition. (*NARA*)

Bibliography

Allen, Louis, *Burma: The Longest War 1941–45* (Phoenix Press, Guilford, 2000).

Bidwell, Shelford, *The Chindit War: Stilwell, Wingate and the Campaign for Burma: 1944* (MacMillan Publishing Co., New York, 1979).

Callahan, Raymond, *Burma 1942–1945* (University of Delaware Press, Newark, 1979).

Chinnery, Philip D., *March or Die* (Airlife Publishing Ltd, Shrewsbury, 1997).

Colvin, John, *Not Ordinary Men: The Story of the Battle of Kohima* (Pen & Sword, Barnsley, 2003).

Diamond, Jon, *Orde Wingate* (Osprey Publishing Ltd, Oxford, 2012).

Diamond, Jon, *Archibald Wavell* (Osprey Publishing Ltd, Oxford, 2012).

Diamond, Jon, *Stilwell and the Chindits: The Allied Campaign in Northern Burma 1943–1944* (Pen & Sword, Barnsley, 2014).

Diamond, Jon, *Combat: Chindit Versus Japanese Infantryman 1943–1944* (Osprey Publishing Ltd, Oxford, 2016).

Diamond, Jon, *Burma Road* (Osprey Publishing Ltd, Oxford, 2016).

Frank, Richard B., *Tower of Skulls: A History of Asia-Pacific War. July 1937–May 1942* (Norton, New York, 2020).

Hickey, Michael, *The Unforgettable Army: Slim's XIVth Army in Burma* (Spellmount, Staplehurst, 1998).

Holland, James, *Burma '44: The Battle that Turned Britain's War in the East* (Corgi Books, London, 2016).

Jeffreys, Alan, *The British Army in the Far East 1941–45* (Osprey Publishing Ltd, Oxford, 2005).

Katoch, Hemant Singh, *Imphal 1944. The Japanese Invasion of India* (Osprey Publishing Ltd, Oxford, 2018).

Lyman, Robert, *Japan's Last Bid for Victory: The Invasion of India* (Praetorian Press, Barnsley, 2011).

Lyman, Robert, *Kohima 1944: The Battle That Saved India* (Osprey Publishing Ltd, Oxford, 2010).

McLynn, Frank, *The Burma Campaign: Disaster into Triumph 1942–45* (Yale University Press, New Haven and London, 2011).

McManus, John C., *Fire and Fortitude: The US Army in the Pacific War, 1942–1943* (Caliber, New York, 2019).

Sacquery, Troy J., *The OSS in Burma: Jungle War Against the Japanese* (University Press of Kansas, Kansas, 2013).

Thompson, Julian, *The Imperial War Museum Book of the War in Burma 1942–1945* (Pan Books, London, 2003).

Tuchman, Barbara W., *Stilwell and the American Experience in China: 1911 1945* (MacMillan, New York, 1970).

Woodburn Kirby, S., *The War Against Japan. Volume IV. The Reconquest of Burma* (Naval and Military Press Ltd, Uckfield, 2004).

Young, Edward M., *Meiktila 1945: The Battle to Liberate Burma* (Osprey Publishing Ltd, Oxford, 2004).